M@NH☎TAN

USER'S GUIDE

M@NH@TT@N
USER'S GUIDE

THE GUIDE TO NEW YORK
FOR NEW YORKERS

CHARLES A. SUISMAN WITH CAROL MOLESWORTH

HYPERION

NEW YORK

*A portion of the illustrations was produced by Chesley McLaren;
photographs, where credited, are the work of Christopher Lovi;
the Zip Code map on p. 239 was created by Kris Tobiassen.*

Library of Congress Cataloging-in-Publication Data
Suisman, Charles, 1958–
Manhattan user's guide : the guide to New York for New
Yorkers / Charles Suisman with Carol Molesworth.—1st ed.
p.   cm.
ISBN 0-7868-8152-6
1. New York (N.Y.)—Guidebooks.
I. Molesworth, Carol. II. Title.
F128.18.S85   1996
917347' 10443—dc20   96-21582
CIP

Book design by Jessica Shatan

FIRST EDITION
2 4 6 8 10 9 7 5 3 1

FOR RAINER

CONTENTS

ACKNOWLEDGMENTS

Many thanks to those who were so generous with their time and expertise in providing information and insights for the articles in this book. Special thanks to Charles Molesworth for his support and encouragement, to our *Manhattan User's Guide* newsletter readers who have given us invaluable feedback, to our agent John Wright, to Hyperion for their enthusiastic support, and especially to our great editor Rick Kot.

INTRODUCTION

This isn't a guide book. It's not, at any rate, a conventional guide book about New York, because it's written for New Yorkers.

It came about like this. We started publishing the *Manhattan User's Guide* newsletter in 1992 as a resource guide, a way for our readers to thread through the amazing variety of the city. We write about anything we think worth a look, worth the money, worth remembering. *MUG* has found ways to help ensure a good move, ways to keep things peaceful as a tenant. We've eaten the food of great chefs like Gray Kunz, Rocco DiSpirito, and Anne Rosenzweig and at small restaurants that offer big flavors or value like Il Bagatto and Jackson Diner. And more: We discovered how to get your passport renewed, the best views and worst spaces in Manhattan. Where to learn juggling. Where to volunteer. The best pizza, the best furniture restorers, the best cocktails. Where to swim, launch a kayak, learn kendo. In the past five years we've also covered some wonderfully skilled and fascinating people. There's Ho-

race Weeks, whose skilled hands clean and restore hats. There's Olga Bloom, who took a barge in the East River and transformed it into the best place to hear chamber music in the city. There's Jack Flosso, a magician's magician who really does know every trick in the book. Putting the newsletter together each month has convinced us that we have the best job in the world.

We had never intended to turn the newsletter into a book but, in 1995, when Hyperion said they wanted to publish *MUG* in book form, we knew a free lunch when we saw one. We figured that all we had to do was collect the best of the articles we'd already published. Exactly one year of intensive work proved us wrong. While some of the articles in this book originated in the newsletter, virtually every one has been extensively researched again. The material has also been completely reorganized so that it falls more logically into this format.

The rules of the game, though, stayed the same: To be included in an article, a subject must be in New York or available here and accessible to the public. Our emphasis is on

Manhattan, though we've made occasional forays to some of the more exceptional spots around the boroughs. We make no claim to being comprehensive (which isn't remotely possible, in any event) and have left out anything that hasn't made a strong impression on us. We've also omitted many obvious subjects (both obvious-wonderful and obvious-dull) that every New Yorker is familiar with. Others have been dropped for any number of reasons (a dry cleaner on the East Side, for example, that wants references before they'll accept your clothes).

When we research something, we try it, buy it, experience it to the extent that it's possible. By and large, we remain anonymous and we pay for everything. After we feel we've got a good handle on what the establishment has to offer, we may do interviews for background. We aren't always able to test out some of the entries (services in particular) to the degree we would like. In those cases, we use a variety of approaches to satisfy ourselves of a company's reliability. The method works pretty well, but it's not infallible.

We include some negative pieces when we feel they're deserved— ripoffs, places that are expensive and overrated, anywhere with a bad attitude. On the things we haven't discovered yet, we hope you'll set us straight. And while we have made every effort to check every fact, with so many thousands of pieces of information there are certain to be errors. These are our errors alone (not Hyperion's) and we hope you'll point them out to us so they can be corrected for a future edition. In some cases, owners, chefs, quality, or merchandise will have changed since we did the research. That's a frustration of doing a user's guide but the excitement of living in this city.

For the most timely info, subscribe to the monthly newsletter, which offers the very latest on restaurants, shopping, services, good deals, sports, and much else. If you'd like to subscribe or give us feedback about this book, our address is P.O. Box 772, Ansonia Station, New York, NY 10023. Our phone is ☎ 724-4692, our fax is ☎ 496-2681.

ARTS & DIVERSIONS

ART GALLERIES

Here are a few of our favorite galleries. These are all in Soho, but note that West Chelsea, with its calmer atmosphere and lower rents, is exerting a pull on many of them.

When Ivan Karp opened the first gallery in Soho in 1969, followed soon after by Paula Cooper, he was trying to get away from the velvet-rope atmosphere of the uptown art world at that time. He wanted a "big, wide, democratic space where everyone feels comfortable and the gallery owner and staff were in full view" of the people coming to visit. The **OK Harris Gallery,** 383 West Broadway [Grand/Broome] ☎ 431-3600, is exactly that and has been the model for many of the 250 plus galleries in the area. New and established artists exhibit side by side—five new shows every five weeks in the largest gallery space in Soho. Mr. Karp says he could never have predicted that Soho would evolve from artists living in raw loft spaces hanging out the sign A.I.R. (Artist in Residence) for the Fire Department to a free

entertainment for all—part art world haven, part scene, a stopping place for visitors from around the world.

Bill Maynes took a small space in 1994 at 225 Lafayette St. [Spring] ☎ 431-3952, and was, for a year, the only gallery in this building on the eastern fringe of the neighborhood. He felt that being "in a modest space off the beaten track suits my personality." He shows mostly paintings and some sculpture by artists headed toward mid-career. Looking at a show of paintings by KK Kozik, Mr. Maynes says, "They have an immediacy that feeds into your sensory part, and after a little time they start opening out on other levels." Mr. Maynes now talks about finding a larger space closer to other galleries.

At **TZ'Art & Co.,** 28 Wooster St. [Grand] ☎ 966-9059, Tom Zollner and Frederieke Taylor combine their gallery and not-for-profit experiences in running a much larger gallery than Mr. Maynes's.

Animal Anomaly by Bill Scanga at TZ'Art & Co.

Work is often displayed on the floor, hanging from the ceiling, or using the large center part of the room. The gallery is distinguished by the Testwall, a freestanding wall visible from both inside the gallery and outside through the Wooster St. windows, on which artists can try things out. They show "young, emerging artists who are conceptually influenced" and tend to like ones "whose work crosses boundaries" using material from literature or science or "photography that uses video in the final work."

Across the hallway from TZ'Art & Co. is **Basilico Fine Arts,** 26 Wooster St. [Grand/ Canal] ☎ 966-1831. Stephano Basilico spent a year or so curating shows on a month-to-month basis, moving from space to space before settling on this one large and one small room that was "carved out of the remains" of a restaurant and some artists' studios. He likes to "create a space where the work is presented in an appropriate manner for it. Sometimes that means painting the walls white and sometimes turning it into a vinyl dungeon," as he did for an exhibition by Toland Grinnell. When talking about the kind of work he shows, and this is another gallery where the photography, sculpture, or conceptual pieces can be on or off the walls, he says, "This is less about dictating the right answers but giving interesting questions to the viewers."

Andrea Rosen, 130 Prince St. [Wooster/ W. Bway] ☎ 941-0203, opened her gallery in January 1990 with a show by Felix Gonzalez-Torres, whose characteristic "stacks"—large printed multiples piled up on the floor (he intended for you to take one

home), are somehow emblematic of this space. Ms. Rosen "does not want to sustain the mystery of the underground. Galleries are truly public spaces" and become more and more so all the time as museums and, in some cases, parks, now charge admission. "Most of what we do in the gallery is give people information. Most people don't come here to buy, and I don't want to eliminate the public aspect of what we do. If art is to serve a function, it needs to serve a larger audience." The works here are always a little adventuresome—most of the artists are in their thirties, and their work centers on psychological and sexual concerns. "And then there is John Coplans," a mature artist who has been photographing the aging process as it works itself out on his own body. Ms. Rosen likes being in Soho, because "the neighborhood grew up around an idea of openness."

Michael Klein opened his gallery on lower Broadway in 1985 and moved to 40 Wooster St. [Grand] ☎ 431-1980, after five years. Mr. Klein came to gallery ownership reluctantly. "Personally, I was diametrically opposed to the art world of the '80s. I wanted a gallery that was homier." The street-level space has a garage-style door that is open in warmer weather so you can step off the pavement into the gallery space. "Galleries are mini-museums. It's always supposed to be a show. I like people to be treated well and I want people to come constantly and I want them to be surprised. I don't want them to say 'I know what's going to be there.'" Mr. Klein shows more established artists working in traditional and non-traditional media: video monitors on the floor, knitted representations of buildings, site-specific constructions, as well as paintings and drawings. "And the great part of the gallery system is it's free."

MORE A list of galleries worth exploring but, given the amount of flux in the art world, you might want to check addresses before starting out on a viewing expedition.

Leo Castelli, 420 West Broadway
  [Prince/Spring] ☎ 431-5160
Charles Cowles, 420 West Broadway
  [Prince/Spring] ☎ 925-3500
Sonnabend, 420 West Broadway
  [Prince/Spring] ☎ 966-6160

Edward Thorp, 103 Prince St.
  [Greene/Mercer] ☎ 431-6880
Luhring Augustine, 130 Prince St.
  [W. Bway/Wooster] ☎ 219-9600
Tanya Bonakdar, 130 Prince St.
  [W. Bway/Wooster] ☎ 925-8035
James Danziger, 130 Prince St.
  [W. Bway/Wooster] ☎ 226-0056

American Fine Arts, 22 Wooster St.
  [Grand/Canal] ☎ 941-0401
The Drawing Center, 35 Wooster St.
  [Broome/Grand] ☎ 219-2166
Peter Blum, 99 Wooster St.
  [Prince/Spring] ☎ 343-0441
Gagosian, 136 Wooster St.
  [Houston/Prince] ☎ 228-2828

Paul Kasmin, 74 Grand St.
  [Wooster/Greene] ☎ 219-3219
Deitch Projects, 76 Grand St.
  [Wooster/Greene] ☎ 343-7300

Postmasters, 80 Greene St.
  [Spring/Broome] ☎ 941-5711
Jay Gorney Modern Art, 100 Greene St.
  [Prince/Spring] ☎ 966-4480
Sperone Westwater, 142 Greene St.
  [Houston/Prince] ☎ 431-3685

John Weber, 142 Greene St.
  [Houston/Prince] ☎ 941-8727
Pace Wildenstein, 142 Greene St.
  [Houston/Prince] ☎ 431-9224

Ronald Feldman, 31 Mercer St.
  [Canal/Grand] ☎ 226-3232
Holly Solomon, 172 Mercer St.
  [Houston/Prince] ☎ 941-5777

Petra Bungert, 225 Lafayette St.
  [Spring/Kenmare] ☎ 925-0200

Thread Waxing Space, 476 Broadway
  [Broome/Grand] ☎ 966-9520
P.P.O.W., 532 Broadway
  [Prince/Spring] ☎ 941-8642
Max Protetch, 560 Broadway
  [Prince/Spring] ☎ 966-5454
Julie Saul, 560 Broadway
  [Prince/Spring] ☎ 431-0747
Jack Shainman, 560 Broadway
  [Prince/Spring] ☎ 966-3866
Janet Borden, 560 Broadway
  [Prince/Spring] ☎ 431-0166
Monique Knowlton, 568 Broadway
  [Prince] ☎ 966-2625
John Gibson, 568 Broadway
  [Prince] ☎ 925-1192
Leo Castelli, 578 Broadway
  [Houston/Prince] ☎ 431-6279
Lowinsky, 578 Broadway
  [Prince] ☎ 226-5440
Jose Freire, 580 Broadway
  [Houston/Prince] ☎ 941-8611

Paula Cooper, 534 W. 21st St.
  [9th/10th] ☎ 674-0766
Matthew Marks, 522 W. 22nd St.
  [10th/11th] ☎ 243-1650
Pat Hearn, 530 W. 22nd St.
  [10th/11th] ☎ 727-7366

Annina Nosei, 530 W. 22nd St.
[10th/11th] ☎ 741-8695
Barbara Gladstone, 513-523 W. 24th St.
[10th/11th] ☎ 431-3334
Metro Pictures, 513-523 W. 24th St.
[10th/11th] ☎ 206-7100
Greene/Naftali, 526 W. 26th St.
[10th/11th] ☎ 463-7770

Mary Boone, 745 Fifth Ave.
[57th/58th] ☎ 752-2929

Joseph Helman, 20 W. 57th St.
[5th/6th] ☎ 245-2888
Galerie Lelong, 20 W. 57th St.
[5th/6th] ☎ 315-0470
Galerie St. Etienne, 24 W. 57th St.
[5th/6th] ☎ 245-6734
Marian Goodman, 24 W. 57th St.
[5th/6th] ☎ 977-7160

Marlborough, 40 W. 57th St.
[5th/6th] ☎ 541-4900
Tibor De Nagy, 41 W. 57th St.
[5th/6th] ☎ 421-3780
Janis, 110 W. 57th St.
[6th/7th] ☎ 586-0110

Pace Wildenstein, 32 E. 57th St.
[5th/Mad] ☎ 421-3292
Andre Emmerich, 41 E. 57th St.
[5th/Mad] ☎ 752-0124
Marisa Del Re, 41 E. 57th St.
[5th/Mad] ☎ 688-1843
Robert Miller, 41 E. 57th St.
[5th/Mad] ☎ 980-5454
Schmidt Bingham, 41 E. 57th St.
[5th/Mad] ☎ 888-1122
Zabriskie, 41 E. 57th St.
[5th/Mad] ☎ 752-1223

ARTS ARCHIVES & LIBRARIES

ANTHOLOGY FILM ARCHIVES

Anthology Film Archives, 32 Second Ave. [2nd] ☎ 505-5181, considers itself "a museum of the cinema." The collection contains over 10,000 independent and avant-garde films that are screened Thursday through Sunday evenings. The closed-stack library is available to scholars on request.

ARCHIVES OF AMERICAN ART

Archives of American Art, a part of the Smithsonian Institution, maintains a regional research center at 1285 Ave. of the Americas [51st/52nd] in the Paine Webber building ☎ 399-5015. Over 12 million items relating to the visual arts, including a number of oral histories, are on microfilm. The lobby area of the archives has a small ex-

hibition area where they show the most recent acquisitions. On a recent visit, some letters from Barnett Newman to Clifford Styll advise Mr. Styll of the arrival of Mark Rothko in NY. M–F, 8:30–4:30. No appt. is necessary.

FRICK LIBRARY

The Frick Library, 10 East 71st St. [5th/Mad] ☎ 288-8700, used to limit its use to art professionals and academics. It's an incomparable resource of photographs and information on European (and some American) paintings, sculpture, and drawings from the fourth through the twentieth century. And it's open to the public.

The idea for the library came from Helen Clay Frick, daughter of Henry Frick, and was designed as a memorial to her father. Inspired by Miss Frick's visit to Sir Robert Witt's library in London (now at the Courtauld), she started her own collection in the bowling alley of the original residence. Later it was moved to a building on what became 71st St., and finally to its current location, adjacent to the Frick Collection. It was begun in 1920 and has grown to include over 750,000 photographs of art. These images, mounted on board, have pertinent information about the artist, dates, period, references, provenance, where the work is now, and so on. Everything is exhaustively cross-referenced. Photos are divided by school: British, Spanish, French, etc., and then subdivided: Women in Profile, Group Portraits from 19th century Italy, Paintings of Dogs from Germany in the 18th century, etc. It also has one of the largest collections (64,000) of auction sale catalogs in the world, sometimes useful in tracing the provenance of a painting. The library has 177,000 books devoted exclusively to art.

To use the library, you will need to have identification, fill in a short card, and sign in and out. Though there is no dress code, a certain decorum is still expected, and you will be asked what you are researching. If it is your first visit, the librarians ask that you come before 2:30 in the afternoon so that you can take the required orientation tour. You must check your coat downstairs, along with all briefcases, bags, even pens. Only pencils and the barest necessities may be brought in. Nothing from the collection ever leaves the library. Photocopies are available with many restrictions, depending on the book, though photos of the mounted images are not restricted. If you are working on a project, books can be reserved for you for a period of time. Two or three librarians are on duty at all times for assistance. The room itself is elegant, contains four long tables, and holds 32 people. There are two Guardis on the wall and five large windows that let in a lot of light. The librarians are formal, knowledgeable, but not especially endearing. Once they get to know you, they'll loosen up a bit. M–F, 10–4; Sat., 10–Noon; closed August and Saturdays in June and July.

NY PUBLIC LIBRARY FOR THE PERFORMING ARTS

NY Library for the Performing Arts, ☎ 870-1630, at Lincoln Center next door to the Beaumont, is one of the most exten-

LOUIS ARMSTRONG ARCHIVE

Louis Armstrong fans (and who's not?) take note: The **Louis Armstrong Archive,** open to the public, is located in The Rosenthal Library on the Queens College Campus. All of Mr. Armstrong's personal effects and the home he lived in in Corona, Queens, were left to Queens College (his home is expected to open to the public in a few years).

There are 5,000 personal photographs, 85 scrapbooks, and 600 reel-to-reel recordings that Mr. Armstrong personally made, as well as diaries, letters, and five of his trumpets. The archive is run by Michael Cogswell, who can be reached at ☎ 718-997-3670. The space is small, so visits need to be arranged on an appointment basis.

sive collections of theatre, film, music, dance, and other performing arts materials in the world. If you're researching the arts, you'll find it here: books, magazines, clippings, records, and music scores. M, 12–8; T, W, 12–6; Th, 12–8; Fr, Sa, 12–6; Su, closed.

POETS' HOUSE

Begun in 1984 with seed money from Stanley Kunitz, **Poets' House,** 72 Spring St. [Crosby/Lafayette] ☎ 431-7920, could be called poets' haven. They maintain a library of over 30,000 volumes of poetry and keep current issues of many small poetry magazines that can be used on the premises. No appointment is necessary to sit in one of the comfy old chairs of this quiet space, reading for pleasure or researching. Each fall they exhibit all of the poetry books published in the United States in the previous calendar year.

SHUBERT ARCHIVES

The Shubert brothers, Broadway theatre owners and producers, built what became the largest theatre organization on Broadway (and around the country). During the decades when they were active, beginning in 1900, they amassed a large collection of correspondence, business records, scripts, architectural plans, costume designs, and so on. The collection is available to serious researchers on application to the **Shubert Archives,** ☎ 944-3895, at the top of the Lyceum Theatre.

BIRDWATCHING

The **National Audubon Society** is at 700 Broadway [E. 4th] ☎ 979-3000. Each year they organize two bird counts. The Birdathon takes place in the spring and, in winter, there is the Christmas Bird Count. A library here can be visited by appointment.
NYC Audubon Society, 71 W. 23rd St. [6th/7th] ☎ 691-7483, conducts birdwatching outings in Central Park, Jamaica Bay, and other nearby locations. Each outing is $4 for nonmembers. They also have a small, noncirculating library.
Rare Bird Alert, ☎ 979-3070, has recorded daily announcements of bird sightings.
The **Urban Park Rangers,** ☎ 800-201-6275, lead birdwatching tours in the city parks. Call for a schedule.

BOATING

The Loeb Boathouse, 74th and East Drive ☎ 517-2233. The Gondola can be reserved for groups up to six. $30 for half an hour. Rowboats are $10 per hour.
Circle Line, Pier 83 Hudson River [43rd] and at South St. Seaport Pier 16 ☎ 563-3200. Three-hour trip around the island, $18.

Cloud 9, ☎ 718-428-5003, is a 95-foot yacht built for entertaining. It leaves from the World's Fair Marina near Shea Stadium. Four-hour dinner cruises with open bar, deejay entertainment. $69.95. Can be chartered for weddings and other parties up to 149 guests.

Great Hudson Sailing Center's Sunset Cruises leave every Fri., Sat., and Sun. in season from Chelsea Pier, the Hudson River and 23rd St. It's a two-hour sail with wine and cheese on a 43-foot sailboat. A bargain-priced $49. Six people max. They also rent sailboats. ☎ 741-7245.

Honey Fitz, World Financial Center ☎ 742-0233. Used by five U.S. Presidents, but mostly associated with JFK, the boat has been restored and can be rented for private functions. A three-hour dinner cruise for 40 guests is approximately $6,500.

Jack's Bait & Tackle, 551 City Island Ave. [Cross] the Bronx ☎ 718-885-2042, has motorboats seating four. $40 for a full day weekdays, $50 weekends.

The **Lettie G. Howard,** ☎ 748-8590, is a restored two-masted fishing boat originally launched in 1893. It is docked now at the South St. Seaport and takes amateur sailors on weekend sails, sometimes up the Hudson. $250 puts you on the boat from Friday evening to Sunday afternoon. You sleep in bunks and get meals on Sat. and Sun. There are no showers on board, but facilities are available at marinas along the way.

NY Waterways, ☎ 800-533-3779, has a day cruise to Sleepy Hollow. $35 takes you past the Tappan Zee onto a bus to Philipsburg Manor and Sleepy Hollow. (Admissions are included.) Their boat to Kykuit, the Rockefeller home in Pocantico Hills, is $50 for the full day trip. They also run short ferry services to Port Imperial, Hoboken, Jersey City, and Hunter's Point. Fares are $2–$4.50.

The Petrel, ☎ 825-1976, is a 70-foot ex–ocean racing boat that holds 36 people. There are a variety of public cruises during the day and evening, leaving from the southeast corner of Battery Park. A 45-minute ride can be taken during the lunch hour. Prices range from $9–$26 for evening cruises. Season is from May 15–Oct. 1. Any time that the Petrel is not conducting public cruises, it can be booked for private sails.

The Pioneer Schooner, ☎ 748-8786, built in 1885 and restored several times since then, is docked at the South St. Seaport. In season, May–Sept., it makes tours of NY Harbor, Ellis, Liberty, and Governor's Islands and runs tours on Memorial Day, July 4th, and Labor Day to see fireworks. It can be chartered for private affairs of up to 40 people. A two-hour charter is $850.

Royal Princess and Excalibur, ☎ 718-934-1014. Dinner cruise around Manhattan with live music. $60 weekdays, $70 Saturdays.

Spirit of New York, Pier 62, the Hudson at W. 23rd ☎ 727-2789. A dinner theatre cruise where the waiters and waitresses perform a Broadway revue. Sun.–Fri. $59, Sat. $72.

Staten Island Ferry ☎ 442-7070. Thirty minutes, 50¢.

Statue of Liberty/Ellis Island Ferry ☎ 269-5755. Adults, $7. Children, $3.

Ventura Yachts, ☎ 516-944-8415, represents a number of private yachts that can be hired for parties, weddings, and corporate events. Prices vary by boat.

World Yacht Cruises, Pier 81 Hudson River and 41st St. ☎ 630-8100. Four-course dinner cruise with dancing. $65 weekdays, $75 Saturdays.

For more on Sailing, see the Sports chapter.

CHAMBER MUSIC

Bargemusic, Fulton Ferry Landing in Brooklyn ☎ 718-624-4061, pulls off the feat of presenting first-rate classical music twice a week in a small town setting with spectacular views of Manhattan. It's the best place for chamber music in New York. The secret ingredient? Olga Bloom. Ms. Bloom, who was 75 in April of 1995, has run this enterprise since 1977, and her touch is all over it. Ms. Bloom and her late husband both played violin, she under Stokowski, he under Toscanini. When her husband passed away, Ms. Bloom, who was born in Boston and always lived near water, decided to provide an intimate atmosphere where people could come together to play and listen to chamber music. So she did what anyone would do: She set up shop on a barge in the East River. You won't think much of the barge from the outside, but inside is a different matter: It's enchanting. So, too, when you listen to the musicians who, since there is no stage, perform within arm's reach. The barge tends to sway a bit, sometimes in tempo, usually not.

Bargemusic artists come from all over to play in these most unusual surroundings, and the quality of playing is exceptional. Programs usually involve at least a piano, violin, cello, and well-known composers. Sometimes the musicians will introduce the works and say a few words about the pieces.

Before the concert and during intermission, a dedicated corps of volunteers has some snacks and beverages ready. People then wander on to the deck to enjoy the view of Manhattan, though you can enjoy the skyline behind the musicians while they play. (In fact, we think the front row here is one of the great views in the city.) You could certainly have a nice Sunday by having

brunch at River Cafe (next door) and then going to Bargemusic. Bargemusic does a few candlelight dinners, cooked by volunteers, with cocktails, supper, a concert, and dessert at intermission. It's $75, $50 of which is a tax-deductible contribution to Bargemusic. Regular tickets are $24.

Strictly speaking, the concerts at the **Cloisters** are not chamber music. But the combination of the setting—the stone Fuentidueña Chapel (brought to Fort Tryon Park from the church of San Martin, north of Madrid)—and the small groups who play here one or two Sundays each month—is often quite transporting. You will find lutes, plainchant, polyphony, morality and mystery plays, and a yearly Christmas program by the Waverly Consort. The simple musical lines, with their unusual harmonies, relax and unburden the modern listener. The chapel seats 265, and sells out quickly, so reserve tickets by phone ☎ 650-2290. They're $17–$30.

One or two Sundays each month, **The Frick Collection,** 1 E. 70th St. [5th] ☎ 288-0700, presents free concerts of classical music. String quartets, small vocal ensembles, and pianists perform in the 200-seat round music room, part of John Russell Pope's 1930s addition to the original mansion. The room has patterned velvet walls, a skylight, three panel paintings by Fragonard, and wonderful acoustics. It's chamber music in a proper chamber. The low, shallow stage provides little barrier between the musicians and the audience. And when the guards slide the pocket doors closed, there is a sense of being sealed off from the world. Unfortunately, luck and planning are required to acquire the free tickets for these concerts. The

Frick's version of crowd control is that they need to receive your written request (include a SASE) for tickets (no fax, no hand deliveries, no overnight mail) on the third Monday before the concert.

When classes are in session, **The Juilliard School** presents student and faculty concerts several times each week. Classmates, who make up part of the audience, cheer lustily at the end of the piece. The concerts are free and come in two categories: either no ticket required (you can just show up) or ticket required (you go to the Juilliard Box Office, ☎ 769-7406, up to two weeks before the performance to pick up a free ticket). There are some afternoon concerts, but most take place in the evening.

From time to time, **The Knitting Factory,** 74 Leonard St. [Bway/Church] ☎ 219-3006, presents chamber music for those who have both ears in the 20th century and their desire for musical surprise intact. Musicians play original compositions or improvise on what once were called the Great Masters, mostly on electrified instruments. Music is often roguishly tongue-in-cheek (like Dave Douglas's two-minute composition "Invasive Procedures"), rhythms can be broken, harmonies come and go. You can hear much fine musicianship and sometimes achingly beautiful pieces. Tradition takes a walk when a quartet can be made up of violin, bassviol, drums, and trumpet.

The Chamber Music Society of Lincoln Center performs a full schedule of programs at **Alice Tully Hall** each season. They offer sophisticated thematic concerts, occasional symposiums, lectures, and, once in a while, pre-concert wine and cheese. Performers from other chamber groups join them from time to time. Ticket prices are around $35 ☎ 875-5788. During the hall's construction

Ms. Tully insisted that the seating be comfortable here. It is and the sound is as soothing as warm soup.

Merkin Concert Hall, 129 W. 67th St. [Bway/WEA] ☎ 362-8719. This small auditorium, in the shade of Lincoln Center, rewards listeners with imaginative programming (like the Jewish Chamber Music Series or all of Bartok's quartets played in one day), there are some early (6 P.M.) concerts, modest ticket prices, good acoustics, and a musically savvy audience.

Concerts at the **Metropolitan Museum of Art** take place mostly in the Grace Rainey Rogers Auditorium, in front of the Christmas tree at holiday times, and, occasionally, in the Temple of Dendur. Generally, concerts are produced in series, sometimes thematic (Music in the Age of the Enlightenment), sometimes presenting a single composer, though tickets are often offered on a single-concert basis. The "Speaking of Music" series, given on late Saturday afternoons, starts with a discussion followed by a concert. Musicians, like the Juilliard and Guarneri String Quartets, are world class. The sound in the 708-seat auditorium, while clear, loses a sense of presence in the balcony. Occasionally, if the artists permit, there are seats on the stage. To get a schedule of events and ticket information ☎ 570-3949.

The **Miller Theater at Columbia University,** 116th and Broadway ☎ 854-1633, has won the Chamber Music America/ASCAP Award for Adventurous Programming. You are likely to hear rigorous moderns like Carter, Crumb, or Wourinen played most often by musicians who have devoted themselves to this repertoire. It's a wide, shallow auditorium, and you will feel close to the stage unless you are in the absolute outermost seats.

Three times each year, Eugenia Zuckerman hosts an event that is part concert, part reading, and part music-appreciation class. These civilizing respites of flute and piano take place in the **Celeste Bartos Forum at the New York Public Library,** a marble-walled beauty with a cast iron framed oval skylight. Held on Tuesdays at 6 P.M., the concert catches you after the rigors of the workday, and in an hour and a quarter shakes the clang of the city out of you and sends you out into the evening with the words and the music of great composers in your ears. Pianist Anthony Newman appears with Ms. Zuckerman and gives a cunning piano demonstration before each piece. Tickets, $8.50, can be obtained from the Public Library Education Dept. ☎ 930-0571 or by stopping in the Library shop. No phone sales. 500 unreserved seats.

Nicholas Roerich, an artist, philosopher, and explorer born in Russia, spent time in France and America. He believed in a relationship between culture and world peace. To that end, the **Nicholas Roerich Museum,** 319 W. 107th St. [Bway/RSD] ☎ 864-7752, offers free chamber concerts most every Sunday at 5 P.M. Sitting in the second floor music room, with about 80 seats, is like visiting a cultured home in Eastern Europe. The walls are covered with Mr. Roerich's paintings, and his sculptures of Buddhas and Shivas are displayed on the heavy wooden furniture. Music students, Russian emigrés, and Upper West Siders attend this almost unknown venue. The performers, who often come from the Philharmonic, are playing music that they don't get a chance to perform in the larger group.

DANCING

Au Bar, 41 E. 58th St. [Park/Mad] ☎ 308-9455. Recorded music with deejay from Sinatra to rap. $15–$25 admission, 9 P.M.–4 A.M. Food: dinner, late-night breakfast. 7 days a week. Dress: Black tie to leather.

Cafe Pierre in the Pierre Hotel, Fifth Ave. and 63rd St. ☎ 940-8185. A trio plays music from the '30s to the '50s with a jazz overtone. If you don't dine there, it's a $10 cover. Thurs., Fri., Sat. dancing from 9 P.M.–1 A.M. Food: fine French in a formal setting. Dress: jacket and tie for men, "elegant for women."

Contra Dance ☎ 459-4080. Call for schedule of events, held most often at Metropolitan Duane Hall Church, 201 W. 13th St. [7th]. It's something like British square or country dancing. $7–$11, generally from 8 P.M. Beginners should come at 7:45 and the caller will talk them through basic moves. Food: light refreshments. Dress: casual.

Dance Manhattan, 39 W. 19th St. [5th/6th], 5th fl. ☎ 807-0802. Ballroom, R & B, tango, and Latin. $4–$10. Classes most nights at 8. Dances held a couple of times each month at 9 P.M. Food: refreshments. Dress: neatly casual.

Delia's, 197 E. 3rd St. [Ave. A/B] ☎ 254-9184. Recorded music, lots of styles. $10 cover, Fri., Sat., from 10 P.M. on. Food: At 8 P.M., a four-course meal is served. Dress: pearls to nose rings.

Denim & Diamonds, 511 Lexington Ave. [48th] ☎ 371-1600. Dancing from 6 P.M. to 4 A.M. Country music with deejay, live bands sometimes on weekends. $5–$10 cover. Classes at 7 P.M. and 8 P.M. Food: bar food. Dress: casual.

The Hideaway, 32 W. 37th St. [5th/6th] ☎ 947-8940. Live duos (e.g., piano, guitar). No cover, no min. Mon.–Sat., variable hours. Food: full menu available. Dress: jacket required. Small dance floor, not hip and intends to stay that way.

The Latin Quarter, 2551 Broadway [95th/96th] ☎ 864-7600. Live top Latin bands. Call for schedule. Food: none. Dress: casual.

Les Poulets Cafe, 16 W. 22nd St. [5th/6th] ☎ 229-2000. Two floors with a deejayed disco on one and Latin music on the other. Live music on the Latin floor on most weekends. Admission, $5–$15, Wed.–Sun., 5 P.M. to late (2–3–4 A.M.). Food: Spanish. Dress: neat casual, no sneakers or T-shirts.

Marc Ballroom, 27 Union Square W. [16th/17th] ☎ 867-3789. Deejayed ballroom and Latin. $10. Every other Sunday night from 7 P.M.–12 A.M. Food: snacks. Dress: all types.

Midsummer Night Swing, in the fountain Plaza at Lincoln Center Plaza ☎ 875-5102. Live bands play a different music each night: waltz, swing, salsa, Cajun, etc. $8. July and August Wed. to Sat. from 8:15–11 P.M. Food: available at the Fountain Cafe. Dress: all types.

Mike Cerrati's, 225 58th St. [2nd/3rd] ☎ 688-8889. Mike Cerrati trio plays Fats Waller to Billy Joel. No cover, no min. Nightly from 8 P.M. (9 P.M. Fri., Sat.). Food: Italian. Dress: jacket required.

Nell's, 246 W. 14th St. [7th/8th] ☎ 675-1567. Mostly live, hip music. $7–$15. Dancing from 11 P.M. Food: supper menu. Dress: no jeans, no sneakers.

New York Swing Dance Society, Irving Plaza at 17 Irving Place [15th] ☎ 696-9737. Live swing $13 for nonmembers. Dancing every Sun., 8–midnight. Call for details about practice nights and lessons.

North River Bar, 145 Hudson St. [Hubert/Beach] ☎ 226-9411. West Coast swing with deejay John Festa. $6. Tues. evenings 9–12. Food: none. Dress: casual.

Rainbow Room, 30 Rockefeller Plaza ☎ 632-5100. The Rainbow Room Orchestra plays swing and alternates with a Latin band. Dinner and dancing Tues.–Sat., 7:30 P.M.–1 A.M.; Sun., 6 P.M.–9 P.M. On Tues., Wed., and Thurs. you can skip their dinner and dance after 11 P.M. (but you must have a reservation, which you make the same day you want to dance). $20 cover. Food: classic continental. Dress: jacket and tie.

Red Blazer Too, 349 W. 46th St. [8th/9th] ☎ 262-3112. Live music every night and Sunday brunch. Type of music changes each night. Tuesdays, George Gee and his 17-piece orchestra from 8–12. $5 cover, two drink min. If you are dining there, no min. Full bar and restaurant service. Dress: informal.

Roseland Ballroom, 239 W. 52nd St. [Bway/8th] ☎ 247-0200. Ballroom dancing, recorded and live music. Thurs. and Sun. 2:30–11 P.M. Admission $7–$11. Food: cafeteria. Dress: jacket required. Call ahead because sometimes the dancing is bumped by the concert schedule.

SOBs, 204 Varick St. [7th Ave. S.] ☎ 243-4940. Always live, mostly throbbing, Brazilian and world music. Call for schedule. Cover: $15. Food: Brazilian/ Caribbean. Dress: casual.

Supper Club, 240 W. 47th St. [Bway/8th] ☎ 921-1940. Live '40s-style big band. $15 music charge. $12–$20 min. Fri. and Sat., 8 P.M.–midnight. Food: American. Dress: jacket and tie.

Tatou, 151 E. 50th St. [Lex/3rd] ☎ 753-1144. Deejay spins "fast pop" after 11 P.M., six nights each week. $10–$20 cover. Dinner served from 5:30 to 11:30. Food: American/French. Dress: jacket and tie required. Out-on-the-town decor.

Tavern on the Green, Central Park West and 67th St. ☎ 873-3200. Recorded music with deejay. Cover $5–$10. Tues.–Sun., dancing from 9 P.M., outside in the summer months only. Food: full menu. Dress: casual.

Tea Dancing, Park Ave. Plaza, 55 E. 52nd St. [Park/Mad]. Swing band. Free. Third Sat. of every month, 3 P.M.–6 P.M.

Times Squares, at the Lesbian and Gay Community Center, 208 W. 13th St. [7th/8th] ☎ 620-7310. Square dancing to recorded music with a live caller for experienced dancers. Mostly for lesbians and gays, but all are welcome. $6. The second and fourth Friday of each month at 7:30

P.M. Food: none. Dress: casual. Lessons are offered from Sept. to May. Write to POB 1229, Ansonia Station, 10023 for info.

View at the Marriott Marquis, 1535 Broadway [45th/46th] ☎ 398-1900. Sun., Mon., recorded, Tues.–Sat., live jazz and top 40. After 9 P.M., $5 cover, 1 drink min. Food: full dinner or buffet available. Dress: no jeans or sneakers.

World Yacht Cruises and other boats: See Boating in this chapter.

MORE **Worldtone Music,** 230 Seventh Ave. [23rd/24th] ☎ 691-1934, which has a kind of '40s, black-and-white movie, pleasantly musty feel, specializes in dance items. Owner Kenneth Spear has been here since 1980, and he sells a lot of ballroom shoes for men and women ($65–$110). Mr. Spear spent 40 years teaching international folk dancing, so he also has a lot of CDs, tapes, and some 45s of dance music for folk and ballroom dancing, as well as Hawaiian, Romanian, African, and Latin dance music. Ballet and tap shoes are available for children and adults, and Mr. Spear will also sell you the taps and recommend a shoemaker who will put them on the shoes.

FOLK MUSIC

Folk Fone, ☎ 674-2508, for a list of singers and groups and their dates and locations around the five boroughs.

GO

Go is a 4,000-year-old game that originated in India but spread to China and other Asian nations. It has changed very little. It's a game of skill and strategy like chess and has no element of chance in it. Unlike chess, you begin with an empty board on which you place and move black and white pieces. A player tries to surround, and thus win, territory. According to Michael Simon, publisher of *Learn to Play Go: A Master's Guide to the Ultimate Game* by Janice Kim and Jeong Soo-hyn, "You can learn the rules in five minutes, but it takes a lifetime to master." A good place to learn is the **New York Go Center,** 323 E. 52nd St. [1st/2nd] ☎ 223-0342. You can stop in and ask the club manager, Jun Umebayashi, to get you started, or you can attend one of their beginner classes (once a week for six weeks, $30). The club is the three floors of a very pleasant-looking town house, complete with a backyard. They've got 100 or so members, about half Asian and half American.

JAZZ

While the appeal of jazz continues to go global, New York City remains the capital of the form. In any given week, you can see a dozen world-class performers in the clubs. The focus of this article is some of the city's steady gigs. These were originally booked during the off times (Monday nights and weekend brunches), but have now become events in their own right. Three other series have been in existence so long that they are very much a part of the jazz scene. Most of these performances sell out on a regular basis, so reservations are needed. Tiny tables, group seating, perfunctory drink service are the norm.

SUNDAYS

It's practically a love fest for **Doc Cheatham** at Sweet Basil, 88 Seventh Ave. S. [Bleecker/W. 4th] ☎ 242-1785. He's been performing here since 1976 at the "oldest jazz brunch in the country." He plays the trumpet as sweetly as ever and sings "These Foolish Things" and other standards. Expect to be reminded of New Orleans and listen for the stride piano of Chuck Folds. No music charge, $10 minimum for each set. Brunch starts at noon, Doc plays sets from 2 to 6.

Jay Leonhart and "his friends," an ad hoc quartet, created each week from 10 or so of Mr. Leonhart's favorite sidemen, have been at the Blue Note, 131 W. 3rd St. [6th/Bleecker] ☎ 475-8592, every Sunday afternoon since 1986. Mr. Leonhart does two shows, at 1 P.M. and 3:30 P.M., mixing his "little poems" with some jazz standards. The vernacular poems are really songs about the exasperations and exhilarations of daily life—alternate side of the street parking, cholesterol levels, or relationships. In one number, he explains why it is impossible to sing and play the bass at the same time (while, in fact, doing it). Mr. Leonhart's introductions may be oblique, but you're being set up. $14.50 gets you a humdrum brunch, a drink, and the show.

MONDAYS

Michael Dorf, the owner of the cutting edge Knitting Factory, 74 Leonard St. [Church/Bway] ☎ 219-3055, says, "The **David Murray Big Band** can play here every Monday night into perpetuity as far as I'm concerned." This is the best band playing in New York at this time—the hottest, the meanest, and, at times, the fastest. It is Mr. Murray's unique style as a composer and as

F. NATALICI

The David Murray Big Band.

a saxophonist to alternate and sometimes overlap the usually opposing camps of swing and progressive jazz. While he does not conduct every week, the band (we've counted as many as 20 musicians onstage, and there is always a tuba and French horn) delivers his original compositions with high energy. When he does conduct, the musicians seem positively driven. Shows at 8 P.M. and 10 P.M., $12 and $14 admission, no minimum.

Maria Schneider is the star on Monday nights at Visiones, 125 MacDougal St. [W. 3rd] ☎ 673-5576, where she leads a 17-piece Jazz Orchestra. She approaches the bandstand (which is actually the end of one of the long tables running the length of the room) with an armload of music and a sense of assurance. Ms. Schneider writes her own charts for standards and composes original pieces. She has an astonishing range of compositional skills: elements of bebop, French impressionism, rock and roll, and flamenco are likely to be heard in any set. Soloists are often supported by small combos within the band, rather than just the rhythm section. Every Monday since 1986. Sets at 9 P.M. and 11 P.M. $5 music charge, $10 minimum at tables, $10 charge at bar includes 1 drink.

The Village Vanguard, 178 Seventh Ave. S. [W. 11th] ☎ 255-4037, is the final stop for the jazz pilgrim. Max Gordon opened it in 1935 and his widow, Lorraine Gordon, now presents the great and the legendary weekly. The **Vanguard Jazz Orchestra** sits on the enlarged stage every Monday night. Started in 1966 by Thad Jones and Mel Lewis, it is currently under the laid-back leadership of Ray Mosca (instead of conducting, Mr. Mosca calls out a tune number, waits for everyone to find the music, and

counts off from the middle row). Part of the enjoyment of an evening there is listening to his dry commentary between songs. They play charts from the Thad Jones/Mel Lewis era, as well as from current members like Jim McNeely. A good listening, swinging band with mellifluous and tight ensemble playing. Sets at 9:30 P.M. and 11:30 P.M. $12 cover, $10 minimum.

THURSDAYS

In the low-ceilinged basement of Fez, 380 Lafayette St. [Great Jones/E. 4th] ☎ 533-7000, the regular bookings are a mixed bag of pop performers, poetry slams, and some jazz, but every Thursday night since 1991, **The Mingus Big Band** has played two sets (9:30 P.M. and 11:15 P.M.). When bassist

CHRIS MILITSCHER

The Mingus Big Band performing at Fez.

Charles Mingus died in 1979 of Lou Gehrig's disease, he left behind over 300 compositions. The band works from a list of over 40 pieces, taking on the longer suites (like "The Black Saint and the Sinner Lady") and some of the more difficult works. Moody, lyrical, cacophonous, sometimes consecutively, this is densely textured music. Sue Mingus, his widow, sets up the 14-piece band that draws from a 150-member pool of musicians. There is no telling who will be there—we have heard David Murray, Kenny Drew, Jr., and Randy Brecker. Mr. Mingus is a tough act to follow, but Andy McKee, onstage most weeks, is a strong bassist. $18 cover with two drink minimum.

SEASONAL

Four times a year, **Dr. Billy Taylor** does a very good job of turning the Grace Rainey Rogers Auditorium at the Metropolitan Museum of Art, of all places, into a comfortable room to listen to jazz and to talk about it. Playing with his trio, the inventive Chip Jackson on bass and Steve Johns on drums, Dr. Taylor invites a guest performer, often a horn player, but sometimes a vocalist, to play along. The musicians play and talk among themselves on stage, and the audience has an opportunity to ask questions. The relaxed and sophisticated grace of Dr. Taylor makes this one of the most civilized events in town. ☎ 570-3949 for the $25 tickets and info on dates.

Bobby Short's tenure at the Cafe Carlyle, 35 E. 76th St. [Mad] ☎ 744-1600, is in its third decade. Mr. Short isn't strictly a jazz singer, and, in fact, calls himself "a saloon singer." He has two extended engagements in the room each year. Seated at the Baldwin, under the "surprise pink, special lavender" lights, Mr. Short's runaway train performance is fueled by a percussive piano style, stoked by articulation. The one-hour set has station stops at American Standards, Down-and-Dirty Blues, and Cole Porter. Service at the Carlyle is rushed, and you can find yourself in some pretty uncomfortable positions trying to see Mr. Short. It's $45 ($25 at the bar), dining and drinks additional, no minimum.

Jack Kleinsinger began producing his joyous **Highlights in Jazz** series in 1973, making it the longest-running series (and at $17, the cheapest) in town. Concerts take place at Pace Auditorium, Spruce St. [Park Row/Gold] ☎ 346-1715. Mr. Kleinsinger produces eight concerts a year loosely based around a theme like "The Art of Swinging." The guests can include anyone in town or passing through. We've seen Jane Jarvis, Marian McPartland, Jon Faddis, Ruth Brown, and Steve Turre. Each concert features a surprise guest. Since Mr. Kleinsinger has known most of these musicians for many years, he gets some great combinations for all-star jam sessions. To get on the mailing list, call ☎ 982-3697 or write to Highlights in Jazz, 7 Peter Cooper Rd., New York, NY 10010.

MORE Les Paul has taken up residence at Iridium, 44 W. 63rd St. [Col/Bway] ☎ 582-2121, on Monday nights. Sets are at 8:30 and 10:30. $20 cover, $10 min.

MOVIES, THEATRE, TV, & VIDEO

BOOKS

Applause, 211 W. 71st St. [Bway/WEA] ☎ 496-7511, **Drama Bookshop,** 723 Seventh Ave. [48th/49th] ☎ 944-0595, and **Richard Stoddard Performing Arts Books,** 18 E. 16th St. [5th/Union Sq. W.] ☎ 645-9576.

FILM MAGAZINES

In addition to Jerry Ohlinger's store, listed on p. 17 under Memorabilia, **Jay-Bee,** 134 W. 26th St. [6th/7th] ☎ 675-1600, has been hoarding magazines for decades. There's no browsing, but they have back issues of all kinds of publications from the last

100 years and fan and movie mags from the '30s–'50s, with 20,000 movie mags in all. If you know what you're looking for, they'll get it for you.

FILM & VIDEO SERIES & SCREENINGS

American Museum of the Moving Image, 35th Ave. and 36th St., Astoria ☎ 718-784-0077.

Anthology Film Archives, 32 Second Ave. [2nd] ☎ 505-5181. Thurs.–Sun. evenings. Independent and avant-garde films.

Bryant Park, ☎ 512-5700. Monday evenings in summer.

Charas, 605 E. 9th St. [B/C] ☎ 982-0627. May–Sept. International and student films dealing with social, often controversial, issues.

City Cinematheque on CUNY-TV, Channel 75. For more than ten years, Professor Jerry Carlson has been bringing unknown and classic films to local TV audiences.

Context Studios, 28 Ave. A [2nd/3rd] ☎ 505-2702. Occasional screenings of independent films and some animation.

Film Forum, 209 W. Houston St. [Varick/6th] ☎ 727-8110.

Harlan Jacobson's Talk Cinema is a series of screenings of independent films that have not yet been released. Mr. Jacobson, who was film critic at *Variety* for a number of years and the editor-in-chief of *Film Comment,* says he wants to bring us the kind of movie experience available "before the marketers took over film advertising." When you attend Talk Cinema, you will have nothing more than a list of credits in your hand—no advertising hype and no reviews. After each showing, there is a discussion. Mr. Jacobson invites a guest who is connected to the film (often the director or a performer) or a critic. ☎ 795-9221.

Human Rights Watch Film Festival, The Walter Reade, Lincoln Center Plaza ☎ 875-5600. June.

Japan Society, 333 E. 47th St. [1st/2nd] ☎ 832-1155, devotes screenings to Japanese film, historical programming, retrospectives, and current releases.

Knitting Factory, 72 Leonard St. [Bway/Church] ☎ 219-3006. Video, silent films, and other independents.

Le Madri, 168 W. 18th St. [7th] ☎ 727-8022. Sunday evenings in summer.

Lesbian and Gay Film Festival, The Public Theater, 425 Lafayette St. [Astor/E. 4th] ☎ 254-7228. June.

Margaret Mead Film Festival, The Museum of Natural History, Central Park West and 79th St. ☎ 769-5100. Late spring.

Millennium Films, 66 E. 4th St. [Bowery/2nd Ave.] ☎ 673-0090. Experimental and independent films.

MoMA, 11 W. 53rd St. [5th/6th] ☎ 708-9480. Daily screenings and the New Directors New Films Festival in March and April.

Museum of Television and Radio, 25 W. 52nd St. [5th/6th] ☎ 621-6800. TV on tape.

NY Film Festival, Lincoln Center ☎ 875-5610. Late September, early October.

NY Jewish Film Festival, The Walter Reade, Lincoln Center Plaza ☎ 875-5600. January.

NY Underground Film Festival, The NY Film Academy, 100 E. 17th St. [Park Ave S.] ☎ 674-4300. March.

NY Video Festival, Lincoln Center ☎ 875-5610. Late July, early August.

Symphony Space, 2537 Broadway [95th]

☎ 864-5400, shows double features of the classics.

Walter Reade, Lincoln Center Plaza ☎ 875-5600. Serious films, international series, independent nights. Schedule available in front of the theatre.

William Wolf, who's been teaching film courses at NYU for over 15 years, previews first-run movies—a mix of independents, commercial, and foreign films, shown just before or just at their release. There's a discussion, once in a while with a guest. ☎ 998-7171, for information.

GIFTS

The gift shop at the **American Museum of the Moving Image,** 36-01 35th Ave. [36th St.] Astoria ☎ 718-784-0077, is a great source of film-related gift items. You can find here, for example, books on film history, star bios, criticism, reference books, boxed sets of George Hurrell photos as postcards, movie camera lamps, posters, T-shirts, salt and pepper shakers—all movie- or TV-related . . . **Television City,** 64 W. 50th St. [5th/6th] ☎ 246-4234, for television-themed gifts.

M E M O R A B I L I A

Jerry Ohlinger's Movie Material Store, 242 W. 14th St. [7th/8th] ☎ 989-0869. The back room of Jerry Ohlinger's store is filled with files and boxes of star photos, magazines, postcards of celebs, and they sell posters of everything from *Babette's Feast* to *The Terminator*. There are loose-leaf reference binders. Some subjects, like Doris Day, have their own binder . . . **Movie Star News,** 134 W. 18th St. [6th/7th] ☎ 620-8160, is a garage space crammed full of color and black-and-white publicity stills of just about any star you'd want. When we were there, a customer came in and asked Paula, whose father started the place 50 years ago, for a shot of Julie Andrews in *The Sound of Music*. Paula shouted, "Jennifer, get me 2177!" There is also a good collection of movie posters . . . **J. Field's Gallery,** 55 W. 17th St. [5th/6th] ☎ 989-4520, for thousands of movie posters . . . **Motion Picture Arts Gallery,** 133 E. 58th St. [Park/Lex] ☎ 223-1009, is an upscale gallery that specializes in rare and older movie posters. Big

sellers include Louise Brooks, Cary Grant, Carole Lombard, and Veronica Lake, but not, interestingly, Bette Davis and Joan Crawford. Lobby cards are quite popular since many sell for around $200. They have many horror film posters . . . **Silver Screen,** 124 W. 36th St. [Bway/7th] ☎ 967-2419, is the place to call (it's not for browsing) for autographs, posters, and 1 1/2 million color and black-and-white photos from the '20s on. They're categorized by name and also by subject (stars with sunglasses, Art Deco, directors, and so on) . . . **Triton Gallery,** 323 W. 45th St. [8th/9th] ☎ 765-2472, is the best place in the city to buy theatrical posters and especially "window cards." These are the small placards that shows have printed to advertise themselves that you see in deli windows around Times Square. They can become collector's items if the show, star, or design are memorable. Window cards for shows start at $12. They also have large posters and postcard-sized souvenirs.

HANDICAPPED INFORMATION

See Wheelchair Access in the Information Chapter.

RESOURCES & RESEARCH

See Arts Archives & Libraries in this chapter.

SOUNDTRACKS & ORIGINAL CAST ALBUMS

Footlight Records, 113 E. 12th St. [3rd/4th] ☎ 533-1572, is almost certain to have the original cast recording or soundtrack to any show or movie you'd want, as well as albums by Yma Sumac, Mabel Mercer, or Nancy Walker.

THEATRICAL INFORMATION

Theatrical Index, published weekly, has the dope on virtually all current and upcoming NY shows and those around the country. It's $8 for a single issue at the Drama Bookshop or by subscription. Call ☎ 586-6343 . . . For London theatre you can subscribe to *London Theatre News* ☎ 517-8608 (see more in the Anglophilia article in the Feature chapter).

TICKETS/HOUSE SEATS

TKTS Booth, Bway and 47th St. Hours: M–Sa, 3–8; Wed. and Sat matinees: Tickets are available from 10–2; Sun. matinee:

from noon. TKTS in the World Trade Center, mezzanine, M–F, 11–3:30; Wed. and Sat. matinees: Tickets are available from 11 A.M. on the day before . . . **The Actor's Fund** has four house seats to every Broadway show, available to anyone, if you are willing to pay double the face value of the ticket and call within 48 hours prior to performance. Half of the ticket price is even tax deductible as a contribution to the Actor's Fund. Call ☎ 221-7300, ext. 133.

VIDEO

The chain with the most interesting videos is **Kim's,** with locations at 85 Ave. A [5th/6th] ☎ 529-3410; 133 Second Ave. [St. Mark's] ☎ 505-0311; 144 Bleecker St. [LaGuardia] ☎ 260-1010; and 350 Bleecker St. [10th] ☎ 675-8996. They're a bit grungy but completely savvy about films, and they include many foreign and independent movies. The stores are organized largely by *directors,* though there are categories such as "mindless action and senseless violence" . . . Rare videos can also be found at **Evergreen Video,** 228 W. Houston St. [Varick] ☎ 691-7362. They have over 5,000 titles and specialize in the hard-to-find and out-of-print . . . For obscure titles, also try **International Film & Video Center,** 989 First Ave. [54th/55th] ☎ 826-8848.

MUSEUMS

MAJOR MUSEUMS

Brooklyn Museum, 200 Eastern Parkway ☎ 718-638-5000. M, Tu, closed; W–Su, 10–5. Suggested contribution, $4.

Ellis Island ☎ 363-3200. Daily 9–5. Ferry tickets (includes admission) are $7, $3 for children.

The Frick Collection, 1 E. 70th St. [5th] ☎ 288-0700. M, closed; Tu–Sa, 10–6; Su, 1–6. Admission, $5. Seniors and students, $3. Children under 10 not admitted, ages 10–15 only with an adult.

Solomon R. Guggenheim Museum, 1071 Fifth Ave. [88th/89th] ☎ 423-3500.

Su–W, 10–6; Th, closed; Fri, Sa, 10–8. Admission, $7. Students and seniors, $4. Members and children under 12, free. **Guggenheim Museum Soho,** 575 Broadway [Prince] ☎ 423-3500. M, Tu, closed; W, Th, F, 11–6; Sa, 11–8; Su, 11–6. Admission, $5. A combination pass that gets you into both museums (valid for seven days) is available for $10.

Metropolitan Museum of Art, Fifth Ave. and 82nd St. Info line ☎ 535-7710, switchboard ☎ 879-5500. M, closed; Tu–Th, 9:30–5:15; Fr, Sa, 9:30–8:45; Su, 9:30–5:15. Suggested admission, $7.

MoMA, 11 W. 53rd St. [5th/6th] ☎ 708-9400. M, Tu, 11–6; W, closed; Th, F, 12–8:30; Sa, Su, 11–6. Admission, $8. Seniors and students, $5. Children under 16, free. Pay what you wish Th and F after 5:30.

Whitney Museum of American Art, 945 Madison Ave. [75th] ☎ 570-3676. M, Tu, closed; W, 11–6; Th, 1–8 with free admission after 6; F–Su, 11–6. Admission, $7. Seniors and students, $5. Children under 12 and members, free. The Whitney has a space in the Philip Morris Building, 120 Park Ave. [42nd] ☎ 878-2550. Admission is always free. M–W, 11–6; Th, 11–7:30; F, 11–6; Sa, Su, closed.

AFRICAN-AMERICAN

The Studio Museum in Harlem, 144 W. 125th St. [Lenox/ACP] ☎ 864-4500. M, Tu, closed; W–F, 10–5; Sa, Su, 1–6. Admission, $5. Seniors and students, $3. Children under 12, $1.

AMERICAN HISTORY

Fraunces Tavern Museum, 54 Pearl St. [Broad] ☎ 425-1778. M–F, 10–4:45; Sa, 12–4; Su, closed. Admission, $2.50.

Intrepid Sea Air Space Museum, Pier 86, 46th St. and Twelfth Ave. ☎ 245-2533. M, Tu, closed; W–Su, 10–5. Admission, $10. Children under 12, $5.

Museum of American Folk Art, 2 Lincoln Square [65th/66th] ☎ 977-7298. M, closed; Tu–Su, 11:30–7:30. Admission, free.

South Street Seaport Museum, 12 Fulton St. [South] ☎ 669-9400. M–Su, 10–5. Admission, $6. Children, $3.

ANIMALS

Bronx Zoo/Wildlife Conservation Park, Bronx River Pkwy and Fordham Rd. ☎ 718-367-1010. M–Su, 10–5. Admission, $5.75. Children, $2. Free on Wednesdays and reduced rates in winter months. Certain areas inside the park have additional fees.

Aquarium for Wildlife Conservation, West 8th and Surf Ave., Brooklyn ☎ 718-265-3474. M–F, 10–5; Sa, Su, 10–7. Admission, $6.75. Children, $3.

Central Park Wildlife Center, Fifth Ave. at 64th St. ☎ 861-6030. April–Oct., M–F, 10–5; Sa, Su, 10:30–5:30; Nov.–March, daily, 10–4:30. Admission, $2.50. Seniors, $1.25. Children ages 3–12, 50¢. Under 3 years, free. All children under 16 must be accompanied by an adult.

CHILDREN

Children's Museum of Manhattan, 212 W. 83rd St. [Bway/Amsterdam] ☎ 721-1234. M, 1:30–5:30; Tu, closed; W, Th, 1:30–5:30; F, Sa, Su, 10–5. Admission, $5.

Children's Museum of the Arts, 72 Spring St. [Bway/Crosby] ☎ 941-9198. M, closed; Tu–Su, 11–5. Admission, $4 weekdays, $5 weekends.

CONTEMPORARY MUSEUMS & ALTERNATIVE SPACES

Alternative Museum, 594 Broadway [Houston/Prince] ☎ 966-4444. M, closed; Tu–Sa, 11–6; Su, closed. Not open between exhibitions. Contribution requested.

Art in General, 79 Walker St. [Cortlandt/Lafayette] ☎ 219-0473. M, closed; Tu–Sa, 12–6; Su, closed. Occasional admission fees.

Dia Center for the Arts, 548 W. 22nd St. [11th] ☎ 989-5912. M–W, closed; Th–Su. 12–6. Suggested donation, $3.

The Drawing Center, 35 Wooster St. [Grand/Broome] ☎ 219-2166. M, closed; Tu, 10–6; W, 10–8; Th–Sa, 10–6; Su, closed. Admission, free, some shows have a suggested admission.

Grey Art Gallery, NYU, 33 Washington Place [Washington Sq. E.] ☎ 998-6780. M, closed; Tu, 11–6:30; W, 11–8:30; Th, F, 11–6:30; Sa, 11–5; Su, closed. Admission, free.

The New Museum of Contemporary Art, 583 Broadway [Houston/Prince] ☎ 219-1355. M, Tu, closed; W, Th, F, 12–6; Sa, 12–8, free from 6–8; Su, 12–6. Admission, $4. Artists, students, and seniors, $3.

P.S. 1, The Institute for Contemporary Art, 46-01 21st St. [46th] Long Island City ☎ 718-784-2084. Under renovation, scheduled to reopen spring, 1997. M, Tu, closed; W–Su, 12–6. Suggested admission, $2.

Queens Museum of Art, NYC Building in Flushing Meadows-Corona Park. ☎ 718-592-9700. M, Tu, closed; W–F, 10–5; Sa, Su, 12–5. Admission, $3, Students and seniors, $1.50.

CRAFTS

American Craft Museum, 40 W. 53rd St. [5th/6th] ☎ 956-3535. M, closed; Tu, 10–8; W–Su, 10–5. Adults, $5. Seniors and students, $2.50. Children under 12, free, accompanied by an adult.

FASHION & DESIGN

The Bard Graduate Center for Studies in the Decorative Arts, 18 W. 86th St. [CPW/Columbus] ☎ 501-3000. M, closed; Tu–Su, 11–5. Admission, $3. Closed in summer.

Black Fashion Museum, 155 W. 126th St. [Lenox/ACP] ☎ 666-1320. Noon–8 P.M., by appt. Admission, $3. You must take the guided tour.

Cooper-Hewitt—see National Design Museum.

F.I.T., Seventh Ave. at 27th St. ☎ 760-7760. M, closed; Tu–F, 12–8; Sa, 10–5; Su, closed. Admission, free.

Museum of American Illustration, 128 E. 63rd St. [Park/Lex] ☎ 838-2560. M, closed; Tu, 10–8; W, Th, F, 10–5; Sa, 12–4; Su, closed. Admission, free.

National Academy of Design, 1083 Fifth Ave. [89th] ☎ 369-4880. M, Tu, closed; W, Th, 12–8; F, 12–8; Sa, Su, 12–5. Admission, $5.

National Design Museum (Cooper-Hewitt), 2 E. 91st St. [5th] ☎ 860-6868. M, closed; Tu, 10–9; W–Sa, 10–5; Su, 12–5. Admission, $3. Seniors and students over 12, $1.50. Free for children under 12 and to all on Tuesday from 5–9.

The New York School of Interior Design, Sherill Whiton Gallery, 170 E. 70th St. [Park/Lex] ☎ 472-1500. M–F, 11–5; Sa, Su, closed. Free admission.

FINANCIAL

The Museum of American Financial History, 24 Broadway [Morris] ☎ 908-4110. M–F, 11:30–2:30; Sa, Su, closed.

The American Numismatic Society, Broadway and 155th St. ☎ 234-3130. M, closed; Tu–Sa, 9–4:30; Su, 1–4. Admission, free.

HERITAGE

The Americas Society, 680 Park Ave. [68th] ☎ 249-8950. M, closed; Tu–Su, 12–6. Admission, free.

The Asia Society, 725 Park Ave. [70th] ☎ 288-6400. M, closed; Tu, W, 11–6; Th, 11–8; F, Sa, 11–6; Su, 12–5. Admission, $3. Students and seniors, $1. Free, Th, 6–8.

China Institute, 125 E. 65th St. [Park/Lex] ☎ 744-8181. M, 10–5; Tu, 10–8; W–Sa, 10–5; Su, 1–5. Suggested admission, $5. Students and seniors, $3.

El Museo del Barrio, 1230 Fifth Ave. [104th] ☎ 831-7272. M, T, closed; W–Su, 11–5. Suggested contribution, $4.

The Hispanic Society of America, Broadway and 155th St. ☎ 690-0743. M, closed; Tu–Sa, 10–4:30; Su, 1–4. Admission, free.

Japan Society, 333 E. 47th St. [1st/2nd] ☎ 715-1223. M, closed; Tu–Su, 11–5. Suggested contribution, $3.

The Jewish Museum, 1109 Fifth Ave. [92nd] ☎ 423-3230. M, 11–5:45; Tu, 11–8; W, Th, 11–5:45; F, Sa, closed; Su, 11–5:45. Admission, $7. Tuesday after 5 P.M., free.

Museum of Chinese in the Americas, 70 Mulberry St. [Canal/Bayard] ☎ 619-4785. M, closed; Tu–Su, 10:30–5. Admission, $3.

The Museum for African Art, 593 Broadway [Houston/Prince] ☎ 966-1313. M, closed; Tu–F, 10:30–5:30; Sa, Su, 12–6. Admission, $4. Children, students, seniors, $2.

National Museum of the American Indian, U.S. Custom House, 1 Bowling Green [State/Whitehall] ☎ 668-6624. M–Su, 10–5. Admission, free.

Ukranian Museum, 203 Second Ave. [12th/13th] ☎ 228-0110. M, Tu, closed; W–Su, 1–5. Admission, $1.

LIBRARIES WITH EXHIBITIONS

The New York Public Library, Fifth Ave. at 42nd St. ☎ 661-7220. M, 10–6; Tu, W, 11–6; Th–Sa, 10–6; Su, closed. No admission charge.

The Pierpont Morgan Library, 29 E. 36th St. [Mad] ☎ 685-0610. M, closed; Tu–F, 10:30–5; Sa, 10:30–6; Su, 12–6. Admission, $5.

MEDIEVAL

The Cloisters, Fort Tryon Park ☎ 923-3700. M, closed; Tu–Su, 9:30–4:45 (Nov.–Feb.), 9:30–5:15 (Mar.–Oct.). Suggested admission, $7.

NEW YORK CITY

The Abigail Adams Smith Museum, 421 E. 61st St. [1st/York] ☎ 838-6878. M–F, 12–4; Sa, closed; Su, 1–5. Museum is shown by guided tour only. Closed during August. Adults, $3. Seniors and students, $2. Free for children under 12.

Brooklyn Historical Society, 128 Pierrepont St. [Clinton/Henry] ☎ 718-624-0890. M, closed; Tu–Sa, 12–5; Su, closed. Admission, $2.50. Free on Wednesday.

Dyckman House, 4881 Broadway [W. 204th] ☎ 304-9422. M, closed; Tu–Su, 11–4. Free admission.

Fraunces Tavern, 54 Pearl St. [Broad] ☎ 425-1778. M–F, 10–4:45; Sa, 12–4, Su, closed. Admission, $2.50. Students and seniors, $1.

Gracie Mansion, 88th St. at East End Ave. ☎ 570-4751. Tours every Wed. by appt. Admission, $3. Seniors, $2.

Lower East Side Tenement Museum, 90 Orchard St. [Broome] ☎ 431-0233. M, closed; Tu–Su, 11–5. Admission, $7. Seniors, $6.

Merchant's House Museum, 29 E. 4th St. [Lafayette/Bowery] ☎ 777-1089. M–Th, 1–4; F, Sa, closed; Su, 1–4. Admission, $3.

Morris-Jumel Mansion, Edgecombe Ave. at W. 160th St. ☎ 923-8008. M, Tu, closed; W–Su, 1–4. Admission, $3.

Museum of the City of NY, Fifth Ave. and 103rd St. ☎ 534-1672. M, Tu, closed; W–Sa, 10–5; Su, 1–5. Suggested admission, $5.

New York City Police Museum, 235 E. 20th St. [2nd/3rd] ☎ 477-9753. M–F, 9–3; Sa, Su, closed. Admission, free.

New York Historical Society, 2 W. 77th St. [CPW] ☎ 873-3400. M, Tu, closed; W–Su, 12–5. Suggested admission, $3.

New York Transit Museum, Boerum Place and Schermerhorn St., Brooklyn ☎ 718-243-3060. M, closed; Tu, 10–4; W, 10–6; Th, F, 10–4; Sa, Su, 12–5. Admission, $3. Children, $1.50.

PHOTOGRAPHY

ICP Uptown, 1130 Fifth Ave. [94th] ☎ 860-1777. **ICP Midtown,** 1133 Ave. of the Americas [43rd] ☎ 768-4680. Hours and admission are the same for both locations. M, closed; Tu, 11–8; W–Su, 11–6. Admission, $4. Seniors and students, $2.50. Tuesday after 6 by voluntary contribution.

SCULPTURE

Socrates Sculpture Park, Broadway at Vernon Blvd., Long Island City ☎ 718-956-1819. M–Su, 10–sunset. Admission, free.

The Isamu Noguchi Garden Museum, 32–37 Vernon Blvd., Long Island City ☎ 718-721-1932. Open April–Oct. M, Tu, closed; W, Th, F, 10–5; Sa, Su, 11–6. Suggested admission, $4.

The Chaim Gross Studio Museum, 526 LaGuardia Place [Bleecker/3rd] ☎ 473-3341. Sa, 11–6; other times by appt. Admission, free.

SCIENCE

American Museum of Natural History, Central Park West and 79th St. ☎ 769-5100. M–Th, 10–5:45; F, Sa, 10–8:45; Su, 10–5:45. Suggested admission, $6.

Hayden Planetarium, 81st at Central Park West ☎ 769-5100. Closed from March 1997 until the year 2000.

New York Academy of Medicine, 1216 Fifth Ave. [103rd] ☎ 876-8200. M–F, 9–5. Sa, Su, closed. Admission free.

New York Hall of Science, Flushing Meadows-Corona Park, Queens ☎ 718-699-0005. M, Tu, closed; W–F, 10–5; Sa, Su, 11–5. Adults, $4. Children, $3.

UNUSUAL MUSEUMS

African-American Wax Museum, 316 W. 115th St. [8th/Manhattan Ave.] ☎ 678-7818. M, closed; Tu–Su, by appt., 1–6. Admission, $10. Children, $5. Raven Chanticleer, founder, director, curator, and fabricator of the exhibition, opened it in 1989 "to give a visual impact to black heritage." There are currently 25 wax figures (including Malcolm X, Josephine Baker, Harriet Tubman, Frederick Douglass, and David Dinkins), and Mr. Chanticleer adds new ones each year. When we last spoke with him, he was working on Bob Marley.

American Museum of the Moving Image, 35th Ave. at 36th St., Astoria ☎ 718-

784-0077. M, closed; Tu–F, 12–4; Sa, Su, 12–6. Admission, $7. Children, $4. AMMI manages to be a lot of fun while fulfilling its mission of being a museum of the "art, history, and technology of motion pictures, television, and video." They look at the magic of movies through technology. There are many hands-on interactive exhibits that will let you do things like make your own video animation, create a flip book of yourself, or see your head on the projected body (in costume) of actors. Using artist Gregory Barsamian's piece *Feral Fount*, a drop of water transforms into a bomb, which is caught by a hand, which then drops a letter, which becomes a paper airplane that breaks a dish in the dishpan on the floor, all using strobe light—an ingenious way to make us see how easily the eye is fooled. There are stations where you can use an editing machine or hear actors tell what they were thinking of during the filming of specific scenes. The whole place is engrossing, fun, and when you leave you want to see a movie—which you can do here on weekends . . . **Museum of Television and Radio,** 25 W. 52 St. [5th/6th] ☎ 621-6800. M, closed; Tu, W, 12–6; Th, 12–8; Fr, Sa, Su, 12–6. Admission, $6. Children, $3. Founded by the late William Paley of CBS, this museum, buttoned up as it is, isn't nearly as much fun as AMMI. The core of the MTR is the collection of tens of thousands of television and radio programs and other broadcasting media items, all available for viewing. There are also daily screenings of things like *Alfred Hitchcock Presents,* a profile on Laurence Olivier, and presidential commercials. A radio listening room provides access to a vanished era. There are seminars, talks, and discussion series. The MTR is obviously valuable as a resource, but the place is weirdly austere.

Dahesh Museum, 601 Fifth Ave. [48th] ☎ 759-0606. M, closed; Tu–Sa, 11–6; Su, closed. Admission by contribution. Dr. Dahesh was a Lebanese scholar who collected 19th century realist paintings and sculpture. Curated shows from his collection.

Fisher Landau Center, Long Island City. This three-story former parachute manufacturing facility was resurrected in 1991 and renovated as a museum/gallery for the art collection of Emily Fisher Landau. Working with her curator, William Katz, Ms. Landau exhibits changing highlights from her collection of contemporary American and European art. Currently containing work from the 1940s to the present, there is a concentration of pieces from the late '70s and '80s. On a recent visit, works by Donald Baechler and St. Clain Cemin were shown together. The Independent Study Program of the Whitney Museum presented its 1995 exhibit at FL, and it is hoped that the collaboration between the ISP and the Fisher Landau Center will continue. The FL Center can be visited by appointment, which should be requested by letter, and you must tour with a guide. Call ☎ 718-937-0727 for more information.

The Forbes Magazine Galleries, 60 Fifth Ave. [11th/12th] ☎ 206-5548. M, closed; Tu, W, 10-4; Th, tours only; Fr, Sa, 10-4; Su, closed. The Forbes is the only museum we have visited that has its own soundtrack. Appropriately stirring anthems play behind the displays of toy soldiers. Mechanical platforms move the little marchers around and around as tiny flags fly and trains run in the backdrop. Other displays are of model boats, Fabergé eggs, Monopoly games, and some historical presidential papers.

The New York City Fire Museum, 278 Spring St. [Varick/Hudson] ☎ 691-1303. M, closed; Tu–Su, 10–4. Suggested admission, $4. A visit here is like hanging around a firehouse, in this case, one built in 1904 and renovated to hold a collection of old engines and newer equipment like the jaws of life. Photographs take you through the history of the Fire Department, celebrating some fire dogs as well as firemen.

Nicholas Roerich, 319 W. 107th St. [Bway/RSD] ☎ 864-7732. M, closed; Tu–Su, 2–5. Admission, free. This beautiful town house contains some of the 6,000 paintings Mr. Roerich made in his lifetime (1874–1947). Most of these are oils of mountaintop landscapes, some of which have a mystical bent. Mr. Roerich was the set designer for the original presentation of *The Rite of Spring* in 1913, and some of his sketches for this are on display. A free chamber concert (see more in the Chamber Music article in this chapter) or poetry reading is given just about every Sunday.

The Old Merchant's House, 29 E. 4th St. [Lafayette/Bowery] ☎ 777-1089. Su–Th, 1–4; F, Sa, closed. Admission, $3. The Old Merchant's House offers an excellent opportunity to transport yourself back a century or so to see how people lived (the upper middle class, anyway). It's revealing but not entirely so: There's a secret trap door whose purpose is a matter of speculation. The house was built in 1832 by merchant Joseph Brewster and became the home of Seabury Tredwell and family from 1835–1933. The youngest daughter, Gertrude, lived at the house her entire life and never married. She died owing money, and a nephew had the foresight to turn the house into a museum before things were sold off. The Federal-style house has a Greek revival interior (filled with Tredwell family furniture and artifacts), which has been restored to its mid-19th century peak. The twin parlors are probably the most memorable rooms, but there are many delightful details throughout—from the bell system for the servants to the way the commodes were camouflaged. If you do the self-guided tour, you won't get to see the trap door, but you can ask a staff member. Whoever needed to use this secret passage entered into it from the hallway between the two bedrooms on the bedroom floor. It was hidden by drawers. Once in, you would climb down two flights and then through an opening in the wall to the outside. The house was apparently built to accommodate the passage as the cellar is narrower than the rest of the house. Curator Mimi Sherman says that many theories have been put forth to explain this passage. "We do know that in the 1820s and 1830s, a great many people made a great deal of money from smuggling." At holiday time, there are candlelight tours and readings of Christmas stories in front of the tree.

Rose Museum at Carnegie Hall, M, Tu, 11–4:30; W, closed; Th–Su, 11–4:30, and just before concerts and during intermissions. Admission, free. Enter 154 W. 57th St. just to the left of the main entrance. The intimate space called the Rose Museum most often holds items having to do with the history of Carnegie Hall—things like Benny Goodman's clarinet and Toscanini's baton. Once a year there is a show on a composer (like a recent one with manuscript copies of Beethoven's sonatas).

Theodore Roosevelt Birthplace, National Historic Site, 28 E. 20th St. [5th/Mad] ☎ 260-1616. M, Tu, closed; W–Su, 9–5. Admission, $2. This is the site of Roosevelt's birth, but the original house was demolished. This reconstruction, done with the help of Roosevelt's sisters, produced an accurate representation of the home. You'll find things here from all periods of his life. You must take a tour through the five period rooms, which are given on the hour. There are chamber concerts on most Saturdays.

100 THINGS TO DO WITH KIDS

THE ARTS

1. NightLights at The Drawing Center, 35 Wooster St. [Grand/Broome] ☎ 219-2166. Readings of contemporary and classic stories for kids by celebrated authors, actors, and artists.

2. Art classes at the School of Visual Arts, 209 E. 23rd St. [2nd/3rd] ☎ 592-2600.

3. Children's Choice concerts at the Met ☎ 570-3949.

4. Readings at Bank St. Bookstore, 610 W. 112th St. [Bway] ☎ 875-4550, and Books of Wonder, 132 Seventh Ave. [18th] ☎ 989-3270.

5. Feld Kids Dance at the Joyce, 175 Eighth Ave. [19th] ☎ 242-0800.

6. Little Orchestra Society, at various venues ☎ 704-2100.

7. Growing Up with Opera, November to March, various venues ☎ 769-7008.

8. Interactive moviemaking exhibits at the American Museum of Moving Image, 35th Ave. at 36th St. Astoria ☎ 718-784-4520.

9. Art talk and sketching at the Met ☎ 879-5500.

10. Jazz for Young People at Lincoln Center with Wynton Marsalis ☎ 875-5299.

11. Kids at the Kaye Playhouse, 68th St. [Park/Lex] ☎ 772-4448. Theatrical performances on weekend afternoons.

12. Opera in Brief—a Saturday morning program for families at Amato Opera Theatre, 319 Bowery [1st/2nd] ☎ 228-8200.

13. IMAX at Sony, 1998 Broadway [68th] ☎ 336-5000, and at the Museum of Natural History ☎ 769-5100.

14. International Festival of Puppet Theatre, each September at The Public Theater, 425 Lafayette St. [Astor Pl./E. 4th] ☎ 539-8500.

15. The New Victory Theatre, 209 W. 42nd St. [7th/8th] ☎ 564-4222. Theatrical performances for kids.

16. The Gilbert and Sullivan Players at Symphony Space, 2537 Broadway [95th] ☎ 864-5400.

TOURING THE CITY

17. Warm weather months only: Breakfast at Belmont for kids ☎ 718-641-4700.

18. NBC tour ☎ 664-4444.

19. The Park Rangers tour of the Little Red Lighthouse ☎ 800-201-7275.

20. Helicopter ride, 34th St. and the East River ☎ 925-8807. Several routes available.

21. The Aquarium, W. 8th St. and Surf Ave., Brooklyn ☎ 718-265-3474, in winter, when the walruses, seals, and penguins are active.

22. Take a boat ride from the Seaport around the harbor on the *Pioneer* ☎ 748-8590.

23. Take the ferry to the Colgate clock ☎ 800-533-3779.

24. A walk over Brooklyn Bridge.

25. On Sundays, walk up the belltower of Riverside Church ☎ 222-5900.

26. Panorama of NYC at the Queens Museum in Flushing Meadows-Corona Park ☎ 718-592-5555.

27. Tram to Roosevelt Island.

28. Warm weather months only: Boat up to Sleepy Hollow ☎ 800-533-3779.

29. Wave Hill, 675 W. 252nd St. [Independence], the Bronx ☎ 718-549-3200.

30. Carousel ride in Central Park.

31. Grand Central Station, right outside the Oyster Bar, the whisper gallery (stand in opposite corners, face the wall, and whisper to each other).

32. Visit the Mounted Police Stables, 621 W. 42nd St. [11th/12th] ☎ 239-9352 for an appt.

33. Castle Clinton and lower Manhattan: free walking tour with a National Park Service Guide ☎ 344-7220.

34. See the park from the ground up with "Wildman" Steve Brill ☎ 718-291-6925.

35. How does "All the News That's Fit to Print" get printed? The *New York Times* tour ☎ 556-1234, ext. 4650.

SPORTS ✍

36. Play Ping-Pong at Mammoth Billiards, 114 W. 26th St. [6th/7th] ☎ 675-2626.

37. Running for kids with the NY Roadrunners ☎ 860-4455.

38. Ride a horse at Riverdale Equestrian Center, W. 254th and Broadway ☎ 718-548-4848.

39. Kid's Rollerblading class with Joel Rappelfeld ☎ 744-4444.

40. Bowling at Bowl-Mor Lanes, 110 University Place [12th/13th] ☎ 255-8188.

41. A day at Chelsea Piers ☎ 336-6500.

42. Ice skating at Rockefeller Center ☎ 332-7654 or at the piers ☎ 336-6100.

43. Swimming at Asphalt Green, 555 E. 90th St. [York] ☎ 369-8890.

44. Go to Shea on Dynamets days ☎ 718-507-8499.

45. Sailing lessons at the Great Hudson Sailing Center, 23rd St. and the Hudson River, at the Chelsea Piers ☎ 741-7245.

46. Rent a bike at the Boathouse, 74th and East Drive ☎ 861-4137, and ride in Central Park.

47. Vigorous dancing at Djoniba Dance and Drum Center, 37 E. 18th St. [5th/6th] ☎ 477-3474.

48. Batting cages and mini-golf on Randalls Island ☎ 427-5689.

MUSEUMS & LEARNING 🚂

49. The Children's Museum of Manhattan, 212 W. 83rd St. [Bway/Amsterdam] ☎ 721-1234.

50. Learn circus skills at Circus Gymnastics, 2121 Broadway [74th] ☎ 799-3755.

51. Manhattan Chess Club, 353 W. 46th St. [8th/9th] ☎ 333-5888, has chess lessons for kids.

52. Learn to sculpt at the Sculpture Center, 167 E. 69th St. [Lex/3rd] ☎ 737-9870.

53. Fun hands-on science at Liberty Science Center, Liberty State Park, NJ ☎ 201-200-1000.

54. Paint pottery at Pull Cart, 31 W. 21st St. [5th/6th] ☎ 727-7089.

55. NY Hall of Science, 47-01 111th St. Flushing ☎ 718-699-0005.

56. Museum of the American Indian, 1 Bowling Green [State/Whitehall] ☎ 668-6624.

57. Learn papermaking at Dieu Donné, 433 Broome St. [Bway/Crosby] ☎ 226-0573.

58. Gardening for kids at the NY Botanical Garden, Southern Blvd. and 200th, in the Bronx ☎ 718-817-8700.

59. Cooking workshops for kids at the New School ☎ 255-4141.

60. David Lasday teaches story telling through film animation, multimedia, and video ☎ 595-1549.

61. Toy display at Museum of the City of New York, 5th Ave. and 103rd St. ☎ 534-1672.

62. Wonderful old fire engines at the New York City Fire Museum, 278 Spring St. [Varick/Hudson] ☎ 691-1303.

63. The Transit Museum, Boerum Place and Schermerhorn St., Brooklyn ☎ 718-243-3060.

64. Ellis Island ☎ 363-3200.

65. Dinosaurs at the Museum of Natural History, Central Park West and 79th St. ☎ 769-5100.

66. The Tenement Museum, 90 Orchard St. [Broome] ☎ 431-0233, and a dog at Katz's Deli, 205 E. Houston St. [Ludlow] ☎ 254-2246.

67. John Grimaldi teaches juggling ☎ 260-1365.

68. Mice antics and other fun topics at Fordham University's Science Development Program for kids ☎ 864-4897.

69. *Intrepid* Sea, Air and Space Museum, Pier 86 [46th/12th] ☎ 245-2533.

70. Visit the Anne Frank Center, 584 Broadway [Houston/Prince] ☎ 431-8249.

71. Picnic at the Socrates Sculpture Park, Broadway and Vernon Blvd., Long Island City ☎ 718-956-1810.

72. The Children's Museum of the Arts, 72 Spring St. [Crosby/Lafayette] ☎ 941-9198, has daily programs, workshops, and exhibits of children's art.

THE HOLIDAYS ⚲

73. Candlelight tour and stories in front of the tree at the Old Merchant's House, 29 E. 4th St. [Lafayette/Bowery] ☎ 777-1089.

74. Holiday Garden Railways at the NY Botanical Garden, Southern Blvd. and 200th St. in the Bronx ☎ 718-817-8700.

75. Hannukah celebration at the 92nd St. Y ☎ 996-1100.

76. The holiday windows of Lord & Taylor and Saks.

77. Winter holiday events at the Morris-Jumel Mansion, Edgecombe Ave. at W. 160th ☎ 923-8008.

78. Make origami animals at the Natural History Museum, next to the Christmas tree ☎ 769-5100.

79. Attend the Lincoln Center Tree Lighting in early December ☎ 875-5000. Less crowded.

80. Purim Pageant at the Jewish Museum, 1109 Fifth Ave. [92nd/93rd] ☎ 423-3200.

81. The Day of the Dead celebration, November 1. El Museo del Barrio, 1230 Fifth Ave. [104th] ☎ 831-7272. Sugar skulls and papercutting workshops.

82. The Museum for African Art, 593 Broadway [Houston/Prince] ☎ 966-1313, has Kwanzaa festivities and storytelling for kids.

FOOD 🥞

83. Frozen custard at Custard Beach, 33 E. 8th St. [University] ☎ 420-6039, or frozen hot chocolate at Serendipity, 225 E. 60th St. [2nd/3rd] ☎ 838-3531.

84. Pancakes at one of the Royal Canadian Pancake Houses, 2286 Broadway [82nd/83rd] ☎ 873-6052, 1004 Second Ave. [53rd] ☎ 980-4131, or 180 Third Ave. [16th/17th] ☎ 777-9288.

85. Dim Sum at Triple Eight Palace, 78 E. Broadway [Market] ☎ 941-8886.

86. Pizza at kid-friendly Two Boots, 37 Ave. A [2nd/3rd] ☎ 505-2276 and several other locations.

87. Brooklyn Diner, 212 W. 57th St. [Bway/7th] ☎ 977-1957, for, among other things, great hot dogs.

JUST FOR FUN 🎩

88. NY Firefighter's Friend, 263 Lafayette St. [Prince/Spring] ☎ 226-3142, for toy fire engines, helmets, etc.

89. Saturday entertainments at the Knitting Factory, 74 Leonard St. [Bway/Church] ☎ 219-3006.

90. 10,000 toy soldiers at the Forbes Galleries, 60 Fifth Ave. [12th] ☎ 620-2389.

91. The play area in Hudson River Park.

92. Listen to New York Kids and Rabbit Ears Radio on WNYC 93.9 FM.

93. East and West side Playspaces: indoor playgrounds ☎ 769-2300.

94. Baseball cards at Collector's Stadium, 214 Sullivan St. [W. 3rd/Bleecker] ☎ 353-1531.

95. Weekends at Asphalt Green: Puppet Playhouse, 555 E. 90th St. [York/EEA] ☎ 369-8890.

96. Tannen's Magic Studio, 24 W. 25th St. [Bway/6th] ☎ 929-4500.

97. Watch the ants on closed circuit TV at the Central Park Zoo, 5th Ave. and 64th St. ☎ 861-6030.

98. Movies for Kids series at Lincoln Center's Walter Reade ☎ 875-5600.

99. Westminster Kennel Club Show at Madison Square Garden the second Monday and Tuesday in February ☎ 682-6852.

100. Watch the chocolate being made at Martine's on the sixth floor of Bloomingdale's ☎ 705-2000, ext. 2347.

OPERA

There are several dozen small opera companies in New York City that provide valuable stage experience for singers on their way up. LeRoy Lehr, who sings with the Met, says, "They are important because young people who are arriving get some exposure." Michael Spierman, director of The Bronx Opera Company, says, "What does 'the toast of Shreveport' do when they arrive here?" He "produces singers when they are unknown enabling them to develop their careers." Teresa Cincionne sang with The Bronx four years ago. Philip Cokorinos (Met), Joyce Cuyer (Met), Philip Booth (Met), Dennis Peterson, Ronald Naldi (Met) are Bronx alumni. Opera directors Cynthia Edwards, Albert Sherman, and Jack Edelman spent some time with The Bronx. Barbara Elliott, artistic director of the Piccolo Teatro dell'-Opera, ☎ 718-643-7775, based in Brooklyn, says she "scouts and auditions singers. Then I present them on their way up in works that serve them well." Sometimes that means doing shorter works in smaller houses like the Sylvia and Danny Kaye Playhouse, sometimes in a full production with a small orchestra, and sometimes in her free Prospect Park concerts in the summer. Renée Fleming (Met), Douglas Perry, Victgoria Livengood (Met), John Daniecki (NY), and Andre Salmon Glover (Showboat) have all passed through her company. Mr. Lehr says that smaller companies give you a chance to hear things that are not going to be put on in the big houses where the pressure is to perform the tried and true. He goes on to note that composers especially need these companies, "since they can't audition" and they "need a way to hear themselves."

The Amato Opera, 319 Bowery [1st/2nd] ☎ 228-8200, was founded in 1948. The Amato packs a lot of creative talent into a small space. They give fully staged performances, with clever sets and costumes. There is no orchestra—they use a piano and a few other instruments. The five yearly productions, mostly from the Italian repertoire, are under the direction of Anthony Amato, who also gives pre-curtain explanations of the plot. Some performances are in English. Ticket prices are $18, gala performances are $35.

American Opera Projects, 463 Broome St. [Greene/Mercer] ☎ 431-8102, develops contemporary American operas by "established composers and people working in other genres." They sponsor readings, workshops, outdoor public performances, sampler performances (where they showcase three or four companies in an evening), and back-to-back performances during the days of the Soho Festival each October. Productions are done without costumes and sets because of the small size of their facility. They make their performance space available to unusual companies like Play It by Ear, which combines opera and improv.

The Bronx Opera Company, 5 Minerva Place [Jerome] Bronx ☎ 718-365-4209, was established in 1967. Under the direction of Michael Spierman, they put on two productions each year, always in English, in the new performing arts center at Hostos Community College, Grand Concourse and 149th and at the good, medium-sized house at John Jay College, Tenth Ave. and 59th. Each January, they perform a rare work and, in May, a well-known work. The Bronx has been a bridge for singers between their apprenticeship stage and the major companies.

The Dicapo Opera Theatre, 184 E. 76th St. [Lex/3rd] ☎ 288-9438, under the direction of Michael Capasso and Diane Martindale, is a joyous experience. In the lower level of the St. Jean Baptiste church is a new 208-seat theatre designed and built for them. It has a pit for the 23-piece orchestra, and banked seats with great sight lines. They mount four full productions each year. The intimacy of this theatre allows you to hear things you may not have heard before.

The artistic director of **Opera Manhattan,** ☎ 799-1660, is Gabriel Guimaraes, who presents French and Italian pieces, often giving New York premieres. Operas are fully staged with a real chamber orchestra and surtitles are used. In summer, they can be found at Marymount Manhattan College, 221 E. 71st St. [2nd/3rd] ☎ 517-0400. There is a second performance in the fall. Singers to look for here are sopranos Tamara Wright, Sarah Johannsen, and Rosemary Barens. Dierdre Howley, the general director, says, "Barton Green and Neil Harrelson are talents moving up." Fifty percent of the gross box office goes to AIDS research and care organizations.

MORE Each summer, Vincent LaSelva and the New York Grand Opera produce two Verdi operas in Central Park at Summer-Stage ☎ 360-2777. Mr. LaSelva's intention is to produce them all in chronological order, which, if all goes well, will conclude with the *Requiem* in 2001.

PRIVATE ART DEALERS

WHAT TO KNOW Generally speaking, private art dealers don't have galleries with regular shows, don't have openings, and frequently have no catalogs. They do offer a level of privacy and discretion to clients, whether they are selling or buying works, that some feel is not available elsewhere. A wide range of periods, styles, media, and price ranges are available. In contemporary work, many dealers work in the "secondary market." This is work that is changing hands after the first sale by the artist or the gallery. These dealers may work from their homes, from offices that look like offices, from offices that look like galleries, or from warehouse spaces.

Karen Amiel, ☎ 439-1924, has worked as the curator for the Arts Council of Great Britain and has run a gallery of her own. In 1985, she decided to become a private dealer. She operates from her home selling post–WWII American and European works. She has had Joseph Cornell boxes, early work by Tom Wesselmann, Doug and Mike Starn's experimental photography, a mirror painting by Roy Lichtenstein, and a motorized wall piece by German artist Rebecca Horn. Ms. Amiel also has prints by Jasper Johns, Robert Rauschenberg, and Lichtenstein. Prices from $5,000 to $500,000.

Timothy Baum, ☎ 879-4512, became a private dealer in the '60s after meeting Man Ray. Already an admirer of Dada and Surrealism, he was astonished that Man Ray, in his eighties at the time, was "quite broke." In "a humble and devotional way," he set out to reverse the lack of understanding in America for this group. For 30 years, Mr. Baum has been dealing in the works of Man Ray, Marcel Duchamp, Max Ernst, Kurt Schwitters, and Yves Tanguy, as well as lending works to exhibitions, curating shows, and writing catalogs and essays. Works on paper include the collages and frottages (from the French word for rubbing) of Ernst. He also has paintings by Tanguy and the wittily puzzling constructions of Duchamp and Man Ray. There are many photographs by Man Ray, whom Mr. Baum describes as the century's "greatest portrait photographer and, with the rayograms and solargrams, the greatest experimental photographer of the 20th century." $300–$300,000.

Robert Dance, ☎ 977-5612, has been dealing in Italian Old Master (15th–18th centuries) paintings and drawings since 1982. He showed us two recordi by Francesco Solimena representing the Christian Virtues—Chastity (holding a belt) and Christian Dogma. A recordo was a sketch that the artist kept for his own filing system after the actual work was placed in a church or sold. He also sells American sculpture from 1900–1940. A tabletop-sized piece by Paul Manship, *Indian Hunter with Dog,* is a smaller version of the one in a public park in St. Paul, Minnesota. Old Master drawings start at $10,000 and paintings at $40,000. Mr. Dance is the president of the Private Art Dealers Association (some of the dealers in this article are members of it), which is intended to provide some structure to private art dealing. If you want more info or a list of their members, ☎ 741-7264.

Markel/Sears Works on Paper, 560 Broadway [Prince] ☎ 966-7469. Kathryn Markel and Marcie Sears represent about 40 contemporary artists and show only work on paper—monotypes, pastels, watercolors, collages, and oil. These works are generally less expensive than oil paintings, and the price range here is $400–$2,500. Ms. Markel has been selling art privately to corporations for thirty years, but their Soho-gallery-like space is open by appointment to individuals. The setting is pretty—Victorian sofas, plenty of space to lay out the work.

Karen McCready Fine Art, ☎ 677-3732. Ms. McCready was the director of Crown Point Press for 12 years. When they closed their gallery space in Soho in 1994, she decided to specialize in works on paper by contemporary artists. These include William Wegman, whose "Table Setting" has the weimaraners balanced like stacked wineglasses. Ms. McCready also has work by Terry Winters, Sol Lewitt, Wayne Thiebaud, Richard Diebenkorn, Sandy Gellis, and Agnes Denes. Prices from $250–$75,000, with much at the lower end.

Samson Fine Art, ☎ 369-6677, is located in a private home, and the works are shown as if they belong to the owner's collection. Maeve Gyenes brings 10 years of gallery experience to her new business. She specializes in "emerging artists" and spent months researching to find artists with little or no representation in New York who meet her standards of aesthetic pleasure. "I didn't want to show just pretty pictures, but I didn't want to show things that are distasteful." The space between these two poles is currently occupied by 12 artists ranging in age from 22–55 who work in a variety of media from pencil drawings to oil paintings. Works are available framed or unframed. Price range is $950–$12,000.

Schiller and Bodo, ☎ 772-8627, is, more precisely, Schiller, Schiller, and Bodo. Lisa and Tina Schiller, sisters, are partnered with Susan Bodo. They're all specialists in the mid-19th Century Barbizon school of painters. Barbizon, near Fontainebleau, outside of Paris, is where this group returned painting to the out of doors. There are many tree-filled landscapes, including several by Narcisse de la Peña. A portrait by Jules Breton of a young girl who seems to be posing while working in the fields, one arm full of wheat, was once in Chicago's Art Institute collection. An unusually peaceful Courbet from 1863 has a small figure fishing in a river. The showroom here is set up like a comfortable salon. Much research is done on each painting, and there is a library of books to consult. $20,000–$100,000.

READINGS

Biblio's Cafe, 317 Church St. [Lispenard/Walker] ☎ 334-6990. The bookshop/coffee house/neighborhood center has scheduled poetry and book readings and open-mike nights.

Books & Co., 939 Madison Ave. [74th/75th] ☎ 737-1450. A well-attended series by contemporary writers and poets.

The Drawing Center, 35 Wooster St. [Grand/Broome] ☎ 219-2166. The monthly NightLights series presents contemporary writers reading from their own works.

Poetry series at the **Knitting Factory,** 74 Leonard St. [Bway/Church] ☎ 219-3055. Every Friday evening at 7 P.M.

The New Dramatists, 424 W. 44th St. [9th/10th] ☎ 757-6960. Occasional readings of new plays.

Nuyorican Poet's Cafe, 236 E. 3rd St. [B/C] ☎ 505-8183. Poetry slams and open rooms with hosts. High-energy readings by mostly young poets.

The revivification of Bryant Park has also reintroduced the **NY Public Library**'s outdoor reading series. Mid-afternoon readings by poets and novelists are free. Inside the library, the Public Education Department presents interviews, lectures, and discussions by the world renowned (Carlos Fuentes), the well thought of (Adam Gopnik), and the New York–centric (Jimmy Breslin). Most are at 6 P.M. $7 tickets can be obtained by mail, not by phone. ☎ 930-0571 for a recorded schedule and ticket availability.

Readings of plays are given at the **NY Public Library for the Performing Arts** at Lincoln Center Plaza, ☎ 870-1630, about once a month on Monday evenings in the Bruno Walter Auditorium. The Reading Room Series offers playwrights an opportunity to try out works in progress. Past presenters have been John Guare, Jon Robin Baitz, and Susan Sontag.

92nd St. Y, 1395 Lexington Ave. [92nd/93rd] ☎ 996-1100. The Unterberg Poetry Center has been presenting the best of poetry and literature in live readings since 1939. Events weekly from October to May.

The Poetry Calendar, ☎ 260-7997, comes out monthly and gives listings of poetry and fiction readings, as well as public events run by PEN. Some months there are over 350 readings. A one-year subscription is $20.

Poetry Society of America, ☎ 254-9628, conducts events in theatres, concert halls, museums, and bookstores around the city. Some are free, others have an admission fee. Poets read from their own works or read in tributes to earlier writers like T.S. Eliot or Emily Dickinson. You can get a copy of their calendar of events by sending a SASE to 15 Gramercy Park South 10003.

Poets House, 72 Spring St. [Bway/Lafayette] ☎ 431-7920, hosts regular readings. All events are open to the public. $5 admission.

The **St. Mark's Poetry Project,** St. Mark's Church, Second Ave. [10th] has been presenting readings and performance events since 1966. Three readings each week. Admission is $6. You can get a schedule by calling ☎ 674-0910.

Symphony Space, 2537 Broadway [95th] ☎ 864-1414, is the home of Selected Shorts, where fine actors and actresses (Rene Auberjonois, Anne Meara, and Tony Roberts) read well-known (Edgar Allan Poe, Isaac Bashevis Singer, Isak Dinesen) and contemporary (Chinua Achebe, Edwidge Danticat, Louise Erdrich) short stories. Tickets $16.

The Manhattan Theater Club's **Writers in Performance** is a series of playwrights reading their own work. City Center, 131 W. 55th St. [6th/7th] ☎ 645-5848.

SCULPTURE

We sat one afternoon to talk about **public sculpture** with sculptor Tom Otterness, whose playful and witty works, *The Real World* in Hudson River Park, and *Life Underground* in the 8th Ave. and 14th St. subway station, are pieces that always seem to occasion interaction. People look, stop, and often talk to each other in front of an Otterness work. We asked him what sculptures around the city he particularly admires. He says it's hard to talk about sculpture without feeling the presence of three works by John Ahearn and Richard Serra's *Tilted Arc.* Public sculpture, he says, used "to make an image of the society." We used to have agreement on what the image was, "now we have no universal image of ourselves," so when new public works go up, "there is a lot of heated debate."

Mr. Ahearn and his assistant, Rigoberto Torres, live and work in the South Bronx. Under Mr. Ahearn's direction, they make life casts of neighborhood people. *Double Dutch, Back to School,* and *Life on Dawson* were greeted with a neighborhood street party when they were placed as permanent wall sculpture on the exterior of a Bronx apartment building. Several of his works are in the collection of the Brooklyn Museum. So no one expected difficulties with three life-sized, highly realistic figures cast from young people he knew in the neighborhood. *Cory* stands with his foot on a boom box holding a basketball. *Daleesha,* a young girl, wears a Batman T-shirt and is on roller skates, and in *Raymond and Toby,* a young man crouches, his arm around his pit bull. In 1990, they were placed in a triangle of land in front of the local police station. Mr. Ahearn's intention, to memorialize the current residents, was not appreciated by his neighbors, who felt a basketball, boom box, and hooded sweatshirt were not images they wanted to see of themselves. Sensitive to the community, he withdrew the pieces from the site. The works, made more famous in a *New Yorker* piece by Jane Kramer (now a book), were displayed at P.S. 1, and are cur-

rently on display at the Socrates Sculpture Park, 31–34 Vernon Blvd. [Bway] LIC ☎ 718-956-1819. They are expected to return to P.S. 1 when the renovation (and new sculpture park) is complete.

Richard Serra's *Tilted Arc* (1981) was removed from 26 Federal Plaza [Court] after complaints from workers in the area, who felt the work was an obstruction in the courtyard. There were public hearings and a civil court case. Mr. Otterness describes the work as "a splinter he [Mr. Serra] put in this big federal body, an irritant that allowed the venting of anger from the general public. It condensed contradictions in the society as a whole, heightened problems, and brought them to the surface and the sculptor got blamed." Now, *Tilted Arc* is in permanent storage. Mr. Otterness says Richard Serra is "arguably the most important sculptor of the last 25 years." Of *Tilted Arc,* he says, "even the ghost of it, the crack in the ground" where it used to be, is a major public work.

Two figures associated with protest and independence were on Mr. Otterness's mind for different reasons. The statue of *Nathan Hale* (dedicated 1893) by Frederick Mac-Monnies is on an inscribed pedestal in City Hall Park, near Broadway and Murray. The Brits executed Nathan Hale as a spy, without benefit of trial. He stands with feet and arms bound with ropes. Mr. Otterness remarks on the loosely chained arms, bound from behind, and his posture, romantic and yearning. He says it's hard not to see eroticism here, with the clothing undone at neck and upper chest, even homoeroticism. You frequently find striking juxtapositions in Mr. Otterness's work; here he observes the placement of an "erotically bound man in front of City Hall." Contrast this with the sculpture of *Mohan-*

das Gandhi (1986) on a waist-high pedestal by Kantilal B. Patel. A lean Gandhi strides forward using his walking stick, wearing sandals, eyeglasses, and a dhoti, a compassionate expression on his face. Gandhi often led Indians in marches during the campaign for independence. "It is beautiful where it is placed (in a garden triangle off the northwest corner of Union Square) in an isolated island with traffic flowing around it. You often see it with bouquets of flowers on it." While Mr. Otterness, whose own sculptures are often at foot- and knee-level, would "like it more at ground-level, it's almost there."

Four Trees by Jean Dubuffet (dedicated 1972) mushrooms up some 42 ft. high in front of 1 Chase Manhattan Plaza in the square bounded by William, Pine, Nassau, and Liberty Streets. Mostly white with heavy black painted lines, they are all dips and odd angles, as though they are shaking out the rectilinear objects that surround them. Mr. Otterness reacts to the scale as well. "It makes you feel enormously small. Walking through it shrinks us, and it changes the way you look at the buildings around it."

Greg Wyatt's *Peace Fountain* was commissioned by the Episcopal Diocese of NY and installed in the Peace Garden next to the Cathedral of St. John the Divine. It is "so huge and so eccentric" that you marvel at the sculptor's ability "to get that personal eccentricity out there without being too washed over" by the process of making a commissioned work. Atop a large swirling base symbolic of DNA sits a giant crab reminding us of life's beginnings in the sea. Several giraffes, an animal which the sculptor has chosen to represent peace, clamber over a sun and moon disc. One is being tenderly caressed by the Archangel Michael's right hand. In his left hand, he holds a large

sword with which he has decapitated a devil. Michael's huge wings arc back and up into the sky. "I have a lot of sympathy for this kind of work. The artist bites off more than he can possibly chew—trying to represent a state of mind." The garden itself also contains the work of NYC schoolchildren on the subject of peace. Their small animal sculptures and personal heroes have been cast in bronze and circle the larger work. Mr. Wyatt has another smaller work using some of the features of the Peace Fountain, called *Fantasy Fountain,* in the southeast corner of Gramercy Park.

Tony Smith is represented by two public pieces in New York. *Tau* is a black welded steel work at the entrance to Hunter College on the southwest corner of 68th and Lex. It is made up of simple, large planes that are subtly angled. Walk around it, raking your eye from top to bottom—there are constant small adjustments in shape and mass. *Throwback,* a black-painted aluminum piece in the courtyard that runs between W. 45th and W. 46th behind 1166 Ave. of the Americas also rewards the viewer who walks around it. Planes and angles make beautiful intersections and projections. Mr. Smith "generated his forms from crystals, he built off their geometric structure. He made models and studied at the American Museum of Natural History." He wanted to see the "ways the surfaces will relate to each other. This gives his work an intellectual underpinning and an organic feel. It had a rationale, not just abstraction made to look well balanced."

Alice in Wonderland, by Jose de Creeft, "was a revolution" in 1959 when it was installed near the Conservatory Pond in Central Park. Sculpture "came off the pedestal and onto the ground. It's meant for people to crawl on it." Mr. Otterness says there was a plaster model in the studio, and "de Creeft must have tested it with kids" because the handholds and the crawling and climbing distances are so right for little bodies. "It's a constant performance piece and a built-in photo opportunity as people engage with it in a tactile way. You can see the areas where the bronze gets polished from being touched so often, a mark of people's affection. The irony of it is that no one knows his [de Creeft's] other work, but everyone knows Alice." . . . Stay in Central Park and walk to just south of the Met. Recently installed is a group of **Three Bears** by Paul Manship. "They are already nicely polished even though they have

Three Bears by Paul Manship.

only been out for a short time. Manship also did the **Lehman Zoo Gates** at the 66th St. entrance to the Children's Zoo. (Probably the most seen work of Paul Manship in NY is the *Prometheus* in Rockefeller Center.)

At South Cove of Battery Park City is a landscaped installation by Mary Miss called **South Cove** (1988). Heaped rocks define the garden edges and boulders sit in the middle of the boardwalk. The greenish poles and pilings have blue light fixtures on them. At the southern edge there is a metal structure with ramps leading up to an observation site. Below, a wooden jetty sways slightly with the movement of the river. It seems to "spiral half out into the water and half up into

the air. The abstraction entwines with nature." Many of the benches provided are intended for two. "It's a very romantic site and seems to be often used for that purpose. I often see people necking there." . . . Two new pieces on high poles have been installed at the water's edge in North Cove Park. Called **Lighting Pylons,** they are by Martin Puryear (1995). A brushed-metal spiral and its companion, a kind of ziggurat, are frames for the water and the atmosphere. "I think he must have been working with intuitive proportions. The measurements appear to be slightly off, and that's what gives it life." The color of both pieces, a gray, "absorbs the sky."

The New Ring Shout, a collaboration among Houston Conwill, Joseph De Pace, and Estella Conwill Majozo, is located in the lobby of 290 Broadway [Duane], on the site of the African Burial Ground. A 40-foot diameter of polished stone, it is divided into three concentric circles and contains a map of NYC marked with evocative and celebratory sites, lines from songs, the names of the tribes of the slave trade, and quotes from 14 men and women on the subject of freedom. "It's a rational structure, but when you walk through it, you only get a piece of it. You make assumptions from the fragments, from the five different rationales working together, and the result is poetic." Mr. Otterness picks up the words Speech, Vision, Balance, and Grace set in four circles at the compass points of the cosmogram. "If you just walk through and see those words, they are a flattering vision of a person. There are a hundred different angles on a kind of unification, an almost ungraspable kind of complication. But it has a structure spiraling toward the center, which gives it a unity. There is a sense (when you stop) that the whole world seems to be pinned on the place where you are standing."

William Butler Yeats's words *"In Dreams Begin Responsibilities"* stream out of a coffee cup in Elizabeth Murray's mosaic room in the Lexington Ave./59th St. subway station. Rolf Olhausen, the architect overseeing the project, says the interchange between the N, R, and the 4, 5, and 6 lines, "one of the most Kafkaesque spaces in the system, has been transformed by art." It's the first place in the subway system where art has been used floor to ceiling, wall to wall. An almost child-like tree, some rising suns, birds and many shoes are mixed in with coffee and tea cups. At one point you walk through a large teacup doorway. Mr. Otterness marvels, "You are walking through a total environment on this large artery between all the lines. You will physically have to walk around and through it and turn in order to see it. You have to remember what you've seen before in order to understand what you are seeing now. It is like being inside of a sculpture, having to walk around on the inside of it, rather than around the outside of it. These coffee cups will meet the bleary-eyed in the morning. Every commuter will understand it."

Over the entrance to the law school at Columbia University, Amsterdam Ave. [116th/117th] on a two-story-high pedestal, is a 40-foot-high work by Jacques Lipchitz, *Bellerophon Taming Pegasus.* Bellerophon has found the horse, Pegasus, drinking from his fountain and is determined to tame the horse. Pegasus's neck is pulled out and down by a coil of rope, which you can see in front of the man's right leg. The sculpture shows the struggle without making it clear who will win. Mr. Otterness says it is a good sculpture, worth seeing. From the street level on Amsterdam Ave., looking up at the dense mass of figures, the work is flattened out. You can get a better sense of the dimensions and the relief by approaching the piece on the elevated walkway from the campus.

MORE **The Socrates Sculpture Garden,** 31–34 Vernon Blvd. [Broadway] Long Island City ☎ 718-956-1819, was recently voted one of 63 Great American Public Places by a national panel of architects, designers, and writers. It wasn't always a great space. It took sculptor Mark di Suvero and local volunteers a year to reclaim the land that had been used as a waste dump. Stones (some appear to be road markers, others have big initials on them), unearthed during the excavation of the Q line subway tunnel, have been turned into a low wall. Now the four and a half acres along the river in Long Island City is both a working site for sculptors and an exhibition area. Each year a sculptor is given a small grant to work there. Welding, marble and wood carving may be under way when you visit. Among the permanent pieces is the *Sound Observatory* by Bill and Mary Buchen, which sits in a hollow by the water's edge. A series of metal drums, some high, some low to the ground, can be played on. There are two shows each year that bring works from all over the world to LIC.

STARGAZING

For reports on what's visible in the night sky, call the Hayden Planetarium's Sky Reporter ☎ 769-5917.

COPING

⟵⟶

CARS

CAR RENTAL
BY EVELYN KANTER

WHAT TO KNOW In New York State, a car's owner, not the driver, is responsible in an accident. To cut liability lawsuits, national chains now check your license. Rules vary by company, but two or more moving violations in the previous 24 months or one accident in 36 months gets you rejected in NYS and at those companies' locations in other states. It is illegal in NYS to discriminate against young drivers. The NYS Attorney General even won a '94 lawsuit against firms that turn away drivers 25 and under. But they still refuse such licensed drivers under the pretext that no insurance is available. Not true: Chains don't want to pay for extra insurance or pass it on. Either rent under a corporate account or forget the biggies. Or, call Enterprise, which charges 25-and-unders a hefty daily surcharge. It is also illegal in NYS to charge extra for collision insurance, so it's buried inside higher rates. Some independents rent only to a credit card that covers the collision damage waiver (CDW) as a membership perk. You are liable for the first $100 in damage unless your credit card contract says they'll pay.

COMPARING COSTS Rental companies are charging for mileage again at 10¢–29¢ per mile over what's allowed free. So, get out your calculator and map to figure out the best deal. It may cost less to keep the car an extra day or buy the unlimited-mileage package. More important, cut costs by traveling out of Manhattan for a bargain rental. We quote prices from the day we did the research, but even though rates change all the time, we think they're still useful as a comparative guide. Prices are also before tax but include CDW except where noted. Seven-passenger minivans are about $65 daily everywhere checked. All major credit cards accepted except where noted; rental companies normally freeze $500 against your card to cover anticipated costs.

NATIONALLY ADVERTISED COMPANIES

Chains like Hertz, Avis, Budget have more prices for the same car than NYC has pot-holes. Want a Tercel for a summer weekend?

Hertz charges $84 daily in Manhattan, $73 if you pick it up at LaGuardia (100 miles free at both), minus 5% if you have an airline frequent flyer number. Take MetroNorth to Stamford and the same car is $46 plus $15 CDW, with unlimited mileage. On a corporate account, the Tercel is $82 in Manhattan after noon Thursday (100 miles free), $52 and unlimited mileage before noon. Or, $38 (unlimited mileage) from Stamford and $44 if you pick it up in Stamford and return it to Manhattan.

INDEPENDENTS Such a dizzying menu of deals may drive you to rent from an independent. The trade-off to their lower rates is few are open past 8 P.M. At **Aamcar,** 303 W. 96th St. [WEA/RSD] ☎ 222-8500, daily rates are $50 weekdays, $70 weekends, and a three-day minimum during the summer at $200. Drivers aged 23–25 are charged $10 a day additional; younger drivers cannot rent or drive. You get unlimited free mileage but no tape deck or power windows. Aamcar's vehicles have a theft-reducing keypad device; don't forget the number, the car won't start without it ... **Manhattan Ford/Lincoln/Mercury,** 555 W. 57th St. [11th] ☎ 581-7850, offers a fully loaded (tape decks, some sun roofs, etc.) current-model Taurus at $70 a day, $240 a three-day week-

end with 200 free miles per day. Drivers 21 and over may rent ... If you don't mind driving an older model with dings and dents, but nothing more serious, **Rent-A-Wreck** offers '89–'91 Ford Tempos at $50 daily, $165 for three-day weekends (50 free miles daily), but a better deal is $279 a week with 1,200 free miles. Nearest location is 205 State St., downtown Brooklyn (near Court St.), ☎ 718-237-0200 ... Bypass the rapid-fire recorded message listing rates for a live person at **Queensboro Toyota,** 77-12 Northern Blvd. [77th], Queens ☎ 718-335-8600. Corollas and Camrys are $48 a day and $149 for a three-day weekend (100 free miles per day), $270 a week (1,000 miles free). They'll rent to any driver who has had a license for four years ... At **Elite,** 1041 Coney Island Ave. [Foster Ave.], Brooklyn ☎ 718-859-0825, the rate is $40 a day for fewer than seven, $30 for more (50 free miles daily), or add $10 daily for 300 daily free miles. Minivans are $66 daily. They rent to those 23 or older with a credit card ... Taking the bus to New Jersey is sensible only if you rent with an American Express or gold MasterCard or Visa because **Sensible,** 2085 Lemoine Ave. Ft. Lee, waives the $15 daily insurance, making a $46 a day Taurus (150 miles free) quite a bargain ... The best deal around may be a 10-minute hike from the Port Jefferson LIRR station. At **Ramp Chevrolet,** 1395 Rte. 112 ☎ 800-731-7267, GEO Prizms are $40 a day (100 miles free), $130 a three-day weekend (500 free miles). No additional charge for an extra driver—they'll accept a photocopy of that driver's license if the driver isn't with you at rental time. Drivers 21–25 are okay. Bonus: there's an after-hours key drop.

UNUSUAL CARS Roarin' Roadsters Rentals, ☎ 201-569-4793. Want a Ferrari for a weekend? A Jag, Maserati, '66 T-Bird, or a Miata? Roarin' Roadsters has them all. You can rent by day or week (all rentals have a 2-day minimum), and prices start at $99 per day for the Miata and go up to $349 for the Ferrari. They deliver to you in Manhattan for $25 each way.

CAR ROUTES

For the best car routes to the airports, see the Travel section in the Feature chapter. For time-saving maps to get you around traffic in the tristate area, buy Joshua B. Isaacson's *No Time for Tie-Ups.* It's available at most bookstores or from ☎ 718-549-0728.

DRIVER'S LICENSE

The DMV offices at 141–155 Worth St. [Centre/Baxter] or 2110 Adam Clayton Powell Jr. Blvd. [125th/126th] ☎ 645-5550, used to be the only places in town to renew your license, and it was invariably a bad experience. Matters have improved somewhat, especially if you know about **License Express,** 300 W. 34th St. [8th/9th] ☎ none. Hours are Mon.–Wed., 8–5:30; Thurs., 8–7. Closed Fri.–Sun. With much smaller lines, this office is likely to save you quite a bit of time. License Express is for renewals only. If you want a service to expedite license renewals, see the Time-Saving article in the Services chapter. If your license is lost or stolen, see the Wallet, Lost or Stolen article in this chapter.

INSURANCE

The state of New York ranks 60 insurance companies each year. You can get a copy of the report, at no charge, by writing to the NY State Insurance Dept. Research Bureau, 160 W. Broadway, New York, NY 10013.

LEASING

The Department of Consumer Affairs has a good six-page guide to automobile leasing. It helps you calculate the actual costs of a lease and how to identify hidden charges. Send a SASE to DCA Publications, 42 Broadway, New York, NY 10004. For more info, ☎ 487-4270.

TOWING

Voluntary. Regulated by the city: $50 for first mile, $3.50 each mile thereafter. If the car needs to be stored before being serviced and the tower takes it from a storage space, it's $10 a day storage for the first three days, $15 a day thereafter. If the car is disabled in a private parking lot, the fee is $100, which includes the first three days of storage. According to the Dept. of Consumer Affairs, you should make sure you use a tow company licensed by the DCA. The license medallion is a small, red plate generally on the rear fender. The truck should also have rates posted right on the truck.

Involuntary. If your car is towed because it is parked illegally, call ☎ 971-0774. They'll tell you where your car is. You'll need $150 for towing plus the amount of the ticket— cash, certified check, money order, or Discover card. If  you have outstanding tickets or liens, you will have to pay those up, too, before you get your car back. The pound is at Pier 76, West Side Highway at 39th Street.

CRIME & SAFETY

BURGLAR ALARMS Isaac Papier, manager of Engineering Services at Underwriters Laboratories, says that the basic requirement for home security products (which includes smoke detectors and home alarm systems) "is that they be inherently reliable." UL has three levels of listings when it comes to security systems. First, the actual products are tested for reliability—much the same as the guarantee on your Christmas lights. Second, installing companies are listed based on a company's ability to install specific categories of alarm equipment. Mr. Papier points out that there are "somewhere between 14,000 and 15,000 installers listed in phone books across the country. Only 1,200 have made the grade of UL." And, lastly, the central monitoring group is listed if they meet the requirements. If they do, they are granted a certificate by UL. They are subject to further "random inspection" by UL. Each level of listing causes the price of a home alarm system to go up. Using a registered installer may give you additional credit on your homeowner's insurance, but Mr. Papier says it will probably not be enough to pay for the alarm system. "The biggest portion of your premium goes for liability (maybe as much as 80%–90%). You will be getting a discount on the remaining 10%–20% of your insurance bill."

Having an alarm system won't necessarily stop someone from breaking into your apartment, but it can be a deterrent. It can also provide a lot of peace of mind. Alan Apo, technical manager with American Insurance Services Group, a company that provides information to insurance companies, says the thing you need to remember about residential alarm systems is that "they are designed to tell someone, either the resident or the alarm company, that there is a problem. They are not designed to keep the criminal out." He says your alarm should be UL listed for residential monitoring service, and that the UL listing on all of the equipment used is a mark of how reputable the company is. You will want an alarm with an outside monitoring station. The monitoring station should be one that "initiates some action on your behalf when an alarm signal is received." The Central Station Alarm Association requires their members to be UL listed. "These are the premium companies."

Steve Doyle, executive vice president of the Central Station Alarm Association, says the technology is such today that "you can get all kinds of bells and whistles on the alarm system, including emergency medical notifications." Members of this association install alarm systems for businesses like furriers, jewelers, and banks, but the bulk of their work is residential. All members use UL listed products, and the central stations are UL inspected. "In an apartment where there is only one way to get in and out, the system does not need to be elaborate to be effective. You may just have contacts on the door that is the only way in." Mr. Doyle says that the price of alarm systems has been dropping and that a single-contact system wired to a central panel should cost less than $1,000. The deterrent value is important. Residences with alarms "have a 25% less chance of being burgled that those without. A thief knows he has only one minute before the alarm goes off." You can get a list of CSAA members in Manhattan by calling ☎ 301-907-0045.

Some things to consider before getting an

alarm. There are **do-it-yourself** alarm systems, and these make sense if you know you will not be living in the apartment for any length of time, since you can take it with you. However, one of the keys to an effective home security system is its link with a central monitoring station, which won't come with a do-it-yourself system. Starting at about $100 (even less for just a door alarm), though, they're considerably cheaper than dealer-installed systems. Canal Alarm Devices, 387 Canal St. [W. Bway] ☎ 431-5066, specializes in these.

For a **dealer-installed system,** you want your doors and, depending on the apartment, windows wired and a glass-break sensor. The systems usually come with a siren and, of course, signs saying your apartment is protected and monitored. You may want to add motion detectors and a fire alarm. Central station monitoring shouldn't cost much more than $20 a month. Your insurance company may offer a discount, up to 20% or so, with a monitored home-security system. As always, read the fine print since you may think you're *buying* the system when it may be a lease-purchase agreement.

LOCKS The Police Department recommends dead-bolt locks with a one-inch throw-bolt or a heavy duty drop-bolt lock. They also say to install a pick-resistant cylinder and a guard plate over the cylinder. Make sure the hardware used to install the locks is top quality, or you will have defeated the purpose of the lock (or, more to the point, the burglar will). Double-cylinder locks (which use a key on both sides of the door) are illegal. **Medeco** and **Mul-T-Locks** are considered especially good locks. Generally, they run

upwards of $120. Medeco has what they call the Biaxial line, which they consider a "high security" lock. The lock is designed so that the pins need to be both lifted and rotated before disengaging the lock. It comes with a restricted keyway system. Locksmiths who have the equipment to cut the keys also have a magnetic reading device. They cut only for those who present a signature card that is issued from the plant when you buy the lock ($125 and up). Mul-T-Lock also manufactures high quality, high security locks . . . If you want a **Fox Lock,** 40 W. 21st St. [5th/6th] ☎ 924-0211, the lock with two horizontal sliding bars, your hardware store will sell you one and install it. But watch out here. If you buy the lock directly from Fox and install it yourself, you'll spend $85. If you buy it from your hardware store, you could spend as much as $325 for the same thing. Some hardware stores will install a Fox Lock you have bought yourself, but still charge you $100–$200. There are locksmiths in town that will charge under $100 for installation. One is Superior Locksmith, 150 W. 34th St. [Bway] ☎ 736-4049.

WINDOWS & GATES Be sure to choose a "ferry," or **safety gate,** not one that's combination locked or padlocked. You don't want to be scrambling for a key or trying to remember a combination should you need to get out fast.

OTHER OPTIONS The Crime Prevention Division of the NY City Police Dept. offers a free home security survey. Call ☎ 614-6741 or your local precinct (see the Police Precincts list in the Information chapter) to arrange for an officer to visit you at home. They will write a confidential security report and hand deliver it to you . . . Safety experts recommend the use of **light timers** when you are away. There are timers available now that turn lights on and off at random rather than set times . . . To start a **neighborhood watch** program, call your local precinct . . . **Self Defenses,** 246 W. 54th St. [Bway/8th] ☎ 541-5400. This store specializes in products having to do with personal safety and protecting your property. While experts caution that these may give you a false sense of security, there are many items for enhanced security at home, on the street, or when you travel.

CLASSES & LECTURES The Crime Prevention Division of the Police Department gives **safety lectures** to groups. Call ☎ 614-6741 for more info . . . Since women can be especially vulnerable in the city, we list a few classes in self-defense geared toward women. Officer Lorelei Sander of the Crime Prevention Division warns against expensive self-defense classes that promise to teach you self-defense methods in a few lessons since "self-defense takes constant practice." **Prepare Inc.** ☎ 719-5152. Director Karen

Chasen says they teach "tools and skills so that women have options beyond submission." A 20-hour session costs $395. Openhouse classes are offered, and she will run self-defense courses at your place of business . . . **Resources for Personal Empowerment.** Laine Jastrom teaches at both The Learning Annex, 116 E. 85th St.[Park/Lex] ☎ 570-6500, and the Open Center, 83 Spring St. [Bway/Lafayette] ☎ 219-2527. The Learning Annex calls the seminar "Street Power" and charges $49. The threehour program explores the "interior and exterior" aspects of self-defense. Ms. Jastrom founded Resources for Personal Empowerment, which teaches her techniques in businesses, schools, churches, etc. . . . At the **YWCA** at 53rd St. and Lexington Ave. ☎ 735-9722, Agnes Violenus teaches the Horan method of self-defense, based on judo techniques. The basics are taught in nine one-hour sessions. $77 . . . **Allan Apo** of the American Insurance Services Group, ☎ 669-0482, consults with and speaks to businesses on violence in the workplace and business travel safety.

ENVIRONMENTAL ISSUES

ASBESTOS The Environmental Protection Agency's Asbestos Ombudsman, ☎ 800-368-5888, can be helpful to individuals or groups about asbestos problems, regulations, or complaints. The city's asbestos line is ☎ 718-595-3730.

BATTERIES You're required to exchange your car battery when you buy a new one. Other batteries are a problem. The city does not want mercury or nickel cadmium batteries in the landfill, but there is no recycling

program for them at this time. Button batteries (the small circular ones) can be brought to many stores that sell cameras or watches for recycling—they're not required to take them, but some do. Alkaline batteries aren't recycled.

CHRISTMAS TREES Christmas tree recycling is an "on-call" program, which means that when a Dept. of Sanitation foreman sees enough trees on streets in an area, he will dispatch a truck to pick up trees for recycling.

GREEN NY Here are some of the groups working to keep NY green: Central Park Conservancy ☎ 315-0385, Environmental Action Coalition ☎ 677-1601, Green Guerillas ☎ 674-8124, Neighborhood Open Space Coalition ☎ 513-7555, Operation Green Thumb ☎ 788-8059, and Trees NY ☎ 227-1887.

HAZARDOUS WASTE Just about anything you'd want children to keep out of is considered hazardous waste: oven and glass cleaners, polishes, paints, glues, disinfectants, fireworks, bullets, explosives, or radioactive waste, if you happen to have any lying around. The city is selecting a site on Staten Island for dumping, in the unlikely event that you are willing to make the interborough effort to dispose of hazardous waste.

LIGHTBULBS Consider using compact fluorescent lightbulbs, because fluorescent light is not the same sickening light it used  to be and no longer buzzes and flickers. They cost more to buy but last ten times as long as a regular bulb and use a quarter the amount of energy. Con Ed figures you can save as much as $2 per bulb per month on your bill. They can't be used with dimmers, though, and will fit into many, but not all, fixtures. Find them at Whole Foods, 117 Prince St. [Greene/Wooster] ☎ 982-1000, Earth General, 147 Eighth Ave. [17th] ☎ 929-2340, and Just Bulbs, 938 Broadway [21st/22nd] ☎ 228-7820.

MATERIALS FOR THE ARTS This program is sponsored by the Dept. of Cultural Affairs and the Dept. of Sanitation (now *there's* a combo). It's designed to get businesses and individuals to donate goods that Materials for the Arts will then match up to performance centers, social services, museums, and arts companies. Free pickups arranged. ☎ 255-5924.

MOTOR OIL State law forbids pouring it down the sewer or throwing it away. Service stations are required to accept up to five gallons of used motor oil per person per day for recycling.

PILOT PROGRAMS Additional recycling requirements are being phased in neighborhood by neighborhood across the city for mixed paper (junk mail, all cardboard, milk and juice cartons), small metal items (old pots and pans, small appliances, piping), and large metal items (large appliances). Some neighborhoods are already recycling these items; the entire city should be doing so by some time in 1998.

STORES The places to go are **Terra Verde,** 120 Wooster St. [Prince/Spring] ☎ 925-4533, and **Earth General,** 147 Eighth Ave. [17th] ☎ 929-2340. Both stores offer household and personal products that are earth-friendly.

WATER

BY EVELYN KANTER

New York City residents and businesses drink up, cook with, wash with, and flush down some 1.5 billion gallons of water daily. It may take a month for water to flow from as far away as 125 miles upstate through some of the 6,000 miles of pipe beneath city streets to your faucets. While many feel New York has some of the best tasting water in the country, people are concerned about what they can't taste—lead, microscopic organisms, as well as chlorine.

MICROORGANISMS Microorganisms such as *giardia, cryptosporidia, microsporidia,* or the bacteria *E. coli* come from the feces of farm animals, wild animals, or human waste. It's a growing worry as upstate areas become more populated and developed. If you have a compromised immune system—i.e., HIV, AIDS, are undergoing chemotherapy, or are taking immunosuppressive medication following an organ transplant, you should consider a home filtration system. Others may also want to consider this, particularly given the reports of *E. coli* having turned up in the city's system. The DEP's spokesman, David Golub, says, "There has been no coliform incident since 1994. The city believes they've isolated the source as birds." They have set up a water fowl harassment system to keep birds off the reservoirs and have put safeguards in place to control and minimize storm and sewer runoff. Also, a 1995 agreement between NYC and upstate communities protects vital watershed land; in essence, NYC pays them for development opportunities sacrificed. The EPA has given NYC a waiver through the end of the century, which means in the year 2000, the EPA will look again at the water purity and determine whether NYC must build a water treatment facility.

The Centers for Disease Control and Prevention, the EPA, and the NYC Dept. of Environmental Protection recommend that those with impaired immune systems boil their water. (Although boiling will not kill *cryptosporidia.* For that you need a filtration system. Be sure

that the filtration system you use filters to at least 5 microns or less. This is said to get rid of 98% of the *crypto.*) In healthy people these parasites may cause flu-like symptoms or diarrhea; for those with weakened systems, they can be life-threatening. David Golub at the NYC DEP claims NYC has "exceedingly low" traces of *crypto* and *E. coli,* even less than in other municipal systems.

LEAD NYC water doesn't contain lead, but lead can leech from old pipes and brass faucets. NYC is one of some 50 U.S. cities adding calcium orthophosphate to the water supply—it coats the insides of pipes to prevent lead leeching. There's more health risk if a child ingests old lead-based paint chips. However, if you're concerned about lead, let water run 30–60 seconds before using. Never use water from the hot water tap for drinking, cooking, or mixing baby formula, because lead leeching is worse in hot water pipes.

CHLORINE The EPA requires its use in surface water sources as a disinfectant. Quantities are not currently regulated, but the EPA has proposed a maximum allowable limit of 4mg per liter. It can be removed by NSF certified home filters. See below.

NSF STANDARDS The NSF (the National Sanitation Foundation) is a non-profit standards group that certifies filtration systems, domestic and imported bottled waters, and packaged ice for purity and compliance with federal and local regulations. If you are concerned about the water you drink, you can call them at ☎ 800-673-8010, and they will send you, at no charge, information on which filtration systems do what: whether they just remove "esthetically displeasing" stuff (things floating in the water that look gross but won't hurt you) or whether they will remove more serious contaminants.

FILTRATION SYSTEMS All reduce unpleasant taste, odor, or discoloration, but not all control harmful contaminants, according to Nancy Culotta, manager of the Drinking Water Treatment Program at NSF International. The statement "Tested to NSF Standards" is *not* a guarantee that manufacturers claims are true. If the system has the NSF logo in a blue circle, it has been certified that contaminant-reduction claims are true.

In one sense, reverse osmosis is the most effective way to purify water (by pressuring the flow through a micron filter), but it is slow, expensive, and wasteful (five gallons of water create one purified gallon). It also doesn't necessarily make sense in NYC since it is designed to remove things that aren't a problem here. Besides, the resulting water is said to be very flat tasting. If you want more info on the system, try Better Waters, ☎ 675-7300, which has a $399 version or Culligan, ☎ 472-9700 (they have an $850 version).

Carbon filters are less expensive but also less effective. Neo Life, ☎ 874-6640, and Sanitary Water Filtration, ☎ 734-5000, sell systems for about $175 that process up to 900 gallons before replacement. Brita is NSF-certified to filter lead, copper, and most particles. The $19.95 unit includes one fil-

ter and processes 35 gallons, replacement filters are $7. Most of the inexpensive units use granular carbon for filtering. You need to be vigilant about replacing filters since the water that flushes through creates channels in the filter itself. After a time, the water goes through the channels without being properly purified. An alternative to this type of filter is the compressed carbon block filter which eliminates the possibility of channels forming. This technology is available from Amway ☎ 505-2117.

BOTTLED WATER NSF also certifies domestic and imported bottled waters and packaged ice for purity and compliance with federal and local regulations. Call NSF ☎ 800-673-8010, ext. 5181.

HELP

The city will test your water for free. ☎ 718-337-4357 (it's a 24-hour hotline). If you can't wait for an appointment (it could take weeks), Independent Testing Labs, ☎ 718-961-8530, tests running and standing water for $80–$175. Results within 5 days.

The EPA has a Safe Drinking Water hotline—a live person answers questions or directs you to the next information source. ☎ 800-426-4791. Request a copy of "Protecting Your Kids From Lead Poisoning" from the NYC DEP ☎ 718-595-3486. For other information, call the main number, ☎ 718-699-9811.

FIRE

SMOKE DETECTORS Smoke alarms have so drastically reduced the number of fatalities from fire that the Fire Department says that 90% of fatalities are now in

places where there is a smoke alarm, but the alarm's battery has died or been disconnected. Marilyn Mode of the Fire Department says, "When you go to sleep, your sense of smell goes to sleep with you. By the time you smell something, it can be too late." The alarms are best placed "between the kitchen and your bedroom. If there is more than one sleeping area in an apartment, place a detector near each. Most sleeping fatalities come from smoke inhalation, not from the actual fire." Gregory Thomas, Public Safety Education Commissioner of the Fire Department, says the smoke detector "gives you two minutes of 'heads-up' time, which is enough to get you out of the house." Some of the new detectors have a tamperproof 10-year lithium battery and a reset switch. Be sure that the smoke detector has a nationally recognized laboratory rating on it, like UL. You should test them periodically and replace regular batteries at least once a year.

DOCUMENTING POSSESSIONS Allan Apo at American Insurances Services Group says you should document your possessions in case of any emergency, so that "you have some proof of what needs to be replaced." You can either make a written inventory list or a videotape. Give some idea of the value of the item either in writing or by a voice commentary on tape. "There are also possessions that are irreplaceable," like deeds to property and other important papers. These he advises keeping "off property" in a safe deposit box. The videotape and inventory list should also be in the safe deposit box. You can also use a UL listed fire-resistant safe. They are rated for the number of hours of protection they provide, and one with a UL listing "should provide sufficient protection."

DRILLS Everyone at the Fire Dept. we spoke with stressed having family drills. Apartment dwellers should plan exit routes. Don't use the elevators. Be sure "you and your children know two means of exit" from the building. If there is a fire, everyone is disoriented. If you've practiced, you'll lose less time looking for family members and pets.

FIRE EXTINGUISHERS These are "strongly advised for everyone." They are filled with a dry chemical under pressure. They should be labeled as "ABC" type. This means it will put out three categories of fires. A—paper, furniture, other household materials; B—petroleum products, cooking oil; C—electrical. In case of an electrical fire, shut off the power first, then use the extinguisher. A 5-lb. extinguisher is a good size for the home. It's small enough to store away and a "12-year-old child should be able to handle this." Most extinguishers have a pressure gauge on them. "If you don't use it and the gauge goes to green, you need a new one."

DAMAGE Daniel Gersh is the president of Maxons Restoration, ☎ 447-6767, a 50-year-old company that comes in after a fire or smoke or water damage to clean up. They are most often called in by insurance companies but respond to individuals as well. They have done jobs in some big buildings like the Empire State Building in 1990, but also work in residences. "In apartment buildings, if there is a fire in one apartment, smoke seeps into others and the firemen use a lot of water," so it's possible to suffer damage even when there has been no fire in your apartment. Crews clean smoke residue off walls and ceilings and determine how to handle other damaged items. In severe cases, where the building is no longer habitable, they clean and pack and put items into storage. If they are called "within 24–48 hours, there is a good chance of salvaging things. After that, mildew and mold start to grow, and then things can't be restored." In emergency restorations, they do water extraction, remove wet padding and carpeting, and set up dehumidifiers. They can often save rugs if the only damage has been by water. Mr. Gersh cautions that in cases of smoke damage, people should try to walk on rugs or sit on upholstered items as little as possible as this causes the smoke residue to go deeper into the fabric, and it becomes harder to clean out. Products like Fantastik will cause smoke stains to set into certain paints rather than remove them.

ADJUSTER　After a fire, your insurance company will send an adjuster to look over the damage and to make a settlement offer. You may want to consider hiring a private adjuster (actually called public adjusters because they're hired by the public). The reasons people do this is because you want to get everything to which you are legally entitled and the adjuster hired by the insurance company is serving a different interest. Adjusters are licensed by the State of New York and are paid by you. They take a percentage of your settlement (there is a legal limit of 12½ % of a settlement and generally the percentage goes down if the settlement is expected to be a large one). Their fees are negotiable. These adjusters fill out forms, put together claims, and negotiate with your insurance company on your behalf.

FUNERALS, BEREAVEMENT COUNSELING, ORGAN DONATION

FUNERALS

Bill Hartgrove of Frank Campbell Funeral Chapel says that one of the most important things you can do at any age is to make funeral prearrangements—sparing family and friends a lot of problems. From experience he knows it's not enough to *tell* people what you want, you need to put it in writing. Otherwise, someone else's wishes may prevail. It doesn't have to be in the will, it can simply state in the will to follow instructions on file at a particular funeral home.

THINGS TO CONSIDER　The Funeral Service Consumer Assistance Program, ☎ 800-662-7666, suggests you consider the following:

1. Do you prefer burial, entombment, cremation, or body donation?

2. Do you want an open-casket viewing?
3. How many days of visitation do you want?
4. What type of religious or secular service would you like?
5. Do you want a funeral procession to the cemetery?
6. Is there any special music or reading you would like?
7. Do you want flowers or memorial donations?
8. How much money do you wish to spend?

CONSUMER INFORMATION　The regulations and laws set by the Federal Trade Commission and NY City and State help ensure fair practices from funeral homes. These are briefly summarized as:

1. A funeral home must give **price information over the phone** as well as available services.
2. A funeral home must, when you visit in person, supply you with a **price and options list.**
3. **Embalming** is *not* required by law, except in some special cases. It may not take place without your authorization.
4. **Cash advance sales.** These are goods or services that the funeral home pays for up front on your behalf (things like flowers, obit notices, pallbearers). In NY, it is not permissible to charge more than the actual amounts for these services.
5. **Cremation.** When direct cremation is desired (no viewing of the body), no casket is required, and an unfinished wood box or alternative container are options you may choose.
6. **Required Purchases.** You have the right to choose only those goods and services you desire; where the law requires you to make a purchase, the funeral provider must disclose this on the Statement of Goods and Services, citing the specific law. The funeral provider must give you a written, itemized statement (with complete costs) of the goods and services. A "presentation sheet" must be made available describing all goods and services.
7. **Complaints.** Contact the Dept. of Consumer Affairs, ☎ 487-4398, or Funeral Service Consumer Assistance, ☎ 800-662-7666.
8. **Living Wills.** Choice in Dying, Inc., ☎ 366-5540, is a not-for-profit organization that, among other things, supplies information on "advance directives"—a Health Care Proxy (authorizing some-

one to make medical decisions on your behalf if you become incapacitated) and a Living Will, which allows you to express your wishes if you become incapacitated by an irreversible condition. They will send an advance directive if you request one.

ORGAN & TISSUE DONATION

Eye-Bank for Sight Restoration ☎ 980-6700. Over 37,000 people have had their sight restored through corneal transplants made possible by donations to the Eye-Bank. Most people can be eye donors. Corneal transplants are the most successful kind of transplant, with a success rate of better than 90%.

New York Regional Transplant Program, ☎ 870-2240 (24 hours), coordinates organ donor referrals. Anyone is eligible for organ donation, and many organs and tissues can be donated. They will not, however, transplant organs or tissues from those with HIV. Donation does not delay the funeral, and you can have an open casket since the procedures do not alter the appearance of the donor's body. The donor family incurs no cost for the donation.

New York Firefighter's Skin Bank at NY Hospital ☎ 746-7546. The money to establish this burn center was provided by firefighters to help firefighters and other burn victims. Transplanting skin is a temporary lifesaving measure for burn victims. It decreases their pain, maintains temperature, and helps to protect them against infection.

DEATH CERTIFICATES

In Person: Bring $15 in cash, personal check, or money order for each certificate and a pen to 125 Worth St. Get an application form at the information desk in the lobby. Certificates will be mailed to you in 3–4 weeks.

By mail: Send the required information (call the number below for details) with a personal check or money order for $15 for each certificate and a SASE to Dept. of Health, Vital Records, 125 Worth St., New York, NY 10013. The copy should be mailed to you in 3–4 weeks. If the death took place before 1949, the records are in the Municipal Archives, 31 Chambers St. [Centre/Elk] ☎ 788-8580. In the case of a recent death, it may take 6–8 weeks to receive a certificate. Certificates can be ordered from the funeral director at the time of death.

BEREAVEMENT COUNSELING

Cancer Care, ☎ 302-2400, has been offering bereavement counseling programs for more than 50 years for groups, including partners support, relatives support, and many others. They also give workshops dealing with living wills, last wills, power of attorney, health care proxies, and other legal aspects that can arise. There is no cost.

Center for Loss and Renewal, 168 W. 86th St. [Columbus/Amsterdam] ☎ 874-4711, is run by R. Benyamin Cirlin, who is also coordinator of bereavement services at the Jacob Perlow Hospice (see below). Individual counseling and weekly group sessions. There are groups for children and adolescents, and they specialize in adult children mourning the loss of a parent. $40 per group session with a sliding scale.

Friends in Deed, 594 Broadway [Houston/Prince] ☎ 925-2009, has a weekly grief support group for people with AIDS and their loved ones.

Lesbian & Gay Community Service Center, 208 W. 13th St. [7th/Greenwich] ☎ 620-7310, offers ten-week grief support programs. There's no charge.

Gay Men's Health Crisis, 129 W. 20th St. [6th/7th] ☎ 337-3477, has a drop-in group that is open to all on Wednesday evenings at no charge.

Jacob Perlow Hospice, First Ave. and 16th St. ☎ 420-2844 (affiliated with Beth Israel), has drop-in grief support groups—there is no commitment to attending additional sessions. Their Grief Reconciliation Seminars are a more "intensive group experience," and you make a commitment to attend (though you are never forced to speak) for eight weeks.

Marble Collegiate Church, 1 W. 29th St. [5th] ☎ 686-2770, runs a ten-week Grief Support discussion group led by Michael Clifford. There is no charge. It is not a religiously based group, and one need not be a member of the Marble Church.

Compassionate Friends, ☎ 517-9820, is an organization for bereaved parents and siblings. Drop-in meetings are held on the second Tuesday of the month at the Marble Collegiate Church. No charge.

Area hospitals offer bereavement counseling or referral. The deceased generally needs to have been a patient at the hospital. One exception is **Mount Sinai's Bereavement Group,** ☎ 241-0733.

JUNK MAIL

Feeling bombarded by junk mail and annoying solicitations? Some relief is available from the Mail Preference Service and the Telephone Preference Service. They'll cut down the volume of mail and calls you'll get for unwanted solicitations. Just send your name, address, area code, and phone number to: The Direct Marketing Association, Mail Preference Service, P.O. Box 9008, Farmingdale, NY 11735.

JURY DUTY

EXEMPTIONS

As of January 1, 1996, state law made automatic exemptions history. No more jury service exemptions for those in certain occupations—clergy, doctors, lawyers, physical therapists, nurses, police officers, firemen, even judges. There is no automatic age limit of 70 for jury service. Being the sole proprietor of a business does not get you an automatic exemption, either. Tom Munsterman, director of the Center for Jury Studies, says that half of the states have already eliminated the list of exemptions for jury service. "New York had the longest list of exemptions," the result of strong lobbies in Albany for their members.

DEFERRALS

No more multiple chances to mail in deferrals, buying another six months each time. When you receive your summons to serve, you have two choices: 1) serve, or 2) figure out when, in the next six months, you can clear your calendar for two weeks. Then you call the Jury Clerk's office where you will reach an automated telephone service that will ask you to key in the date you will serve. You will be called within a day or two of that date. The computer will tell them if you're trying to get a second postponement. Some discretion to give a second postponement will operate at the time of actual service for "people starting a new job or if a death has occurred." "We will listen to hardship," says Vincent Homenick, Chief Clerk of the Jury Division, but a train ride to Chambers St. will not constitute hardship. The only hardships, besides a medical condition that "renders you incapable of performing jury service," they will consider are for 1) someone who has the care of a child "where other arrangements cannot be made" or "because of the special needs of the child" and 2) financial hardship, in which 3–5 days of service will "significantly compromise their ability to support themselves." Proper documentation has to be submitted in each case. There will be some flexibility on a case-by-case basis. But "it does not make sense to eliminate all of the exemptions and then to reinstate them one by one," according to Judge Jonathan Lippman, Deputy Chief Administrative Judge of NY State.

RECIPROCITY

If you have served on a federal jury and are called for state service within two years of the federal service, you can be excused for a period of two years from the end of the federal service.

BACKGROUND

There are more jury trials in Manhattan than anywhere else in the world. Two thousand potential jurors are needed each day to keep the system running. There had been a proportionally small pool of citizens eligible for jury duty—800,000 in Manhattan. The elimination of the automatic exemptions adds one million names to the jury roles statewide. The law says you should have to serve only once in four years, but, in Manhattan, the pool had been so reduced that those who served found themselves being called every two years.

Who's behind it? Judith Kaye, the Chief Judge of New York State, has, in her years as a trial lawyer and now judge, heard all the grumbling about jury duty. She told us she is determined to make jury service (as she prefers) a "positive encounter with the justice system." Judge Kaye convened a "blue ribbon" panel to study the issues and make recommendations on how to increase the size of the pool, streamline the process, and improve the experience. Judge Lippman says, "The public view of the judicial system comes from jury service. The fundamental premise of the new law is that all are treated equally."

Jury Duty!

PENALTIES

A new Non-Compliance Unit has been established. If you ignore the first summons, you will be fined up to $250, and you will be "ordered to serve." If you do not appear to serve then, a default judgment of $250 will be entered against you, which will appear on your credit record (you can also be held in contempt of court). This carries a possible $1,000 in fines and/or 30 days in jail. A recent case in which someone sent a surrogate in for jury duty caused a judge to sentence the called juror to 500 hours of community service, which was worked out in the jury clerk's office.

THE GOOD NEWS

Manhattan has moved to a three-day, one-trial period of service. Some, most, or all (they're still working that out) who are not serving on a jury by the end of three days will be excused . . . An attempt is being made to speed along the voir dire process in civil cases. Voir dires now have a judge presiding or supervising and there is a pre–voir dire settlement conference with attorneys and the judge . . . Mandatory sequestration during deliberation has been eliminated as a matter of course, but can still can occur in felony cases . . . $750,000 has already been put into upgrading the jury areas. Judge Kaye says, "Amenities are so important. All airless, dilapidated rooms do is agitate and annoy jurors." In the Central Jury Room, some work stations have been installed, but bring batteries for your laptop since there are not as many outlets as work stations. New, more comfortable chairs have been added around the sides of the room, some new lighting has been added (more is planned), and deliberating rooms have been painted. Judge Kaye says of jury service, "It's a right that we have, a centerpiece of the American jury system. Come participate and you will help us make it better. We will make the burden as light as we can, as short, as educative, as pleasant as we can."

OMBUDSERVICE

The OmbudService has been instituted by Judge Kaye to assist jurors. The Vera Institute of Justice, working with the Office of Court Administration, maintains a table outside the Central Jury Room, Mon.–Wed., 9–11. They are there to listen to juror complaints and to resolve problems.

TERM OF SERVICE

Grand Jury. There are 13 Grand Juries impaneled each month for a 30-calendar-day term. You can serve from 10–1 or 2–5 each day, and they try hard to give you your preference. Most people put the other half day in on their jobs. There is no plan to shorten the term of service for Grand Jury Duty.

Regular Jury Duty. Your period of service is still technically for two weeks, the experiment of the three days/one trial period of service could reduce it to three, but figure on a week. The first day you are called, you need to be there at 8:30 for orientation. Otherwise, the hours are generally 9–4:30.

YOUR EMPLOYER

Chances are your boss will now be serving, too. But state law says you cannot be disciplined, fired, or penalized for serving on jury duty. If your company has more than 10 employees, your boss has to pay you $15 a day for the first three days of your service. This is the same as the state's rate of payment. Most employers do pay their salaried employees, but many, such as waiters and independent contractors, lose out.

RESTAURANTS Jury duty offers one noncivic consolation—being near some excellent Asian food: **Thailand Restaurant,** 106 Bayard St. [Baxter] ☎ 349-3132 (try the pad Thai); the cluster of Vietnamese restaurants on Baxter Street (try **Nha Trang,** 87 Baxter [Canal/Bayard] ☎ 233-5948), and **Excellent Dumpling,** 111 Lafayette St. [Canal/Walker] ☎ 219-0212.

SHOPPING **Anbar Shoe Steal,** 60 Reade St. [Church/Bway] ☎ 227-0253, for women, five minutes from 60 Centre St. Name-brand shoes heavily discounted. Donna Karan and Joan and David are mixed in with Via Spiga . . . **Century 21,** of course . . . Large display areas at **Fountain Pen Hospital,** 10 Warren St. [Church/Bway] ☎ 964-0580, are fun even if you are not buying . . . **J & R,** 15 Park Row ☎ 238-9100 . . . **Ruby's Bookstore,** 119 Chambers St. [W. Bway/Church] ☎ 732-8676.

HISTORY In the **Municipal Archives** at 31 Chambers St. [Centre/Elk] ☎ 788-8580, there is a reference library in room 112 with newspapers, magazines, and books having to do with NYC. You can just go in and read for a while. If you go to room 103 and ask to be taken to the Archives, you can see the permanent exhibit, which has a photographic reproduction of the paper authorizing the sale of Manhattan from the Indians to the Dutch. The original is in Amsterdam. It is in Old Dutch, signed by Peter Minuit, and marked by the Indians.

MOVING

BROKERS AND LANDLORDS

Brokers Fees: They're negotiable and not regulated by law. They can run from a month's rent to 20% of the year's rent. If you're going to be doing a lot of the legwork, negotiate the fee down . . . If you want your landlord to **paint** before you move in, get it in writing. In stabilized buildings, they're required to paint every three years, not when there's a vacancy—though many landlords do paint then . . . **Rent stabilized and controlled:** In a stabilized building, the landlord is required to inform you of the previous tenant's rent, and the amount that the landlord can increase the rent is set by law. The Rent Guidelines Board, ☎ 349-2262, meets each summer to set the percentages for the increases that become effective October 1. Forget about rent controlled. If you're looking for an apartment, you can't get a rent-controlled place, and if you're in one, chances are you're not moving. A building is rent stabilized if it falls into one of several categories having to do with when the building was built, whether it got special tax benefits, etc. Stabilization means that your rent is regulated, certain building services are mandated, you are entitled to renew your lease, and you can't be evicted unless you deserve it . . . **Security Deposits:** One month is legal, not two. Sometimes landlords ask for two anyway. The deposit must be kept in an interest-bearing account. You get the deposit back, if there is no damage, when you leave, minus 1% . . . **Subletting:** See Tenants Issues article in this chapter.

MOVING COMPANIES

WHAT TO LOOK FOR

Make sure the mover is **licensed** by the Dept. of Transportation. Ask for their certificate number. You can verify it with the DOT at ☎ 718-482-4815. Moving companies must have liability insurance, cargo insurance, and be in compliance with workman's compensation regulations. (If you hire

a mover who doesn't have workman's comp and there's an accident, you may be involved in a lawsuit.) The best way to find out if your mover is okay here is to call the DOT at the number above and ask.

The most common type of move within the city is the **hourly rated move.** For short moves (usually 40 miles or less), the mover will estimate based on the number of workers needed, the number of hours needed, and the charge for the van. If the final charges exceed the estimate by more than 25%, the mover is required to give you back your things after you give them the estimate plus 25%. The balance of the payment is due within 15 days. **Weight-rated moves** are generally used for long distances. **Lowball estimates** can be a sign of trouble. Don't accept a phone estimate. If the company is too busy to give you an **estimate in your apartment,** they are too busy to give you a good move. A new regulation from the DOT says that if your apartment is over 400 square feet, the moving company *must* come for an on-site estimate if you request them to do so.

Not all movers will give a **written binding estimate,** but it is often the best method. This is a flat rate that the mover gives you after looking over your things and calculating manpower and hours. Movers will often tell you that this kind of an estimate is likely to be higher than an hourly estimate, but many people prefer this type. Be careful, though, because a written binding estimate may exclude items. The written binding estimate should be binding, but sometimes there are disagreements during the course of the move. The mover is required to deliver your goods after you pay the amount of the estimate plus 10%. You are required to pay the balance within 15 working days.

Packing charges should be on a per carton basis, not hourly. If furniture and cartons are being moved on a time basis, *packing* should be done on a per carton basis before the furniture and cartons moved on a time basis. *Unpacking* should be done after furniture and cartons moved on a time basis. Even though the DOT says that if the mover accepts cartons you have packed, they are responsible for damage, the reality is that if you have packed the boxes, movers are going to be unwilling to accept this responsibility.

Be sure to find out what **extra charges** you may incur. Besides packing and unpacking charges, watch out for packing-material charges, travel time, and whether they charge extra for something like a piano. Move **valuables** such as cash and jewelry yourself. If you're moving into a high-rise, be sure to ask the building if there are **elevator restrictions, time and/or day restrictions,** whether you need a **certificate of insurance,** and whether **masonite** needs to be put over the floors. **When to move:** Summer and the end of the month are the busiest times for movers. If you can move at other times, do.

Most of the time, **payment** will be in the form of cash or a certified check. Don't forget that you may need 25% over the estimate for hourly rated moves and 10% for written binding estimates. **Tipping:** Figure at least $5 per man per hour.

More info: Call the **Better Business Bureau** to verify the company's rating. ☎ 900-225-5222. You are charged 95¢ a minute. Get the DOT's useful booklet called the *Summary of Information for Shippers of Household Goods.* Get it early in the process from your mover, or call the DOT at ☎ 718-482-4815. **The Dept. of Consumer Affairs** has a guide to moving. Call ☎ 487-4444 to get it.

RECOMMENDED MOVERS

No moving company is perfect, but the following companies should give you a good move.

Big Apple Moving, 88 Third Ave., Brooklyn ☎ 505-1861. In business since 1980.
Big John's, 1602 First Ave. ☎ 734-3300. In business since 1980.
Brownstone Brothers, 426 E. 91st St. ☎ 289-1511. In business since 1976.
Careful Moving and Storage, 251 E. 137th St. ☎ 718-585-3031. In business since 1961. Some of the preceding information about moving was supplied by Fred Feddeck of Careful Moving. Since they have been in business for so long, they have compiled a booklet of "suggestions for a successful moving experience."

MOVING SUPPLIES

Here's why we like **West Side Movers** supply store, 644 Amsterdam Ave. [91st/92nd] ☎ 874-3800. Their prices are a bit better than most of the other places we visited. It's usually only fifty cents or a dollar less than other places, but that can add up. On some items, though, such as a whole roll of bubble wrap, West Side charges $75 for a roll of 500 feet (2 feet wide), while Big John's charges $375. Small difference in bubble sizes (3/16″ for the former, 1/3″ for the latter), but a big difference in price. We like that they have free reprints available on moving, including one on helping children through a move. Free delivery on orders of $30 or more . . . **Wolf Paper and Twine,** 680 Sixth Ave. [21st/22nd] ☎ 675-4870, sells the 3/16″ bubble wrap for $67 . . . **Robert Karp Container,** 618 W. 52nd St. [11th/12th] ☎ 586-4474, is in a funky, to be polite, area, but this warehouse is a place to consider not so much because their prices are a bit lower than elsewhere (which they are), but because they have double-wall heavy-test boxes that will help ensure your things arrive the way you packed them. Free delivery with $100 minimum . . . **Pathe Shipping Supplies,** 547 W. 20th St. [11th] ☎ 691-0326, also carries a full selection of boxes and other accessories at good prices. Free deliveries on orders of $75 or more, often on the same day.

VALUATION

When you move, you don't buy insurance from the mover, you have, instead, a number of coverage options.

1. You get **Minimum Coverage** (or Limited Movers Liability) automatically—free protection that is basically worthless. If this is the only insurance you have, you will get 30¢ for every pound of damaged goods (60¢ for interstate).
2. **Standard Coverage** means you pay 50¢ per $100 of declared value, with a minimum of $2,500 coverage. If something breaks, the movers are responsible for having it fixed or paying based on *depreciated* value.
3. This option may be offered through your mover. For **Full Replacement Value,** figure about $8.50 per $1,000 of declared value. Your mover must do the packing. If something breaks, the company will try to fix it. If they can't, you get the full replacement value.
4. You can buy your own. (Your homeowner's insurance may provide coverage—but don't count on it. Check your policy.) The DOT can answer questions here. ☎ 518-457-6503.

COMPLAINTS

If the move occurred within the state, the complaint is handled by the DOT. Call ☎ 718-482-4810 for details. If you have a problem and can get something written on your inventory or bill of lading, this will prove useful. The Dept. of Consumer Affairs, ☎ 487-4398, takes moving company complaints and the Better Business Bureau can help resolve problems, ☎ 533-7500.

HELP

When you can't do it alone, see our list of people who can help in the Organizers article in the Services chapter.

NOISE

THE LAW

While noise codes exist (offering some protection if you live over a dance club, for example), most noise issues fall under the Warrant of Habitability section of the law. This means you should be free from unreasonable interference from other tenants. If, say, your upstairs neighbor/drummer is going at it in the wee hours, your landlord is supposed to intervene on your behalf. There are some laws that deal with decibel levels, but the laws set these allowable levels so high that it is unlikely any noise, aggravating as it may be, will exceed those levels in your apartment. Things like hours when someone may practice an instrument may be spelled out in your lease. If not, the generally accepted hours for practice are 6 A.M.–10 P.M.

TO COMPLAIN

Call the DEP to make a complaint ☎ 718-699-9811.

WINDOWS

Neil Woolf at Apple Architectural Windows, ☎ 643-0080, says windows can go a long way toward reducing noise. Renters must get permission from the landlord and bear the expense. **Thermal windows** are composed of three sections: 1) glass, 2) a space of air that reduces noise, your heat and air conditioning bill, and dust, 3) more glass. There are different kinds of thermal glass; the most effective (and expensive) uses two pieces of glass laminated together to form each pane. In a landmark building or when a landlord won't grant permission, you can install an **interior window,** identical to the exterior window, that will give you the effect of a thermal window . . . CitiSilence, 247 E. 83rd St. [2nd/3rd] ☎ 874-5362, also installs interior windows. Prices are based on the size of the window and the kind of glass used, but a 30" x 36" window starts at $200 . . . Richard's Interior Designs, 1390 Lexington Ave. [91st] ☎ 831-9000, has **upholstered walls** in both residences and restaurants to cut down on noise and further suggests using draperies with a black-out lining.

SOUND MACHINES

Hammacher Schlemmer, ☎ 421-9000, has 4 **sound machines** ranging in price from $49.95 to $159. The simplest is just white noise, the most expensive has waterfall sounds, birds, and the ocean . . . Brookstone, 18 Fulton [in the Seaport] ☎ 344-8108, sells "Tranquil Moments" that has six different sounds for $90.

TENANT ISSUES

We spoke with several experts in the field of New York tenant laws, and what follows is a brief rundown of the most common issues tenants face. Most of the information is related to regulated apartments. Much background for this article came from William Rosen of the Metropolitan Council on Housing and attorneys Arlene Boop and Steven Smollens, who specialize in tenant law.

EVICTION It takes work to get evicted. **Nonpayment:** If you don't pay your rent for an extended period of time and don't have the means to pay it, the owner will most likely win the right to evict. However, Mr. Smollens says, "judges are not anxious to evict if it looks like you can pay it." The NYC Marshal's office has special rules when they are evicting someone over 65, providing they know the age. They must notify Adult Protective Services, who will send someone out to determine "how the person has gotten himself into this situation." Many elderly ignore court papers because they feel exempt from the consequences—they are not. Mr. Smollens cautions, "Don't ignore the court papers. The court does not know about your special circumstances unless you bring it to their attention." **Primary Residence:** In rent stabilized apartments, the owner has the right not to renew the lease if he can prove the apartment is not your primary residence. He'll use public records such as voter registration cards, Post Office forwarding notices, and property deeds. **Non-Profit Use:** If the building is owned by a not-for-profit agency and they want to use it for their own purposes, you can be evicted. **Owner's Personal Use:** This usually happens in smaller brownstone-type buildings. The owner has to be an individual (not a corporation or a group) and intend to live there or use it for a family member. He does not have to provide you with another place to live. **Nuisance Cases:** Courts act on the principle that most nuisances can be cured, but make enough noise, leave enough garbage in the halls, and it can form the basis of an eviction proceeding. **Use of the Apartment for Illegal Purposes:** Selling drugs or conducting other criminal activity can get you the boot.

HARASSMENT Most times harassment occurs because the landlord wants to retrieve the apartment. Mr. Smollens says harassment usually takes these forms: 1) repeated **telephone calls** demanding that you give up your apartment without follow up with legal notices; 2) a **decrease in services** that may be construed as dangerous; 3) a threatened or actual carrying out of an illegal **lockout or eviction;** 4) challenging the tenant for having children. Rent regulated tenants can file complaints with NYS Division of Housing and Community Renewal ☎ 718-563-5678. The bureau can order the landlord to desist; if he or she persists, a formal proceeding can follow. In egregious harassment cases, the matter may be turned over to the State Supreme Court. Unregulated tenants must bring a criminal harassment complaint against the landlord. In cases of non-payment of rent or when rent is late, the landlord can make rent demands in the form of written legal notices that he mails to you and can put on your front door. Multiple notices of this type are not considered harassment. Note: If the landlord starts proceedings for non-payment, the tenant must take it seriously. "The only time a tenant can feel safe is if he has received a signed notice from the landlord discontinuing the suit," according to Mr. Smollens. Even with a discontinuance in your hands, you can find a 72-hour notice of eviction on your door. "Do not ignore it. You must go to court, see a lawyer if you can, get an order to show cause, and a restraining order which will temporarily stop the proceedings until you can straighten them out. Don't ignore anything that looks like it comes from the courts."

HELP AND ADVICE Public information number for the **NYSDHCR** (NYS Division of Housing and Community Renewal): ☎ 718-563-5789 . . . **Metropolitan Council on Housing,** 102 Fulton St. [William] ☎ 693-0550, is a tenants' rights organization. They give practical free advice over the telephone M, W, and F, 1:30–5, explaining the law and giving specifics, advice on heat, water damage, plumbing and electrical problems, even going so far as to tell you how to word a letter to your landlord. They also give advice on cases of eviction and rents . . . A **video guide** to NYC Housing Courts produced by the NY Bar Association is set up at 111 Centre St. [White/Leonard] outside room 225. It takes you step by step through a landlord/tenant case . . . Two attorneys who specialize in tenant issues: **Arlene Boop,** partner in Alterman & Boop, 35 Worth St. [W. Bway] ☎ 226-2800, works mostly in tenant law and employment discrimination cases. **Steven Smollens,** a partner in Smollens Guralnick and Frazer, 15 Maiden Lane [Bway/Nassau] ☎ 406-4454, has been practicing housing law for 20 years, representing tenants and landlords (mostly small property owners) . . . The Open Housing Center, 594 Broadway [Houston/ Prince] ☎ 941-6101, publishes *The Housing Resource Guide,* for $20.

HOUSING COURT Landlord and Tenant Court, 111 Centre St. [White/Leonard] is a busy place. You have to go through a security check when you enter the building. This can be time-consuming as it is a thorough check, and, most often, there are lots of people on line. In the early morning there are long waits for the elevator, so factor in these things if you have an early court date (the judges aren't happy if you're late).

LEASES **Before signing:** 1) There are 1 million rent stabilized apartments in NYC, and Mr. Rosen advises strongly that you rent nothing else. He points out that in unregulated apartments there are no controls over lease renewal—in other words, they can throw you out. 2) Any verbal promises made to you before you move in or sign the lease are not binding on anyone. 3) If there are any portions of the preprinted lease (and most landlords use the preprinted form because it is "a tried and true document that will stand up in court") that you want to

change (you want to bring your dog with you but the lease says no pets) or any verbal agreement that is important to you (redoing the floor) before you take occupancy of an apartment, it must be in writing. It must appear either in the lease or in a rider. Mr. Smollens points out that "even experienced renters are unlikely to remember from lease to lease that there is a clause in most leases that says all representations made that are not in the lease don't exist." **High Rent, High Income Deregulation:** If your rent is over $2,000 and you make more than $250,000 for two consecutive years, your apartment can become deregulated. Mr. Rosen says, "Many tenants think, 'Well, I'll just pay the market rent.' They don't realize they are then liable to eviction at the end of a lease." **Renewals:** Rent Increase Guidelines from Oct. 1, 1996–Sept. 30, 1997 were: one-year lease: 5% and 2-year lease: 7%. **Services:** In rent regulated apartments, the landlord has to file an information sheet with the NYSDHCR that tells what services are part of the condition of the rental. This includes things like stove, refrigerator, dishwasher, air conditioning, video intercom, doormen, etc. These services must be maintained in your apartment. A tenant can check with DHCR to find out what these services are, ☎ 718-739-6400. If your refrigerator gives up, the landlord must replace it. If your refrigerator is just old and unsightly and you want a new one, you can ask the landlord to provide it. If he agrees, he can pass along the cost of the new item as part of your rent. This becomes a permanent part of the rental cost of your apartment. **Subleasing:** It's legal, but you have to do it carefully. It requires written consent from your landlord, which the law says he cannot withhold unreasonably. You can sublet only two out of every four years, and you have to show intention to return. The sublessee has no right to renew the lease if you do not come back. Rent *controlled* tenants do not have the right to sublease. If you sublet a furnished apartment, the tenant can legally charge you only 10% above the legal rent—though this is, needless to say, often ignored.

REPAIRS Many things don't get repaired because landlords don't know about them. If no repairs are made after a verbal request, notify the landlord in writing. Keep a good copy for yourself and get proof that you sent the request. If you mail it, do so by certified mail, return receipt requested. If you hand deliver it, have the original and the copy stamped with the date received. If, after waiting a reasonable amount of time for repairs to be made, nothing happens, a tenant can begin a **Housing Proceeding.** This can be done with or without an attorney. Visit the HP Clerk at 111 Centre St. [White/Leonard], room 225. You fill out forms with what you believe to be the violations. Mr. Smollens advises writing everything down (peeling paint and plaster, leaks, running water, inadequate heat and hot water, broken windows, etc.) before you leave home so you don't leave anything out. You will have to pay $35 for an index number (your case number). After this, things happen relatively quickly. An inspector should be at your home in 8–10 days to document any violations; following that, a court date is set. The court can issue an "order to correct" that sets out a timetable for compliance. If the landlord defies this, he is liable for contempt of court. The HP is "effective and efficient and does not take a lot of time. It will achieve results that the tenant has not been able to achieve with the landlord." Arlene Boop says that the HP is an "excellent alternative to withholding rent."

ROOMMATES The law is complicated here. The Sharing Law allows anyone to have one unrelated person and their depen-

---

P E T S

Many leases in NYC have a no-pets provision. Dogs are generally more objectionable to landlords than cats, because dogs need to be in the public spaces of the building. If you move in with a dog, you should have the clause removed from your lease and get special provision to bring the dog in. However, if you bring in a pet and *openly display the pet*, the landlord has 90 days to bring action to remove the dog. If the landlord brings suit within 90 days, he will most likely win the suit. If you openly display the dog for 90 days and the land- lord does nothing, you will most likely win the suit should there be one. "Sneaking the dog in and hiding it does not satisfy the three-months notice rule." The 90-day rule has been enacted to prevent "arbitrary and capricious action on the part of landlords" in removing pets that people may have had for years. You will have some idea of the landlord's attitude toward pets by the number you see in the building, though some may be there because they are grandfathered in.

dent children in the household without the landlord's permission. The second person's name does not have to appear on the lease. You can establish tenancy without a lease if the second person signs the rent checks and the landlord accepts them for a reasonable amount of time.

SERVICE DECLINE Tenants can pool rent money to care for the public spaces of a building or pay a utility bill if the landlord has not. In most situations (provided the utilities know it is a residential building), the utilities will post a notice in the building when non-payment by the landlord is about to result in termination of service. These notices contain information on how tenants can start the process to pay for utilities using rent money. According to Ms. Boop, this "has been working reasonably well." Tenants do not pay the arrears, only the cost of running the building going forward. This does not apply to oil companies. However, she says, "judges generally condone tenant arrangements for oil delivery if they can prove that the service was not provided and that the landlord had reasonable opportunity to provide it." Tenants should show that "reasonable notice was given to the landlord that there was no oil there." Ms. Boop advises that you always send notice to the landlord in at least two ways. Certified return receipt requested mail doesn't always work, because some landlords have

been known not to pick it up. Use regular mail, take written complaints directly to the landlord or maintenance company (where you get a date-stamped copy of receipt), or fax information from a fax that gives you a verification. It's wise, in cases of chronic no-heat complaints, for two or more tenants in the building to keep a diary showing the temperature outside and inside the apartment, with the time and date the readings were taken.

SUCCESSION RIGHTS The law on succession rights continues to be clarified. Mr. Smollens says cases are "constantly arising because the landlord disputes a succession, or the successor tenant institutes a proceeding to have the rights declared. Most of the current cases have to do with children remaining after the parents move out or die, or children moving back in two or three years before the parents leave the apartment." Don't jump to any conclusions on succession without consulting a lawyer. "In general, these are not peacefully resolved, because the apartment is a valuable recovery for a landlord. Many are contested in co-op buildings." Ms. Boop says succession "requires real occupancy," and the courts are left with the problem of weeding out the opportunists. The law requires a two-year residency to establish succession. The succeeding party needs to show "the bona fide nature of the family relationship" and that they "participated as a member of the household." Judges have been upholding the rights of unmarried straight or gay partners, although the issue has not been resolved conclusively. Generally, if you can prove financial and emotional interdependence, the court will treat you as a married couple. For financial interdependence, judges look for a life insurance policy or a will naming the other as beneficiary, things owned in common, and joint bank accounts.

TENANT INSURANCE Tenant's Insurance (or renter's insurance as it is sometimes known) exists to protect us urban dwellers against personal belonging loss and provides coverage for liability. The Tenants Form Policy (HO-4) is a "package" policy because it combines loss and liability coverage, though for some companies, the liability part of it is optional. In addition to coverage against loss, the policy will include the legal costs of defense if you're sued in a liability case and will pay for increased living expenses, up to a predetermined limit, should you be forced, by disaster, to live in a different apartment or a hotel. The HO-6 is for co-ops and condos.

Personal Belongings: To obtain a policy, you'll need to inventory furniture, clothing, major personal belongings, and assess their cash value. Photographs of major items will aid in the process. Major personal belongings like furs, jewelry, silver, and, sometimes, other items will require an addition to the standard policy (read: more money). Here's a rundown of what disasters your policy would cover (they list volcanic eruptions, but MUG thinks this is unlikely): fire, lightning, smoke, burst steam pipes, roof collapse from snow and ice, rioting, vandalism, vehicles, and a few other calamities. These are known as the Perils, and you should be covered for about 17 of them. Be sure to read the Exclusions section. Some, for example, do not cover you for any water damage un-

less the water damage causes a fire, explosion, or theft.

Liability: In addition to paying up to the limit of their liability (usually between $100,000 and $300,000) for damages in a suit if someone is injured in your apartment, the insurance company will also pay for medical expenses if a guest is injured on your premises (there may be some limits from your insurer). This applies only to guests, not to you or to any "regular residents," but would cover residence employees, provided the company knows they are there.

Specific Plans: We checked with three major companies: Allstate, Aetna, and State Farm. They each asked a series of questions relating to the neighborhood and size and construction of the building. All quotes are the annual cost based on $33,000 coverage and $100,000 liability and full replacement value of goods with a $250 deductible. Allstate: $345; Aetna (Aetna's minimum is $300,000 liability): $224; and State Farm (requires a smoke detector, a dead-bolt lock, and a fire extinguisher): $272. The theft insurance may extend beyond your apartment to include loss as a result of holdup or pickpocketing.

There is a toll-free National Insurance Consumer Helpline that can answer questions, provide information, and channel complaints: ☎ 800-942-4242.

WALLET, LOST OR STOLEN

Some numbers you may need if your wallet is lost or stolen.

AIRPORTS LOST AND FOUND
Check with your carrier or try:
JFK ☎ 718-244-4225

LaGuardia ☎ 718-533-3988
Newark ☎ 201-961-6230

BANK CARDS
Apple ☎ 472-4545 M–F, 9–5; Sa, 9–2
Bank Leumi ☎ 343-5475

Bank of NY ☎ 914-899-6777
Chase ☎ 800-632-3300
Chemical ☎ 800-648-9911
  (credit cards) ☎ 935-9935
Citibank ☎ 627-3999
EAB ☎ 800-556-5678 (credit
cards) ☎ 516-296-5500 (ATM cards)
East NY Savings ☎ 800-724-3697
First Federal ☎ 800-556-5678 (credit
cards) ☎ 800-462-3047 (ATM cards)
Greenpoint Savings ☎ 953-8330, until 9
P.M. weekdays. Sa, 9–2
Marine Midland ☎ 800-462-1874
Republic Bank ☎ 718-488-4050, 9–5
only. ☎ 800-745-2265 24 hrs.

CARD PROTECTION SERVICES
You give them the info ahead of time, and
if disaster strikes, you call one number to
have your cards canceled.
American Express ☎ 800-227-2639. $15
per year or $36 for 3 years.
Credit Card Hotline (Chase)
  ☎ 800-468-5463. $15 a year.
Diners Club Protection Service
  ☎ 800-633-3985. $25 a year with many
extra features.
Discover ☎ 800-347-2683. Basic service
$4.99 for 1 year, $12.99 for 3 years.
Protection Plus (Citibank)
  ☎ 800-338-3815. $15 for 1 year.
Sentinel Services (Chemical)
  ☎ 800-423-5166. Basic service: $9/yr,
$24/3 yrs. VIP level: $18/yr, $45/3 yrs.
This has extra features like a cash advance and emergency transportation
funds, and it allows you to register other
documents as well.

CAR RENTAL CARDS
Avis Wizard ☎ 516-222-3000, from 8–5;
after 5 ☎ 800-352-7900

Budget Rapid Action ☎ 214-404-7941
Dollar ☎ 800-800-0088
Hertz #1 ☎ 405-721-6440

CREDIT CARDS
American Express/Optima
  ☎ 800-528-4800
Diners/Carte Blanche ☎ 800-234-6377
Discover ☎ 800-347-2683
Visa/MasterCard:
Chase ☎ 800-632-3300
Chemical ☎ 800-648-1911
Citibank ☎ 800-843-0777
Midland ☎ 800-462-1874

CREDIT REPORTS
To clean up a credit report when cards or
numbers are stolen, contact the three credit
agencies for copies of your reports. Detail
what charges you are not liable for and return
to them. Keep accessing these reports until
they are clean. It may take awhile until all false
charges are reported to the credit companies:
1. **TRW,** P.O. Box 8030, Layton, Utah
  84041 ☎ 800-422-4879.
2. **Trans Union,** P.O. Box 390, Springfield,
  PA 19064 ☎ 718-459-1800.
3. **Equifax,** P.O. Box 105873, Atlanta, GA,
  30348 ☎ 800-685-1111.

DEPARTMENT STORE CARDS
Barneys ☎ 800-926-5393
Bendel's ☎ 800-888-3614
Bergdorf's ☎ 872-8851
Bloomingdale's ☎ 355-5900, after hours
  ☎ 800-950-0047
Brooks Brothers ☎ 682-8800
Lord & Taylor ☎ 827-5200
Macy's ☎ 800-743-6229
Saks ☎ 800-221-8340
Tiffany's ☎ 201-971-3511 (you can call
  collect) or ☎ 800-827-1396

DRIVER'S LICENSE

You need 6 "points" of I.D.—anything that you can find: passport, canceled checks, utilities bills, etc. These all have different point values. Call for more info ☎ 645-5550 and especially to make sure you have enough I.D. when you go in. Fill out the MV44 form, have photo taken ($7.25), pay with cash, check, or money order, and you'll get a temporary license; the regular one will be mailed. They're at 141–55 Worth [Centre/Baxter] M–F, 9–4:30.

FREQUENT FLYER CARDS

American Airlines ☎ 800-882-8880
Continental ☎ 713-952-1630
Delta ☎ 404-715-2999
Northwest ☎ 800-447-3757
TWA ☎ 800-325-4815
United ☎ 605-399-2400
USAir ☎ 800-872-4738

GAS CARDS

Amoco ☎ 800-247-0067
Exxon ☎ 800-344-4355
Gulf ☎ 800-321-9902
Mobil ☎ 800-552-1223
Shell ☎ 800-331-3703

Texaco ☎ 800-552-7827 or
☎ 713-567-7827 if you don't have your card number.

PASSPORT

☎ 800-688-9889

PHONE CARDS

AT&T ☎ 800-225-5288
MCI ☎ 800-444-2222
NY Telephone ☎ 890-2350 M–F, 8–8;
Sa, 8–4 (or call operator)
Sprint ☎ 800-877-4646

SOCIAL SECURITY CARDS

☎ 800-772-1213, to get application, form SS5

SUBWAY LOST AND FOUND

☎ 718-625-6200. Open only M, T, W, F from 8–noon and Th, 11–6:45.

TAXI LOST AND FOUND

☎ 302-8294. Try this, but cabbies will often deposit the lost item with the police precinct closest to where you got out.

Districts & Spaces

←――――――――――――――――――――――――――→

THE BON VIVANT

BY ADAM GOPNIK

The attraction of rows of booths in coffee shops is a hard one for a New Yorker to explain, except in terms either depressingly nostalgic or else just as depressingly homey. Nonetheless, my own favorite vista in New York is the one presented by the two booths that sit inside the west side windows at the **Bon Vivant** coffee shop on 12th and Broadway. My first morning in New York (setting aside a first run-through in 1964, aged seven: the "Small World" ride, twice, sinister devil dolls, shrieking world peace) was in August 1978, when my true love took me to a coffee shop on Madison. A real New York coffee shop—a row of booths along the north wall; a quilted aluminum console; separate menu for breakfast, two eggs with Virginia ham. It taught me an essential New York lesson—that cramped and generous aren't necessarily opposites. That place, the Gardenia,

is gone now—well, not gone, but all dolled up, with hard-backed chairs and a short wine list and the waiters, Nick and Joe, trained to sprinkle cocoa on your cappuccino. It defined a zone of pleasure for me, though, and the few little Greek coffee shops that are left still seem to me to be the hearths of the city, especially now that this plague of espresso bars is driving them all away (why should New York take lessons in style from *Seattle?*).

There are, by my doubtless idiosyncratic count, only about three coffee shops worth the name left—Gracie's Corner, up on 86th, which for a little while in the eighties was my Café de Flore; I did my writing there and thought about doing it; the Palace, all the way east on 57th St. (odd that it survives; it's a bit tony, but authentic: They have a wine list on which some of the wines are called "fruity" and some "nutty," but only one is called "nutty and fruity"), and the Bon Vivant, on Broadway near 12th St. The interior of the Bon Vivant is one of my favorite places around the city; it was done over, sometime back in the early eighties, in a kind of candied postmodern palette, sort of what you might expect from somebody who once visited a house that had been decorated by Michael Graves's nephew. There are candy apple colors, and sour grape colors, and off-aquas all over. It is those two big booths near the front, which look west onto Broadway, that I love most. The pleasure of booths on a street window is, I think, if not limited to New York, at least especially rich here. Out in the real world, America, whenever I travel, I notice that all the booths are stowed away in the back, away from the street and the noise. But there is no back, no *room,* in New York. (Notice how the coffee shop on *Seinfeld* is just a big phony; the space is too big, and the booths sit inside, away from the street.) Space costs too much here, so the booths line up by the window.

This is where the uncanny brightness of the decor inside the Bon Vivant has a wonderful effect. The theory, I'm sure, was that the bright colors would brighten things up inside, without anyone stopping to think that what it would really do is darken things up *outside*—make lower Broadway look even dingier and more shadowy than it did before, like a woodcut from an Expressionist novel-in-pictures, long shadows trailing the angst-ridden hero home. But this is a

The booths at the front of the Bon Vivant.

blessing, too: Now, when you're inside the Bon Vivant on an average winter Saturday, around three o'clock, eating your Yankee bean soup with white toast and a soda, it *always* looks as if it is about to snow. The dark sky, the dim light, the gray pallor that hangs over everything—you think . . . *snowstorm coming,* six inches on the way . . . all that white, tomorrow morning. Then you step outside and, your eyes no longer tuned to the dazzle of all those bright leatherette booths, you become accustomed again to the New York palette running its usual spectrum from Pigeon Feather Purple-Gray to Olde Chewing Gum Off-White, and you realize, no, no snow. But for a little while you thought that by the time you got home, the city would be beautiful, which is no small gift for the price of soup.

Adam Gopnik writes for The New Yorker.

BROOKLYN

It's awfully hard to get some of us to cross the bridge, but here are some reasons, beyond the more well-known ones (BAM, the Brooklyn Botanic Garden, Peter Luger, Prospect Park, and the Promenade) to go to Brooklyn. Highlights for us are John

Cashman's tours of Green-wood Cemetery and the moving phoenix of Weeksville.

SPACES

BROOKLYN HISTORICAL SOCIETY

If the idea of visiting an historical society makes you think that you will spend a lot of time speaking in hushed tones and weighed down by dust, you haven't been to **The Brooklyn Historical Society,** 128 Pierrepont St. [Clinton/Henry] ☎ 718-624-0890. There are many compelling reasons to visit: the lovely George B. Post designed building, the permanent exhibition on Brooklyn is great fun and informative, and their temporary shows can be extremely relevant to contemporary life.

CARROLL GARDENS

Walking through many sections of Brooklyn rewards those interested in architecture and history. Brooklyn Heights, Park Slope, Fort Greene and Clinton Hill, Prospect Park South, and Cobble Hill are favorites of ours. **Carroll Gardens** doesn't have the splendor of some of these other neighborhoods, but the sense of community is strong—you feel it just by spending a little time here. The area (parts of which have been designated an historic district) was conceived by Richard Butts in 1846, and the houses were built from 1869–1884. It is particularly the gardens fronting each house that give the small district its special character. There is a sizable Italian presence in the area, reflected in the stores and restaurants along Court Street. After a tour of the area, we'd stop at **The Fall Café,** 307 Smith St. [President/Union] ☎ 718-403-0230, which seems to us perfectly in keeping with the area—it's a storefront coffeehouse with chairs, sofas, magazines, and newspapers. They encourage you to linger, do the crossword, schmooze.

EMPIRE FULTON FERRY STATE PARK

At the **Empire Fulton Ferry State Park,** you get the noise in stereo from both the Brooklyn and the Manhattan Bridges, and to call it a state park seems to be stretching the point. Even so, we like Brooklyn's newest park because you share great views of New York with few of your fellow New Yorkers—or anybody else for that matter.

WEEKSVILLE

There is something haunting about **Weeksville.** These are the houses, located at 1698–1708 Bergen Street and built between 1840 and 1883, that are the vestiges of the community built by free blacks in what is now the Bedford-Stuyvesant section of Brooklyn.

Weeksville was named for James Weeks, who bought land from the Lefferts family in 1838. Around him grew a close-knit community of several hundred, consisting of houses, churches, and a school. Out of Weeksville came a number of distinguished citizens, including Moses P. Cobb, the first black policeman in Brooklyn, as well as Dr. Susan Smith McKinney-Steward, one of the first black female physicians in the country. Although slavery was abolished in New York state in 1827, communities like Weeksville provided a refuge against intolerance, particularly after the Draft Riots of 1863. Eventually the community became absorbed into Bed-Stuy, and it wasn't until 1968 when the historian James Hurley led a workshop on Brooklyn neighborhoods at Pratt Neighborhood College that anyone looked for remains of Weeksville. He, with engineer and pilot Joseph Haynes flew over Brooklyn looking for lost Weeksville. Since the colonial Hunterfly Road, on which these houses were situated, predated and did not conform to the borough's street plan, Messrs. Hurley and Haynes discovered from the air the four remaining clapboard houses. In August 1970, the houses were landmarked and the Society for the Preservation of Weeksville and Bedford-Stuyvesant History was formed. The houses are being restored (by Li/Saltzman Architects), and it is now an historical society. In the planning stage is a new facility to include *The New Merengue,* an art installation by Houston Conwill, Joseph De Pace, and Estella Conwill Majozo that was exhibited in the lobby of the Brooklyn Museum. The artists have donated the large installation to Weeksville.

A walk around the simple setting, in a neighborhood fallen on hard times, makes you feel the bittersweet history of African-Americans in New York. It stays with you. Weeksville's executive director, Joan Maynard, is passionate about the importance and relevance of the houses. She says, "We have an opportunity and obligation to preserve Weeksville for future generations."

The Weeksville Lady.

From a tintype found at the site, the society chose an unidentified woman to symbolize Weeksville, and she is known as "The Weeksville Lady." Rather than a symbol of the past, she seems to be gazing proudly into the future. The same might be said of Weeksville. For more info, call ☎ 718-756-5250.

GREEN-WOOD CEMETERY

Take a walking tour with John Cashman, expert on and passionate guide to **Green-wood Cemetery,** and you get an incredibly interesting walk through American history. Consider a few of the people buried here: De Witt Clinton, Duncan Phyfe, Lola Montez, Samuel F. B. Morse, "Boss" Tweed, Louis Comfort Tiffany, Leonard Bernstein, Charles Ebbets, Horace Greeley, Henry Steinway, Elias Howe, and Currier and Ives, among many other notables in every walk of life and others with equally interesting stories beyond the ornate mausoleums and simple stone markers. Before Prospect and Central Parks, New Yorkers used the 478-acre Green-wood as an ersatz park, strolling, picnicking, and enjoying the idyllic setting with its wonderful views of Manhattan (it's the highest point in Brooklyn). If you go on a tour, you might want to go when the cherry blossoms are in bloom at the end of April. Whenever you go, you are certain to catch some of Mr. Cashman's enthusiasm for this remarkable spot. Mr. Cashman is a retired New York City police officer who started mowing the lawns in Green-wood when he was young because he thought he'd pick up a little extra cash and "a great tan." It has turned into a lifelong passion, this digging into the history of Green-wood. Nowadays, you can visit only on an official tour. Mr. Cashman's tours are given on Sundays from April–June and September–November. Call ☎ 718-469-5277 for more info and to reserve a spot. The tour is $5.

THE ARTS

In the 1980s, many artists, feeling pushed out of Soho by rising rents, took the L train one stop into Brooklyn to the traditionally Polish and Italian neighborhoods of Williamsburg and Greenpoint. Coffee shops, thrift shops, new small restaurants, and small galleries are developing around Bedford and Berry streets, side by side with the Polish bakeries and Italian delicatessens. **Pierogi 2000,** 167 N. 9th St. [Bedford/Driggs] ☎ 718-599-2144, pays tribute to both groups of residents in their name. Pierogi 2000 mounts regular shows and maintains portfolios on at least 200 Brooklyn artists that you can browse through . . . **Art Moving,** ☎ 718-782-4206, specializes in 24-hour shows. Location changes from show to show. The art is often accompanied by music from local bands, poetry readings, and performances. **Sauce** (so named because it is above a pasta warehouse), 173A N. 3rd St. [Bedford/Driggs] ☎ 718-384-9271, often coordinates its shows to occur around an Art Moving event . . . **Momenta Arts,** 72 Berry St. [9th/10th] ☎ 718-218-8058, has gallery hours, Th–Su, 12–6, when a show is up . . . Closer to Borough Hall is **Rotunda Gallery,** 33 Clinton St. [Cadman Plaza/Pierrepont] ☎ 718-875-4047, which specializes in shows by contemporary artists who "live, work, or were born in Brooklyn." . . . You can visit **Urban Glass,** 647 Fulton St. [Flatbush] ☎ 718-625-3685, and watch the process of glassmaking. In their Robert Lehman Gallery, artists who work in glass are exhibited. Classes are offered . . . **Brooklyn Waterfront Artists Coalition,** ☎ 718-596-2507, is a group of several hundred artists who either live or work in Brooklyn. They hold several exhibitions each year which are open to the public. Each May the Pier Show is held in the pre–Civil War warehouses at 141 Beard St. [Richards/Van Brunt] in Red Hook. Later in the summer BWAC sponsors an outdoor sculpture show at the Empire Fulton Ferry State Park . . . The only time **Rene Murray** has spent outside of Brooklyn was the six years at the University of Michigan, where she got her M.A. in ceramics. She has been practicing her skill back in the borough ever since. Ms. Murray has a distinctive sculptural style even when her pieces are utilitarian. She prefers handbuilt to wheel-thrown pieces, which means that her range of shapes is striking. She recently exhibited 60 small teapots, each different. Ms. Murray also makes her own glazes, develops her own colors, and does not use commercial products. Her work is in gallery shows, but you can go to her twice yearly sale on the second Saturday in December and the second Saturday in June. Call ☎ 718-875-7153 for directions . . . Each year from mid-July to mid-September, the Brooklyn Bridge itself becomes a venue for theatre and musical performances, literary readings and art installations. The **Creative Time Company** programs events inside the base of the Bridge on the Brooklyn side [Cadman Plaza W./Old Frontage]. You can get a schedule by calling ☎ 206-6674 in season.

GOOD DEALS

Lots of good deals in the borough. Here are a few of them: **Aaron's,** 627 Fifth Ave. [17th] ☎ 718-768-5400, is well worth a trip for women's clothes. Searle raincoats at Aaron's were $210, $390 at Saks. Clothes are arranged by designer, are clearly organized, and the selection is large. Sale racks, where the discounts are 70% off the off-price, contain some amazing things like Bill Blass and Scaasi dresses for $75. You'll find names like Eileen Fisher, Tahari, and Tomatsu . . . **Domsey,** 431 Kent Ave.

[Bway/8th] ☎ 718-384-6000, seems like the world's biggest thrift store. Lots of stuff you don't want with a few things you do to justify the effort . . . **Frankel's Discount Store,** 3924 Third Ave. [40th] Sunset Park ☎ 718-768-9788, has some great prices on boots—less than half of what you'd pay for the same thing in Soho, but selection is limited. 20% off most Timberland shoes . . . If it's been a while since you went **antiquing** on Atlantic Avenue (especially between Hoyt and Nevins), you'll be surprised at the number of good stores here. Most specialize in 19th century American and English furniture . . . **Marshall's Smoked Fish,** 23 Anthony St. [Morgan/Vandervoort] ☎ 718-384-7621, is difficult to reach except by car, but if you come here (weekdays only), you'll get high-quality salmon, sable, and other smoked fish at lower prices than just about anywhere.

FOOD

Joe's Busy Corner, ☎ 718-388-6372, has been on the corner of Driggs Ave. and North 7th St. since 1933. The current Joe, Joe Nespole, lived above the store as a child, worked there from the age of 12, and took over as proprietor in 1959. His partner is his nephew, Tom Prevete. Joe's makes it a point to have Italian specialties year round and for holidays. Mr. Nespole makes his own mozzarella, both fresh and smoked, and, with one assistant, makes things like raviolette with pesto, stuffed artichokes, and pasta with basil salad. Around Easter time, they make pizza rustica, a thick, cheese pie containing salami and proscuitto, and pizza grano, a sweet ricotta and cream cheese cake with grains of wheat. It's all good. For Christmas, Joe says many of the old timers come back for the baccalà salad. But Joe's is more than a place to buy Italian specialties. Need to leave your key somewhere your visitors can pick it up? Need to leave a message for someone? Need someone to take care of your mail while you're away? If you live in Joe's neighborhood, he'll handle it. Diligently working the front of the shop is the 79-year-old Jo Jo, an unpaid volunteer and no relation, who keeps things shelved and in proper order. Perennially chomping on a cigar, Jo Jo was a member of the Sym Phony, the Dodgers' band. Stop by, he'll tell you all about it.

For Brooklyn restaurants, see the Brooklyn section of the Restaurants chapter.

MORE Other reasons to visit are scattered throughout this book. They include the Aquarium, Architectural Salvage Warehouse, Bargemusic, Brooklyn Botanic Garden, the Brooklyn Museum, the Brooklyn Promenade, J. Schacter Co., The New York Transit Museum, Nordic Delicacies, and Sahadi Trading.

CARNEGIE HILL

What's strikes us about about Carnegie Hill isn't the number of benches you'll find there, but that you find any at all. You do find benches in and around the city's parks, but rarely within city neighborhoods. You find them in Carnegie Hill, though, as if the residents and merchants know you'll want to linger, to enjoy the distinctive character of their piece of the island. About the district: We're not being precise. This is a *section of*

Carnegie Hill, which actually covers, more or less, Fifth Ave. to Lexington between 86th and 96th. We've narrowed the definition to Madison Ave. between 86th and 96th, since this is Carnegie Hill's Main Street.

HISTORY

Manhattan got its name from the Indians, of course, who called the place Manhatta, which meant "hilly island." Carnegie Hill is among the highest points. The village of the 60 or so Weckquaesgek Indians who settled here is now buried beneath the pavement around Park Ave. and 98th Street. The Dutch and the English were slow to settle this area (though quick to draw the Weckquaesgeks into conflict) because the area was too hilly for farming. Transportation improvements, the first being the NY and Harlem Railroad and then the announcement of the Third Ave. El in 1868, started the development of much of the East Side. It didn't happen quickly, though: When Andrew Carnegie, in 1898, bought the land between East 90th and 91st, squatters were living on it, as they did on many of the undeveloped plots. His mansion encouraged other wealthy New Yorkers to move north. The houses in the area became grander, and even today, the feel of the French château is evident in many of the designs. There are two historic districts in this area: E. 90th–92nd between Madison and Park, as well as E. 92nd–94th between Fifth and Madison. (Only parts of the blocks are landmarked, but when you stroll, it's not hard to determine what is and is not designated.)

STORES

BOOKS

The Corner Bookstore, 1313 Madison Ave. [93rd] ☎ 831-3554, a prime example of a neighborhood bookstore, and one that feels very much at the center of the community . . . For military aficionados, there's the **Military Bookman,** 29 E. 93rd [5th/Mad] ☎ 348-1280.

FOR KIDS

Greenstones, Too, 1184 Madison Ave. [86th/87th] ☎ 427-1665, for kids' parkas and knapsacks, outerwear and cool hats . . . **Bonpoint & Jacadi,** 1281 Madison Ave. [91st/92nd] ☎ 369-1616. Charming children's clothes next to the ever-popular **Penny Whistle Toys** . . . Expensive French and Italian clothes for kids at **Au Chat Botte,** 1192 Madison Ave. [87th/88th] ☎ 722-6474, and **Catimini,** 1284 Madison Ave. [90th/91st] ☎ 987-0688 . . . **Wicker Garden for Children,** 1327 Madison Ave. [93rd/94th] ☎ 410-7001, has clothes, lots of white wicker, plus wicker cribs and chairs (see more in children's furniture) . . . **Dollhouse Antics,** 1343 Madison Ave. [94th] ☎ 876-2288, sells wonderful dollhouses and everything for the inside. They also have classes in construction . . . **Art and Tapisserie,** 1242 Madison Ave. [89th] ☎ 722-3222, does customized gifts—they'll add a child's name to rocking chairs, clocks, bookends.

CLOTHES

Nancy & Co., 1242 Madison Ave. [89th] ☎ 427-0770, has stylish women's clothing . . . **Ann Crabtree,** 1310 Madison Ave. [92nd/93rd] ☎ 996-6499, sells clothes, mostly from Italy and France, with an eye to good fabrics . . . **J. McLaughlin,** 1311 Madison Ave. [92nd/93rd] ☎ 369-4830, is a good source for clothes to wear on the Vineyard . . . **Ann's Boutique,** 1306 Madison Ave. ☎ 410-5339, specializes in limited editions of one-size-fits-all clothing with arty details . . . **Veronica Delachaux,** 1321 Madison Ave. [93rd/ 94th] ☎ 831-7800, carries upscale, attractive maternity wear.

OBJECTS

Mark Milliken, 1200 Madison Ave. [87th/88th] ☎ 534-8802, is a popular neighborhood stop for its funny, whimsical art objects . . . **Marjory Warren—The Studio,** 1225 Madison Ave. [88th/89th] ☎ 876-9777, has funky earrings, necklaces, bags, sweaters, and pillows . . . **Keesal and Matthews,** 1244 Madison Ave. [89th /90th] ☎ 410-1800, for not inexpensive but tasteful gifts: glasses, bowls, china, candles . . . **Works Gallery,** 1250 Madison Ave. [89th/90th] ☎ 996-0300, has jewelry and handblown glassware . . . The **Frank J. Miele Gallery,** 1262 Madison Ave. [90th] ☎ 876-5775, specializes in folk art.

RESTAURANTS, FOOD, SPIRITS

Bistro du Nord, 1312 Madison Ave. [93rd] ☎ 289-0997, is probably the most stylish of the restaurants in the area, and features a Provençal menu . . . **Cafe Equense,** 1291 Madison Ave. [91st/92nd] ☎ 860-2300, for pasta . . . **Table d'Hôte,** 44 E. 92nd [Mad/Park] ☎ 348-8125, looks like the neighborhood: a small, cozy, New England–looking restaurant with tasty food. The tables themselves are small, service is friendly, the whole thing satisfying . . . **Schatzie's Prime Meats,** 1200 Madison Ave. [87th/88th] ☎ 410-1555, looks like a regular neighborhood butcher but, in fact, carries an unusual range of meats from alligators to zebras . . . **Ecce Panis,** 1260 Madison Ave. [90th/91st] ☎ 348-0040, with its distinctive aquamarine ex-

terior and some of the better bread in the city . . . **Canard & Co.,** 1292 Madison Ave. [92nd] ☎ 722-1046, has benches outside for you to sit on in good weather to enjoy one of their sandwiches or gourmet items . . . **La Fromagerie,** 1374 Madison Ave. [95th/ 96th] ☎ 534-8923, for very good sandwiches and cheese . . . **K & D Wines,** 1366 Madison Ave. [95th/96th] ☎ 289-  1818, is an unpretentious liquor store with quite a few wine bargains . . . Popular pizza at **Pintailes,** 26 E. 91st St. [Fifth/Mad] ☎ 722-1967, and top it off with a stop in at **Mr. Chips,** 27 E. 92nd St. [Fifth/Mad] ☎ 831-5555, for a scoop of ice cream . . . Reliable and tasty brunches at **Sarabeth's,** 1295 Madison Ave. [92nd/ 93rd] ☎ 410-7335.

SPACES

Be sure to walk by **120, 122,** and **160 E. 92nd**—landmarked frame houses on the south side of the street, built in 1859, 1871, and 1852, respectively. They are clapboard houses that are complete anomalies in today's New York landscape, but how inviting they are! You can find another at 128 E. 93rd . . . **Hotel Wales,** 1295 Madison Ave. [92nd] ☎ 876-6000, see more in the Smartest Hotels article in the Hotels chapter . . . Note the remains of **The Squadron A Armory,** and have a few moments of quiet in the **public space behind the Carnegie Hill Tower** at 40 E. 94th Street—a nice, shady spot in one of the most graceful districts in the city.

FIREPLACES

If you don't have a fireplace, here are places in town that have genuine, wood-burning hearths. You might want to call to make sure they're stoked up.

RESTAURANTS & BARS **All State Cafe,** 250 W. 72nd St. [Bway/West End Ave.] ☎ 874-1883 . . . **Beekman Bar and Books,** 889 First Ave. [50th] ☎ 980-9314 . . . **Chumley's,** 86 Bedford St. [Grove/Barrow] ☎ 675-4449 . . . **I Trulli,** 122 E. 27th St. [Park Ave. S./Lex] ☎ 481-7372, an Italian restaurant with a great glassed-in fireplace, seen from two rooms . . . **Keens,** 72 W. 36th St. [5th/6th] ☎ 947-3636, in the Pub Room and the Bull Moose room . . . **Marylou's,** 21 W. Ninth St. [5th/6th] ☎ 533-0012, has one in the library room, one in the garden room . . . **Molly's,** 287 Third Ave. [22nd/23rd] ☎ 889-3361 . . . **Pierre au Tunnel,** 250 W. 47th St. [Bway/8th] ☎ 575-1220 . . . **Rene Pujol,** 321 W. 55th St. [8th/9th] ☎ 246-3023, in the back room . . . **Savoy,** 70 Prince St. [Crosby] ☎ 219-8570 . . . **7th Regiment Mess,** 463 Park Ave. [66th] ☎ 744-4107, in the 4th-floor dining room . . . **21,** 21 W. 52nd St. [5th/6th] ☎ 582-7200, in the lounge . . . **Vivolo,** 140 E. 74th St. [Park/Lex] ☎ 737-3533 . . . **Water Club,** 500 E. 30th St. [East River] ☎ 683-3333, has two . . . **Ye Waverly Inn,** 16 Bank St. [Waverly Place] ☎ 929-4377, two wood-burning fireplaces.

HOTELS **Inn New York City,** 266 W. 71st St. [Bway/West End Ave.] ☎ 580-1900 has two: one in the Parlor suite bedroom, the other in the Loft suite on the top floor . . . **The Lowell,** 28 E. 63rd St. [Park/Mad] ☎ 838-1400, has 33 rooms with fireplaces . . . **The Mayfair,** 610 Park Ave. [65th] ☎ 288-0800, has 14 suites with wood-burning fireplaces.

FLEA MARKETS

Well enough has not been left alone. It's not enough that Sixth Avenue in midtown has been stripped of so much character by an endless succession of undistinguished skyscrapers. Now, Sixth Avenue in Chelsea has been rezoned for a mix of commercial and residential use. This means that the flea markets, and these days that almost always means the area around Sixth and 26th, are likely to be relocated. The district can largely be traced back to Alan Boss, who opened the first parking lot between 24th and 25th street as a flea market in 1976. Mr. Boss says that one owner of a lot has decided to develop, but other owners are taking a "wait and see" attitude before removing the weekend fleas. He does think that within 5 to 10 years the fleas will be relocated.

OUTDOORS

W. 24th–27th: The **Annex Antiques Fair and Flea Market** is on Sixth Ave. from 24th

to 27th. The east side of Sixth Ave. between 24th and 25th is the biggest of the flea spaces. The Annex is Sun. only. The Antiques Fair (Sat. and Sun.) between 25th and 26th is the only area that charges admission—$1. Mr. Boss says that, technically, all of the lots are open from 9–5 for retail, but in reality antique dealers "are buying oil paintings by flashlight at 4:30 in the morning," often not waiting until the trucks are fully unloaded. Interior decorators, on the other hand, generally prefer to wait until it's light. Another of Mr. Boss's fleas is in the dogleg parking lot on the west side of Sixth Ave. between 26th and 27th . . . Under different management is **The Grand Bazaar,** 25th [6th/Bway]. It cuts through the block between 25th St. and 26th St. and has 100–200 dealers.

INDOORS

W. 18th: The Metropolitan Book Center, 123 W. 18th St. [6th/7th], housing antiquarian and rare-book dealers, also holds special book fairs.

W. 19th: The **Metropolitan Antiques Building,** 110 W. 19th [6th/7th] has special shows and auctions (vintage clothing, book fairs, and 20th century), 10 months of the year. It's closed July and August. Call ☎ 463-0200 for a schedule of events at both places.

W. 25th: The Indoor Antiques Fair has moved and changed its name to **Showplace,** 40 W. 25th St. [Bway/6th] ☎ 633-6063, 8–5, Sat., Sun. There's a small cafe downstairs . . . The twelve floors of The **Chelsea Antiques Building,** 110 W. 25th [6th/7th] ☎ 929-0909, are now full with 75 large and small dealers. Some current floor by floor highlights: On 6, an estate jewelry dealer and a specialist in old photos of

NYC. On 8, a woman who specializes in vintage luggage, a specialist in black Americana, and a store with a lot of Elvis Presley (the snack bar is here, too). On 9, the Antiquarian Book Arcade gives space to 65 different booksellers. On 10, the Lubin Galleries holds auctions of estate merchandise every other Thursday evening at 6 P.M. Previews are on Tues. 10–6 and Wed. 10–8 ☎ 924-3777. The basement is now carpeted and is full of vendors. The glass cases on the main floor hold consignment merchandise from dealers in other states who want a presence in NYC . . . **The Garage,** 112 W. 25th St. [6th/7th] Sat. and Sun. Another Alan Boss operation. Two floors of a covered garage for vendors with more fragile merchandise, more prints, textiles, and small items. There's often good silver downstairs.

W. 26th: International Antiques and Collectibles, 30 W. 26th St. [6th/Bway] ☎ 255-7615, is open Tues.–Sun., and currently has mostly large furniture pieces.

STORES **The Old Paper Archive,** 122 W. 25th St. [6th/7th] ☎ 645-3983. They sell movie posters, prints, magazines, lobby posters, postcards, sheet music, and theatre programs—all from the private collection of the owner, Ron Wershba . . . **Lucille's Antique Emporium,** 127 W. 26th St. [6th/7th] ☎ 691-1041, is run by Lucille Buckalter, who oversees her domain from behind a capacious desk. Her linen collection includes '40s and '50s printed tablecloths, damask bedcovers, and European 100% linen sheets. There is vintage designer clothing, millinery, select costume jewelry, and some large furniture pieces. Lucille's is open Tues.–Fri. noon–7:30 as well as flea days. On Sundays there is live jazz in the afternoons.

OTHER FLEAS The **Columbus Ave. Flea Market** between 76th and 77th, Sun. . . . **P.S. 183 Flea Market,** 419 E. 67th, every Sat. . . . **SoHo/Canal Street Flea Market** on the NW corner of Bway and Grand, Sat. and Sun.

GARDENS

As urban dwellers, we admit we're pretty easy to please when it comes to greenery and flowers, but there are some surprisingly bucolic spots in and around Manhattan that offer various combinations of flowers, vistas, and tranquillity.

Abigail Adams Smith Museum Garden, 421 E. 61st St. [1st/York] ☎ 838-6878. This is a secluded and enticing place, even if the noise of the 59th St. Bridge never abates. There isn't exactly a profusion of flowers, just a spot of green you may have to yourself.

Brooklyn Botanic Garden, 900 Washington Ave. [Eastern Parkway] ☎ 718-622-4433. Don't miss it when the cherry blossoms are in bloom in early May, in spite of the throngs of fellow New Yorkers who will be there with you. We're always delighted by the lovely, at times breathtaking, series of gardens. There is an extensive Japanese garden, a well-known bonsai collection, a rose garden (5,000 bushes, 1,200 varieties—best viewing is in June), and a rock garden with big sprays of basket-of-golds, dozens of varieties of narcissus, and huge golden parade tulips. There's also a large indoor conservatory of tropical plants and trees.

Central Park has two gardens: **The Shakespeare Garden,** north of the 79th St. transverse, which is small but quite pleasant. All of the plants in it are mentioned in Shakespeare . . . **The Conservatory Garden,** at 105th and Fifth, is one of the most idyllic spots in the city. It's named for the large greenhouses that were built there in 1899 before Robert Moses replaced them with gardens. The crab apple allees are glorious, as are the two gardens with fountains on the north and south ends. Best of all is the serenity afforded by its design and by the fact that it is relatively uncrowded. Highly recommended.

You could make the case that the herb garden at **The Cloisters,** Fort Tryon Park, ☎ 923-3700, is the prettiest in the city. Not for the flowers and trees there, though they're pleasant enough (the 250 or so types of plants here were all cultivated during medieval times), but for the sum of the parts, the effect of the whole setting. You're above the river, you get a glimpse of the bridge, and the whole thing has a transporting southern European feeling. It's restful and exhilarating at the same time. Though the herb garden is well loved, the heather garden, outside the entrance to the Cloisters, features daffodils, azaleas, heather, of course, as well as more views to the river.

We think **The New York Botanical Garden,** Southern Blvd. and 200th St., in the Bronx ☎ 718-817-8700, is one of the treasures of New York. We've also found that it's one of those places that many New Yorkers haven't visited. A shame. In our book, any place with over 100 kinds of lilac trees is okay. And azaleas! Their azalea lane is extraordinary, especially in May. The 250-acre garden includes pristine woods with trails (this really gives you the feeling of being away), the E.A. Haupt Conservatory (set to reopen in mid-1997 after a major renovation), a rose garden, rock garden, waterfall, and research library. Skip the tram ride and just walk.

Morris-Jumel Herb and Rose Garden, 1765 Jumel Terrace [160th] ☎ 923-8008. MUG loves the Morris-Jumel (see the article on Harlem in this chapter) and the small herb and rose garden behind the house provides another excuse to head up to this special place.

Ninth Street Community Garden and Park, 144 Ave. C [9th], celebrated their 15th anniversary in 1995, and it's one of the most successful community gardens in the city. Forty people do the gardening, not counting the area set aside for children to grow things, and there is much community involvement. The garden has won many awards.

Rusk Garden Institute, First Ave. and 34th Street, isn't exactly a garden but it's worth including anyway. It's a greenhouse garden with a small outdoor area, open to the public, the primary purpose of which is to provide patients undergoing rehabilitation with a nice atmosphere in which to stroll and to enjoy the benefits of caring for plants. They have birds, fish, and various types of plants, including orchids. Many of the plants are for sale.

St. Luke's Garden, Hudson St. [Barrow/Christopher], is a green oasis in a part of the city shortchanged on that color. Go in at the sign for the school and keep going until you come upon the quiet garden where

people like to read, sun, and relax in this pretty and protected space.

United Nations Garden, offers a sense of open space, with the towers at a remove. Despite the fact that you're over the FDR, it's fairly quiet. An appropriately peaceful place.

Wave Hill, 249th St. and Independence Ave., Riverdale ☎ 718-549-3200, is the most beautiful spot in the five boroughs. The house, which has been home to Mark Twain, Teddy Roosevelt, and Toscanini, is worth a look, but it's the grounds that are so enchanting. There is a greenhouse filled with unusual and magnificent flowers and a nearby herb garden. We wonder if there is a better seat in town than the bench under the cupola in the wild garden with its view over the garden and to the Hudson. If you can tear yourself away, take a walk in the woods and around the perimeter of the grounds or lounge on the lawns. Take the 1 or 9 to 231st and then use the car service just outside of the subway stop to get you the rest of the way, or take the 7 or 10 bus to 252nd St. While you're up here, **Riverdale Park** must be one of the loneliest parks anywhere. It's really more of a pathway through a wooded area in Riverdale. It may not, by itself, justify a trip

Wave Hill: the best seat in town.

up here, but if you're visiting Wave Hill, this makes for a most pleasant walk afterward. The park starts at about 233rd Street along the Hudson River, and runs to 254th. It affords you the rare (in New York) peaceful, natural setting in which you will hardly encounter another living soul. Just a pleasant walk through the trees, with the occasional glimpse of the water. You *are* over the Conrail tracks, so you may hear a passing train, but it is otherwise undisturbed. You won't confuse a walk here for a walk in England's Lake District, but it is rather nice.

A small garden carrying a potent message. When you're next in Battery Park, just east of Castle Clinton, you might want to pause by the **Hope Garden.** Opened in 1988 on the first World AIDS Day, it was intended as a reminder and symbol of hope for people with AIDS. There are 1,500 Betty Prior rosebushes, a pink flower that begins blooming in June and continues all the way into December. Each rosebush has been dedicated to a person who has died of AIDS.

HARLEM

Harlem is so rich in history and anecdote that as Marvin Gelfand, who gives occasional tours of Harlem, says, "You gather the group on a corner and begin to point out in a 360-degree pattern what is important at that crossroads. Three hours later, you realize you haven't left the corner." What follows are some of the highlights of the area. Our suggestion is to go by day—not because, as conventional "wisdom" has it, Harlem is wildly unsafe. We've spent a lot of time up there, perfectly unscathed and warmly welcomed. The reason to go by day is simply that you can see and experience more: the beautiful terra cotta on St. Aloysius, the murals by Aaron Douglas, the joyful noise of a Canaan choir, see the "beautiful castle" of Harlem, and stroll the streets of Hamilton Heights and Strivers' Row, two of Manhattan's loveliest sections.

116TH STREET You might not expect to see echoes of a French château, the Pitti Palace, and the Doge's Palace near 116th Street, but you can. The **Wadleigh Junior**

High School, 215 W. 115th St. [AC Powell, Jr. Blvd./F. Douglass Blvd.], once a top high school in the city and recently renovated for nearly 50 million dollars, is the château. The Pitti Palace is evoked by the 1908 McKim, Mead & White **115th St. Branch Library,** with its rusticated limestone exterior. The landmarked **First Corinthian Baptist Church,** 1910 Adam Clayton Powell, Jr. Blvd. [116th], was a movie showplace of Roxy Rothafel. Thomas Lamb designed it in 1913, and the Doge's Palace is a clear inspiration . . . The **Graham Court Apartments,** 1923–1937 Adam Clayton Powell, Jr. Blvd. [116th/117th], was home to Zora Neale Hurston. The building (along with 409 Edgecombe in Sugar Hill) is considered Harlem's top-of-the-line apartment building. It was commissioned by William Waldorf Astor and was designed by Clinton and Russell, who later did the Apthorp— which much resembles the Graham Court . . . At **Mt. Nebo Baptist Church,** 1883 AC Powell, Jr. Blvd. [114th] ☎ 866-7880, note the Stars of David in the frieze and Ferdinand, Isabella, and Christopher Columbus in the tiles, reflecting the change of ownership (and faiths) as the temple, and then church, was erected. The church's 10 choirs rotate Sunday services (11 A.M.) and frequently tour Paris and elsewhere . . . **Canaan Baptist Church,** 132 W. 116th St. [AC Powell, Jr. Blvd./Lenox], also boasts several choirs and a vigorous, well-attended service, but you may want to opt for the church's Gospel Express ☎ 865-3597. On some Sunday afternoons, the choirs, with guests, perform traditional gospel, and there's an all-you-can-eat buffet—$25 . . . **Minton's Playhouse,** 206-210 W. 118th St. [AC Powell, Jr. Blvd.], birthplace of bebop music, now owned by Drew Nieporent, may reopen as a jazz club, though details are sketchy.

125TH STREET The echoes around 125th Street are not European, but of Harlem's own past. Looking at the **State Office Building,** 163 W. 125th St. [AC Powell, Jr. Blvd./Lenox], you'd never know that it was once a gathering point for the community, the site of **Lew Michaux's** beloved bookshop and art gallery. It was also a center of political argument—Michaux, according to Jan Morris in *Manhattan '45,* being "the best known arguer in Harlem" . . . There was a lot of arguing and orating here at **Bug House Corner,** 125th and Adam Clayton Powell, Jr. Blvd., where orators of all stripes used to hold forth. Among the most popular: A. Philip Randolph, who founded the railroad porter's union, and "Pork Chop" Eddie Davis . . . The **Theresa Hotel,** 2090 Adam Clayton Powell, Jr. Blvd. [125th], is the work of George and Edward Blum from 1910. It's now an office building, but be-

came known as a place where jazz musicians stayed. Castro also stayed in 1960 when he spoke at the U.N. Most people tell you he chose to stay here rather than the more capitalist hotels in midtown, but apparently he turned up first at the Waldorf with a retinue that included a flock of chickens for dinner. The Waldorf couldn't guarantee the safety of Castro or his chickens, so he left for the Theresa . . . The **Langston Hughes House,** where the writer lived and worked from 1947 to 1967, is at 20 E. 127th St. [5th/Mad], but you won't see so much as a plaque. Nearby, at **17 E. 128th St.,** from 1864, is a vestige of old New York—the wooden house is one of the few remaining in the city . . . **The Apollo,** 253 W. 125th St. [AC Powell, Jr. Blvd./F. Douglass Blvd.], ☎ 749-5838, still has Amateur Night on Wednesdays . . . The **Studio Museum,** 144 W. 125th St. [Lenox/AC Powell, Jr. Blvd.] ☎ 864-4500, showcases black artists past and present. The museum's gift shop is a good source for books on African-American history and artists . . . The **United House of Prayer,** 124th & F. Douglass Blvd., was evangelist Daddy Grace's church. (He and Father Divine, you'll remember, offered salvation and food to attract many thousands of believers. Father Divine claimed to be God, a claim that got a P.R. boost when he was in jail on a minor charge and the judge who landed him there died of a heart attack. Father Divine's famous comment: "I hated to do it.") . . . **The Black Fashion Museum,** 155 W. 126th St. [Lenox/AC Powell, Jr. Blvd.] ☎ 666-1320, by appt., founded in 1979, is a townhouse museum that celebrates black women who sewed for themselves and others. You can see a dress sewn by Rosa Parks, a debutante gown with hand-sewn roses designed and made by Ann Lowe (who made all of the dresses for Jacqueline Bouvier's wedding party), as well as contemporary designers. There are two shows each year . . . Before leaving the 125th Street area, be sure to stop in at **Georgie's Pastry Shop,** 50 W. 125th St. [5th/Lenox] ☎ 831-0722. Doughnut lovers make pilgrimages here from all over for their plain and jelly doughnuts—far superior to any in the city, and a match for doughnuts anywhere . . . Don't miss the gorgeous exterior (the AIA guide likens it to Belgian lace), or the interior, for that matter, of **St. Aloysius,** 209 W. 132nd St. [AC Powell, Jr. Blvd./F. Douglass Blvd.], done by Renwick in 1904 . . . **All Saints R.C.** at E. 129th St. [Mad], is a fine Renwick, Aspinwall and Russell church . . . **Astor Row,** W. 130th St. [5th/Lenox], was built starting in 1880, at the instigation of William Astor. His grandfather, John Jacob Astor, had bought the land several decades earlier. It's a distinctly un-Manhattan streetscape (some of the houses have wooden porches) and a beguiling one. The street is undergoing rehabilitation.

Astor Row.

135TH STREET The **Schomburg Center for Research in Black Culture,** 515 Lenox Ave. [135th] ☎ 491-2200, is the place to research any information on Harlem or black culture in general. While at the Schomburg, go to the atrium just beyond the main entrance. The terrazzo and brass cosmogram on the floor, **Rivers** by Houston Conwill, Estella Conwill Majozo, and Joseph DePace, is built over a tributary of the Harlem river.

Quotes from *Rivers* by Langston Hughes are used in the piece. Mr. Hughes's remains are buried under the words "My soul has grown deep like the rivers." If you're going to the Schomburg, by all means make an appointment, ☎ 491-2241, to see the Aaron Douglas murals. Two of the four panels of **Aspects of Negro Life** (1934) can be seen. The shop at the Schomburg contains some African craft work and books on race relations and African-American topics. There is another Douglas mural in the barbershop at the YMCA, of all places, 180 W. 135th St. [AC Powell, Jr. Blvd./F. Douglass Blvd.], called **Evolution of the Negro Dance.** It was a gift of Mr. Douglas to the Y, and he painted it directly onto the wall there in 1933. Art and hair care don't mix: the chemicals used in the hair salon are deteriorating the oil paint . . . More murals: At Harlem Hospital, in the Women's Pavilion on E. 137th St. [Lenox/5th], enter the street door marked Dental Clinic. On either side of the doorway are two WPA murals by Charles Alston. **Magic in Medicine** and **Modern Medicine** trace the history of healing from traditional African methods to germ theory. They are worth the trip. Charles Alston also directed a group of WPA mural artists at the hospital. In the Nurses Residence, E. 136th St. [Lenox/5th], take a left after the entrance. At the end of the hall is a multipaneled history of African-Americans, beginning with African tribesmen and ending with a Cab Calloway–like entertainer dancing in a white suit . . . At the corner of what was then Seventh Ave. and 135th was **Small's Paradise,** 2294 Adam Clayton Powell, Jr. Blvd. [135th], the famous nightclub. It's a languishing site, but there is talk of reopening a club on the spot . . . **Jungle Alley,** 133rd St. [Lenox/AC Powell, Jr. Blvd.], was home to jazz clubs and restaurants like the Clam House, The Nest, and Tillie's Inn, the latter a magnet for Harlem artists of all kinds during the Renaissance . . . At 131st and Lenox, the **Liberation Bookstore** has been selling books by and about African-Americans and related topics since 1967. The sign in the windows says: "If you don't know, learn. If you know, teach" . . . **Williams Christian Methodist Episcopal Church,** Adam Clayton Powell, Jr. Blvd. [131st/132nd], was originally the **Lafayette Theatre,** a significant legit theatre for African-American performances in the '30s. In the median across the street from the theatre used to stand **The Tree of Hope.** People used to lean against it or rub it for the luck it was supposed to bring. There's a sculpture on the spot . . . The **Renaissance Casino,** 2351 Adam Clayton Powell, Jr. Blvd. [138th], has fallen on hard times. It was once a hopping casino and ballroom and the place where Mayor Dinkins was married . . . Both **Mother A.M.E. Zion,** 140 W. 137th St. [Lenox/AC Powell, Jr. Blvd.], and the **Abyssinian Baptist Church,** 132 W. 138th [Lenox/AC Powell, Jr. Blvd.], have distinguished histories in the community and both are well worth visiting. Abyssinian is perhaps Harlem's best known church because of its ministers past (Adam Clayton Powell, Sr. and Jr.) and present (the Rev. Calvin Butts). Abyssinian has gospel service Sundays at 11, and you'll find a lot of international visitors there . . . **Strivers' Row,** 138th to 139th [AC Powell, Jr. Blvd. to 8th], was home to many Harlem notables (W.C. Handy, Eubie Blake, Vertner Tandy) and is made up of houses designed by James Brown Lord, Bruce Price, and McKim, Mead & White. You can't miss the fact that these houses have back alleys (in Manhat-

Strivers' Row.

tan!); that the streets are cut through mid-block, north to south, with ways for horses (WALK YOUR HORSES is still painted on some of the gates); and that these are among the prettiest streets on the island.

SUGAR HILL A must-visit in Harlem is the **Hamilton Heights Historic District,** from W. 141st–145th along Convent Ave. On what was Alexander Hamilton's estate, you'll find an exceptionally lovely neighborhood made up of houses in many styles, including Flemish and Dutch, Art Deco, and Tudor. Be sure to walk down **Hamilton Terrace** on your way to **Hamilton Grange.** The Grange, Hamilton's 1802 house by John McComb, Jr. (who designed City Hall), was plopped unceremoniously on Convent Ave. [141st/142nd] over 100 years ago as a "temporary" stop on its way to a permanent site as a national monument. The house is closed at the moment, and plans are under way to move it to St. Nicholas Park so that it can be sited properly (right now its side is fronted to the street). Hamilton lived in the house for only two years before being killed in the duel with Aaron Burr . . . Hamilton Heights is part of the area called **Sugar Hill,** loosely from the high 130s to 160th, Amsterdam to Edgecomb, so nicknamed in the thirties because the area was inhabited by successful and affluent blacks living, it was said, the "sweet life." . . . **Essie Green Galleries,** 419A Convent Ave. [148th] ☎ 368-9635, by appt. Ms. Green and her husband, Sherman Edmiston, moved their 18-year-old Park Slope gallery to Harlem in 1989. Mr. Edmiston spent his childhood in Harlem and missed the "village quality" of the neighborhood. Originally encouraged to go into business by Romare Beardon and his wife, Ms. Green specializes in black masterworks. This includes artists of the Harlem Renaissance, such as Charles Alston (who taught Jacob Lawrence, Mr. Beardon, and Robert Rauschenberg), William Carter, an artist of the Chicago Renaissance, and Charles Ethan Porter (one of the earliest black painters in America—born around 1820), the collagist Alan Stringfellow, and Mr. Beardon . . . At 10 St. Nicholas Pl. [W. 150th], is the Romanesque **Bailey House,** once owned by the circus impressario. It's now a funeral home. Of the house, architect and Harlem expert Anthony Bowman says, "It's a beautiful castle in Harlem." . . . **Dance Theater of Harlem,** 466 W. 152nd St. [St. Nicholas] ☎ 690-2800, founded in 1969 by Arthur Mitchell, was recently renovated by Hardy Holzman Pfeiffer to include new classrooms, four studios, and office space. The second Sunday of each month, from November to May, they hold open-house performances at 3 P.M. Singers, dancers, and sometimes students, perform.

JUMEL TERRACE HISTORIC DISTRICT

The Morris-Jumel Mansion, 1765 Jumel Terrace [160th] ☎ 923-8008. Born in 1774, the daughter of a sailor and a prostitute, Eliza Jumel was beautiful and brilliant and ended up the richest widow in New York. Beautiful, brilliant, and *shrewd*. Unwilling to remain Stephen Jumel's mistress, she be-

came gravely ill while he was away on a business trip. On his hasty return, she asked to be married to him before she died, and he immediately agreed. Her recovery was rapid and complete. Whether or not Gore Vidal's hilarious portrait of her in *Burr* is accurate, she's an intriguing figure and is just part of the fascinating history of the Morris-Jumel Mansion. This is a terrific Sunday afternoon outing (any day will do) that combines the mansion, the small but interesting Jumel Historic District, and, a couple of blocks away, a meal at Wilson's. The Morris in the name is Roger Morris, son of the famous architect of the same name, who built the house in 1765 as a summer place for himself and his wife. Jumel bought the house in 1810. It is Manhattan's oldest residential structure, and an excellent example of the Palladian style. George Washington had his headquarters here for a time, and it is easy to picture the great man in the small but fine office on view. (Don't miss, outside his office, the laundry list in GW's own hand, written two days before his inauguration, which includes his hair net.) Aaron Burr figures into the history of this house, but you'll have to go there to find out how. The herb and rose garden in the rear is lovely . . . Right by the mansion are some wonderful row houses that comprise the **Jumel Terrace Historic District.** Foremost among these is Sylvan Terrace, between Jumel and St. Nicholas. Built in 1882, this pristine, incredibly evocative street will transport you to old New York the moment you enter it. The Jumel Terrace houses between W. 160th and W. 162nd and on W. 160th between Edgecombe and St. Nicholas are also beautiful 19th century row houses in good condition . . . Two blocks from the Jumel District is **Wilson's Bakery and Restau-**

rant, 1980 Amsterdam Ave. [158th] ☎ 923-9821. In business for over 40 years, it's a nondescript place that promises "good home cooked meals" and they do deliver. Savory biscuits, ribs, potato salad—you can't go wrong. Service is as sweet as the baked things.

MORE The **Audubon Ballroom,** Broadway at 165th St., is known as the site where Malcolm X was shot in 1965. Saved from destruction, it has been incorporated into a new science and technology building for Columbia. The site is expected to include a memorial to Malcolm X . . . You can take a **tour** (highly recommended) with Anthony Bowman. His company is A La Carte NY Tours ☎ 410-2698. You can also tour the area with Michael Henry Adams ☎ 283-4965.

HENDERSON PLACE & GRACIE MANSION

Henderson Place Historic District consists of 549–553 E. 86th St. [East End Ave.], 6–16 Henderson Place, 140–154 East End Ave., and 552–558 E. 87th St. Although there is a terribly intrusive high-rise that is responsible for having lopped off part of Henderson Place for all eternity, you can still feel the presence of an earlier era here. The cul-de-sac was completed in 1882, the development of fur importer and hatmaker John C. Henderson (Lamb and Rich were the architects). It was conceived as a housing group for "persons of moderate means," and the Queen Anne houses, 24 of which remain, were modest for the time, though they are certainly charming. Alfred Lunt and Lynn Fontanne lived here . . . Across the street is an entrance to **Carl Schurz Park,** named for the German immigrant Carl Schurz (1829–1906), who served in the Lincoln and Hayes administrations, and who later became an editor of the *New York Evening Post* and *Harper's Weekly.* The park's most notable feature is the promenade along the East River . . . The park connects to **John Finley Walk,** where the great views continue. This walk was named after John Finley (1863–1940), a former City College president and *New York Times* editor-in-chief. Finley, in addition to his many other accomplishments, was the original power walker . . . Archibald Gracie built the Federal-style **Gracie Mansion,** 88th St. [East End Ave.] ☎ 570-4751, in 1799. The city bought it in 1887, but it didn't become the mayor's residence until 1942. When Mrs. Wagner lived here, she was unhappy with the ambience and small size of the house, and got money raised to add a wing (1966). The small room with her portrait is the nicest spot in the house—of the public rooms, anyway. The public areas were renovated in 1984—the patterned carpet, painted floors, and painted baseboards give a busy and not exactly elegant impression. When we visited, we asked if departing mayors were asked to leave something behind for the mansion. Our tour guide looks at us in disbelief and asks, "Like *what,* you mean some of their *personal furniture?*" Yes, we say. She: "Honey, when they're gone, they're gone." Tours available Wednesdays, and you must reserve.

ILLUMINATED BUILDINGS

In the wings, behind the flood of light that gives the buildings of New York their glow and washes the city with romance, are a handful of designers who have created the night skyline. This is a look at some of our favorite illuminated buildings in Manhattan, with comments from the designers responsible for them.

MIDTOWN

When you look at the story of illuminated buildings in New York, you have to start with Douglas Leigh. Mr. Leigh began his career in advertising and became known for his Broadway spectaculars in which billboards became events: the Times Square smoking Camel sign was one, a Pepsi billboard with a block-long waterfall out of electric bulbs was another. You also have to start with the **EMPIRE STATE BUILDING,** which Mr. Leigh says he has been infatuated with for decades. When the ESB was finished in 1931, it was nearly vacant, and even at the start of WWII was only one-third rented. Mr. Leigh had the idea of getting Coca-Cola to take the top floors and use the mooring mast and radio antenna as part of their corporate identity. He also proposed that the tower have changing lights that would indicate what the weather was going to be. Coke would package bottles with a small guide to decipher the colors. By late 1941, Coke had agreed, but following Pearl Harbor, the lights of the city were darkened. The government suddenly needed a lot of office space, filling up much of the Empire, and the Coke deal fell by the wayside. After the war, they decided to use a different, simpler lighting scheme. More than three decades passed before Mr. Leigh had another crack at the

Empire. In 1976, he was made chairman of City Decor to welcome the Democratic convention and visitors for the Bicentennial. This time, he suggested to the ESB's owners, Harry Helmsley and Lawrence Wien, that the lights be colored red, white, and blue. It was an instant success, and they were left that way until the end of '76. Mr. Leigh then offered the idea of tying the lights to different holidays, rather than the weather.

THE CHRYSLER BUILDING "Hey, can you do something about the top" is how Bill DiGiacomo, who redid the electrical and air conditioning systems at the Chrysler when it was bought by Mass Mutual, said management approached him near the end of the job. The results have been enchanting New Yorkers ever since. Floodlights were not used because there is no real access to the exterior of the dome, and the dome is made out of gunmetal, which absorbs lamp light. They decided back lighting was the answer and tried many variations, ending up with the simplest fluorescent tubing. Mr. DiGiacomo knows that the Chrysler has a special place in the city's heart and that people take the illumination personally. Should it be a few minutes late in lighting up, he says people call and ask where the lights are.

THE HELMSLEY BUILDING 230 Park Ave. When we talked to the lighting designers for this article, we asked all of them which building *they* liked most in town, and the Helmsley was mentioned by almost everyone. This is a Douglas Leigh lighting design on the Warren and Wetmore building. We told Mr. Leigh that nearly all the other designers we spoke with had picked

CHRISTOPHER LOVI

The Helmsley Building.

the Helmsley as their favorite, but he insists that it's a "good building to start with." He said that they added a lot of gilding (23 karat gold) when they decided to illuminate the building, including gilding the sculptures and clock and adding a gold band around the lower part of the pyramid roof. Adding gold to the cupola would be overdoing it, they thought, so they didn't. The yellow (high-pressure sodium) light is focused on the tower from beneath and glows through the balustrades and onto the cupola. It gives a spectacular focus to the vista down Park Avenue.

GRAND CENTRAL was lit by Sylvan R. Shemitz Associates (who also lit the Jefferson Memorial in Washington). The idea, according to Mr. Shemitz, was to approach the Warren and Wetmore and Reed and Stem building as a "daytime composition." He explains that when sun shines on a building, it is warm, directional light that casts shadows. These shadows are not black because of ambient light from the sky—actually a mix of blue and magenta. A key light is used to mimic sunshine thrown onto Grand Central; fill lights, with magenta filters, cast the shadows. In order to give the effect of the light falling onto the building, they mounted the lighting fixtures on buildings surrounding Grand Central. The shadows fall below the cornices and the projections on the building, so the viewer sees the building and the interesting shadows. Much work went into the specific choice of site of these lights, and they needed to get permission from adjoining building owners, which took about a year. Mr. Shemitz said the building should not look "surprised or decorated" by the light, but should appear as what it is. The lighting of the arches is the "pin on the dress." The general lighting was unveiled in 1991 and completed by uplighting the arches in December 1992, transforming Grand Central from a "dark hole" in the city's center into an inviting area.

ROCKEFELLER CENTER The great Broadway lighting designer Abe Feder also made an enormous contribution to the city at night when he was asked to light Rockefeller Center from four sides. He decided to project light up the building (about 850 feet), but bulbs he used in the theatre projected perhaps 80 feet. Bulbs used in sports arenas projected greater distances, but they were meant to be on for a shorter period of time and were already big in size. In the end, he took these as a prototype and developed a bulb that had the power wattage increased from 400w to 1,500w, without increasing its size. In all, 342 of the lights illuminate Rockefeller Center from many locations, and Mr. Feder focused each one individually. The lighting was unveiled on December 3, 1984, at 5:15 P.M. before the lighting of the Christmas tree. In general, Mr. Feder is pleased by lighting in the city, and says it gives the city a "patina."

THE ROCKEFELLER GROUP, INC.

Abe Feder in action.

CITICORP Lexington Ave. and 53rd. A Douglas Leigh design. The slanted tower had been built with a glass front for solar energy—which did not work out. Just the triangle of the top is lit from the outside of the building, and in misty weather offers strange effects—sometimes fiery looking. When the building was new, there were numerous false alarms to fire departments in inclement weather.

PENINSULA/ST. REGIS vantage point. When you cross Fifth Avenue at 55th Street at night, pause as long as you can in the middle of the avenue and look up. When you do, the combined effect of the illumination of the two hotels provides an exhilarating rush of warm light.

FOUR SEASONS HOTEL 57 E. 57th St. [Mad/Park]. The new hotel was lit by Jules Fisher and Paul Marantz. According to Peter Aaron, an associate partner at Pei Cobb Freed, the Four Seasons is an unusual exterior lighting arrangement in that it uses few floodlights to avoid disturbing hotel guests. There are many corners and setbacks to the building that provide locations for the exterior lanterns developed by Pei. These lanterns (unlike many other buildings, the light sources are visible) are placed to give soft illumination to the building and light only the corners. The designers sought a candlelight quality: soft and atmospheric. Some floodlights are used at the top where there are no guest rooms. Paul Marantz said that as the tallest hotel in Manhattan, they wanted to identify it distinctively.

PARK AVENUE TOWER 65 E. 55th St. [Mad/Park]. The illumination is by two designers: Stephen Margulies at Cosentini Associates did the distinctive pyramid, and

Sylvan Shemitz lit the plaza. Mr. Margulies said they wanted to reinforce the architectural form of the building at night, to give it a night identity, an impact on the skyline and, considering its position in the middle of the block, an illumination that wouldn't be lost from a lot of vantage points. From a logistical standpoint, the pyramid sits over the cooling towers, so they needed lighting that didn't have to be changed (you can't climb on the cooling). The solution, experimental at the time, was to use fiber optics. Mr. Margulies thinks the best vantage point is in front of the Seagrams building or going into the Midtown Tunnel from Queens. When you do, the pyramid lines up with the Chippendale top of the Sony building for an interesting effect. For the plaza, Mr. Shemitz said he illuminated in the corners upward, emphasizing the building's setbacks, so that when you stand in the plaza, it should look like "a flower growing out of the ground."

CROWN BUILDING 730 Fifth Ave. [57th]. Another Warren and Wetmore that was lit by Douglas Leigh. The tower, which was originally green, was gilded to get the effect he wanted. The color of the building below the tenth floor was different from the color above, so he had the top painted to match the bottom. At Fifth and 57th, four buildings are lit, and Mr. Leigh did them all, as well as the holiday snowflake. On this project, he met Philip Johnson who said, "I want to congratulate you on 5th and 57th." Mr. Leigh said, "Oh, you like the way it looks?" And Mr. Johnson replied, "More importantly, for getting four people to agree to the same thing at the same time."

Two more noteworthy illuminated buildings on the northern end of our tour. The first is **JOHN JAY COLLEGE,** 899 Tenth Ave. [58th], a beautiful Douglas Leigh design, done in 1990, on the Flemish baroque building. Mr. Leigh worked from models and gave the school three options: the least expensive and least desirable, the compromise, and Mr. Leigh's preferred design but also the most expensive. The college chose the middle option (we think it is still a success). The lighting is programmable for different seasons of the year for effect and especially to save money.

TRUMP PARC SOUTH 100 Central Park South [6th]. This Douglas Leigh design is only on the older part of this residential building—the part that faces the park. Since it's residential, they developed a special fixture which creates a "pencil of light" that has no spill or glare. The fixtures are placed between the windows about fifteen floors up and the pencil light extends upward.

BELOW 34TH STREET

2 PARK AVENUE [33rd] This Ely Jacques Kahn building, from 1927, was bought by the Mendik Company in the '80s, who restored it. The lighting, by Douglas Leigh, emphasizes the brightly colored Art Deco terra cotta, which, according to Susan Tunick of Friends of Terra Cotta, "uses two types of terra cotta ornament on the upper story setbacks. One is a brightly colored red, green, and blue geometric design, while the other is a more linear banding with beige glaze. The treatment of the terra cotta and the choice of proper colors were so important to Kahn that he had full-scale plaster models made and set on the roof of the unfinished building. These models were painted to match the glaze colors Kahn intended to use on the terra cotta. This ex-

periment gave him the opportunity to see how the color changed under available light conditions and how it looked at a great height."

NEW YORK LIFE 51 Madison Ave. [26th], is a 1928 Cass Gilbert building and a Douglas Leigh light design on the site of the original Madison Square Garden. The tower was lit in 1985 in honor of NY Life's 140th birthday. The octagonal top is made of gold ceramic.

Nearby at Madison and 24th is **MET LIFE,** illuminated since 1980. The tower, completed in 1909 (based on the Campanile of St. Mark's), is the only building we know of that used light effects to indicate the winner of an election. (In the 1908 presidential election, a searchlight would shine northward if Taft won reelection—which he did.) Holidays are now indicated using colored lights.

The **CON ED** building at Irving Place and 14th St. is a Henry Hardenbergh design, but the clock tower is by Warren and Wetmore, completed in 1926, illuminated by Douglas Leigh. Con Ed has installed what is called "light engine" technology, developed by GE, that replaces the incandescent bulbs used to light the tower. Instead of 215 bulbs per clock face, there are 10 fiber-optic devices (with one 70- or 150-watt bulb each) that distribute the light to the points on the clock face. Con Ed, who should know, says the new technology will reduce the electrical demand to illuminate the building by 83%. It is thought to have widespread practical applications in conserving energy . . . A favorite of ours is the Douglas Leigh design for **90 WEST STREET** [Albany/Cedar]. This is a 1907

Cass Gilbert building, and it was lit in 1985 with 224 floodlights onto the top third. The upper part of this building has a lot of ornamentation, and the light was placed selectively to give a play of light and shadow on these ornaments and to give the crown of the building a rectangular halo.

THE EMPIRE STATE BUILDING

The lights on the mast are on panels of fluorescent bulbs. There are five colors on the panels, and they rotate until the desired color faces the building. The two setbacks are illuminated by floodlights and gels. The gels are changed manually, and it is a six-hour job for four electricians working out of doors.

The actual dates on which the lights denote something are not as fixed as you might think. In fact, most of the days that have special lighting do not have a date noted on the ESB schedule.

Sometimes there is a conflict of dates that has to be worked out. Sometimes a group wants the commemorative lights on the same day as a parade (Pulaski Day, for example) that is not the same as the calendar date. Sometimes the lights will commemorate an occasion (blue for Sinatra's 80th) or be paid for by a corporation (as Microsoft did when they launched Windows 95). In any case, when you see the following color combinations, this is what is being honored. The rest of the time, the building's lights are white.

Martin Luther King Day (Jan., mid): *Red, Black, and Green*

Valentine's Day (Feb. 14): *Red*

Presidents' Day (Feb., 3rd week): *Red, White, and Blue*

Greek Independence Day (Mar. 25): *Blue and White*

St. Patrick's Day (Mar., 3rd week): *Green*

Easter Week/Spring: *Yellow and White*

Israel Independence Day (April 15): *Blue and White*

Police Memorial Day (May 15): *Blue*

Armed Forces Day (May 18): *Red, White, and Blue*

Memorial Day (May, end): *Red, White, and Blue*

Portugal Day (June 10): *Red, Yellow, and Green*

Flag Day (June 14): *Red, White, and Blue*

Gay Pride (late June): *Lavender and White*

Independence Day (July 4): *Red, White, and Blue*

India Independence Day (Aug., mid): *Green, White, and Orange*

Labor Day (Sept., 1st week): *Red, White, and Blue*

"Race for the Cure"/Breast Cancer (Sept.): *Pink and White*

Pulaski Day (Sept., 2nd week): *Red and White*

POW/MIA Recognition (Sept., mid): *Yellow*

German Reunification Day (Oct. 3): *Yellow, Red, and Black*

Columbus Day (Oct., 2nd week): *Red, White, and Green*

Fire Prevention Week (Oct., mid): *Red*

United Nations Day (Oct. 24): *Blue and White*

Autumn colors (Oct. 28–Nov. 30): *Red and Yellow*

Veteran's Day (Nov. 11): *Red, White, and Blue*

"Day Without Art/Night Without Lights" AIDS Awareness (Dec. 1): *Dark for 15 minutes*

Christmas (Dec. 1–Jan. 6): *Red and Green*

Most New Yorkers relish Cass Gilbert's **WOOLWORTH BUILDING,** but Mr. Leigh is not happy with the lighting (especially with the peak of the tower). He submitted the plan for the building's illumination, but they had an electrical contractor implement it, so he didn't get to fine-tune it.

AMERICAN INTERNATIONAL 70 Pine St. [William/Pearl]. Horton Lees Lighting has revamped a 60-year-old design. The glass in the spire has been replaced with a white translucent glass and new golden lights have been installed inside, which makes the top glow like a lantern. The refurbished flood-lights on the terrace and setbacks wash the stonework of the building with a "cool, sparkling light." A "wedding cake" effect is achieved by lighting only the columns be-tween the lantern and the terrace with blue/white halide lamps.

THE LITTLE RED LIGHTHOUSE

There are two stories of the Little Red Light-house. The first is the book called *The Little Red Lighthouse and the Great, Grey Bridge* by Hildegarde Swift and Lynd Ward, a chil-dren's favorite since 1942. It's available at the Bank Street Bookstore, 610 W. 112th St. [Bway] ☎ 875-1654, and other book-stores. The other story is the one of the ac-tual Little Red Lighthouse. The 40-foot lighthouse was built in 1880 and served Sandy Hook, New Jersey, before it was moved to its site in Ft. Washington Park in 1921. When the George Washington Bridge was built (complete with its own beacon), the LRL became something of a relic and was decommissioned in 1932. In 1951, when the city was going to auction it off, however, the outcry made it clear that it had become a beloved relic. It was thus turned over to the city's Parks Dept., which promptly let the last light-house on the island fall apart. In 1982, city Comp-troller Harrison Goldin got the city to commit money to restoring the lighthouse and Ft. Washington Park. You can visit the exterior of the lighthouse any time (be sure to walk west from W. 181st St. and not other accesses since this area can be pretty deserted). Or, visit the LRL outside and in with the Urban Park Rangers, who give a tour once a month. Call ☎ 800-201-7275.

The Little Red Lighthouse.

LONG ISLAND CITY

A miniguide to Long Island City, a part of New York that is moments away from Man-hattan, but worlds away in terms of atmos-phere and scale. Come with us as we explore the city in back of the Pepsi sign.

HISTORY
Long Island City (imprecisely: Hunters Point, Ravenswood, Sunnyside, part of Woodside, and parts of Steinway and Asto-ria) was settled by the Dutch in the 1600s,

and then by William Hallet, who built a limekiln factory in 1862 at what is now Hallet's Cove. LIC was named by Captain Levy Hayden in 1853, but the city got going after a push from Thomas H. Todd, who started publishing the newspaper called the *Long Island City Star* in 1865, five years before there even *was* a Long Island City. In 1898, Queens joined New York City, and LIC became its county seat. When the Queensboro Bridge opened in 1909, LIC began its transformation into an industrial hub. By the 1920s, there were a lot of companies here, including Pierce-Arrow, Ford, Daimler, Sunshine Biscuits, Silvercup Bakery, and Chiclets, attracted by the confluence of rail and shipping transportation along its waterfront. Now, you notice the relative peacefulness and the low scale of the buildings first. This, in fact, gets right to the current dilemma of LIC: how to balance its present character, based on its manufacturing past, and accommodate its longtime residents and the artists who have settled here with the developers who all share an appreciation for LIC's special advantages—its small-town feel, its easy commute, its spectacular views of, and proximity to, Manhattan.

SPACES

A brief roundup of the many interesting buildings and public spaces in LIC: **The International Design Center,** 29-10 Thomson Ave. ☎ 718-937-7474, took up residence in several former factories (Sunshine Biscuit and Adams Chewing Gum) and have dramatic interiors from I. M. Pei and Gwathmey Siegel & Assoc. We like visiting the building, but there is no denying a torpor has settled in and there are a lot of vacancies . . . A block away from the IDCNY are two buildings, one called the **Falchi Building**

and one known as **The Factory,** 30-00 & 31-00 47th Ave. [31st St.]. Formerly used as warehouses for Macy's and Gimbel's, they have now been converted into mixed-use spaces, but are most notable for the enormous sculpture installation on the entire ground floor (and in the elevators) constructed with refrigerators, pots and pans, school buses, bowling pins, and kitchen sinks. You may wonder what movie you have walked into. PeeWee meets Blade Runner is the answer. (As we write this, the building's owners are planning to destroy the installation.) . . . For a public spot with a fine view, go to the **Public Pier,** at 44th Drive, next to the Water Club. You face the ruins of the Smallpox Hospital on Roosevelt Island and get the panorama of the East Side of Manhattan . . . **New York Architectural Terra-Cotta Works Building,** 42-16 Vernon Blvd. [Bridge Plaza S.], is a Tudor revival beauty in bad need of care. The company, which was in business until 1928, supplied terra cotta for the Ansonia and Carnegie Hall, among others. It has been vacant since the 1960s . . . The original **NY State Supreme Court Building,** 25-10 Court Square [Jackson Ave.], was built on this site in 1872, but it was destroyed in a fire. The current Beaux Arts building by Peter M. Coco, from 1908,

The current NY State Supreme Court Building.

has had a number of famous trials here, including the sensational 1927 murder trial of Ruth Snyder and Henry Judd Gray. Ms. Snyder, you may remember, was the first woman electrocuted in Sing Sing. Her lover, Henry Judd Gray, after a few cocktails, had bopped Snyder's husband on the head. Seeing that her husband was wounded but still alive, Ms. Snyder finished the job. This was also the courthouse where Willie Sutton, when asked why he robbed banks, said, "Because that's where the money is." The third-floor courtroom has a dramatic and most attractive Tiffany skylight, said to be the largest in the state. The courthouse has been used in several movies, including Hitchcock's *The Wrong Man.* The building isn't really open for touring, but if you want to see it, see if the guards will let you in . . . **The Citicorp Building** (the only skyscraper around) stands opposite the courthouse, but the only reference it and its small park has to the courthouse is its resolute ignorance of its elder and better . . . Walking on 45th Ave. [21st/23rd St.], the **Hunters Point Historic District** is a graceful, well-preserved area, built in the 1870s. Especially noteworthy are the cornices and the iron railings . . . **Sunnyside Gardens** around Skillman [43rd/48th St.] is an example of a planned community that works wonderfully. Built in the '20s, the designers included many alleys that are actually hidden gardens, as are the spaces in back of the buildings. Surprising and delightful.

THE ARTS

Isamu Noguchi Garden Museum, 32–37 Vernon Blvd. [33rd Rd.] ☎ 718-204-7088. Suffice it to say that if you have never been here, the trip out will reward you many times over. This beautiful museum, opened in 1985, is across the street from Mr.

Noguchi's original studio. One assumes he was attracted to the spaciousness of LIC, but a more pragmatic reason for moving here was the proximity to the Vernon Blvd. marble suppliers. You can see over 300 works, the stone pieces, the designs for playgrounds and public spaces, and the light sculptures. The **Socrates Sculpture Park,** 31–42 Vernon Blvd. [Broadway], was started by sculptor Mark di Suvero in 1986. It's well worth a visit, especially paired with the Noguchi Museum a block away. See more in the Sculpture article in the Arts and Diversions chapter . . . **P.S. 1 Museum,** 46-01 21st St. [46th Ave.] ☎ 718-784-2084, the Institute for Contemporary Art, is very much at the center of the LIC art community. It has gallery space and artists' studios, and features exhibitions and performances in many media. You can arrange visits to Long Island City **artists' studios** by calling ☎ 718-784-2935 . . . The film community has made a home in Astoria (part of which is considered LIC) at the **Kaufman Astoria** and **Silvercup** studios. Visit the nearby **American Museum of the Moving Image,** 35th Ave. at 36th St., Astoria ☎ 718-784-0077 . . . **The Thalia Spanish Theatre,** 41-17 Greenpoint Ave. [47th Ave./48th Ave.] in Sunnyside ☎ 718-729-3880, features the work of contemporary Spanish playwrights, as well as the classics . . . The art collection of Emily Fisher Landau, called the **Fisher Landau Museum,** is, under certain circumstances, open for viewing by appointment. See more in the Unusual Museums article in the Arts and Diversions chapter.

FOOD

In addition to **Stick to Your Ribs,** 5–16 51st Ave. [5th St.] ☎ 718-937-3030 (see more in the Barbecue article in the Food chapter), LIC has some other notable eateries . . . **Water's Edge,** 44th Drive [at the East River] ☎ 718-482-0033, is a popular, if expensive, spot with those great views . . . For the same view in an outdoor and less formal setting (not in the same culinary league, of course), the **East River Grill,** 44-02 Vernon Blvd. [44th] ☎ 718-937-3001, at the East River Tennis Club is an alternative to know about . . . **Le Triomphe,** 21–50 44th Dr. [21st] ☎ 718-706-0033, is a small treasure of French food (with Moroccan specialties) in an attractive space that feels like a real escape. Not inexpensive, but we'd still go back in a minute . . . **Don Pelayo,** 39-20 39th Place [Queens Blvd.] ☎ 718-784-4700, is an endearing, if somewhat eccentric, place with good paella, ropa vieja, tapas, and flamenco shows on the weekends . . . **Manducatis,** 13–27 Jackson Ave. [47th Ave.] ☎ 718-729-4602. The tavern exterior gives way to a good-sized restaurant for serious Italian food. Manducatis has many fans, but we think you're likely to eat better here once they know you.

STORES

There is a **Cockpit/Avirex** outlet at 31-00 47th Ave. [Van Dam] ☎ 718-482-1997 . . . You can visit the **Pace Furniture Warehouse Outlet Center** at 11-11 34th St. [11th] LIC ☎ 718-721-8201 . . . For great prices and selection on office furniture, go to **Office Furniture Service,** 47-44 31st St. [48th] LIC ☎ 718-786-7776, and **Adirondack Furniture Outlet,** 31-01 Vernon Blvd. [31st Ave.] ☎ 718-204-4550. See more on these stores in the Furniture article in the Stores chapter.

SPORTS

There are two excellent tennis clubs here: **East River Tennis Club,** 44-02 Vernon Blvd. [44th] ☎ 718-937-2381, and **Tennisport,** 51-24 Second St. [Borden/54th] ☎ 718-392-1880.

MONEY

The Museum of American Financial History, 24 Broadway [Morris] ☎ 908-4110, chronicles in its tiny space the financial development of the country. You may find a history of mutual funds or a display of ticker tape machines. A worthwhile investment of time for those with an interest in the subject. M–F, 11:30–2:30 only.

The American Numismatic Society, Broadway at 155th St. ☎ 234-3130, has, for well over a century, been studying, documenting, and preserving coins and paper money of civilizations extending back 2,500 years. Their

major exhibit "The World of Coins" takes up two small rooms. Though it's small in size, its scope is broad. Again, if you're remotely interested in the subject, you'll find it fascinating. Members of the society (basic membership is $40) get access to its extensive library and to its many programs, conferences, and events.

We love the tour of the **Federal Reserve,** 33 Liberty St. [William/Nassau] ☎ 720-6130, which lasts less than an hour, because it doesn't happen nearly enough that we get to see $16 million in cash and armloads of gold bricks. The landmarked building near Wall Street is a kind of Florentine fortress,

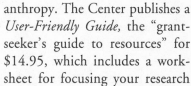

built in 1924 and expanded in 1933 to include the entire block. You enter 33 Liberty Street, get your visitor's pass, go through security, and up to the cash-processing floor. When you look through the windows to the adjoining workspace, you will be looking at about 16 million dollars (depending on the day) in cash. Seeing that much money seems to stimulate even the most jaded New Yorkers. The workers in blue coats are handling the money in what seems to be an old-fashioned process, with a bit of high technology to spot counterfeit notes. They catch about 135 bogus bills a day. Then you go downstairs, 80 feet below street level to look at those lovely trapezoidal gold bricks. Each of the 63 countries (no Communist and few Arabic) has a cage full of gold, and when one country wants to make a gold transfer to another, they just schlep a few bars down the hall. Book five days or more in advance.

Stock Exchange, ☎ 656-5168. Self-guided tours are from 9:15–3 during the week. Get the free tickets at 20 Broad St. (Tickets are usually gone by 2 P.M.)

Stack's Rare Coins, 123 W. 57th St. [6th/7th] ☎ 582-2580, is the best known and largest coin dealer in the city.

The Foundation Center, 79 Fifth Ave. [16th] ☎ 620-4230, isn't a foundation but a non-profit organization that is a clearing-house for virtually anything you want to know about foundation and corporate phil-

anthropy. The Center publishes a *User-Friendly Guide,* the "grant-seeker's guide to resources" for $14.95, which includes a worksheet for focusing your research and much good advice. As for individual grants, if you are involved in a for-profit endeavor, start with the Foundation Center's book *Foundation Grants to Individuals.* The majority of grants to individuals, though, are for educational support. The Center also has all the information you need for proposal writing. The Center here is modern and comfortable (important since, if you're serious, you may spend many hours here doing your homework). They also sell all of their publications at their small bookstore, though the books are generally very expensive: The Foundation Directory costs $185 in softcover. At their website, http://fdncenter.org, you can find a short course in proposal writing and other foundation information.

The Greenpoint Bank, 130 Bowery [Grand/Broome], originally the Bowery Savings Bank, is one of our favorite of Manhattan's commercial interiors. It was built in 1895 by McKim, Mead & White, in the Classical Revival style. It's now occupied by the Greenpoint Bank. It's impossible not to be affected by the sheer calm beauty of the interior. Look at the hand-painted wood columns, and let your eye travel upward to the magnificent domed skylight. ⑤

NEW YORK SOCIETY LIBRARY

Even though the New York Society Library, 53 E. 79th St. [Mad/Park] ☎ 288-6900, is on a major cross street, it keeps a low profile. All well and good. That means, if you

become a member here, you will enjoy the same lovely rooms with the same amount of peace and quiet in your pursuits.

Despite its name, it's not a library for NY

society; rather, it was started by a group that called themselves the NY Society. That was in 1754, and its first location was a room in City Hall, where it was referred to as the "city library." Between 1795 and 1937, it moved several times (Nassau St., Leonard St., University) and, in 1937, to its present site.

The reading and reference room on the ground floor is open to the public. Members, though, may make use of the rest of the library's 12 floors. This means you have access to the stacks, which are divided by subject matter (biography, philosophy, religion, etc.). It also means access to the other reading and study rooms. One of the reading rooms looks like an attractive living room of a home. The Member's Room, on the second floor, is on a grander scale. There's a

children's library on the third floor. A couple of small, quite pleasant private rooms, with a desk and window, can be reserved in advance for a day or a week. They are locked, so you can leave research books and papers out. The library considers its collection's strengths to be in English and American literature, history, art history, and books about NY. They have dozens of periodicals and a complete set of the *NY Times* on microfilm.

There are currently 3,000 members, and you can become one for $135 a year. This membership extends to all permanent members of your household. If you drop by, they will gladly show you around.

NOHO

High society, Walt Whitman, furniture stores, and a couple of juicy murders make up the patch of Noho past and present. For our purposes, it's the small area between Broadway and Bowery north of Houston for about three blocks. A quick tour:

BROADWAY **The Cable Building,** 611 Broadway [Houston], by McKim, Mead, & White, built in 1894 as the cable car business headquarters at just the time the city was committing to a subway system. The first cable car, horsedrawn, had started in 1832, running from Prince to 14th along the Bowery . . . 628 Broadway [Houston/ Bleecker] was **The New York Mercantile Exchange,** built in 1882. You can still see the name prominently lettered on the building (look up) . . . 670 Broadway [Bond], on the NE corner, was the third location of

Brooks Bros., from 1874–1884 . . . On Broadway between Bleecker and W. 3rd on the west side of the street was the **Grand Central Hotel.** At the time it was built in 1871, it was, with 630 rooms, the largest in the world. A year later, it was also the sight of a famous murder. Colonel James Fisk was a rich and extravagant speculator (to put it charitably). After a convoluted scandal with Edward Stokes, both of whom were rivals for one Josie Mansfield, Fisk was shot on the staircase of the hotel by Stokes . . . Also on the west side of the block close to Bleecker was the cafe **Pfaff's,** where the "bohemians" hung out in the 1850s. They spent their time flouting convention and eating and drinking in Charlie Pfaff's place in the cellar. Walt Whitman was central to the group, as were William Dean Howells, Lola Montez, Ada Clare, and Adah Isaacs Menken.

The latter two scandalized society with their combination of affairs, writing, and, in the case of Menken, a sensational, lightly clad stage performance.

BLEECKER STREET You could pass by 65 Bleecker St. [Crosby] many times and not realize what a special building it is. It's the **Bayard-Condict Building,** built in 1899, and the only building in NY designed by Louis Sullivan. The building gets more interesting as your eye travels upward: The top of the building is ornamented with angels, said to have been included because Condict wanted them, though Sullivan did not . . . **Two Boots,** 74 Bleecker St. [Bway/Crosby] ☎ 777-1033, is across the street for good pizza, or stop in one of the neighborhood hangouts, the **Noho Star,** 330 Lafayette St. [Bleecker] ☎ 925-0070.

LAFAYETTE Elan, 341 Lafayette St. [Bleecker] ☎ 529-2724. Jeff Greenberg's store celebrates the "clean and simple lines" of 20th century design in furniture and small decorative pieces. Mostly it's filled with things from the '40s and '50s. Heywood-Wakefield dressers and tables, Eileen Grey chrome and glass tables, Eames, Saarinen, and Knoll pieces can be found here . . . **Marty's Cool Stuff,** next door to Elan, more or less displayed on the street, is flea market merchandise: some junk, some cool stuff . . . **Temple Bar,** 330 Lafayette St. [Bleecker-Houston] ☎ 925-4242, is still a prime, pretty choice for a martini (better during the week) . . . **Small Furniture Co.,** 363 Lafayette St. [Bond] ☎ 475-4396, is "a little mecca for furniture." They repair, restore, and then sell desks, tables, chairs, etc. Ideal for students and first-time apartment dwellers to find inexpensive, good things.

There is a second showroom at 19 Bond St. [Lafayette/Bowery] for higher-end and upholstered pieces.

BOND STREET It's hard to imagine when you look at Bond St. now, but from 1830–1850, it was the preferred address of New York society. **1 Bond** was home of Albert Gallatin, who helped found what became NYU and who served under Jefferson. Now on the site is the cast iron building for Robbins & Appleton, watchmakers from 1880 . . . At 2 Bond is **Avery on Bond,** ☎ 614-1492, owned by Rick Avery, specializing in Americana, both antiques and reproductions. You'll find painted rustic furniture and desks and dressers in mahogany and bird's-eye maple . . . **Elephant & Castle,** 6 Bond St. [Bway/Lafayette] ☎ 254-9604, serves up their tasty "elephant burgers" . . . **24 Bond St.** [Lafayette/Bowery] was Robert Mapplethorpe's studio in the '70s and '80s . . . **Buying the Farm,** 26 Bond St. [Lafayette/ Bowery] ☎ 505-9880, and **Rhubarb Home,** 26 Bond St. [Lafayette/ Bowery] ☎ 533-1817, both have country furniture. Patrick Moultney's home furnishings and antiques store, **30 Bond St.** [Lafayette/ Bowery] ☎ 995-8037, has become a regular stop for decorators. He has a large, eclectic stock of "interesting things at good deals," such as a home bar decorated with a painted rooster ($375) that could be used as a small counter/cutting board in a kitchen . . . **31 Bond St.** [Lafayette/Bowery] was the site of the sensational murder of Dr. Harvey Burdell. It's well chronicled by Jack Finney in his book *Forgotten News* (Finney also wrote *Time and Again*). The building is gone now, but, as Finney points out, 26 Bond looks just like it . . . **Il Buco,**

47 Bond St. [Lafayette/ Bowery] ☎ 533-1932, is an antique shop by day and a most appealing restaurant by night. See more on it in the East Village and Noho section of the Restaurants chapter . . . Susan B. Anthony lived at **44 Bond** [Lafayette/ Bowery] in the late 19th century . . . **Shinbone Alley** [Great Jones/ Bond], which cuts north to south in Noho, was laid out in 1825 and, according to one source, it "owes its name to the bend in the little way that crosses Lafayette St. near Bleecker."

GREAT JONES STREET The street was named by Samuel Jones, "father of the New York Bar," who gave the deed to the city, according to Henry Moscow's *The Street Book,* and then wanted it named for him. Since his brother-in-law, Dr. Gardiner Jones, already had a street named for him, Mr. Samuel played a little one-upsmanship and added the adjective . . . At 44 Great Jones [Lafayette/ Bowery] is the Beaux Arts home of **Engine Company No. 33,** originally built for the chief of the fire department in 1898 by Ernest Flagg and W. B. Chambers.

PIERPONT MORGAN LIBRARY

Each return to the Pierpont Morgan Library, 29 E. 36th St. [Mad/Park] ☎ 685-0610, one of the city's most civilized places, always gives us a new detail to savor. We think the special exhibits of drawings, prints, books, or manuscripts are invariably worth seeing, and their permanent collection includes a Gutenberg Bible and inscribed tablets of Mesopotamia. These are displayed in rooms that are softly lit and never overcrowded. Then we go with pleasure into Mr. Morgan's library, stocked with three tiers of books and ornamented with lunettes by H. Siddons Mowbray, who

also did the mural painting in the entrance hall. After that, the exquisite study, with its deep-red brocade walls on which hang paintings (including a Tintoretto and a Perugino) and its large fireplace. Charles McKim designed the original Renaissance palazzo building and, in 1928, an annex was built. In 1991, the Garden Court was created, and it is a very pleasant spot for a little lunch or for tea in the modern, light-filled atrium among indoor trees and plants. Interesting, civilized, and restorative—you can't ask more than that of a cultural institution.

ST. MARK'S HISTORIC DISTRICT

Body-snatching, Jackson Pollock, a pear tree, and the power of the Stuyvesant family are some of the historical details that make up the small area in the city known as the St. Mark's Historic District. This is essentially East 10th Street and Stuyvesant Street between Second and Third Avenues.

We've expanded southward to include East 9th and eastward to include First Ave. An arbitrary designation, but you can make from it a short walking tour, enjoy some interesting bits of history and the unusual and engaging shops and restaurants of the area.

FIRST AVE. BETWEEN 9TH ST. AND 10TH ST.

Black Hound, 149 First Ave. ☎ 979-9505, is a pretty store with enticing-looking tarts, cookies, and chocolates. We like the little cakes . . . **Angelica,** 147 First Ave. ☎ 529-4335, sells a range of herbs (medicinal and cooking) . . . You never know what you'll find at **Repeat Performance,** 156 First Ave. ☎ 529-0832. Last time we coveted the rhinestone-studded accordion, and their specialty is sets of vintage small lampshades . . . The **First Ave. Pierogi & Deli,** 130 First Ave. ☎ 420-9690, sells blintzes, freshly made pierogis with six or so fillings, kapusta (a browned sauerkraut) to serve with them, bigos (a Polish stew with meat and sausage), and, occasionally, stuffed cabbage leaves. Turning the corner onto 9th, going west:

9TH ST. BETWEEN FIRST AVE. AND SECOND AVE.

The cool, minimalist **Gold Bar,** 345 E. 9th St. ☎ 505-8270, is starting to turn into a long run . . . **Enchantments,** 341 E. 9th St. ☎ 228-4393, sells all manner of potions, new age merchandise, things holistic, and stocks more than you need for spells and curses. It also has one of the more interesting bulletin boards in the city. Last time we looked, there was a card that said "Witch Seeks a Ceremonial Group in NY Area" . . . **Clayworks,** 332 E. 9th ☎ 677-8311, sells the work of owner/potter Helaine Sorgin . . . **Hoshoni,** 309 E. 9th St. ☎ 674-3120, has an attractive collection of Southwest and Southwest-inspired items: lamps, jewelry, pottery . . . **Dinosaur Hill,** 302 E. 9th St. ☎ 473-5850, is a festive toy shop that sells toys like glass marbles and puppets and some creative clothing for children . . . Before crossing Third Ave., you'll pass **Veselka**

Coffee Shop, 144 Second Ave. ☎ 228-9682. Veselka is the Ukranian word for rainbow and is meant to stand for the mix of foods served here—Ukranian, Polish, and American—maybe the only place in town where you can get a plate of potato pierogis and a spinach salad. Cheap prices to an appreciative East Village crowd . . . **Meghan Kinney Studio,** 312 E. 9th St. ☎ 260-6329, designs women's clothing, mostly in stretch and some shiny fabrics; they do some custom work . . . **New York City Custom Leathers,** 312 E. 9th St. ☎ 674-3895, has a few clothing pieces on the racks and more on the staff—hip-hugging pants and midriff-baring tops . . . **Cobblestones,** 314 E. 9th St. ☎ 673-5372. Delanee Koppersmith sings while she works in her attic of a shop. Vintage clothing, old juice glasses, plastic handbags, ashtrays, travel souvenirs . . . **Deus ex Machina,** 324 E. 9th St. ☎ 777-1971, has handmade jewelry by several artisans, much metal, some with stones . . . **Mostly Bali,** 324 E. 9th St. ☎ 777-9049, for masks, wood carvings, textiles, shell ankle bracelets . . . **Fialka Boutique,** 324 E. 9th St. ☎ 460-8615, sells understated clothing for women . . . We like the **Paris Apartment,** 328 E. 9th St. ☎ 780-0232 (mostly the French boudoir), for its painted, carved wood-frame chaises, chairs with smashed cushions, mirrors, and satiny fabrics. Some objets . . . **Gallery Vercon,** 332 E. 9th St. ☎ 473-0506. Unique hats, scarves, and jewelry (some Bakelite) . . . **Archangel Antiques,** 334 E. 9th St. ☎ 260-9313. Don't have the strength to walk the flea markets, but need a quick fix? Large selection of antique cufflinks, buttons, and sewing supplies. Also many vintage eyeglasses, some with cases, much jewelry, postcards, and other small gewgaws . . . **Little Wing,** 334 E. 9th St. ☎ 533-9464, some clothes, some kitsch, new, old, whatever . . . **H,** 335 E. 9th St. ☎ 477-2631, carries small decorative items and small furniture pieces artfully arranged . . . **Geomancy,** 337 E. 9th St. ☎ 777-2733. John Eaton's taste runs to ethnic items that will look well in modern homes, like the burnished Colombian cookware and austerely beautiful Japanese plates . . . **Chartreuse,** 309 E. 9th St. ☎ 254-8477. Everything you would have found in the Beaver's home—pulled glass vases, ovoid cocktail tables, splashy glazed Danish modern pottery, and for when the boys were put to bed, cocktail shakers . . . **Jan Eleni,** 315 E. 9th St. ☎ 533-4396, is a restful shop of carefully chosen antiques. Bakelite-handled cutlery, china cups and saucers, and enamel dental trays with covers . . . **Jutta Neumann,** 317 E. 9th St. ☎ 982-7048, has hip leather bags, wallets, and sandals.

9TH ST. BETWEEN SECOND AVE. AND THIRD AVE.

Cafe Tabac, 232 E. 9th St. ☎ 674-7072, trying to make the adjustment from "You can come in, but you can't sit upstairs" to "So nice to see you" . . . **Col Legno,** 231 E. 9th St. ☎ 777-4650, is an Italian restaurant with quite decent food . . . **Decibel Sake Bar,** 240 E. 9th St. ☎ 979-2733, for sake any way you like . . . If you turn right, you'll be on Stuyvesant Street.

STUYVESANT STREET

The St. Mark's Historic District includes 21–35, 42–46 Stuyvesant Street. This street makes up one side of the Renwick Triangle, completed in 1861. It is thought to be the plan of James Renwick, architect of St. Patrick's and Grace Church. The houses were completed in 1861 as a result of speculation (fueled by proximity to the

Stuyvesants) that this area would become one of the more fashionable areas. It never did. The houses are brick, Anglo-Italianate in style, except for number 21. The Stuyvesant farm extended from what is now 3rd St. to 23rd St., from Ave. C to the Bowery, and had been Stuyvesant-owned since the 1600s, when Peter Stuyvesant was the last Dutch governor of New Amsterdam. As explained in Charles Lockwood's *Manhattan Moves Uptown,* Stuyvesant's grandson, Petrus, mapped his land in 1789 by true east and west rather than the later grid of Manhattan, which matches the island's axis. After the institution of the city's grid in 1811, all of the other streets and houses that did not follow the grid were changed, and houses were demolished. The Stuyvesants, being the Stuyvesants, got to keep their street (at that time the driveway to the mansion) on its original axis, as it remains today. 21 and 44 Stuyvesant housed Stuyvesants when they

Stuyvesant St.: off the grid.

were built. 21 Stuyvesant, the Federal-style **Stuyvesant-Fish residence,** was built in 1804 by Peter Stuyvesant's great-grandson for his daughter Elizabeth's marriage to Nicholas Fish. It is now a National Historic Landmark. The **St. Mark's-in-the-Bowery Church,** ☎ 533-4650, is Manhattan's oldest worship site. The late Georgian church is made of fieldstone and was completed in

1799, though the steeple and the portico came later. Peter Stuyvesant is buried on the church's east side, exactly where his private chapel was before the church was built. A. T. Stewart, who founded the store that became Wanamaker's, was resting in peace here when his body was snatched from its grave and held for $20,000 ransom. After it was eventually paid by his widow the body was returned, but then, understandably, interred elsewhere. The church has a long relationship with poets, dancers, and theatre people. Kahlil Gibran read there in 1919, and Isadora Duncan danced there in 1922. Others who have read or performed are William Carlos Williams, Edna St. Vincent Millay, Martha Graham, and Ben Hecht. Frank Lloyd Wright was a member of the church. The Theater Project (still producing plays), founded in 1964 as Theater Genesis, produced Sam Shepard's first two plays. The Poetry Project (1966) had heavy involvement in its early years from Allen Ginsberg, Anne Waldman, and Paul Blackburn. Currently under the direction of Ed Friedman, they give three readings each week and two workshops. The Dance Project is headed by Laurie Uprichard and performs every Thurs.–Sun. (with the exception of July).

The St. Mark's-in-the-Bowery Church.

10TH STREET

In the 1950s, much of East 10th Street was a significant artists' enclave. The New York School developed here in lofts, galleries, and studios. Many artists who became well known lived, worked, and/or exhibited around this 10th St. community. They include Willem de Kooning, Jackson Pollock, Louise Nevelson, Franz Kline, Helen Frankenthaler, Mark Rothko, Robert Motherwell, and Claes Oldenburg.

10TH ST. BETWEEN FIRST AVE. AND SECOND AVE.

Shabu-Tatsu, 216 10th St. ☎ 477-2972, is a branch of a Tokyo restaurant that we recommend enthusiastically. It's a Japanese barbecue place, and the dish to have is Shabu-Shabu. You get a hot pot, the beef, and vegetables, and you do the cooking. Basic Shabu-Shabu is $24 for two people, but we like the one with a better cut of meat that costs $33 for two. An unusual treat . . . The **10th Street Lounge,** 212 E. 10th ☎ 473-5252, used to be an old ambulance garage that was converted into a bar. The dramatic space is worth stopping into when there's no cover charge . . . **ReGeneration,** 223 E. 10th St. ☎ 614-9577, sells sofas, cabinets, and tables from the '50s.

SECOND AVE. BETWEEN 9TH ST. AND 10TH ST.

The Second Avenue Deli, New York's most popular deli, is at 156 Second Ave. ☎ 677-0606.

10TH STREET BETWEEN SECOND AVE. AND THIRD AVE.

The historic district continues here. Designated are 102–128 E. 10th, 109–129 E. 10th, as well as the house at 232 E. 11th . . . Stanford White grew up on the site where 118 E. 10th is now . . . Finally, the pear tree. On the building at the north corner of E. 10th and Third Ave. is a plaque that reads: "On this corner grew Petrus Stuyvesant's pear tree. Recalled to Holland in 1664, on his return he brought the pear tree and planted it as a memorial 'by which' said he 'my name may be remembered.' The pear tree flourished and bore fruit for over 200 years." The plaque was placed there by the Holland Society in September 1890.

TIMELESS DESIGN

We asked some writers, designers, architects, and others for some examples of timeless design in New York—building, space, area, or object. Here is what they said.

Akiko Busch, contributing editor of *Metropolis:* "I have always thought of design as the graceful intersection of unlikely ingredients. What, then, might be a more perfect and more timeless design than a room that accommodates a Great Blue Whale and a dance floor. These are, of course, the improbable furnishings that cohabit the **lower level of the American Museum of Natural History.** The 94-foot fiberglass whale hovers with absolute grace overhead. And on a section of the floor below is a parquet dance floor. The space is a marvel—at once illogical, incongruous, romantic, sexy, epic, grandiose, and grand. What is more timeless than the human love of dance or than our fascination with the secrets of the deep? Here is a room that accommodates them both, a space in which frivolity cohabits with the mysteries of the deep sea as though they were natural accomplices. This is the basement of my dreams, and it is a room to dance in if there ever was one."

Terence Riley, Chief Curator of Architecture and Design at MoMA: **"The Manhattan Street Grid**—New York's most impressive public and democratic space."

Todd W. Bressi, urban design and planning teacher: **"Broadway north of 59th St.,** where the traffic runs in both directions and there is a mall. The street has been in this configuration for 100 years. This is one of the great streets in the world. It is a great civic space, lively and animated, providing lots of different types of places for people who want to do lots of different types of things. It is constantly changing as the needs of the neighbors change. It doesn't look now the way it did 50 years ago. It provides the city with a place for future inventive uses."

Andrew Dolkart, architectural historian: "The **subway token** is an object that is a very identifiable New York thing. It is so simple and so useful and so readily identifiable as to what it is that New Yorkers don't want them replaced. They are also wonderfully recyclable."

Glenn Gissler, architect: "Walter De Maria's installations **The Broken Kilometer,** 393 W. Broadway, and **The Earth Room,** 141 Wooster, open since 1979 and 1977, respectively. The installations are dramatic and meditative spaces—they remain 'pure' art spaces and stand out as vestiges of the 'original' Soho. For me they live as almost sacred spaces which operate on a plane above the commerce and politics in a constantly changing and increasingly commercial art district."

John Tauranac, mapmaker and urban historian: **"The Empire State Building.** One of the joys of the building is that every time you look at it, you are liable to find some-

CHRISTOPHER LOVI

"The intersection of unlikely ingredients."

thing new and satisfying about it. The buildings that came before it were coarse, unrefined; the buildings that follow lack its style, its panache, its warmth. Now over 65 years old, I am happy to see that local souvenir shops are still happily selling little figurines of the Empire State Building, some with thermometers clinging unceremoniously to its facade or King Kong dangling from its roof. I think that it is safe to say that the building is timeless in all its permutations. Like a Faulkner character, it is enduring. It is a classic."

Hugh Hardy, architect, Hardy Holzman Pfeiffer Associates: "**Rockefeller Center** is timeless. It invented midtown. Its juxtaposition of public spaces and private places makes it an urban ideal. It's all there—the Rockettes, the Rainbow Room, television studios, ice skating, roof gardens, art works, and offices all come together in a place that *is* New York."

Peg Breen, president of the NY Landmarks Conservancy: **"City Hall,** built between 1802 and 1811, was meant to symbolize New York City's emergence as the leading city in the country and New Yorkers' pride in their city's accomplishments. It was the first city hall located within a park. It is prized for its grand interior space and elegant Federal and French Renaissance exterior. It also houses one of the premiere collections of early American full-length portraiture and a statue of George Washington cast from life. President Lincoln's body lay in state at the top of the stairs."

City Hall.

Corliss Tyler, vice-president of Takashi-

maya: "The **Delacorte Clock** in Central Park. Spirited with all the elements of classic design, the pirouetting bronze animals not only complement the past, but function in the present and will undoubtedly withstand the critical eye of future artists and designers. My own enthusiasm is not only supported by the design value, but the fact that so many people derive so much pleasure in seeing and hearing the clock—plus it just makes me feel good."

Joyce Pomeroy Schwartz, Public Art Consultant: "Midtown Manhattan, the tourist center of the city, is defined by commerce—retail shops to street vendors. Yet there is a special street, **W. 54th St. between Fifth and Sixth Avenues,** that confounds generalities. It is identified by its very special character and architecture. Walking down this unique street, we get a sense of what New York was like during another era. Coming from Fifth Ave., one encounters the classical Palladian architecture of the University Club anchoring a handsome row of landmark buildings. Continuing down the street, we pass by Number 5 Petrol House with its fantasy animals ornamenting gates of black iron. Number 7 is the former residence of arts patron Robert Lehman. Its fabled art collection is now installed in its own wing at the Met. Numbers 9 and 11 were sensitively restored by U.S. Trust Co. The red brick McKim, Mead & White buildings have period interior furnishings, mahogany paneling, and flocked wall covering equal to its graciously proportioned facade. Number 13, formerly the Museum of Primitive Art, and 15, were the home and office of Nelson Rockefeller. Known as the Rockefeller Apartments, Number 17 (with 24 W. 55th) is a modern landmark designed in 1935 by architects

CHRISTOPHER LOVI

Harrison and Fouilhoux as pied-à-terre apartments for people who worked at Rockefeller Center. These buildings, grand and well designed, suit New York's urbane diversity. As you continue down the street, you will find clubs, hotels, and MoMA's sculpture garden. Few streets in New York have the ambience of West 54th."

Nicholas Quennell, landscape architect, Quennell Rothschild Associates: "In responding to your question, I find I am divided in my loyalties. My first reaction to your question was almost instantaneous: The most extraordinary example of 'timeless design' in New York is the **Long Meadow at Prospect Park.** And I would be happy to leave it at that. The Long Meadow is certainly one of the greatest manmade landscapes in the world. As three-dimensional sculpture (no, really four-dimensional—it has to be moved through to be experienced); as a place which satisfies spatial needs for social interaction and recreation; as a slice of country brought into the city; and as the perfect climax to the 200-year tradition of picturesque landscape which preceded it.

"At the same time I keep going back to some of the places in New York which satisfy not because they are great works of art or could even be categorized as 'timeless design' but because they stand for what is so wonderful about the City—its ability to constantly surprise you with buildings, neighborhoods, and spaces which are in some way extraordinary. To mention a few: the old terra-cotta factory mansion under the Queensboro Bridge abutment in Queens; the old Steinway mansion overlooking La-Guardia airport, its yard filled with aging automobiles and 'Beware of the Dog' signs; 'Soundview'—a neighborhood of varied houses and splendid views of the Sound at the southern tip of the Bronx; Sailor's Snug Harbor in Staten Island (an architectural gem which could certainly be classified as 'timeless design'), the mysterious remnant of a neo-Egyptian archway hidden behind a Broadway storefront in Inwood; Brighton Beach Boardwalk, as much for its inhabitants as its physical character. My list could go on and on, and will certainly continue to grow as long as I travel around the city. This process of discovery is certainly one of the great pleasures of living in New York."

TOURS

Carnegie Hall ☎ 903-9790
Cathedral of St. John the Divine ☎ 932-7314
Federal Reserve ☎ 720-6130
Fulton Fish Market ☎ 748-8590
Gracie Mansion ☎ 570-4751
Harlem Spirituals ☎ 757-0425
Horticultural Society ☎ 757-0915
Lincoln Center ☎ 875-5350
Madison Square Garden ☎ 465-5800
Metropolitan Opera ☎ 769-7020

New York Times ☎ 556-1234, ext. 4650
NBC ☎ 664-4444, ext. 4000
Radio City ☎ 632-4041
Seagram Building ☎ 572-7000
Steinway Piano Factory ☎ 718-721-2600
Yankee Stadium ☎ 718-293-4300, ext. 552

TOUR GUIDES & TOUR COMPANIES
Adventures on a Shoestring ☎ 265-2663. Emphasizes the offbeat in their walking tours.

Big Onion Walking Tours ☎ 439-1090. Ed O'Donnell met Seth Kamil at Columbia where they both were getting Ph.D. degrees in NYC history. They realized their different backgrounds (Romanian Jewish and Irish Catholic) had many NY neighborhoods and sites in common. They founded Big Onion Tours, the only tour company where all the employees (now four) have an advanced degree in NYC history.

Joyce Gold Tours ☎ 242-5762. Ms. Gold, teacher at NYU, gives popular tours to most areas of the city.

Marvin Gelfand's A Walk of the Town ☎ 222-5343. Customized tours by a historian of New York City, who specializes in politics, journalism, writers, and the connections among them.

Municipal Arts Society ☎ 439-1049. Especially for their tours of Grand Central.

Radical Walking Tours ☎ 718-492-0069. Bruce Kayton gives 11 tours, ranging from Wall St. to Harlem, covering the subjects that many tours leave out: Malcolm X, Margaret Sanger, protest, anarchism, and so on.

Sidewalks of New York ☎ 517-0201. People, gossip, murder, and scandal are their forte.

Signature Tours ☎ 517-4306. Sets up individualized tours after you complete a detailed questionnaire.

Urban Park Rangers ☎ 800-201-7275. The rangers give walking tours in all of the parks, including discussions of birdwatching, ecology, and history.

"Wildman" Steve Brill ☎ 718-291-6825. Mr. Brill, the naturalist, gives tours with an emphasis on the environment, plants, and nature.

TRIBECA

HISTORY

One of the most pleasurable things about our perambulations around the city is looking for flashes of an older New York. When a piece of New York's past survives, it often helps us visualize how the area grew, how it might have felt to have been there in another time, enhancing our understanding of the neighborhood's character. Walking through Tribeca, you can see ghosts everywhere, but it was while walking on Hudson near Laight Street that we wished to do a little time traveling, since our imagination was insufficient. St. John's Park was, for a time, (1820s–1840s) an "Eden," as one newspaper described it. Elegant Federal-style houses surrounded the enclosed park (similar to Gramercy Park), and the centerpiece of the area was St. John's Chapel. Except for the name of the street, here is a part of New York completely and utterly vanished. Now it's the entrance to the Holland Tunnel.

According to Andrew Dolkart, author of *The Texture of Tribeca,* "There are actually two Tribecas: the Broadway corridor, which extends west approximately two blocks, and the Washington market area." The Broadway area was the "mid-19th-century commercial core of New York." It is based on Italian Renaissance precedents and uses a lot of Tuckahoe marble (from upstate), some sandstone, and there are cast-iron storefronts. These buildings were used mainly for stores, lofts, and manufacturing. Mr. Dolkart points out that there is a distinct break when you move to the Washington

Market area, which was built in the 1880s and 1890s. The buildings, frequently Romanesque Revival in style, are of red or yellow brick, and have brick ornamentation. There are lots of solid, arched forms and some terra cotta detail. There is often cast-iron on the ground floor. Elevators had been invented by this time, so the buildings tend to be wider and taller. They were built for the food and paper industries, and there were some refrigerated warehouses.

We don't know what the house of **Mme. Restell,** the well-known mid-19th-century abortionist, looked like (before her move uptown to Fifth and 52nd St.), but it stood at Greenwich and Chambers. Luc Sante, author of *Low Life—The Lures and Snares of Old New York,* told us that for her "infallible French female pills" and "celebrated Preventative Powders for married ladies, whose health forbids a too rapid increase of family," Mme. Restell charged $500–$1,000, which, he says, was "astronomical for the time." But the high fees insured that she would have plenty of business, and she was kept on retainer by roués to care for their changing mistresses. She was eventually "hounded to her death by Anthony Comstock, a self-appointed moral censor of the times." After being released from the Tombs, she slit her throat in her bathtub . . . **The Tombs,** the prison where executions were performed, was torn down in 1974. It was bounded by Franklin, Leonard, Centre, and Lafayette.

BUILDINGS & SPACES

Here are some of the buildings, spaces, and sites worth noting in the district. Starting at **Warren St.,** Andrew Dolkart notes that between West Broadway and Broadway, you see a virtually intact 19th century commercial streetscape . . . At Church and Cham-

bers, the 1857 Cary Building by John Kellum is a prime Italianate cast-iron building . . . In 1846, A. T. Stewart opened the **first department store in America,** at 280 Broadway [Chambers]. Its marble exterior and luxurious merchandise made Stewart rich and famous. The store had no sign since it was so well known. It later

The Cary Building.

became known as the Sun Building, for the newspaper it housed. Now, Modell's is downstairs and city offices are upstairs . . . Walking up Broadway, and looking west on **Reade Street,** you get another glimpse of commercial 19th century New York, as you do if you continue up to **White St.** . . . Continuing to **2 White St.,** the small house on the corner is a survivor from 1809. It's one of the oldest residential houses in Manhat-

The small house at West Broadway and White St.

tan . . . At Franklin and Varick, you'll see the 1887 **D.S. Walton Company**'s Romanesque Revival building on the northwest corner, which we wish still had its original tower . . . **The Mercantile Exchange** still has its tower. The building, at 6 Harrison St., was built in 1884 and is the home of Chanterelle . . . We like the view down Staple St. with the bridge connecting

the old House of Relief (part of New York Hospital) with the ambulance garage . . . Don't miss the lobby of the 1930 **Western Union Building** at 60 Hudson St. [Thomas/Worth]. The beautiful brickwork inside is unlike anything else we know of in the city.

View down Staple St.

The *AIA Guide* tells us there are 19 shades of brick . . . More brick, this time part of the Federal-style **Harrison Houses,** built between 1796 and 1828. These charmers were saved from destruction in the '60s. Most of the houses were relocated to their current sites from Washington St. . . . If you go north at this point on Greenwich, north of Hubert, you can feel an earlier Tribeca rather easily. One building certainly worth noting is the **Fleming Smith** warehouse at 451–453 Washington St. [Watts]. Designed by Stephen Decatur Hatch in 1892, the striking Flemish-style building has Capsouto Frères on the ground floor . . . If you go south from the Harrison Houses, walk through the pleasant **Washington Market Park,** Greenwich St. [Chambers/Duane], even if the glory now goes to the **Hudson River Park,** one of our favorite spots in the city.

SHOPPING

Not your usual shopping district, Tribeca nevertheless has some interesting stores. **Kae's Kids,** 311 Greenwich St. [Reade/Chambers] ☎ 791-6915. A well-selected group of clothing in sizes newborn to 7, mostly for girls. Some handknit sweaters and hats in bright colors and rayon print dresses in imaginative styles . . . **Anbar Shoes/Shoe Steal,** 60 Reade St. [Church/Bway] ☎ 227-0253, has women's shoes at discounts, sizes 6–10, with some small areas devoted to smaller and larger sizes. Shoes are arranged by color in clearly labeled boxes. From casual to dressy, flats and heels, some funky, some glitzy. We saw Sacha of London, Van Eli, and Yves St. Laurent, among others . . . **Tatsuo Tsujimoto & Daughters,** 104 Franklin St. [W. Bway/Church] ☎ 343-2930. Mr. Tsujimoto specializes in rugs, traditional as well as his original designs. His rugs are made in India, and he sells them from this location at wholesale. (A 6' × 9' is $239, smaller sizes available.) There is a line of undyed, earth-friendly designs, too. He will also work with you if you want to design your own rug. Prices average $30 per square foot, plus the fee for the artwork (from $150, depending on complexity) . . . **TriBeCa Potters,** 443 Greenwich St. [Vestry/Desbrosses] ☎ 431-7631, is composed of 10 potters who share a very large studio space. Working in different styles and different media (stoneware, porcelain, earthenware), they produce tabletop items, vases, and mirror frames . . . **Folly,** 13 White St. [Bway/Church] ☎ 925-5012, sells antique, generally large, garden ornaments like urns, sculpture, benches . . . At **Mobilier,** 180 Franklin St. [Greenwich/Hudson] ☎ 334-6197, Patrick Marchand specializes in French designer furniture of the 1950s, but he has other things from the same period, like a Noguchi table, and some small pottery pieces . . . For more on great furniture, see **Wyeth,** 149 Franklin St. [Varick/Hudson] ☎ 925-5278, and **Sing Ken Ken,** 401 Washington St. [Laight] ☎ 226-1641, in the Furniture article in the Stores chapter . . . **Knobkerry,** 211 W. Broadway [Franklin] ☎ 925-1865, is Sara Penn's store with work of artists known and unknown, fine and folk, in a pleasantly jumbled setting. She often displays the witty art of David Hammons.

FOOD AND DRINK

Throughout the 19th century, the Washington Market was the major produce center in the city. It seems fitting that Tribeca is again a food center, with its concentration of wonderful restaurants—these are described in the Restaurants chapter . . . Other noteworthy food purveyors include **Harry Wils Co.,** 182 Duane St. [Hudson/Greenwich] ☎ 431-9731, in business since 1921, and one of the few survivors from the days of Tribeca as the butter and egg center of New York. They continue to supply restaurants and food shops all over town, but they have a cash and carry counter that will sell butter, eggs, yogurt, and other dairy and grocery items to you. Many things such as butter can be bought in quantities small enough for home use . . . **Aux Delices des Bois,** 4 Leonard St. [W. Bway/Hudson] ☎ 334-1230, the mushroom specialist . . . **Washington Market,** 162 Duane St. [Hudson] ☎ 571-4500, is the excellent gourmet shop . . . **Umanoff & Parsons,** 467 Greenwich St. [Watts] ☎ 219-2240, sells cakes, pies, tarts, and quiches retail, right from the bakery

door, even though it's not a retail store as such. Just follow the smell into the anteroom and ask for a list . . . **Moscahlades Bros.,** 28–30 N. Moore St. [Varick/Hudson] ☎ 226-5410, are importers of Greek, Italian, and Spanish products who will sell you liters of inexpensive Spanish olive oil, olives, and dolmades . . . **TriBakery,** 186 Franklin St. [Greenwich/Hudson] ☎ 431-1114, has terrific breads and sweets and it's a pleasant spot for lunch . . . **Puffy's Tavern,** 81 Hudson St. [Harrison] ☎ 766-9159, is a popular, low-key neighborhood hangout, but it's **Walkers,** 16 N. Moore St. [Varick] ☎ 941-0142, that has been a tavern here since 1890.

GALLERIES

Soho Photo Gallery, 15 White St. [Bway/Church] ☎ 226-8571, shows the creative work of New York's commercial photographers . . . **Apex Art,** 291 Church St. [Walker/White] ☎ 431-5270, does some adventurous programming, often turning the gallery over to guest curators . . . **Art in General,** 79 Walker St. [Bway/Lafayette] ☎ 219-0473, so named because it is an art gallery in the General Hardware building, has installations in the street-level windows, sound art in the elevators, and exhibitions in the galleries on the 4th and 6th floors. There are often panel discussions and/or video programs . . . **Franklin Furnace Archives,** 112 Franklin St. [W. Bway/Church] ☎ 925-4671. The archive has been sold to MoMA, but there are regular exhibitions in this space.

CRAFTSMEN & MATERIALS

Friedman & Distillator, 53 Leonard St. [W. Bway/Church] ☎ 226-6400, shares office space with an adhesives company and someone who sells parts for elevators. Make your way past the hardware to Toni Peikes in the back room. This business was established in 1923 to sell trims to the millinery trade, but over the years it has metamorphosed into lampshade fabric and trims. There are silk shantungs, pongees, and linens, as well as linings. The ribbon and braid trims are imported from Europe, and there are many old beauties as well as new trims . . . **Joshua's Trees,** 138 Duane St. [W. Bway/Church] ☎ 349-5671. This is the showroom of Joshua Hoffman, who has been in the rare wood business for more than 20 years. He sells mostly to architectural woodworkers, but will sell to anyone who needs wood for a home renovation or furnituremaking project . . . **Space Metal Surplus,** 325 Church St. [Canal/Lispenard] ☎ 966-4358, is a retail store that sells metal—mostly to artists, students, and construction workers. They have rods, sheets, extruded bars, perforated sheets (like you have in your radiator screen), and screening, and will cut to size . . . **S.A. Bendheim,** 122 Hudson St. [N.

Moore] ☎ 226-6370, has stained glass materials and classes.

DIVERSIONS

MUG loves the **Knitting Factory,** 74 Leonard St. [Bway/Church] ☎ 219-3055, because the music charges are reasonable ($12–$18), there are no minimums, the music is serious and hip and energizing, and they have 20 microbrews on tap (and on cold nights, the waitress will offer to make you hot tea) . . . **Biblio's Book Store and Cafe,** 317 Church St. [Lispenard/Walker] ☎ 334-6990. Biblio's has poetry readings, video screenings, book signings, and music performances—mostly by local talent . . . **Roulette Music Loft,** 228 W. Broadway [Franklin/N. Moore] ☎ 219-8242. Jim Staley and David Weinstein run about 50 experimental music concerts a year in this 75-seat theatre founded in 1980. According to John Schaefer, noted new music authority, this is "the most experimental music being performed—everything from free improvisation to avantgarde rock." In general, composers present their own music. Ticket prices average $7.

VIEWS

Some vantage points around the boroughs that we find irresistible.

BARGEMUSIC

Snag a front-row seat at Bargemusic (see more in the Chamber Music article in the Arts and Diversions chapter), and you are within arm's length of the first-class musicians. Behind them, a glorious window onto the city, which also seems within arm's reach.

BOWERY

Standing at night on the Bowery, roughly at Broome Street, we are always taken with the fantasyland view toward midtown in which the Met Life, the NY Life, the Con Ed, and the Empire State buildings seem to huddle for a group shot of colorful lights.

BROOKLYN PROMENADE

Not exactly news, but never less than thrilling. A little picnic on the benches here

The Bowery, View.

facing Manhattan is pure joy. To us, the Grand Canyon is just a big hole in the ground—these are the canyons we love.

CHELSEA PIERS

The best place in Manhattan to sit in a whirlpool is poolside at the Sports Center at Chelsea Piers ☎ 336-6000. That's because poolside is also right over the Hudson. Sit in the hot tub and watch the sun set over the river.

THE CLOCKTOWER GALLERY

Out on the balcony of the Clocktower, 108 Leonard St. [Bway/Lafayette] ☎ 233-1096, you get sensational 360-degree views of Manhattan from a modest height, with the muf-

The Clocktower.

fled hum of traffic as your sound track. It's the city in all its sprawling splendor: Broadway, the Hudson, Manhattan Bridge, the World Trade Center, the Woolworth Building—just amazing. Best of all, hardly anyone's around, except for the artists who have studio space here, and the views are almost guaranteed to make you giddy.

GREEN-WOOD CEMETERY

You can't stroll or picnic in Green-wood Cemetery, the way New Yorkers did when the cemetery first opened. If it sounds somewhat morbid, it doesn't feel that way when you're there. It's as pleasant as can be, and as it's the highest point in Brooklyn, the view to southern Manhattan is terrific. You can't just show up, you need to be on a tour—try one of John Cashman's ☎ 718-469-5277. See more in the Brooklyn article in this chapter.

HUDSON RIVER PARK

If we only had an hour to explain New York to someone, we'd come here. We'd sit on the lawn and look out to Liberty and Ellis Islands, recalling the settlement of the city and its expansion ever northward. We'd say that development is a recurring theme in New York—balancing out the need for space and the desire for growth. We'd watch the people along the promenade, the walkers, joggers, Rollerbladers, baby carriages, the young and the old. To borrow from E.B. White, here is New York.

LONG ISLAND CITY PUBLIC PIER

At the Public Pier at 44th Drive, next to the Water Club, the Gothic ruins of the Smallpox Hospital on Roosevelt Island and the panorama of the East Side of Manhattan make for a memorable view.

MADISON SQUARE PARK

There is a photograph taken in 1901, which you may have seen at the Ladies Mile exhibit at the Museum of the City of NY, of two stylishly dressed young women walking uptown along Madison Square Park, beneath the trees, next to the horse and carriages. The light filters through the trees onto the sidewalk, and as you become aware of the light, you note the scale of the buildings in the background and how much sky is visible. The photographer was facing southward, and you also see that the Flatiron Building is yet to be built. (It rises the next year.) We like

ROOF GARDEN AT THE MET

See if this works. Go to the Metropolitan Museum. Make your donation. Take the left corridor behind the cashier, then a left before the iron gates. Go straight till you see the elevators on your right. Take the elevator to the roof garden. Doesn't this help? It works for us. It's open more or less from May 1 to late October, and only when the weather's good. It's an anodyne when Manhattan gets the way it does. Lovely during the day and romantic at dusk when the museum is open late (Fri. and Sat.).

the view afforded by entering Madison Square Park toward the east side, and picking a bench facing westward. The buildings are, at most, 20–30 stories high, and you can recreate the scale of an earlier New York.

MUSEUM OF NATURAL HISTORY

Take a break from the dinosaurs and step into the rotunda on the southeast corner of the Museum of Natural History, 79th and Central Park West ☎ 769-5100. Sit on one of the padded benches and enjoy the views over the park to the east and the skyscrapers to the south.

NEW YEAR'S EVE

Here is our way to see the ball drop in Times Square, see fireworks, and still be away from the hordes. We go into the park shortly before midnight at 72nd St. toward Tavern on the Green, where the people doing the midnight run will be warming up. We stand on the patch of grass north of Sheep Meadow, just west of the little concession building. From there, looking southward through the skyscrapers, you will just be able to make out the ball in Times Square. Watch the ball, toast the New Year, enjoy the fireworks, kiss.

PARAMOUNT HOTEL

At the Paramount Hotel, a seat at one of the tables on the balcony is a prime spot for people watching.

PENINSULA BAR

The bar at the Rainbow Room has great views, of course, but at the Peninsula Bar, you can get outside to enjoy all of Fifth Avenue at your feet.

WAVE HILL

If you need a break from all the urban views, sit on the bench under the cupola in the wild garden at Wave Hill, with a view over the garden and to the Hudson. See more in our article on Gardens in this chapter.

THE WALDORF=ASTORIA & THE ROYALTON

THE WALDORF=ASTORIA

Whether or not you have had occasion lately to walk through the sleek and soothing corridors of The Waldorf=Astoria, 301 Park Ave. [50th] ☎ 355-3000, or to delve into its interesting history, what follows is a brief compendium on the history of the hotel, which had its centenary in 1993.

In the last decade of the 1800s, William Waldorf Astor hit upon a plan to inconvenience the aunt he didn't like: Mrs. William Astor, the doyenne of New York society. He built a hotel, the Waldorf, in what was then her backyard: Fifth Avenue and 33rd Street (where the Empire State is now). William won that round: Mrs. Astor moved uptown. Her son, John Jacob Astor IV, who loathed William but couldn't fail to notice the Waldorf's success, then began negotiating with him to build a hotel on his mother's former plot of land. The Waldorf (named after the town in Germany where the Astors came from) and the Astoria became one hotel in 1893. Since the hotel was a marriage of convenience, John Jacob and his mother insisted on a clause in the contract that the two hotels maintain at least 30 inches of air space between them and giving John Jacob and his mother the right to seal up the space and break off into a separate hotel, should the need arise. The Waldorf=Astoria used the "equals" sign between the two names as a way of stating that the two entities were equals. It also represents the walkway between the two hotels that became known as Peacock Alley.

Peacock Alley became a hot spot in a way that restaurants and clubs may today, but public areas rarely do (except, perhaps, the Royalton. See below). All day, every day, and late into the night, people (up to 15,000 a day) dressed up, way up, and went to see and be seen. The more passive spectators took positions on the many comfortable chairs and sofas (lounging at the Waldorf),

and the more active ones attended functions, ate in the restaurants, and promenaded. Someone is said to have remarked that it looked like "an alley of peacocks," and the name stuck. Catering to the needs of the rich and famous was the man known as **Oscar of the Waldorf.** For many years he was the public face, the tone, the style of the hotel. His understanding of social distinctions and his many more practical skills imbued him with a kind of power and aura that became legendary.

The hotel had made its plans to move to the current, larger uptown site and had completed the financing days before the Crash. Construction took two years and the new Waldorf=Astoria opened on October 1, 1931. The new building (47 floors, 1,610 guest rooms—200 of which are in the Towers) was built over tracks now used by Metro North, and so the architects built the structure on stilts to act as a cushion against vibrations. If you look outside at the base, you can see the sidewalk curve up to meet the building.

The new Waldorf remained a vital part of the city's nightlife with the **Starlight Roof Supper Club.** Everyone played there, from Glenn Miller to Ella to Jascha Heifetz. The roof opened and there was dancing under the stars. The hotel closed the roof (not the room) because the air conditioner compressors were placed over that part of the hotel. Looking at the room today, it is hard to make the leap to the glamor that was once associated with it.

The hotel made no money until 1950 because it opened in the Depression, and during World War II, the government restricted room rates. Conrad Hilton had wanted to own the Waldorf, as the story goes, ever since he had seen a picture of it decades before. He is said to have cut out the picture and put it under the glass on his desk. Hilton got his hotel when the Hilton chain acquired the Waldorf in 1977. They've done a lot of restoration to the building. Many of the "improvements" were taken out with a return to the original Deco look. It's the only Hilton hotel without the Hilton name in it.

THE ROYALTON

We weren't around to lounge at Peacock Alley in its time, but the lobby of The Royalton, 44 W. 44th St. [5th/6th] ☎ 869-4400, strikes us as the '90s equivalent. When the hotel first opened, we stopped in from time to time for a look, and the lobby would be empty. Now when you go in, it's almost always filled with people (more locals than hotel guests) having lunch, tea, cocktails, a meeting, a tête-à-tête, a drink after work. It makes us want to *promenade*.

THE WORST SPACES IN MANHATTAN

The J, M, Z, Canal St. Station. Everywhere are scabs of crumbling, filthy, rusty chunks of wall, which are either sodden, oozing, or leaking, and out of which protrude menacing, scummy stalactites. Perhaps it's just as well that the lighting is so bad—the shock of seeing this subway station well lit would probably be too much to bear. The TA is doing work here, but the fact that they let it get into this state in the first place is an utter disgrace. Since you can also transfer here to the N, R, and 6, maybe they'll consider some signage.

The Manhattan Mall, Sixth Ave. [33rd/34th]. From the science experiment ornaments on the exterior to the numbingly banal, aggravatingly laid-out interior, the salmonella pink paint, there isn't a single good reason to shop here when the city offers so many superior alternatives. Much has been written about the "malling" of New York—this is what everyone is afraid of.

Columbus Circle. We think Columbus Circle is the biggest missed opportunity for intelligent urban planning anywhere on the island. It could be such a wonderful urban plaza, a meeting place before a walk in the park, a

place to sit, a locus for activity extending in many directions. As it stands, it's bad for pedestrians and a bottleneck for traffic. The tribute to the continent's discoverer is plagued by some terrible buildings—the Coliseum to the west (the word "access" mysteriously appears on the front of the building 19 times), Donald Trump's building, claiming to be "the most important new address in the world," can only make you roll your eyes, and the Dept. of Cultural Affairs building to the south can only make you avert them. Even so, with thoughtful planning, Columbus Circle could be an appealing place. As it is, it's a place to get through, a paradigm of potential unmet.

The **Calvin Klein Store,** 654 Madison Ave. [60th] ☎ 292-9000. An entrance that appears deliberately unwelcoming, followed by barren, monochromatic rooms with low, shin-bruising cement display tables. You edge up the cheerless, narrow, monastic stairs, note the bad, scuffed paintwork, instinctively duck your head down from the low ceilings. This isn't a place you'd want to linger, not a place you'd want to sit if you could, not a place where you'd want to shop, given the few pieces of clothing that seem strung up without context. We like Mr. Klein's clothes just fine, but the minimalism of the store's environment is punishing.

1 Harkness Plaza, W. 62nd St. [Bway/Columbus]. The shops have given up here, the only signs of life in this interior courtyard are the dozen palms that soldier on under the grimy glass. A jumble of bad design and neglect: burned-out bulbs, missing acoustical tile, the terrible red, orange, and purple color accents, the corrugated metal siding. A piano has a big sign that says "Please do not touch the piano!" but spontaneous group singalongs seem highly unlikely. This is the worst kind of public space, so ugly and deadening that no one would choose to spend a moment here when they could be anywhere else on earth. Truly, hell's waiting room.

Bally Total Fitness, pick any location. The one at Broadway and 74th is ringed with orange neon and mirrors, which give a sickly cast to the cramped space. Health clubs don't need to be elaborate minicities like Reebok, but the Ballys (formerly Jack LaLanne) make sloth an attractive alternative.

What is the one thing, the single thing in the entire world that you cannot put up on the walls of **Penn Station?** Answer: pictures of the *old* Penn Station. Penn Station would easily have qualified for this article in any case, but the recent addition of the achingly beautiful photos of the old Penn Station in the horrible main waiting area is really adding insult to injury. And this station isn't just ugly, it lacks basic amenities. People wait here for their trains, facing the big board, without the benefit of a single chair. (The designated waiting area has seats, but you have to get up and go look at a monitor for train information.) When your train is announced, it's an inevitable pileup at the tiny escalator. There is a new entrance on 34th St., and the lower level, for so many years an oven in the summer, now has benefit of air-conditioning. Still, there's such a long way to go.

The penitentiary-style **Marriott Marquis Hotel,** 1535 Broadway [45th/46th] ☎ 398-1900, has much to be penitent about. As it bulldozed its way into Times Square in the '80s, it cleared out two small theatre jewels, the Morosco and the Helen Hayes. The Morosco was designed by Herbert Krapp, and the intimacy and acoustics of that theatre made it a joy to see plays there. Alas, they made a pile of Krapp. You enter into the garage-like ambience of the Marriott and find your way to the elevators that take you to the 8th floor. If you think Times Square is so terrible that you have to put your lobby eight floors above it, why build there? Within, scraggly plants drip down the walls of the central atrium, against which the tacky elevators and a revolving clock face try to infuse a little kinetic energy into a vacuum. They buried a time capsule here on October 8, 1985, which contains 100 artifacts and historical representations of contemporary life in NYC . . . "to endure for the futurians of 2085 A.D." What about what the presentians must endure? If only they had buried the building and kept the capsules.

YORKVILLE

Earlier in the century, the Jäger Haus was a formal restaurant in the heart of Yorkville, with a German owner, a thriving German community outside its door, and an echo of the Old World within: vaulted ceilings, violins playing, a huge fireplace, potted plants, a horseshoe bar. Above the restaurant were several dance halls with crystal chandeliers. Kathy Jolowicz, the unofficial historian of Yorkville, remembers waltzing with her father there, with her feet on top of his. Yorkville has been a center for many ethnic groups over the years, with large German, Hungarian, and Irish populations. Now, the Kleine Konditorei is owned by a Hungarian, the Budapest Bakery (which had been taken over by a Lebanese) is gone, and the dance halls are, too. The changes in the past few years have been sweeping, but you can still walk in parts of Yorkville, especially near the river, and feel the openness of another, quieter time. We look at Yorkville as it was and is now.

HISTORY

When New York passed from being a Dutch colony to an English colony in 1664, a line was drawn at about 84th St. and the East River to 106th St. and the Hudson River. North of the line was Dutch (New Harlem) and south of the line was British. The Germans that we associate with Yorkville did not come in until after the Revolutionary War. Wealthy Germans like the Rhinelanders (sugar) and the Astors (fur) built mansions here. Each had a sliver of land on the East River, and the estates fanned out as they went inland. In the 1830s, the area began to be gridded up, and the descendants of these families parceled out the land. The next generation of Germans to settle there were people like the Rupperts (beer), the Ringlings (circus), and the Ehrets (beer). In the early 1800s, carriage horse drivers used to race each other up Third Ave. for fun and wind up at one of the taverns around 84th and Third Ave., such as Hazzard House and

Wintergreen's. As coach and rail transportation to the area improved in the mid-1800s (ending the drag racing possibilities, to the coachmen's dismay), the population grew—especially when people like Andrew Carnegie and Archibald Gracie began to build their mansions nearby. (See more in the Henderson Place & Gracie Mansion article earlier in this chapter.) Along with these homes, the great breweries, such as Jacob Ruppert's and Ehret's, were taking up an increasingly large piece of real estate in the area. Yorkville got a sudden population surge following the *General Slocum* disaster. The *Slocum* was a pleasure cruiser that sailed on the East River. One weekday in 1904, it was carrying a church group on its way to a picnic when it caught fire, killing 1,200 German women and children. Many men were left without a family, and they moved from the Lower East Side into the areas around the breweries in Yorkville. By WWI, E. 86th St. was known as the "German Broadway," First Ave. as the "Czech Broadway," and Second Ave. as the "Hungarian Broadway" (also known as "Goulash Avenue"). York Avenue is named for Sgt. Alvin York, one of the great heroes of WWI.

BUILDINGS & SPACES

The **Zion St. Mark's Church,** 339 E. 84th St. [1st/2nd], is over 100 years old and is the last German church in Yorkville—still very much a center of German life in the community. It has an interesting history that is documented by Kathy Jolowicz in a booklet available at the church for $5. They have a service in

The Zion St. Mark's Church.

German every Sunday at 11 A.M., followed by a Kaffeestunde at 12. The church contains rare Munich–style stained glass windows. In addition to services and the popular coffee hours, the church hosts a German film club, opera performances, and a language school . . . Landmark designation has been given to **City and Suburban Homes** at 79th and York. These are model tenements built in 1901–1913 by a company called City and Suburban Homes, founded by a group of prominent families of the time (Astors and others) "to provide good, decent housing to the working poor." Immigrants were eager to settle there, and the complex became known as "the treasure of Yorkville." Along with the breweries, they were one of the most famous features of the neighborhood. It's easy to see why, especially when you consider the type of tenement housing that had been previously available to immigrants. It was most often a cold-water flat, often railroad-style, with little light or ventilation, bathrooms in the hall, and designed to afford little privacy to residents (you usually had to go through one bedroom to get to another). City and Suburban offered an attractive alternative, and with people of all nationalities there, it was one of the first integrated communities in NY. Many rooms had windows, there was an inner court instead of an air shaft, and each flat had a toilet and hot water and steam heat. It's a great site, too—off the river on a wide street, and with a school and John Jay Park next door. "It was a true social housing experiment" according to Betty Cooper Wallerstein, president of the East 79th Association, in that they built four buildings, saw how they worked, then built the next

four . . . At 555 E. 78th St., the City and Suburban Co. and the Junior League built the **Junior League Hotel** for working women. It had a sewing room, a typing room, a library, and a roof garden with pergola, among other amenities. In the 1970s, it was transformed into a luxury building . . . Also across the street are the **Cherokee Apartments,** originally called the Shively Sanitary Tenements, to house people with TB. According to Ms. Wallerstein, "Today the complex is very much like it was. Peter Kalikow bought it in 1984 and had plans to demolish it. He began warehousing apartments and doing little maintenance. The landmark fight took nine years but was successful, and the

The Cherokee Apartments.

building is now owned by the Wasserman family, who are engaged in making the repairs, bringing the buildings up to code, and renting the apartments. When the insides are renovated, they plan to restore the outside" . . . There are **walking tours** of the City and Suburban complex run by Marie Beirne. Call for info ☎ 628-5970.

Other notable buildings and interiors include the city landmarked **NY Public Library Yorkville Branch,** 222 E. 79th St. [2nd/3rd] ☎ 744-5824. This was the first of the libraries funded by Andrew Carnegie (38 would follow), and the building is considered a fine example of Palladian style . . . The vaulted ceiling of **St. Elizabeth of Hungary Church,** 211 E. 83rd St. [2nd/3rd], is exquisite . . . The *AIA Guide* calls the bell tower of the

Church of the Holy Trinity, 312–332 E. 88th St. [1st/2nd], one of NY's "great bell towers."

YORKVILLIANS

You hear frequently from longtime Yorkvillians that they loved growing up here because of the tremendous sense of belonging to a community. Mary Minarik, the manager of Kolping House, a residence for foreign students and young professionals, grew up on 86th St., where there were 13 apartments in the building. In the late '60s, when the developers bought up properties in the neighborhood, they moved from their apartment, where her parents were paying "about $28 a month," all the way to 87th St., "which seemed like it was a world away." Dia Stettmeier is quoted in the *History of Zion St. Mark's Church:* "We used to dance all night. Who can forget the Platzl, The Lorelei, The Brau Haus, The Weinecke (later The Student Prince) all on 86th Street?—and so many more. In our salad days, we danced till 3 A.M. on weekends then listened to the bands jam another hour—then off to Geiger's across the street to have breakfast. It was open at that time until 5 A.M. New York at that stage was truly a night town." From Kathy Jolowicz: "In the mornings I would see the red feather bedding airing on the window sills, sometimes cushioning gawking matrons as they watched the street below. As we strolled in the evening we always ran into some of the guys from the soccer teams, and their friends. We would go to one of the German movies, or to Cafe Hindenburg for coffee and cake, one of my favorite hangouts. Everybody knew everyone. Untouched by war and its wake, this was the only Germany I knew until I visited my parents' homeland. It was a lot like 86th Street, only bigger."

THE SHOPS

These are some of the shops, restaurants, bakeries, and taverns that still exist with ties to the past: The Ideal had been serving up German food for 61 years, until the place burned in December 1993. Now, there's a new Ideal, called **Ideal Food & Bar,** 322 E. 86th St. [1st/2nd] ☎ 737-0795, with eight of the employees from the original and the same cooks who've been serving up the wurst for the past 25 years . . . The owners of the **Yorkville Inn,** 1701 Second Ave. [88th] ☎ 410-0375, are the Kaufhold family; they're related to the owners of the old Bavarian Inn on 86th Street. Some German dishes are served here . . . Still serving German food are the **Heidelberg,** 1648 Second Ave. [85th/86th] ☎ 650-1385, and the **Kleine Konditorei,** 234 E. 86th St. [2nd/3rd] ☎ 737-7130 . . . **Schaller & Weber,** 1654 Second Ave. [85th/86th] ☎ 879-3047. According to Ralph Schaller, the store continues to use the same recipes for the wurst that they used when the store was opened in 1937 by his father and Herr Weber . . . German-owned **Kramer's Pastries,** 1643 Second Ave. [85th/86th] ☎ 535-5955, has been around since 1925 baking, among other things, great schnecken. They also supply a lot of Black Forest cake to neighborhood events . . . The **Herbert Glaser Bake Shop,** 1670 First Ave. [87th] ☎ 289-2562. The Glaser family has been serving pastry for more than 90 years. Dobos torte is their specialty . . . **Yorkville Packing House,** 1560 Second Ave. [81st]

☎ 628-5147, sells Hungarian meat and other Hungarian food items as does **Tibor Meat,** 1508 Second Ave. [78th/79th] ☎ 744-8292, down Second Avenue . . . You can round out your Hungarian meal with pastry from **Rigo,** 314 E. 78th St. [1st/2nd] ☎ 988-0052. Their most popular item is the Rigo cake—a Hungarian chocolate mousse cake. When you want Hungarian food but don't want to prepare it, there's the Old-World-feeling **Mocca,** 1588 Second Ave. [82nd/83rd] ☎ 734-6470 . . . Other shops worth noting are **Elk Candy,** 240 E. 86th St. [2nd/3rd] ☎ 650-1177, marzipan central for 59 years, and **Tal Bagels,** 333 E. 86th St. [1st/2nd] ☎ 427-6811, which makes great bagels, among the very best in the city.

FEATURE

$\longleftrightarrow$

INTRODUCTION

The Feature chapter is a group of articles that cuts across our usual organization of Stores, Services, Info, and so on. What you find here is a broad range of subjects such as Anglophilia, Sleep, Leather, Fish, and Pianos. The approach to the subject varies but may include places to buy whatever's under discussion, related services, relevant consumer information, and profiles and interviews.

AMERICANA

ARTISANS

BASKETMAKER These days, basketmaking isn't always given a lot of respect—unless the person making the basket is Nancy Moore Bess. She exhibits constantly in craft galleries around the country but always has a few pieces in her studio that she will be happy to show you. Ms. Bess makes traditional baskets, art baskets, and wall hangings. Recent studies in Japan have enhanced the Shaker-like simplicity of some of her designs. She

Basket by Nancy Moore Bess.

teaches basketry at the Craft Students' League and at Parson's. Prices for her pieces start at $100 for a small basket. ☎ 691-2821.

FURNITURE MAKER Scott Jordan has a small factory in the Brooklyn Navy Yard with 15 employees. They make solid cherry tables, chairs, beds, and sofas in slightly updated Mission and Shaker styles, using traditional techniques. You can see the pieces at his showroom at 137 Varick St. [Spring] ☎ 620-4682. Mr. Jordan believes that they are in the tradition of craftsmen who take "what's done in the past and forge something of their own out of it." Some items are in stock, others are made to order.

POTTER Jon Waldo paints on familiar forms—plates, bowls, cups, vases—to which simple, bold, sunny images are added. He is fond of using words as images, or adding things like scissors, a lion's head, or an airplane. His commission work tailors pieces to your particular interests: "I'd like to know if your grandfather was a carpenter, if you like a certain favorite poem, if you speak French . . ." He also makes tea sets, butter dishes, candlesticks, and lamp bases. Call him at ☎ 777-4838. A cup and saucer retails for about $50.

QUILTER Chris Bobin is an old-fashioned quilter but her subjects are modern, as is her sensibility. She has an ongoing series of quilts called "Occupations for Women" that show what the career possibilities were for women when she was growing up. So far, she's done an airline stewardess, Miss America, a nurse, a nun, and Barbie. She has made a quilt representing the restaurant what-to-do-when-someone's-choking poster. Ms. Bobin does embroidery work, too—straightforward, traditional work. Quilts run from about $650 for a 2 ft. × 3 ft. up to $3,500. Embroidery is $85 an hour or by the piece. ☎ 475-7268.

WHERE TO BUY

America Hurrah, 766 Madison Ave. [65th/66th] ☎ 535-1930, sells Navajo rugs, Native American beadwork and baskets, hooked rugs, some quilts, books, and toys.

Laura Fisher, 1050 Second Ave. [56th] in the Manhattan Art and Antiques Center ☎ 838-2596. You'll find a very large selection of quilts and other bed toppings—chenille, white work, crochet, knit—large and small hooked rugs, and some printed tablecloths from the '40s and '50s in the $50 range. There's a small selection of American folk art, including Popsicle stick and bottle cap pieces, and a table with a mosaic linoleum top.

Kelter Malcé Antiques, 74 Jane St. [Greenwich/Washington] ☎ 675-7380, was the name of the store Jole Kelter and Michael Malcé had on Bleecker Street for many years. Now they sell their lively collection of Americana from their home on Jane Street. It's Early American painted country furniture and accessories, hooked rugs, folk art, and some sports memorabilia. By appt.

Kentucky, 137 Duane St. [Church/W. Bway] ☎ 349-6577. By appt. Kathy Shorr travels throughout the eastern United States collecting country antiques and modern folk art and also shows contemporary artists who work in the folk art tradition. She is especially attracted to items with a fish motif, and supplies many things to seafood restaurants around town. From Kentucky are gouache paintings of fruits and still lifes by Loftin True framed in antique frames. There are large and small furniture pieces, chests, tables, chairs, some folding screens, which she builds from old window shutters, pottery bowls, pitchers, colored wooden bowls, and mirrors.

Bernard & S. Dean Levy, 24 E. 84th St. [5th/Mad] ☎ 628-7088. This townhouse has been converted into a five-floor shop selling American antiques. You can take the elevator to the 5th floor and work your way down floor by floor, seeing lots of Hepplewhite, Sheraton, and Chippendale. There are mirrors, paintings, clocks (table and grandfather), furniture, candlesticks, and some silver and pottery. All items are tagged with historical information, description, provenance, and price. The staff is exceptionally friendly.

Judith and James Milne, 506 E. 74th St. [York] ☎ 472-0107, sell their eclectic and fine mix of American country antiques out of a good-sized commercial loft. When we visited, there was a very appealing selection of quilts, chairs, hooked rugs, tin lamps, pine cupboards, and a carousel horse among the items. The Milnes have been selling Americana for over 20 years, now including early 20th century pieces.

Pantry and Hearth, 121 E. 35th St. [Park/Lex] ☎ 532-0535. It's clear when you enter Gail Lettick's home and shop that she's been an ardent collector of 18th century Americana for a long time—30 years, in fact. Most of the furniture, china, wall decor, and textiles that you see when you walk through her living room, dining room, kitchen, and bedrooms are for sale. If you don't find what you are looking for, she will "find to order." The furniture, of course, is constantly changing, so the 1740 dining table, the tin kitchen (a kind of early rotisserie), or the 1760 Philadelphia candle stand may be gone by the time you arrive, but they will have been replaced with new old things. Ms. Lettick believes she has the most painted country furniture in the city. It's best to call for an appointment but, if she's in, she's open.

Susan Parrish Antiques, 390 Bleecker St. [Perry/W. 11th] ☎ 645-5020. Ms. Parrish has specialized in selling quilts and painted 19th century and early 20th century furniture for over 20 years. You may also find Navajo weaving, folk art game boards, rocking horses, weathervanes, and whatever else Ms. Parrish is currently interested in. She's always got a great selection of quilts from 1820–1940, selling from $300 into the thousands. She is likely to have many varieties: Amish, patriotic, early chintz, Baltimore album quilts, crib quilts, pictorials, wool, and log cabin quilts. You may find antique flags, there is always a bed for sale (and related bedding items), and some "silly things" like printed tablecloths. Ms. Parrish says she is a purist in that she sells little that is repainted or refinished. She carries the real thing, whatever its value.

Piston's, Manhattan Art and Antiques Center, 1050 Second Ave. [55th/56th] ☎ 753-8322. A good source for pewter. We saw plates from the early 1700s, as well as porringers, beakers, salt cellars, candlesticks, and pitchers. There is pewter from America and Europe.

Israel Sack, 730 Fifth Ave. [56th/57th] ☎ 399-6562. The Sacks, in business for 90 years, have given three rooms of furniture to the Metropolitan Museum of Art American collection, and their knowledge of the subject and their extraordinary collection of 18th century furniture is evident in their very large display area. Each piece has a descriptive label and a price tag. The top of the line for American furniture.

Thomas K. Woodard, 799 Madison Ave. [67th/68th] ☎ 988-2906, sells small pieces of furniture and lots of interesting decorative items, old lettering and shop signs, some glass and china, and a selection of pristine quilts. They make their own cotton area rugs and runners called Woodard Weave. Most are striped and come in soft colors. The simple designs give the rugs a modern look.

MORE

The Museum of American Folk Art, 2 Lincoln Sq. [65th/66th] ☎ 595-9533, is, of course, always a good source of information on Americana. They plan to move back eventually to their home base on W. 53rd, but for the next few years will remain at Lincoln Square, showing the over 3,000 pieces of their permanent collection on a rotating basis. These folk paintings, sculptures, textiles, and decorative arts are exhibited in the gallery that runs off to the right. The main space is usually given over to traveling shows, sometime quilts, sometimes a single artist, sometimes the effect of a particular immigrant experience on American folk art. There is a study collection and a library that are open (by appt.) to members and those studying in the field.

At the **Metropolitan Museum of Art,** Fifth Ave. at 82nd ☎ 535-7710, there's an enormous collection of Americana, thousands and thousands of pieces, in the Henry R. Luce Center for the Study of American Art. Whenever we've visited it, it's been very quiet up there—ideal for viewing and research. Research is made easy by a computer system that has the collection catalogued.

ANGLOPHILIA

Every anglophile imagines a different, invariably mythical, England. Ours is populated with villages of Lucias and Mapps, plotting their latest triumphs of one-upsmanship. Whatever your idea of England is, here are some ways in New York to conjure it up.

FOOD AND TEA Your first stop should be Nicky Perry's **Tea and Sympathy,** 108 Greenwich Ave. [Jane/W. 12th] ☎ 807-8329. Ms. Perry says, rightly, "It *is* England in here as far as I am concerned." Come here for a full English tea from 11–6 weekdays and 1–6 on weekends and some familiar British meals the rest of the time. Ms. Perry's own favorites change from month to month, but two are the shepherd's pie and the roast lamb on Sunday.

When you want to stock up on British foods, **Myers of Keswick,** 634 Hudson St. [Horatio/Jane] ☎ 691-4194, is it. Peter Myers was a butcher in Keswick in the Lake

Anglophilia!

District. He moved to NY and opened his shop over a decade ago because so many Brits were pining for "certain items, baked beans being the foremost, that were not available here." Even though Heinz is an American company, new arrivals from England always say the same thing when they see the English can on the shelf—"They don't taste the same." Mr. Myers prepares bangers, chipolatas, and Cumberland sausage, the recipe for the latter having been inherited from his grandfather. The store also stocks pork pies, Cornish pasties, Scotch eggs, and, at the holidays, mince pies.

More British food products at **Burke & Burke**—the stores are good (though expensive) sources for British candy, some Fortnum & Mason products, and other food items such as Heinz Ploughman's Relish . . . **Farrell's,** 1326 Lexington Ave. [88th/89th] ☎ 860-3925, has a small selection of candy and biscuits, as well as Tayto crisps (from Ireland).

SPIRITS Here are some spots with either a British feel or with a high proportion of British patrons. For actual Brits, try **NW3,** 242 E. 10th St. [1st] ☎ 260-0891, and the **Two I's,** 248 W. 14th St. [7th/8th] ☎ 807-1775 . . . **The North Star,** 93 South St. [Fulton] ☎ 509-6757, has the trappings of a pub and serves eight British beers on draft . . . Moving uptown, **McCormacks Pub,** 365 Third Ave. [26th/27th] ☎ 683-0911, shows English soccer and rugby matches every Sat. starting at 11 A.M. . . . **Manchester NY,** 920 Second Ave. [49th] ☎ 223-7484, has a few British staples such as fish and chips, shepherd's pie, and a ploughman's lunch . . . At the **British Open,** 320 E. 59th St. [1st/2nd] ☎ 355-8467, a pubby feeling with an emphasis on anything golf.

ORGANIZATION **The English Speaking Union,** 16 E. 69th St. [5th/Mad] ☎ 879-6800, is Anglophile central for uptowners. It's an organization started in 1920 with a mission to increase communication in the world through the use of English. The NY branch is situated in a lovely old townhouse. $80 a year allows you use of their 8,000-volume library (mostly British writers), invitations to their many events (movies such as *The Windsors*), various other society meetings (the Brontës, Jane Austen), and speakers. There is a tea every weekday afternoon from 3–5:30, $6 for members ($8 for non-members). There are certain travel benefits as well, including 10% off on any British Airways flights when you book at their Fifth Ave. office. The ESU sponsors many educational programs for students (local and otherwise).

SOAPS, COLOGNE, REMEDIES, ETC.
When we go to England, we always stock up on Lemsip (for colds), Eye Dew (leaves Visine in the dust), D.R. Harris Pick-Me-Up (a potion that does some good the morning after), and Molton Brown products. But they're all available without a boarding pass at **Cambridge Chemists,** 21 E. 65th St. [5th/Mad] ☎ 734-5678, albeit with hefty surcharges. Owner Joseph Policar makes trips to England to develop sources, he says, "for things you find in a good English medicine chest. Anything that is not forbidden by the FDA." They also carry Penhaligon's, Redoxon, badger brushes from John Bull, Floris, Trumper, Czech & Speake, some Boots products, Victorian bone handle toothbrushes from various makers. A catalog of all their products is available for $1.50 . . . Other sources for these products: **Ad Hoc Softwares,** 410 West Broadway [Spring] ☎ 925-2652, carries some Molton Brown and Neal's Yard products (smallish selection). Most of the department stores carry some Floris, Penhaligon's, or Molton Brown. **Floris** has a store at 703 Madison Ave. [62nd/63rd] ☎ 935-9100. For Penhaligon's, the best supplies are at Saks and Bergdorf's.

THE ARTS If London means theatre to you, you should know about the newsletter **London Theatre News,** ☎ 517-8608. Each issue has theatre reviews, interviews, reviews of restaurants near the theatres, and articles on theatre-related books and records. A three-month subscription is $23 (perfect if you're planning a trip), but it's good enough that you may opt for the full year at $51. They also have a theatre ticket service (including discounts on some), and what better people to ask for recommendations? . . . **Mrs. Hudson's Video,** 573 Hudson St. [W. 11th/Bank] ☎ 989-1050, is a good source for British videos. Big renters: *Middlemarch,*

This Sporting Life, Saturday Night Sunday Morning . . . On the telly: Look for British comedy on Comedy Central and there are more Britcoms on WLIW (Ch. 21) . . . A&E often has offerings from the **BBC** . . . The ***Walford Gazette*** is a newspaper for fans of *East Enders.* You can get a free sample issue of either the *Walford Gazette* ($15 for subscription, published quarterly) or **British Television,** a guide to all the English programs that make it to this side of the Atlantic, by writing to 35–50 78th St. #2F, Jackson Heights, NY 11372.

CLOTHING   **Jekyll & Hyde,** 93 Greene St. [Prince/Spring] ☎ 966-8503. Mike and Angie Boyle bring the best of hip Brit menswear to NY each year. All of the clothes are designed by English designers, and you'll find things like Roger Dack's high-buttoned Edwardian suits and John Smedley's fine knit shirts (wool in winter, Sea Island cotton in summer).

NEWS AND POLITICS   You can get your weekly dose of "Order! Order!" from **British Politics** on C-Span and your daily dose of news from **ITN News** on Ch. 21. BBC Worldwide's **The World Service** is broadcast on radio on WNYC am 820, 7 nights a week. British newspapers aren't hard to find: **Hotalings,** 142 W. 42nd St. [Bway/6th] ☎ 840-1868, carries nine major British papers (everything except the *Evening Standard* and the *Mirror*) and **Eastern Newsstand** in the Met Life building, ☎ 687-1198, carries the *Times,* the *Mirror,* the *Independent,* and the *Evening Post.*

PLANNING A TRIP   **British Travel Bookstore,** 551 Fifth Ave. [45th/46th] ☎ 490-6688, is not widely known, but it's worth a stop if you're going to be doing some pleasure traveling in the British Isles. They have every guide book imaginable, videos, and Landranger Maps of every square inch of England and Wales—great for serious walkers.

CITY CLOCKS

Marvin Schneider is the official Clockmaster of New York City. Some years ago, when his path through town took him past the four-sided clock at 346 Broadway [Leonard/Worth], known as the **Clocktower,** he noticed that the clock did not work. He looked inside and realized that he and his friend Eric Reiner could fix it. After the city threw up a million-dollar-liability insurance obstacle, Mr. Schneider got the New York Life Insurance Co., the orig-inal builders of 346 Broadway, to underwrite, along with Lloyd's of London, the million-dollar tab. He worked for 12 years as a volunteer on city clocks before being officially appointed Clockmaster. Mr. Schneider calls the clock at 346 Broadway "the grandest clock in the city." It is a weight-driven clock with three sets of 800-pound weights that need to be raised each week. Most often this can be done by machine, but sometimes it has to be done by hand. Mr. Schneider resets the clock most weeks around noon on Wednesdays. You can make an appointment to be with him when he does this. ☎ 274-4449. Mr. Schneider says this clock "has the distinction of being a landmark both on the inside and on the outside."

Among the other clocks that Mr. Schneider cares for is **Minerva and the Bell Ringers** at Herald Square Park. This clock originally stood on the New York Herald Building, which was torn down in the '20s. The works date from the 1890s and were built weight driven, modified to electricity 40 years ago. Two figures swing hammers and toll the hour—but only between 8 A.M. and 10 P.M. It was felt when the clock was built that it would be too disturbing to have the clock chime for 24 hours, so in an early effort at noise control, the chiming hours were limited to most people's waking hours.

Here are some of the other notable clocks in the city: The sidewalk clock at **522 Fifth Ave.** [44th] was moved to its current location in the 1930s from 43rd St. It used to be in front of the American Trust Company . . . **The Toy Center clock,** at 200 Fifth Ave. [24th] has been there since 1909 . . . The **Sherry Netherland clock** is thought to have been installed when the hotel opened in 1927. The clock at **1501 Third Ave.** [84th/85th] was put up around 1885 outside jeweler Adoph Stern's shop. That was across the street from the clock's current location. When Mr. Stern moved, so did the clock. It's in the shape of a big pocket watch . . . The **Sun Clock** is the green four-faced clock that hangs off the corner of the building that used to house the *New York Sun* newspaper at Broadway & Chambers. It was manufactured by the International Co., which later became IBM. In 1967, the insides were replaced so that now only the case is original . . . The **Col-**

gate clock is not, of course, in the city, it's in Jersey City; nevertheless it is faced to provide the time to city residents. Colgate, for its centennial in 1906, put up an octagonal clock to promote its Octagon soap. In 1924, they replaced it with the current clock, made by Seth Thomas. The clock is 1,963.5 square feet, and it is the world's largest vertical clockface. The minute hand is 26 feet long and weighs 2,200 pounds . . . The **Met Life** building, 1 Madison Ave. [23rd], has a clock that sounds different measures of Handel's *I Know That My Redeemer Liveth* until 9 P.M. After that, the tower flashes the quarter hours . . . The **Red Square** apartment building, 250 E. Houston St., has a large clock on top of the building made by M & Co. The numbers read, clockwise, 12, 4, 9, 6, 1, 10, 5, 11, 7, 2, 3, and 8 . . . It is said that the **Atlas clock** in front of Tiffany's stopped ticking at the exact time of Lincoln's death—April 15, 1865, at 7:22 A.M. Tiffany's says this is the only time it has stopped running (it was reset on the same day) . . . The **Maiden Lane** clock, 174 Broadway [Maiden] ☎ 732-0890, set into the sidewalk, is owned by the William Barthman Jewelers. It was installed by the company around 1915. Originally, it was a drop number clock (numbered cards flipped to give the time) but it is now an electric clock with a Cartier face. The glass covering, which resists scratching, is made from a material designed by NASA for use in the space shuttle.

The Toy Center clock.

COMPUTERS

Some strategies to help buy and maintain computers with much guidance provided by Bruce Stark, who runs Computer Tutor and Mac Tutor (see below under Training and Troubleshooting).

BUYING HARDWARE Unless you're proficient with computers, Mr. Stark says, buy desktop computers, monitors, and printers either from reputable manufacturers directly (rather than from some unknown warehouse) or from a retailer in your area. Otherwise, support is going to be almost nonexistent. Reputable manufacturers? Look at **Micron** (☎ 800-388-6334) and **Dell** (☎ 800-727-3355). For stores, try **Rockwell,** 261 Madison Ave. [39th] ☎ 949-6935, and **J & R** (though service isn't J & R's strong suit) or for the Mac: **PCSI,** 26 W. 23rd St. [5th/6th] ☎ 255-7600, or **MPC,** 4 W. 20th St. [5th/6th] ☎ 463-8585. For laptops, Mr. Stark would never do mail order since the machines are more fragile than desktop models. He likes **Toshiba** and **IBM** here. For all other hardware items, things like modems or backup equipment, try a reputable company such as **PC and Mac Connection** (☎ 800-800-1111).

BUYING SOFTWARE As Mr. Stark says, if you know what you want, buy mail order and buy cheap. If there's a problem and you can't get satisfaction from the mail-order company, you always have recourse from the manufacturer. Again, you can try PC and Mac Connection, listed above. In town, MUG likes **J & R,** 15 Park Row [Beekman/Ann] ☎ 238-9100. Their software floor is easily the most pleasant software environ-ment, and they have the best selection, too. We don't like **CompUSA,** 420 Fifth Ave. [37th/38th] ☎ 764-6224, at all because it's such an awful experience: the aisles are too crowded, service is difficult to come by and the level of knowledge isn't great, and when you leave, they're too busy inspecting your purchases to make sure you haven't stolen anything to thank you for your business. Prices are generally competitive between the two stores, with some variations from item to item. Usually the differences are small, but it does pay to compare on big-ticket items. At one point, PageMaker 5 was selling for $599.95 at J & R, $499.98 at CompUSA. Still, in comparing 8 popular pieces of software (and the Microsoft mouse), the total retail price was over $2,000 but there was only a $34.70 difference between the two stores. Pickups and returns are J & R's Achilles' heel. You are forced to go into the basement, in dire surroundings, where you are likely to face a line and lots of "watch your back"s as deliveries are made into their storeroom area. As for return policies: at CompUSA, for both hardware and software, you have 30 days to return with receipt or invoice and all original packaging. If you don't have the packaging, they charge you a "restocking" fee, which is 15% of the sale. No money back, store credit only. At J & R, you have 10 days to return, only for store credit . . . We'd also shop at **Egghead** (various locations) and **Rockwell,** but we avoid **Software Etc.** because of their limited selection, limited service, and frequently too high prices.

CAFES WITH COMPUTERS **@Cafe,** 12 St. Marks Pl. [2nd/3rd] ☎ 979-5439, **In-**

ternet Cafe, 82 E. 3rd St. [1st/2nd] ☎ 614-0747, alt. coffee, 139 Avenue A [St. Mark's/9th] 529-2233, Cybercafe, 273 Lafayette St. [Prince] ☎ 334-5140.

COMPUTER BOOKS McGraw Hill Bookstore, 1221 Sixth Ave. [48th] ☎ 512-4100, is the first place to check for almost any computer book imaginable, though Coliseum and Barnes & Noble also have good selections. Computer Book Works, 25 Warren St. [Bway/Church] ☎ 385-1616, sells computer books, some at discount.

DONATING USED COMPUTERS Materials for the Arts, ☎ 255-5924, happily accepts IBM compatible used computers, 286 or higher with a hard drive, for use in arts institutions around the city. You can also call Nonprofit Computing, ☎ 759-2368.

NEW YORK ONLINE For information on New York, available online, see NY Online in the Information chapter.

REPAIR First, try the place where you bought it. If not, for IBM compatibles, try Tailored Technologies, ☎ 947-4422. In addition to fixing and maintaining your hardware (and providing, as they say, "peace of mind"), they also can set up a network. The on-site rate is $125/hour. If you bring your equipment in, it's $90/hr. Neither rate includes parts. For Macs, try PCSI (see "Buying Hardware" above) . . . Also for Macs, Tekserve 163 W. 23rd St. [6th/7th] ☎ 929-3645, where David Lerner and his technicians service Macs and Powerbooks, do repair work, upgrades, and data recovery. Unlike many others, Tekserve prefers to re-

pair than to replace parts—which is less expensive for you. Carry-in service only, backed with a one-year warranty.

SOFTWARE REVIEWS If you or your company need to keep up with the latest software in a serious way, Software and CD ROM Reviews on File from Facts on File is a good solution. For $249 a year, the staff culls over 100 publications and then characterizes these reviews in an abstract. You can get a sample by calling ☎ 967-8800.

TRAINING AND TROUBLESHOOTING MUG always recommends PC Tutor ☎ 787-6636 and Mac Tutor ☎ 362-6241, run by Bruce Stark. They do a lot of tutoring, of course, but also consulting, buying, training, installing things like scanners—everything but heavy physical repair. It's $95 an hour, 2-hour min. with a few additional price structures. They have averted disaster for us more than once and they're a pleasure to deal with . . . Ms. Tommy Rupinski at Women in Technology, ☎ 924-7200, has 17 independent consultants with whom she works, and when you call she will spend as much time as you need to ascertain which of her consultants, for IBM or Mac, can help you best. They do hardware support, software support, installation, Internet training, and Web page design. She says, "If I can't fix it, I won't bill you." $80 an hour for training, $95 for installation; she'll quote for network or desktop publishing jobs . . . Eric Rode works with IBM compatibles doing one-person jobs up to medium-sized firms. He can handle networks, train, troubleshoot, and recommend software and hardware. It's $80 an hour plus out of pocket travel expenses ($15–$20 minimum, since he lives in New Jersey) ☎ 908-757-0203.

USER'S GROUPS **Mac User's Group** has classes, seminars, and is an excellent resource for all Mac things. Classes consist of things like Intro to the Mac as well as classes on specific software such as Quark or Photoshop. They're $100 for 5 hour classes (for members, $150 for nonmembers), max of 10 per class. Individual membership to that MUG is $45 per year. ☎ 473-1600 . . . **PC User's Group,** ☎ 533-6972, is $35 a year. Among other things, they hold general meetings, which are free and open to the public, on the third Wed. of each month.

EYEGLASSES

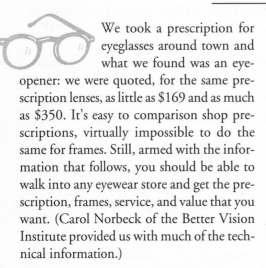

We took a prescription for eyeglasses around town and what we found was an eye-opener: we were quoted, for the same prescription lenses, as little as $169 and as much as $350. It's easy to comparison shop prescriptions, virtually impossible to do the same for frames. Still, armed with the information that follows, you should be able to walk into any eyewear store and get the prescription, frames, service, and value that you want. (Carol Norbeck of the Better Vision Institute provided us with much of the technical information.)

LENSES **Plastic**—weighs less than glass and is less breakable, but can scratch. The plastic lens is the most common. It is lighter weight than glass, easier to tint, and has the same visual acuity as glass . . . **Glass**—resists scratches without a coating. Durable but heavier than other lens materials . . . **Polycarbonate**—thinner than regular lenses, they are impact-resistant and filter out UV rays. Good for children, for glasses worn during active sports, and if you have little or no vision in one eye. Ms. Norbeck says, "They do not give the best clarity because light passes through them slower. They are hard to make, so there can be a wide variety of quality." . . . **High index—**

are lenses made from special plastics or, in some cases, glass. They are thinner than the other lenses and are often used where another material would result in a thick lens. There may be an extra charge for high-power or oversize lenses. While they are thinner and lighter in weight than glass, "visual acuity can be more varied—you may see a little less well than through glass or plastic." This is partly because high index reflects more light away from you than glass or plastic lenses. An anti-reflective coating can increase the amount of light that comes through the lens, thus improving the vision with these lenses . . . **Aspheric lenses**—are thinner, flatter lenses that can be made in polycarbonate or other high index materials. They can be made in all focuses. They improve sight in the periphery by compensating for the difference in distance between the far edges of the lens and the center of the eye. Figure an additional $40–$100. It depends on the power of your prescription, though, whether they will do you any good. Ms. Norbeck says, "If the optical company you are working with can't talk to you about asphericity and all the other options, they are not selling good lenses." . . . **Single-vision lenses**—correct for one field of vision, either close up or far away . . . **Bifocal lenses**—correct for distance and close-up (no mid-range correction), but the line in center of the lens sometimes causes an image to "jump and blur." There is a special kind of bifocal called "double seg" that has a second correction placed higher in the lens for close-up viewing—useful for people who perform a lot of close work . . . **Trifocal lenses**—correct for distance, mid-range, and close-up. Two visible lines on lens. Good for people who need a lot of "arm's length" vision like com-puter operators . . . **Progressive-Addition lenses**—also called no-line bifocals. Progressive lenses give a smooth transition from distance to close-up sight. You will need to rely on the store staff to show you frames that will work with the size lens required for progressive lenses, but you should have "at least 20 mm of depth (about 3/4 in.) from the center of your pupil to the bottom of the frame" to get the best benefit of the lens. Ms. Norbeck notes, "These are the only things to wear now. They are now in their fourth generation of development. Bifocals are a 100-year-old technology." The Varilux brand is state of the art, but some of their patents have expired. There are 42 brands of progressive lenses on the market. Varilux is considered to be the best, but Rodenstock, Sola, Silor, Zeiss, Pentax, Seiko (and others) are making good lenses. Ask which brands of lenses the store carries.

✌ **SPECIAL COATINGS/TINTS** Scratch-resistant—for plastic lenses. This is recommended for people who take their glasses off a lot during the day. Most lenses come scratch-resistant . . . **Anti-reflection coating**—eliminates reflections from both surfaces of the lens. When light is being reflected away from your eyes, less light is entering your lenses. Some people find that the A/R coating helps them to see better, and they

may be of some benefit in night driving. They're sometimes hard to keep clean, but a hydrophobic coating can remedy this. It gives better vision and looks better. A/R coating will add an additional $30–$55 . . . **Polarized lenses**—eliminate reflected glare on regular or sunglasses. They are an expensive option especially helpful for fishermen, for example, who look directly into the water. Contrary to popular opinion, they are not best for driving . . . **Tints**—colors added to the lens, sometimes for cosmetic effect, sometimes for light-sensitive people. Most do not offer UV protection . . . **Gradient lenses**—These are darker at the top than the bottom of the lens for reduction of overhead glare . . . **UV protection**—can be added to plastic lenses to protect eyes from UV rays . . . **Photochromic lenses,** which darken in bright conditions, are available only in glass lenses (and only in gray or brown). They can't be made thinner but can be made in single-vision and progressive-addition lenses . . . **Mirrored lenses**—make you look like the State Police and can reduce infrared rays. They scratch, and so require care in handling. Glass or plastic lenses only. They are necessary to protect from the heat of infrared at high altitudes . . . Other things that can be done to lenses: **Rolling and polishing**—smooths out the lens edges . . . **Beveling and faceting**—thins lens edges and prisms the light. **Grooving and painting**—adds color to the edges of lenses in rimless frames.

✌ **FOR CHILDREN** Safety is a major concern, so polycarbonate lenses should be used. Fitting is very important for children. The frame should also be one that has been especially designed for children, not just a small or "shrunk down" adult frame. The bridge on a child's frame needs to be specially designed. Spring hinges at the temples are advised. If there is a lot of pulling or bumping, they don't go out of adjustment. Look for warranties on children's eyewear.

👓 **FRAMES** It's difficult to comparison shop frames since finding the same frame in two different stores is a long shot. However, frames have a style number and a size stamped on the inside of the temple—if you have these numbers, it's possible to comparison shop or special order. Frames are available in plastic, metal, and rubber (rubber is used mostly in sports frames). Flexible frames are good for people who are very active—they're great for teenagers but expensive. See the section on style below for the stores in town carrying large selections of designer frames. You can spend anywhere from $75–$400 for frames.

👓 **SHOPPING FOR GLASSES** Wherever you go for glasses, you will need to rely on an optician to help sort out the array of technical choices listed above. A good optician will ask you some questions about your lifestyle: Do you play a lot of sports? Do you do close work? How much are you outside? to know what to advise. Ask the store if they have a warranty in case the glasses are imperfect. There are different quality levels in lenses, and a place that is promising to make a complete set of eyeglasses for $39.95 is probably using an inferior lens. Ms. Norbeck says, "You don't have to buy glasses in the place that gives you your prescription. Shopping for eyeglasses is no different than shopping for anything else." When we went shopping for glasses, we asked for the same thing in

each store: Varilux lenses (by name) with a high-index lens in the right eye. The prices we quote for each store were the ones we got for this prescription.

👓 **GOOD VALUES** Quality **Optical Frames,** 50 W. 34th St. [6th] at The McAlpin Hotel #8A12 ☎ 239-5200. Appt. only. No eye exams. This was the best assortment of frames we saw at any of the inexpensive places. Discounted designer (Calvin Klein, Armani) and non-designer frames. Nice service from Harry Levi, who guides you through frame selection and dispenses lots of accurate advice and information along the way. This is not exactly a showroom, more like an office with eyeglass frames. 4–7 working days for glasses. Our lens quote: $169 . . . **Park Avenue Visionary,** 55 E. 52nd St. [Park/Mad] ☎ 751-2020. Eye exams by appt. Inside the Park Ave. Atrium. You might not expect to find value in this good-looking store with its stock of designer frames and up-to-the-minute looks. Considerate and knowledgeable help with frame choice. The Armani frame we liked a lot was priced at $136—a great price for Armani. Lens quote: $199 . . . **Sol Moscot,** 118 Orchard St. [Delancey] ☎ 477-3796 and Sixth and 14th ☎ 657-1550. Eye exams, no appt. necessary. Don't be fooled by the fact that Moscot is on Orchard St. This store has one of the better selection of designer frames in town (as well as glasses for kids). All frames are discounted and Moscot says if you have seen a frame they don't have, they will get it for you at a discount price. Our lens quote: $209 . . . **Unique Eyewear,** 19 W. 34th St. [5th/6th] ☎ 947-4977. No eye exams. You must bring your own prescription, frame selection is strictly self-serve, and there's not a great choice. Still, there are good deals here. 1-week wait. Unique will put lenses into frames you buy elsewhere. Our lens quote: $170.

✿ **STYLE ABOVE ALL** **Leonard Poll,** 40 W. 55th St. [5th/6th] ☎ 246-4452. No eye exams. An extensive selection of frames in a range of styles from conservative wires to European colored plastics to Cartier. Poll also has many nice styles at modest prices. They offered us a choice of Varilux, saying we could use a previous generation at $195 or a later one that costs $295. No one else gave us this choice. A thin lens would be an additional $15. 1 week for glasses . . . **The Eye Man,** 2266 Broadway [81st/82nd] ☎ 873-4114. Eye exams by appt. A great selection of designer frames in many style ranges in this large store. Try-on frames were clean. Helpful, courteous service. They also have a large selection of children's frames. Our lens quote: $325 . . . **The Eye Shop,** 50 W. 8th St. [6th/MacDougal] ☎ 673-9450. Eye exams by appt. Many frames, such as Hanae Mori, that we did not see in other places. Our lens quote: $230 . . . **Myoptics,** 82 Christopher St. [7th/Bleecker] ☎ 741-9550, is the largest store in the Myoptics chain. The frames were among the hippest and best looking we tried and include L.A. Eyeworks, Matsuda, Martine Sitbon, and Tico. Eye exams by walk in or appt. Our lens quote: $293.96.

✿ **THE CHAINS** **For Eyes,** 241 W. 23rd St. [7th/8th] ☎ 741-2020, has opened its first store in NYC. *Consumer Reports,* in a survey of chain optical shops, found them to have the lowest prices. The frames are ticketed with the price for a complete package— frames and single-vision lenses. Glasses start at $50 and go up in $10 increments to the most expensive Cazal frames for $300–$400. Tinting is free and a second pair is discounted. Our lens quote: For Eyes adds $199 to the package price for Varilux lenses and $15 for thinning. They have a good selection of designer frames as well as frames for children. Eye exams by appt. Good advice, too . . . **Cohen's Fashion Optical,** 5 Greenwich Ave. [Christopher] ☎ 645-1395, and many other locations around town. Eye exams on a walk-in basis. Cohen's advertises heavily that a second pair is free. However, the second pair is limited to single-vision lenses and an assortment of leftover-looking frames. Since this was no help in our case, they gave us the option of having $50 deducted from our bill. Selection is just okay. Our lens quote: $290 . . . All the **LensCrafters** stores are set up the same way. There are waist-high cases around the store with trays of frames in them. Plastic and metal frames are sorted according to price, ranging from $50–$200. You are encouraged to select your own frames. Everyone who approached us in the stores we visited was very helpful. There are also information kiosks explaining the various options with lens models and information pamphlets. Our lens quote: $225. They do not, however, use Varilux brand lenses, so this is a different brand than other stores have been asked to quote on. Glasses in an hour (even our prescription) as they advertise. Uniform pricing, uniformly courteous . . . At the four **Pearle Vision**s, there was no consistency in price. Our price quotes went from $272.50–$329, and there was confusion about how much to charge in three of the four stores. Service was poor at three of the four and the store at 6 E. 23rd St. did a lot of pressuring to buy. Pearle Vision Express promised our glasses in 5–15 days—or, as they don't advertise, glasses in about a fortnight. The only Pearle where we thought normal shopping conditions prevailed was at 10 E. 42nd St. [5th/Mad] ☎ 986-2150. Eye exams by appt. Our lens quote: $275. Glasses in 1 week.

👓 **OTHER STORES**   Here are a few other eyewear shops that have things to recommend them. **Eyes on the World,** World Trade Center Concourse ☎ 432-0777. Best to make an appt. for eye exam. Our lens quote: $235. Helpful staff, large selection, but only a few cutting-edge designer frames. Lab on premises . . . **Judith Optical,** 799 Lexington Ave. [62nd] ☎ 838-8739, is a small store with solicitous service. They explain why they are showing you specific frames and give good information about lenses. No eye exams. Our lens quote: $249 . . . **Purdy,** 501 Madison Ave. [52nd] ☎ 688-8050. No eye exams. Lots of frames, lots of designers. Individual boothlets for consultation. Our lens quote: $350. Will work with you if you need glasses right away, otherwise, it's a few days. Also at 1195 Lexington Ave. [81st] ☎ 737-0122 and 971 Madison Ave. [76th] ☎ 794-2020 . . . **Westway Vision,** 645 Ninth Ave. [45th] ☎ 245-0686. Eye exams by appt. or walk in when the doctor is there. Well-chosen, moderate selection of frames. Helpful, good advice. Some antique frames are available, but you have to ask for them. They are not suitable for all types of lenses. Our lens quote: Lenses $225, 3-day wait.

FISH

AQUARIUMS FOR THE HOME   For advice on home aquariums, you can call **The Fish Doctor, Inc.** ☎ 908-290-1547. Kate McClave has a degree in marine biology and knows a lot about filtration and water quality. She advises homes, hospitals, and restaurants on designing and setting up an aquarium. She will consult with you about size of tank, help you to select fish, and establish a good diet for them. She makes house calls if they are necessary ($50–$100 depending on problem and distance) and dispenses lots of advice on the telephone about things like incompatible or sick fish. There are weekly maintenance contracts to keep your tank cleaned and cared for ($75–$350 a week, depending on the size of the system).

BOOKS   James Cummins, 699 Madison Ave. [62nd/63rd] ☎ 688-6441, has rare books dating back to the 17th century, some angling books, and some modern fishing books . . . **Sportswords,** 1475 Third Ave. [83rd/84th] ☎ 772-8729, has lots of current books on all fishing topics, but especially on fly fishing.

FISH & ART   Aquasource Gallery and Seafood, 101 Crosby St. [Prince] ☎ 343-2548. This store (and gallery) specializes in flash-frozen farm-raised fish. In the shop's second room is a gallery that shows fish-related art . . . **Kentucky,** ☎ 349-6577, sells many pieces with a fish motif. See the article under Americana in this chapter.

FISH DECOYS   Antique fish decoys and lures can be found at **Grove Decoys,** 36 W. 44th St. [5th/6th] ☎ 391-0688. Owner Bill Bender also sells a book called *Antique Fish Tackle* for $35.

FISHING & FISHING TOURS You need a license to fish—your best bet is to get it from Manhattan Custom Tackle or Urban Angler (see below) . . . **Pastime Princess** fishing tours, Pier 3 Sheepshead Bay, Emmons & Bedford Sts. ☎ 718-252-4398, has a recorded announcement that tells you what they are fishing for each day. Cost includes rods and tackle. Half-day fishing in summer months with an evening trip for bluefish. All-day fishing in winter months. They also have a 3-hour sunset cruise on Sunday to the Statue of Liberty . . . Also from Sheepshead Bay, Pier 6, **The Brooklyn 5,** ☎ 718-769-9815, in summer when the bluefish are running, boats leave every morning and evening. On Fridays, boats leave at 7 P.M. and sail all night, returning about 5:30 A.M. $32. In winter months boats leave at 6:30 A.M. for bottom fishing ("cod, ling, whatever's out there") and come back between 3:30–5 P.M. . . . **Capt. Joe Shastay,** ☎ 201-451-1988, charters his 19-foot center console *Mako* for evening fishes out of the Liberty Harbor Marina in Jersey City, Wall St., or 23rd St. piers. The boat can take up to 3 people and costs $325. He fishes for striped bass and/or bluefish March–Jan 1. Daytime, evening, and weekend trips can be arranged. He provides tackle and "you don't need a fishing license in tidal waters." You can also fish at **Harlem Meer** in Central Park, catch and release only. They have tackle there, but make sure to bring a photo I.D. or a fishing license with you.

FISHING SUPPLIES Manhattan Custom Tackle, 913 Broadway [20th/21st] ☎

Gone Fishin

CHEYEY

505-6690. Jack Mlyn ties the flies and Phil Koenig builds the rods. They have equipment for both fly and surf fishing. They build custom rods because "factory rods skimp on the components." They help you choose a shaft, then they put on the guides, shape the handle to your hand, even let you select the color wrap you want, and put your name on it. "All of this comes to about 15% more than the factory rod." Mr. Mlyn says that in New York, "we have some of the best, and most diverse, fishing in the country within 1 1/2 hrs of NYC." They also sell licenses . . . **Urban Angler,** 118 E. 25th St. [Park/Lex] ☎ 979-7600. This is a father-and-son team, Steve and Jon Fisher (that's their name). Their clean and airy space is devoted to fly fishing. They sell equipment and give advice, have a line-rigging service and an informative and opinionated catalog. The Fishers also give fly tying lessons for both salt and fresh water fishing. Jon teaches casting in Madison Sq. Park for $50/hr. They have daily reports on conditions in the Catskills and Westchester and can connect you with a licensed guide as well as sell you a fishing license . . . **Orvis,** 355 Madison Ave. [45th] ☎ 697-3133, is another store well known for its fishing supplies.

FULTON FISH MARKET The South Street Seaport sponsors tours of the Fulton Fish Market on the first and third Thurs. of the month from April to October at 6 A.M.: $10 per person. Tour is about 1 1/2 hrs, and you can buy fish. Call ☎ 748-8590 for reservations.

RESTAURANTS Where we'd go for fish: *high end* **Oceana,** 55 E. 54th St. [Mad/Park] ☎ 759-5941, ... *bargain fish* (but good fish) at **Cucina di Pesce,** 87 E. 4th St. [2nd/3rd] ☎ 260-6800, **Pisces,** 95 Avenue A [6th] ☎ 260-6660 ... *bouillabaisse* at **Cafe Crocodile,** 354 E. 74th St. [1st/2nd] ☎ 249-6619, **La Colombe d'Or,** 134 E. 26th St. [Lex/3rd] ☎ 689-0666 ... *brandade* at **Le Pescadou,** 16 King St. [6th Ave./Varick] ☎ 924-3434 ... *fish head casserole* at **Hunan Garden,** 1 Mott St. [Bowery] ☎ 732-7270 ... the *lobster sandwich* at **Arcadia,** 21 E. 62nd St. [5th/Mad] ☎ 223-2900, and the **Lobster Club,** 24 E. 80th St. [5th/Mad] ☎ 249-6500 ... *oysters* at the **Oyster Bar Grand Central,** of course ☎ 490-6650 ... *raw bar* at **Blue Ribbon,** 97 Sullivan St. [Prince/Spring] ☎ 274-0404 ... *red snapper* at **Elias Corner,** 24-02 31 St. [24th Ave.] ☎ 718-932-1510 ... *salmon* at **Christer's,** 145 W. 55th St. [6th/7th] ☎ 974-7224 ... *scallops* at **Lespinasse,** 2 E. 55th St. [5th/Mad] ☎ 339-6719 ... *sea bass tamarind* at **Planet Thailand,** 184 Bedford [N. 7th], Brooklyn ☎ 718-599-5758 ... *seafood sausage* at **Chanterelle,** 2 Harrison St. [Greenwich/Hudson] ☎ 966-6960 ... *sushi* at **Nobu,** 105 Hudson St. [Franklin] ☎ 219-0500, **Hasaki,** 210 E. 9th St. [2nd/3rd] ☎ 473-3327, **Blue Ribbon Sushi,** 119 Sullivan St. [Prince/Spring] ☎ 343-0404, **Sapporo East,** 245 E. 10th St. [1st] ☎ 260-1330 ... *swordfish* at **Park Ave. Cafe,** 100 E. 63rd St. [Park] ☎ 644-1900 ... *sturgeon* at **Barney Greengrass,** 541 Amsterdam Ave. [86th/87th] ☎ 724-4707.

SHARK'S TEETH **Maxilla and Mandible,** 451 Columbus Ave. [81st/82nd] ☎ 724-6173, sells fossil fish, shark teeth, some fish skeletons, and "sea creatures." Your source for freeze-dried piranhas: **Evolution,** 120 Spring St. [Greene/Mercer] ☎ 343-1114.

HAWAII

We're probably among the few who mourned the closing of Hawaii Kai next to the Winter Garden, with its tacky version of everything Hawaii, its dancers of modest talent, the uninspired food. We loved it anyway. Here are a number of other means to get into the spirit of the Islands.

Radio Hula, 169 Mercer St. [Houston/Prince] ☎ 226-4467, is a store filled with reminders of Hawaii: bright tropical printed shirts, blouses and dresses, soaps and scents using tropical flowers and essences. But they are serious about providing information about the culture and heritage of the is-lands. They'll also provide entertainment for a party: Two dancers and two musicians can do a 40-minute show (with costume changes) and then give guests a hula lesson. Slack key and steel guitar players are available, and there is a Hawaiian deejay, who will play from his collection of over 200 LPs of Tahitian, Samoan, Tongan, and Hawaiian recordings. Classes in contemporary hula are given by the folks at Radio Hula, for women and men (the first hula dancers were men), at Dance Space, 622 Broadway [Houston/Bleecker] every Tuesday at 7:30 P.M. You can have them make up fresh leis ($45) for you

and your guests or send you a lei maker with enough materials to teach your guests how to make their own. Many CDs here, including one we like called *Hawaiian Slack Key Guitar Masters*—it's great background music.

At least once a year, WNYC's David Garland plays 70 different versions of the *Hawaiian War Chant*. Until the next Chant marathon, he's picked two of his favorite in-print Hawaiian music CDs: Martin Denny's *Exotica!* and music by Hawaiian crooner Alfred Apaka. If you can't find these, call ☎ 800-756-8742 to order from Public Radio's Music Source.

The Hawaii Tiny Bubble Band, ☎ 718-768-6182, performs authentic music from Hawaii for private parties and corporate events generally as a trio of steel guitar, ukelele, and bass (sometimes with a drum and keyboard, sometimes with dancers).

Throwing a luau is a snap if you know about **Orchids of Hawaii,** ☎ 800-223-2124, way up in the Bronx. You don't need to visit their showroom full of coconut drink glasses, palm tree stirrers, Mai Tai syrup, areca leaf trees, bo-bo platters, grass skirting, lanterns, Maori masks, and fountains. Everything is for sale or rent and can be ordered over the phone from their catalog. They have inexpensive leis, but you can also get the real orchid ones from them, flown in a day before an event. Talk to Kim.

LEATHER

BUYING LEATHER **Leather Facts,** 262 W. 38th St. [7th/8th] ☎ 382-2788, is floor-to-ceiling leather skins—dyed, printed, foiled (printed with metallics), perforated, and embossed—neatly stacked on shelves. Mr. François George specializes in selling small amounts of leather to people like dry cleaners trying to match a color for a repair, upholsterers and designers making samples. He can repair and alter your leather garments and can custom make garments for you. He will also apply leather toggles to your garments, make and sew on leather-covered buttons, and make bound button-holes in leather . . . **Dualoy,** 45 W. 34th St. [5th/6th] ☎ 736-3360, is where to find quality leather for upholstery and interiors. Bill Feigen sells mostly cowhides from Europe. "The European cow is bigger than the American. A European hide is about 60 sq. ft., an American hide only about 40 sq. ft." Bring dimensions of what you're going to cover and Mr. Feigen can dispense good advice. He's got 60–80 colors available, starting at $7 per sq. ft. He also has some unusual items like parchment and shagreen (from sharks) that are being used in art deco interiors . . . They've got so much at **Aadar Leather,** 154 W. 27th St. [6th/7th] ☎ 647-9340, that focusing and selecting can be a problem. Hides, pelts, snakeskins, strips, leather cordage, and some fur tails in an array of colors and patterns. Leather spilling off the shelves and uneven floors add to the charm (and challenge) . . . **Renar Leather,** 68 Spring [Bway/Crosby] ☎ 349-2075, sells mostly wholesale to big manufacturers. However, if "bales are broken" or there are single pieces, they're happy to sell to you. The front showroom has one wall of leather in these categories at good prices.

LEATHER REPAIR **Superior Leather Restorers,** 133 Lexington Ave. [28th/29th] ☎

532-8437. Marvin Rosen has been doing leather repair for decades now, and places like Barneys and Bendel's trust him to do alterations. Twelve supple-handed employees in this busy shop can replace zippers in leather garments as well as handbags, luggage, and all manner of specialized cases. They set snaps and sew on buttons, repair buttonholes, fix tears, replace leather collars, cuffs, even whole panels. They repair baseball gloves and can add straps to bags. His son-in-law runs the dry cleaning and dyeing facility in Queens. They clean, color, refinish, and dye leathers. They work on suedes and shearlings. Redressing a bag starts at $55 . . . Other excellent leather repairers: **Modern Leather Goods Repair Shop,** 2 W. 32nd St. [5th/6th] ☎ 947-7770. Free pickup and delivery in Manhattan. After receiving your items they will call you and give you an estimate. If you decide not to have them do the work, they return your things to you at no charge. $35 and up for redressing a bag . . . **Artbag Creations,** 735 Madison Ave. [64th] ☎ 744-2720, repairs ladies' bags only (starts at $50) . . . Two other leather repair shops that have been around for a long time are **Fordham Repair Center,** 10 E. 33rd St. [5th/Mad] ☎ 889-4553 ($18.50 and up to redress a bag, depending on size and condition), and **Kay Leather Goods Service,** 333 Fifth Ave. [33rd] ☎ 481-5579 (redressing starts at $15).

LEATHER FURNITURE REPAIR The **Robert Falotico Studios,** 315 E. 91st St. [1st/2nd] ☎ 369-1217, can supply you with a wall of false book spines, or they can restore and repair injuries to your leather furniture. A few cat scratches on a newer piece might require only a repair, a deteriorated older piece might require leather replacement and

reupholstery. Mr. Falotico, a second generation leather worker, also repairs leather tops, including the gold-tooled trim on desks and tables. Straight leather replacement is $70 per sq. ft., restoration costs "depend on how bad things are." Mr. Falotico has a number of smaller items that can be made for sale, including leather-covered wastebaskets, legal trays, and boxes. A wastebasket starts at $185 . . . **Michele Costello,** ☎ 410-2083, trained with Mr. Falotico before opening her own business. Ms. Costello does leather repairs and new leather work in about equal measure. She restores, replaces, and puts new leather, parchment, and shagreen on doors, furniture, desks, walls, even floors. You can also get custom leather drawer liners for jewelry and leather jewelry boxes, false book panels, have an old leather trunk restored, have the parchment on a lampshade replaced, or have leather binding stitched on a rug.

LEATHER WORKERS Barbara Shaum **Leather,** 60 E. 4th St. [2nd/Bowery] ☎ 254-4250. You won't see a lot of stock when you visit Barbara Shaum because most of her work is done to order and the shop takes up most of the floor space. There are sample bags and belts and some sandals to try on. Working in leather for 40 years now, Ms. Shaum learned leather working, and sandal making in particular, in Provincetown from Menalkus Duncan, son of Isadora. Average style of sandals is $175 . . . **Shirl B Creations,** 137 Thompson St. [Bleecker/Houston] ☎ 475-2425, features Ms. B's original handbag designs. The leather shop is on the premises, so some colors, strap and belt lengths can be customized. She's made leather coasters ($40/set of 4) and pillows, too . . . **Jutta Neumann Leather Craft,** 317

E. 9th St. [1st/2nd] ☎ 982-7048, makes creatively shaped handbags in pretty colors for women and wallets for men and women. Off the shelf or custom work. . . . **David Samuel Menkes,** ☎ 989-3706, custom tailors leather for people *serious* about leather. Jackets, vests, and lots of very tight pants sport zipper treatments, have corded trims, and use quilted leather. Mr. Menkes also copies garments and does "special repairs" such as shortening sleeves from the top, removing sleeves and binding armholes, or replacing worn out leather sections. Pants start at $360, shirts at $150.

LEATHER CLEANING **Leather Craft Process,** 212 W. 35th St. [7th/8th] ☎ 564-7995 (located inside Marvel Cleaners for decades). Most local dry cleaners are not equipped to clean leather garments, so they send them out; chances are they send to Leather Craft.

Take your garment there directly and Leonard will consult with you as to what can and cannot be done, with an estimate. They clean, redye small areas, and soften the leather at their plant in New Jersey. You get a bill in the mail with the exact charge. When it's paid, your goods are cleaned and shipped back to you. All of this takes about 3 weeks. The estimate at a local dry cleaner for a leather varsity jacket in bad shape was $60. Leather Craft did it for $40. They also do alterations and repairs on leather garments.

GLOVE CLEANING See Clothing Care in the Services chapter.

LEATHER BARS **The Lure,** 409 W. 13th St. [9th/Wash.] ☎ 741-3919, is the leather bar of choice for gay men—dress code (and they mean it) on weekends . . . Also, **The Vault,** Tenth Ave. at 13th St. ☎ 255-6758.

MAPS

ANTIQUE MAPS **Argosy Bookstore,** 116 E. 59th St. [Lex/Park] ☎ 753-4455, has an incredible selection of antique maps. You can find a lot of maps of New York, of course, and of just about everywhere else. The maps are on the second floor, but there's a small bin on the ground floor of $10 maps . . . **New York Bound,** 50 Rockefeller Plaza ☎ 245-8503, also carries maps but theirs are centered around New York. Prices start at $50 or so . . . **Richard B. Arkway,** 59 E. 54th St. [Mad/Park] ☎ 751-8135, specializes in world maps of the 17th century, American maps, early atlases from Dutch 17th century to American 19th century. They also have wall maps that are examples of Early American printing, navigation

maps, and early sea charts . . . **Martayan Lan,** 48 E. 57th St. [Mad/Park] ☎ 308-0018, specializes in early and rare maps, antique globes, and some map-related books . . . **Swann Galleries,** 104 E. 25th St. [Park] ☎ 254-4710, has two major map and atlas auctions each year, generally in May and December. Every Thursday from Sept.–June, Swann holds auctions, some of which may have maps . . . A company called **Maps,** 241 Centre St. [Broome/Grand] ☎ 941-9102, sells exceptionally handsome reproductions of antique maps, framed and unframed. Simple framing starts at $75, but plan to spend $140 and up, depending on the size of the map. As an added service, owner Julie Spriggs will research the map and add some descriptive text when she frames it. About 15 maps of NYC at different historical periods are included in a selection of over 400 titles. By appt.

CURRENT MAPS You can find current maps (as well as guidebooks and other travel items) at: **The Complete Traveller,** 199 Madison Ave. [35th] ☎ 685-9007, **Hagstrom Map & Travel Center,** 57 W. 43rd St. [5th/6th] ☎ 398-1222, **Traveller's Bookstore,** 22 W. 52nd St. [5th/6th] ☎ 664-0995. **Rand McNally,** 150 E. 52nd St. [Lex/3rd] ☎ 758-7488.

SPECIFIC MAPS The Identity Map Co., 55 Bethune St. [Wash] ☎ 627-1994, has a great map of **Manhattan from 65th St. south.** Printed on two sides, it measures 36 in. × 48 in. and costs $25. It's attractive and contains incredible detail, identifying streets, outlines of buildings, museums, parks, schools, hotels, subways, and more. They

have also produced maps with a smaller focus, such as one of **Greenwich Village** . . . For a reproduction of the **earliest known map of Manhattan,** attributed to Johannes Vingboons, c. 1639, send $15 for the map plus $2 postage to the Library of Congress, Information Office, Box A, Washington, DC 20540 ☎ 202-707-5000. Request item C-4 . . . There's a wonderful map of **Central Park** by George Colbert and Guenter Vollath, done for the Greensward Foundation. Mr. Colbert wanted to change the focus of the typical park map from the baseball fields and statues to the trees, meadows, lakes, and hills. He spent some time surveying the park and worked from old surveys to create this topographical map. It can be purchased folded ($3) or unfolded ($10) plus shipping cost, directly from the Greensward Foundation ☎ 473-6283, at the Dairy in the park, and at Urban Center Books ☎ 935-3592 . . . The well-known **Isometric Map of Manhattan** is available from Manhattan Map

MAPMAKERS

Claudia Carlson, ☎ 749-8358, started as a book designer and was encouraged to branch into maps by an art director. Many of her maps appear in books or newspapers, but she also makes personal maps. If you need to show people how to get to "that little clifftop where you are getting married," or how to find your house, she can do it for you.

John Tauranac is a mapmaker who's done (among other things) a persuasive alternative to the TA subway map. His Museum Mile map covers W. 49th St. to E. 105th St. from, roughly, Fifth to Lexington, and is a model of clarity and usefulness. He also has a foldable subway map (for

your wallet), a foldable bus map, a rail map of metropolitan NY, a wall map of Battery Park, and others. The foldables are $1.50, the subway map is $2.50, and the Museum Mile is $3.95. They're widely available but you can also order directly from Mr. Tauranac by sending price of map plus tax and a business-size SASE to Tauranac, Ltd., 900 West End Ave. #8B, 10025-3525.

The Museum Mile map by John Tauranac.

Co., 31 E. 28th St. ☎ 683-5700. It is a map, measuring 28 in. × 38 in., of midtown Manhattan showing the buildings in a 3-D style. The last update was done in 1991. $7.95 folded, $12.95 rolled, plus $5 for shipping.

MAP COLLECTIONS & GROUPS In **The New York Public Library Map Division** (Room 117) ☎ 930-0587, you'll find Alice Hudson, the head of the division, where she has worked since 1970. The collection contains 400,000 loose maps and almost 14,000 atlases. Ms. Hudson showed us the 1891 atlas of Manhattan, which has each building color coded to indicate brick or frame construction. Factories and sites are named, the original water courses and the farm boundaries are shown. All of the maps and materials in this collection are accessible to the public, and help is available from the library assistants. If the size and condition of the map allows, a photocopy can be made. Otherwise, you are permitted to make a pencil tracing of the map or to photograph it. There are currently 12 map software programs available but only one computer in the map room, and it receives pretty heavy use. Some programs require an appointment . . . **The Mercator Society,** ☎ 930-0588, is a support group for the Map Division of the library, helping to raise funds for the ongoing needs of the collection. Members donate $250 annually, receive a newsletter, and are invited to special events.

Just one of the collection: America in 1587 by Ortelius.

The New York Map Society was founded in 1978, and while many of the members are professional geographers and cartographers, there are also many nonprofessional members, including its president, David Starr, a TV producer. They meet on the first Saturday of the month for discussion of things like new mapping systems for automobiles or the history of subway maps in NYC, and go on occasional field trips. You can contact the Society by writing to Mr. Starr at 241 W. 4th St., 10014.

MORE At the Map and Book Store of the Department of City Planning, 22 Reade St. [Bway/Elk] ☎ 720-3667, you can buy **Bytes of the Big Apple,** which are maps of NYC on disc. There are tax blocks, street maps, and other administrative maps that can be used as base maps for larger projects. $50 each.

MYSTERIES

THE BOOKSTORES The Black Orchid, 303 E. 81st St. [1st/2nd] ☎ 734-5980. **Murder Ink,** 2486 Broadway [92nd/93rd] ☎ 362-8905; 465 Second Ave. [76th/77th] ☎ 517-3222; 1 Whitehall St. [Stone] ☎ 742- 7025. **The Mysterious Bookshop,** 129 W. 56th St. [6th/7th] ☎ 765-0900. **Partners & Crime,** 44 Greenwich Ave. [6th/7th] ☎ 243-0440. **Whodunit,** 302 W. 12th St. [8th] ☎ 741-4676.

THE MERCANTILE LIBRARY The Mercantile Library, 17 E. 47th St. [5th/Mad] ☎ 755-6710, is a private library that predates the NY Public Library and specializes in mysteries—claiming one of the best collections of mysteries in the world. To join costs $75 a year for an individual, $90 for a family. The mystery collection is the reason it's the headquarters of the Mystery Writers of America.

EDGAR ALLAN POE You can visit the **Poe Cottage** at Grand Concourse and E. Kingsbridge Rd. in Poe Park, the Bronx ☎ 718-881-8900, on Sat. from 10–4 and Sun. from 1–5. Poe moved up there in 1846 and lived there for three years until he died. Take the 4 or D train to Kingsbridge . . . Before that, Poe lived at **206 W. 84th St.** [Amsterdam], now named "Edgar Allan Poe St.," where he finished *The Raven* in 1844 . . . See the restaurant article on Il Buco for Poe's inspiration for *The Cask of Amontillado.*

FICTION AND TRUE CRIME For true crime, read Luc Sante's *Low Life—Lures and Snares of Old New York,* in paper. It's a kind of history of New York, told from the underbelly . . . *The Mystery Readers Walking Guide* by Alzina Stone Dale lets you know exactly which mystery fictional characters did what where . . . Partners & Crime says that while there aren't many new books coming out with NYC as a setting, three writers who continue to place their detectives in NY are Lawrence Block, with his Matthew Scudder books; Thomas Adcock's Neil Hockady series; and Stephen Solomita and his detective, Stanley Moodrow. Mr. Block told us that he sets so many books in NYC "simply, it's because it's where I live. Even when I moved away for a while I found that I continued to set my books here. It is my spiritual center." He knows that the books set up a whole sensorium for New Yorkers just by the mention of a cross street, but also realizes that a lot of reading is done by people who have never been "east of Denver." It's natural, he says, to anchor a book in a specific neighborhood, and he wanders all over the city looking for locations. We asked for a few Matthew Scudder real-life equivalents and Mr. Block obliged. Scudder lived on 57th between Eighth and Ninth in a hotel that reminds him of the Henry Hudson. He spends a lot of time as an ex-drinker in Armstrong's, which used to be on Ninth Ave., but is now at 57th and Tenth. Elaine lived on E. 50th [1st/2nd], but she and Scudder moved in to the Parc Vendome at 57th and Ninth in *The Devil Knows You're Dead.* Mr. Block publishes an amusing newsletter for his fans once or twice a year. It's free—fax your request to receive it to ☎ 675-4341.

CLUBS & ORGANIZATIONS Wolfe Pack is an organization dedicated to the exploits of one of America's most famous detectives, Nero Wolfe, created by Rex Stout. They have 3–4 meetings and events each year, including a shad roe dinner in the spring. In the autumn, the major event—a full weekend with theatre, speakers, and the Black Orchid banquet—concludes with a Sunday "Brunch Hunt," where you have to locate the correct restaurant. To become a member and to get the *Gazette* (published quarterly), write: PO Box 822, Ansonia Station, NYC 10023 . . . The **Sherlock Holmes societies** are hierarchical: you start by joining one of the Scion Societies. In NYC, it's The Priory Scholars. Write: Bill Nadel, 235 W. 71st St., 10023. These groups meet several times a year in local restaurants for dinner and drinks, the reading of papers, etc. If your interest and scholarship propels you to deeper knowledge of the subject, you may be asked to join The Adventuresses and, finally, the highest honor, The Baker Street Irregulars . . . **The Mystery Writers of America** is primarily a professional organization, but many of their events (dinners, meetings, talks by mystery writers, forensic experts, and so on) are open to the public. For more info, send a SASE to 17 E. 47th St., 6th fl., 10017.

THE EDGARS If you're a mystery buff, you know that the Edgars, sponsored by the Mystery Writers of America, are the mystery world's top award in the U.S. The awards banquet is open to the public. It's usually in April. For more info, write The Mystery Writers of America at the above address.

HOSTING A MURDER MYSTERY Bogey's Mystery Tours was started in 1981 by Karen and Bill Palmer, ☎ 362-7569. They set up interactive Agatha Christie–style whodunits with prizes for the winners. Groups can be as small as ten and can be private or corporate. They also give monthly dinner parties on a Fri. or Sat. night at the Yankee Clipper. $59.95 is the price for dinner and mystery evening . . . Murder mystery games are available at **Game Show,** 474 Sixth Ave. [12th] ☎ 633-6328 and 1240 Lexington [83rd] ☎ 472-8011. They usually involve 6–8 people and have names like "The Class of '54" and "The Wall St. Scandal." About a dozen titles are available from $19.98–$29.98.

ORCHIDS

Hatleberg/DeCastro Orchids, 43 Eighth Ave. [Horatio/Jane] ☎ 463-9577. Earl Hatleberg, an orchid grower (not a florist), runs this vest-pocket-sized shop. He stocks about 50 orchid plants at a time from his greenhouse about 100 miles north of the city. Hours are somewhat irregular since Mr. Hatleberg is often out making his wholesale rounds to shops around town. Tracking him down, though, is worth the effort. Not only is he very good at talking about and describing the flowers you are looking at—he will point out the tiny details of structure that may be missed by the novice—but he's a pleasure to talk with, period. Orchids start at $35.

The Manhattan Orchid Society meets each second Wednesday of the month at the N.Y. Horticultural Society at 128 W. 58th St. [6th/7th] ☎ 718-389-6033. Ask for

Mark Farran. This is a group of about 200 hobbyists who grow orchids in their own homes. There are speakers, demonstrations, and frequent plant sales. **The Greater New York Orchid Society** is also a large, active orchid society that meets in Throgs Neck in the Bronx ☎ 718-931-3000.

The Orchid Show, generally in March in the Winter Garden of the World Financial Center, is the largest show of its kind in the country. They have 100 exhibitors, there are plants for sale, workshops, and demonstrations. Admission is free. If you want to see what extraordinary plants these are, the Orchid Show is the ideal place. For more info, call the Manhattan Orchid Society.

Two places where you can see orchids are the **New York Botanical Garden,** 200th St. at Southern Blvd. in the Bronx ☎ 718-817-8700, where they have 5,000 orchids with about 40 on display at any one time. The NYBG offers beginning and advanced courses on orchid growing . . . **The Brooklyn Botanic Garden,** Eastern Pkway/Empire Blvd. ☎ 718-622-4433, has orchids on display when they're in bloom and sells orchids in the gift shop.

Two florists who specialize in orchids are **Miho Kosuda,** 310 E. 44th St. [1st/2nd] ☎ 922-9122, and **Zeze,** 398 E. 52nd St. [1st] ☎ 753-7767.

PAPER & PENS

ART AND WRITING PAPER New York Central Art Supply, 62 Third Ave. [10th/11th] ☎ 473-7705. This store has a wide range of extraordinary papers, mostly handmade, from all over the world, including some of the papers from the Living Treasures of Japan. The staff, under manager David Aldera (who has been working with papers for 15 years), are all working artists, and they know a lot about what they sell. NY Central sells Lost Link Papers, a group of 24 designs of swirls and geometrics, many using subtle metallics, made in New York by Virginia Buchan and Nora Ligorano . . . Other places with good paper displays are **Kate's Paperie,** 561 Broadway [Prince] ☎ 941-9816, and **Pearl Paint,** 308 Canal [Church/Bway] ☎ 431-7932 . . . The **Dieu Donné Papermill,** 433 Broome St. [Crosby/Bway]

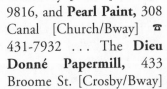

☎ 226-0573, teaches papermaking classes at all levels and has a retail space, where they sell their own handmade papers, as well as a gallery. They show the work of artists—like Chuck Close and Duane Michaels—who use Dieu Donné papers . . . **Il Papiro,** 1021 Lexington Ave. [73rd] ☎ 288-9330 and 250 Vesey St., World Financial Center ☎ 385-1688, sells Florentine-style hand-marbled papers by the sheet ($23 for 20 in. × 20 in.) and other items made from the papers . . . When you want the most beautiful writing paper anywhere, you want **Pineider** from Italy. Bergdorf's has a small selection. $25 gets you 10 envelopes and sheets.

OTHER PAPER Your local stationer probably doesn't have a big selection of paper on hand because it takes up too much shelf space. Buying in large quantities is no problem; lots of suppliers can help you. Your stationer can order paper for you, but you may not have the time. Just about the only place in Manhattan that will sell you, from stock on hand, as little as one ream of paper is **Limited Papers,** 80 Washington St. [Rector] ☎ 797-7022. In a rush or tight spot, they're a good resource to know about. They sell most of the well-known brands, such as Crane's, Mohawk, Strathmore, and Hammermill. They stock colored paper, recycled paper, and envelopes. Prices and service are good. This isn't a store, exactly. It's on the 7th floor of an office building. Your best bet is to call ahead and give them your order. It will be waiting for you when you turn up. They'll deliver for $15. Check or cash only . . . **Jams,** 611 Sixth Ave. [18th] ☎ 255-4593 and other locations. Lots of papers, many in 100 sheet put ups, with matching envelopes . . . **The Paper Peddler,** 119 W. 26th St. [6th/7th] ☎ 242-4776, plenty of colors and fancies along with plain whites (these are primarily business papers). They have a price list and will sell as few as 100 sheets in some styles.

STATIONERY, INVITATIONS, & ANNOUNCEMENTS Mrs. John L. Strong,

699 Madison Ave. [61st/62nd] ☎ 838-3848. Mrs. Strong set up a table in her sister's trousseau shop in the early '30s, from which she sold hand-engraved stationery. She developed her own paper recipe with a small papermill for a heavy, creamy white cotton stock, and she selected engravers who could do the exacting work of cutting steel plates to produce the sharp line she wanted in her lettering. When Joy and Robert Lewis bought the business from Mrs. Strong's heirs in 1986, they wanted to maintain the tradition in a way that "simplified without cutting off from the past." The same rich paper

and hand engraving is used on invitations, announcements, personal stationery, place and calling cards.

Creative, yet correct, stationery products are the forte of Linda Stein at **Calligraphy Studios,** 100 Reade St. [Church/W. Bway] ☎ 964-6007. By appt. Ms. Stein is an expert on contemporary protocol and the situations of address in the fractured, extended family. She designs monograms and can produce an entire "stationery wardrobe" that can be hand- or machine-engraved. She also provides sophisticated personal mementos to be given to guests at weddings, birthdays, and other events. Hand calligraphy in all languages and many styles is done by her 15 calligraphers.

Ellen Weldon Design, 273 Church St. [Franklin/White] ☎ 925-4483. Ms. Weldon's calligraphy (she works in 16 styles and hand engraves her own plates) is one element in her repertoire for creating striking and personal invitations. She offers a wide range of paper selection, various printing methods, and ways to embellish the paper (watercolor painting, ribbon ties, etc.). Everything—invitations, personal stationery, menu cards, seating cards, testimonials—is done to order.

Miriam Schaer, ☎ 718-788-2029, acts as a freelance art director for small companies. In this capacity, she designs and prints promotional materials—postcards, notices, invitations, and holiday greeting cards using fine papers and her own whimsical, sometimes retro artwork. She does baby announcements and invitations to private events. A consultation begins at $250, deductible from the job.

CALLIGRAPHERS Anna Pinto, ☎ 201-

656-7402, will meet with you at your home

or office for consultation on invitations, scrolls, testimonials, awards, and menus in many styles—both historical and contemporary. Ms. Pinto works on fine papers and will letter a poem or quotation, often using watercolor on the background. She has designed a group of lively, contemporary decorated initials that can be used as the basis of note cards.

The Gabriel Guild, ☎ 718-625-4610, is made up of approximately 50 members who study and practice medieval book arts. They teach courses in gilding, calligraphy, and panel painting and give one-day workshops. They happily accept private commissions for cards, signs, or original artwork.

PRINTING We are often asked at MUG for a printer and always recommend, with enthusiasm, our own: **Westprint,** 873 Washington St. [13th/14th] ☎ 989-2948. Tim Bissell, the proprietor, wanted to be a printer since he was a newsboy at age 12, going to the newspaper office of the *Willamantic Daily Chronicle.* He started Westprint, which specializes in work for nonprofits and small businesses, in 1986. This isn't the place to go for a "quick and dirty" job, but they do orders as small as a thousand pieces and much larger runs. They can design a small business package and offer mail shop services. Typesetting and graphic design are additional services, and they will work from a disk or traditional mechanicals. They'll quote on the phone.

The Center for Book Arts, 626 Broadway [Houston/Bleecker] ☎ 460-9768, teaches courses in either traditional or contemporary bookbinding and letterpress printing. Classes are small (6–10 people) and you can get a copy of their catalog by calling them or stopping in to their 5th-floor

gallery where they exhibit books made by contemporary artists . . . **Nadja Press,** ☎ 866-5595, is located in an impossibly small space inside the Center for Book Arts. Carol Sturm and Douglas Wolf turn out impressive small editions of fine books and personalized invitations and announcements. Working with fine papers, hand-set type, and hand bindings, they have printed editions of poetry by some of America's finest poets, including James Merrill and Robert Creeley. All books are signed by the author and, if illustrated, signed by the artist as well and are available only through the Press. They take the same care with personal announcements and invitations, business cards, personal stationery, thank you notes, and birth announcements . . . **Solo Impression,** 520 Broadway [Spring/Broome] 925-3599, is the fine print shop of Judith Solodkin, the first woman Master Lithographer in the U.S. Using her 20 years experience, she collaborates with artists who may or may not have done lithography before to produce fine prints and art books. Her equipment spans two centuries of technique, from the traditional Bavarian limestones (a material which gives the best quality print) to aluminum plate, photo plates, and lasers. The papers are often luxurious. Ms. Solodkin shows her prints by appointment. Dotty Attie, Petah Coyne, William Wegman, Robert Rauschenberg, and Ed Koren have had work on display there. Ms. Solodkin also hand prints invitations, birth notices, table cards, and menus. She will help you choose paper and type face. Unlike a commercial printer, she prefers to work in small editions and quantities.

BOOKBINDING Carolyn Chadwick, ☎ 865-5157, by appt. Ms. Chadwick hand makes very beautiful small and large note-books and albums for many purposes. Books in her line start at $20, custom work is more, depending on labor and materials involved. Ms. Chadwick also repairs and rebinds old books. In cases where rebinding is not a good idea—rare books or first editions, for example—she makes slipcases and clam shell boxes to hold and protect them. She can do gold lettering, and binding is done in leather or paper (or both).

Without any formal training in book-binding, Richard Hackett's **Tactile,** ☎ 242-4320, has developed highly crafted, hand-made journals, photo albums, and frames. One, with a beaded spine, brings the threads that hold the pages together to the outside of the book. Most of his work is for corpo-rate events, but he also does gifts for private parties—with a minimum of 30 pieces.

PAPERWEIGHTS Leo Kaplan Ltd., 967 Madison Ave. [75th/76th] ☎ 249-6766, has a large collection of antique and new glass paperweights, starting at $98. There are many traditional millefiori models, but there are a number of works by contemporary glass craftsmen.

PENS—BUYING The best deals on new pens are to be found at the **Fountain Pen Hospital,** 10 Warren St. [Church/Bway] ☎ 964-0580, **Joon** in the Trump Tower and at 782 Lexington Ave. [61st] ☎ 935-1007, and **Pearl Paint . . .** The **Fountain Pen Hospital** has contemporary and vintage pens. Not all the vintage pens are on display. If you ask Terry or Steve Wiederlight (third-generation owners of this business estab-lished in 1946), they will show you pens kept in leather cases that they don't have room to display. Every other month they

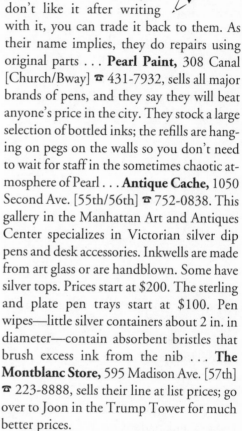

print a brochure showing ap-proximately 175 vintage pens for sale. There is a one-year guarantee on all vintage pens they sell, and if you don't like it after writing with it, you can trade it back to them. As their name implies, they do repairs using original parts . . . **Pearl Paint,** 308 Canal [Church/Bway] ☎ 431-7932, sells all major brands of pens, and they say they will beat anyone's price in the city. They stock a large selection of bottled inks; the refills are hang-ing on pegs on the walls so you don't need to wait for staff in the sometimes chaotic at-mosphere of Pearl . . . **Antique Cache,** 1050 Second Ave. [55th/56th] ☎ 752-0838. This gallery in the Manhattan Art and Antiques Center specializes in Victorian silver dip pens and desk accessories. Inkwells are made from art glass or are handblown. Some have silver tops. Prices start at $200. The sterling and plate pen trays start at $100. Pen wipes—little silver containers about 2 in. in diameter—contain absorbent bristles that brush excess ink from the nib . . . **The Montblanc Store,** 595 Madison Ave. [57th] ☎ 223-8888, sells their line at list prices; go over to Joon in the Trump Tower for much better prices.

PENS—REPAIR In addition to the Foun-tain Pen Hospital noted above, you can try **Authorized Repair Service,** 30 W. 57th St. [5th/6th] ☎ 586-0947. Richard Weinstein and Vanessa Cardenas repair (and sell) new and vintage pens. "Pens take a lot of wear and tear," and the folks at Authorized are pre-pared with hundreds of drawers of replace-ment parts that they have been collecting for 40 years. In new pens, they like Parker be-cause of the lifetime warranty and that company's after-sale service. "We don't see many of them coming in for repairs." It costs about $35 to recondition an old pen. They replace the fill system and adjust the ink flow to be compatible with modern inks, as well as polish and clean. Cracks in the body can't be repaired, but just about everything else can.

Geoffrey Berliner, 928 Broadway [21st/22nd] ☎ 614-3020 (best by appt.). The day we visited Mr. Berliner, he had 5 fountain pens in his shirt pocket. Mr. Berliner is especially fond of pens from the "Golden Age of the Fountain Pen" (1915–1940). During this period companies "were trying to outdo each other by creating a better filling mechanism, more nib styles," and in creating new designs and using different materials for the barrels of the pens. Mr. Berliner appraises and buys old pens. Many stationers around town send their pens to him for repair. Since many parts for old pens are no longer available, Mr. Berliner makes replacements on special lathes in the back room. He offers a search service for old pens.

PHOTOGRAPHY

AUCTIONS Swann Galleries, 104 E. 25th St. [Park/Lex] ☎ 254-4710, **Sotheby's** ☎ 800-444-3709, and **Christie's** ☎ 546-1063, all have photography auctions in the fall.

BOOKS AND PUBLICATIONS *Photography in NY,* a bimonthly gallery guide available at the International Center of Photography and the Museum of Modern Art bookshops, gives a rundown on photo exhibits and dealers in NYC and elsewhere . . . Robert Persky publishes the newsletter *The Photograph Collector,* which gives auction and trade show dates, listings of lectures and seminars, and info on new publications and catalogs. $125/year. ☎ 838-8640 . . . **Aperture Book Center/Burden Gallery,** 20 E. 23rd St. [Mad/Park] ☎ 505-5555. Aperture was founded in 1952 by Minor White and others as a journal for photographers. They have never shied away from controversial photojournalistic or artistic subjects. They publish the journal *Aperture* and many photography books. The recent *Aperture 40* celebrated their 40th anniversary with photographs and statements from each of the 70 photographers who have been published in the journal since its founding. The bookstore sells all the books and publications. They manage the Paul Strand Archive . . . **A Photographer's Place,** 133 Mercer St. [Prince/Spring] ☎ 431-9358, is owned by Harvey Zucker and Gene Bourne. Mr. Zucker was a commercial photographer who decided to keep his hand in by selling photography books. New and used, technical and esthetic books are on hand. They have many rare and out-of-print books that are not available for browsing. A catalog is available. A few old cameras are for sale, and there is a small selection of 19th century daguerreotypes and tintypes . . . **Chartwell Booksellers,** 55 E. 52nd St.

[Park/Lex] ☎ 308-0643, carries current and out-of-print photography books. Often, they are signed. The building allows them exhibit space in the lobby where, in the last 12 years, they have exhibited many of the 20th century greats: Brassai, Atget, Walker Evans.

CAMERA BUYING If you know exactly what you're looking for and don't need questions answered, **B & H Photo,** 119 W. 17th St. [6th/7th] ☎ 807-7474, is usually the place to go for the biggest discount. We found a complete Pentax 6×7 elsewhere for $2,612; at B & H: $2,038. Closed Saturdays . . . **Calumet,** 16 W. 19th St. [5th/6th] ☎ 989-8500, has been in business for almost 50 years as a mail-order company. The shop on 19th St. has a staff of 11 manning the counter, each an expert in a field—lighting, large format, 35 mm, used and classic cameras. Darkroom supplies, film and photo shoot equipment are available, and there is a large rental department for cameras, lenses, lighting, and studio supplies (including wind and smoke machines). On occasional Saturdays, manufacturers present equipment seminars.

CAMERA   REPAIR Top of the line repair: **Jeff Akbarzadeh,** 920 Broadway [20th/21st] ☎ 777-5900. He's been a camera technician for 25 years, six of them with Ken Hansen's now-shuttered store. He works only on what he calls "professional cameras," from 35 mm to large format but no point-and-shoot mod-

els. Mr. Akbarzadeh brings his training in physics and engineering to the cameras that come his way. Aside from routine cleanings and tune-ups, he creates "photographic gadgets" when a customer needs something. He has created mounts that attach, say, a Zeiss lens to a Hasselblad body, while retaining the full features of both pieces. He has been wrestling with the problem of how to get the Pentax 6×7 to double expose without losing other features of the camera. Recently, he figured it out. Basic maintenance $40–$125, according to the equipment, lens cleanings vary based on number of features and parts in lens . . . **Swiss Camera and Optic Service,** 38 W. 32nd St. [5th/6th] ☎ 594-6340. Before Joe Valgoi began fixing cameras in 1963, he worked with surveying instruments. He says that this kind of mechanical work "suits my hands." Mr. Valgoi services mechanical cameras, as opposed to the newer self-adjusting ones with electronic circuits. He specializes in many brands of still and movie cameras. Mr. Valgoi says a movie camera should be serviced every 200,000 feet or every 3–5 years, whichever comes first. A still camera should come in for an overhaul every 200 rolls of film. With proper care and maintenance, he says a good camera can last 50 years. A mechanical overhaul, which includes cleaning and lubrication, runs $90–$150. Lens cleanings and lubes are an additional $58–$88. Parts are extra . . . **Nippon Photo Clinic,** 920 Broadway [20th/21st] ☎ 982-3177, is strictly a repair shop. Eight technicians work on most major brands of professional cameras. They will "partially open" your camera and give you an estimate before starting work. "Depending on the condition of the inside" general overhauls can run from $80–$150, says Casey Akagi, who runs the place. Lens cleaning $25–$150, depending on the complexity of the lens. They do no modification work and no movie cameras. Generally, repairs take a week.

CLASSES **The International Center of Photography** has the widest range of classes, from beginning darkroom techniques to computer and electronic imaging. Some courses are weekend seminars and some last 10 weeks. The education department, ☎ 860-1776, can give you a full listing. All are given at the uptown location Fifth Ave. and 94th St. . . . **Pratt Manhattan,** 295 Lafayette St. [Houston] ☎ 925-8481, offers a handful of photography courses.

CLUBS **The Camera Club,** 853 Broadway [13th/14th] ☎ 260-7077, is the oldest (107 years) club of its type in the country, with a history that includes a sometimes stormy relationship with Alfred Stieglitz, exhibitions that brought the work of Man Ray to NY, and a long record of service in WWII. Stieglitz was instrumental in promoting the club's quarterly publication, *Camera Notes.* Currently written by the club members, it contains reviews of gallery photo shows and short essays on aspects of photography. The 130 members are a diverse group of enthusiasts that include professional and nonprofessional photographers. All members share in the duties of running the club as well as having access to the 7 darkrooms (2 for color), a studio space, and a small library. A public gallery shows work by members and nonmembers. Membership is $600/year . . . **The Park West Camera Club,** 5 W. 63rd St. [CPW/Bway], inside the West Side Y, ☎ 592-4700, was established in 1937 and holds meetings each Monday with presentations and workshops by professional photographers. They go on field trips, maintain

a circulating library, and host social occasions. There are 2 dark rooms (B&W or color) that are available to members 24 hours a day, 365 days a year. To be a member you first join the Y (the lowest membership package is $100), then pay $65 a year dues to the camera club.

GALLERIES *Upper East Side:* **Bonni Benrubi Gallery,** 52 E. 76th St. [Mad/Park] ☎ 517-3766, **Houk Friedman,** 851 Madison Ave. [70th/71st] ☎ 628-5300, **Robert Mann Gallery,** 42 E. 76th St. [Mad/Park] ☎ 570-1223, **The Sander Gallery,** 19 E. 76th St. [5th/Mad] ☎ 794-4500, **Howard Schickler Fine Art,** 52 E. 76th St. [Mad/Park] ☎ 737-6647. *Midtown:* **Pace/ Wildenstein/MacGill,** 32 E. 57th St. [5th/Mad] ☎ 759-7999, **Zabriskie,** 41 E. 57th St. [Mad] ☎ 752-1223. *Union Square/ Gramercy:* **Aperture Book Center/Burden Gallery,** 20 E. 23rd St. [Mad/Park] ☎ 505-5555. *Soho:* **Jayne H. Baum Gallery,** 588 Broadway [Houston/Prince] ☎ 219-9854, **Janet Borden Gallery,** 560 Broadway [Prince] ☎ 431-0166, **James Danziger Gallery,** 130 Prince [Wooster/W. Bway] ☎ 226-0056, **Howard Greenberg Gallery** and **Gallery 292,** 120 Wooster St. [Prince/ Spring] ☎ 334-0010, **Lowinsky Gallery,** 578 Bway [Prince] ☎ 226-5440, **Julie Saul Gallery,** 560 Broadway [Prince] ☎ 431-0747, **The Witkin Gallery,** 415 West Broadway [Prince/ Spring] ☎ 925-5510. *Tribeca:* **The Soho Photo Gallery,** 15 White St. [W. Bway/ Varick] ☎ 226-8571. It is run as a cooperative gallery by commercial photographers in NYC who show only their creative work there.

PHOTO RESTORATION See Photo Restoration under Services.

PIANOS

Whether it's the restless syncopation of Gershwin, the sound of a 1950s piano bar, or Geri Allen at the Vanguard, when we hear a piano, it's the sound of Manhattan.

🎹 **MICHAEL FEINSTEIN** There are a lot of performers who sing Irving Berlin's "I Love a Piano," but when Michael Feinstein sings it you know he means it. He told us, "The role of the piano has changed. In the 'teens and '20s, having a piano was necessary for having music in the home and was the hallmark of the home. The success of a song was based on how much sheet music it sold. Now, success of a song is related to how many recordings it sells." Mr. Feinstein also related Ira Gershwin's reaction as a little boy when they hauled the family's first piano in through the window—he said he couldn't believe they were rich enough to afford it. Mr. Gershwin, who figures so prominently in Mr. Feinstein's history, also figures in the new lyrics to "I Love a Piano." Mr. Feinstein is a Baldwin artist and thought it "absurd" to sing the lyric "I know a fine way/to treat a Steinway." One night after a performance, the Amazing Kreskin suggested, "I'm appalled when/it's not a Baldwin"—which is what Mr. Feinstein now sings. Ira Gershwin wanted to expand this verse to include other pianos and suggested, "I'm never bickering/when at a Chickering." When Feinstein asked what he would do with a Yamaha, Gershwin said, "Well, of course you know it's not pronounced YAmaha, it's YaMAha." After the briefest pause, Gershwin came up with "Your Daddy's rich and/YaMAha's good looking."

🎹 **DAVID DUBAL** David Dubal, a piano teacher at Juilliard and author of *The Art of the Piano,* was a friend of Vladimir Horowitz, and says the Horowitz piano, a Steinway, was "regulated like a race horse." Playing on it, one feels the notes are "ready to take off." Mr. Dubal should know since he toured with Horowitz's piano to dozens of cities in the U.S. The story, Mr. Dubal says, of Mr. Horowitz pounding a nail into the floor of Carnegie Hall to mark the place where his piano sounded best is a true one. Look for his course, **The World of the Piano,** open to the public, at Juilliard. Call ☎ 799-5000 for more details.

🎹 **MARIAN MCPARTLAND** Nowadays, club owners are very careful about the pianos they provide performers, according to jazz pianist Marian McPartland. In the old days, she told us, club owners thought it was funny to say, "What's the matter with the piano, we just had it painted." Ms. McPartland has been playing since she was a young child and was an "absolute addict" about practicing (sometimes eight hours a day). When we asked how much she practices now, she laughed and said the practicing she did as a child "is standing me in good stead now" because time to practice is in short supply. Part of that time is taken up with her weekly radio show called "Piano Jazz" on WBGO fm 88.3, Thursdays at 8 P.M. It's a totally improvised show in which Ms. McPartland talks to jazz pianists, in addition to solo and duet playing from Ms. McPartland and her guests.

🎹 **BUYING A PIANO** If we were in the market for a piano, we'd do two things. The first would be to buy *The Piano Book* by Larry Fine. In it, Mr. Fine tells you everything you need to know about buying and owning a piano. If you want more personalized advice, Mr. Fine does an over-the-phone consultation for $30 (for half an hour) in which he will discuss your needs and budget and answer your questions. ☎ 800-545-2022. The book is available at Patelson's Music House, 160 W. 56th St. [6th/7th] ☎ 582-5840, and from the 800 number . . . The second thing we'd do is ask a piano technician (technicians have more training than tuners) to accompany us to the store, especially important if you're buying a secondhand piano. Some unscrupulous dealers sell pianos that seem okay but have, for example, a cracked soundboard. Evan Giller, ☎ 249-4398, is a well-respected technician as well as a piano restorer. He charges $100 for a normal tuning of a modern piano (and $100 and up to inspect a piano).

🐦 **UNUSUAL PIANOS TO BUY** The **Piano Exchange,** 150 School St. in Glen Cove, Long Island ☎ 516-671-6515, claims to have the largest selection of pianos in the country, many of which are for sale. The rest make interesting viewing. These include a transposing piano (the kind Irving Berlin used) and the first electric piano ever made, played by Earl Hines at the 1939 World's Fair in Flushing Meadows. Call for an appt. . . . At **Maximiliaan's House of Grand Pianos,** 200 Lexington Ave. [32nd/33rd] ☎ 689-2177, they sell historic pianos and Bösendorfers.

🐦 **UNUSUAL PIANOS TO SEE** At the **Metropolitan Museum of Art:** A broad collection of pianos dating from the inception of the piano to the 1850s. Pianos of note include the oldest surviving piano in the world, built by Bartolomeo Cristofori in Florence in 1720. They also have a piano with a Duncan Phyfe workshop case and a beautiful grand that belonged to Napoleon's second wife, Marie Louise. Though not currently on display, the Met has a piano of the kind used by Mozart, which has extra bass notes, operated by a footboard . . . **At the Waldorf:** Cole Porter, a resident of the Waldorf Towers for many years, was given a piano by the hotel and he is said to have composed many of his classics on it. When he died, he left the piano to the hotel. You can hear it played nightly in the lobby from 4 P.M.–8 P.M. . . . **Wendell Castle Pianos:** at Peter Joseph Galleries, 745 Fifth Ave. [57th/58th] ☎ 751-5500. Wendell Castle, the well-known art furniture maker, was

A Wendell Castle piano.

commissioned by Steinway to build the 500,000th Steinway, which recently toured. He's made other sensational pianos, including the stunning "Ivory Spirit," which can be seen in the gallery catalog . . . **On 23rd St.:** If you walk along 23rd St., you may wonder what a piano is doing in the lobby at 120 E. 23rd. This piano, made by Smaldi 'Andreas Christensen and designed by Poul Henningsenin in 1931, was bought by Jerry Cohen of Williams Real Estate at Sotheby's auction in Monaco. He thought it would make a nice addition to the lobby.

🐦 **THE NEW PLAYER PIANOS** You can get your piano retrofitted with what looks like a CD player. This will turn your piano into a player piano. You can buy pre-

S T E I N W A Y   T O U R

You can take a (*long*) tour of the Steinway factory and see the extraordinary amount of labor (not to mention 12,000 parts) that goes into a Steinway piano. Watching the workers bend the wood to make the frame is memorable, as is the sight of dozens of grand piano frames curing (which they do for months) before they're ready to move back into the assembly process. The factory makes about 2,000 pianos a year (there is one other Steinway factory—in Hamburg, Germany) and uses a lot of machines and techniques developed by Steinway over 100 years ago. If you go, wear comfortable shoes because the factory is large and the tour lasts a good two hours. You need to call for a reservation at ☎ 718-721-2600.

recorded discs—of George Gershwin at the piano, for example—pop it into your player, and have the effect of Gershwin playing your piano. Incredible. While the Bösendorfer and the Yamaha Disklavier are state of the art, the Bösendorfer costs over $100,000 (you get the piano with the machine) and the Yamaha machine comes only as part of a Yamaha piano. The popular alternative, from $4,500, is the **PianoDisc,** a digital piano player. Not only will it play back from a selection of discs, you can record and play back your composition. Your piano needs to go into the shop for installation of the machine. It's available at most piano sellers.

🎹 **PIANO TEACHERS** No shortage of wonderful piano teachers in the city. The best way to find them is to use the music schools: **Juilliard** (☎ 799-5000), the **Manhattan School of Music** (☎ 749-2802), and the **Mannes School** (☎ 580-0210) have lists of teachers that tell you what degrees they hold, whether they'll come to you, whether they teach children, and so on. You can also try the **Third Street Music School** ☎ 777-3240 and the

Harlem School of the Arts ☎ 926-4100, which specializes in jazz instruction.

🎹 **PIANO TUNERS** In addition to Evan Giller, mentioned in the Buying a Piano entry, **Bill Garlick,** ☎ 516-363-7364, is another excellent tuner. He also gives unusual piano weekends—see below. $85 for a tuning ... **Linnea Johnson** ☎ 982-8635 charges $65 for tuning.

🎹 **PIANO GUEST WEEKENDS** Bill Garlick knows as much about the piano as anyone—he worked at Steinway for a number of years, has been a consultant to the Smithsonian and the Met Museum on the subject, and has lectured extensively on the piano. For piano enthusiasts, he does a Piano Bed and Breakfast: you start with a tour of the Steinway factory, then check into Mr. Garlick's home on Long Island. There you will learn everything you've ever wanted to know about the piano: history, tuning, repairs, and there's lots of listening. He has many antique keyboards that you can see. Cost is $125 per day, includes breakfast and lunch. Call ☎ 516-363-7364.

SLEEP

"... sore labor's bath, balm of hurt minds, great nature's second course, chief nourisher in life's feast ..." A few ways to help you sleep.

IN GENERAL We sought some general, practical advice on sleep from Dr. Eli Bryk, head of orthopedics at Beth Israel Hospital. He advises getting the "firmest possible mattress you're comfortable with." While there are wide variations among people who suffer back pain, he says one of the predisposing elements is often a soft mattress. "If you feel you need a bedboard, you probably need a new mattress." If that's not possible, Dr. Bryk says, a bedboard is a good stopgap measure. People with neck pain, he says, often find relief with a cervical pillow. People with lumbar pain sometimes find relief by putting a pillow against the small of the back. Water beds are "sensuous but not necessarily good for your back." Much has been written about a proper sleeping position, but there is no evidence that any position is better or worse for your back. Futons, he says, are good for young people with strong backs, but most older people find them too hard.

MATTRESSES Generally speaking, bad news for consumers. The Department of Consumer Affairs says that "mattress manufacturers and retailers are in bed together—conniving to make comparison shopping virtually impossible by offering 75 or more mattress model names *exclusive to each retailer.*" Nancy Butler, director of the Better Sleep Council, says, "In competitive markets like NY, retailers demand exclusive mattresses from manufacturers, which they [comply with] because if they say no, the retailer will simply get it from someone else.

So, forget model names and look for things like coil count."

The three largest manufacturers are Sealy, Simmons, and Serta and, according to the director of marketing at Dial-a-Mattress, Danny Flamberg, the three American mattress makers are "parity products," meaning the differences are minimal. In fact, coils for all three are made by the same manufacturer, Leggett and Platt. (When we spoke to L & P, they clarified that Sealy makes their own coils for Posturepedic, and Simmons makes their own for Beautyrest. Virtually all of the rest of the coils are made by L & P. These are the interlacing helical coils called "Bonnell's" after their inventor.) Kathy Fanning, who purchases mattresses for the Millenium hotel, looks for brand-name reliability and a good warranty period. She buys very, very firm and says the biggest mistake consumers make is to be swayed by good-looking ticking—ignore the ticking or the color and go for quilted tops with no buttons.

WHAT TO LOOK FOR An **innerspring** is better than a foam mattress. The **thicker** the mattress, the more comfortable. It should be at least 7 ins. Extra thick mattresses, 9 ins. or more, are more comfortable but more expensive. About **coils:** Generally, the more the better. Bare minimums: 300 coils in a full size, 375 in a queen size, and 400 in a king. While the Better Sleep Council says that, for example, a full-size bed should have no fewer than a 300-coil count, practically speaking, good mattresses have over 400. Ask about the **gauge** of the steel in the coil. Lower gauges are stiffer and therefore better (10 is better than 12). The same applies to the gauge of the **border wire.** This is the wire around the mattress border that helps the mattress maintain shape. The more **padding,** the better. For the **top** of the mattress, Dacron is considered the best material. Ask to see the "bun" or sample section of the mattress. Ignore **firmness** terminology. Everything's called firm. According to Consumer Affairs, "Consumers should be wary of paying more than $1,000 for a mattress set in NYC."

WHERE TO BUY There are plenty of places to buy mattresses in the city, but as far as we're concerned, the best place is **Frederick,** 107 E. 31st St. [Park/Lex] ☎ 683-8322. It's been in business since 1928, mostly in the Rizick family, whose brothers, Stuart and Robert, are the current owners. The narrow-fronted store has three floors displaying mattresses from all the major brands, as well as water beds, electric beds, sofa beds, latex mattresses, and futons. They provide special mattress sizes and special-cut box springs for antique beds. For people who do not like, or are sensitive to, spring mattresses, they can get you a horsehair mattress. Very fair prices and good service . . . Royal Pedic, in business since 1946, makes a mattress in many sizes from all-natural materials, with all-cotton padding and covers and a natural rubber latex pad. It's available at **Earth General,** 147 Eighth Ave. [17th] ☎ 929-2340. **Terra Verde,** 120 Wooster St. [Prince/Spring] ☎ 925-4533, sells an all-natural, all-organic (!) mattress from Crown City, with coil counts from 250–1000.

OTHER BEDS For old-fashioned **bunk beds,** see Children's Furniture in the Stores chapter or try North Carolina Furniture Showroom, 12 W. 21st St. [5th/6th] ☎ 260-5850. The disadvantage here is that there are

no bunk beds on the floor (you select from a catalog). The prices seem fair to us, but you can't see the bed before it arrives, and once you've bought it, it's yours. Bloom & Krup, 206 First Ave. [13th] ☎ 673-2760, has simple metal tubing bunk beds painted red, white, or black. You can get them with two same-size beds or a double bottom and twin top. $449 for a single-single and $549 for a double-single, including mattresses . . . **Joe Biunno,** 129 W. 29th St. [6th/7th] ☎ 629-5630, makes custom four-poster beds. He has a large library of post and finial styles and can finish or paint them in virtually any color. For a **foam bed** try Foam Tex, 150 W. 22nd St. [6th/7th] ☎ 727-1780. It's a bare bones operation (that's been around since 1952) in terms of retail display, but they will custom make any size mattress, including daybeds and their covers. They have a number of orthopedic products, including knee-lift pillows, wedges for your back or knees, anti-snore pillows, cervical pillows, lumbar cushions, and acoustical foam (used on walls to absorb sound). When looking for a foam mattress: 2 pounds per cubic foot density is the minimum you should look for—the higher the pounds per cubic foot, the better the foam . . . You can **rent** a bed at AAA U Rent, 861 Eagle St. ☎ 923-0300. A folding bed with a steel frame and a 5 in. foam mattress is $35 a week, plus $15 pickup and delivery, plus tax. Closed weekends, and they need one- to two-day's notice.

BEDDING Between **Bed Bath and Beyond,** 620 Sixth Ave. [18th] ☎ 255-3550, and **ABC Carpet & Home,** 888 Broadway [19th] ☎ 473-3000, ABC tends to have a much broader selection of sheet patterns and certainly more higher-end stuff. BBB has some unusual offerings such as sofa bed sheet sets, cot sheets, and an inflatable bed. But if you're shopping at BBB, information is in short supply: the goose down pillows don't tell you much about down content, etc. ABC sells dozens of different sheet brands and has an excellent selection of flannel sheets, throws, blankets, and down comforters. They provide a lot of useful information on the down contents . . . For **antique linens,** Françoise Nunnallé, ☎ 246-4281, sells fancy European embroidered and lace-trimmed linen sheets starting at about $500. Heavily embellished pillow shams start at $400 a pair or $250 for a single. Trouvaille Française, ☎ 737-6015, also sells Eurolinens at more modest prices (figure $135 and up for sheets; pillow shams start at $65). Jana Starr Antiques, 236 E. 80th St. [2nd/3rd] ☎ 861-8256, has a large supply of cotton and linen sheets starting at $75. The Italian ones can be large enough for a king size bed. They can restore pillowcases ($45 and up) and shams ($60 and up) when you buy them and will have a pillow made to fit. Alice Underground, 380 Columbus Ave. [78th] ☎ 724-6682, has pillowcases from $5 . . . You can find **good deals on sheets** at: J. Schachter Co., 5 Cook St. [Manhattan/Graham], Brooklyn ☎ 718-384-2732. They sell discount sheets and bedding. If you call them with a pattern that you've seen, they'll give you a quote (and if you want it, they'll UPS it). Schachter's does custom work, making a comforter cover or dust ruffle from your sheet pattern.

They can also goose up your old goose down comforter . . . **Natural sheets** at ABC, BBB, Terra Verde, and Earth General.

PILLOWS Pillow specialists include: **J. Schachter Co.** (see above) and **Mike and Misha Pillow,** 114 E. 1st St. [1st/A] ☎ 260-7270. They custom make bed pillows in down and feather. And there's **Izzy Itzkowitz,** 174 Ludlow St. [Stanton/Houston] ☎ 477-1788. Mr. Itzkowitz is a NY institution, working under what can charitably be called Dickensian circumstances. He makes feather pillows and comforters.

ALLERGIES AND BEDDING Dr. Paul Ehrlich, an allergy and asthma specialist, says dust mites, microscopic insects that live in mattresses (as well as carpeting and elsewhere), excrete a protein that can cause allergic problems, as well as irritate people with eczema. These, in turn, can cause sleeping problems. They are impossible to get rid of if the mattress has them. Instead of throwing away the mattress, Dr. Ehrlich suggests covering the mattress with a hypoallergenic mattress cover that seals the mites inside. Plastic covers don't do the trick (they're porous enough not to solve the problem). There are hypoallergenic pillow covers as well. Dr. Ehrlich says he's done a lot of comparison pricing of these items and says the best deals are from a company called **Allergy Home Care Products** ☎ 800-327-4382 . . . **J. Schachter** (see above) also makes a faux down pillow that's almost as comfortable as real down, but without the sneezing.

COPING WITH NOISE See Noise article in the Coping chapter.

NIGHTLIGHTS Try **Just Bulbs,** 938 Broadway [21st/22nd] ☎ 228-7820, for an assortment of whimsical nightlights: moons, pigs, cowboys, a lizard, a skull, all with light sensors, starting at $12.50 . . . **Alphabets,** 115 Avenue A [7th/8th] ☎ 475-7250, has these nightlights: trailers, trouts, a man on a horse, log cabins, sunflowers, cowgirls, and others.

TEDDY BEARS **Zona,** 97 Greene St. [Prince/Spring] ☎ 925-6750, has an adorable handmade bear for $10, **Distant Origin,** 153 Mercer St. [Prince/Houston] ☎ 941-0024, has an American Flag teddy. **The Enchanted Forest,** 85 Mercer St. [Spring/Broome] ☎ 925-6677, has several charming teddys; **A Bear's Place** 789 Lexington Ave. [61st/62nd] ☎ 826-6465, has handmade English bears; and **Housing Works Thrift Shop,** 143 W. 17th St. [6th/7th] ☎ 366-0820, has a tiny, waiflike teddy for $12. The entire cost is a donation

to Housing Works, which provides housing for people with AIDS.

WHERE TO GET MORE INFO **The Center for Medical Consumers,** 237 Thompson St. [3rd/4th] ☎ 674-7105, has files crammed with info from medical journals, newspapers, and magazines on a wide range of sleep topics: sleeping, dreaming, snoring, insomnia, etc. See more under Medical Information in Information.

WHERE TO GET HELP **NYU Sleep Center** at Bellevue, 462 First Ave. [27th] ☎ 263-8423 . . . **The Sleep Disorders Center** of the City College of New York, 138th St. and Convent Ave. ☎ 650-5396 . . . **The Sleep Disorders Center** at Columbia-Presbyterian, 161 Ft. Washington Ave. ☎ 305-1860 . . . **The Sleep Disorders Institute** at St. Luke's Roosevelt Hospital, 1090 Amsterdam Ave. [114th] ☎ 523-1700 . . . **The Sleep-Wake Disorders Center** at Montefiore Hospital, 111 E. 210th St. ☎ 718-920-4841.

TRAINS

The Transit Authority may not always inspire warm feelings, but the **NY Transit Museum,** 130 Livingston St. [Boerum/Smith], Brooklyn ☎ 718-330-3060, is a museum that will have anyone with the slightest interest in trains excited. You enter below ground, as if you are entering a subway station, which, in fact, you are. (It's a decommissioned IND station.) Inside, examples of everything from tokens, maps, turnstiles to (the best part) many old trains (from 1904 on) that you can walk through. Even without an interest in trains, it's hard to resist the sense of time travel these relics evoke. There is a terrific gift shop here where you can buy an as-

sortment of transit-related gifts (also satellite stores at Grand Central and Penn Stations). The Museum has an archive of photos, drawings, and documents of public transportation, which is open for research by appointment. Call ☎ 718-694-1068.

Red Caboose, 23 W. 45th St. [5th/6th] ☎ 575-0155. *The* place to buy model trains and all the accouterments. They also have tools to build the trackside structures like the Brach's candy factory. No trains are set up, and the charm comes from the mania and sheer number of items offered for sale. Lots of books on model and real railroading. They also buy old models.

In Grand Central, the **Sprague Memorial Library** has a trove of info on all aspects of electric railroads. Frank Julian Sprague developed the first successful electric trolley car in 1888, and this library in his name has his collection plus books, magazines (from all over the world), academic papers, photos, and Transit Authority materials. It's pleasantly chaotic, and you have the sense that there are many hidden treasures still to be unearthed. Up a different set of elevator banks is the **Williamson Library,** home of the Railroad Enthusiasts, with thousands of books and other materials on railroading. Mr. Williamson was the president of the NY Central, and his collection started this library over 50 years ago. On the floor is a carpet they used to roll out for the 20th Century Limited. Around this dusty clubhouse is a wide variety of railroad-related materials, including an original Strickland Report from 1826 on the advantages of railroads versus canals for freight transport. For info on the Williamson: write PO Box 040320, SI 10304. Dues are $25 annually. For the Sprague, write to Electric RR Association, PO Box 3323, NYC 10163-3323. It's $15 a year plus $1 initiation.

In each issue of *NY Streetcar News,* you'll find convincing argument for the redevelopment of trolley use in the city and interesting articles on light rail in the city's past. Recommended for anyone interested in city planning or simply a more livable city. Published 6 times a year, subscriptions are $16. Call ☎ 718-875-7102.

For a few weeks around Christmastime, look for the **Holiday Garden Railways** at the NY Botanical Garden. It's 6,000 feet of large model trains, mountains, forests, castles, waterfalls, bridges, tunnels (the trains go on and through them), and scale model buildings of NY. ☎ 718-817-8700.

TRAVEL

AIRLINES

	RESERVATIONS	ARRIVAL/ DEPARTURE	FREQUENT FLYER CLUB	LOST LUGGAGE
Aer Lingus	557-1110	557-1110	557-1110	718-553-4205
Aeroflot	265-1185	265-1185	NONE	332-1044
Aerolinas Argentinas	800-333-0276	718-632-1700	800-333-0276	718-656-2554
Aeromexico	800-237-6639	800-237-6639	800-247-3737	718-656-6177
Air Afrique	586-5908	586-5908	586-5908	541-7518
Air Canada	800-776-3000	800-488-1800	800-361-8253	LGA: 718-476-5278 NWK: 201-961-1724
Air France	800-237-2747	800-237-2747	800-375-8723	JFK: 718-553-2450 NWK: 201-961-2285
Air India	751-6200	407-1376	751-6200	718-632-0111
Air Jamaica	800-523-5585	800-523-5585	718-830-0622	718-656-2826
Alaska Airlines	800-426-0333	800-426-0333	800-654-5669	800-426-0333

	RESERVATIONS	ARRIVAL/ DEPARTURE	FREQUENT FLYER CLUB	LOST LUGGAGE
Alitalia	582-8900	582-8900	582-8900	800-905-9992
Aloha Airlines	800-367-5250	800-367-5250	800-367-5250	808-837-6817
America West	800-235-9292	800-235-9292	800-247-5691	JFK: 718-632-5737
				LGA: 718-334-7099
				NWK: 201-961-1514
American Airlines	800-433-7300	800-223-5436	800-882-8880	800-535-5225
Asiana	800-227-4262	800-227-4262	800-227-4262	718-244-7077
Austrian Airlines	800-843-0002	800-843-0002	800-221-8125	800-843-0002
Avianca	800-284-2622	800-284-2622	800-284-1758	718-632-1466
British Airways	800-247-9297	800-247-9297	800-955-2748	800-422-9499
Canadian Airlines	800-426-7000	800-426-7000	800-426-7000	800-426-7000
Carnival Airlines	800-824-7386	800-824-7386	800-824-7386	800-359-2538
Cathay Pacific	800-233-2742	800-233-2742	800-762-6403	310-417-0244
China Airlines	800-227-5118	718-553-0600	399-7892	718-553-8202
Continental	319-9494	800-784-4444	713-952-1630	NWK: 201-961-1750
				LGA: 718-334-7099
Delta	239-0700	800-325-1999	404-715-2999	JFK: 718-632-5664
				LGA: 718-565-3964
				NWK: 201-430-3900
El Al	800-223-6700	800-223-6700	852-0604	JFK: 800-223-6700
				NWK: 201-643-3042
Finnair	800-950-5000	800-950-9529	800-950-3387	718-656-7477
Iberia	800-772-4642	800-537-2316	713-952-1630	718-656-2553
Icelandair	800-223-5500	800-223-5500	800-223-5500	718-917-0648
Japan Airlines	800-525-3663	800-525-3663	800-525-6453	718-244-5213
Kiwi International	800-538-5494	201-622-3232	NONE	201-961-3489
KLM	800-374-7747	718-632-2603	800-374-7747	718-632-2613
Korean Air	800-438-5000	800-438-5000	800-438-5000	718-632-8731
Ladeco	800-825-2332	718-244-6281	305-670-6705	718-244-6281
Lan-Chile	800-488-0070	718-995-6962	800-488-0070	718-995-6962
Lot Polish	800-223-0593	800-223-0593	852-0254	718-632-3079
Lufthansa	800-645-3880	800-645-3880	800-581-6400	JFK: 718-632-7180
				NWK: 201-961-7438
Mexicana	800-531-7921	800-531-7921	800-531-7901	201-961-3488
Midwest Express	800-452-2022	800-452-2022	800-452-2022	800-233-2830
Northwest	800-225-2525	800-441-1818	800-447-3757	JFK: 718-244-5615
				LGA: 718-476-7411
				NWK: 201-961-4624

	RESERVATIONS	ARRIVAL/ DEPARTURE	FREQUENT FLYER CLUB	LOST LUGGAGE
Olympic Airways	838-3600	A: 838-3825 D: 838-4165	NONE	718-632-7180
Philippine Airlines	800-435-9725	800-435-9725	800-635-8653	800-524-6667
Qantas	800-227-4500	800-227-4500	800-227-4500	310-215-4495
Royal Air Maroc	750-6071	750-6071	750-5115	750-5115
Royal Jordanian	949-0050	949-0050	949-0060	718-632-8512
Sabena	800-955-2000	800-873-3900	800-955-2000	800-274-2552
Scandinavian	800-221-2350	800-221-2350	800-221-2350	800-650-2247
Singapore Airlines	800-742-3333	718-632-2078	800-742-3333	718-632-2078
South African Airways	826-0995	826-0995	826-0995	718-632-3086
Swissair	800-221-4750	800-221-4750	800-241-4141	800-221-4780
TAP	800-221-7370	800-221-7370	800-221-7370	JFK: 718-632-4290 NWK: 201-624-6363
Thai Airways	800-426-5204	800-426-5204	800-426-5204	800-426-5204
Tower Airways	718-553-8500	718-553-8500	NONE	JFK: 718-553-7800
Turkish Airlines	339-9650	339-9650	NONE	JFK: 718-553-7100
TWA	290-2121	290-2121	800-325-4815	JFK: 718-656-8750 LGA: 718-803-6827 NWK: 201-961-3059
USAir	800-428-4322	800-943-5436	800-872-4738	JFK: 718-553-5867 LGA: 718-533-2491 NWK: 201-642-5506
United	800-241-6522	800-241-6522	800-421-4655	800-221-6903
Varig	682-3100	682-3100	682-3100	718-632-0800
Viasa	800-468-4272	800-468-4272	800-468-4272	800-468-4272
Virgin	800-862-8621	800-862-8621	800-365-9500	JFK: 718-995-2920 NWK: 201-961-3481

AIR COURIERS

BY KELLY MONAGHAN

If you're interested in flying round the world at unbelievably low fares, you're in the right place. New York is the air courier capital of the country, if not the world. Every week, more than 100 air courier flights leave Kennedy and Newark, offering $300 trips to London and $600 trips to Rio. Because you live in New York, you can take advantage of last-minute specials that can put you in Brussels for $50 or send you to Singapore for $250. And those are all round-trip fares!

THE BASICS An air courier is someone who accompanies time-sensitive business cargo checked as passenger's baggage on regularly scheduled international flights. Ordinary air cargo must arrive at the airport hours before flight time and then go through cumbersome customs procedures on arrival at the destination. Passengers' baggage, in contrast, can go on the plane up to the last minute and is cleared through customs as soon as the plane lands. Shipping important materials as passengers' baggage can mean the difference between overnight and two-day delivery.

To take advantage of this little loophole in international shipping regulations, however, the shipper needs a passenger. That's where folks like you and me come in. In exchange for giving up our checked baggage allotment for the use of overnight shippers and for serving as their "air courier," we get a break on the fare. And what a break it can be!

As a rule of thumb, you can figure on saving one-half to two-thirds the unrestricted coach fare. For example, I once flew to London for $250 round-trip when the actual cost of the ticket was $920 round-trip. Unlike regular air fares, courier fares go *down* as the flight date approaches and the courier company starts to worry that they may not fill the seat. Last-minute deals usually offer fares of $100 to $150 to Europe. It's even possible to fly for free, although that is becoming rare out of New York. West Coast courier companies still regularly offer free flights to places like Tokyo, Singapore, and Bangkok. In exchange for these super fares, you do remarkably little (other than travel light). Your main job is to carry an envelope with the paperwork for the shipment to be handed over to a courier representative at your destination. You never have to handle, and may never even see, the cargo you are accompanying. And don't worry, it's all perfectly legal and aboveboard. Customs makes sure of that.

So what's the catch? There are a number of trade-offs involved in courier travel. Usually there is only one courier seat per flight (exception: Madrid), but the companies listed below will work with you to arrange for two people to travel together. As noted, you will be restricted to carry-on luggage only (although there are exceptions to this rule, too). Most courier trips are limited to one- or two-week stays. This makes it easy for the courier companies to keep track of things; after all, they are in the freight business, not tourism. Again, there are exceptions that will let you stay for up to 30 days.

It's also pretty much a cash-and-carry business. Some companies take plastic, but coin of the realm is preferred. You pay up front but don't see your ticket until minutes before flight time when you meet a total stranger (shades of John Le Carré!) at a prearranged spot in the airport. Until you get used to it, this cloak-and-dagger uncertainty can be a bit unnerving.

Air couriers come in all shapes and sizes, from business people with six-figure incomes to cash-starved students. Courier travel is perhaps best suited to retirees with plenty of free time, freelancers who can be flexible about when they travel, and the adventurous traveler of any age or station. Best strategy: set a time period during which you'll travel and then, as the date approaches, start shopping for last-minute bargains. If you're willing to take potluck on the destination, you should be able to find a super-low-cost trip.

GETTING BOOKED The biggest courier company in New York is **Halbart Express** ☎ 718-656-8189, located out by JFK. They fly to a dozen or so European cities and also serve Santiago, Chile; Tokyo; Hong Kong; and Singapore. There are other local companies that serve niche markets like Tel Aviv, Puerto Rico, Australia, and several South American destinations, but Halbart is by far the largest and can get you to most places you want to go. While you can deal directly with Halbart, you may find it more convenient to book through one of the Manhattan booking agencies that specializes in courier travel. These agencies also offer flights from other companies besides Halbart. Usually there's no difference in the fares (although one charges a "registration fee") . . . My favorite is **Discount Travel International** (DTI), 169 W. 81st [Columbus/Amsterdam] ☎ 362-3636. Owned by Dawn McCaffrey, DTI pioneered the value-added service that is becoming more common in the courier business. They will make regular airline bookings so a friend can fly with you on your courier trip, book connecting flights into NY, and get you a great deal on a hotel in Rio and elsewhere. Once they get to know you, they will call with news of last-minute specials (as I was putting the finishing touches on this article, I had to turn down a $200 trip to Singapore!) . . . The doyenne of courier travel is Julie Weinberg's **Now Voyager,** 74 Varick [Canal/Grand] ☎ 431-1616. Now Voyager charges a $50 annual registration fee, which adds a significant amount to your fare if you fly only once. Their best feature is the extensive voice mail listing of currently available flights and fares. Getting through to a human being, however, takes patience. You're often better off simply showing up at their office.

Kelly Monaghan's book, Air Courier Bargains: How to Travel Worldwide for Next to Nothing, *lists scores of air courier companies across the U.S. and around the world, along with dozens of tips for getting the lowest courier fares. $14.95 plus shipping,* ☎ *800-356-9315.*

THE AIRPORT GUIDE

For anyone who does any travel planning for companies or groups: The Port Authority publishes ***The Airport Guide—A Professional Travel Planner's Reference,*** and it has an enormous amount of good info in addition to being beautifully designed. It contains airport layouts, details of transportation services, information for handicapped travelers, including specs on height of dining tables at the airports, ramp slopes, and bathroom measurements. Fax a request to ☎ 435-6782.

CAR TRIPS & KIDS

About **motion sickness,** Dr. Bradley A. Connor (an expert in travel medicine—see Travel/Medical section below) offers the following advice: The human body was built for walking, not riding in a car at 55 mph. For many people, the structures in the inner ear that control the sense of balance cannot tolerate the horizon flying by. Some people are helped by riding in the front seat of the car. Reading makes things worse. Adults who are affected can use Dramamine or the new Scopolamine patch. This can be placed directly on the skin (most people put it behind their ear) and can be worn for several days at a time. This helps to control the balance center and many people have good results with it. While Dramamine is not recommended for children under 12, some pediatricians may permit it for some children. For very young children who are affected, stopping the car and walking for a while may help. There does seem to be a connection between some foods and motion sickness. Avoid fatty foods. If possible, try not to drive right after eating if you are prone to motion sickness . . . **Game Show,** 1240 Lexington Ave. [83rd/84th] ☎ 472-8011, suggests the travel version of Boggle Jr., Guess Who, and Memory (all under $12), and they say these games provide "interesting play and have no loose pieces to roll around the car." . . . You might consider a **portable VCR,** available at Sound City, 58 W. 45th St. [5th/6th] ☎ 575-0210. They've got a 9 in. Magnavox you can plug into the cigarette lighter that comes with a car battery cord—$400. You can rent one at Video Overseas, 249 W. 23rd [7th/8th] ☎ 229-9110, for about $20 a day.

CONSOLIDATORS

BY KELLY MONAGHAN

Let's say you have to be in Milan next week to seal a big business deal. Your excitement is equaled only by your horror at the exorbitant "unrestricted" coach ticket you are going to be forced to buy—after all it's too late to qualify for those super-saver fares. Before you say, "There go the profits," reach for the phone and call **Moment's Notice** (☎ 486-0500). They'll give you a fare at or close to the super-saver fare the airline says you can't have. Or perhaps you're planning a vacation overseas. You want to go some place different, a bit off the beaten path. You check your copy of my book *The Insiders Guide to Air Courier Bargains* and find there's just nothing for Transylvania. Do you forget about it? No, you pick up the phone and call **Pennsylvania Travel** (☎ 800-331-0947), which specializes in Eastern

Europe, and get the lowest possible fare. Or, let's say you simply want to squeeze a little extra money out of the airline on which you have just reserved a flight at the best possible fare. You pick up the phone and call Hans Ratzenstein at **British European** (☎ 800-747-1476) and tell him what you've got. In exchange for getting the ticket through him, Hans will (in most cases) be able to give you an additional 5% off the fare you've booked.

Hans is a *consolidator*. Like the folks at Moment's Notice and Pennsylvania Travel, he is one of a small but growing group of entrepreneurial businesspeople who are bringing the time-honored strategy of mass marketing to the travel industry.

WHAT IS A CONSOLIDATOR? In simplest terms, a consolidator is someone who buys wholesale and sells below retail. In this case, the commodity is airplane seats. Consolidators buy large blocks of seats from the airlines at steep discounts. They then turn around and sell those seats to you (or to travel agents) at a price that is well below the ticket's "face value" but still high enough to earn them a profit.

WHEN TO USE THEM In **high season,** when tickets are normally inflated because of increased demand. **When you have to fly on short notice.** Be aware, however, of the difference between courier companies and consolidators. As the flight date approaches, the courier company gets more and more nervous they'll have no one to fill the seat; consequently the fare goes down to lure someone into taking it. For a consolidator, on the other hand, a ticket becomes, if anything, more valuable as the flight date approaches. That's because the consolidator knows his best customers are those people who must purchase tickets on short notice. **When you're looking for an offbeat, bargain vacation. When you're looking at a high-priced trip,** such as one around the world or with many family members.

TRADE-OFFS Don't expect any great deals on First Class or Business Class. You're locked in to the airline on the ticket. Very few consolidator tickets allow you to change airlines. Refunds aren't always available and, if they are, they are available only through the consolidator. Many airlines treat consolidator tickets differently than they do "regular" tickets. Most of these differences are minor: no frequent flyer mileage credit, no advance seating assignment, a direct rather than a nonstop flight, no special meals, no refunds.

DEALING WITH CONSOLIDATORS The easiest way to deal with consolidators is not to—deal with a travel agent instead! Some consolidators will not deal directly with the public, so going through a travel agent automatically gives you access to a bigger market. Travel agents are more convenient, too. Most consolidators, though, are very much like travel agents. That is, you can pick up the phone, tell them what you want, book a flight, pay for it with a credit card, and have it mailed to you.

RISKS AND REMEDIES I am often asked, "Are consolidators reliable?" Well, sure, some consolidators go out of business, but then so do some airlines. Nothing is for certain, and I can't guarantee nothing awful will happen to you if you call one of the consolidators listed here. On the other hand,

they've all been around for a while, and they have all sold thousands and thousands of tickets to people who had perfectly uneventful trips. Some precautions: Use your credit card to pay for your ticket, find a consolidator close to home that you can visit in person, and get your tickets as soon as possible. If something is wrong, you'll have time to get it fixed.

NEW YORK CONSOLIDATORS **Air Travel Discounts** ☎ 922-1326 (Central America, worldwide). **Asensio Tours** ☎ 213-4310 (South America). **Cedok Central** ☎ 689-9720 (Europe, Middle East). **Cheap Tickets** ☎ 570-1179 (Coast-to-coast, Asia, Europe). **Council Charter** ☎ 661-0311 (Western Europe, Martinique). **Council Travel** ☎ 661-1450 (Student travel). **CWT** ☎ 695-8435 (Worldwide, last-minute tickets). **Dial Europe** ☎ 758-5310 (Worldwide, specializing in First and Business Class). **Discount Travel International** ☎ 362-3636 (U.S., Europe). **E. European Travel Center** ☎ 718-339-1100 (Eastern Europe). **Fly Wise Travel** ☎ 869-2223 (U.S., worldwide, last minute). **Flytime Tour & Travel** ☎ 760-3737 (Europe, U.S., Asia). **Globe Travel** ☎ 843-9885 (Europe, Asia, hotels). **Hari World Travels** ☎ 957-3000 (India, worldwide, U.S.). **Homeric Tours** ☎ 753-1100 (Greece, Portugal, Morocco). **International Travel Exchange** ☎ 808-5368 (U.S., Europe, Africa, Middle East). **Jet Vacations** ☎ 247-0999 (France, England, Italy, Portugal). **Jetset Tours** ☎ 818-9756 (Pacific rim, round-the-world, hotels). **Lotus Travel** ☎ 213-1625 (Europe, Mediterranean). **Magical Holidays** ☎ 486-9600 (Europe, Africa, South America, Middle East). **Moment's Notice** ☎ 486-0500 (Worldwide). **New Frontiers** ☎ 779-0600

(Europe, France, Italy, charters). **P & F International** ☎ 718-383-5630 (Eastern Europe, Middle East, South America, hotels). **Persvoyage** ☎ 719-0900 (Europe, Middle East). **Pino Welcome Travel** ☎ 682-5400 (Italy, South America, Asia, Africa). **Service Travel** ☎ 779-1600 (Europe, U.S.). **STA Travel** ☎ 627-3111 (Student and youth travel). **Sunrise Tours** ☎ 947-3617 (Europe, Baltic, Russia). **TFI Tours** ☎ 736-1140 (Worldwide, U.S., South America, Europe, 61 airlines). **The French Experience** ☎ 986-3800. **Tourlite International Inc.** ☎ 599-2727 (Middle East, Greece, Turkey, Costa Rica, South America). **Travac Tours** ☎ 563-3303 (Europe, some Africa). **Travel Today International** ☎ 447-6565 (Middle East, Saudi Arabia, Worldwide). **Tulips Travel** ☎ 490-3388 (Southeast Asia, worldwide). **United Tours Corp.** ☎ 245-1100 (Eastern Europe, Russia via Aeroflot). **Up and Away** ☎ 889-2345 (Europe, Africa, Middle East). **Zohny Travel** ☎ 953-0077 (Middle East, Asia)

Kelly Monaghan's book Consolidators: Air Travel's Bargain Basement *contains a complete listing of consolidators across the country and reveals the secret of buying consolidator tickets at the even lower "net" fares reserved for travel agents. $6.95 plus shipping,* ☎ *800-356-9315.*

FALL FOLIAGE

New York: 800-225-5697
New Jersey:
   Northern Region: 201-948-3820
   Central Region: 609-737-0623
   Southern Region: 609-561-0024
Connecticut: 800-282-6863
Massachusetts: 413-443-9186
Pennsylvania: 800-847-4872

GAY & LESBIAN TRAVEL

There are a number of books and travel agencies that specialize in the gay and lesbian market but the best source is **Out and About,** an informative and smartly designed newsletter. 10 issues are $49. ☎ 800-929-2268.

GETTING TO THE AIRPORTS

BY TAXI JFK: Taxis should cost $30–$35 from JFK to midtown. (The TLC tested, which may or may not be in effect when you read this, a $30 flat rate *from* JFK to anywhere in Manhattan, exclusive of tolls and tips. There is no nighttime charge, no charge for extra baggage. If riders request multiple stops in Manhattan, the $30 fare is good to the first stop, then the driver puts on the meter. The metered fare is collected at the last stop.) LGA: $15–$20 from LGA to midtown. NWK: $50 or so. You are charged meter fare plus $10 plus tolls and tips. These are, clearly, just estimates, but we've been in a number of taxis lately with souped-up meters, so be aware. The number for lost articles is ☎ 840-4735 and complaints is ☎ 221-8294. From Teresa Marracello in the Aviation Department at the Port Authority, who thought readers should know this about **gypsy cabs:** "Many Manhattanites know that the gypsy cabs at the airports are unauthorized and illegal. Most Manhattanites also feel savvy enough to weed out the more dangerous drivers, and to even strike a good deal with these cabs/limos. They should know that many of the cab drivers, well dressed though they may be, will lock a passenger's luggage in the trunks of their cars, increase the originally agreed upon price, and not release the luggage until the price is paid. Some incidents are even more dangerous: passengers are dropped off on abandoned streets and the driver takes off with their luggage . . ."

SUBWAYS TO JFK Take the **A** train (direction: Far Rockaway) to the Howard Beach Station. Transfer to the free shuttle bus. It operates approximately every 10 minutes and stops at each airport terminal. Allow at least 90 minutes from 42nd and Eighth Avenue to the terminal . . . Take the **A** train (direction: Far Rockaway) to the Lefferts Boulevard Station. Transfer to the Q-10 bus, the Green Bus line . . . Take the **3** train to the New Lots Ave. station. Then take the B15 bus . . . Take the **E** or **F** train to Queens, exit at Union Turnpike Station. Take the Q10 bus from there.

BUSES TO JFK **Carey Bus,** ☎ 718-632-0529, runs between JFK and 6 midtown stops: Park Ave./41st (this is the first stop in Manhattan and last stop on the way to the airport), Port Authority, NY Hilton Sixth/53rd, Sheraton Seventh/52nd, Marriott Marquis Bway/45th, Holiday Inn Crowne Plaza Bway/48th, Grand Central, and Penn Station. Buses leave every 20 minutes between 1 P.M. and 7 P.M. and every 30 minutes at other times. $13 . . . **Gray Line Air Shuttle,** ☎ 315-3006, leaves hourly from NY to JFK from dozens of NY hotels. From JFK, they leave every 20 minutes or so. $16 one way.

HELICOPTER TO JFK **New York Helicopter** no longer offers regular scheduled service, but you can book a helicopter from the East 34th St. heliport to JFK, seating 5 for $299. At Kennedy, the helicopter stops at the General Aviation Terminal, which is not associated with any of the airlines. You

will have to take the airport shuttle bus or have NY Helicopter arrange a limo service ($50) for you.

SUBWAY TO LAGUARDIA Take the **7** to Broadway/74th or the **E, F, G,** or **R** to Roosevelt Ave. and transfer to the Q33 bus. For meeting people or when traveling light, you can take those trains and then grab a cab from there. This cuts out most of the traffic, and it turns out to be a cheap, fast trip (cheaper than a cab from the city, faster than Carey). Or, take the **A, B, C, D, 2, 3, 4, 5,** or **6** train to 125th St. or the **1, 9** to 116th St. (and Adam Clayton Powell Blvd.); there you can get the M60 bus, which stops at all LGA terminals. It runs every 30 minutes (and stops at most of the avenues on 125th St.) . . . Take the **N** train to Astoria Blvd., where you can catch the M60 bus.

BUS TO LAGUARDIA **Carey Bus,** ☎ 718-632-0529, runs between LGA and 6 midtown stops: (see above under JFK). Buses leave every 20 minutes between 1 P.M. and 7 P.M. and every 30 minutes at other times. $10 one way . . . **Gray Line Air Shuttle,** ☎ 315-3006, leaves hourly from NY to LGA from dozens of NY hotels. From LGA, they leave every 20 minutes or so. $13 one way.

WATER SHUTTLE TO LAGUARDIA ☎ 800-543-3779. **Fare:** $20 one way, $30 round-trip. **From:** Wall Street's Pier 11 and the East 34th St. Heliport. **To:** LaGuardia's Marine Air Terminal. **Operates:** M–F (no weekend or major holiday service) during business hours. **Notes:** Service is timed to meet arrivals and departures of Boston and Washington shuttles. It's 25 minutes from the 34th Street stop and 40 minutes from Pier 11. You need not be flying Delta to use the service. If you're not flying the shuttle, you will need a shuttle bus to the other passenger terminals.

TRAIN TO NEWARK From the World Trade Center, take the PATH train to Newark Penn Station ($1). From other PATH stations in Manhattan, you'll have to change trains. At street level, take the Air Link shuttle bus run by New Jersey Transit. It runs every 20 minutes or so and costs $4. PATH ☎ 800-234-7284. NJ Transit ☎ 201-762-5100.

BUSES TO NEWARK · From Penn Station (corner of 34th & Eighth) **Olympia Trails** ☎ 964-6233, runs every 20 minutes, except early morning when it runs every 30 minutes. $7 one way. From Grand Central (41st and Park), take Olympia Trails, which runs every 20 minutes. $7 one way. From 1 World Trade Center [West], next to the Vista hotel, runs every 30 minutes. From NWK, runs every 20 minutes to Penn Station and Grand Central, every 30 minutes to WTC . . . **NJ Transit Airport Express Bus** ☎ 201-762-5100, runs every 15 minutes from Port Authority to NWK, operates 24 hours (less often during overnight hours), and takes approximately 30 minutes. $7 one way, $12 round trip . . . **Gray Line Air Shuttle,** ☎ 315-3006, leaves hourly from NY to NWK from dozens of NY hotels. From NWK, they leave every 20 minutes or so. $18 one way.

BEST CAR ROUTES TO THE AIRPORTS

BY JOSHUA ISAACSON

TO NWK VIA THE GW BRIDGE Note: The NJ Turnpike is divided into two parallel segments between Newark Airport and the GW Bridge called the "Eastern and Western

Spurs." Both spurs will take you to Newark Airport. In fact, they merge just above the airport. The advantage to knowing how to get onto either spur of the turnpike is that if you hear a traffic report of a problem on one, you can take the other and avoid the delay. After crossing the GW Bridge, you have two choices: **1.)** follow the signs to I-95 South (NJ Turnpike). When you do this, you'll be placed onto the Western Spur of the NJ Turnpike. Take the turnpike to Exit 14 and follow the signs to Newark Airport. **2.)** follow the signs to Rte. 46. After a few minutes on Rte. 46, you'll see signs to I-95 South (NJ Turnpike). When you take this route, you'll be placed onto the Eastern Spur of the NJ Turnpike. Take the turnpike to Exit 14 and follow the signs to Newark Airport. ☞ I generally prefer to take Rte. 46 to the Eastern Spur because I feel that this way is slightly shorter than the Western Spur, and there are several very inexpensive gas stations along Rte. 46. Please note, Rte. 46 currently has some reconstruction activity.

TO NWK VIA THE LINCOLN TUNNEL After you come out of the Lincoln Tunnel, you'll be on the 495 Viaduct. Just follow the signs to the NJ Tpke. Southbound. You'll be placed onto the Eastern Spur. Take the turnpike to Exit 14 and follow the signs to Newark Airport. Sometimes the 495 Viaduct gets very backed up heading into the Toll Plaza entrance to the turnpike. There are two options you could try while on the 495 Viaduct: **Option 1:** Instead of following the signs to the Tpke. Southbound, follow the signs to Rte. 3. Just after you bear right toward Rte. 3, you'll see an Exit sign saying, "West 3-Local-Secaucus." Bear right at the sign to get onto the service road of Rte. 3. You'll pass directly in front of Tops Appliance Center and you'll see a sign that says, "Secaucus, 800 feet." Continue a few hundred feet and you'll drive under Paterson Plank Road. Just before you drive under Paterson Plank Road, you'll see an exit sign which says, "North Bergen." Then you'll pass under PPR and make an immediate right turn. There are no signs to identify PPR, so just make the right turn after you pass the "North Bergen" exit. Take this exit and it will put you onto Paterson Plank Road toward Secaucus. Shortly, you'll see an entrance sign to the Tpke. Southbound! This is also for the Eastern Spur. **Option 2:** Instead of following the signs to the Tpke. Southbound, follow the signs to Rte. 3. Continue on Rte. 3 for a while and as you near the Meadowlands Sports Complex, you'll see the entrance signs to the Tpke. Southbound. This will put you onto the Western Spur of the NJ Tpke. Southbound.

TO NWK VIA THE HOLLAND TUNNEL
You have two options: **Option 1:** After you exit the Holland Tunnel and pass all the gas stations, follow the signs to Rtes. 1 & 9 to the Pulaski Skyway. The Pulaski Skyway is actually "Express" Rtes. 1 & 9 (cars only). The elevated Pulaski Skyway ascends above Kearny and descends near the northern edge of Newark Airport. At this point, you should begin to watch for signs to Newark *very carefully.* There will be lots of curves and turns, but if you follow the signs correctly, you'll end up at Newark Airport. (The Highway Authority has a very poorly designed symbol for the airport. It's supposed to look like a plane but, to me, looks like a triangle divided into blue, red, and green segments.) There are no tolls via this route! **Option 2:** After you exit the Holland Tunnel and pass all the

gas stations, follow the signs to the New Jersey Turnpike. This puts you on what's known as the NJ Turnpike Extension. Follow the signs to Newark Airport.

TO LGA VIA THE TRIBOROUGH BRIDGE
After you cross the Triborough, you'll be on the Grand Central Parkway Eastbound. Exit 7 is for LaGuardia Airport. If the parkway becomes backed up before you reach Exit 7, here are some options: **Option 1:** Take Exit 3 or Exit 5. Both will put you on Astoria Blvd. Eastbound. Continue on Astoria and make a left onto 82nd St. (there's an Exxon station on the far right corner of this intersection). Make a right onto 23rd Ave. Make a left onto 94th St. and drive into LaGuardia. **Option 2:** Take Exit 6 and make a left turn onto 94th St. and drive into LaGuardia.

TO LGA VIA THE 59TH ST. BRIDGE If you take the **upper level**—follow the signs to "Northern Blvd. and 21st St." At the traffic light at the end of the exit ramp, make a right turn onto 21st St. Continue about a mile on 21st St. and make a right onto Astoria Blvd. (You'll see the Triborough Bridge.) Soon you'll see the entrance to the Grand Central Parkway, which goes to LaGuardia. This is a popular route with taxicab drivers. If you take the **lower level**—follow the signs to Northern Blvd. Continue on Northern for about 1.5 miles and make a left onto 68th St. or 69th St. If you make a left onto 68th St., you can immediately get onto the BQE and then take Exit 39 to the Grand Central Parkway. If instead you stay on 68th St. or 69th St., they will merge into Boody (there's a Mobil gas station at this merge). Boody runs into Astoria Blvd. and then you'll see the entrance to the Grand Central Parkway to LaGuardia.

TO LGA AND JFK VIA THE WILLIAMS-BURG, MANHATTAN, OR BROOKLYN BRIDGES After crossing the lower Manhattan bridges into Brooklyn, the drive to LaGuardia Airport is actually a fairly straight line via the BQE Eastbound. Unfortunately, the BQE constantly suffers from traffic jams. Equally unfortunate is that there are no really efficient ways to reach Kennedy Airport from lower Manhattan. The drive from lower Manhattan is basically like traveling the circumference of a large circle rather than cutting across its diameter. This is because Brooklyn has no central highway, save for the very short Prospect Expressway.

The following are ways to reach the BQE Eastbound from the three "lower" bridges. After that, there are explanations of how to reach the two airports once you're on the BQE Eastbound. **1.)** Crossing the Williamsburg Bridge, stay to the left and drive onto the BQE Eastbound. **2.)** Crossing the Manhattan Bridge, stay toward the right and just before you reach the end, make a right onto Concord St. If Concord is closed, then make a right onto Tillary St. Then make a right onto Jay St. and a right onto Sands St. In a moment, you'll see the entrance to the BQE Eastbound. **3A.)** Crossing the Brooklyn Bridge, stay toward the right. Take the Cadman Plaza West Exit and keep bearing toward the right onto Cadman Plaza West and then make the first right onto Prospect St. After a few blocks, make a right onto Jay St. and then a quick left on Sands St. In a moment, you'll see the entrance to the BQE Eastbound. (If you can find and read the small and occasional signs that say "To Kennedy and LaGuardia Arprts," you'll find the BQE entrance just the same . . .) **3B.)** Crossing the Brooklyn Bridge, stay toward the left. Make a left onto Tillary St.

and after a few blocks, you'll see the entrance to the BQE Eastbound. ☞ NOW . . . To reach **LaGuardia Airport,** you must take the BQE Eastbound up to Exit 39 to the Grand Central Parkway Eastbound to LaGuardia Airport. To reach **Kennedy Airport,** you must take the BQE Eastbound to Exit 35 to the LIE Eastbound to the Grand Central Parkway Eastbound to the Van Wyck Expressway Southbound to Kennedy Airport.

If you would like one method of traversing **straight across Brooklyn to Kennedy Airport,** here it is . . . It actually takes only 30–35 minutes from the Brooklyn side of the Williamsburg Bridge when the traffic's light. However, how does one know when it is or isn't light? . . . Crossing the Williamsburg Bridge, stay to the right and get off at the very first exit—"Local Streets" (you need to bear right and then left), which will put you onto Broadway. After about 12 blocks, make a left onto Flushing Ave. Then make a right onto Beaver St. Beaver will merge into Bushwick Ave. (Please note: Broadway and Bushwick Ave. run parallel, so . . . if you miss the left turn onto Flushing, you can always make a left turn on virtually any street, go one block, and then make a right onto Bushwick Ave.) Continue about 2 miles on Bushwick and watch for a very large Sunoco gas station. You must make a left turn just before the gas station onto Highland Blvd. (Be sure not to get on the Interboro Parkway!) After Highland Blvd. flows out of the park, continue straight onto Highland Place. After a few blocks, make a left onto Atlantic Ave. Quickly, get over to the right lanes because just after passing Logan and Fountain Avenues, you must bear right onto Conduit Ave., and there is no sign to indicate Conduit. After this, the "traffic signs" and "forks" are a bit confusing, but in almost any case, you will end up at Kennedy.

For clarity, Conduit Ave. becomes the "service road" to the Belt Parkway and the Nassau Expressway just as all three pass in front of Kennedy. (All three run parallel and almost touch as they pass in front of Kennedy.) If you end up on the *Nassau Expressway,* you will see the exit to the Van Wyck South to Kennedy. If you end up on *Conduit Ave,* you'll see the exit to 150th St., Kennedy Airport. If you end up on the *Belt Parkway,* take the 150th St. exit to the airport. (Please note—Bushwick Ave. and Broadway go through a pretty rough area of Brooklyn. I don't recommend this "local route to Kennedy" if you're afraid of getting lost—as it is always possible to get lost. I also don't recommend women driving this route solo.)

As an aside, you can take the Brooklyn-Battery Tunnel into the BQE/Gowanus Expressway down to the Belt Parkway, which goes to Kennedy Airport. However, the Belt follows the entire shoreline perimeter of Brooklyn, making it very scenic but also making it like driving two-thirds around the circumference of a very large circle rather than cutting across the diameter—neither efficient nor fast.

TO JFK VIA THE TRIBOROUGH BRIDGE
Take the Triborough Bridge into the Grand Central Parkway Eastbound to the Van Wyck Expressway Southbound to Kennedy Airport.

TO JFK VIA THE 59TH ST. BRIDGE Take the 59th St. Bridge to Queens Blvd. to the LIE Eastbound to the Grand Central Parkway Eastbound to the Van Wyck Expressway Southbound to Kennedy Airport.

Note 1: If you think that Queens Blvd. is moving well and are unsure about the situation on the LIE and the Grand Central, you can continue on Queens Blvd., and just as you pass the Maple Grove Cemetery (on your right) you can turn right onto the Van Wyck Service Road (southbound). Shortly, you will see an entrance ramp to the Van Wyck Southbound.

Note 2: If you take the "express" or center lanes of Queens Blvd. and want to get onto the LIE, you must watch carefully for the sign to the LIE (for the crossover from the "express" to the "local" lanes), because access to the LIE Eastbound entrance ramp is only possible from the "local" right-hand lanes of Queens Blvd.

TO JFK VIA THE QUEENS MIDTOWN TUNNEL Take the Queens Midtown Tunnel, which exits into the LIE Eastbound, into the Grand Central Parkway Eastbound into the Van Wyck Expressway Southbound to Kennedy Airport.

☞ Note: The LIE Eastbound intersects both the Grand Central Parkway Eastbound and, just a minute later, the Van Wyck Expressway Southbound. Normally, a driver would exit the LIE Eastbound onto the Grand Central Eastbound and then onto the Van Wyck Southbound—however, one could exit from the LIE Eastbound directly onto the Van Wyck Southbound. If this sounds confusing, it's because the Grand Central Parkway makes a big "S" curve as it goes through central Queens. It runs east-west from the Triborough Bridge to LaGuardia, but then it runs north-south from LaGuardia to Kew Gardens and then turns east-west again—just at the point it intersects the Van Wyck Expressway. So, actually the Grand Central (Eastbound) and the Van Wyck (Southbound) run almost parallel from north central Queens until they intersect in Kew Gardens.

Joshua Isaacson is the author of No Time for Tie Ups, *available from Herruth Publishing, PO Box 1140, Bronx, NY 10471,* ☎ *718-549-0728.*

INSPASS

Anything to get you out of lines at International Arrivals has to be considered a good thing, so we thought you might want to know about INSPASS. The Immigration and Naturalization Service, which always has your comfort in mind, instituted a program some time ago for frequent business travelers. The way it works is this: You fill out an application in which you state that you make three or more business trips a year and you've never been a spy, terrorist, or Nazi (among a few other questions), send it in, and wait a long time for the INS to respond. If you qualify, you get a card that allows you to bypass the normal inspection line after you get off an international flight. You go to the INSPASS lane, insert your card, allow the machine to read your hand "geometry," and that's it. You still have to wait for your bag and go through the regular customs process. Currently, while the INSPASS is in its pilot phase, there is no fee. You can get an application (with a lot of patience) by calling ☎ 800-870-3676 or picking up the form (I-833) at International Arrivals at JFK or Newark.

LUGGAGE REPAIR

See Leather in this chapter.

PASSPORTS

NEW: You've never had a passport or not had one within the past 12 years. You must apply in person, fill out the brown form, and bring four things: **1.**) Proof of U.S. citizenship: previous passport or certified birth certificate. "Notification" of birth certificate doesn't cut it. If you have no birth certificate, other records that suggest you exist may be used: baptism or circumcision certificate, hospital birth records, and other personal, school, census, or family Bible records. You also have to bring a "letter of no record" from your state saying that the birth certificate is not on file. Those born in NYC can get a copy of their birth certificate at 125 Worth St. See Licenses, Permits and Certificates in the Information chapter. **2.**) Proof of Identity: Driver's license, previous passport, government I.D., or an identifying witness. (If you bring an identifying witness, that person must have "good primary I.D." and the applicant must bring signature I.D.) **3.**) 2 Photos. Black-and-white or color from the past 6 months. 2 in. × 2 in. in size. **4.**) Fees: $65 for 18 and older, valid for 10 years. $40 for under 18 years, valid for five years.

You can apply at the following post offices: GPO, Eighth Ave. & 33rd St.; Ansonia Station, 40 W. 66th St. [CPW/Columbus]; Church St. Station, 90 Church St. [Barclay/Vesey]; Cooper Station, 93 4th Ave. [11th]; FDR Station, 909 Third Ave. [54th/55th]; Manhattanville Station, 365 W. 125th St. [Manhattan/Morningside]. You can also apply at the New York County Clerk's Office, 60 Centre St. [Pearl/Hamill] ☎ 374-8359.

RENEW: You must have had a passport in the past 12 years and been 18 or older when it was issued. Fill out the pink form. Send in your old passport. You need two photos (see above). The form recommends a "pleasant natural pose." Make out the check for $55, payable to Passport Service. If you are using the U.S. Postal Service, mail to: National Passport Center, PO Box 371971, Pittsburgh, PA 15250-7971. If you are using another mail service (FedEx, etc.), send to: Mellon Bank, Attn: Passport Supervisor, 371971, 3 Mellon Bank Center, Room 153-2723, Pittsburgh, PA 15259-0001. You can take renewals to the post offices listed above and they will "accept them as a courtesy," but it will slow things down. Better to mail them yourself.

RUSH: Normally, the processing time takes 3–4 weeks. If you need to get a new passport or renew in less time, it is possible if you have a plane ticket. Bring it with you and the passport office (in Rockefeller Center) will issue you a passport within the amount of time remaining before your flight, even if it is within 24 hours. There is an additional expedite fee of $30 for every passport issued or renewed in less than 10 days.

LOST OR STOLEN: If your passport is lost or stolen while you're in the U.S., and you need a replacement right away, apply in person with a detailed statement of what happened. You should report the loss on form DSP64. Fill out form DSP 11, bring two photos, your driver's license for I.D., and $65. The State Department treats this as if you are applying for a new passport. If you

lose your passport while you are out of the U.S., you are advised to go to the nearest U.S. embassy or consulate.

TOO BUSY OR LAZY: See Time-Saving Services in the Services chapter.

MORE INFO: Federal Information Center ☎ 800-688-9889; NY Passport Office ☎ 399-5290; State Department ☎ 202-647-4000; National Passport Office ☎ 603-334-0500; Internet home page: http://travel.state.gov (Passport and travel safety information).

SNOW REPORTS
See the Sports chapter.

TRAVEL/MEDICAL ADVICE
For people who do a lot of international traveling, **Travel Health Services,** 50 E. 69th St. [Mad/Park] ☎ 734-3000, may be helpful to know about. It's run by Dr. Bradley A. Connor, a gastroenterologist and an expert in travel medicine. After a consultation, they will provide information on everything from jet lag to malaria, and give advice to people with existing medical conditions such as diabetes or heart disease, as well as to those traveling when pregnant. Travel Health Services administers vaccinations, will sell you a small medical kit to take along, and has a booklet of information on health and travel. You also get access to their network of English-speaking doctors around the world if you get sick.

THE WORLD'S FAIRS

Spend a few minutes looking at photos in one of the books on the New York World's

Fairs and it's easy to understand their allure to collectors, historians, designers, and dreamers. From John Kriskiewicz, who teaches a course on the World's Fairs: "World's Fairs have a hold on the imagination . . . They are a mix of the academic, scientific, and technological and personal nostalgia—this is a powerful cocktail."

1939 The 1939 World's Fair has become synonymous with a kind of optimism and belief in the future not much in vogue today. Its theme was "building the world of tomorrow," and much of the magic of the fair came from the fair's own design principles. These principles evolved from the fair's Board of Design, which governed pavilion design, color, layout, lighting, style, zoning, and so on. It helped frame the fair's vision of the streamlined future—the participation of designers and artists from all fields, including Norman Bel Geddes, Raymond Loewy, Isamu Noguchi, Walter Dorwin Teague, Russell Wright, noted architecture firms, and top talent in many fields infused the sense of that future with genuine wonder.

Some of the more popular attractions: Surely the most striking image was the Trylon and Perisphere. The Perisphere housed, as the guidebook stated, " 'Democracity'— symbol of a perfectly integrated, futuristic  metropolis pulsing with life and rhythm and music." The Futurama ride at the GM pavilion, in which people in seats moved over the enormous scale model of the landscape of 1960, was the hit of the fair. Other popular attractions were the large animated Ford production turntable; Raymond Loewy's streamlined train; the 10-million-volt flash at the GE building; the time capsules buried on the fairgrounds; the Life Savers Parachute Tower; the extremely

A vintage postcard of the DuPont Pavilion at the 1939 World's Fair.

popular and elaborate water shows (with Eleanor Holm) at Billy Rose's Aquacade; and some quite un-P.C. (but well-attended) attractions in the amusement zone, including nude painting and Midget Town.

Behind the scenes, Grover Whalen, one of the prime movers of the '39 Fair, had managed to rustle up 60 international exhibitions and vital corporate participation. But never far from the center of the action was Parks Commissioner Robert Moses, who saw the fair as a means of turning Flushing Meadows into a New World Versailles. After the first season ended in October, it was clear that the fair was not a financial success. In the second year, there was a change of management and tone. It was decidedly more populist, and so the more carnival-like amusement area, given scant attention by the fair's designers, became a focal point. When the fair closed down, though, it had lost money and Moses had to bide his time for the chance to turn the site into a showpiece park.

1964 Robert Moses was chosen to head up the '64 fair and he felt that this fair could avoid the mistakes of the earlier one and provide funding for Flushing Meadows Park, or

"Central Park for the 20th Century" as he said. As Mr. Kriskiewicz points out, though, the '64 fair was "planned during a period of great consensus—the late '50s—then opened in a period of great conflict—the mid-'60s." As Rosemarie Bletter, contributor to *Remembering the Future: The New York World's Fair from 1939 to 1964,* says, there was more distrust and defensiveness as a response to the Atomic Age and a loss of "belief in progress and the future." That accounts, in part, for the fair's less enthusiastic reception by the public and critics.

Another complaint was the lack of a centralized design committee. Moses was opposed to such a committee for the fair, and he got, predictably, a broad range of pavilions and exhibits—some praised, many not. In a much-condemned mix of art, theatre, and religion, the Vatican pavilion showcased Michelangelo's *Pietà,* which was placed in a theatrical (and bullet-proofed) setting by Broadway designer Jo Mielziner. There was also the maligned Illinois pavilion that featured Lincoln reciting some of the Gettysburg Address, courtesy of Disney Audio-Animatronics. On the plus side, the '64 fair had the appealing Unisphere, by Gilmore Clarke, sited where the Trylon and Perisphere stood. (The concept for the general layout of the '39 fair and the plan for Flushing Meadows was also by Mr. Clarke.) There was Saarinen and Eames's IBM egg-shaped pavilion; another Futurama; George P. Nelson's Chrysler pavilion; the Tower of Light pavilion; Bel-Gem waffles; and commission work from Roy Lichtenstein, Andy Warhol, and James Rosenquist. Many visitors singled out the Spanish pavilion as especially memorable, and it won that fair's gold medal for architecture.

WHAT YOU CAN SEE NOW Following a three-year and 15-million-dollar renovation, the Queens Museum (located in the NYC building of both fairs) now houses a permanent exhibition on the fairs called **A Panoramic View.** You will get a history of the site from 17th century Indian grounds; its years as an enormous garbage dump; the '39 fair; the temporary headquarters of the U.N.; the '64 fair through to its current incarnation as Flushing Meadows Corona Park . . . Part of the permanent installation is the spectacular **Panorama of the City of New York,** a scale model of the entire city from the '64 fair that has been upgraded with over 60,000 additions. It was one of the hits of the fair. At that time, you sat in a car and were transported "around the city." Now, no car, just an overview on a walkway that goes around (and, in places where the walkway turns to glass, over) the city. As you watch, the lights go from day to night. The model is huge (it's the largest architectural model in the world), so rent binoculars in the gift shop ($1) . . . There are prettier parks in the city than **Flushing Meadows Corona Park** but not many with as interesting a history. The site was an infamous ash dump (which Fitzgerald described in *The Great Gatsby* as a "valley of ashes—a fantastic farm where ashes grow like wheat into ridges and hills and grotesque gardens"). The land was reclaimed for the '39 fair. Since that fair lost money, ambitious plans for the park were halted. From 1946–1950, Flushing Meadows served as temporary home to the United Nations (during an eventful international time—the birth of Israel, the Korean conflict, the blockade of Berlin). When the '64 fair lost money as well, progress on the park again

The Unisphere.

slowed, but in 1967, Flushing Meadows Corona Park finally became one of the city's parks . . . You can see the recently refurbished **Unisphere,** looking as good as new. It was declared a landmark in 1995, and now sports some dramatic night lighting. The surrounding **fountains,** with 96 spigots that shoot water 22 ft. high, have also been restored and are working. The **reflecting pools** are next on the restoration list . . . Between the Unisphere and the reflecting pools, new **murals** by Matt Mullican have been sandblasted into the pavement. These murals celebrate the site's history, and Mr. Mullican said his view of the Fair as an "allegorical city" is reflected in its design . . . **The Queens Theater** in the park has been refurbished and the **Hall of Science** has gotten a 12-million-dollar overhaul . . . On the grounds, of course, are also **Shea Stadium** and the **National Tennis Center**. The original plan for Flushing Meadows Park had pitch and putt golf—which the park now has . . . You can see the **Fountain of the Planets** . . . If you look through the fence at the NY State Pavilion, you can see some of the floor mosaic, a 144 sq. ft. **map**, provided in '64 by Texaco, of New York state highways. There's a chance this could be repaired . . . Be sure to walk about 300 yards south of the museum to see where the **time capsules** are buried (they contain a "comprehensive cross section of today's civilization" from both fairs. The '64 capsule contained things like a bikini, a Beatles record, freeze-dried foods, a Bible, and graphite from the first nuclear reactor). They are supposed to

be opened in 6938 . . . You can see sculptor Donald Delue's **Rocket Thrower** from '64 and the Jetson-like **benches** from that fair are still in use or have been replaced with the same design . . . The art deco **flagpoles** with the eagles are from '39 . . . The Spanish Pavilion from '64 won much praise for its design. It's now in St. Louis as the base for that city's Marriott Pavilion hotel. The Billy Rose Aquacade is scheduled for demolition in 1996.

A GALLERY R. Anthony Munn is a 3-D photographer with a passion for the two World's Fairs. At his **Depthography Virtual Image Gallery**, 122 E. 27th St. [Park/Lex] ☎ 679-8101, he has a collection of 3-D slides of the fairs that he shows from time to time. Call the gallery to get a schedule. He will also arrange showings for educational and other groups.

A CLASS John Kriskiewicz teaches a course called **A Panoramic View: A Look at NY World's Fairs**, offered every few years at Cooper Union. He also offers walking tours and lectures through the Queens Museum ☎ 718-592-7800.

COLLECTIBLES **Mood Indigo,** 181 Prince St. [Sullivan/Thompson] ☎ 254-1176. The items in Diane Petipas's shop all come from the '30s to the '50s, so the '39 World's Fair falls in her calendar. She has tabletop items, most of which were souvenirs of the exhibitors. The Trylon and Perisphere logo of the fair is on many of the items . . . **Darrow's Fun Antiques,** 1101 First Ave. [60th/61st] ☎ 838-0730, is a narrow, overstuffed shop of antique toys and games. There is a shelf devoted to fair memorabilia . . . **New York**

Bound, 50 Rockefeller Plaza ☎ 245-8503, has some books on the fair, as well as a box of fair ephemera: photos, postcards, and so on . . . Best books to read on the fair: *Remembering the Future* (excellent essays), *Trylon and Perisphere* (exceptional photos and reminiscences of people who attended), *Dawn of a New Day,* and *The NY World's Fair 1939/1940.* Look for books and memorabilia at **The Queens Museum** . . . *The World of Tomorrow,* and how can you resist it with Ethel Merman singing the title song? is a video available at the **Museum of the City of NY** ☎ 534-1672 . . . You might also want to subscribe to *Fair News,* put out by the World's Fair Collectors Society. Write to P.O. Box 20806, Sarasota, FL 34238. There is also a quarterly journal called ***World's Fair.*** Call ☎ 415-924-6035 for more info.

FOOD

BANANAS

You *can't* get everything in New York. This wounds our civic pride, but it's true. You can't buy a bottle of gin on Sunday, you can't play decent miniature golf, and you can't buy Haa Haa bananas.

THE FRUIT

We wondered why, with all the wonderful food shops in the city, there are, at most, only two or three varieties of bananas available. When we asked why they don't carry many kinds of bananas, the fruit manager at Dean & DeLuca told us "there isn't much call for that." In other words, yes, we have no bananas. But we think most people would be surprised at the types (hundreds) of bananas that exist and the differences in flavor, aroma, texture, and appearance. We became intrigued by the names alone, which are quite evocative: **Jamaican red** (beautifully red inside), **Ice cream** (which has the creamy texture and

Bananas!

taste of ice cream), the **Chinese Golden Aromatic** (called Go San Heong, which means "you can smell it from over the next mountain"), and the **Haa Haa.** These are worlds apart from the standard-issue Valery or Grand Nain you find at local stores. Since the exotics are impossible to find in Manhattan stores, here are two growers from whom you can mail order these exotic varieties: **Seaside Banana Garden** ☎ 805-643-4061 in California (in certain seasons, as many as 15 varieties at one time) and **W.O. Lessard Banana Farm** ☎ 305-247-0397 in Florida. They will also send you fascinating (truly) information on the bananas they carry. Mr. Lessard, who has written *The Complete Book of Bananas* (available for $35 plus shipping), offers the better deal of the two: 15 lbs. for $40. Seaside sent us fewer bananas, but 9 varieties as opposed to Mr. Lessard's 4. Lessard ships fruit in summer and early fall, when it's ripe.

MADE WITH BANANAS

Here are some suggestions for dishes with bananas from **Robert Sietsema,** who writes the wonderful newsletter *Down the Hatch.* (*Down the Hatch* can be purchased at Kitchen Arts and Letters, 1435 Lexington Ave. [93rd/94th] ☎ 876-5550.) **Banana pudding** at Mississippi Barbecue, 172–14 Baisley Blvd. [172nd] in Jamaica, Queens, no phone. Open Thu.–Sat., 6:30–11 P.M. only. Old-fashioned southern banana pudding, made with vanilla wafers and topped with browned meringue. Delicious. (Their second location is at 201–05 Murdock Ave. [201st] St. Albans, Queens ☎ 718-776-3446) . . . **Fried green plantain appetizer** at Keur N'Deye, a Senegalese restaurant at 737 Fulton St. [Elliott/Portland], Brooklyn ☎ 718-875-4937. Ask for the homemade hot sauce that's sometimes served with it . . . **Banana batida** (milkshake) at Los Mariachis, a Mexican restaurant serving food from the state of Puebla, located at 805 Coney Island Ave. [Cortelyou/Dorchester], Brooklyn ☎ 718-826-3388 . . . Patio Place, a Jamaican restaurant (quite good) at 593 Flatbush Ave. [Midwood/Rutland], Brooklyn ☎ 718-693-4502, has a breakfast item called **banana porridge,** which is a drink consisting of green banana mashed with hot water. It's thick and delicious.

MUG would add the tart and refreshing **banana lassi** at Indian Cafe, 201 W. 95th St. [Bway/Amsterdam] ☎ 222-1600 . . . Union Square Cafe, 21 E. 16th St. [5th/Union Sq. W.] ☎ 243-4020, serves a warm **banana tart** that has bananas under a thin, crackly, caramel-y crust. On top, USC's own honey vanilla ice cream, underneath, a crème anglaise strewn with bits of macadamia nut brittle. Sweet banana nirvana . . . **Banana ice cream** at Chinatown Ice Cream Factory, 65 Bayard St. [Elizabeth/Bowery] ☎ 608-4170, must be the best around . . . For **banana bread,** we like the very straightforward (and tasty) version served during weekend brunch at Home, 20 Cornelia St. [Bleecker/W. 4th] ☎ 243-9579. They don't officially sell loaves of the bread to take out, but if you call and ask for Jill, she will try to bake an extra loaf. ($6) . . . Dean & DeLuca carries Busha Brown's Jamaican **banana chutney.** $6 for 12 oz. . . . For a **banana daiquiri,** there's Bayamo, 704 Broadway [W. 4th/Washington] ☎ 475-5151.

BARBECUE

For great ribs, you need to travel south and west in the U.S. Closer to home, you need to be heading north or east.

Eastwards, **Stick to Your Ribs,** 5–16 51st Ave. [5th/Vernon], Long Island City, ☎ 718-937-3030, delivers the goods. A different sort of fusion in the culinary world: Robert Pearson, a Brit, makes sensational Texas-style ribs just across the river in Long Island City. Well worth the very short trip there for the pork ribs, pork sandwiches, beef brisket, and an occasional exotic, like rattlesnake.

Almost as far east you can go and still be in Queens is **Mississippi Barbecue,** 172–14 Baisley Blvd. [172nd], no phone, Thu.–Sat., 3–12. Here you get sensational ribs cooked on little round grills next to a small wooden shack at the edge of a field.

It's like taking a trip down South. The ribs are slightly sweet and spicy, with all kinds of sides available: macaroni and cheese, collard greens, candied yams, pigs feet, corn, banana pudding, and lemon icebox cake. A second location is open every day but Monday at 201–05 Murdock Ave. [201st] St. Albans ☎ 718-776-3446. Both places are takeout only.

Up north, Sylvia's, Snooky's, Londel's, and Emily's all make some excellent ribs.

See more in the Harlem article in the Restaurants chapter.

When you want the barbecue to come to you (in a big way), call **Smokin' Joe's True Blue Texas Barbecue** ☎ 718-948-3340. Joe Mizrahi, born in Brooklyn, felt that what New York needed was a 16-foot mobile wood-burning barbecue oven. He will bring his "traditional down home Texas-sized cookout" to your party. A minimum of fifty people. Prices start at $30 per person and up.

BREADS

There are the old bakeries, like D & G, Morrone, and Orwasher's, and the new wave of breadmakers, like Columbus Bakery, Tribakery, Amy's Breads, and Sullivan Street Bakery. In between are some top bakeries, like Tom Cat, Ecce Panis, Bread Alone, and Rock Hill, that haven't been around forever, but long enough to perfect what they do. We did a comparison tasting of some of these breads, but we're not including any of the tasting notes because each entry is some variation of "Wow, great bread." With the preceding list, you can't miss. Here are some specific favorites in various categories.

BAGELS We like our bagels modestly portioned, crusty, and flavorful enough to eat plain right from the store. We have no use for ones that are soft, flabby, elephantine. **Columbia Hot Bagels,** 2836 Broadway [110th] ☎ 222-3200, does a fine job, but our favorite bagels are from **TAL,** 979 First Ave. [53rd] ☎ 753-9080 and at 333 E. 86th St. [1st/2nd] ☎ 427-6811.

BAGUETTES Plenty of good ones to choose from, but we're partial to the ones from

Columbus Bakery, 474 Columbus Ave. [82nd/83rd] ☎ 724-6880. They've got an olive and rosemary version, too.

BIALYS Kossar's Bialystoker Kuchen Bakery, 367 Grand St. [Essex/Norfolk] ☎ 473-4810, has been doing bialys for over 50 years, and they continue to be so good, in part, because they grind fresh onions by hand down in the basement. The bialys are also available at Zabar's.

BISCUITS You won't find a lot of biscuits at the city's bakeries. Fortunately, **The Bread Shop,** 3139 Broadway [123rd] ☎ 666-4343, has the matter well in hand with their buttermilk version and another with cheese on top.

BRIOCHE The appeal of brioche eluded us for a long time—until we tasted the big, rectangular brioche loaf baked at **Ecce Panis,** 1120 Third Ave. [65th/66th] ☎ 535-2099 and 1260 Madison Ave. [90th/91st] ☎ 348-0040. Now we get it. We're still looking, though, for an outstanding brioche à tête (the common brioche shape).

CROISSANTS Is this one category we have to concede to the French? Perhaps it's just not possible to do perfect croissants outside that country. Here are some croissants, though, that don't suffer much by comparison. Our favorites are from **City Bakery,** 22 E. 17th St. [Bway/5th] ☎ 366-1414. We think they're the best in the city . . . There are big, flaky ones at **Lipstick Cafe,** 885 Third Ave. [53rd/54th] ☎ 486-8664; buttery ones at **Ceci Cela,** 55 Spring St.

[Lafayette/Mulberry] ☎ 274-9179; and good ones from **Bonté,** 1316 Third Ave. [75th/76th] ☎ 535-2360.

FOCACCIA Sarah Black's focaccia continues to be our favorite. Her breads are baked at the Tom Cat Bakery in Long Island City and are sold under the name Companio. Try some at **Dean & DeLuca,** 560 Broadway [Prince] ☎ 431-1691; **Positively 104,** 2725 Broadway [104th] ☎ 316-0372; and **Marché**

BREADS THE FOODIES EAT

Gael Greene, *New York* magazine: The bread she has "every day with lunch when I don't go out is Eli's onion ficelle." The one she asked for on her birthday was Amy's olive twist. (There is a party and everyone brings a dish, but "the bread person gets specific instructions.") Ms. Greene likes the nut raisin rolls at Columbus Bakery and "many other things there."

Maury Rubin, City Bakery: A bread he loves is the sourdough pullman from Sullivan Street Bakery. "It's a beautiful shape . . . I love its form and I love ripping it apart . . . I wouldn't take a knife to that thing."

Howard Glickman, Fairway: "Besides Eli's? The whole wheat and white Italian breads from D & G. It's not a fancy bread . . . it's a basic, wholesome bread, reasonably priced . . . still made in a brick oven."

Chip Fisher, Lamalle Kitchenware and Mr. Chips: Mr. Fisher likes Orwasher's cinnamon raisin and Eli Zabar's seven grain bread and rolls, which he calls "the best rolls around."

Fred Ferretti, *Gourmet:* Mr. Ferretti is partial to Tom Cat bread and the regular round Italian loaf from Zito's. He buys "all the time" at Trio, 476 Ninth Ave. [36th/37th] ☎ 695-4296, waits for the

bread to get stale, cuts it thin and bakes it in the oven until it gets hard. "I'm partial to any bread that has a crust that is almost two inches thick."

Ed Levine, *New York Eats:* Another vote for the olive twist at Amy's; "Ecce Panis, of course," and Bruno's, 506 LaGuardia Pl. [Bleecker/Houston] ☎ 982-5854, which makes their bread in Brooklyn. They have one that is softly Tuscan, a crusty sourdough that is good, peasant-y bread." Mr. Levine says that Georgie's Pastry Shop, 50 W. 125th St. [5th/Lenox] ☎ 831-0722, makes "phenomenal" Parker House rolls, "too labor intensive for many other bakers to make. I'm currently in love with the Portuguese rolls from Viera's in Newark that are sold in the West Side Supermarket, 2171 Broadway [76th/77th] ☎ 595-2536. They are slightly airy, have a nice, crusty texture without being too hard, and Robert Pearson uses them for his barbecue at Stick to Your Ribs."

Eric Asimov, *New York Times:* Mr. Asimov says he likes the brick oven bread from Policastro in NJ (available at Dean & DeLuca), Tom Cat, Ecce Panis, "of course there's Zito's," where he thinks the Italian and wheat are good, but the prosciutto bread is what he really likes.

Madison, 931 Madison Ave. [74th] ☎ 794-3360 and 36 E. 58th St. [Mad] ☎ 355-3366. Marché is the only retail place in town to carry her ciabatta panini rolls—they show up in the late afternoon, just in time for supper.

FRENCH Soutine, 104 W. 70th St. [Bway/Columbus] ☎ 496-1450, does many things well, but we're particularly enamored of their French bread. With some good olive oil and fresh herbs, it's a perfect light meal.

ITALIAN BREAD Though the old Italian neighborhood has changed around **Morrone & Sons,** 324 E. 116th St. [1st/2nd] ☎ 722-2972, the bakery remains a beloved institution. One former neighbor remembers that going to Morrone, located below street level, was called "going down the hole." ("I'm going down the hole—you want to walk me?") Their breads are available at **Balducci's.** Also, **D & G,** 45 Spring St. [Mulberry/Mott] ☎ 226-6688; **Zito's Bakery,** 259 Bleecker St. [6th/7th] ☎ 929-6139; and **Vesuvio,** 160 Prince St. [Thompson/W. Bway] ☎ 925-8248.

ONION BREADS **Morrone** makes great onion rolls, and we're also crazy about **Ecce Panis**'s onion stick, which has long strands of onion topped with a liberal dusting of Parmesan—it couldn't be more delicious.

OLIVE BREAD Amy of **Amy's Breads,** 672 Ninth Ave. [46th/47th] ☎ 977-2670, is Amy Scherber, and we dote on two of her breads. One is the olive bread (see Gael Greene's view in the sidebar) and the other is the semolina raisin and fennel.

PROSCIUTTO BREAD At **D & G,** the prosciutto bread and the provolone bread, well-known favorites here, are as good as ever.

PUMPERNICKEL Orwasher's, 308 E. 78th St. [1st/2nd] ☎ 288-6569, has been baking breads for New Yorkers since 1916. These include several excellent pumpernickels—we like the dark better than the light, and the one with raisins most of all.

RYE Orwasher's, again, bakes first-rate rye bread. **Burke & Burke**'s rye is also fine—unusual in that it contains cumin seeds in addition to the caraway.

SODA BREAD The **Traditional Irish Bakery,** 3120 Bainbridge Ave. [205th/206th] ☎ 718-547-4174, in the Bronx, makes a classic soda bread studded with big, plump raisins. They're also in Woodside, Queens, at 61-10, Woodside Ave. [61st] ☎ 718-565-7492.

SCONES Olives, 120 Prince St. [Wooster/Greene] ☎ 941-0111, has wonderful, lighter-than-the-usual scones, most often with cranberry, once in a while with currants.

SEMOLINA Amy's Breads makes a semolina with raisins and fennel that is hugely and deservedly popular. Ours often doesn't make it home.

SEVEN GRAIN Bread Alone, available at the Union Square Market (Wed. and Fri.), Zabar's, Balducci's, and both Fairways, does our favorite seven grain. It's made with honey, and it's so moist and tasty that you'll never think it could be good for you.

SOURDOUGH For a long time we wouldn't eat anything but **Tom Cat** sourdough (available at Grace's, Balducci's, and Dean & DeLuca, among many others). We still think it's wonderful, but **Bread Alone's San Francisco** loaf may be the best sourdough available in the city. We also like **Rock Hill**'s, available at the Union Square Market (Sat.) and would eat the pugliese and the pullman from **Sullivan St. Bakery,** 73 Sullivan St. [Spring /Broome] ☎ 334-9435, any day with pleasure.

WHITE There are no tricks to **D&G**'s white bread, but it's good enough to give white bread a good name.

ZAHTAR Damascus Bakery of Brooklyn was started in 1930 by Hassan Halaby, who had emigrated from Syria and who the company says introduced pita to America. Today, his grandson, David Mafoud, is running the company, and they continue to sell their pita bread all over the country. It's their zahtar, though, that we find completely irresistible. It's a circular, soft, flatbread flavored with zahtar (thyme), sesame, and a little vinegar. It's available at **Damascus Bakery,** 195 Atlantic Ave. [Court] in Brooklyn ☎ 718-855-1456, many supermarkets, and most of the gourmet shops.

BUTTER & EGGS

BUTTER

We did a little side-by-side comparison of some of the better butters available in the gourmet shops. **Plugrá** is the butter widely used by chefs and bakers because it has an 82% butterfat content, rather than the usual 80%. That doesn't sound like much of a difference, but you can certainly taste the difference. In addition, there's less water content in it and top-quality cream has been used. Plugrá is unbeatable . . . **Celles sur Belle** is, as one chef said to us of this bright yellow butter, "perfect for putting on bread and it smells great." . . . **Egg Farm Dairy** also makes a quality butter. All these butters are available at Balducci's and many other of the gourmet stores . . . The Vinegar Factory and Gourmet Garage make their own butter, good for everyday use.

EGGS

Fresh eggs from **Knoll Krest Farm** are courtesy of chickens that have been floor-raised. They're hormone-free, and their feed has no additives or any artificial substances. Look for the eggs at the Union Square Market on Wednesdays and Saturdays. You get the eggs within a couple of days of their being laid. They're also available at Gentile Brothers, 1045 Madison Ave. [79th/80th] ☎ 879-2717, and Simchick Meats, 944 First Ave. [52nd] ☎ 888-2299.

CHEESE

Here are some of the best and most unusual cheeses from the city's cheese purveyors.

We've left out many of the big names (Explorateur, Livarot, Reblochon), but think any combination of the cheeses described would make a great cheese plate. Where would we buy? Most of the following stores offer good selection and quality, but we think Murray's, Dean & DeLuca, and Ideal do it best.

Agata and Valentina, 1505 First Ave. [79th] ☎ 452-0690, has a decent selection of cheeses, and most of the big names: a Fiore de Sardegna, the mild Sardinian cheese; a six-year-old Gouda (Gouda is a common cheese, but when it's aged see how uncommonly good it can be—this one has a wonderful sherry flavor); and a farmhouse Brie.

The emphasis at **Balducci's,** 424 Sixth Ave. [9th/10th] ☎ 673-2600, is on French cheeses, with a big selection of goat cheeses. We are partial, though, to their domestic offerings. They carry several of the Egg Farm Dairy cheeses, including the mild and buttery cow's milk Muscoot. The Blue Goat from Illinois is excellent, with a slightly sweet first taste followed by a swift kick from the goat. From Washington State, Sally Jackson's aged sheep's milk is even better. It has a strong barnyard flavor and smell, with a smooth consistency.

Dean & DeLuca, 560 Broadway [Prince] ☎ 431-1691. Not the biggest selection in town, but certainly choice. D & D has about 150 cheeses at any one time, and one of their specialties is English farmhouse cheese, mostly from Neal's Yard. Jon Strober, their buyer, says, "It's hard to get unpasteurized milk cheeses, especially in goat and sheep, so whenever we find them we take them." Keen's Farmhouse cheddar is an unpasteurized cheddar. Kirkham's Lancashire is a "buttery, crumbly cheddar that's a good melting cheese and good for Welsh rarebit." Benleigh Blue is a limited-supply sheep milk cheese from England. Birkswell (sheep) "is a hard,

very nutty, and a little fruity cheese with an aged Gouda-like texture and an aged pecorino-like taste." They have Irish farmhouse cheeses, including Gubeen (cow's milk) and Croghan (goat's milk). Croghan is "a semi-soft cheese with a washed rind. It's a good table cheese and is nice with crusty bread and fruit, like pears or apples." Dean & DeLuca does well with domestic cheesemakers. Mr. Strober says, "Cheesemakers are popping up all over the U.S." They carry the Vermont Shepherd, a slightly sandy, earthy cheese that we like, and Sally Wienenger's goat cheese from Hunter Mountain, NY. You can also find Sally Jackson's superb goat and sheep cheeses from Oroville, Washington. Westfield Farms in Massachusetts sends some "very goaty, but rich and creamy" fresh goat cheeses as well as a soft and rich goat blue. D & D sells Crowley cheese from Vermont. Crowley is the oldest cheese producer in the country (the Crowleys were making cheese in their barn in 1824), and the cheese, technically a Colby, is usually just called Crowley cheese. That's because it's full of flavor, unlike most Colbys.

DiPalo, 206 Grand St. [Mott] ☎ 226-1033. Louis DiPalo goes to Italy every two years or so to pick out the Parmesan cheeses he will offer at DiPalo's in Little Italy. They bring in fresh sheep's milk ricotta from Rome, which is mild, light in color, and doesn't taste salty. But the pride of place here belongs to the aged Parmesans. It is now possible to get the Invernigno, made from the winter milk. They are lighter in color, sweeter, more delicate, have less fat and less bite than other Parmesans. They're at peak between 2 and 2 1/2 yrs., and DiPalo usually sells the batch that is ready by the end of March each year. They make their own "fresh dairy," i.e., their own mozzarella, which has a lovely, delicate milk flavor. They are incredibly nice here.

Fairway, 2127 Broadway [74th/75th] ☎ 595-1888. Cheese is no longer the star of the Fairway show, but you can still find many good offerings. They don't carry many farmhouse or artisanal cheeses, but they do have the Capriole Banon, a fine goat's milk cheese wrapped in chestnut leaves that have been soaked in brandy. They also sell Teleme, the wonderful, mild, California cheese, something like a Monterey Jack, with a hint of caramel flavor.

Gourmet Garage, 453 Broome St. [Mercer] ☎ 941-5850, was the first to carry Wabash Cannonball, a goat cheese from the Capriole Farms in Indiana. This is an alarming-looking cheese, a small lobe of blue and white rivulets. But it is sensational, with a first taste something like an eau de vie, which then softens into a pungent cream. It was named "Best Cheese Made in America" in 1995 by the American Cheese Society. Gourmet Garage has a good but inexpensive sharp raw milk cheddar made for them. The Garage has no cheese counter, though— everything is precut or prewrapped.

Grace's Marketplace, 1237 Third Ave. [71st] ☎ 737-0600. Look especially among their 200 or so cheeses for the Italian cheeses from La Bottera ("The Cottage"). These are limited-production cheeses made to order. The Tuma is a name for the shape, about the size of a Camembert, but in texture is more like a Muenster. Made from cow's milk, they come plain or seasoned with truffles or red pepper. The Murazzano is a fresh sheep's milk cheese, semisoft with a natural rind and natural mold, which is a little sharp. El Caprino del Piemonte (goat milk), also from La Bottera, comes plain or flavored with mushrooms, olives, or peppers. Bianco Sot-

tobosco is made from cow and goat and is a cylinder seasoned with truffles. They carry the Colston Basset Stilton from Neal's Yard, a top Stilton.

Ideal Cheese, 1205 Second Ave. [63rd/64th] ☎ 688-7579. When you taste the Brie de Meaux at Edward Edelman's store (changes in the law now allow Brie de Meaux to come in), you understand why Brie became popular in the first place. It's completely unlike the ubiquitous rubbery and tasteless Bries you mostly encounter. Ideal carries the real (as opposed to the French) Vacherin Mont d'Or from Switzerland, which had been unavailable since 1987 (a problem with organisms has been solved). It's a seductive mix of creaminess and woody flavor.

Joe's Dairy, 156 Sullivan St. [Houston/Prince] ☎ 677-8780. Joe Campanelli makes fresh mozzarella every day the store is open. He's not permitted to make the curd in the city, so that comes from elsewhere. He makes his first batch about 8:30 in the morning and continues until six at night. It takes him about ten minutes to make a 35-lb. batch. There's no recipe, just "knowledge and the feel of the hand." Fresh, smoked, in a roll with prosciutto, in a roll with roasted peppers and capicolla, and marinated bocconcini. Their mozzarella is extraordinary.

It's easy to pick well at **Murray's,** 257 Bleecker St. [Cornelia] ☎ 243-3289, since they have already done so. At any one time there are likely to be 150 cheeses in the store. The Pavé d'Affinois, a double crème from the Ile de France, ripened by cheese master Chantal Plasse, is heavenly. When you see her name on a cheese, buy it. The Foglia di Noce, from a single farmer in Italy, is a leaf-wrapped pecorino. Duckett's Caerphilly, a Neal's Yard cheese, gives you a clear idea why Caerphilly was a staple of Welsh miners. We can never get enough Cheshire, and the raw milk Appleby's Cheshire is everything you want from that great cheese.

People's Gourmet, 198 Eighth Ave. [20th] ☎ 691-3948. A nice selection, including many domestic cheddars. People's carries some Spanish cheeses, among them the sheep's milk favorite, Manchego. They also have Iberico, another hard cheese that is light and buttery, slightly fruity, and the salty Cabrales—a Spanish blue that mixes all three milks.

At **Russo's Mozzarella & Pasta,** 344 E. 11th St. [1st/2nd] ☎ 254-7452, Jack Russo makes 150 lbs. of fresh mozzarella each day and "anywhere from 200–500 lbs. a day during the holidays." Fresh, salted, smoked, marinated bocconcini (bite-sized) and ciliegine (cherry-sized), sometimes braids, rolls with prosciutto, sundried tomatoes, and sometimes they put cherry tomatoes in it.

Somewhere in the neighborhood of 300 cheeses are available at **The Vinegar Factory,** 431 E. 91st St. [1st/York] ☎ 987-0885. You can do well here, but it's not our favorite place to buy cheese since everything is precut and wrapped.

Zabar's, 2245 Broadway [80th/81st] ☎ 787-2000. Zabar's carries three of the Peekskill Egg Farm Dairy cheeses: the Muscoot, the Hollis, which they describe as similar to a Limburger without so much aroma (we'd say without so much flavor as well), and the Amelia, a goat cheese made in Portugal, which Egg Farm ripens. You can get cheese from Louisiana, including the strong-smelling Catahoula, a raw cow's milk from Chicory Farm. Zabar's has a cheese called Malvern, which is made from ewe's milk. They fly in fromage blanc from France with 0%, 20%, and 40% fat.

CHEESE COURSES

Some of the city's restaurants that regularly offer a cheese course:

Chanterelle, 2 Harrison St. [Greenwich/Hudson] ☎ 966-6960 . . . **Gramercy Tavern,** 42 E. 20th St. [Bway/Park Ave. S.] ☎ 477-0777 . . . **Il Buco,** 47 Bond St. [Bowery/Lafayette] ☎ 533-1932 . . . **Mad.61,** 10 E. 61st St. [5th/Mad] ☎ 833-2200, offers several plates, including one called "England" with Colston Basset Stilton, Appleby, Cheshire, Somerset Cheddar, and another of Spanish cheese. They have a small retail cheese counter as well . . . **Picholine,** 35 W. 64th St. [Bway/CPW] ☎ 724-8585. Picholine is the only restaurant in the country to have its own cheese cave. They have a selection of 30 cheeses at any one time from a separate cheese menu. Spanish, Italian, French, and American cheeses are available.

MORE You can't write about cheese in NY without talking to Steve Jenkins, who put Fairway's cheese department on the map and then worked as a consultant to some of the other gourmet shops in town. He doesn't do much cheese consulting anymore, because the cheese departments that were set up in stores like Fairway some years ago now can run on their own. The importers will offer the supply to anyone, and there is no more exclusivity to stores. We are in "a situation of demand." Americans who have traveled want to "re-create the situation where they were at the source. Cheese fills the bill. Once people have done any traveling at all they understand what the cheese should taste like and want to have that experience."

"There is interest in artisanal cheeses made in America and elsewhere." Of these, he particularly likes Sally Jackson's from Washington State, Cindy Major's sheep cheeses from Vermont, and Lettie Kill-moyer's goat cheeses from Hubbardston, MA. France and Spain are producing many artisanal cheeses; Italy is lagging behind.

The fact that we can't import cheese made from unpasteurized milk "prevents us from having soft, ripened cheeses like Camembert and Brie. You can buy Roucoulon (French for warbler), which tastes like real Camembert. It is made from a new process that adds back the bacteria to the curd after pasteurization." The bacteria puts the flavor back in. The 60-day rule (FDA regulation says a cheese has to be aged 60 days if it is made from unpasteurized milk before it can enter

the country) prevents us from getting some goat cheeses, and we don't get the washed rind cheeses like Époisses. ("Ones here are phony.") Brie de Meaux is made from raw milk and boxes are not marked "Brie." They are marked "fromage de Meaux"—a trademark given before the appellation was granted. Only three factories in France are now making Brie in the traditional way. Three "acceptable brands of pasteurized Brie" are Hutan, Ermitage, and Vitelloise.

With cheese, "you can judge a book by its cover. A good cheese should have a rustic rind, rough texture, be neutral-colored, and have a mottled appearance. The more colorful the less good. No paraffin, no plastic around it."

COFFEEHOUSES

Here are a few old-time coffeehouses that have a dance in the old dame yet. The following are selected because they've stood the test of time and because they pass the coffee house test: eat and drink as little as you want, stay as long as you want. (Veniero's, has, on occasion, been known to break this rule.)

Caffè Roma, 385 Broome St. [Mulberry] ☎ 226-8413, established in 1891, makes everything they sell. It really is pretty in here, with the dark green walls, pressed tin ceiling, and pendulum clock at the back. Good cappuccino, coffee for real coffee lovers. The rum babas are a special treat—the secret is they use baker's Jamaican rum and old-fashioned yeast they get from Budweiser. Definitely the powerhouse rum baba of New York. Excellent ricotta cheesecake, too.

De Robertis, 176 First Ave. [10th/11th] ☎ 674-7137, has been here since 1904 and also in the same family (John De Robertis is the current proprietor). It's brighter than most of the other coffeehouses and dotted with photos charting the history of the place. They serve a full range of Italian pastries, biscotti, and cakes. We like the fig tarts a lot and the strong, rich, slightly bitter coffee. We also like the mix of people that the neighborhood brings, and that they're happy for you to sit there forever and talk (though there is a sign asking you not to lie across booths). The baking is done on premises by six bakers.

The Peacock Caffè, 24 Greenwich Ave. [6th/7th] ☎ 242-9395, established in 1946 and located originally on W. 4th Street, claims to be the first Florentine coffee shop in NYC. Everything is just where it was the last time you were there. And it's just as dark—all tans and browns—including the brown ceramic floor. There are still the heavy carved wooden tables and pews along the wall to sit in, the stained glass peacock over the coffee machine, and classical music playing. The menu says the cappuccino is made with espresso, and they mean it. They do all their own baking and their signature cakes are the Venetian chocolate rum delight and the Florentine apple torte. The owner says you come with your friends and stay as long as you want, and they promise not to "bowl you over with new ideas." Light meals are available.

Veniero's, 342 E. 11th St. [1st/2nd] ☎ 674-7264. Established in 1894, Veniero's

(of the coffeehouses listed) has the biggest variety of pastries, all of which are baked on the premises. They also supply pastry to many other specialty stores and coffee shops. The owner especially recommends the chocolate mousse cake, and they make their own gelato.

Caffé Dante, 81 MacDougal St. [Bleecker/Houston] ☎ 982-5275, has been around since 1915, and while they get most of their baked goods from Veniero's, they do make excellent cappuccino and espresso. We'd fix the choice of music, though (one day "The Sound of Music"—not exactly ideal coffeehouse listening).

COOKING CLASSES

See the Cooking article in the Learning chapter. You can also check the bulletin board at

Kitchen Arts and Letters—see more on the store in this chapter.

ETHNIC SOURCES

ASIAN

Asia Market Corp., 71 1/2 Mulberry St. [Canal/Bayard] ☎ 962-2028
Kelley and Ping, 127 Greene St. [Houston/Prince] ☎ 228-1212

CHINESE

Kam Man Food Products, 200 Canal St. [Mulberry/Mott] ☎ 571-0330

DUTCH

Chocolada, 125 Second Ave. [St. Marks/7th] ☎ 533-2133

GERMAN

Schaller & Weber, 1654 Second Ave. [85th/86th] ☎ 879-3047

GREEK AND MEDITERRANEAN

International Grocery, 529 Ninth Ave. [39th/40th] ☎ 279-5514
Ninth Avenue Cheese Market, 615 Ninth Ave. [43rd/44th] ☎ 397-4700

INDIAN

Foods of India, 121 Lexington Ave. [28th/29th] ☎ 683-4419
Kalustyan's, 123 Lexington Ave. [28th/29th] ☎ 685-3451
Patel Brothers, 37–46 74 St. [37th] Jackson Heights ☎ 718-898-3445

INDONESIAN

Udom, 81 Bayard St. [Mulberry/Mott] ☎ 349-7662

IRANIAN
Iran Super, 1729 Second Ave.
[89th/90th] ☎ 348-8080
Nader International Food, 1 E. 28th St.
[5th/Mad] ☎ 686-5793

IRISH
Traditional Irish Foods,
3120 Bainbridge Ave. [205th/206th]
the Bronx ☎ 718-547-4174 and
4268 Katonah Ave. [235th]
☎ 718-994-0846
Kircher's Colonial Market, 1711 Second
Ave. [88th/89th] ☎ 722-4004

JAPANESE
Katagiri, 224 E. 59th St.
[2nd/3rd] ☎ 755-3566

JEWISH
Murray's Sturgeon, 2429 Broadway
[89th/90th] ☎ 724-2650
Barney Greengrass, 541 Amsterdam Ave.
[86th/87th] ☎ 724-4707

KOREAN
Han Ah Rheum, 25 W. 32nd St.
[Bway/5th] ☎ 695-3283

MEXICAN
Stop 1, 210 W. 94th St.
[Amsterdam/Bway] ☎ 864-9456
Kitchen Market, 218 Eighth Ave.
[21st/22nd] ☎ 243-4433
Mi Mexico Pequeno, 157 Allen St.
[Stanton/Rivington] ☎ 254-4914

Las Poblanitas, 78-03 Roosevelt Ave.
[78th/79th] Jackson Heights
☎ 718-672-7114

POLISH
First Avenue Pierogi & Deli, 130 First
Ave. [9th/10th] ☎ 420-9690
Kurowycky Meats, 124 First Ave.
[St. Marks/7th] ☎ 477-0344

RUSSIAN
White Acacia, 679 Coney Island Ave.
[Cortelyou/Ave. C] ☎ 718-284-5393

SCANDINAVIAN
Nordic Delicacies, 6909 Third Ave.
[Bay Ridge], Brooklyn ☎ 718-748-1874

SOUTH AMERICAN
Los Paisanos, 79-16 Roosevelt Ave., Jackson Heights ☎ 718-898-4141

THAI
Bangkok Center Market, 104 Mosco St.
[Mott] ☎ 349-1979
Udom, 81 Bayard St. [Mulberry/Mott]
☎ 349-7662

VIETNAMESE
Tan Al Hoa Supermarket, 81 Bowery
[Hester/Canal] ☎ 219-0893

See also Herbs and Spices in this chapter.

FISH

LOWER MANHATTAN/CHINATOWN
AEG Seafood, 206 Centre St.
[Hester/Howard] ☎ 966-6299

Hong Keung Seafood and Meat Market,
75 Mulberry St.
[Canal/Bayard] ☎ 267-6961

TRIBECA
Petrosino & Sons, 161 Duane St.
[Hudson] ☎ 732-8131

SOHO/LITTLE ITALY
Aquasource, 101 Crosby St.
[Prince/Spring] ☎ 343-2548
Dean & DeLuca, 560 Broadway
[Prince] ☎ 431-1691

WEST VILLAGE
Balducci's, 424 Sixth Ave.
[9th/10th] ☎ 673-2600
Jefferson Market, 450 Sixth Ave.
[10th/11th] ☎ 533-3377

GRAMERCY/UNION SQUARE
Catch 21, 31 E. 21st St.
[Bway/Park Ave S.] ☎ 475-8770

MIDTOWN WEST
Central Fish, 527 Ninth Ave.
[39th/40th] ☎ 279-2317

MIDTOWN EAST
Pisacane, 940 First Ave.
[51st/52nd] ☎ 752-7560

UPPER WEST SIDE
Barney Greengrass, 541 Amsterdam Ave.
[86th/87th] ☎ 724-4707
Best Fish Market, 2510 Broadway
[93rd/94th] ☎ 866-5800
Citarella, 2135 Broadway
[74th/75th] ☎ 874-0383
Jake's, 2425 Broadway
[89th] ☎ 580-5253
Murray's Sturgeon, 2429 Broadway
[89th/90th] ☎ 724-2650

UPPER EAST SIDE
Holland Court, 1423 Lexington Ave.
[93rd] ☎ 289-8490
Leonard's, 1241 Third Ave.
[71st/72nd] ☎ 744-2600
Rosedale, 1129 Lexington Ave.
[78th/79th] ☎ 288-5013
Catalano's at the Vinegar Factory,
431 E. 91st St.
[1st/York] ☎ 987-0885

HARLEM
Fairway, 132nd St. and 12th Ave.
☎ 234-3883

FLAVORS

At **Flavors,** 8 W. 18th St. [5th/6th] ☎ 647-1234, they call their salad bar a "market table" but, as far as we're concerned, it's a salad bar and the best one in New York. (If you're looking for a market table, it's the best one of those, too.) This place, primarily takeout, was started in January 1994 by Pamela Morgan. Ms. Morgan, who continues to run the catering company that spawned Flavors, is making some *really* tasty and flavorful food. Hard to go wrong at the salad bar: They do a lot of different beans, almost always slightly underdone, which would surely convert bean-haters. We like the white beans with oregano, the spicy black bean salad, and you'll probably agree that chickpeas (with a Moroccan dressing) never tasted this good. The pastas are excellent, but change all the time, so it's difficult to recommend any in particular. Unlike most salad bars, the Caesar salad here needs no apologies. Try their Mediterranean grilled chicken salad with capers, thyme, and little strings of lemon peel. If this is too healthy-sounding, indulge in the ham and cheddar tarte. The noodles here, soba or cold sesame, are completely satisfying and whatever potatoes they're serving, don't miss them (the ones with bacon are deliriously good). In fact, they also have a potato bar, where you can get a hot baked potato and add a number of toppings. In the area where hot food is served, you get great mashed potatoes. The salad bar is $6.95/lb., and Flavors also has prepared sandwiches and other goodies. Most of their business is to go, but you can eat here at the few tables in the front.

FOIE GRAS, PÂTÉ, CHOPPED LIVER

FOIE GRAS

BLOC DE FOIE GRAS

For top-quality foie gras, **Petrossian,** 182 W. 58th St. [7th] ☎ 245-2217, has foie gras that is creamy, subtle, flavorful, rich (and rich you must be): It's $154/lb. with truffles, $122/lb. without . . . Next best, **Dean & DeLuca,** 560 Broadway [Prince] ☎ 221-7714, has a demi-cuit goose foie gras without truffles, $94/lb., that isn't assertive but it's got all the foie gras flavor you could want, with a hint of vinegar . . . For a more intense, earthier flavor, try the D'Artagnan, $80/lb. at **Balducci's,** 424 Sixth Ave. [9th/10th] ☎ 673-2600 . . . With a couple of days notice, you can get a terrine de foie gras from the restaurant **C.T.,** 111 E. 22nd St. [Park/Lex] ☎ 998-8500. It's $130/lb.

MOUSSE DE FOIE GRAS

The mousse of duck foie gras from D'Artagnan, a much more affordable $28.80 for 8.5 ounces, is not quite the same thing as a having bloc de foie gras, but it is a great value (and even better when you pay $16.95 for it at Gourmet Garage). It has the forward taste of foie gras and a creamier consistency, but lacks in nuance.

FRESH FOIE GRAS

When you want fresh foie gras, you'll do well with D'Artagnan duck foie gras, which comes from Hudson Valley Farms. It can be ordered directly from D'Artagnan, ☎ 800-327-8246, or by having Balducci's special-order it for you. It is $45/lb., and each one is approximately 1 1/2 lbs. . . . Urbani brings in fresh shrink-wrapped goose and duck foie gras from Bizac, France, when they can get it. It's available at **Terramare,** 22 E. 65th St. [5th/Mad] ☎ 717-5020. Goose is approximately $65/lb. and duck is $63/lb.

PÂTÉ

Not many places these days make their own pâté. It's too labor-intensive for a product that is currently out of favor. You'll find the excellent quality pâtés from D'Artagnan at most of the city's better food shops. Dean & DeLuca makes one pâté in house—salmon and dill . . . For delightful, country-style, homemade-tasting pâtés, go to **Chez Bernard,** 323 W. Broadway [Canal/Grand] ☎ 343-2583.

CHOPPED LIVER

Russ and Daughters, 179 E. Houston St. [Orchard/Allen] ☎ 475-4880, makes smooth and pleasant chopped liver. Down the street at **Katz's Delicatessen,** 205 E. Houston St. [Ludlow] ☎ 254-2246, they make chopped liver that is sweeter, more moist, and chunky with eggs . . . We have two favorite chopped liver sources. One is at **Second Avenue Deli,** 156 Second Ave. [10th] ☎ 677-0606, where they really chop it, unlike places that grind because it's faster. It's creamy, rich, and delicious. At **Barney**

Greengrass, 541 Amsterdam Ave. [86th/87th] ☎ 724-4707, it's a light-colored mash of liver, pieces of egg, and marinated onions. It's great chopped liver.

FOOD DELIVERY

CAVIAR We hop on the subway for just about anything, but for caviar it just won't do. Let **Petrossian,** ☎ 245-2217, deliver to your door. It's an extra $12.50 weekdays with a surcharge of $25 for weekend delivery (and you must notify them by Friday afternoon for weekend service) . . . **Caviarteria,** ☎ 759-7410, will also deliver on weekdays (only) with a $10 delivery charge.

DESSERT Rugelach, brownies, cakes, ice cream, and other goodies are just a phone call away from **Dessert Delivery** ☎ 838-5411. $6 minimum, delivery is $10 . . . A lot of people are partial to **Eileen's Cheesecake.** Delivery is $5. No delivery on weekends. Call ☎ 966-5585.

FRUIT Spectacular fruit is available from **Manhattan Fruitier,** ☎ 686-0404, for $50 a basket and up. There are other choices that include dried fruit, chocolates, and so on. $10 delivery charge in Manhattan.

MEALS You can get home delivery from about 50 of Manhattan's restaurants, including La Côte Basque, Arcadia, Akbar, China Grill, and March, by calling **Dial-a-Dinner** ☎ 779-1222. They charge 20% over the menu price. Call them for a catalog . . . **Private Foods,** ☎ 334-6169, offers healthy

food delivered to the home. Richard Markstein, one of the principals, started Nosmo King and moved on to this service. You can have things like free-range chicken with turnips and leeks, vegetable tofu lasagna, and red snapper with ginger, lime, and miso.

MILK **Milkman** is a service from Mitchell Newspapers that delivers Elmhurst Dairy, Lactaid, and Juniper Valley organic milk as well as the *New York Times.* They service the East and West Sides to about 100th St. twice each week and are there before 7 A.M. You can also get juices, colas, Snapple, and waters. No minimum. ☎ 279-6455.

ORGANIC **Herban Kitchen,** ☎ 627-2257, will send you prepared meals, organic produce and/or groceries. Each week there is a new menu, which has about 10 choices for prepared meals (peppers stuffed with couscous or Kentucky un-fried free-range chicken with mashed potatoes), from which you choose five. Soup and salad comes with the meals. An assortment of five vegetarian meals (fish and poultry are also available) for one person costs $60. As far as produce goes, you choose what you want from the approximately 35 items on the list. They can bring you Organic Cow of Vermont milk, fresh eggs and organic sourdough bread, olive oils, juices, and cereals. There is a $5 delivery charge for Manhattan below 96th St., slightly higher for other areas, and they deliver in the evening . . . Organic Meals from **Inside Out.** Lucienne de Mestre sends out boxes once a week containing five meals. You can have one- to three-course boxes. All foods used are certified organic, and your meals can contain meat, fish, and poultry, or be wheat-, dairy-, yeast-, and pepper-free. They also have weekly fruit and vegetable boxes should you want to do your own cooking. Boxes start at $31.50. Once you are receiving a box, you can order from a large array of other organic and health-related products. Delivery in Manhattan is Tuesday evening from 6 P.M. to 10 P.M. ☎ 800-394-6655 . . . **Urban Organic,** ☎ 718-499-4321, delivers boxed assortments of fruit and vegetables once a week. Each box contains between 16 and 22 fruits and veggies (there are always carrots, potatoes, a leafy green salad vegetable and a leafy green cooking vegetable, apples, bananas, oranges, and grapefruits). The remainder of the items are what's fresh and available in the market. Three different-sized boxes (1–2 people, $27; 2–4 people, $37; and family, $52), and there is no delivery charge in Manhattan and Brooklyn. Dietary restrictions are kept on file and taken into account when they are making up your box. Deliveries are in the evening between 4 and 10. Also available is a complete line of healthy groceries and dairy products.

WATER We'll never forget the time we were visiting L.A. and asked our friend's mother for a glass of water. Mom: "Oh, I'm sorry, but the Sparklers man hasn't come yet this week." We settled, of course, for the healthier alternative: a can of Tab. New Yorkers can wait for their own water delivery courtesy of **Dream Beverages,** ☎ 718-655-5200, which delivers an intriguing variety of sparkling and still waters at no charge to your door (or office), with a $50 minimum. They also carry Snapple beverages: 24 16-oz. bottles for $18.

GREENMARKETS

The Greenmarkets are made up of 220 farmers, bakers, and fishermen who sell directly to you. Except for fishermen, who must catch part, but not all, of their fish, the farmers and bakers must have grown, raised, or otherwise produced all of their goods themselves. The perishable produce must be picked 24 hours or less before they sell it. (This doesn't apply to root crops or apples.) Most of the markets are open from 8–3, but there is a certain amount of latitude here. Go early.

Bowling Green [Bway/Battery Pl.]. Thursdays, July–Oct.
World Trade Center [Church/Fulton]. Tuesdays, June–Nov. Thursdays, all year
City Hall [Chambers/Centre]. Tuesdays, all year. Fridays, all year

Washington Market Park [Greenwich/ Reade]. Saturdays, all year
Federal Plaza [Bway/Thomas]. Fridays, all year
Smith Barney Plaza [Greenwich/N. Moore]. Wednesdays, all year
Petrocelli Park [Bway/Spring]. Thursdays, July–Nov.

Tompkins Square Park [7th/A]. Sundays, May–Dec.

St. Mark's Church [E. 10th/2nd Ave.]. Tuesdays, June–Nov.

Abingdon Square [W. 12th/8th Ave.]. Saturdays, May–Dec.

Union Square [17th/Bway]. Mondays, Wednesdays, Fridays, Saturdays, all year

Sheffield Plaza [W. 57th/9th Ave.]. Wednesdays and Saturdays, all year

West 70th St. [Amsterdam/WEA]. Saturdays, June–Nov.

I.S. 44 Columbus Avenue [W. 77th/Columbus]. Sundays, all year

W. 97th St. [Amsterdam/Columbus]. Fridays, June–Dec.

Minisink Townhouse [W. 143rd/Lenox]. Tuesdays, mid-July–Oct.

West 175th St. [Bway]. Thursdays, June–Dec.

HAMBURGERS, HOT DOGS, & CONDIMENTS

HAMBURGERS

Aggie's, 146 W. Houston St. [MacDougal] ☎ 673-8994. A generous burger of flavorful meat, slightly on the dry side, but very decent. $6.95 ... **Bar 89,** 89 Mercer St. [Spring/Broome] ☎ 274-0989. A burger the size of a stack of pancakes with a little pat of butter melting on the beef. You'll know you've had a burger. $8 ... **Broome St. Bar,** 363 W. Broadway [Broome] ☎ 925-2086, makes compact, juicy burgers inside a pita. $6 ... **Cal's,** 55 W. 21st St. [5th/6th] ☎ 929-0740. Their large (10-oz.) oval burgers come between two slices of thick bread. The meat is juicy and charred well. An excellent burger— one of the city's best. $12 ... **The Corner Bistro,** 331 W. 4th St. [Jane] ☎ 242-9502, has one of the town's more generous burgers. It's a dripping, messy hunk of beef ... **Elephant and Castle,** 68 Greenwich Ave. [Charles] ☎ 243-1400 and 6 Bond St. [Bway/Lafayette] ☎ 254-9604. We like coming here for the "Elephant" burger, decent meat under a slathering of sauce with some curry in it and a couple of slices of bacon. $8.50 ... **44,** at the Royalton, 44. W. 44th St. [5th/6th] ☎ 944-8844.

We aren't the first to say that this is the best burger in town, but we couldn't agree more. A juicy round of meat, a perfect amount of salt and seasonings under a small English muffin. It comes with lots of good sides: peppery cole slaw, caperberries, and their homemade potato chips. $15.75, not listed on the menu ... **Gotham,** 12 E. 12th St. [5th/University] ☎ 620-4020. The Jerry Burger (named after owner Jerry Kretchmer) is a thick puck of fresh, well-seasoned meat under a big hat of a sesame bun. Lunch at the bar, with one of Gotham's good wines by the glass is, for us, a lunch of perfect contentment. $14 ... **Home,** 20 Cornelia St. [Bleecker/W. 4th] ☎ 243-9579. A great burger. The oval-shaped patty is perfectly cooked, the meat is noticeably fresh-tasting and juicy, and it's set between thick slices of buttered rye. With it, Home's first-class onion rings and original ketchup. $6 ... **Keens Chophouse,** 72 W. 36th St. [5th/6th] ☎ 947-3636. In an atmospheric setting like Keens' Pub Room, any burger would taste good, but this burger is pretty good to begin with, and it's nicely char-broiled. Have it with a dollop of their sour cream and horseradish, and wash it down with a pint of Keen's ale. $8.75 ... **Prime Burger,** 51 E. 51st St. [5th/Madison] ☎ 759-4729. These aren't the best burgers in town, but the staff here is as sweet as can be and the place has a kind of well-worn gentility to it. We like sitting at the counter or in one of the funny chairs that are something like highchairs for adults. $2.95 ... **Union Square Cafe,** 21 E. 16th St. [5th/Union Sq. W.] ☎ 243-4020. Both the beef and the tuna burgers are worth a stop here any time, as if an excuse were needed. Sit at the tightly packed bar and tuck into one of these big beauties. $11 ... **Zoë,** 90 Prince St. [Bway/Mercer] ☎ 966-6722. A large disk of beef flame-broiled, served in a sesame-studded bun. Beefy, dripping, delicious. Try it with smoked mozzarella from Joe's Dairy. $10.

HOT DOGS

Brooklyn Diner, 215 W. 57th St. [Bway/7th] ☎ 977-1957. An obscenely large and thick all-beef frank, in no way contained by the wrinkly little buns. Probably the best dog in the city ... **Leo's Famous,** 861 Sixth Ave. [30th/31st] ☎ 564-3264 and 100 W. 32nd St. [6th] ☎ 695-1099. The southernmost of the two Leo's is the original. It's smaller and hasn't got any place to sit, but it has got Leo, working his Hebrew National "tube steaks," as he has for over 50 years to the perfect point of crispness and juiciness ... **Hallo Berlin,** 402 W. 51st St. [9th/10th] ☎ 541-6248 and from the pushcart at Fifth and 54th at lunchtime during the week. You get currywurst and other authentic (and *lecker*) German wurst ... **Katz,** 205 E. Houston St. [Ludlow] ☎ 254-2246. Perfectly straightforward, old-fashioned, and enjoyable dogs ... Also recommended are the dogs from **Papaya King,** 179 E. 86th St. [3rd] ☎ 369-0648.

CONDIMENTS

Gra Habns Farms comes to the Union Square greenmarket every Friday and Saturday in the persons of Virginia and Carl Jensen. They bring herbal (mixed, basil, garlic, dill, tarragon, and opal basil), red, and white **vinegars** made from grapes that grow around Seneca Lake. Mr. Jensen, a baseball fan, more specifically a Dodgers fan, has developed his own recipe for Ebbets Field **mustard.** It's on the grainy side and has a nice punch from the vinegar. They also sell **bread and butter pickles** and **garlic mustard pickles,** as well as **salsa** ... Home, 20 Cornelia St. [Bleecker/W. 4th] ☎ 243-9579, bottles their **ketchup** and their **barbecue sauce** ... Martin Anthonisen from Scarborough Fields Farm sells **herbal vinegars.** He's at the Union Square Market on Mondays and at the World Trade Center market on Thursdays.

HEALTH & VEGETARIAN FOOD

BY BARBARA AND TAMAR HASPEL

For anyone determined to eat a healthful diet, a good rule of thumb (although it's one we've broken a few times in compiling our own list of favorites): Stay away from any place with the word "health" in its name or prominent in its self-description. You want purveyors of food to think "taste" before any other considerations enter their minds. Once you know you're in a place where eating and its pleasures are the top priorities, you can start to look around, and negotiate, for foods that fit into your diet. Ask about ingredients and, if you can't get a satisfactory answer, don't buy. Also, if your restaurant meal arrives containing something your server neglected to mention when you asked (like a lot of cheese) or with a fatty sauce on the food (and the waiter swears he didn't hear you say "sauce on the side"), send it back. Good eating in New York is easy. Prudent eating is much more difficult. Here's a sampling of possibilities. These places have provided us with a lot of great food. They can do the same for you.

TAKEOUT

Citarella, 2135 Broadway [75th] ☎ 874-0383. Perfectly fresh fish, unusual meats, such as extra lean buffalo, and much more. They make their own fresh sausages—not only seafood but low-fat chicken and turkey varieties. Citarella can't tell you just how much fat their sausages contain, but they render very little when they're sautéed and just one or two of the spicy poultry kind can flavor a big pot of beans or pasta sauce.

Bruno the King of Ravioli, 249 Eighth Ave. [22nd/23rd] ☎ 627-0767, 653 Ninth Ave. [45th/46th] ☎ 246-8456, and 2204 Broadway [78th] ☎ 580-8150. Not all Bruno's raviolis taste royal, but the ones filled with shiitake mushrooms are delicious, not to mention virtually fat-free. We like the carrot-spinach-mushroom-filled kind, too. They also bake great traditional biscotti—the hard low-fat kind that you can dunk in your coffee. Try the ones that are loaded with dried fruit.

Jake's Fish Market, 2425 Broadway [89th] ☎ 580-5253. An excellent fresh-fish selection, plus better gefilte fish than your grandmother ever made. There's also a good selection of healthful prepared foods. The roasted and grilled vegetables are well worth taking home, and the poached salmon makes a wonderful dinner entree on a warm night.

Dean & DeLuca, 560 Broadway [Prince] ☎ 431-1691. Avert your eyes from the cheese department and make your way to the back of the store, just west of the cooking utensils, where you'll find one of the finest selections of high-quality dried legumes in the city. If you come just before closing time, you can get for half-price any produce that the produce manager thinks won't meet his standards by the next day.

Whole Foods Market, 117 Prince St. [Wooster/Greene] ☎ 982-1000 and 2421 Broadway [89th] ☎ 874-4000. We are somewhat offended by health-food stores: the worthless supplements, the cardboard snacks, the touting of alternative sweeteners, the overpriced organic produce. However, we find ourselves in Whole Foods at least once a week. Yes, they purvey all of the above, but they also make delicious fresh hummus, baba ghanoush, and any number of other salads and dips. (Watch out, though. By no means is everything here low in fat.) Our favorite—and very healthful it is, too—is their spicy sweet-potato salad/dip with raw vegetables. We like it spread on breakfast toast, or just nibbled straight out of the container. It's even macrobiotic, if that means anything to you.

Broadway Health Food, 2333 Broadway [84th/85th] ☎ 874-6048. Only four blocks down Broadway, but a world away from the bustle of Whole Foods, this is a health food store like health food stores used to be, with a slightly seedy, unprofitable look and a vaguely medicinal odor. However, they sell some of the same items as Whole Foods for a little less and, most important, they are the only place we know in New

York where you can still grind your own peanut butter. This means not only that your peanut butter is perfectly fresh (provided the peanuts are—and they always seem to be) with no salt, sugar, or additives, but that you can opt for a very small amount if you want. We don't know about you, but we find it a lot easier to settle for very little peanut butter in the store than we do when it's sitting on the kitchen counter next to a loaf of crusty bread. If we've bought only 43¢ worth, even if we do eat it up in one day, the damage is minimal.

PLACES TO EAT IT

Angelica Kitchen, 300 E. 12th St. [1st/2nd] ☎ 228-2909. The only vegan restaurant we know where there's as much respect for food as there is for vegetarian principles. Everything is carefully prepared and assertively flavored. They avoid the error of relying on sweeteners in main courses, and they eschew ersatz meat. The space is bright and pleasant and the servers are happy to explain the menu, which is posted on a blackboard and changes daily. Try the great cornbread, the walnut pâté, and the dragon bowl with its perfect vegetables. You can even have their dairy-free desserts and not be disappointed. (Just don't expect them to be low in fat.) We've eaten terrific bread pudding here and cake that wasn't half bad.

Josie's, 300 Amsterdam Ave. [74th] ☎ 799-1000. We have a little trouble understanding restaurants that use no dairy products but serve meat (unless, of course, they're kosher, which Josie's emphatically is not). Health? Philosophy? No explanation seems to fit. But for anyone avoiding saturated fat, it's nice to know there's no butter or cream lurking in the mashed potatoes. And Josie's

turns out tasty fare that's mostly low in fat. Vegetable preparations are interesting, fish are competently grilled. The butter-free mashed potatoes are excellent. Pastas, however, are just all right—it's best to make some other choice. At dessert, they relax their anti-dairy strictures to good effect. Try the lemon ribbon pie made with Mattus ice cream.

Republic, 37 Union Square West [16th/17th] ☎ 627-7172. All of the dishes here are very low in fat but, typically for Asian fare, rather high in sodium. However, if salt's not a concern for you, you can get a very satisfying, guilt-free meal for about $10.

New World Grill, 229 W. 49th St. [8th/9th] ☎ 957-4745. If you want a delicious and healthful pre-theatre meal, there's no better place. In nice weather, when you can eat outside near the fountain in the plaza, it's a truly memorable dining experience, worth seeking out even if you have no theatre tickets. It's well-executed American food—try the roasted and grilled vegetables, the grilled tuna with Asian salad, or the rigatoni with an addictive smoked tomato sauce. There are wonderfully creative fruit desserts (we love the grilled pear slices) and a good selection of sorbets.

Barbara and Tamar Haspel, a Manhattan-based mother/daughter team, write, edit, and publish Dreaded Broccoli, *a quarterly food-letter dedicated to making low-fat cooking and eating feasible, perhaps even pleasurable, that includes recipes, food strategies, nutrition news, product and restaurant reviews, and irreverent commentary. It's $14 per year (4 issues), $26 for 2 years. Mail to 121 W. 92nd St., New York, 10025. Visa/MC info can be mailed to the same address or faxed to ☎ 663-2407.*

MORE MUG would also add a few places to the Haspels' good list: The large and attractive "natural market" in Soho called **Grassroots,** 520 Broadway [Spring/Broome] ☎ 334-2444 for prepared foods, good-looking organic produce, and many other natural and healthy goods . . . **Blanche's Organic,** 22 E. 44th St. [Mad] ☎ 599-3445 and 972 Lexington Ave. [70th/71st] ☎ 717-1923. We think this is appealing healthy food—good soups, greens, and daily specials . . . **Mavalli Palace,** 46 E. 29th St. [Mad/Park Ave. S.] ☎ 679-5535, has wonderful vegetarian Indian food, and **Hangawi,** 12 E. 32nd St. [5th/Mad] ☎ 213-0077, is a delight of vegetarian cooking, Korean-style. See more on Mavalli Palace and Hangawi in the Restaurants chapter . . . **Urban Organic, Herban Kitchen,** and **Inside Out** are three companies that deliver organic produce (and other items). See more in the Food Delivery article in this chapter.

HERBS & SPICES

Adriana's Caravan, ☎ 718-436-8565, mail order for virtually any herb or spice you could need.

Angelica's, 147 First Ave. [9th] ☎ 529-4335, more health herbs than cooking and a large collection of reference books.

Aphrodisia, 264 Bleecker St. [6th/7th] ☎ 989-6440, for herbs, spices, and peppers in glass jars. You scoop, they weigh.

Foods of India, 121 Lexington Ave. [28th/29th] ☎ 683-4419.

Garlic: Keith Stewart is the farmer at the Union Square Market who sells rocambole garlic. This variety, according to Mr. Stewart, is "closer to the original wild garlic from Asia." It doesn't store quite as well, but has a richer flavor and is easier to peel. Unlike the California garlic that is in most stores, the rocambole is a "hard neck" variety. The cloves do not overlap, but form around a tough central stem, the "neck." There are about seven wedges per boll. It is especially good roasted. Mr. Stewart is at the market summers every Wednesday, Friday, and Saturday.

Herb plants: At the northwest corner of the Union Square Market on Mondays is Martin Anthonisen from Scarborough Fields Farm. He's got seven different types of thyme plants, including lemon thyme, coconut thyme, and caraway thyme. He sells only herbs in pots: $2.50 for a small pot. He also carries many other herbs (including different types of basil and rosemary). He's also at the World Trade Center market on Thursdays.

The Herb Place, 690 Washington St. [Charles/Perry] ☎ 255-1213.

Kalustyan's, 123 Lexington Ave. [28th/29th] ☎ 685-3451. Indian spices—the next best thing to a trip to Jackson Heights.

Patel Brothers, 37–46 74th St. [Roosevelt/37th] Jackson Heights ☎ 718-898-3445.

Sahadi Importing Co., 187 Atlantic Ave. [Court/Clinton] Brooklyn ☎ 718-624-4550.

Spice House, 99 First Ave. [6th] ☎ 387-7812. Spices, mostly Indian, open 24 hours.

KITCHEN ARTS AND LETTERS

Kitchen Arts and Letters, 1435 Lexington Ave. [93rd/94th] ☎ 876-5550, is invaluable as a store that carries food and wine books, books on kitchen antiques, food scholarship, fiction with food themes, and, of course, cookbooks. It is further distinguished by the knowledge and dedication of owner Nahum Waxman and his staff, who provide information on a wide range of food-related topics. In fact, they have on staff a specialist "searcher" who, for no charge or obligation to the customer, will look for out-of-print materials. Mr. Waxman says, when it comes to finding an answer to a question, they "never give up."

Kitchen Arts has an international clientele of food pros ("they tincture the atmosphere") who come to do serious and pleasurable historical research into food, as well as restaurateurs looking for new menu ideas and nonprofessional food and wine lovers. They carry current and out-of-print cookbooks (many of which are stored in the basement, so ask) as well as imported books you will have difficulty finding elsewhere. When we were there, Mr. Waxman showed us a book called *Fermented Fish in Africa,* published by the Food Agricultural Organization of the U.N. and a copy of the 1949 classic *History and Social Influence of the Potato.* The atmosphere in the store is most welcoming.

KITCHENWARE

Bridge Kitchenware, 214 E. 52nd St. [2nd/3rd] ☎ 688-4220. The outside of the building may be spiffed up, but inside things are, thank goodness, just as they have been—not spiffed up. The knives are behind the same glass protector. The chipped blue-painted drawers contain utensils and gadgets for wine service and for baking and pastrymaking. Imported French baking pans for tarts, madeleines, and sables are stacked on metal shelves. Large pots and roasters are up near the ceiling. There are as many odd, cheap dishes here as at Fish's Eddy. A good deal is the over 100 styles of serviceable glassware for daily use or for specialties like pint English pub glasses ($2 each).

Broadway Panhandler, 477 Broome St. [Wooster] ☎ 966-3434, has been around since 1976 and makes a point of carrying seasonal equipment and cake-decorating supplies as well as classic kitchenware. There is less of a stress on classic French cuisine here—more woks, steamers, and ginger graters. They have a large cake and candymaking section, with supplies for making multilayer cakes, and a lot of specialty molded cake pans.

NY Cake and Baking Distributors, 56 W. 22nd St. [5th/6th] ☎ 675-2253, has things for the serious baker as well as the party thrower. Commercial-weight baking pans in all sizes, including graduated pans for tier cakes, are shelved alongside the (at last count) 63 designs for shaped cakes. To ice the cake there are piping tools, spreaders, combs, and food colors. Cake toppers and plastic figurines cover a wall. There are press-on sugar decorations and sugary letters to spell out happy birthday to anyone. Gum paste orchids, daisies, and roses are made up and boxed as if they came from the florist. Valrhona chocolate is available in bars or in bulk, and there are all manner of colored sugars and sprinkles and gold and silver dragees. They teach courses in cake decorating, and every fall they hold a cake contest.

Lamalle Kitchenware, 36 W. 25th St. [Bway/6th] ☎ 242-0750. Formerly a supply house for professional chefs, it now has kitchenware for professionals and home cooks. Most of the items sold here are made in France, one exception being the Wüsthof knives (which are always 25% off retail). Mauviel copper pots in two different qualities (the dinner line and the professional line), lots of pastry tools, and much bakeware. White porcelain ramekins, soufflé, and quiche dishes, but no dinner plates or glassware.

MEAT & POULTRY

LOWER MANHATTAN/CHINATOWN
Bayard St. Meat Market, 57 Bayard St. [Bowery/Elizabeth] ☎ 619-6206

East Broadway Meat Market, 36 E. Broadway [Catherine/Market] ☎ 941-5530

Hong Keung Seafood and Meat Market, 75 Mulberry St. [Canal/Bayard] ☎ 267-6961

TRIBECA
Polarica, 73 Hudson St. [Jay/Worth] ☎ 406-0400

SOHO/LITTLE ITALY
Dean & DeLuca, 560 Broadway [Prince] ☎ 431-1691

Pino's Fine Meats, 149 Sullivan St. [Houston/Prince] ☎ 475-8134

WEST VILLAGE
Balducci's, 424 Sixth Ave. [9th/10th] ☎ 673-2600

Faicco's Pork Store, 260 Bleecker St. [6th/7th] ☎ 243-1974

Florence Meat Market, 5 Jones St. [Bleecker/W. 4th] ☎ 242-6531

Jefferson Market, 450 Sixth Ave. [10th/11th] ☎ 533-3377

Ottomanelli Brothers, 285 Bleecker St. [7th/Jones] ☎ 678-4217

EAST VILLAGE
East Village Meat Market, 139 Second Ave. [St. Mark's/9th] ☎ 228-5590

Kurowycky Meats, 124 First Ave. [7th/8th] ☎ 477-0344

GRAMERCY/UNION SQUARE
Les Halles, 411 Park Ave. South [28th/29th] ☎ 679-4111

Quattro's Poultry, Union Square Market, Wed. and Sat.

Todaro Brothers, 555 Second Ave. [30th/31st] ☎ 532-0633

Tom's Meat Market, 214 Third Ave. [18th/19th] ☎ 475-0395

MURRAY HILL
Center Meat Market, 514 Third Ave. [34th/35th] ☎ 689-5090

MIDTOWN WEST

Esposito and Sons, 500 Ninth Ave. [38th] ☎ 279-3298

MIDTOWN EAST

Empire Purveyors, 901 First Ave. [50th/51st] ☎ 755-7756

Simchick Meats, 944 First Ave. [52nd] ☎ 888-2299

UPPER WEST SIDE

Broadway Butcher, 2446 Broadway [90th/91st] ☎ 769-2500

Citarella, 2135 Broadway [74th/75th] ☎ 874-0383

Nevada Meat Market, 2012 Broadway [68th/69th] ☎ 362-0443

Oppenheimer, 2606 Broadway [98th/99th] ☎ 662-0246

UPPER EAST SIDE

Agata and Valentina, 1505 First Ave. [78th/79th] ☎ 452-0690

Akron Prime Meats, 1424 Third Ave. [80th/81st] ☎ 744-1551

Albert's Prime Meats, 836 Lexington Ave. [63rd/64th] ☎ 751-3169

Holland Court Market, 1423 Lexington Ave. [93rd] ☎ 289-8490

Kircher's Colonial Market, 1711 Second Ave. [88th/89th] ☎ 722-4004

Leonard's, 1241 Third Ave. [71st/72nd] ☎ 744-2600

Lobel's, 1096 Madison Ave. [82nd/83rd] ☎ 737-1372

Ottomanelli Brothers, 1549 York Ave. [82nd] ☎ 772-7900

Park East Kosher Butchers, 1163 Madison Ave. [85th/86th] ☎ 737-9800

Schaller & Weber, 1654 Second Ave. [85th/86th] ☎ 879-3047

Schatzie's Prime Meats, 1200 Madison Ave. [87th/88th] ☎ 410-1555

Tibor Meat, 1508 Second Ave. [78th/79th] ☎ 744-8292

HARLEM

Fairway, 132nd St. and Twelfth Ave. ☎ 234-3883

M U S H R O O M S

The gourmet stores certainly will have a selection of mushrooms, but we like going to the specialists. That means **Aux Delices des Bois,** 4 Leonard St. [Hudson/W. Bway] ☎ 334-1230. You can find as many as two dozen fresh varieties, plus many other dried mushrooms ... At **Green Village,** 1457 Third Ave. [82nd] ☎ 734-7687, eight or nine kinds are generally available ... The very nice **Hans Johansson,** ☎ 914-232-2107, sells retail by mail order. He's likely to have 25–35 varieties fresh and 13 dried. He ships UPS overnight ($25 minimum), so you'll be sure to get them as fresh as possible. He does sampler boxes and can arrange a gift basket. Everything comes with an information brochure.

OYSTERS

THE OYSTER BAR Sandy Ingber begins his day at 4 A.M. at the Fulton Fish Market buying oysters for the **Oyster Bar** in Grand Central Station, ☎ 490-6650, where he purchases only about 50% of his needs. The rest come to him from around the world. When he buys oysters he is looking, of course, for freshness, checking the "tags" (see below). He carries his oyster knife with him and opens a few from each bag. He looks for a "shiny, watery texture" and a good color ("no green or brown"). The OB serves over 4,000 raw oysters each day and sometimes has up to a dozen varieties. The difference between the East Coast and the West Coast is significant. The indigenous West Coast varieties were wiped out in a blight and were replaced by imported Japanese stock. So, while there are "some small characteristic differences," there is a sameness to them: a sweet, mild flavor. On the East Coast, the oysters have great variety. Oysters from as little as a mile apart can "be distinctively different." His current favorites are the Belons from Maine, "a European flat variety, metallic and very briny"—becoming rarer; the Kumamoto, "no bigger than a quarter with a deep cup that has a sweet cucumber aftertaste"; and the Wellfleet, "very briny and smooth." . . . **Blue Ribbon,** 97 Sullivan St. [Prince/Spring] ☎ 274-0404, has one of the most popular raw bars in the city. You will find either bluepoints or Malpeques there . . . **Docks Oyster Bar,** 2427 Broadway [89th] ☎ 724-5588 and 633 Third Ave. [40th] ☎ 986-8080, has a daily assortment of four East Coast and four West Coast varieties . . . **Oceana,** 55 E. 54th St. [Mad/Park] ☎ 759-5941, has three varieties and **Aquagrill,** 210 Spring St. [6th] ☎ 274-0505, four to six kinds daily.

BUYING OYSTERS **Jake's Fish Market,** 2425 Broadway [89th] ☎ 580-5253, has Connecticut bluepoints on sale just about every day. Bill Bowers, buyer and owner of Jake's, says when you're buying oysters, you have every right to ask to see the **tag.** This comes with every bag of oysters (and clams), and it tells you three things: the date of the harvest, the place of the harvest, and the name of the harvester. If a vendor refuses to show you this tag, you should be "very leery" of these oysters. Five or six days is okay from the date of harvest, "one week tops."

EQUIPMENT **Lamalle Kitchenware,** 36 W. 25th St. [5th/6th] ☎ 645-8219, can protect you in chain mail gloves for $45. They also have $14 white porcelain oyster plates (with indentations), oyster stands, and oyster knives. **Dean & DeLuca** has an ergonomic oyster knife with a big, contoured handle for $9.50.

MORE The "Diamond Jim" Brady Club was founded to pay homage to the bivalve and also to raise money for Citymeals-on-Wheels. Mr. Brady and his friend Lillian Russell were known to consume six dozen oysters before lunch, dinner, and as a late evening snack. Aspirants to the club qualify for membership by a onetime test of eating six dozen oysters. They hold a yearly festive dinner in which oysters play a major role. The acting president, or Maître Klaxoneur, is Roger Yaseen. Mr. Yaseen can be reached at ☎ 492-6150 for further information.

PIZZA

The history of pizzamaking in New York dates from 1905. That's when Gennaro Lombardi fired up his oven on Spring Street, introduced pizza to New York, set the pie standard, and, in time, trained many of New York's famed pizzamakers, including the men who later opened Totonno's and John's of Bleecker Street. It's a somewhat complicated lineage.

Patsy's, 19 Old Fulton St. [Front/Water] Brooklyn Heights, Brooklyn ☎ 718-858-4300. Patsy Grimaldi makes superlative pies—our favorite in the city. He opened up here after selling the Patsy's at First Avenue and 117th St. (*That* Patsy's was named after his uncle Patsy who started the place in 1931. *That* Patsy's now has a second location at 509 Third Ave. [34th] ☎ 689-7500. They make excellent pizza, too, with a thin, crisp crust, delicately topped.) There is no connection between the Patsy's in Manhattan and Brooklyn and, in fact, there's some disagreement about who has the right to use the name. In any event, the Brooklyn restaurant is in a league of its own. The coal oven produces blistery crusts with a slight char taste, a friend of Patsy's produces the mozzarella, and the restaurant roasts the peppers in the coal oven, going through 18 bushels a week. Patsy loves music and pizza but you don't have to love music to love Patsy's.

Also in Brooklyn is the famed **Totonno's,** 1524 Neptune Ave. [15th/16th], Coney Island ☎ 718-372-8606. The way the story has usually been told is that Totonno's was started in 1924 by Anthony (Totonno) Pero, who had been trained by Gennaro Lombardi. After his death, his son, Jerry Pero, kept up the tradition until he passed away in 1994. Now, Joe Ciminieri, the husband of Anthony Pero's granddaughter, is keeping up the tradition. He says he is "making pizza the way it was before it became fast food." The dough is made daily and it's not kept overnight. (When the pizzeria opened in 1924, no one had a refrigerator so you couldn't keep the dough overnight, and they never changed the practice.) They use a coal oven which heats up to 850° (gas only goes to about 500°). No one disputes Totonno's great pizza. Joe Ciminieri says, though, that Gennaro Lombardi didn't teach Anthony Pero pizzamaking, that it was the other way around. Lombardi had a grocery store and Totonno asked if he could make pizza in it. We're staying out of it (though Gennaro Lombardi's grandfather made pizza in Naples. And, his great-grandfather worked for Raphael Esposito, who originated the margherita pizza on July 10, 1889, in honor of Queen Margherita di Savoia's visit to Naples. The three ingredients—cheese, tomato sauce, and fresh basil—were chosen to represent the colors of the Italian flag). Totonno's is open Thurs.–Sun.

Back in Manhattan, the best pies are at **John's,** 278 Bleecker St. [6th/7th Ave. So.] ☎ 243-1680, 48 W. 65th St. [CPW/Columbus] ☎ 721-7001, and 408 E. 64th St.

[1st/York] ☎ 935-2895, and at **Lombardi's,** 32 Spring St. [Mott/Mulberry] ☎ 941-7994. It's appropriate for a story having to do with pizza to come full circle. The name Lombardi's, as a pizzeria, passed into history in 1971. Gennaro Lombardi, the originator's grandson, ran a restaurant using the family name from 1978–1987. He decided to re-open the restaurant as a pizzeria in 1992 "to keep the name alive." Mr. Lombardi says that "part of my after school duties were to help my father make dough." He and other neighborhood boys "worked on a long wooden table in the basement of the pizzeria." The original site at 53½ Spring St. didn't work out. The number 6 train runs below it and the oven had cracked and was beyond repair. The new Lombardi's is across the street from the original, and the oven (a bread baking oven) was found at 32

The original Lombardi's at 53½ Spring St.

Spring—it was part of the Parisi bakery. After reconditioning, it was pressed back into service, now for pizzas. "There's no secret to good pizza," Mr. Lombardi says. "Use a coal oven, fresh dough, and high-quality ingredients." Lombardi's is back, serving pies that would make Gennaro Lombardi senior, we think, very happy.

SOUP

Al Yeganeh is generally referred to as the Soup Man at **Soup Kitchen,** 259A W. 55th St. [Bway/8th]. No phone. He's notoriously cranky, but his soup is pure joy. This place is a hole-in-the-wall (takeout only and closed during the summer), but from these unprepossessing surroundings comes a choice of amazing soups, chock full of ingredients that are transformed into liquid gold—pure alchemy. We are partial to the seafood bisque, the corn chowder, the Cuban black bean, the lima bean, and the goulash. Each order comes with bread, usually challah or French, fruit, and a mint or some touch like that. You will know you are in the right spot by the line snaking down the block. After eating this soup, we are always reminded of the Lily Tomlin routine in which a charac-

ter explains that a Campbell's soup can is soup, a Warhol Campbell's soup can is art. The character meticulously explains, "this is soup, this is art." Eat the soup here and the distinction melts away: This soup *is* art . . . Across town at **Daily Soup,** 21 E. 41st St. [5th/Mad] ☎ 953-7687, the people here are giving Soup Man some real competition. They always have 10–12 soups, including at least one vegetarian. As with Soup Man, you get bread and fruit and a cookie they've baked on the premises. We haven't had anything we didn't like: good chicken soup, vegetarian chili, New England clam chowder, wild mushrooms with kale, and pea with Parmesan . . . Down a few steps into a tidy little shop in Mott Street, potions are being brewed. At the **Sweet-n-Tart Cafe,** 76 Mott

St. [Canal/Bayard] ☎ 334-8088, you can have some inexpensive, fortifying, and excellent noodles in soup, but the most interesting thing here is what's called "Tong Shui"—these are hot or cold  soups meant to be eaten after a meal or as a snack with tea. There are said to be health benefits to them, and even if we haven't eaten our way back to eternal youth, we can say we've been intrigued with things like walnut with lotus seed tong shui, served hot, that was sweet but not too, with the chestnut-like bite of the lotus seeds. The Tong Shui average $2 a bowl . . . We have a soft spot for the cheery bustle of a lunch at **La Bonne Soupe,** 48 W. 55th St. [5th/6th] ☎ 586-7650, with red gingham on the walls and red-and-white-checked tablecloths, efficient French staff, and satisfying, inexpensive food. For $11.95 you can have a bowl of their onion soup, salad with a garlicky dressing, and a chunk of a baguette. Add a glass of red wine and you have optimal fortification against the meanest possible Nor'easter . . . One of New York's favorite minestrones is still available

at **Trattoria Spaghetto,** 228 Bleecker St. [Carmine/Downing] ☎ 255-6752. It's the recipe of Rene Batista and the sustenance of many customers of the Bleecker Street Luncheonette, as this place was known previously . . . **Shopsin's General Store,** 63 Bedford St. [Morton] ☎ 924-5160, is a quirky family-run restaurant—Dad does the cooking, Mom and the kids run the front of the house. A long list of soups is available made from a combination of rich stocks and sometimes exotic ingredients. Closed weekends . . . Our favorite takeout place, **Flavors,** 8 W. 18th St. [5th/6th] ☎ 647-1234, makes soup as fine as the rest of their offerings. The creamy mushroom has no cream, but an intense mushroom flavor; there's a robust split pea; a minestrone with vegetables fresh enough to retain some crispness; and a sensational seafood bisque . . . For authentic Japanese soups, you always eat well at **Menchanko-Tei,** 39 W. 55th St. [5th/6th] ☎ 247-1585, 131 E. 45th St. [Lex/3rd] ☎ 986-6805, and 5 World Trade Center Concourse ☎ 432-4210 . . . **Franklin Station Cafe,** 222 W. Broadway [Franklin] ☎ 274-8525, is a favorite of ours for sometimes spicy, invariably delicious Malaysian noodle soups.

SWEETS

BROWNIES

When we want a great brownie, we go to **Sarabeth's,** 423 Amsterdam Ave. [80th/81st] ☎ 496-6280 and 1295 Madison Ave. [92nd/93rd] ☎ 410-7335. These moist squares are unsurpassed in the city, we think, because they are so moist, not too sweet, with little clumps of chocolate adding texture.

CAKE

CAKEMAKERS
Baked Ideas ☎ 925-9097. It's in the details that Patti Page's cakes (chocolate or yellow butter cake) distinguish themselves. She uses lots of colors and can create something as startling (which she did for an Australian bride) as a wedding cake in the shape of the Sydney Opera House. Most cakes are $200

and up, and two weeks' notice is usually needed.

Ron Ben-Israel ☎ 627-2418. The basis for Mr. Ben-Israel's cakes is seven layers—four of cake, three of buttercream. Often the cake is moistened with a liqueur like Grand Marnier or Amaretto. He says that people come up with crazy ideas, and he tries to accommodate them. He did a wedding cake in the form of the NY skyline, complete with lighted windows. He's done a grand piano with chocolate flowers cascading out of it. The cost averages $9–$10 per person. Book as far ahead as possible.

Cakes by Margaret Braun ☎ 929-1582. On dense chocolate tortes, butter pound cakes, or devil's food cakes, Ms. Braun does

Margaret Braun's bejeweled crown cake.

painting with food coloring and adds intricate piping. She doesn't do floral designs but does create three dimensional "fruits." She's made cakes in the shape of a jeweled crown on a pillow and a three-dimensional cheeseburger. Cakes begin at $250, generally it's about $10 per guest. Order "way ahead" during wedding season, otherwise at least two weeks. See more below about Ms. Braun's exceptional work with sugar.

Chelsea Baking Co. ☎ 989-9800. The cakes here are the work of George Todd. Working with carrot, strawberry, or different kinds of chocolate cake, Mr. Todd does theme cakes (one time he did a cake drum set). In our carrot cake tasteoff (see below), Chelsea Baking's cake won handily. Figure $65–$80 for a very basic cake, more for a theme cake. They like a week's notice.

Creative Cakes ☎ 794-9811. Bill Schutz has turned chocolate fudge with buttercream

frosting into personalized Monopoly boards and some nontraditional wedding cakes—for a bride and groom who liked to jog, he did a cake of two joggers whose running shoes were tied together. The smallest cake serves 25, and starts at $200. Two weeks' notice appreciated.

Cheryl Kleinman ☎ 718-237-2271. Customizing for corporate logos or biographical details for individuals is much of what Ms. Kleinman does in chocolate, pound, or carrot cakes. Her wedding cakes tend to be "antiquish"—off-white with flowers in muted colors. She also does cupcakes and petit fours. Prices start at $6.50 a portion, and two weeks' or more notice needed for a party, longer for a wedding.

Rosemary Littman ☎ 201-833-2417. A basket of flowers with roses and lilacs overflowing the sides is Ms. Littman's signature cake. You won't know it's a cake until you taste the buttercream, chocolate, and yellow pound cake. She's done a cake in the form of a champagne bottle in an ice bucket. Small cakes start at $150, a basket of roses cake, which yields 50–60 pieces, is $350. Generally, a week's notice, longer for theme cakes.

Colette Peters ☎ 366-6530. "Eggs, bacon, and coffee"; luggage; and shopping bags are a few of the unusual cakes made by Ms. Peters. She says every cake is different, and she uses a variety of ingredients to achieve her effects. Pricing starts at $8 a person, generally three weeks' notice needed, more for wedding cakes. See more on Ms. Peters below in Gingerbread Houses.

Gail Watson Custom Cakes ☎ 967-9167. Ms. Watson does mostly wedding cakes in 13 different flavors and with 25 different fillings. Some of the cakes are designed with buttercream flowers, some with fresh flowers. She needs at least a month's notice for weddings; figure $4.25 a serving. No theme cakes.

Sylvia Weinstock Cakes ☎ 925-6698. Known for botanically correct, realistic flowers on her chocolate, hazelnut, and yellow cakes, Ms. Weinstock is the doyenne of NY cakemakers. She's done replicas of a college library, a stack of medical journals, and the World Trade Center, in addition to countless wedding cakes. $350 minimum, a couple of days' notice for wedding cakes, longer for theme cakes.

CARROT CAKE

One gray Friday morning, we fanned out across the city, from Chelsea to 246th Street, gathering up slices of (and whole) carrot cakes. We had selected seven entrants and did a blind tasting to find out who makes the best carrot cake in town. We revived from a bad case of sugar shock and found consensus as follows. The runner up: **Les Friandises,** 972 Lexington Ave. [70th/71st] ☎ 988-1616, has the most elegant of the cakes we tasted: moist, nutty, not too sweet, with a slightly lemony frosting. $3.25 a slice. The winner: **Chelsea Baking Co.** ☎ 989-9800. A pretty, if conventional-looking cake, very moist with lots of strips of carrots, coconut, plump raisins, a cream cheesy frosting that's not too sweet. An easy pick. A 10-inch cake is $22, serves 10–12. Not a retail store, call ahead, one day's notice.

COFFEE CAKE

Rudy's Pastry Shop, 905 Seneca Ave. [Myrtle] Ridgewood, Queens, ☎ 718-821-5890. It's a long way from Manhattan's gourmet stores—exactly what we love about Rudy's. This is the kind of wonderful, old-fashioned bakery that still has hanging cylin-

ders filled with string that they use to wrap up your haul. It's a bakery where the ladies behind the counter are sweeter than the coffee cake, which tastes the way coffee cake used to taste. The last time we were there, we said to the lady who helped us that we were taking our things back to Manhattan. "Manhattan," she said somewhat wistfully, as some might say of Paris, "I don't get there too often." She then packed up a few goodies, on the house, for the subway ride home.

CHOCOLATE

A sampler of our favorite chocolates in the city.

Most chocolate lovers would start with the irresistible edible jewels of chocolate master Robert Linxe at **La Maison du Chocolate,** 25 E. 73rd St. [5th/Mad] ☎ 744-7117. They're not long on visuals the way Richart chocolates are. In fact, they're virtually unadorned, but what amazing chocolate it is! Whether you go for the bittersweet ganache, called Caracas, or any of the flavored chocolates (the Valencia has orange peel and orange liqueur), they are intense sensory experiences and, for many, the last word in chocolate. There isn't a day that can't be improved with some of M. Linxe's creations. A box of 45 pieces is $45.

Ortrud Münch Carstens' chocolates. Ms. Carstens says she is a great admirer of M. Linxe, and it shows in her dedication to creating the ideal truffles and other chocolates. Once you spend some time lolling them around in your mouth, you'll never go back to the insipid, the uninspired, the too sweet. We like Angelina chocolate in Paris and have been known to finish a pot of their hot chocolate. But if you have done the same, you know that a subsequent tour of the Louvre is rendered impossible—you must lie down for an hour. Angelina chocolate is thick and overwhelming. Ms. Carstens' is just the opposite. This is no rococo cocoa. It's great chocolate because, as she says, "I try to distill everything down to the vital components and to get to the top of the taste." She says ten years with an architectural firm has contributed "a purist component" to her chocolates.

The way she accomplishes this is by making chocolate as if she were a "19th century chocolatier," using machines to cool and dehumidify the room but none in the making of the chocolate. When she makes a coffee-flavored ganache, she does not grind the beans, but crushes them with her rolling pin. Her current array of a dozen or so flavors includes the "rusty tools" first made in honor of her father, who asked if she couldn't do something "more masculine." Originally she cut each tool by hand from the block of chocolate, now she uses a mold for them and spends "ten times the molding time creating the rust." Ms. Carstens takes great care in the selection of ingredients, using organic produce wherever possible, artisanal cognacs, and low quantities of sugar—this preserves the star quality of the chocolate she is using. Ms. Carstens works with Valhrona mixes exclusively. Most of the world's cocoa beans come from Africa, South America, and South Asia, and the overwhelming amount (85%) of production is a bean called the *forastero*. The remaining 15% is divided between the *criollo*, which has a flowery, fruity flavor, and the *trinitario*—a bean which is a cross between the forastero and the criollo, which she calls "well balanced and assertive." These two beans are the "Grand Crus." Ms. Carstens worries about the size of each piece—it should be small enough for you to let it melt in your mouth before you bite into

Complete with (edible) rust: Carstens' "rusty tools."

it, but large enough to give you the maximum impact of flavor.

Ms. Carstens delivers her products to Dean & DeLuca three or four times each week (during holidays, she brings in fresh candy each day). They cost $2 each, the tools are $4. If she is bringing truffles, she makes them the night before so that they are as fresh as possible. "A truffle is a fresh product. The texture and taste curve goes down from the day it is made." These truffles have two enrobings to be sure they are completely covered, but she likes the shell on the truffle to be "paper thin." All this passion about the details of a single piece of chocolate pays off when you taste it. It's the most elegant chocolate imaginable.

Manon chocolate, from Belgium, is available on the 7th floor of Bergdorf Goodman ☎ 753-7300. We are fans of this chocolate, and particularly like the Feuille, chocolate cream, and crème frâiche, the rum caramel, and the Almond Masse Pain, subtle and creamy and about as far from marzipan as you can get.

Richart Design et Chocolat, 7 E. 55th St. [5th/Mad] ☎ 371-9369. Richart is known for their beautifully designed, understated geometrics. The essences of the flavors are quite subtle, and while we don't get a chocolate high from Richart, this is fine chocolate. The caramel is a particular favorite.

When we think of **Teuscher,** 25 E. 61st St. [Mad/Park] ☎ 751-8482 and at 620 Fifth Ave. [49th/50th] ☎ 246-4416, it's especially for their champagne truffles, though there are other good choices. Still, we've never walked out with anything but their round, sugar-dusted, champagne-filled beauties.

Michael Rogak can tell when he shakes your hand whether or not you have what it takes to be a candymaker. That's because, besides coordination and dexterity, you need cool palms. If they're too warm, you'll flunk swirling. He should know since he's a third-generation Brooklyn candymaker. His grandfather, Julius Rogak, opened the House of Fine Sweets in the 1920s, which specialized in penny and 2¢ candy—things like jelly bars, chocolate-covered twists, and coconut balls. When his son, Martin, went into business in 1946, he decided to make better-quality chocolates and opened, with his partner, Joseph, **JoMart Chocolates,** 2917 Ave. R [E. 29th/Nostrand], Brooklyn ☎ 718-375-1277. The small candy factory, behind the shop in Brooklyn, turns out about 150 varieties of chocolates. They specialize in what Mr. Rogak calls "Old World" candies—things like chocolate with their flavored homemade marshmallow. (Marshmallow flavors include vanilla, maple, coffee, chocolate, and chocolate caramel.) The "caranut," which they developed, is coconut and caramel covered with chocolate. They also specialize in nut patties, whole nuts covered by chocolate, which Mr. Rogak says is a very American candy. The peanut butter cup they make is much better than Reese's.

The butter crunch is wonderful. JoMart makes their own marzipan, and their chocolate-covered raspberry jelly (they make their own jelly) was developed by Michael's grandfather. They'll ship anywhere and are happy to do special items, even in small quantities. If they don't have a mold for it, they'll make it—so you can have your logo in chocolate or just about anything else. JoMart's candies are available at the Brooklyn location and in Manhattan at the **Be-Speckled Trout,** 422 Hudson [St. Luke's/ Morton] ☎ 255-1421, **Economy Candy,** 108 Rivington [Ludlow/Essex] ☎ 254-1531, and **Broadway Nut,** 2246 Broadway [80th/81st] ☎ 874-5214.

Li-Lac, 120 Christopher St. [Bleecker/ Bedford] ☎ 242-7374, has been making their popular old-fashioned candy for Villagers and others for over 70 years.

5th Ave. Chocolatière, 510 Madison Ave. [52nd/53rd] ☎ 935-5454, does personalized molds. See more in the Gifts and Collectibles article in the Stores chapter.

COOKIES

It's just not a cookie city. We think most of the offerings around town are okay, not bad, run-of-the-mill. We'd like to see a place, call it Cookie City, that's not a chain but a shop with an artisanal cookiemaker. This is someone who dreams cookies the way Maury Rubin dreams tarts or Ortrud Carstens dreams chocolate. Anyone out there? Having said that, Mr. Rubin at **City Bakery,** does, in fact, make good cookies (particularly the small sugar and cinnamon, as well as the peanut butter). **Taylor's,** 523 Hudson St. [W. 10th/Charles] ☎ 645-8200 and 228 W. 18th St. [7th/8th] ☎ 366-9081 and 175 Second Ave. [14th] ☎ 674-9501, makes an exceptionally fine oatmeal cookie with lots of cinnamon that is large, moist, and studded with raisins.

CUPCAKES

There are other cupcakes around, but you might as well go to the source. New York's cupcake central is the **Cupcake Cafe,** 522 Ninth Ave. [39th] ☎ 465-1530. You can always find the chocolate, vanilla, and walnut in the store. Call them to special order lemon, orange, lemon poppy, or carrot with vanilla, chocolate, maple, mocha, lemon, orange, or cream cheese icings.

CUSTARD

Nobody makes custard much these days, but **Custard Beach,** 33 E. 8th St. [University] ☎ 420-6039, is upholding the tradition beautifully. There are special flavors every day.

DOUGHNUTS

Fisher and Levy makes doughnuts we like, and there are wonderful jellies from Rudy's Pastry Shop (see above under Coffee Cake). For incomparable doughnuts, though, you want **Georgie's Pastry Shop,** 50 W. 125th St. [5th/Lenox] ☎ 831-0722. The doughnuts are available after 12 noon or so until about 6 P.M. You get a choice of the plain or jelly, and they're both sensational.

FUDGE

Luise Wykell's fudge is sweet but not cloying, with a notably smooth consistency. Ms. Wykell offers two basic types: the "Traditional" is chocolate with or without nuts and the "Classic" is mint chocolate with no nuts. She says she uses an enhanced version of her mother's recipe, but is otherwise tight-lipped about the ingredients. Ms. Wykell does mail order (and assures us that fudge travels well, having shipped as far as Africa), though if you want to pick some up, it's available at Dean & DeLuca. It's $25 for a one-pound box. Her mail order business is call **Luise's Favorite Fudge,** and once you try it, it's very likely to be your favorite fudge, too. ☎ 226-1105.

GINGERBREAD HOUSES

Colette Peters, cakemaker extraordinaire, (see above) creates gingerbread houses—a Swiss chalet in gingerbread is $175. If you give her a photo, she will make a gingerbread version of your house (figure $175 and up). Ms. Peters doesn't use a lot of candy but gets architectural effects with shaped dough pieces, colored icings, nuts, and extraordinary piping abilities. Chocolate shortbread can be substituted for the gingerbread, if you prefer. ☎ 366-6530 . . . For more traditional-style gingerbread houses, try **Elk Candy,** 240 E. 86th St. [2nd/3rd] ☎ 650-1177, or **Kleine Konditorei,** 234 E. 86th St. [2nd/3rd] ☎ 737-7130, which gets theirs directly from Germany at holiday time.

ICE CREAM

We can't get enough of the ice cream and sorbet of **Chelsea Ice** ☎ 989-9800. We think it's the best ice cream and sorbet in town. It's not a retail store, so you have to buy 2 1/2-quart containers, but once your crowd tastes the chocolate truffle, with its big chunks of truffles, or the very grapefruity grapefruit Campari, you'll have no trouble getting through them. They're $10–$16 each . . . The other excellent ice cream maker is **Ciao Bella,** widely available in pints. Popular flavors are cinnamon, hazelnut, and passionfruit orange sorbet . . . We also like the Italian ice creams and sorbets from **Sant Ambroeus,** 1000 Madison Ave. [77th/78th] ☎ 570-2211 . . . For flavors with a Far Eastern spin, we go to the **Chinatown Ice Cream Factory,** 65 Bayard St. [Elizabeth/Bowery] ☎ 608-4170, especially for the lychee, the almond cookie, and the ginger.

PIES

Pies from these places make us happy: **The Little Pie Co.,** 424 W. 43rd St. [9th/10th] ☎ 736-4780, which makes pies like sour cream apple walnut, pear-apple crumb, and banana cream coconut; **Bubby's,** 120 Hudson St. [N. Moore] ☎ 219-0666 (call to order), whose signature pie is the caramel apple; and pies from the **Cupcake Cafe,** 522 Ninth Ave. [39th] ☎ 465-1530 . . . Sue Houghtaling's chocolate mousse pie is available at **Houghtaling Mousse Cafe,** 389 Broome St. [Centre] ☎ 226-3724, and comes in several flavors (though the straight chocolate with the chocolate crust is really out of this world) and sizes, from $8.50–$22 . . . For sweet potato pie, **Georgie's Pastry Shop,** 50 W. 125th St. [5th/Lenox] ☎ 831-0722.

SCHNECKEN

We think the best places to satisfy schnecken cravings are at **Greenberg's,** 1100 Madison Ave. [82nd/83rd] ☎ 744-0304, 2187 Broadway [77th/78th] ☎ 580-7300, and 518 Third Ave. [34th/35th] ☎ 686-3344, Macy's ☎ 494-1091, and at **Kramer's Pastries,** 1643 Second Ave. [85th/86th] ☎ 535-5955.

TARTS

We vowed we wouldn't endlessly plug the newsletter version of *Manhattan User's Guide* in this book, but allow us a brief anecdote. After every issue of MUG is completed, we give ourselves one treat and it is always a tart from **City Bakery,** 22 E. 17th St. [5th/Bway] ☎ 366-1414. City Bakery has been open since December 1990, and its baker and owner, Maury Rubin, has been turning out a succession of beautiful-looking and better-tasting tarts in often surprising flavors. Yes, there's a lush chocolate and an ideal apple, but we've had, over the years and among many notables, blueberry coconut, crème brûlée, milky way, and cranberry almond. Mr. Rubin uses only the freshest local ingredients. Fruit tarts, for example, are available only when the fruit is locally available. They use farmstead products exclusively. That means, they get the milk, cream, and butter from farms that do all the steps from milking to bottling. And you do taste the difference. One time, one of the staff told us that the baker made white chocolate baby tarts because "he's in a good mood." Judging by his work, he's in a good mood a lot.

MORE When **Margaret Braun,** ☎ 929-1582, one of the city's notable cakemakers (see above), was in art school, she paid for it by working in bakeries. She liked the baking so much that she found a way to combine it with her love of art. She makes extraordinary cakes, but is also a sugar artist. Combining sugar, water and vegetable gums, she creates a sugar that can be rolled and cut and transformed into sculpture. She then applies her skills as a painter to designing directly onto the sugar with food coloring. She makes boxes, place cards, keepsakes, party favors, and ornaments out of sugar, as well as specialized toppers for wedding cakes. When it's dry, the sugar is like a bone china (durable unless you drop it), and the boxes can be kept for years. They can be monogrammed or otherwise personalized.

TEA

UPTOWN

Carlyle Hotel, 35 E. 76th St. [Mad]
☎ 570-7192. High tea from 3–5:30.

English Speaking Union, 16 E. 69th St. [5th/Mad] ☎ 879-6800.
3–5:30, 3–7:30 on Tues.

Kings' Carriage House, 251 E. 82nd St. [2nd/3rd] ☎ 734-5490. Mon.–Sat. 3–4:30.

Lowell Hotel, 28 E. 63rd St. [Park/Mad]
☎ 838-1400. 3:30–6:30.

MacKenzie-Childs, 824 Madison Ave. [68th/69th] ☎ 570-6050. 2–6.

Mad.61, 10 E. 61st St. [5th/Mad]
☎ 833-2200. Tea and the dessert menu can be ordered all day long.

Mark Hotel, 25 E. 77th St. [5th/Mad]
☎ 879-1864. 2:30–5.

Mayfair Regent, 610 Park Ave. [65th]
☎ 288-0800. 3–5:30.

The Pierre, 2 E. 61st St. [5th]
☎ 838-8000. 3–5:30.

Plaza Athénée, 37 E. 64th St. [Mad/Park]
☎ 734-9100. A choice of teas is available all day long in the lounge.

Toraya, 17 E. 71st St. [5th/Mad]
☎ 861-1700. Japanese green tea and pastries from 11–5:30.

Trois Jean, 154 E. 79th St. [Lex/3rd]
☎ 988-4858. Tea and pastries from 2–5.

MIDTOWN

Algonquin, 59 W. 44th St. [5th/6th]
☎ 840-6800. Tea, coffee, and little snacks served in the lobby any time.

Bendel's, 721 Fifth Ave. [56th]
☎ 247-1100. 2:30–5.

Felissimo, 10 W. 56th St. [5th/6th]
☎ 247-5656. 3–5.

Fitzpatrick Hotel, 687 Lexington Ave. [56th/57th] ☎ 355-0100. 3–5.

Four Seasons Hotel, 57 E. 57th St. [Mad/Park] ☎ 758-5700. 3–5.

Le Train Bleu at Bloomie's, 1000 Lexington Ave. [59th/60th]
☎ 705-2100. 3–5.

Peacock Alley at the Waldorf, 301 Park Ave. [50th] ☎ 355-3000. 2–5.

Peninsula, 700 Fifth Ave. [55th]
☎ 247-2200. 2:30–5.

Pierpont Morgan Library, 29 E. 36th St. [Mad] ☎ 685-0610. In the Morgan Court. Tues.–Fri., 2–4; Sat.–Sun., 2–5.

Plaza, 768 Fifth Ave. [59th]
☎ 759-3000. 3–6.

Royalton, 44 W. 44th St. [5th/6th]
☎ 869-4400. Informal service in the lobby.

Stanhope, 995 Fifth Ave. [81st]
☎ 288-5800. 1–5:30.

The Tea Box at Takashimaya, 693 Fifth Ave. [54th/55th] ☎ 350-0100. 3–5.

DOWNTOWN

Thé Adoré, 17 E. 13th St.
[5th/University] ☎ 243-8742.
Informal, served after lunch.

Anglers and Writers, 420 Hudson St.
[St. Luke's Pl.] ☎ 675-0810. 3–7.

CIII, 103 Waverly Pl. [MacDougal]
☎ 254-1200. 3:30–5.

Danal, 90 E. 10th St. [3rd/4th]
☎ 982-6930. Fri. and Sat., 4–6.

 Inn at Irving Place,
56 Irving Pl. [17th/18th]
☎ 533-4600. 3–6.

Kelley and Ping, 127 Greene St.
[Houston/Prince] ☎ 228-1212.
Informal service of Asian teas with
Asian sweets.

T Salon, 142 Mercer St. [Prince]
☎ 925-3700. Tea all day, but "Proper
Tea" is served 3:30–6. A New York Tea,
which includes a glass of port is served
from 6–8.

Tea and Sympathy, 108 Greenwich Ave.
[W. 12th] ☎ 807-8329. 11:30–6.

Yaffa's, 353 Greenwich St. [Harrison] ☎
966-0577. 2–5.

HOTELS

<————————————————————————————————————>

INTRODUCTION

When the demand for your sofabed or guest room exceeds supply, here are some of the city's options for putting up family, friends, or colleagues. We list rack rates to give you a relative idea of the hotel's prices, though they are frequently more than you need to pay. Rates vary considerably, depending on day of the week, season, and whatever promotional rates the hotel is offering. The prices quoted are the starting rates for standard doubles during the week, unless otherwise indicated.

THE DORALS

A tip sheet on the Dorals. **Doral Tuscany,** 120 E. 39th St. [Lex/Park] ☎ 686-1600. This is the nicest of the Doral properties in the city. It's in good but not perfect condition. The rooms are comfortably sized, but the bathrooms are disproportionately small. It could be a jewel with more care. $195. **Doral Court,** 130 E. 39th St. [Lex/Park] ☎ 685-1100. Larger than its neighbor just down the block with less character, for less money. $174. **Doral Park Avenue,** 70 Park Ave. [38th] ☎ 687-7050. About the same grade as for the Doral Court, passable rooms, though not remotely special and ridiculously small bathrooms. $174. **Doral Inn,** 541 Lexington Ave. [49th/50th] ☎ 755-1200. The runt of the litter. The lobby is a sea of luggage, the rooms have dirty carpets, drab brown and mousy gray furniture, little closet space. The renovated "executive level" floors are a bit better. $129 for standard rooms; executive level starts at $160.

HIPPEST HOTELS

CARLTON ARMS

The Carlton Arms, 160 E. 25th St. [Lex/3rd] ☎ 679-0680, is a glorious flophouse. The brochure for the hotel notes that the place isn't for everyone, and that is certainly the case. Though not located in the East Village, it's East Village in spirit, and there's something of Amsterdam as well. Amenities are at an absolute minimum; bathrooms are shared. There are artists' murals covering most of the walls (giving each room its unique character) and a red-light feel to the corridors. This is for young visitors, at least in spirit and probably in flesh. $57–$65.

FRANKLIN

Read more about **The Franklin,** 164 E. 87th St. [Lex/3rd] ☎ 369-1000, in the article in this chapter on NY's smartest hotels and the man who's responsible for transforming the property from blight to bloom.

GERSHWIN

Like the Carlton Arms, you'd send people to **The Gershwin,** 7 E. 27th St. [5th/Mad] ☎ 545-8000, provisionally. The accommodations are more Kurt Weill than Gershwin. But a lot of work has gone into a place that had gone to seed. Now, European and other international travelers keep the place busy, undeterred by things like little or no closet space and a pronounced funkiness. Standard rooms are $65, "designer rooms" are $82 (these have a phone, TV, a bit more stylish furniture). "Dorm rooms" (which sleep 4–8) are available for $20.

PARAMOUNT

The Paramount, 235 W. 46th St. [Bway/8th] ☎ 764-5500, continues to be one of the top NY choices for hip travelers, though it's well out of the budget range. We love spending time in the lobby here since it's a space with the sleekness of Deco and the shadows of film noir. Sitting on the balcony while having a bite to eat makes for great people watching. The rooms obviously suffer from the constraints of the original physical plant. Still, with their Think Big versions of Vermeer and many deft touches—the masking of a radiator, the detail on a pull cord—you may be able to adjust to the lack of space, both in the room and the bathroom. Doubles run from $190–$205.

ROYALTON

The Royalton, 44 W. 44th St. [5th/6th] ☎ 869-4400. The style here provides a Starck contrast to the routine, familiar, cookie-cutter formula of so much of American lodging. The staff is famously good-looking, their restaurant, 44, is a power lunch spot, and the lobby is, perhaps, the modern day equivalent of the Waldorf's Peacock Alley. You wouldn't call the rooms spacious, but they aren't tight the way they are at the Paramount. This is not a hotel particularly geared for the business person. A small desk with a not-so-great light means you're not likely to spend a lot of time going through contracts here. Do we love it, though? We do. Cool, sleek, a temple of fabulousness. $285.

MORE There's nothing quite like **The Chelsea Hotel,** 222 W. 23rd St. [7th/8th] ☎ 243-3700, where a stroll down the corridors is full of ghosts. $135 . . . **The Mercer,** 99 Prince St. [Mercer] ☎ 226-5656, is supposed to open. Someday. When it does, it's sure to be a magnet for hipsters.

HOTEL ELYSÉE

Mel Marvin, at the piano of the Monkey Bar before its renovation in 1994, used to crack jokes about **The Hotel Elysée,** 60 E. 54th St. [Mad/Park] ☎ 753-1066, referring to it as the Hotel Easylay. No more jokes, no more Mel. It's now one of New York's more attractive boutique hotels. The 99 rooms (modest in size, comfortable, and tastefully, if not memorably, decorated) have queen-sized beds, marble baths, and VCRs. Guests get a free continental breakfast, and compli-mentary wine and hors d'oeuvres at cocktail hour. There are three rooms with working fireplaces, and a few have terraces. The $700 presidential suite (a bargain as far as top suites go) has a fireplace, a terrace, a grand piano, and a service kitchen. Back-of-the-building rooms tend to be quieter, though a bit smaller. The restored Monkey Bar still has monkey murals, bar stools that look like olives, and the restaurant features the well-liked cooking of John Schenk. $245.

INN AT IRVING PLACE

The Inn at Irving Place.

The Inn at Irving Place, 56 Irving Pl. [17th/18th] ☎ 533-4600, is enchanting, with the ambience of those inns you think about escaping to in the country for a long fall walk. 12 rooms (7 suites), most with (nonworking) fireplaces, have been done up with period antiques, Frette linens, and lots of nice little touches, such as 2-line phones and CD players. No kids or pets allowed. Rates from $250 (includes conti-nental breakfast), but for that you have a genuinely discreet and gra-cious atmosphere. They serve tea in their parlor from 3–5, Wed.–Sun.—open to any-one. It's around $20 per person.

INN NEW YORK CITY

There are people who like to stay in large, looks-the-same-wherever-you-are-but-has-24-hour-room-service hotels, and those who seek lodging that is unique and mem-orable. For the latter, there is **Inn New York City,** 266 W. 71st St. [WEA] ☎ 580-1900. There are four suites total in the hotel, each different, individual, lovely. The Parlor Suite on the ground floor is spa-cious—there's plenty of room to accom-modate the piano and the Jacuzzi. You get your own terrace. The Loft Suite has an-tiques and reproductions, a fireplace, what they call a kitchenette (but you may call a kitchen), and a cedar closet. The Vermont Suite is a duplex with lots of pine and its own entrance. Our favorite is the Spa Suite, which takes up the whole floor, and comes with a spa room with glass brick, a sauna, and a very large Jacuzzi. You wouldn't go wrong with any of the four, though perhaps you'd opt for the Vermont last. Three of the suites have washers and dryers, all have dish-washers and lots of closet space, and many small and thoughtful touches. Prices start at $195 a night, add $50 for an additional guest. There's a two-night minimum, and monthly rates are available.

THE LOWELL

The Lowell, 28 E. 63rd St. [Mad/Park] ☎ 838-1400, is less well known than some of the flashier hotels in town, though that is precisely the point. Consider the Lowell for its restful atmosphere, its lovely rooms (especially the suites), and excellent service. There are 61 rooms, 48 of which are suites. Everything seems to have been fitted with enormous care. Many of the suites have wood-burning fire-

The Garden Suite at The Lowell.

places, and all have kitchens. The Gym Suite has an exercise room, but it is the Garden Suite that is considered the prize of the hotel. It's a one-bedroom suite with two terraces, one of which has a fountain and rose bushes, the other of which has an outdoor dining area. Closets have real wood hangers, there are bathrobes, ties racks, and an umbrella in the umbrella stand. Bathrooms, though they're quite small, have good amenities. For dinner, the Post House is next door, and you can meet for tea in the Pembroke Room. Rates from $275. The Garden Suite is $755.

THE MILLENIUM HILTON

The Millenium Hilton, 55 Church St. [Fulton/Dey] ☎ 693-2001. The single biggest asset of the hotel is its views. It can be an astonishment just walking off the elevator to your room, and if you're on the upper floors of the 55-floor hotel, you may find it hard to tear yourself away from the window. Everything about this place works smoothly. There's a swift check-in and check-out. Elevators are frighteningly fast. Rooms are small,

and we're not wild about the design, but it is an effective use of the space. Given the right view, you won't care anyway. There are nice touches in the room and bathroom: lighted makeup mirror, bathrobes, fax, 2-line phone, iron and ironing board, a copy of the current *New York* magazine. The mattress is perfect. The staff is extremely friendly. The heated swimming pool has a nifty view of St. Paul's Chapel. $280.

MORGANS

"Warm," "cozy," and "homey" are words used in a press release on the hotel **Morgans,** 237 Madison Ave. [37th/38th] ☎ 686-0300. They aren't the adjectives that first come to our mind. The hotel was redone by Andree Putman, and it is true that where there was gray, black, and white there is now camel, but whether the whole effect is soothing or ster-

ile depends on your own sense of what makes a space inviting. You could also describe it as modern monastic, but the fact that the windows are not double-glazed works against the construct of serenity. We like the Balcony Suite, with two balconies and lots of light. In sum, mixed feelings about Morgans. $220. The Balcony Suite is $475.

OMNI BERKSHIRE

The Omni Berkshire, 21 E. 52nd St. [5th/Mad] ☎ 753-5800. There are enough reasons to stay at the renovated Berkshire to overlook some of its weaknesses: a plain lobby, armoires rather than closets, a serious price tag for the room. But those rooms are stylish and pleasing. There's a business cen-ter, a small but satisfactory health club, and many extras: phones that double as infor-mation centers, marble bathrooms (they nar-rowed the hallways to increase the size of the bathrooms), free shoeshine and *NY Times,* etc. There's also the attraction of chef Elka Gilmore downstairs at Kokachin. $295.

OTHER LODGING

5 BED AND BREAKFASTS

The artist who runs **Soho B & B,** Crosby St. [Bleecker] ☎ 925-1034, sees to it that when you enter either the high-ceilinged loft or the carriage house you'll forget the back-street quality of Crosby St. The loft bedroom and bath are located just above the painter's stu-dio. The bedroom window looks out on Louis Sullivan's Bayard-Condict Building. There are fresh flowers, and a breakfast is provided for $90 per night. The carriage house has its own entry, a small sitting room, a double bed, and a kitchenette. Fresh flow-ers but no breakfast for $95 per night. Both accommodations are decorated with artifacts collected from Africa, the South Seas, and Mexico.

In the West Village is the three-room **Abingdon B & B,** 13 Eighth Ave. [12th] ☎ 243-5384. Located upstairs over the Brew Bar (coffee, not beer), these three nicely decorated rooms, with private phone lines, answering machines, and TVs (in a no-smoking environment), run from $75–$135. You get a $5 voucher for breakfast at the Brew Bar. This is an unhosted B & B, so it feels like having your own apartment. One room has the bath en suite, the other two share. The only downside might be if you're a light sleeper, since you're right over 8th Ave.

Upper West Side B & B, W. 77th St. [Bway/WEA] ☎ 472-2000. This beautifully restored landmarked 1891 townhouse on the Upper West Side has four bed and breakfast units in a setting that includes in-laid wooden floors and a carved woodwork stairway. Each unit has a large bedroom, sit-ting area, and antiques. Amenities include TV, separate phone lines, answering ma-chines, kitchenettes with pots and pans, dishes and glassware, toaster, coffeemaker, and microwave. One room has a small gazebo with a grape arbor in summer. No smoking. $120 per night.

The Gracie Inn, 502 E. 81st St. [York/East End] ☎ 628-1700. Twelve rooms range in size from a small studio to a two-bedroom penthouse suite with a roof terrace. Each room has a private bath, cable TV, VCR, telephone, and kitchenette. The country-style rooms have rag rugs, flowered curtains, and hand-stenciled borders on the walls. Most have some convertible furniture (both sofas and chairs), which can increase the sleeping space. $99–$169 for studios, $249–$449 for penthouse. Rates vary ac-cording to day and length of stay.

On **E. 93rd** [5th/Mad], ☎ 472-2000, an entire building of B & Bs with large bed-sitting rooms and bathrooms; microwaves, toaster ovens, separate phone lines, cable, dishes and glasses; queen-sized beds, love seats, and chairs. Rooms in the back look out over a small garden. $99.

Le Refuge Inn B & B, 620 City Island Ave on City Island, the Bronx ☎ 718-885-2478. The warmth of the welcome, the pleasant old sea captain's house on the main strip of City Island, and the chamber concerts on Sundays are the best reasons to visit Pierre Saint-Denis's inn in the far reaches of the Bronx. M. Saint-Denis is also the proprietor of Le Refuge, a restaurant on the Upper East Side that MUG likes very much. Though we have stayed at the inn, we have not tried the prix fixe dinner here, but we expect it is up to M. Saint-Denis's usual high standards. For us, City Island allows you to feel far removed from many aspects of city life, yet you can stand at the water's edge and see the twin towers on the far horizon. The island is often described as a bit of New England in New York, a description that may be stretching a point. We can't say we're enamored either of the restaurants on the island: The Lobster Box, 34 City Island Ave. [Rochelle/Belden] ☎ 718-885-1952, or Johnny's Reef, 2 City Island Ave. [Belden]

☎ 718-885-2086. After a lobster at The Lobster Box, we left longing for Ogunquit, and at Johnny's Reef, nearly everything is fried. If you take your fried foods outside to eat, you may feel like Tippi Hedren—the gulls here are relentless and incontinent.

B & B COMPANIES
City Lights, ☎ 737-7049, has the right attitude. Yedida Nielsen, who's been doing this for more than a decade, screens all the apartments for "safety, privacy, comfort, and the personal warmth and friendliness of staying in a real home." You'll be asked about budget, whether you want hosted or unhosted, number and size of beds, part of town, and any special requirements or preferences. B & Bs have minimum stays. Each guest gets an evaluation form at the end. We'd start our search for a B&B with City Lights . . . You might also try **Urban Ventures** ☎ 594-5650.

FURNISHED APARTMENTS
The Sutton, 330 E. 56th St. [1st/2nd] ☎ 752-8888, specializes in stays of a month or longer. Furnished apartments in sizes from studios to two-bedroom suites run $4,000–$12,500 a month. Kitchens have everything you need, except food; there is maid service, a concierge, and a health club.

SEAPORT INN

Not that you want your guests to think that the South Street Seaport is New York, but if you want to give them a different perspective on the city, try Peck Slip (named for mer-chant Benjamin Peck who, in the 1760s, built the building that became the Peck Slip Market). That's where Best Western has their **Seaport Inn,** 33 Peck Slip [Front] ☎ 766-6600, and though the neighborhood doesn't exactly look like the plaza in front of the Plaza, it's a great base from which to explore Manhattan's history. The rooms are only adequate in size, but are nicely done, and come with queen- or king-sized beds, standard bathrooms (though a few have steam or whirlpool), and some rooms have views toward the East River or the Brooklyn Bridge. From $139.

SMARTEST HOTELS

In an age when you often get less for more, hotelier/real estate attorney Bernard Goldberg is giving more for less. His philosophy is to "buy the property at the right price and put the money into the things the consumer wants and enjoys. Fill up the hotel and give the best value." His moderately priced hotels have well-designed rooms and original art in the public areas, and don't charge extra for videos for the VCR, CDs, the specially bound volumes of literary classics, fresh flowers, breakfast, concerts, and after-theatre dessert buffets. "I have a phobia about charging for extras. I hate checking out of a hotel and finding a minibar charge for pretzels for $2.50 when you know you could have bought them for 35¢. That's why we provide free Perrier and don't have minibars in our rooms. A hotel makes its money on the price of the bed, not every which way. An empty room can't be regained." MUG asks about the free concerts. Mr. Goldberg replies, "Oh, of course! People say I should charge something. Charge $1 they say. Why? It's a nice feeling to come into a hotel lobby when you are away from home and hear music."

The Franklin, 164 E. 87th St. [Lex/3rd] ☎ 369-1000. The Franklin was so run down that Mr. Goldberg's daughter avoided the block on her way to and from school. His family's reaction to his announcement that he was going to buy it was concern for his mental state. "Crannies in the walls were full of crack vials, there were bullet holes in the walls." Now, there is an Elie Nadelman in the lobby, the hotel offers free parking to its guests, and, Mr. Goldberg says, "Even I can't get a room there." The place is a textbook example of how to take a property with tiny rooms and gussy it up with a lot of style and not a few freebies. If you need a lot of space, stay elsewhere. If you like the Paramount, you'll like the Franklin. $149.

The Hotel Wales, 1295 Madison Ave. [92nd/93rd] ☎ 876-6000. The Wales was the first hotel that Mr. Goldberg bought. "I'm a real estate lawyer. I lived near there and walked by it. It was a run-down dump. I kept saying to myself, 'I don't get it. It's a great building, a European boutique-type of hotel.' " So he bought it. "We didn't do anything, no major architectural work, just cleaning and furnishing." Stripping 80 years of white paint off the interior, though, revealed beautiful woodwork. MUG thinks it's an ideal hotel for the neighborhood: quiet and pleasantly old-fashioned. The rooms aren't extraordinary (the hallways are even dowdy), but they have lots of wood pieces and details and a comfortable feeling. Not for your cutting-edge friends or those who require much luxury, but for just about anybody else. There are free chamber concerts there every Sunday. $165.

The Mansfield, 12 W. 44th St. [5th/6th] ☎ 944-6050. The Mansfield was built in 1904 and had become a monument to

The stylish Hotel Mansfield.

sheetrock. When they started stripping it away, "treasures of iron and steelwork were discovered," as well as other pleasant surprises. These include a steel-structured glass dome, an elevator with iron and glass doors, copper sheathing on the windows, and terrazzo floors. A glass skylight has been repaired. The rooms are, again, quite small, but are so beautifully designed that they are extremely inviting and pleasing. A beautiful restoration, and quite an appealing hotel. $145.

The Roger Williams, 131 Madison Ave. [31st] ☎ 684-7500. At the time this book was being prepared, Mr. Goldberg had an-nounced plans to renovate this 211-room hotel in an "Arts and Crafts style, because that's when it was built." He's chosen Rafael Viñoly to do the renovation, which is scheduled to be completed in early 1997. If we were the betting types, we'd bet this is going to be another success. Post-renovation rates are expected to be in the $125 range.

The Shoreham, 33 W. 55th St. [5th/6th] ☎ 247-6700. For so many years the Shoreham seemed to us a lost soul. It was neither a good hotel, a good bargain, nor a good character study. Now, it's streamlined and soigné, with Warren McArthur furniture, a Winold Reiss mural in the lobby, and cool, clean rooms that only lack Carole Lombard in them. $215.

TOP HOTELS

THE FOUR SEASONS

At most hotels, you get out of the taxi, go through the doors, walk to the front desk, and pull out a credit card. You don't just go into I. M. Pei's **The Four Seasons**, 57 E. 57th St. [Mad/Park] ☎ 758-5700, you make an entrance. Rather than reaching for your wallet, you are likely to be gazing up at the geometric, soaring expanse of the lobby; instead of the mundane concerns of checking in, you are almost compelled to make conclusions about space and scale and comfort. We find it vastly preferable to the timid or the overly familiar, and the stouthearted may find the scale amusing even as it arm wrestles them to the ground in easy domination. As New Yorkers, we find sitting in the lobby lounge (for tea or a drink) soothing, since it offers our greatest luxury in abundance: space. We easily warm up to the comfortably sized rooms that are filled with lots of English sycamore and all the amenities you'd expect and some touches you wouldn't: e.g., drapes that open automatically from a switch next to the bed. The views from many of the rooms are wonderful, and the service throughout the hotel is of exceptional calibre. Room rates from $550.

THE ST. REGIS

The St. Regis, 2 E. 55th St. [5th/Mad] ☎ 753-4500. You stay here for the service, Lespinasse, and the King Cole Bar. In some ways, we think the lobby here is even less welcoming than the Four Seasons. The Four Seasons says Public Space, while this one, small and with few chairs, says Private quite as forcefully. Other spaces in the hotel, most notably the King Cole Bar, are meant for you to install yourself. (There's also the small, delightful, mahogany-paneled Cognac room and the Astor Court for tea.) The St. Regis has rich, Old World rooms with marble baths, but you are more likely to come away remembering you had a butler (one per floor) than the specifics of the room. The St. Regis is a popular place for weddings and other events in their banquet and meeting facilities, with the St. Regis Roof being the most well known. Prices from $383.

MORE Other top hotels in the city include: **The Carlyle,** 35 E. 76th St. [Mad] ☎ 744-1600. Rates start at $325 . . . **The Mark,** 25 E. 77th St. [5th/Mad] 744-4300. Rates start at $325 . . . **The Peninsula,** 700 Fifth Ave. [55th] ☎ 247-2200. Rates start at $340 . . . **The Pierre,** Fifth Ave. and 61st ☎ 838-8000. Rates start at $335 . . . **The Regency,** 540 Park Ave. [61st] ☎ 759-4100. Rates start at $285 . . . **The Plaza Athenée,** 37 E. 64th [Mad/Park] ☎ 734-9100. Rates start at $295 . . . **The Ritz Carlton,** 112 Central Park South [6th] ☎ 757-1900. Rates start at $299 . . . **The NY Palace,** 455 Madison Ave. [50th] ☎ 888-7000, could be among the top hotels in the city after renovation by its current owner, the Sultan of Brunei, is complete. We saw model rooms (and renderings) for the towers, which are done in two schemes: modern and classic. They're quite handsome, with much attention to detail. The whole place has been thoroughly de-Leona-ized. With Le Cirque slated to take over much of the Villard Houses, this property, with its prime location, may be one of the most sought-after hotels in the city. Rates from $325.

UNDER $150

UPPER EAST SIDE

Barbizon Hotel, 140 E. 63rd St. [Lex] ☎ 838-5700. Only the single tiny "studios" qualify here at $130. These are bed-sized rooms, but are worth considering for the neighborhood. There aren't many amenities, and rooms on Lexington can be a bit noisy.

UPPER WEST SIDE

Hotel Beacon, 2130 Broadway [75th] ☎ 787-1100, and the **Milburn Hotel,** 242 W. 76th St. [Bway] ☎ 362-1006, are two somewhat similar properties, a stone's throw from each other, both (partly) residential, with remodeled, small rooms, good beds, and kitchenettes. A good value for the money; a slight edge to the Beacon for ambience. The Beacon starts at $115, the Milburn, $119.

MIDTOWN

The Martha Washington, 30 E. 30th St. [Mad/Park] ☎ 689-1900. *"We've learned what women want"* says the Smithsonian-worthy, earnestly unfashionable brochure for the old Martha. The hotel is for women only, and this odd throwback is often frequented by young European woman in possession of more humor than cash. A single room without bath is $40. A double with bath is $80, but there are very low weekly rates (the same double with bath is $290 by the week).

　　The Roger Williams, 131 Madison Ave. [30th/31st] ☎ 684-7500. See the Smartest Hotels article in this chapter.

　　Herald Square, 19 W. 31st St. [Bway/5th] ☎ 279-4017. Outside, the former Life Building has been restored to high lustre. Inside, you'll find simple, clean, small rooms (though the lighting is terrible), *very* limited closet space (a 2-foot rack in some cases), firm mattresses, good water pressure. $95.

The Manhattan, 17 W. 32nd St. [Bway/ 5th] ☎ 736-1600, was formerly the decrepit Aberdeen hotel, but you'd never know it by walking into the lobby, now rather sleek. In fact, after the overhaul, we had to ask to make sure it was really the same place. Rooms don't have the style of a hotel like the Franklin, and they're not large, but it's still a place worth knowing about. $115–$165.

Stanford Hotel, 43 W. 32nd St. [Bway/ 5th] ☎ 563-1480. The lobby here is China-town-restaurant-bright, but the hallways and rooms, which are small, are much more tasteful and serene, with lots of earth tones. Bathrooms are old-fashioned (some with pink and black tiles) but in decent shape. Some of the mattresses were less than su-perfirm. $99.

Madison Towers, 22 E. 38th St. [Mad] ☎ 685-3700. A possibility, but our most re-cent visit was less favorable than previous ones. Rooms don't feel cramped, but they can be dark and can have a residue of smoke from the previous occupant. The front desk is considerably less considerate than we re-membered. $150.

Hotel Metro, 45 W. 35th St. [Bway/5th] ☎ 947-2500. They buried the old Colling-wood, and not a moment too soon. The Metro has arisen in the same physical plant—not that you'd ever know it. The new Deco de-sign rightly spruces up the place—this is a smart choice for a modestly priced hotel in the area. As usual in this price range, neither rooms nor bathrooms are big, but

for about $125 a night, with continental breakfast, it's a good deal. If you get the right room on a high floor, you get closeup views of the Empire State Building. There's a small exercise room, rooftop terrace, library, and a lounge with a fireplace.

The Mansfield, 12 W. 44th St. [5th/6th] ☎ 944-6050. See the Smartest Hotels arti-cle in this chapter.

The Wentworth, 59 W. 46th St. [5th/ 6th] ☎ 719-2300. Another in the hearten-ing increase of modest-but-decent afford-able hotels. No awards for style, but with prices mostly under $115, this place can be recommended for value.

Portland Square, 132 W. 47th St. [Bway/ 6th] ☎ 382-0600. Unadorned hospital-like rooms, but clean, with firm mattresses. Bath-rooms are pretty hoary; minimal closets. $79.

Pickwick Arms Hotel, 230 E. 51st St. [2nd/3rd] ☎ 355-0300. You will not get pretty or cheerful rooms here, but you get a good midtown neighborhood and a well-run hotel. $99, less for rooms with shared baths.

Wyndham Hotel, 42 W. 58th St. [5th/6th] ☎ 753-3500. When we think of the Wyndham, we think of Bertie Wooster's Aunt Dahlia. The hotel has plenty of ec-centric splash and color, is firmly rooted in an earlier, indeterminate era, and lacks only Wodehouse's hilarity, though that is cer-tainly arguable. So the beds are a little soft, the water pressure a little weak. The quirk-iness appeals to a lot of show-biz types (and others) who love the Wyndham like an ec-centric favorite aunt. Rooms are $145.

CHELSEA

Chelsea Inn, 46 W. 17th St. [5th/6th] ☎ 645-8989. Perfect for some, but not for everyone. There are 13 spartan rooms, many with a shared bath, most with kitchenettes. No elevator or amenities to speak of. $80.

VILLAGE

The Larchmont, 27 W. 11th St. [5th/6th] ☎ 989-9333. A 50-room hotel with tiny rooms, but each one has many nice touches, including books in each room, TV, AC, a desk, and good lighting. Downtown could use a dozen more Larchmonts. Bathrooms are shared. $85.

Washington Square Hotel, 103 Waverly Pl. [Wash Sq.] ☎ 777-9515. You won't fall in love with the spare rooms, but they are clean and you might get one with a view over Washington Square Park. $110.

SOHO

Off Soho Suites Hotel, 11 Rivington St. [Bowery/Chrystie] ☎ 353-0860. Off Bowery is more accurate, but if the neighborhood isn't a problem for you, you can have functional, clean, decent-looking rooms at a modest price. $85 for a suite for two (shared kitchen and bath), $139 for a private kitchen and bath (up to 4 adults).

MORE See Other Lodging in this chapter for information on Bed and Breakfasts.

THE WALDORF=ASTORIA

The Waldorf=Astoria, 301 Park Ave. [50th] ☎ 355-3000. Spacious rooms and fairly quiet, though it is possible to hear the garbage trucks in the middle of the night. The staff is polite and service is good, but when the hotel is busy, room service can get behind. The biggest drawback, and for us a major one: the shower is terrible. The knob is on the opposite end of the tub from the showerhead, particularly inconvenient because you'll need to make frequent trips to it to try to get a decent shower—unlikely in any case. The pressure is low except when the dial is turned all the way to hot. That improves the pressure, but makes the water too hot. Readers who have stayed at the Savoy in London know they have incredible showers, perhaps the shower of your life. The Waldorf, on this count, is pretty far at the other end. From $325 . . . **The Towers** is deservedly famous as a kind of hotel within a hotel. It has its own entrance, a separate check-in, separate concierge, butlers, and bellmen, and is one of the most deluxe hotel spaces around. There are permanent residents, too, who enjoy the same security and privacy as the large number of dignitaries and celebrities who have stayed or lived here over the years. From $369.

THE WARWICK

The Warwick, 65 W. 54th St. [5th/6th] ☎ 247-2700 $230. Very spacious rooms for the price, though the decorating lacks excitement. Roomy, walk-in closets and pretty bathrooms. If you're looking for a midrange midtown hotel with a little extra leg room, try the Warwick. $260.

INFORMATION

AUCTIONS

Christie's, 502 Park Ave. [59th] ☎ 546-1000. High season is May and November. **Christie's East,** 219 E. 67th St. [2nd/3rd] ☎ 606-0400, auctions less expensive merchandise—high season is June and December.

Federal Auctions. The GSA (General Services Administration) sells cars and other items, sometimes by auction, sometimes by sealed bids. The hotline for auction information is ☎ 800-488-7253.

F.I.T. Each year in April F.I.T. holds an auction to benefit the student scholarship fund. The auction is the idea of furniture conservator Eli Rios, who collects donated antiques all year. The students restore and refinish the pieces for the auction, thereby getting some practical experience and working for a good cause. ☎ 670-7823.

Leland's Auction House, ☎ 545-0800, says it is the "only sports memorabilia auction house in America." They have twice-yearly events at the Southgate Towers Hotel near Madison Square Garden. Leland's is the company that auctioned Babe Ruth's uniform, Jackie Robinson's hat, and, for New Yorkers, the "how sweet it is" ball that rolled through Bill Buckner's legs in the fifth game of the 1986 World Series, keeping the soon-to-be-champion Mets alive. Auction days at Leland's are festive family events, since bidders and nonbidders bring the kids to the viewing. Each auction lasts two days. For those who wish to consign items, Joshua Leland Evans is a licensed sports memorabilia appraiser.

Morrell & Co., 535 Madison Ave. [54th/55th] ☎ 688-9370, held, in 1994, the first live public auction of wines since prohibition. They are scheduling wine auctions four times a year at the Union League, 37th and Park. They stress the old and the rare, and not just French. They will send you a pamphlet that explains their bidding procedures (you don't have to be present to bid).

Police Auctions. The Police Department

auctions off seized property that includes everything from costume jewelry to cars and vans. By calling ☎ 406-1369, you can get a recorded schedule of auctions as well as directions to the inspection areas in Queens. Auctions are held in the auditorium at 1 Police Plaza. You make "payment in full right away" and buy all items "as is, no refunds, no warranties, no guarantees."

Sotheby's, 1334 York Ave. [71st] ☎ 606-7000. Over 500 auctions each year with the most intense months being May and November. You need a ticket for evening sales, and if you have a successful bid, expect to pay the hammer price plus the buyer's premium—15% up to $50,000 and 10% after that.

Swann Galleries, 104 E. 25th St. [Park/Lex] ☎ 254-4710, specializes in American rare books, including maps and atlases, autographs, manuscripts, photographs, and works of art on paper. They hold approximately 35 auctions a year on Thursday evenings. Works to be auctioned are on view the preceding Saturday and Monday through Wednesday. If you wish to consign something for sale, send in a description with a photocopy, if possible. The staff at Swann is small, so it may take them a while to get back to you. Generally, the minimum consignment accepted is $1,000, but this can be made up of more than one item. Map auctions generally occur in May and December.

Tepper and Lubin Galleries have a uniquely NY character—they're more like Zabar's than Sotheby's. "Yell out if I don't see ya," says the auctioneer. At one Saturday morning auction, a large old William and Mary–style GE Radio is shown briefly. "Take out the radio and make it a bar," advises the auctioneer before the bidding starts.

"Anyone need a zither? $10. Real cheap." One item, a coffee table, is expected to go for $40–$60. "Do I hear 20? 20? 10? Do I hear 10? No? Throw it out!" Everything imaginable goes on the block, including furniture of every period and varying degrees of quality, to rugs, paintings, silver, and china. At Tepper, go to look at the pieces (there are usually over a thousand lots per auction) on view the day before the auction, usually Friday. The catalogs are free, except for some specialty auctions. The auctions start at 10 A.M. on Saturday and go for most of the day. They average 100–120 lots per hour. You don't register, just raise your hand to bid. Have cash or a personal check (if you're a first-time

buyer, you will need a certified check), and be prepared to put down a deposit of 30% on the spot. The balance is due on pick-up, either within 30 minutes after the auction finishes or until the following Tuesday. A 10% premium of the successful bid price goes to the house. This means if you buy something for $100, you will pay $110 (plus sales tax). Lubin works essentially the same way, though they require a $50 deposit to bid and they accept major credit cards, personal checks, and cash. "Important" estate auctions mean higher quality items and a more serious atmosphere. Tepper is at 110 E. 25th St. [Park Ave. S./Lex] ☎ 677-5300. Lubin is at 110 W. 25th St. [6th/7th] 10th fl. ☎ 924-3777. Tepper auctions about twice a month, always on Saturday at 10 A.M. Lubin auctions are monthly on Thursday evenings at 6 P.M.

William Doyle, 175 E. 87th St. [Lex/3rd] ☎ 427-2730. They hold three or so auctions each month, with special ones in

Lalique, majolica, Belle Epoque, and couture scheduled once a year. The Tag Sale, next to the main auction house, has "treasure auctions" of more affordable items. On Tuesdays, 9:30–12:30, you can walk in with an item and have it appraised. There are public lectures on aspects of collecting and restoration. ☎ 427-4885 for a recorded announcement of upcoming auctions.

SELLING AT AUCTION Auction houses accept items on consignment. They all have minimum dollar amounts that they accept. If they take your items, you may have to pay a fee for the catalog listing, and the auction house takes a percentage of the hammer price. This is on a sliding scale depending on the value of the item. Since your consigned item actually belongs to you even while it is in the auction house, it's a good idea to carry insurance on it. You should work out with the auction house what the reserve amount is. This is usually the lowest bid they'll accept for the item. You may be charged if the lot does not reach the reserve. Since many auctions are of thematically grouped materials (maps and atlases, for example), it may take a few months until your item is actually auctioned.

BUILDINGS & ARCHITECTURE

An assortment of resources to learn more about the buildings and architecture of the city.

AIA Guide. The building-by-building bible by Elliot Willensky and Norval White. $24 at bookstores.

Building Codes. A binder of info on the city's building codes, available from Citybooks, 61 Chambers St. [Bway/Centre] ☎ 669-8245.

Building Information. ☎ 900-463-6362 is a number to call ($1.95 a minute) for specific city lot numbers, actions, DOB violations, and landmark status.

Municipal Art Society, 457 Madison Ave. [51st] ☎ 935-3960, has many walking tours conducted by architectural experts. The Information Exchange is a small library within the MAS containing books, periodicals, and clippings (they have been gathering these since the mid-'70s) organized by topic. M–F, 10–1 or by appt. MAS sponsors public programs on architecture and preservation and gives occasional courses.

Museum of the City of NY, Fifth Ave. and 103rd St., ☎ 534-1672, ext. 262, is the place to go for city photographs of all vintages. By appt.

NYC Landmarks Preservation Commission. 100 Old Slip [Water/South] ☎ 487-6800.

NY Historical Society, 2 W. 77th St. [CPW] ☎ 873-3400, has an extensive collection of architectural materials, plans, and drawings. They have the archives of many architectural firms, most significantly Cass Gilbert. You need to make an appt. at ext. 228. Hours are usually W–F, 12–5.

NY Landmarks Conservancy, 141 Fifth Ave. [21st] ☎ 995-5260, has a Technical Services division that answers telephone questions on the technical matters of architectural preservation. They will give referrals to craftsmen and contractors. They publish *The Restoration Directory,* which contains information on restoration contractors, masons, metalworkers, architectural woodworkers, and the like.

Stores. NY Bound, 50 Rockefeller Plaza ☎ 245-8503, and Urban Center Books, 457 Madison Ave. [51st] ☎ 935-3592.

Tours. Many tour guides of the better walking tour companies are excellent sources of information on NY buildings. See Tours in the Districts and Spaces chapter.

CENTRAL PARK

Administration: ☎ 360-8236.

Ball Field Permits: ☎ 408-0277.

Belvedere Castle and the Henry Luce Nature Observatory: mid-park at 79th St. ☎ 772-0210.

Bike Rental: Loeb Boathouse ☎ 861-4137 M–F, 10 A.M.–dusk; Sa & Su, 9 A.M.–dusk. $6–$12, I.D. needed.

Boathouse Cafe: 74th St. and East Drive ☎ 517-2233.

Carousel: 64th St. mid-park ☎ 879-0244 10:30–5 weekdays; 10:30–6 weekends. 90¢. Weather permitting.

Central Park Conservancy: ☎ 315-0385.

Concerts: 2 Philharmonic concerts and 2 Met operas on the North Meadow (while the Great Lawn is being restored) ☎ 875-5700. SummerStage schedule ☎ 360-2777.

Conservatory Garden: 105th St. and Fifth Ave., 8 A.M.–dusk. Tours on Sats. at 11, Apr.–Oct.

Croquet/Lawn Bowling Permits: north of Sheep Meadow ☎ 360-8133.

Charles A. Dana Discovery Center: 110th St. near Fifth Ave. ☎ 860-1370. Family workshops, education programs. Call for their calendar.

The Dairy: mid-park at 65th St. has current information about the park as well as its history and design ☎ 794-6564.

Gondola Rides: Loeb Boathouse 74th St. and East Drive ☎ 517-3623. Evening hours for up to 5 people through Nov. 1. $30/1/2 hour. Reservations are suggested.

Horseback Riding: Claremont Stables, 175 W. 89th St. [Amsterdam/Columbus] ☎ 724-5100. M–F, 6:30 A.M.–one hour before dusk, Sa & Su, 6:30 A.M.–4 P.M., $33 per hour. You need reservations.

Horsedrawn Carriages: 59th St. and Fifth Ave. or Sixth Ave. ☎ 246-0520. $34 for the first 20 minutes, $10 for each additional quarter hour.

Ice Skating: Lasker Rink mid-park at 106th St., Wollman Rink mid-park at 62nd St. ☎ 396-1010. $6.50 adults, $3.25 children, $3.25 skate rentals.

Information: At the Dairy, mid-park at 65th St. ☎ 794-6564.

Loeb Boathouse: 74th St., mid-park ☎ 517-2233.

Lost and Found: There isn't one.

Model Boats: Conservatory Water at E. 72nd St. [5th] ☎ 360-8133. You can get a permit to store your boat.

Parks Commissioner: Henry J. Stern ☎ 360-1305.

Pedal Carriages: Tavern parking lot from May–Oct. 9:30 A.M.–dusk, $15 per hour.

Police: 86th St., mid-park ☎ 570-4820.

Rock and Wall Climbing: North Meadow Recreation Center, mid-park at 97th St. ☎ 348-4867.

Rowboats: Loeb Boathouse, 74th St., mid-park. M–F, 10–5:30; Sa & Su, 10–6:30. $8 per hour. $20 deposit ☎ 517-2233.

Running: The reservoir is 1.58 miles around. The NY Road Runners Club holds weekly races or group runs ☎ 869-4455. Front-runners is the gay running group ☎ 724-9700.

Shakespeare in the Park: Delacorte Theater, 79th St., mid-park ☎ 861-8277. Tickets available on the same day in the park and at the Public.

Shakespeare Garden: mid-park at 79th St.

Special Events Infoline: ☎ 360-3456.

SummerStage: ☎ 360-2777.

Swedish Cottage Marionette Theater: mid-park at 79th St. ☎ 988-9093.

Swimming: Lasker Pool, mid-park at 106th St. ☎ 396-1010. Open July and Aug., 11–7.

Tavern on the Green: ☎ 873-3200.

Tennis: 7 A.M.–dusk. Permits at the Arsenal ☎ 360-8133. Full season adult permit is $50. Reservation line for permit holders, M–F, 1–4 ☎ 280-0205. Reservations are $3 each.

Traffic: In summer, roads closed weekends 7 P.M. Fri.–6 A.M. Mon. Weekdays, closed 10 A.M.–3 P.M. and 7 P.M.–10 P.M. (59th St. & Sixth Ave. to 72nd St. and Fifth is closed only from 7 P.M.–10 P.M.).

Trolley Tours: ☎ 397-3809. 90-minute tour leaves from Grand Army Plaza, 59th St. and Fifth Ave. weekdays 10:30, 1, and 3. $14.

Zoo: 64th St. & Fifth Ave. M–F, 10–5; Sa & Su, 10:30–5:30. Adults $2.50, 3–12-year-olds 50¢ ☎ 861-6030.

CHARITIES & VOLUNTEERING

CHARITIES

A few worthy charities among many. The Better Business Bureau publishes a useful *Charity Giving Guide.* Write to the BBB, 257 Park Ave. South, 10010.

Anti-Violence Project, 647 Hudson St. [13th/14th] ☎ 807-6761, is, more particularly, the New York City Gay and Lesbian Anti-Violence Project. They are a crime assistance agency that provides services for victims of bias crime, HIV/AIDS–related violence, sexual assault, and domestic violence. Services include a hotline, accompaniment to police or hospital, and counseling. They generally work to reduce public tolerance of anti-gay and -lesbian assaults.

Lawyers for Children, 110 Lafayette St. [Canal/Walker] ☎ 966-6420, provides legal representation and social workers for children who are either voluntarily placed into foster care by their parents, or in cases of neglect, abuse, termination of parental rights and custody and adoption. Even though judges may appoint lawyers for these children, it is not automatic. Without their advocacy, children may be left longer in institutional care. With it, children feel they haven't been forgotten. They expect to represent 4,000 children this year, and their goal is to see that the children end up in stable and happy homes.

Sanctuary for Families, POB 3344, Church St. Station, 10008 ☎ 349-6009, provides legal and social services for battered women and their children. They have a crisis shelter where women can stay for 90 days and then move to one of their transitional residences. Other services include counseling, legal services, art and play therapy for children.

Sprout Inc., 893 Amsterdam Ave. [103rd/104th] ☎ 222-9575, provides travel and recreation opportunities for developmentally disabled adults. Weekend trips to ten-day trips, as close as the Catskills and as far away as Paris.

These are some of the charities that see to it that the homebound, the homeless, and the hungry are fed all year round: **City Harvest** ☎ 463-0456. 15,000 pounds of food per day, left over from restaurants, events, and other food sources, is transported by City Harvest to places throughout the city that feed the homeless. **Citymeals-on-Wheels** ☎ 687-1234. Citymeals delivers hot, nutritious meals to the homebound elderly . . . **Food & Hunger Hotline** ☎ 533-7600. Offers an array of referral, counseling, and coordinating services for the homeless and hungry and the emergency food providers . . . **Food for Survival** ☎ 718-991-4300. This group gets food that is "cosmetically damaged" or that for other reasons would not be sold and distributes it to soup kitchens and other emergency food sources . . . **God's Love We Deliver** ☎ 294-8100. God's Love makes meals and then delivers them to hundreds of homebound people with AIDS, as well as providing nutrition counseling . . . **Holy Apostles Soup Kitchen** ☎ 807-6799. This soup kitchen has provided over two million meals in the dozen years since it started.

CHARITIES THAT PICK UP

These charities that pick up do so under certain conditions and circumstances. Most won't pick up for one or two items unless they're especially valuable. They also divide into two groups: some give your donations directly to needy people; other places accept only goods they can sell. These must, therefore, be of higher quality. No one will repair donated items and most places don't want mattresses. It may take time for the items to be picked up since charities often need to make special arrangements for a truck.

Council Thrift Shop ☎ 439-8373. Pickups in Manhattan only from 8th St.–96th St. They will take a maximum of five sealed boxes (no bags) of clothing in "very good condition." They do not give clothing away; they make their money from resales. No upholstered or large furniture. Waiting time for pickups is 2–4 weeks. Benefits the National Council of Jewish Women.

Furnish a Future is run by The Partnership for the Homeless ☎ 718-875-5353. They give donated items directly to clients who choose things in their warehouse. They help people make the transition from the shelter to permanent housing. They pick up only complete households or "major donations," i.e., ones that will fill a truck. Otherwise, you can call them and they will advise you where you can drop things off.

Goodwill Industries, ☎ 718-721-2900, picks up in Manhattan, Queens, and the Bronx. They'll take furniture in salable condition. They accept resalable clothing and household items only with furniture. Items are sold in their thrift shops or occasionally given directly to the handicapped.

Harlem Restoration Project, ☎ 864-6992, pickup in Manhattan only from 9–12. They accept clothing, household goods, books, bric-a-brac, and furniture. They will take bedding. Items are sold in their thrift shop and are donated to other agencies.

The Irvington Institute for Immunological Research, ☎ 879-4555, will pick up in Manhattan from 8th St.–96th St. They take furniture, clothing, appliances and electronics (in working order), and household items. Clothing and small items need to be packed in cartons, and there is a three-carton minimum for pickups. Benefits the Irvington Institute, which funds medical research on cancer, diabetes, AIDS, and other diseases.

Materials for the Arts, ☎ 255-5924. Not a charity but an organization that provides materials for the not-for-profit cultural community of NYC. About 1,500 groups are registered with them as recipients—everyone from a children's art project to Lincoln Center. Donations can be used as stage props, reception room furniture, and so on. They do not take clothing or bedding but will accept just about everything else. They have their own truck and pick up in the five boroughs. There is a two-week wait. If they cannot use what you are donating, they will try to refer you to another group.

Memorial Sloan Kettering Thrift Shop ☎ 535-1250. Things have to be really, really good before they will rent a truck: furniture, paintings, jewelry, china, clothing.

Nazareth Housing ☎ 777-1010. Sister Mary Agnes doesn't have much storage space, so whatever they pick up has to go directly into a formerly homeless person's new apartment. They have a small van, pick up in Manhattan, and will take decent household items and furniture.

Repeat Performance Thrift Shop ☎ 684-5344. Again, not a charity but donations benefit the New York City Opera. They take only *large* donations of furniture. They generally pick up only in Manhattan,

but for large donations will make arrangements in the other boroughs.

Salvation Army, ☎ 757-2311, picks up generally from 8–3. They will take furniture that's free of rips, tears, or stains, bagged clothing, bric-a-brac, and appliances. They climb two flights for furniture and three flights for clothing. They will come for clothing with no furniture. If you donate an item for which you will claim more than a $500 value, it must be accompanied by an appraisal form and tax form #8283.

Spence-Chapin Thrift Shop, ☎ 718-347-2953, does regular pickups in Manhattan of resalable furniture (if you call, you'll get their moving company). Money goes for their programs assisting children and families.

St. George's Thrift Shop, ☎ 979-0420, picks up furniture only, in Manhattan on Tuesdays. If it's upholstered, it must be in excellent condition. Proceeds go to a food program and a homeless shelter.

St. Luke's Thrift Shop, ☎ 924-9364, accepts furniture in good condition. Allow a couple of weeks for pickups. Some of the proceeds go to a scholarship fund for the school and an AIDS food service.

St. Vincent de Paul Society, ☎ 718-292-9090. There is a two-bag minimum for pickup in Manhattan. All furniture must be in usable condition and require no repairs. Donations go into thrift shops and directly to needy families.

VOLUNTEERING

Robert Schmehr, ☎ 459-8433, is in charge of an **Art and Recreational Therapy** program at St. Clare's Hospital, 51st St. [9th/10th]—the largest designated AIDS center on the East Coast. According to Mr. Schmehr, over 50% of the hospital is centered around HIV, and many of the patients are very poor. "Some have been incarcerated, some have had substance abuse problems. Since HIV gets people sick during their most productive years, most of the patients are between 20 and 40." They have extensive hospital stays and not many visitors. Through art classes and social events, the volunteers try to create a supportive community. Over the holidays, there is an additional need for one-day volunteers.

Dr. Evelyn Lipper, a pediatrician, has developed a language program at NY Hospital where over 10,000 patients come into the pediatric clinic each year. Called **Heads Up: Children Read Listen and Learn,** volunteers teach parents the importance of reading to their children and teach them *how* to read to their children. Dr. Lipper believes that reading aloud stimulates speech and language development in young children. They look for people who have had experience with children and who can donate one afternoon a week consistently for a year. Call ☎ 874-7261.

New York Association for New Americans, 17 Battery Place [Washington] ☎ 425-2900, is an immigrant services and refugee reresettlement agency. NYANA help starts at the airport, continues with assistance learning English, finding a place to live, a place to work—the whole socialization process. NYANA needs volunteers to help new Americans, in informal settings, improve their English, among other things. Call volunteer services at ☎ 425-5051, ext 8111.

At Bellevue Hospital, 27th St. & First Ave., the Patient Advocate Volunteer Emergency Room Service **(PAVERS)** program trains volunteers and medical students to act as liaisons between patients, doctors, and family in ER situations. Volunteers look to basic, nonmedical needs of patients and offer emotional support for family. PAVERS with additional training also screen women 16 and over for domestic violence (25% of the women seeking ER care are victims of domestic violence), refer them to resources in and outside the hospital, and see that their cases are documented in the hospital records. ☎ 561-4858.

The Hospital for Special Surgery is a specialty hospital on E. 70th St. [York] where people with rheumatic diseases and joint problems come for care. The **VOICES** Program (Volunteer Outpatient Community Empowerment Information Services) uses volunteers to conduct needs assessments, provide information on Medicaid and SSI, and referrals to community resources to the patients in the clinics. There has been some staff cutback, making the volunteers more important than ever. ☎ 774-2467.

CLEARINGHOUSES New York Cares, ☎ 228-5000, in addition to their yearly coat drive, produces a monthly calendar of opportunities for volunteers, which you receive after a bit of training. Some are one-day programs (distributing toys or planting bulbs), other are for longer commitments . . . The **Mayor's Voluntary Action Center,** ☎ 788-7550, maintains a computer database of volunteer opportunities in about 3,000 agencies in all five boroughs . . . The **Volunteer Referral Center,** 161 Madison Ave. [32nd/ 33rd] ☎ 745-8249, refers volunteers to not-for-profit institutions in Manhattan. There are many opportunities to work with children, "hospitals are always in need," visiting the elderly, "clerical work is always in demand," and there are now many opportunities for teaching English as a second language.

COMPLAINTS

Better Business Bureau ☎ 533-7500; Dept. of Consumer Affairs ☎ 487-4444.

Air Pollution: Dept. of Environmental Protection ☎ 718-699-9811.

Banks: Federal Reserve System ☎ 202-452-3693.

Doctors: NY State Dept. of Education Office of Professional Discipline ☎ 951-6400. NY County Medical Society Peer Review ☎ 684-4670.

Dry Cleaning: Neighborhood Cleaners Assoc. ☎ 967-3002 ext. 239.

Garbage: Sanitation Action Center ☎ 219-8090.

Heat: Central Complaint Bureau ☎ 960-4800.

Insurance: NY State Insurance Dept. ☎ 602-0203.

Lawyers & Judges: Bar Assoc. Departmental Disciplinary Committee ☎ 685-1000.

Mail: Postmaster ☎ 330-3668.

Movers: Dept. of Consumer Affairs ☎ 487-4444. The BBB releases a report each year naming the most-complained-about movers ☎ 533-7500.

Noise: Dept. of Environmental Protection ☎ 718-699-9811.

Potholes: Dept. of Transportation ☎ 442-7939.

Real Estate Agents: NY Dept. of State, Div. of Licensing ☎ 417-5748.

Schools: NYC Board of Education ☎ 510-1500, for fraud, corruption, criminal activities in public schools. NYS Dept. of Education for private and parochial schools ☎ 518-474-3879.

Sidewalks: Dept. of Transportation ☎ 442-7148.

Stores: Dept. of Consumer Affairs ☎ 487-4444. BBB ☎ 533-7500.

Street Cleaning: Sanitation Action Center ☎ 219-8090.

Street Lights: Dept. of Transportation ☎ 442-7070.

Subway: Transit Authority ☎ 718-330-3322.

Taxis & Car Services: Taxi & Limousine Commission ☎ 221-8294, but all complaints must be in writing: T&L C, 221 W. 41st St., NYC 10036.

Tenant Issues: For stabilized or rent-controlled apts. ☎ 718-739-6400, info and complaint line.

Water: Dept. of Health ☎ 442-1999.

DEPARTMENT STORE HOURS

ABC Carpet & Home
888 Broadway [19th] ☎ 473-3000.
M–F, 10–8. Sa, 10–7. Su, 11–6:30

Barneys (downtown)
106 Seventh Ave. [17th] ☎ 593-7800.
M–Th, 10–9. Fr, 10–8. Sa, 10–7.
Su, 12–6

Barneys (uptown)
640 Madison Ave. [61st] ☎ 826-8900.
M–F, 10–8. Sa, 10–7. Su, 10–6

Bergdorf Goodman
754 Fifth Ave. [58th] ☎ 753-7300.
M–W, 10–6. Th, 10–8.
Fr & Sa, 10–6

Bergdorf Goodman Men
745 Fifth Ave. [58th] ☎ 753-7300.
M–W, 10–7. Th, 10–8. Fr, 10–7.
Sa, 10–6

Bloomingdale's
1000 Third Ave. [59th] ☎ 705-2000.
M–W, 10–6:50. Th, 10–9. Fr,
10–6:50. Sa, 10–6:30. Su, 11–6:30

Century 21
22 Cortland St. [Church] ☎ 227-9092.
M–F, 7:45–7. Sa, 10–7

Henri Bendel
712 Fifth Ave. [55th/56th]
☎ 247-1100. M–W, 10–6:30. Th,
10–8. Fr & Sa, 10–6:30.
Su, 12–6

Lord & Taylor
424 Fifth Ave. [39th] ☎ 391-3344. M,
10–8:30. Tu & We, 10–6:30. Th,
10–8:30. Fr & Sa, 10–6:30. Su, 12–6

Macy's
151 W. 34th St. [6th/7th] ☎ 695-4400.
M, 10–8:30. Tu & We, 10–7.
Th & Fr, 10–8:30. Sa, 10–7. Su, 11–6

Saks
611 Fifth Ave. [50th] ☎ 753-4000.
M–W, 10–7. Th, 10–8. Fr & Sa, 10–7.
Su, 12–6

Takashimaya
693 Fifth Ave. [54th/55th]
☎ 350-0100. M–W, 10–6. Th, 10–8.
Fr & Sa, 10–6

KIDS

The Parents League of NY, 115 E. 82nd St. [Lex/Park] ☎ 737-7385, was established in 1913 and has three main concerns: education, entertainment, and safety. In terms of education, you can look at files of information on the over 125 independent schools in Manhattan. There is also a directory of schools that you can take home with you. They offer a one-on-one advisory service. After making an appointment, you meet with a "knowledgeable parent who has been through the process." They hold an Independent School Day in the fall of every year. Representatives from the schools attend, and parents and children can ask questions and get information. In the spring, there is an early childhood education event. The same type of service is offered for summer camps.

They keep extensive files on birthday party sites and entertainers, after-school activities, family travel, babysitters, and tutors. Especially useful are the parents' feedback cards. Whenever someone uses a party service or after-school program, they are asked to fill out one of these cards describing their experience. These cards are on file at PL for others to read to help in determining whether a service or activity will be useful to them. They have established the Safe Haven program—mostly on the Upper East and Upper West Sides (though they are working to expand it). Stores and shops that participate in this program display a yellow decal. Children who feel threatened know they can go into one of these shops to wait out the threat. There is a yearly health program and a series of workshops. Topics covered are things like Homework and Study Skills, Parent/School Communication, and Changing Schools.

You can join the Parents League for $35 a year. You then have access to their files and publications, you receive their Calendar and Guide to New York, and, if you have a toddler, *The Toddler Book,* which lists programs for children under the age of three.

The Early Childhood Development Center, 163 E. 97th St. [Lex/3rd] ☎ 360-7893, has been around for over 20 years. The parenting program here can begin when a child is four weeks old. Parents come with their children once a week for a professionally led one-hour group session. The emphasis is on answering the questions of new parents and focuses on "what is developmentally appropriate" for children of a given age. The program was developed by Dr. Nina Lief, whose three books, *The First [Second, Third] Year of Life,* are available as parent guides. Director Becky Thomas wants "to help parents enjoy their parenting." Groups are limited to 10 parents with their babies. There are family night sessions where both parents attend and special evening meetings for working mothers. Dr. Thomas says, "We want to support parents in their effort to do the best job and to give them the best information." The ECDC is affiliated with the New York Medical College.

Children with Special Needs, 200 Park Ave. S. [17th] ☎ 677-4650, is primarily a research and referral agency for parents of kids with disabilities. They don't deliver direct services and don't give direct financial help, but they can point parents in the right direction. They advise where to go for things like independent evaluations (second opinions) and school transportation, maintain information on private boarding schools and summer camps, and, under certain circumstances, act as an advocate with the public school system. There is a one-time fee on a sliding scale up to $50 (which may be waived for hardship), if you need to visit them in their office. Telephone information is always free.

Kid's Culture Calendar. Great for parents and for those of you who have to keep nieces and nephews and friends' children happy. It's called the *Kid's Culture Calendar,* published by the Alliance for the Arts and it's a 15-page pamphlet (very nicely designed) with dozens of the most noteworthy events, exhibitions, activities, and programs around the five boroughs that will especially appeal to kids. History, puppets, Muppets, holiday events, storytelling—all kinds of good stuff. The KCC costs $2.75 and is available at bookstores and museums or by calling the Alliance for the Arts at ☎ 947-6340.

The Corner Bookstore, 1313 Madison Ave. [93rd] ☎ 831-3554, features books on parenting and child development and carries *The Manhattan Directory of Private Nursery Schools* by Lina Faulhaber and *The Manhattan Family Guide to Private Schools* by Catherine Hausman. These books are also available at other city booksellers.

LICENSES, PERMITS, CERTIFICATES

Birth Certificate: 125 Worth St. [Lafayette/Centre], Room 133 ☎ 442-1999 for recorded information.

Construction Permits: Dept. of Buildings, 60 Hudson St. [Thomas/Worth] ☎ 312-8501.

Death Certificate: Dept. of Health, 125 Worth St. [Lafayette/Centre] ☎ 442-1999. See also Funerals in the Coping chapter.

Dog License: ☎ 566-2456.

Domestic Partners Registration: 1 Centre St. [Chambers], Room 265 ☎ 669-2400, 8:30–4:30 M–F.

Driver's License: Motor Vehicles offices, 155 Worth St. [Centre/Baxter] and 2110 Adam Clayton Powell Blvd. [126th] ☎ 645-5550 for both locations. The License Express office, 300 W. 34th St. [8th/9th] is for license renewals only. No phone.

Film Shoot Permit in NYC: ☎ 498-6710.

Fishing and Hunting Licenses: ☎ 718-482-4987.

Liquor License: 11 Park Place [Bway/Church] ☎ 417-4002.

Marriage Licenses: 1 Centre St. [Chambers], City Clerk's office, Room 252 ☎ 669-2400, 8:30–4:30 M–F.

Motorcycle License and Registration: Dept of Motor Vehicles info line ☎ 645-5550.

Passports: See information under Travel in the Feature chapter.

Street Fair Permits: 51 Chambers St., Room 608 ☎ 788-7439 for info, although you must start with the local Community Board.

Tennis Permits: In the Arsenal, 830 Fifth Ave. [64th] ☎ 360-8111.

MEDICAL INFORMATION

CENTER FOR MEDICAL CONSUMERS

At 237 Thompson St. [3rd/4th] ☎ 674-7105, there is a small library that has books and files of articles from medical journals, newspapers, and magazines. Things are arranged by topic, and the librarians are helpful in pointing you in the right direction. You can't take things out, but there are tables for note-taking and a Xerox machine. M–F, 9–5; W, 9–7.

KARPAS CENTER

The Karpas Health Information & Education Center at Beth Israel, 311 First Ave. [18th] ☎ 420-4247, is set up as a drop-in storefront. There are brochures and pamphlets and much information on cancer and cancer therapies. A computer data bank helps to locate information not in the storefront. They have a program of lectures and do screenings (high blood pressure, skin cancer, etc.).

PRESCRIPTIONS

Block Pharmacy, Third and 74th ☎ 288-2224, is aptly named if it's information you're seeking. We had called and asked for a price on the prescription drug Seldane. "We don't give out prices on the phone, you'll have to come in." We have come in. "Do you have your prescription?" No. "I can't give that out," and the conversation is terminated. We'll tell you why we think they're not talking: It's because of all the pharmacies we've tested, Block's prescription prices have been

Drug	Strength	Quantity	BLOCK price	PRICE MARK price
Dilantin Kapseals	100 mg	100 tablets	79.85	24.99
Feldene	20 mg	15 tablets	119.85	44.99
Lotrisone cream	—	45 g	89.95	45.99
Nicorette	2 mg	96	89.95	44.99
Seldane	60 mg	60 tablets	149.85	93.99
Tagamet	300 mg	100 tablets	199.85	89.99
Valium IV	2 mg	90 tablets	99.85	43.99
Voltaren	75 mg	60 tablets	199.85	81.99
Zovirax ointment	5%	15 g	79.85	42.99
Total			**1,108.65**	**513.91**

the highest by serious margins. Even if a pharmacy refuses to quote prices, they are required by law to *post* the prices of some of the most common prescription drugs—which Block does. Block is perfectly within the law not to quote on the phone and to charge whatever they can get for the prescription. It seems to us, however, that requiring pharmacies to quote on the phone would be helpful to those who may be least able to comparison shop: the elderly, the ailing, and the indigent. The above prices, in all cases, are what Block charges for the brand name drug. Generic prices are lower.

NY ONLINE

Some places to look for NY info online.

GENERAL In the *New York Times* section on America Online (keyword: @times), you can read many of the top stories of the day or go to one of the sections such as the arts, science, or computers and technology. Their photo gallery has a selection of celebrities, sports figures, and so on, but also has things like a shot of the platform of Penn Station from 1911 and a 1928 photo of the inauguration of a sprinkler system on Sheep Meadow. The whole thing is well designed (as is usually the case on AOL), and, best of all, there's good information available. The *Times* has their own Web page, which you must pay to use: www.nytimes.com . . . *New York* magazine's (Go: NYMAG) spot on CompuServe is very easy on the eye but hasn't yet got much meat on its bones. It's divided into the cover story, the Cue section, talk, shopping, and a guide section. There's not much happening in the library sections, and the shopping and the "guide" section are too thin at this point to be of real use . . . The service that goes by the name **NY Online** can be reached at http://www.nyo.com. You can then download their software for Windows or Mac. The reason to do this is they have a wide range of discussion threads, everything from health, spirituality, food, sports, sex, subways, and black politics . . . The **Pipeline** service, ☎ 267-3636, is a New York–based and –centered approach to the Internet. Among other services offered, there's a wide range of NY information here—restaurants, Barnes & Noble reading schedules, arts, local news, and weather . . . **Echo,** http://www.echonyc.com, calls itself a virtual salon, and that's probably the most precise definition of this service that focuses on group discussions on the arts, politics, and many other subjects . . . **Total NY,** http://www.totalny.com, is more a small slice and not one that has a clear profile (a little bit on music, on models) but is worth a look . . . **Paperless Guide to NY,** http://www.mediabridge.com:80/nyc, has info on dining, hotels, museums, and other events . . . **AddressFinder,** http://www.mediabridge .com:80/nyc/locator/only does addresses along major avenues.

THE ARTS *NY Times* on AOL for gallery and museum listings and reviews, reviews of film, dance, theatre, home video, etc. . . . *New York* magazine on CompuServe for reviews and listings . . . Art: **The Whitney,** http://www.echonyc.com:80/~whitney . . . Ballet: **NYC Ballet,** http://www.nycballet.com for schedule and subscriptions . . . Opera: **NYC Opera,** http://www.interport.net/nycopera . . . Movies: http://www.777film.com, to buy tickets . . . For contemporary music, check out http://www.sonicnet.com . . . Theatre: AOL has Playbill: Bway & Off Bway listings of schedules, cast lists, musical numbers, prices, and sometimes production history, and a plot summary. On AOL, you can also read the *NY Times* reviews.

GAY **NYC Net** is an online service focused on gay and lesbian life in the city. Forums, the arts, organizations, and Virtual Christopher St., a collection of NY-based professional, political, and community groups.

JOB HUNTING Check the *NY Times* classifieds (AOL), where you can search by job title.

LIBRARY For a look at the future of libraries, see the NY Public Library's info network, http://www.nypl.org.

REAL ESTATE www.nyrealty.com, a searchable database of apartments . . . You can search the *Times* on AOL for rentals and co-ops or condos with some additional keywords and location limiters.

RESTAURANTS Since eating out is a major pastime of so many New Yorkers, there are plenty of chat groups on the various services. You can also read reviews by Ruth Reichl or Eric Asimov of the *Times* on AOL . . . On CompuServe, you can read Gael Greene at *New York* mag.

SPORTS MetroSports Magazine, http://virtumall.com/metrosports/. **Jets and Giants,** http://www.flhome.com/teams/team.html ... **Yankees,** http://grove.ufl.edu/~katl52/nyy.html.

TRANSPORTATION Subways, http://www.mediabridge.com/nyc/transportion/subways/. This site is several gifs of the subway map of Manhattan broken down into sections ... **LIRR map,** http://pavel.physics.sunysb.edu:80/RR/LIRR.gif ... **Amtrak,** http://www.amtrak.com ... **Transit Museum,** http://www.nytransit .com:80/nytm/.

YELLOW PAGES http://www.niyp.com:80.

NY PUBLIC LIBRARY INFO LINE

☎ 340-0849. This number is busy a lot because it's so handy for getting answers to questions on the order of: Who was president when . . . ? Where do you put the apostrophe . . . ? What is sloe gin . . . ? It seems to us they know the answer to everything, and even if they don't it's a comforting thought.

OPEN LATE/24 HOURS

All are open 24 hours a day, seven days a week, unless otherwise noted.

Animal Emergency
Animal Medical Center, 510 E. 62nd St. [York] ☎ 838-8100.

Billiards
Chelsea Billiards, 54 W. 21st St. [5th/6th] ☎ 989-0096.

Car Rental
Avis, 217 E. 43rd St. [2nd/3rd] ☎ 593-8378.

Copying
• Kinkos, 24 E. 12th St. [5th/University] ☎ 924-0802; 191 Madison Ave. [34th] ☎ 685-3449; 16 E. 52nd St. [5th/Mad] ☎ 308-2679; 2872 Broadway [112th]

☎ 316-3390; 245 Seventh Ave. [24th]
☎ 929-2679.
• Village Copier, 20 E. 13th St. [5th/University] ☎ 924-3456.
• Copy USA, 491 Amsterdam [83rd/84th] ☎ 580-8666.

Florist
Not Just Roses has not just roses until 5 P.M. and then just roses thereafter. They will deliver in Manhattan 24 hours a day. ☎ 247-6737.

Gas Stations
Upper East
Mobil, 1730 First Ave. [90th] ☎ 369-3365.
Upper West
Amoco, 2040 Eighth Ave. [110th] ☎ 864-5003.

Downtown
- Exxon, Tenth Ave. [23rd] ☎ 675-7646.
- Gulf, FDR Drive [23rd] ☎ 686-4546.
- Gaseteria, 800 Lafayette St. [Houston] ☎ 274-1191.
- Mobil, 290 West St. [Canal] ☎ 925-4602.

Gym
- Crunch, 404 Lafayette St. [E. 4th/Astor] ☎ 614-0120. M–F, 24 hrs.
- WorldGym, 1926 Broadway [64th] ☎ 874-0942. M–F, 24 hrs.

Messenger
Bullit Courier ☎ 855-5555.

Music
Performances at Small's, 183 W. 10th St. [7th] ☎ 929-7565, begin when most other jazz clubs close—at 2 A.M. Groups play bebop and neo-bebop until 8 A.M. Musicians in the audience are invited to take solos, making it a true jam session. Club owner Mitchell

Borden wants people "to be able to come to a jazz club more than once a year," and he has set the admission price accordingly. It's $10. No alcoholic beverages are served, but you are permitted to bring your own. Nonalcoholic beverages are included in the admission charge. No waitress service. You take care of yourself, hang out, listen.

Package Delivery
Airline Delivery Services, ☎ 687-5145, will pick up anywhere in the tristate area and deliver anywhere in the tristate area 24 hours a day.

Pharmacy
- Kaufman Pharmacy, Lexington and 50th, ☎ 755-2266.
- Genovese Drugs, 1299 Second Ave. [68th] ☎ 772-0104.

Post Office
James A. Farley Post Office, 421 Eighth Ave. [32nd] ☎ 967-8585.

Restaurants
Lots of restaurants are open very late. These are open 24 hours:

- Around the Clock, 8 Stuyvesant St. [3rd Ave.] ☎ 598-0402
- Big Nick's, 2175 Broadway [77th] ☎ 362-9238
- Brasserie, 100 E. 53rd St. [Park/Lex] ☎ 751-4840
- Coffee Shop, 29 Union Square West [16th] ☎ 243-7969
- David's Pot Belly, 94 Christopher St. [Hudson] ☎ 242-8036
- Empire Diner, 210 Tenth Ave. [22nd] ☎ 243-2736
- Florent, 69 Gansevoort [Washington/ Greenwich] ☎ 989-5779 (closed 5 A.M.–9 A.M., M–F)
- French Roast, 458 Sixth Ave. [11th] ☎ 533-2233; 2340 Broadway [85th] ☎ 799-1533
- Gam Mee Ok, 43 W. 32nd St. [5th/Bway] ☎ 695-4113
- The Good Diner, 554 Eleventh Ave. [42nd] ☎ 967-2661
- Han Bat, 53 W. 35th St. [5th/6th] ☎ 629-5588
- Kang Suh, 1250 Broadway [32nd] ☎ 564-6845
- Kiev, 117 Second Ave. [7th] ☎ 674-4040

• Manatus, 340 Bleecker St. [Christo-pher/W. 10th] ☎ 989-7042
• Market Diner, 572 Eleventh Ave. [43rd] ☎ 695-0415
• M & G Diner, 383 W. 125th St. [Manhattan/8th] ☎ 864-7326
• Skyline Restaurant, 1055 Lexington Ave. [75th] ☎ 861-2540
• Westway Diner, 614 Ninth Ave. [43rd/44th] ☎ 582-7661
• Wo Hop, 17 Mott St. [Canal] ☎ 267-2536
• Woo Chon, 8–10 W. 36th St. [5th/6th]

☎ 695-0676
• Yaffa Cafe, 97 St. Marks Place [A/1st] ☎ 674-9302

Spices
Spice House, 99 First Ave. [6th] ☎ 387-7812

Translations
All-Language Service, 545 Fifth Ave. [45th] ☎ 986-1688 . Translations into and from 58 languages around the clock.

PASSPORTS

See Travel in the Feature chapter. See also Time-Saving Services in the Services chapter for help with passport renewal.

POLICE PRECINCTS

1st precinct ☎ 334-0611, 16 Ericsson Place [Varick]. W. Houston south, Bway to 12th Ave., south of Frankfort.
5th precinct ☎ 334-0711, 19 Elizabeth St. [Bayard/Canal]. E. Houston south to Frankfort, Bway to Allen.
6th precinct ☎ 741-4811, 233 W. 10th St. [Bleecker/Hudson]. W. Houston to W. 14th, west of Bway.
7th precinct ☎ 477-7311, 19 1/2 Pitt St. [Broome]. E. Houston south, east of Allen.
9th precinct ☎ 477-7811, 321 E. 5th St. [1st/2nd]. E. Houston to E. 14th, east of Bway.
10th precinct ☎ 741-8211, 230 W. 20th St. [7th/8th]. W. 14th to W. 43rd, 7th Ave. and west, west of 8th Ave. above W. 29th.

13th precinct ☎ 477-7411, 230 E. 21st St. [2nd/3rd]. E. 14th to E. 29th, east of 7th Ave.
Midtown South ☎ 239-9811, 357 W. 35th St. [8th/9th]. 29th to 45th, Lex to 9th Ave.
17th precinct ☎ 826-3211, 167 E. 51st St. [Lex/3rd]. E. 29th to E. 59th, Lex and east.
Midtown North ☎ 767-8400, 306 W. 54th St. [8th/9th]. 45th to 59th, west of Lex.
19th precinct ☎ 452-0600, 153 E. 67th St. [Lex/3rd]. E. 59th to E. 96th, 5th and east.
20th precinct ☎ 580-6411, 120 W. 82nd [Columbus/Amsterdam]. W. 59th to W. 86th, CPW and west.
Central Park ☎ 570-4820, 86th [Transverse]. The Park.
23rd precinct ☎ 860-6411, 164 E. 102nd St. [Lex/3rd]. E. 96th to E. 114th, 5th and east.

24th precinct ☎ 678-1811, 151 W. 100th St. [Columbus/Amsterdam]. W. 86th to Cathedral Pkwy, CPW and west.

25th precinct ☎ 860-6511, 120 E. 119th St. [Park/Lex]. E. 115th to E. 133rd.

26th precinct ☎ 678-1311, 520 W. 126th St. [Bway/Amsterdam]. Cathedral Pkwy to W. 133rd, Morningside and west.

28th precinct ☎ 678-1611, 2271 Eighth Ave. [W. 122nd/W. 123rd]. Central Park North to W. 127th, 5th to Morningside.

30th precinct ☎ 690-8811, 451 W. 151st St. [Amsterdam/Convent]. W. 133rd to W. 155th, Edgecombe and west.

32nd precinct ☎ 690-6311, 250 W. 135th St. [8th/ACP]. W. 127th to W. 155th, 5th to Edgecombe.

34th precinct ☎ 927-9711, 4295 Broadway [W. 181st/W. 182nd]. W. 155th and north.

POST OFFICES

General & Zip Code Info: ☎ 967-8585

Stamps by Phone: ☎ 800-782-6724

24-Hour General Post Office: ☎ 967-8585

Postal Answer Line (automated, no zip code info): ☎ 330-4000

Express tracing and supplies: ☎ 800-222-1811

LOCATIONS (Hours are for window service. Lobby and vending machine hours may be longer):

25 Broadway [Battery Pl.] **Bowling Green** ☎ 363-9490. M–W, F, 8–6, Th, 8–8, Sa, closed

73 Pine St. [William] **Wall Street** ☎ 269-2161. M–W, F, 7:30–6, Th, 7:30–8, Sa, closed

130 E. Broadway [Division] **Knickerbocker** ☎ 227-0089. M–W, F, 8–6, Th, 8–7, Sa, 9–4

1 Peck Slip [Water] **Peck Slip** ☎ 964-1054. M–W, F, 9–5:30, Th, 9–6:30, Sa, 9–4

6 Doyers St. [Bowery] **Chinatown** ☎ 267-3510. M–F, 9–5:30, Sa, 9–4

90 Church St. [Vesey] **Church Street** ☎ 330-5247. M–F, 7–midnight, Sa, 9–5

350 Canal St. [Church] **Canal Street** ☎ 925-3378. M–W, F, 8–5:30, Th, 8–6:30, Sa, 8–4

185 Clinton St. [Bway] **Pitt** ☎ 254-9270. M–F, 9–5, Sa, 9–4

103 Prince St. [Greene] **Prince** ☎ 226-7868. M–F, 9–5:30, Sa, 9–4

201 Varick St. [King] **Village** ☎ 989-9741. M–W, F, 9–5:30, Th, 9–6:30, Sa, 9–4

527 Hudson St. [Charles] **West Village** ☎ 989-5084. M–F, 9–5:30, Sa, 9–4

244 E. 3rd St. [B/C] **Tompkins Square** ☎ 673-6415. M–F, 9–5:30, Sa, 9–4:30

70 W. 10th St. [5th/6th] **Patchin** ☎ 475-2534. M–F, 9–5:30, Sa, 9–4

93 Fourth Ave. [11th] **Cooper** ☎ 254-1389. M–W, F, 8–6, Th, 8–8, Sa, 9–4

432 E. 14th St. [1st/A] **Peter Stuyvesant** ☎ 677-2112. M–W, F, 8–6, Th, 8–8, F, 8–6, Sa, 9–4

76 Ninth Ave. [15th] **Port Authority** ☎ 929-9296. M–F, 9–5:30, Sa, closed

217 W. 18th St. [7th/8th] **Old Chelsea**
☎ 675-2415. M–W, F, 8–6, Th, 8–8,
Sa, 9–4

232 Tenth Ave. [24th] **London Terrace**
☎ 242-8248. M–F, 9–5:30, Sa, 9–4

149 E. 23rd St. [Irving/3rd] **Madison
Square** ☎ 673-3771. M–W, F, 8–6,
Th, 8–7:45, Sa, 8–3:45

40 W. 32nd St. [Bway/5th] **Greeley
Square** ☎ 244-7055. M–F, 9–5:30,
Sa, closed

Eighth Ave. & 33rd St. **J.A. Farley
General Post Office** ☎ 967-8585. 24
hours

115 E. 34th St. [Park/Lex] **Murray Hill**
☎ 689-1124. M–W, 8–5, Th, 8–8,
F, 8–6, Sa, 7–4

19 W. 33rd St. [5th/Bway] **Empire State**
☎ 736-8281. M–F, 9–5:30, Sa, closed

223 W. 38th St. [2nd/3rd] **Midtown**
☎ 944-6597. M–F, 7:30–6, Sa, closed

340 W. 42nd St. [8th/9th] **Times Square**
☎ 502-0420. M–W, F, 8:30–5:30,
Th, 8:30–7:30, Sa, closed

5 Tudor City Place [1st/2nd] **Tudor**
☎ 697-8656. M–F, 9–5, Sa, 9–4

405 E. 42nd St. [1st] **United Nations**
☎ 963-7353. M–F, 9–5:30

23 W. 43rd St. [5th/6th] **Bryant**
☎ 279-5960. M–F, 9–5:30, Sa, closed

450 Lexington Ave. [45th] **Grand Central**
☎ 330-5768. M–F, 8–9, Sa, 8–1

610 Fifth Ave. [49th] **Rockefeller Center**
☎ 265-3854. M–F, 9–5:30, Sa, closed

322 W. 52nd St. [8th/9th] **Radio City**
☎ 265-6677. M–W, F, 7:30–6,
Th, 7:30–8, Sa, 9–5

909 Third Ave. [54th] **FDR**
☎ 330-5549. M–F, 8–8, Sa, 9–4

27 W. 60th St. [Bway/Columbus]
Columbus Circle ☎ 265-7858.
M–F, 9–5:30, Sa, closed

40 W. 66th St. [CPW/Columbus]
Ansonia ☎ 362-7486. M–F, 8–8:30,
Sa, 9–4

221 E. 70th St. [2nd/3rd] **Lenox Hill**
☎ 879-4401. M–W, 8–6, Th, 8–8
F, 8–7, Sa, 9–4

1483 York Ave. [78th/79th] **Cherokee**
☎ 288-3724. M–W, F, 9–5, Th, 9–7,
Sa, 9–4

131 W. 83rd St. [Col/Amst] **Planetarium**
☎ 873-3701. M–W, 7:30–6,
Th, 7:30–8, F, 7:30–7, Sa, 8:30–4

229 E. 85th St. [2nd/3rd] **Gracie**
☎ 988-6681. M–W, 8–6, Th, 8–8,
F, 8–7, Sa, 9–4

1619 Third Ave. [90th] **Yorkville**
☎ 369-2230. M–F, 8–6, Sa, 9–4

693 Columbus Ave. [95th] **Park West**
☎ 866-7322. M–F, 8–6, Sa, 9–4

215 W. 104th St. [Bway/Amsterdam]
Cathedral ☎ 662-9191. M–W, 8–6,
Th, 8–8, F, 8–7, Sa, 8–4

153 E. 110th St. [Lex/3rd] **Hell Gate**
☎ 860-3557. M–F, 8–5, Th, 8–6,
Sa, 8–4

1123 Amsterdam Ave. [115th] **Columbia**
☎ 864-1874. M–F, 9–5, Sa, 9–4

232 W. 116th St. [ACP/St. Nicholas]
Morningside ☎ 864-6968.
M–F, 8:30–5:30, Sa, 9–4

167 E. 124th St. [Lex/3rd] **Triborough**
☎ 534-0865. M–W, F, 8:30–5,
Th, 8:30–6, Sa, 9–4

365 W. 125th St. [Morningside/Manhat-
tan] **Manhattanville** ☎ 662-1901.
M–W, F, 8–5, Th, 8–6, Sa, 8–4

2266 Fifth Ave. [138th] **Lincolnton**
☎ 281-9781. M–F, 8–5, Sa, 8–4

217 W. 140th St. [ACP/8th] **College**
☎ 283-2235. M–F, 9–5, Sa, 9–4

521 W. 146th St. [Bway/Amsterdam] **Hamilton Grange** ☎ 281-8401. M–F, 8–5, Sa, 8–4

99 Macombs Place [154th] **Colonial Park** ☎ 368-4211. M–F, 8–5, Sa, 8–4

3771 Broadway [157th] **Ft. Washington** ☎ 368-7302. M–F, 9–5, Sa, closed

511 W. 165th St. [Amsterdam/Audubon] **Audubon** ☎ 568-3311. M–F, 8–5, Sa, 8–4

555 W. 180th St. [St. Nicholas/Audubon] **Washington Bridge** ☎ 568-7601. M–F, 8–5, Sa, 8:30–4

90 Vermilyea Ave. [204th] **Inwood** ☎ 567-3032. M–F, 9–5, Sa, 8–4

4558 Broadway [Hillside] **Ft. George** ☎ 942-0052. M–F, 8–5, Sa, 8–4

TRANSIT & COMMUTING

Adirondack Trailways ☎ 967-2900
Amtrak ☎ 800-872-7245
Bridge & Tunnel Construction Schedule ☎ 800-221-9903
Capitol Trailways ☎ 800-333-8444
Fire Island Ferry ☎ 516-589-0810
Greyhound ☎ 800-231-2222
Hampton Jitney ☎ 800-936-0440
Hoboken Ferry Service ☎ 908-463-3779

LIRR ☎ 718-217-5477
Mass transit updates ☎ 976-6277. Cost: 35¢ per call
Metro-North ☎ 532-4900
NJ Transit ☎ 201-762-5100
NYC Transit Authority ☎ 718-330-1234
PATH ☎ 800-234-7284
Short Line Bus ☎ 736-4700
Staten Island Ferry ☎ 718-727-2508

VOTING

Call ☎ 800-367-8683 for voter registration. The only rules are that you be an American citizen, 18 years old or older, and have lived at your address for at least 30 days. Register if you have moved or have not voted for four consecutive years. To find out where to vote, call the NYC Board of Elections ☎ 487-5300.

WHEELCHAIR ACCESS

GENERAL Very helpful is the **Access Guide for People with Disabilities** from the Mayor's Office for People with Disabilities. ☎ 788-2830. This guide gives you a good overview of access to theatres, hotels, department stores, restaurants, and public transportation. It indicates accessibility of parking, entrances, ramps, doors, aisles, elevators, restrooms, telephones, water fountains, rooms, and special seating. There are also lists of special conditions for specific sites.

Access for All, published by Hospital Audiences and WCBS Newsradio 88, is somewhat narrower in its focus—it includes theatres, museums, and tourist sites but goes into useful depth for each site. For City Center, say, you get the number to call for access information, auxiliary aids and services, whether or not there's a passenger loading zone, where the nearest parking garages are and where the curb ramps from the parking to City Center are located. The guide tells you there are nine sets of double doors, how many inches wide, and the steps involved. It notes whether there are alternate entrances, the counter height of the box office, specific bathroom dimensions, water fountains, telephones, and wheelchair locations inside the theatre.

AIRPORTS See the Airport Guide in the Travel article in the Feature chapter for information on handicapped facilities at the three airports.

SUBWAYS **Subway Info for People with Disabilities:** ☎ 718-596-8585 **MTA Elevator/Escalator Hotline:** ☎ 800-734-6772

THEATRE **Theatre tickets:** The Shubert Organization charges $7.50 for a wheelchair location and the same for an accompanying guest, but these allocations are limited. At Jujamcyn, it's half-price (half of the orchestra price), when available. When using TeleCharge, ask for the Wheelchair Hot Line ☎ 239-6200. The Nederlanders haven't roused themselves to create a chain-wide policy. Call the individual theatres.

ZIP CODE MAP

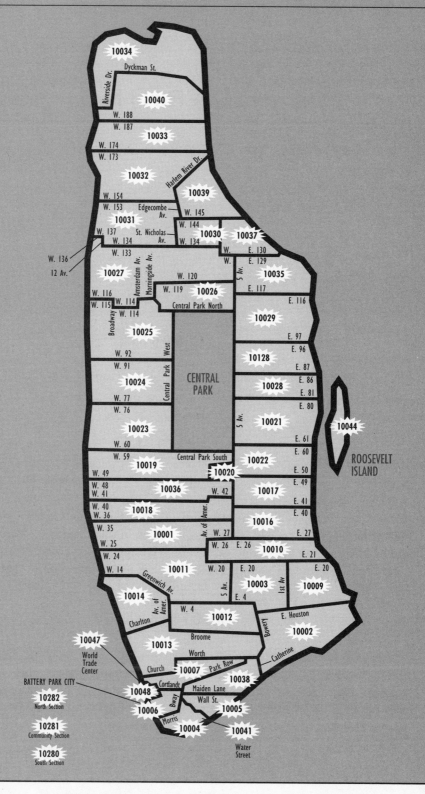

LEARNING

$\longleftrightarrow$

ACCORDION

Charlie Giordano, ☎ 627-8651, teaches French, Italian, Mexican, Irish, classical, or rock accordion styles. $40 for a 50-minute lesson.

ANTIQUES

Sotheby's Education Department, ☎ 606-7000, gives lectures and holds one- to three-day seminars on topics like American furniture or setting a holiday table with antique dishes. There is also a nine-month accredited course on American Arts, many graduates of which go on to work in the antique or auction fields . . . You can attend lectures at **Bard Graduate Center.** See more on design in this chapter . . . **Parsons School of Design,** 66 Fifth Ave. [13th] ☎ 229-5690, has an Antiques Connoisseurship program.

BOOKBINDING

The Center for Book Arts, 626 Broadway [Houston/Bleecker] ☎ 460-9768, teaches courses in either traditional or contemporary bookbinding and letterpress printing. Classes are small (6–10 people), and you can get a copy of the class schedule by calling them or stopping in at their 5th-floor gallery, where they exhibit books made by contemporary artists. Courses start at $175, $35 for materials.

BRIDGE

Here's our list of bridge clubs, many of which offer classes:

Beverly Bridge Club, 130 E. 57th St. [Park/Lex] ☎ 486-9477

Culbertson Club, 24 Fifth Ave. [9th/10th] ☎ 254-5754

East End Temple Bridge Club, 396 Second Ave. [22nd/23rd] ☎ 254-8518

Harmonie Bridge Club, 4 E. 60th St. [5th/Mad] ☎ 355-7400

Kings and Queens, 130 E. 57th St. [Park/Lex] ☎ 486-9477

Manhattan Bridge Club, 27 W. 72nd St. [CPW/Columbus] ☎ 799-4242

Riverside Bridge Club, 400 Riverside Drive [112th/113th] ☎ 749-2251

Town Bridge Club, 9 E. 86th St. [5th/Mad] ☎ 876-6020

For more info, try the American Contract Bridge League ☎ 800-467-1623. You might also want a subscription to *Bridge World Magazine,* ☎ 866-5860 for details.

CALLIGRAPHY

The **Craft Students League** inside the YWCA, Lexington and 53rd St. ☎ 735-9731, teaches italic and copperplate calligraphy. Twelve two-hour sessions are $160. Materials are extra . . . **The China Insti-**tute, 125 E. 65th St. [Park/Lex] ☎ 744-8181, teaches Chinese calligraphy and Chinese brush painting at beginning and advanced levels. Ten two-hour sessions for calligraphy are $225.

COMPUTERS

To learn about computers, see the training and troubleshooting section of the Computer article in the Feature chapter.

COOKING

BY DORLENE KAPLAN

If you'd like to improve your cooking skills—to save money on restaurants or to make the most of our city's extensive variety of edibles—you'll find more cooking courses in Manhattan than any other city in the country. Venues range from private homes to professional kitchens, with classes for every cuisine. The following individuals and schools offer instruction for cooks of all levels of ability. If you're a beginner, start with a participation course, where you'll practice handling utensils and preparing recipes. Demonstration classes are better for the experienced cook who's seeking new recipe and menu ideas. Whichever you choose, you'll come away with new friends, new skills, and renewed enthusiasm for your time in the kitchen.

Native Italian cookbook author **Anna Teresa Callen,** 59 W. 12th St. [5th/6th] ☎ 929-5640, has taught the cuisine of her homeland in Greenwich Village for more than a dozen years. Her 5-session course ($615) is limited to six students and meets one evening a week in a home kitchen equipped with commercial appliances.

One block west, the nonprofit **James Beard Foundation,** 167 W. 12th St. [6th/7th] ☎ 627-2308, offers members ($60 and up per year) more than 200 dinners a year prepared by well-known chefs from around the world. Saturday morning demonstrations ($45), scheduled once or twice a month and limited to 20 participants, feature noted chefs and cookbook authors.

Around the corner in a restored landmark townhouse, the **New School's Culinary Center Arts Program,** 100 Greenwich Ave. [Jane/12th] ☎ 255-4141, offers more than 150 different courses taught by a 50-member faculty of experienced culinary professionals. Each trimester, programs include walking tours of ethnic neighborhoods, behind-the-scenes tours of the city's finest restaurants, demonstrations by noted chefs, two- to eight-session participation courses on a variety of topics, hands-on classes for youngsters, and wine instruction. Tuition ranges from about $70–$80 per session, and class size is limited to 20 for walking tours, 14 for cooking classes.

In addition to the vacation programs he offers in Florence, noted cookbook author **Giuliano Bugialli,** ☎ 966-5325, conducts participation classes in his Soho townhouse from November to February. The 4-session courses ($400) are limited to 12 students and meet mornings or evenings in a large, professionally equipped Tuscan kitchen. All students must enroll in the First Series—four sessions covering basic techniques—before proceeding to the Continuation Series, which features new menus each season.

For more than 20 years, cookbook author and caterer **Karen Lee,** 142 West End Ave. [66th] ☎ 787-2227, has taught New Yorkers and out-of-towners traditional and nouvelle Chinese cuisine. Her 4-session hands-on courses ($400) are limited to 9 students and meet one morning or evening a week in a Lincoln Center–area well-equipped kitchen.

Since 1978, chef **Henri-Etienne Lévy,** 216 W. 89th St. [Bway/Amsterdam] ☎ 362-0638, has taught more than 20 courses a year that are devoted to French cuisine, with emphasis on the Provence region. The hands-on classes—limited to 4 students and held in a well-organized Upper West Side kitchen—promise to teach you how to cook well, efficiently, and without recipes. The calendar includes the 6-session basic course and 5-session courses on breadmaking, fine pastry, desserts, soup and buffet, and the regions of Provence and Alsace. Each course is $450.

Arlene Feltman Sailhac brings the top chefs and cookbook authors to her series of evening demonstrations, **De Gustibus** at Macy's, ☎ 439-1714. About a half-dozen one- to five-session courses are offered each season in a specially designed space that seats 70. Students can enroll in individual sessions ($60–$90) on a space-available basis. Many well-known New York chefs demonstrate their specialties.

Those with a sweet tooth will find a variety of participation classes at **The Chocolate Gallery School of Confectionary Arts,** founded in 1978 and located in Chelsea at 34 W. 22nd St. [5th/6th] ☎ 675-2253. More than 100 4-session and one-day cake decorating courses ($80) are scheduled annually, each limited to 15 students. Course content ranges from the basics to intricate borders and designs. One- and two-session workshops cover chocolate, wedding cakes, French pastries, baking, and advanced decorating topics.

Cookbook author Annemarie Colbin heads the 20-member faculty at **The Natural Gourmet Institute for Food and Health,** 48 W. 21st St. [5th/6th] ☎ 645-5170, where health-conscious cooks can choose from more than 50 evening and weekend classes ($55–$60) devoted to the creative preparation of whole grains, beans, and fresh produce. The 10-session core program ($405), for those considering a vegetarian lifestyle, is supplemented by classes devoted to techniques, ethnic cuisines, baking, and health-related topics. The $22 five-course Friday Night Dinner, prepared by a student in the Chef's Training Program,

may be the best health food bargain in town.

Dedicated to teaching cooking as a fine art in the European tradition, **Peter Kump's School of Culinary Arts,** 307 E. 92nd St. [2nd] ☎ 410-4601 and 50 W. 23rd St. [6th] ☎ 242-2882, offers career and recreational programs in cooking, pastry, and baking. Recreational courses that meet throughout the week cover a wide range of topics ($125–$260). A demonstration series features well-known chefs and other culinary experts ($45–$75). The school's core courses consist of 5-session courses ($475) that cover cooking and baking methods. Classes are taught by a 50-member faculty in the eight kitchen facilities.

Dorlene Kaplan is the author of The Guide to Cooking Schools, *a comprehensive book on cooking schools all over the world. It's available at Coliseum Books and Kitchen Arts & Letters. You can order the guide by mail ($19.95 plus $3 postage) from ShawGuides, P.O. Box 1295, Ansonia Station, New York, NY 10023 or by calling* ☎ 800-247-6553.

DANCING

MANY STYLES The following three studios teach just about any step and style you could want. All three have tap, ballet, and jazz, but you'll also find yoga, hip-hop, and hula. **Broadway Dance,** 1733 Broadway [55th/56th] ☎ 582-9304; **Dance Space,** 622 Broadway [Houston/Bleecker] ☎ 777-8067; and **Steps,** 2121 Broadway [74th] ☎ 874-2410. Classes are all day every day, and they range in price from $9–$12, with discounts for a package of classes.

PRIVATE Cha-cha, tango, fox-trot, waltz, rhumba, salsa, or meringue with **Pierre Dulaine,** artistic co-director of The American Ballroom Theater Co., who is a wonderful dancer and extremely charming. He will teach individuals or couples. $150 for a consultation and an hour lesson. ☎ 532-8091.

BELLY DANCING As Andrea Beeman, an instructor at the **Anahid Sofian Studio,** 29

W. 15th St. [5th/6th] ☎ 741-2848, told us: "It looks easy but it's really quite a workout. It's good for the body, natural to it. It's great for muscle tone since it's a dance of isolation. Some men take belly dancing, too." Classes are $8.50 for 90 minutes . . . **Serena Studios,** 939 Eighth Ave. [55th/56th] ☎ 245-9603. Serena was the youngest student of Ruth St. Denis and studied with Alwin Nikolais. She has been teaching belly dancing since 1964. Only women are permitted in these classes, but ages range from 20–60 . . . Another good teacher for beginners is **Jajouka,** ☎ 686-0774, who has been teaching and performing for over 20 years. She gives a beginner's class every Thursday evening from 6:30–8. There are "more aspects to the dance than the night club entertainment part of it. It's a wonderfully expressive form." $12 per class, men welcome . . . The extraordinary **costumes** worn by dancers are the expertise of Stella Grey, a former commodities broker who got hooked on the dance during a tour of Morocco. A costume consists of an intensely colored skirt, belt, bra top, and veil—they're elaborately beaded, appliquéd, and use lots of beaded fringe. The amount of handwork that each costume requires means that Ms. Grey can usually make only two each year. She also travels to Egypt several times a year to buy costumes from special tailors. She has some full costumes and various coin belts and coin trimmed veils that are just right for use in dance classes. ☎ 541-5054.

HULA See Hawaii in the Feature chapter.

DESIGN

The Bard Graduate Center for Studies in the Decorative Arts, 18 W. 86th St. [CPW/Columbus] ☎ 501-3000. The classes here are for matriculating students. However, they give lectures and hold symposiums that are open to the public. The topics are related to the exhibitions in their gallery space. Visit or call for a program.

F.I.T., Seventh Ave. and 27th St. ☎ 760-7650, has many courses in design that are open to anyone: interiors, jewelry, accessories, menswear, packaging, and textiles.

NY School of Interior Design, 170 E. 70th St. [Lex/3rd] ☎ 753-5365. The main purpose of the school is to offer a full program of courses leading to certification in design, though some classes are open to the general public on a noncredit basis. They range from Historical Styles 101 through Art Deco to more technical things like Introduction to Lighting. A small gallery on the ground floor is open to the public from 12–5, M–F.

Parsons School of Design, 66 Fifth Ave. [13th] ☎ 229-5690, teaches continuing education courses in interior, product, textile, and theatre design.

FASHION & COSTUMES

MUSEUMS AND COLLECTIONS The **Costume Collection** at the Museum of the City of New York, Fifth Avenue at 103rd St. ☎ 534-1672, has over 40,000 pieces in its collection, some of which are always on view. These might include a white and silver gown worn by Marian Anderson, ostrich feather fans used by Sally Rand, or bits of NY history—things like the doorman's uniform worn by Buster at Henri Bendel or the Civic Wreath presented to the Marquis de Lafayette. Scholars can study the collection by calling Phyllis Magidson at ext. 215.

The following three resources are in the Met Museum. The **Irene Lewishon Costume Reference Library,** ☎ 650-2723, is the study collection. If you have a research project, you can use the library. Dierdre Donohue, the Library Coordinator, asks that you try to narrow down your field of inquiry—"If you ask for '18th century dress' you will be there for a year." **The Met Costume Institute,** ☎ 879-5500, is managed by Dennita Sewell, ☎ 650-2663, and can be visited by scholars with an appt. . . . **The Antonio Ratti Textile Center** consolidates the textile collections of all the other departments except for the Cloisters and the Costume Institute. It is a storage and conservation area. Scholars and researchers can work there by appt. ☎ 650-2310.

The **Museum at F.I.T.,** ☎ 760-7760, mounts several shows each year, often with accompanying lectures or talks that are open to the public.

The **Brooklyn Museum,** ☎ 718-638-5000, has a costume collection strong in 20th century French and American couture. The library has two significant sketch collections—one of French couture done for Henri Bendel's in the '30s and another of Hollywood designers such as Adrian and Edith Head. Make appointments with Patricia Mears, the curator at ext. 311.

CLASSES **Parsons School of Design,** ☎ 229-5690, offers a wide range of courses both for career garmentos and civilians. There are basics like sewing, patternmaking, and draping, computer textile design, fashion illustration, courses for designing shoes, hats, and sweaters, and fashion history. For career pointers, there are the courses "Fashion Design Portfolio" and "How to Get Hired in the Fashion Industry."

Andrew Burnstine, executive v.p. of Martha's for many years, usually teaches a course on fashion at **NYU** called "The Business of Fashion"—7th Ave. executives and designers are guests at each class. Call ☎ 998-7133 for info. $265.

At **F.I.T.,** Seventh Ave. and 27th St., ☎ 760-7650, many fashion design classes on a continuing-education basis. For those starting a business, there are Saturday and evening classes geared to learning the economics of a successful business.

BOOKSTORES **Fashion Books & Magazines,** 1369 Broadway [37th] ☎ 695-0490, has a selection of imported fashion magazines and also carries a good assortment of books on aspects of fabric design and embellishment . . . **Fashion Design Books,** 234 W. 27th St. [7th/8th] ☎ 633-9646, caters to the students at F.I.T. There are textbooks and some technical manuals. There is plenty for the nonstudent: foreign fashion magazines, books on historical figures in fashion, and others on narrower subjects like ties or buttons. Some art and sewing supplies . . . **F.I.T. Bookstore,** Seventh Ave. and 27th St., ☎ 760-7717. In addition to textbooks, there are over 200 titles on jewelry, textiles, fashion, as well as magazines and supplies.

FISHING

To learn fly tying and casting, see Urban Angler in the Fish article in the Feature chapter.

FLORAL ARRANGING

There are flower arranging classes at **The NY Horticultural Society,** 128 W. 58th St. [6th/7th] ☎ 757-0915. These are taught by Nancy Kitchen, who has done the arrangements for two presidential inaugurations. $140 for three sessions . . . For dried floral arranging, see **Cut and Dried,** 968 Lexington [70th/71st] ☎ 772-7701, under Florists in the Service chapter.

GARDENING

RESOURCES **New York Horticultural Society,** 128 W. 58th St. [6th/7th] ☎ 757-0915, offers Saturday and evening classes, some of which are specifically about city gardening. The 15,000-book library is available to everyone for reference purposes, though only members may borrow books. A small greenhouse faces onto 58th St., where they sell plants brought in from nearby nurseries. Books and seeds are also for sale here. Many plant societies hold their meetings at the NYHS, including the Indoor Gardening Society. Members have a sale table where plants that have been grown in city apartments are sold. Many of the plants are rare and not available elsewhere in town. The Gardening Society also buys supplies at wholesale and sells them at a small markup on meeting nights and provides a monthly six-page bulletin. All are welcome to attend a meeting. To join, it's $15 a year . . . Linda Yang's book on city gardening, *The City and Town Gardener—A Handbook for Planting Small Spaces and Containers* ($18 in paper), is considered an ideal primer on urban gardening.

WHERE TO BUY **Chelsea Garden Center,** 401 W. 22nd St. [9th] ☎ 929-2477 . . . **Dimitri's Nursery,** 1992 Second Ave. [101st/102nd] ☎ 831-2810. Worth the trip for price and variety . . . **Farm & Garden Nursery,** 2 Sixth Ave. [White] ☎ 431-3577 . . . **NY Botanical Garden** plant shop, Southern Boulevard and 200th (the Bronx) ☎ 718-817-8705 . . . **Smith & Hawken,** 394 W. Broadway [Spring/Broome] ☎ 925-0687, sells plants, though not exclusively for indoors but chosen with NYC in mind. They also have enough misters, gardening gloves, and interesting containers to keep any gardener or gardener-to-be happy . . . **Union Square Market.**

THE GREEN MAN Scott D. Appell is that rarest of homegrown creatures, a native New York horticulturist. He's been hooked on gardening since age nine when he was part of the Brooklyn Botanic Garden's program for children. Now, with twenty years of horticultural and teaching experience, walk with him through a Manhattan nursery and he still talks about each plant with enthusiasm. His business is called **The Green Man.** For $100 an hour, Mr. Appell will come prepared to give you a personal horticultural lesson—a plant-by-plant tour of your home or terrace. If you have no plants, he will make recommendations about what will grow where, as well as teach you how to care for them, including how to grow an herb garden indoors. Mr. Appell can be reached at ☎ 966-4745.

GLASSWORKING

You can visit **Urban Glass,** 647 Fulton [Flatbush] in Brooklyn ☎ 718-625-3685, and watch the glassworkers blowing and forming vessels through window walls. Classes are offered in all forms of glasswork, including neon. The Robert Lehman Gallery at the same location exhibits artists who work in glass.

S. A. Bendheim, 122 Hudson St. [N. Moore] ☎ 226-6370, has a basic stained-glass course, teaching layout to patina, which they offer several times each year. Seven weeks, two hours a week. $110. Tools and supplies cost $80–$130, depending on the project. Classes limited to 12.

GUITAR

Jack Baker runs the **Fretted Instruments School of Folk Music,** 32 Cornelia St. [Bleecker/W. 4th] ☎ 243-7957, where they teach not only guitar but mandolin, banjo, and fiddle. They teach finger picking blues guitar, and contemporary acoustic guitar.

$20/half hour . . . **Eve Silber,** ☎ 242-9096, teaches mostly beginners and children and works in most styles—classical to rock. $25 for a 45-minute lesson if you go to her, more if she comes to you.

JUGGLING

John Grimaldi, ☎ 260-1365, has been juggling for more than 25 years, and teaching it for almost as long. He's a firm believer that coordination is something you learn. At the end of a one-hour lesson, and with a little practice, a person should be able to juggle three objects, usually balls or scarves. You don't need any special equipment. Lessons can be in your own home (or elsewhere) and cost $45 for one hour.

Mr. Grimaldi is the artistic director of the NY Lyric Circus, which can be hired for parties.

The New York Jugglers meet weekly on Thursdays at 7:30 in the gym at the Carmine Recreation Center, Seventh Ave. S. at Carmine St. ☎ 242-5228. It's a very informal group of street performers, professionals and amateurs who practice, observe, and assist one another.

WHERE TO BUY Brian Dubé, 520 Broadway [Spring] ☎ 941-0060. In this showroom and shop, sized for practicing and attached to his offices and assembling operation, Brian Dubé sells juggling equipment. These are pieces he has designed and manufactured with durability and balance in mind. The shop contains a small shelf of books with titles such as *Three Ball Digest: All You Ever Need to Know About Juggling Three Balls* or *Will Rogers Rope Tricks.* Mr. Dubé's juggling balls, clubs, Devil Sticks, hats, twirling plates, and stackable cigar boxes are also available. Mr. Dubé says that juggling "really doesn't require lessons" or a teacher. The basic skills can be learned from books and videos.

KITE FLYING

See the Kiting article in the Sports chapter for information on where to buy kites, fly kites, and learn more.

LANGUAGES

NYU, ☎ 998-7030, teaches 25 different languages in many different kinds of programs. You can learn 16 languages at **The New School,** 66 W. 12th St. [5th/6th] ☎ 229-5690, including sign language, and 10 at the **World Trade Institute Language Center,** 1 World Trade Center ☎ 435-4074. **Alliance Française,** 22 E. 60th St. [Mad/Park] ☎ 355-6100, has a full range of French classes . . . In addition to NYU's classes, that school's Office of Student Employment, ☎ 998-4757, can supply you with a grad student whose rate will be between $15 and 20/hr. An automated phone system asks you to fax in a job description.

CHINESE
The China Institute, 125 E. 65th St. [Lex/Park] ☎ 744-8181, teaches Mandarin, some Cantonese, and has a children's program.

ENGLISH AS A SECOND LANGUAGE
You can get classes in English as a second language at the **English Speaking Union,** 16 E. 69th St. [5th/Mad] ☎ 879-6800, the **World Trade Institute** (see above), **Hunter College,** 695 Park Ave. [68th/69th] ☎ 772-4290, and at **Columbia University,** 505 Lewisohn Hall, ☎ 854-3584.

FRENCH
Aline Baehler, ☎ 334-8497, a native speaker and an assistant professor at NYU, generally tutors in her office. Conversational level students read articles in French publications and discuss them. This is used as a springboard to improve grammar and vocabulary. She teaches all levels. $30/hr. at her office, $40 if she comes to you.

Carmen Coll, ☎ 517-0520, has been teaching French for 20 years. She teaches all levels, conversation and business French. In most situations she comes to you. The method she uses is tailored to the individual and the situation. $50/hr.

Michel Lalou, ☎ 289-7193, a graduate of the École Normale Supérieure, has been teaching French in NYC for over 15 years, some of them at the United Nations. He is the author of *Le Français Actif,* a conversation book. He tutors adults and children 14 and up from his home on the Upper East Side on a one-to-one basis. Five one-hour lessons cost $175.

Guitty Roustaï has expanded La Croisette, ☎ 861-7723, her French school for children. There is an after-school program for children 2 1/2–12 years at 22 E. 95th St. Children start by learning through songs and games and progress to more regular lessons in a relaxed atmosphere. Mme. Roustaï also tutors adults privately, ☎ 888-7408, tailoring her teaching to your specific needs. $50/hr.

Thierry Torlai, ☎ 886-1876, has been tutoring since 1990. He prefers to go to the student's home or office. Sometimes, if it's a conversation class, he meets the student in a cafe. Materials and methods are adjusted to the student's level and interests. A 75-minute lesson is $30.

GERMAN

Elliot Junger, ☎ 734-0587, is a bilingual speaker who learned German in early childhood. He is a professional translator who does private tutoring in German in the evenings. "I assume no prior language knowledge in beginning students," a useful attitude when teaching a language with not only genders but cases. "I don't assume you have remembered them from your Latin class." He uses a primer text with beginning and intermediate students and adds some methods of his own, such as a color system for the genders. Advanced students read from newspapers and work on translating articles. The cost per hour is $45–$50, depending on whether you go to him or he comes to you.

Deutsches Haus at NYU, 42 Washington Mews ☎ 998-8660, teaches German-language classes at beginning and intermediate levels and gives conversation classes based on themes or topics. Classes follow the semester schedule of NYU. $400 for ten weeks—3 hours and 15 minutes each week. Day and evening schedule available.

ITALIAN

Parliamo Italiano, 132 E. 65th St. [Lex/3rd] ☎ 744-4793, run by Franca Lally, is situated in a lovely townhouse. The school has an Italian-family-at-home feel to it. There are 50 classes a semester at 12 levels with 12 all-native teachers. The maximum class size is 14, which some may find over the optimal level. Classes are taught during lunch hour, evenings, and Saturday mornings. The method, developed by Ms. Lally, is one in which no English is ever spoken. The emphasis in the school is on having fun while learning Italian. 10-week classes start at $225 for 1 1/2 hour lessons . . . At **Scuola Italiana,** in Our Lady of Pompeii, 240 Bleecker St. [Carmine/Leroy] ☎ 229-1361, the approach is more traditional, with a course, developed at the University of Perugia, emphasizing reading, writing, and speaking. All teachers are natives who have taught in Italy. Courses run two months and the director, Beatrice Muzi, says that after five sessions of the two-month courses, you should be "proficient, conversant, and comfortable." Twice a week, 6–8 P.M., is $295. Sat., once a week (16 hours) is $180. 12 people max to a class.

JAPANESE

Accent on Language, 160 E. 56th St. [3rd/Lex] ☎ 355-5170, teaches Japanese on a private basis, one teacher to one student. All teachers are from Japan and are trained in teaching to English speakers. They talk to you to determine your goals and how much time you feel you can devote to learning Japanese. Meetings are arranged to suit your schedule. The fee of $38 per hour is based on 1 1/2-hour classes and a minimum of 24 hours. The price goes down if you are willing to sign up for more hours. They use *Japanese for Busy People,* a text using the English transcriptions of Japanese characters called *romaji.*

IBEC, 11 E. 44th St. [5th/Mad] ☎ 867-2000, specializes in teaching Japanese to Americans and American English to Japanese. They emphasize listening and speaking comprehension and are strong on conversational skills. Mr. Endo, the president, says that at first, it is possible to learn Japanese without learning to read and write it. After you are able to communicate, you can then study reading and writing. IBEC teaches lots of business people. There are some classes, but most instruction is private. Lessons are $36 for one 45-minute session—with an eight-session minimum.

Ichiro Kishimoto, ☎ 718-625-7756, teaches privately and in small groups. He will come to your office for group lessons. He says the hardest thing for Americans to do when learning Japanese is to find 15 minutes a day to study. Even this small amount of time can make a big difference. He stresses conversation, because "if you can speak, you can enjoy the language." A one-hour weekly private lesson at his house is $50.

Japan Language Forum, 342 Madison Ave. [43rd/44th] ☎ 338-0113, gives private and group lessons, or they can arrange for someone to come to your business or home. The beginner classes are limited to seven people, and some of the advanced classes have no more than three students. The beginning text is *Learn Japanese.* They teach survival Japanese to the first-time traveler, but beyond that it has an academic orientation, teaching simplified characters *(kanji)* in the beginning classes. They conduct some cross-cultural business seminars. You are invited to a free lesson. $410 for 10 lessons.

Japan Society, 333 E. 47th St. [1st/2nd] ☎ 715-1256, has been running their language school for more than 20 years. It is now the largest Japanese program in the U.S. Twelve levels of Japanese are taught, from beginning Japanese to advanced *kanji.* Simplified forms of the Japanese syllabaries—*hiragana* and *katakana* as well as simple *kanji*—are included in the beginning instruction. Special intensive weekend courses are taught for those who plan to move to Japan. Classes can have as many as 20 students. Cost is $220 for an 18-hour course.

Mieko Makishima, ☎ 718-832-3533, says, "In the beginning Japanese is not very hard. The pronunciation and the structure is not hard." In advanced lessons, cultural things, such as levels of formality, are introduced. These can be trickier. She uses *Japanese for Busy People* for beginners, and after that will use newspapers and magazine articles. Ms. Makishima teaches private and group lessons in her home in Park Slope, or she will come to your office. If she comes to you the cost is $50/hr., lower if you go to her.

SPANISH

Spanish Institute, 684 Park Ave. [68th/69th] ☎ 628-0420. A full range of classes from beginners to "superior." They stress the "natural approach," which emphasizes conversation. They teach standard Spanish—idiomatic expressions can vary considerably from country to country and within some of them. Beginners start with three hours a week for 14 weeks. $625. They can arrange private lessons for $50/hr., with a minimum of 10 hours.

LEIMAKING

See the entry on Radio Hula in the Hawaii article in the Feature chapter to learn about leimaking.

MAGIC

Tannen's Magic Studio, 24 W. 25th St. [Bway/6th] ☎ 929-4500, gives a series of magic classes in the shop. Four evening lessons are $198. They will arrange for private magic lessons starting at $135/hr., depending on what you want to learn. Each August they run a magic camp for children ages 12–20.

Irving V. Gonzalez, ☎ 332-0791, teaches magic classes for adults at the New School and privately teaches adults and children as young as age six. Lessons generally start at $65.

See also Magic Stores in the Stores chapter.

MANUSCRIPT ILLUMINATION

The Gabriel Guild gives classes and workshops in all aspects of the medieval book arts—preparation of parchment, gilding, making quills and medieval inks, calligraphy, pigmentmaking from the original sources, and painting. They teach in rented spaces in Soho and in their workshop in Port Chester. Call Patricia Miranda or Karen Gorst at ☎ 718-625-4610. A catalog of handmade medieval art supplies is available.

PAPERMAKING

Dieu Donné, 433 Broome St. [Bway/Lafayette] ☎ 226-0573, is a nonprofit papermill that manufactures paper for artists and conservators. They offer classes in plain and fancy papermaking. Eight-week classes are around $400, and workshops start at $90.

PIANO

For information on how to buy a piano and how to find a piano teacher, see the Piano article in the Fetaure chapter.

PRINTMAKING

Manhattan Graphics Center, 476 Broadway [Broome/Grand] ☎ 219-8783, teaches etching, silkscreen, monotype, mezzotint, intaglio, lithography, and other printmaking styles at their workshop space. Beginner and advanced classes. You can rent workspace if you are an artist member—membership is $25/year. Workshops start at $60, 12-week courses at $360.

QUILTING

Quilter's Passion, 531 Amsterdam Ave. [85th/86th] ☎ 580-2621, teaches beginning quilting in eight two-hour sessions. $150 for the eight two-hour sessions lessons. Supplies are extra.

SCIENCE

KIDS **The American Museum of Natural History,** ☎ 769-5310, offers an ongoing series of children's workshops. Many are hands-on. Workshops are $30 . . . **The Science Development Program,** over 20 years old, under the auspices of Fordham University, offers weekend morning sessions where scientists lecture and give demonstrations. Four classes are $85, with an annual $20 registration fee. ☎ 864-4897.

NY Hall of Science, 47-01 111th St., Flushing Meadows ☎ 718-699-0005. Of the spruced-up exhibits, we think you and the kids will think some are merely exciting and some are exciting and instructional. There is a drop-in area where, for $2, a child can make a project that is coordinated with *Magic School Bus,* an animated science program on Channel 13. One-hour DARTS (Discovery Activities Related to Science) workshops are offered most every Saturday and Sunday afternoon for small additional fees.

TEENS The Junior Academy of the **NY Academy of Sciences,** 2 E. 63rd St. [5th] ☎ 838-0230 ext. 422, is a leadership and scientific organization for students in grades 7–12. The young academicians plan their own lecture series, organize field trips, and hold social events. They meet and interact with prominent scientists and learn not only about science but about the educational, career, and personal choices scientists have to make. Scientists such as Russell Hulse, a Nobel Prize–winning physicist, have lectured and spent some additional time with the students. There is an annual College and Career Fair where colleges with strong science programs come to talk to prospective students. It's open to the public. The yearly membership fee is $15.

ADULTS Scientific meetings at the **NY Academy of Sciences,** 2 E. 63rd St. [5th] ☎ 838-0230, are free and open to the public. While many of the topics would require spe-

S E W I N G

Sew Fast Sew Easy, 147 W. 57th St. [6th/7th] ☎ 582-5889. In the pink and turquoise brownstone opposite Carnegie Hall, Elissa Meyrich runs a complete teaching sewing center. Classes start with a beginner making a pull-on skirt or workout pants and proceeds through four levels to making an unconstructed jacket. The four sessions cost from $160–$200, depending on level. Each two-hour and 45-minute class is limited to no more than eight sewers. If you don't have a sewing machine or space for cutting, Ms. Meyrich offers rental of cutting tables and machinery at the shop, $6–$6.50/hr. Sew Fast has a small shop with an assortment of patterns and notions and some instructional videos that can be viewed free on your lunch hour. Elna machines are sold here, and repair work is done on all kinds of machines. Other services include custom fitting a muslin pattern—$35 for 90 minutes. People attending class here get a 10% discount at Poli Fabrics across the street.

cialized knowledge, others are of general interest . . . The **American Museum of Natural History,** ☎ 769-5310, gives lectures, courses, behind-the-scenes tours, and sponsors field trips geared to adults . . . **NYU** offers serious science courses to laymen in their Continuing Education department. ☎ 998-7133.

SPORTS

You can get instruction in more sports than you might think in the city—everything from kayaking to golf. See the individual listings in the Sports chapter.

WATCHMAKING

The Joseph Bulova School, 40–24 62nd St., Woodside ☎ 719-424-2929, offers watchmaking and watch repair programs that run from 9–17 months. Classes are geared for people who want a career in watchmaking.

WEAVING

The Handweavers Guild of NY, ☎ 864-6151, has a mentoring program in which a handweaver will give private instruction in your home for $30/hr., two-hour minimum. Members of the Guild also teach classes at School Products, 1201 Broadway [28th/29th] ☎ 679-3516.

WINE

Executive Wine Seminars, P.O Box 1791, Old Chelsea Station, NY, NY 10113 ☎ 800 404-9463, was the result of a conversation between Howard Kaplan and Robert Millman while they were both working for Morrell & Co. Mr. Millman, who teaches philosophy at LaGuardia College (and spent some of his graduate student days learning about wine), and Mr. Kaplan, who is in the wine business, felt there were people who knew about food but were shy about ordering wine in restaurants. They began offering seminars geared to "business needs and business situations" and then added "the consumer-oriented seminars." Tastings are focused around "high level, extravagant, and luxurious wines." The introductory two-session course (limited to 20) tastes 24 wines, including a Chateau Yquem. Robert Parker makes a yearly appearance. Membership is $60 per person or $100 per couple. For this you get advance mailings about events, a 10% reduction in the cost of each event, and access to members-only events. Prices for individual tastings run from $60–$125. EWS offers about 40 events each year; members' events are limited to 18 people, open events may have as many as 55. Members-only dinners take place at restaurants like JoJo.

Willie Gluckstern spends most of his time providing wine lists for restaurants and training waitstaff in wine service. He also teaches at both the Learning Annex and Peter Kump's Cooking School. Classes at the Learning Annex ☎ 570-6500 are $55 a

session. There is a white wine, red wine, and a Champagne evening where 25 to 30 wines are tasted at each. The lessons at Peter Kump's ☎ 410-4601 are given in the working kitchen classroom. A chef prepares a nine-course tasting meal. Each course is served with between 3 to 6 different wines and there is discussion on how to match wine with food. A white wine, a red wine, a dessert wine, and a Champagne evening are offered for $75 each. All of the classes are on Friday evenings.

Harriet Lembeck, ☎ 718-263-3134, teaches a serious academic wine course in the NY Helmsley Hotel. The ten-week class has about 50 students. Each week Ms. Lembeck surveys the wines of a country with a one-hour lecture, after which there is a one-hour tasting. A textbook, reading assignments, and "open-book tests" are part of the curriculum. (The class has been filling up regularly since the mid '70s, so it can't be too onerous.) Many of the people who take the course are interested in entering the wine and spirits industry. A Certificate of Completion is offered, provided you can pass the blind tasting test. (You get the names of the wines beforehand, so much of the mystery is dispelled.) The survey class is $525. Four additional classes on beers and spirits is $200. Ms. Lembeck is also the Wine Director for the **New School.** She gives three- and four-week introductory courses (limited to 32 people, $225) that introduce tasting terms, talk about restaurant wine service, how to buy in a wine shop, and how to store wine, decant Port, and open Champagne. There are also one- and two-night sessions such as "Chardonnay Around the World." You can get information on these by calling ☎ 255-4141.

Mary Ewing Mulligan, the director of the **International Wine Center,** 231 W. 29th St. [7th/8th] ☎ 268-7517, is the first American woman to earn the Master of Wine degree, the British title open only to members of the wine trade. The International Wine Center's name connotes an imposing institution, but the physical premises are unassuming. Indeed, Ms. Mulligan stresses enjoyment of wine over learning facts. (You won't be crammed with information about soil types.) There is, though, much one can learn here in the courses that run the range from "Discovering the Pleasures of Wine" (three two-hour classes for $140) to "Best-Selling Restaurant Wines" ($40 for one class). Class size is 15–30. You don't have to be a member to attend the classes. You can also join the International Wine Club at the Center, which gives you access to members-only tastings (about 50 a year) with winemakers or wine authorities. There are two levels of membership—$125 for Select and $400 for Full. All members have access to members-only tastings held every week. You have to register for each tasting and select members pay a higher per tasting fee than full members. Full members can go to some tastings free. Guests have included Piero Antinori, Robert Parker, Georges Duboeuf, Christian Pol-Roger, and Clive Coates.

Kevin Zraly of the **Windows on the World Wine School,** who came by his interest in wine when he was a waiter in a fine restaurant near New Paltz, believes that learning about wine is sometimes too technical. He wants it to be fun. The eight two-hour sessions parallel his book *The Windows on the World Complete Wine Course,* which every student receives. The first lesson is on the white wines of France. After that, you taste your way through whites from New York, California, and Germany before moving to five lessons on red wines. About 10 wines are tasted in each session. The goal is to "gain a little confidence and not be intimidated with restaurant wine lists." Since most of the students (there are about 100 in each class) are also wine buyers, there is information on how to not feel lost in a good wine shop. Classes are $475. There is a beginner- and an advanced-level course. Graduates are eligible for membership in the Wine Buyer's Circle. A $400 yearly fee gets you audio and video tapes, bottles of wine, and invitations to wine and food dinners in restaurants and trips to Europe. ☎ 914-255-1456.

WOODWORKING

Garrett Wade, 161 Sixth Ave. [Spring/Vandam] ☎ 807-1155, offers classes in various aspects of woodworking, including veneering, restoring, learning to French polish, and so on. These are generally two-hour classes, and many are $20. The French polish classes are $80 and limited to 10 people.

Albert Constantine and Son, 2050 Eastchester Road in the Bronx ☎ 718-792-1600, has the best collection of wood and related materials around, though it's not easy to get to without a car (the best way with public transportation is to take the NY Bus Service's Morris Park Bus, ☎ 718-994-5500. Picks up along Madison Ave., $4). They also give classes on Sats. on wood finishing, carving, veneering, and so on. $25 per class; classes run 9 A.M.–1 P.M.

The Craft Students League at the YMCA, Lexington Ave. at 53rd St. ☎ 735-9731, teaches woodworking courses. Basic carpentry courses (hanging shelves, using portable power tools, and applying molding) alternate semesters with furnituremaking classes. There are courses in finishing and refinishing that start with stripping and go to faux finishes. 12 three-hour classes are $310.

RESTAURANTS

←——————————————————————→

INTRODUCTION

This chapter distills our journeys around the city in search of good food to just over 125 restaurants. We've included restaurants because we love them, because we think the experience is interesting, because they're a great value, because we think they're overrated. We've left out many worthy places but have tried not to include any about which we are indifferent.

A brief word about our methods. We are always anonymous and we accept no free meals (or free anything). In evaluating a restaurant, the quality of the food is more important, for us, than atmosphere, service, value, or a great wine list—though we certainly try to take all of those into consideration. You'll note that we demand more from places that charge more.

For many in this city, restaurants are a favorite pastime, and everyone has their list of favorites. This is ours:

Alison on Dominick
Blue Ribbon
Cascabel
Chanterelle
Elias Corner
Follonico
Hangawi
Hasaki
Home
Honmura An
Jackson Diner
Le Refuge
Oyster Bar
Planet Thailand
Pó
Roetelle A.G.
Savann
Union Square Cafe

There are many wonderful chefs in the city but when we are asked for our favorite, it is

Rocco DiSpirito's food we eat with more pleasure than any other. At deadline for this book, he was making preparations for his new restaurant but details weren't available. Here's what we can tell you about this exceptionally talented chef.

Rocco DiSpirito.

Mr. DiSpirito was born in New York in 1966. For as long as he can remember, everything centered around dinner in his family and he would often help his mother in the kitchen. His grandmother, who lived in the country, "grew everything. She made her own wine, her own preserves. And my uncles used to hunt. When I was 11, I started working in a pizzeria, making the pizza, grating the cheese. At 14, I started working at the New Hyde Park Inn. It's a German restaurant where I made head cheese, potato dumplings, they made their own sausages, all their own soups." After that, he spent six months cooking at a seaside resort in Israel before starting at the Culinary Institute of America. After graduating from the CIA, he traveled in France and remembers being in a French home when the host went to the kitchen, took out a bottle of black truffles that he had preserved, and poured the juice over the salad. "*That* opened my eyes." He also remembers the delight of eating oysters and drinking Chablis at four in the morning and then going to the Rungis market. Returning to the U.S., he went to Boston University (as a teaching assistant there, he met his wife, Natalie, in Advance Food and Beverage Management). In 1991, he moved to New York and went to work for Gray Kunz at Lespinasse, where, he says, all of his basic skills developed a layer of finesse. He learned how to make sure "everything is carefully chosen, the flavor, texture, and color, so the plate is greater than the sum of the parts."

Mr. DiSpirito has been the chef at two restaurants in the city and we have eaten a few dozen of his creations. Some of the highlights that you may find at his next restaurant are a meltingly tender veal chop, a wild mushroom soup that he calls "simple" (you've never had such a "simple" soup), and a sublime seafood risotto. His striped bass, with fava beans, sweet corn, and a black truffle vinaigrette, is a perfect combination of sweetness, ocean, earthiness, and texture. When he adds cubanelle peppers, mango, and lime pickle to a delicate steamed cod, it's a marriage of delicious friction and heat. His calamari with watermelon and avocado sounds awful but see what alchemy can be wrought by so much talent and passion.

"I don't have any rules about what goes with what. I think there are two sides to cooking. One side has to be heavily disciplined and the rules have to be really well adhered to, but on the other side, there are no rules—anything can go with anything as long as it tastes good." The greatest pleasure in cooking? "The instant gratification of watching someone enjoy it."

LOWER MANHATTAN/CHINATOWN

BRIDGE CAFE

The Brooklyn Bridge seems to tuck **The Bridge Cafe,** 279 Water St. [Dover] ☎ 227-3344, in its vest pocket. It is hard to think about the old, ramshackle building that houses the restaurant without the context of the bridge's shadow. It's roughly analogous to the Little Red Lighthouse and the George Washington Bridge, except here you can eat. Once you're inside, though, the Bridge Cafe seems to have its own light source. Unbuffeted by trends or thrill-seekers, it is free to be a sunny and cheering restaurant. The bartender smiles. The waitress counsels you on the menu. Corn and red onion fritters are set on your red-checked tablecloth. There's good beer on tap and a nicely chosen wine list. Order the chicken pot pie or the mafalda pasta (chicken, pancetta, and broccoli rabe) or one of the specials, and you can be sure everything will taste fresh and homemade. This is a place to catch up with a friend, have a low-key dinner with your mate, or sit on the sidelines of the city before diving back in. Entrees average $15.

CHINESE

MUG asked Chinese food expert Eileen Yin-Fei Lo to look at the Chinese restaurants around the city and write about some of the authentic Chinese dishes to be found. (More of her findings are in the Shun Lee Palace article in the Midtown East section and in the Queens section.)

BY EILEEN YIN-FEI LO

It is possible, I am happy to report, to eat true Chinese cooking in New York. This is no minor circumstance. Often, the proprietors of Chinese restaurants are either unwilling to explain what is authentic about the four regional cuisines of China or are careless with their definitions. The result most often is that the information passed on to the public is either poor or wrong. Dishes from one region are labeled as being from another; schools of cookery are interchanged willy-nilly; and we still hear and

read about "mandarin" cuisine when there is no such thing. Thus the eating public is woefully under-informed about the many accents of what, in my opinion, is the greatest cuisine in the world. What follows is a modest compilation of some unusual, and authentic, Chinese cooking available in the city, some of it rare, much of it largely unknown, all of it fine.

SHANGHAI At **Hunan Garden,** 1 Mott St. [Bowery] ☎ 732-7270, where, despite its name, the accent is on the foods of Sichuan, with a few from Shanghai, it is possible to eat the best Shanghai-style fish head casserole in the city. As prepared, this soup in a clay pot contains the head and half the body of a carp cooked in chicken stock with black mushrooms, sliced pork, chunks of fried bean curd, scallions, ginger, coriander, and chiles. It is a marvelous mix. There are fish head casseroles available elsewhere in the city, virtually all under the same name, *yue tau sah wah,* in the Cantonese style—with only the fish head chopped up and stewed in a broth flavored with ginger, scallions, coriander, and rice wine. The Shanghai casserole is different indeed and at Hunan Garden, perfect. Entrees average $10.

SICHUAN Hunan Garden, with its chef Xu Wei from Chengdu, cooks authentic Sichuan food as well. Its version of a Sichuan classic, which goes by the intriguing name, "Intimate Couple," could not be better. Very thin slices of beef, beef tongue, tripe, and tendon are cooked, tossed with minced garlic and ginger, scallions, ground Sichuan peppercorns, sesame seeds, chiles, and crushed peanuts. It is searingly hot, undeniably delicious. Its name, *fu chai fai pin,* translates as

"Husband and Wife Hugging Together." I know of no other restaurant where this dish is available.

FUJIAN One of the more exotic pockets of Chinese cookery lies in Fujian, formerly Fukien, a province in south China midway between Shanghai and Canton. It relies heavily on the sea, on fish, eels, crabs, conch, clams, oysters, and shrimp, all of which are cooked, often with noodles, in thick, aromatic soups, occasionally with a red puréed sauce base known as *hung tsao* made from fermenting red rice. The cooking of this region often bears the name of its capital, Foochow, now Fuzhou, and it is possible to find representative Fujian food these days in a number of restaurants. One must be wary, however, for often the appellation "Foochow" will be added to dishes that are not of that region.

In Chinatown, one of these newer Fujian restaurants is **Long Shine,** 53 East Broadway [Catherine/Market] ☎ 346-9888. The menu lists a braised lamb soup, which fails totally to describe this well-prepared traditional soup from Fuzhou, known as *sah tsao yeung yuk,* or "casserole red rice lamb." It consists of a thick broth based on that fermented rice sauce, in which chunks of lamb, bean thread noodles, black mushrooms, and scallions are cooked. The rice colors the soup red, and the mingling of the residual taste of rice wine with the meat and pungent vegetables is exceptional. Average dish, $9.

CANTONESE Cantonese cooking has for some time been taken for granted by those who do not understand it. For those who do, the Cantonese table—the richest in China, the most varied, ever in flux and now so influenced by Hong Kong—offers great satis-faction. I recommend the unusual, often unique, preparations at **Golden Unicorn,** 18 East Broadway [Catherine/Bowery] ☎ 941-0911, surely the best traditional Cantonese restaurant in the city, with the best dim sum around, yet with a most daring kitchen. Entrees average $13.

Until recently, veal was an unknown in the Chinese kitchen. It was introduced, as have been so many other ingredients from other countries, to the Chinese in Hong Kong. Golden Unicorn—with its antennae attuned to the waves from Hong Kong—offers it prepared two ways: sautéed in a thick, faintly sweet brown sauce laced with crushed black pepper; and recently in a way found nowhere else—slices of veal cooked with Dragon Well green tea and rare and expensive yellow tree fungus, with scallions and thin slices from the stems of Chinese broccoli. It is a triumph of tastes and textures. Hong Kong in New York.

Eileen Yin-Fei Lo teaches regional Chinese cuisine at China Institute in America and is the author of several cookbooks.

JOE'S SHANGHAI

Eat at Joe's. **Joe's Shanghai,** 9 Pell St. [Doyers/Bowery] ☎ 233-8888, is the Manhattan branch of the Flushing original, and this restaurant, no beauty contest–winner, serves delicious Shanghai food. You'll certainly want the steamed buns to start, especially those with crabmeat. When you bite in, you get a spurt of the soup along with the filling. The chive and shrimp wonton are almost as good. In fact, we've liked nearly everything we've tried here—prawns with spicy pepper salt, noodle dishes, and the fish head casserole. We'd eat here happily anytime, but because it's so good, you may have to wait for a table—if you're on jury duty, this may rule out Joe's. Come back for dinner. Dishes average $10. Cash only.

NHA TRANG

When we first visited **Nha Trang,** 87 Baxter St. [Bayard/Canal] ☎ 233-5948, in 1992, there were few Vietnamese restaurants in the city. That's changed considerably, much to our delight, though we still think Nha Trang one of the best. We have enjoyed many dishes here but particularly like the bún dishes. These consist of rice vermicelli, often in a broth, with a variety of accompaniments. A popular meal in Vietnam is Bún Bo, which adds sliced beef, onions, and curry. This revivifying bowl of noodles, broth, coriander, crushed peanuts, and heavenly curry costs $3.50. Add some nuoc cham, the fish sauce with chiles, for a higher heat factor. The place is plain-looking, the staff friendly. Bún Bo and some Vietnamese coffee make a perfect lunch. Cash only.

NEW YORK NOODLETOWN

At **New York Noodletown,** 28 1/2 Bowery [Bayard] ☎ 349-0923, bypass menu items like the ordinary Beef Chow Fun and go for the specials, which are carefully prepared and delicious. When the Chinese flowering chives are available, don't miss them, they're wonderful, particularly when mixed with roast duck. Three Jewels is chicken, barbecued roast pork, and duck. Especially appealing are the slightly sweet exterior of the pork and the condiment that comes with the chicken. It's finely minced ginger, scallions, and oil, and it is addictive. The salt-baked dishes are worth having (though the salt-baked shrimp have had their shells removed and are less succulent than those done with shells). The congee here is pacifying, particularly when it's done with pork and preserved egg. The usual Chinatown decorating standards. Most dishes are under $10. Cash only.

TAI HONG LAU

Tai Hong Lau, 70 Mott St. [Bayard/Canal] ☎ 219-1431. Easier on the eyes than some of the other Chinatown restaurants, but don't come for the atmosphere. Come instead for the Cantonese cooking. Have the baked scallop, with bits of bell pepper and cucumber, or the smoky pig's knuckle with jellyfish. The deep fried bacon seafood roll should probably come with a warning from the Surgeon General, but what it lacks in salutary effect is made up for in flavor. Don't miss the lobster with ginger and scallions or the Peking duck, which is first-rate here, prepared into a kind of sandwich rather than rolled, using a fluffy bread that looks like a shoe insert. Come Monday to Wednesday with a friend and you will each pay $18 for this treat, not a bad deal for Peking duck. Otherwise, dishes average $14. AmEx only.

THAILAND RESTAURANT

Thailand Restaurant, 106 Bayard St. [Baxter] ☎ 349-3132. This is more than a jury duty restaurant, though it is a perfect choice for that. Thailand Restaurant serves exceptional Thai food, some of the very best in the city. You could have nothing more than their gold medal Pad Thai and be perfectly content. Any of the curries are worth having. They have two other restaurants in the city under the name Pongsri Thai. Dishes average $10. AmEx only.

MORE **Sweet 'n' Tart Cafe,** 76 Mott St. [Canal/Bayard] ☎ 334-8088, for "tong shui"—something like dessert soups—and other good food . . . **20 Mott St.,** 20 Mott St. [Pell/Chatham Sq.] ☎ 964-0380, for

Cantonese food, **Triple Eight Palace,** 78 East Broadway [Market] ☎ 941-8886, for dim sum.

TRIBECA

BOULEY

Mr. Bouley is on the move, so we omit any thoughts on his cooking until he's settled in. We'll miss the trim and handsome dining room on Duane St., the staff marching out with a procession of plates, and, perhaps most of all, the magical (and affordable) lunches. We look forward to eating his food again.

BUBBY'S

Sarah Vaughan for you, Etch-A-Sketch for the kids, breakfast any time, caramel apple pie, **Bubby's,** 120 Hudson St. [N. Moore] ☎ 219-0666, practically begs for your approval. Okay, we love you. Bubby's doesn't have a squeaky screen door snapping shut, but that's the feel of the place—with windows out onto the former warehouses and buildings designed for manufacturing. For the food, an open door policy—pork chops, crab cakes, shepherd's pie (with corn!), salmon in Thai sauce. Have pie for dessert. Dishes average $15.

Karen and David Waltuck.

CHANTERELLE

Norbert Elias, in his book *The Civilizing Process,* says that civilization "refers to something which is constantly in motion, constantly moving 'forward.' " Yet Mr. Elias puts the word *forward* in quotes, as if to say, "Well, that's the idea, anyway." In the 50 years that have elapsed

since Mr. Elias wrote his classic, confidence in the idea of an increasingly civilized world may be undermined daily. In all of the metropolis, the best emollient for this is a visit to **Chanterelle,** 2 Harrison St. [Hudson] ☎ 966-6960. Much of the appeal of the restaurant comes from the old-fashioned sense of care gentling the spareness of the room. Yet "spare" isn't quite right, since the wood columns, the sunset warmth of the wall color, the trademark enormous vats of flowers, the unwavering attention to details are judged so exactly as to induce that particular Chanterelle sense of well-being. This is surely due to Karen Waltuck, who doesn't seem to run the place as much as guide, tend, anticipate, minister, engage, and enhance. Your fellow diners do their part, too, in appreciation of the artfully constructed ambience: the noise level is neither hushed nor hysterical, everyone's attention seems to be on the people they're dining with, and you may find that each of your fellow diners is clad in black, white, or gray.

We've been a fan of David Waltuck's cooking since the early days of the restaurant on Grand Street and think it's better than ever. We have had the occasional dish we didn't love, but when Mr. Waltuck wants to make you faint away, oh, he can—take one bite of his ravioli with a fricassee of wild mushrooms—that will do it. So will the seafood sausage, which has been on the menu since the Grand Street days. Have you eaten so much salmon that you've forgotten how wonderful it can be? Try Mr. Waltuck's poached salmon with basil butter that comes with bite-sized pea pods and green beans. Generally, when he cooks seafood, it seems an especial labor of love.

Among the many pleasures of an evening at Chanterelle are the outstanding (for New York, at any rate) cheese trays that you could choose to be the last course of your meal. You'd miss, though, desserts such as poached apricots with Burgundy granita or a caramelized peach with rum sabayon. Menus are $73 and $89.

The wine list is filled with many treasures, though we'd like to see a few more on the lower end and some more half bottles. Having said that, with a full wallet you can have a great wine experience here, aided by Roger Dagorn, a very knowledgeable and most agreeable sommelier.

Whatever the state of the world, Chanterelle is itself a civilizing process.

FRANKLIN STATION CAFE

The only thing we don't like about **Franklin Station Cafe,** 222 W. Broadway [Franklin/White] ☎ 274-8525, is that there's only one. We'd like a few of these small, simple restaurants sprinkled around the city so we'd never have to travel far to eat some of their French and Malaysian food. It's the Malaysian part that we're partial to (though they make fine ham, turkey, and other sandwiches in the "French" division), but you can't go wrong with any of the selections: satays, Rendang or curry chicken, and especially the noodle soups. Shrimp and chicken feature prominently in these, and there are quite a few daily specials and variations. FSC bakes their own cakes and cookies, and they make a mean lemonade. Dishes average $7.

MONTRACHET

A number of acclaimed chefs have spent time in the small kitchen of **Montrachet,** 239 W. Broadway [Walker/White] ☎ 219-2777. It's now Chris Gesualdi who is turning out the fine dishes, particularly the squab and the salmon, that pair well with the Burgundies that Drew Nieporent's restaurant emphasizes. Entrees average $28.

Mr. Gesualdi started his restaurant career at age 15 washing dishes in a steakhouse. He was 18 when he went to the Culinary Institute of America, graduating in 1982. He worked in Connecticut with Raymond Perone at The Inn at Ridgefield, a country French restaurant. Mr. Gesualdi says, "It is where I really got started, butchering, making pastries, working the line. After a year, Raymond Perone said, 'I've taught you all I can, now it's time to go to NY.' " Once here, he says, "I walked around town and looked at menus. If I saw something on it I didn't recognize, I offered to work there free to learn." After stints in many of the city's major restaurants, he came to Montrachet in 1991, starting as sous chef and becoming chef de cuisine in 1994. There are two major pleasures at Montrachet: one of the city's great wine lists and Mr. Gesualdi's cooking.

NOBU

A writer for a food magazine wrote an article about the best way to eat at **Nobu,** 105 Hudson St. [Franklin] ☎ 219-0500. Start with this, move to that, have this before that. Don't have that until you've finished this. Spare us. There are many ways to put together a meal at Nobu. You would, of course, be perfectly content to have just sushi. You won't find better fish on the island. Among the most memorable from a recent visit were the freshwater eel, the delicate "live" scallop, and the yellowtail with scallion. You can do what most do here, which is to mix it up—some sushi and some of the other inventive offerings from chef Nobuyuki Matsuhisa. The style of the kitchen is, in fact, to mix things up, adding ingredients to sushi that must be considered heresy by traditionalists, but certainly are wonderful inventions. From the other sections of the menu, we'd skip the tempura (never a favorite) but have most anything else: a creamy, spicy crab dish, the beef skewer, or any of the specials the house is cooking up. Things like the ginger parfait cone and the Asian pear tart finish off a meal here simply and well. Average dinner price, $60.

MORE French food at **Capsouto Frères,** 451 Washington St. [Watts] ☎ 966-4900 . . . **Layla,** 211 West Broadway [Franklin] ☎ 431-0700, Drew Nieporent's spot for Middle Eastern food and belly dancing . . . **The Odeon,** 145 West Broadway [Thomas] ☎ 233-0507, probably due for recognition from the Landmarks Commission and still going strong . . . **Rosemarie's,** 145 Duane St. [Church/W. Bway] ☎ 285-2610 for Italian food . . . and more Drew Nieporent restaurants: **Tribeca Grill,** 375 Greenwich St. [Franklin] ☎ 941-3900, and **Tribakery,** 186 Franklin [Greenwich/Hudson] ☎ 431-1114, where you can sit to have a light lunch or take away the baked goods. It makes nightly transformations into an Italian restaurant called **Zeppole.**

SOHO/LITTLE ITALY

ALISON ON DOMINICK

We've never seen children at **Alison on Dominick,** 38 Dominick St. [Hudson/Varick] ☎ 727-1188, though we're sure that since everyone is well treated, they would be, too. Still, leave them home. This is a restaurant for grown-ups. The mostly black-and-white decor doesn't dance for your attention. Yet it's just sophisticated and romantic enough to frame your evening. The food isn't architectural, and it doesn't borrow spices from every emerging nation on the planet. Yet it's fine food from chef Dan Silverman, and we doubt if we made a weekly visit that it would diminish its appeal.

Mr. Silverman has a sure hand with fish. He does a nice riff on brandade, wrapping the salt cod up in phyllo and adding little squirts of tapenade and rouille. In general, the only thing we want a kitchen to do with an oyster is to shuck it, but Mr. Silverman's oysters, prepared with a brunoise of Granny Smith apples, cucumber, mint curry oil, and Calvados sabayon, are most enjoyable (though we'd have preferred a little less apple and a brinier oyster). We like his pan-roasted sea bass with marjoram sauce and capers very much and prefer his monkfish to the one at Le Bernardin. When duck is undercooked, as it is here, it can be hard to distinguish from beef, but the kitchen prepares the Long Island breast with juniper and Chartreuse, which seems to coax the flavor forward. The squab with red cabbage and fingerling potatoes in walnut oil offers warm and earthy flavor without any coarseness. There are occasional missteps (a potato, celery root, and leek soup that's bland, or a mushroom daube with an herb spaetzle that's been overlemoned), but they are infrequent. We don't know why the chocolate soufflé with honey banana and cinnamon ice cream isn't cloying, but it's not. A beggar's purse of caramelized apple with warm sour cherries and Calvados ice cream is given a real snap by the sourness of the cherries, and the white pepper ice cream with the raspberry Napoleon makes a pleasing conflation. The wine list emphasizes Burgundies, but you can still find bottles for as little as $19. And anyplace with three Pineau des Charentes—how bad can it be? Dishes average $28.

BLUE RIBBON

People tend to gravitate to the raw bar offerings of **Blue Ribbon,** 97 Sullivan St. [Prince/Spring] ☎ 274-0404, and they are superb. We have been equally delighted with the prepared dishes. Blue Ribbon, for instance, does a commendable paella Basquez, with chicken, mussels, shrimp, clams, and spicy sausage. Things like striped bass are prepared sensitively, and the smoked trout is very good. You don't often see beef marrow and oxtail marmalade on the city's menus, but this is a wonderful dish and Blue Ribbon does right by it. They don't take reservations, so arrive early or be prepared to hang out. Entrees average $20. More fresh fish a few doors away at **Blue Ribbon Sushi,** 119 Sullivan St. [Prince/Spring] ☎ 343-0404. Blue Ribbon Sushi serves until 2 A.M., Blue Ribbon until 4 A.M.

CASCABEL

Cascabel, 218 Lafayette St. [Spring/Broome] ☎ 431-7300, is the most protean of restaurants in the city. A confluence of factors make it so: location (slightly off), decor (stylish but not overdone), attitude (relaxed and accommodating), and, most of all, Tom Valenti's food, suitable for any palate, season, whim, or occasion. Thus, a restaurant flexible enough to come to for a celebration or to enjoy casually.

If you have eaten Mr. Valenti's food, you know about his braised lamb shank. You also know that he is unafraid of rich, bold flavors, isn't shy with seasoning, doesn't swear you can cook without salt. But this isn't heavy cooking—broths are frequently substituted for sauces. Agnolotti stuffed with foie gras in a leek and truffle broth is a case in point, brimming with game and the earth. His cooking is so vigorous that you wonder what use he could have for puff pastry, but he's got the right dish for his style of cooking—the puffs are filled with smoked eel and potatoes and surrounded by horseradish cream. As much as we like rabbit, it always strikes us as food for a Barbara Pym character. We can remember few better versions of rabbit than his rabbit with asparagus and morels, and not once while we ate did Ms. Pym come to mind. Nothing but praise for the gravlax, the pan-roasted herbed striped bass, and the ragout of mussels with white beans and artichokes. Entrees average $23.

Cascabel is intensely loose and relaxing, however oxymoronic that sounds, because there's a major chef in the kitchen and a dedicated and considerate staff out front. Without any pretension or straining for effect, it's a delight.

CHEZ BERNARD

Chez Bernard, 323 West Broadway [Canal/Grand] ☎ 343-2583. A simple place with some excellent country French food. Come here for Bernard Eloy's merguez sausage, one of his pâtés, the house-smoked salmon, and the lamb chop, which comes with great mashed potatoes. Twenty or so years ago, the

Burgundy-born Mr. Eloy had a restaurant called L'Ecrivisse on 56th St., but he is better known for his butcher shop, now closed, on Thompson St. At Chez Bernard, he is making 12 different pâtés, (including pistachio, country, maison, pork, vegetable, and salmon), 12 kinds of sausages, and curing hams. Much of this is available to take out.

COUNTRY CAFE

Country Cafe, 69 Thompson St. [Spring/Broome] ☎ 966-5417. A very sweet place. There's wonderfully goofy music that you have to fight singing along with—the proprietor puts up no such fight. The front door seems to pop open and closed without warning—we hope they never fix that. Excellent bistro offerings: calves' liver and mashed potato, fish soup with strong aioli, tasty mussels, both the steak and coq au vin are notably tender. Country Cafe just feels good. Entrees average $15. Cash only.

CUB ROOM

You may leave humming the scenery from **Cub Room,** 131 Sullivan St. [Prince] ☎ 677-4100, but, in any event, you're likely to leave humming. The design and lighting of this restaurant, cafe, and bar are so singularly attractive and the real estate so prime, that you may fear dreary food and lots of attitude.

The bar/lounge area of the Cub Room.

Instead, nice food, no attitude. Henry Meer, the chef-owner, says he would describe what he does as "elegant comfort food." The cub steak—sautéed filet mignon with shallots, green peppercorns, golden raisins, Cognac, Madeira, and veal stock—has been on the menu from the beginning (Mr. Meer says he's surprised at the amount of meat that they sell in general). Other signature dishes include the salmon Caesar and the lobster salad with grilled Maine lobster, with organic baby greens, confit of duck, grilled Vidalia onions, baby candy cane beets, and mangoes. When shad roe, soft shelled crabs, and halibut are in season, they are on the menu (or as daily specials). Dover sole is also very popular here. Cub Room makes their own bread and ice cream. The wine list, which starts at $22, stresses small American vintners from California and Long Island. Entrees average $26. AmEx only . . . **Cub Room Cafe,** 183 Prince St. [Sullivan] ☎ 777-0030, the lower-priced annex, serves things like meat loaf, macaroni and cheese, and fresh organic salads.

FRONTIÈRE

We're crazy about **Frontière,** 199 Prince St. [Sullivan/MacDougal] ☎ 387-0898. The staff is welcoming, and, though the room is fairly crowded, it manages to be both romantic and full of cheer. Chef Andrew Nathan turns out robust and honest food—whether it's a pan-fried rockfish, a poussin, or a bacon and leek tart with Roquefort cheese. Our favorite from the kitchen, that we dream about many nights before going there and many after, is the côte de bœuf. It's sliced at the table and served with a tasty béarnaise and gratin dauphinoise. The meat melts tenderly in your mouth, the charred crust is swoon-worthy, and the bone is worth fighting over. That's the only discord you should encounter in this good-natured place. Entrees average $20.

HELIANTHUS

"Food" with "quotes" around it makes us "nervous." When we see "chicken," "ham," and "meat" balls on a menu, we usually look for the "exit." But we're at peace at **Helianthus,** 48 MacDougal St. [Houston/ Prince] ☎ 598-0387, and so are the vego-skeptics at our table, because what comes out of the kitchen here is fresh and flavorful. Try the Japanese barbecue, a meatless shish kebab, or the Helianthus Forest—a roll-your-own dish that includes minced shiitake mushrooms, water chestnuts, and sunflower seeds. Spoon it into a lettuce leaf and roll. Sunflowers are of the genus helianthus, and you'll find the sunflower theme carried to amusing extremes—they're *everywhere.* Everywhere, that is, except on the table which, alas, has pink carnations. Entrees $9.

HONMURA AN

Honmura An, 170 Mercer St. [Houston/Prince] ☎ 334-5253, is a wonderful New York outpost of the Tokyo original. It's a large loft space on the second floor with a modern, restful design. At the back, you can watch the soba, the heart and soul of the place, being made in a glass-enclosed room. The $43 tasting menu is highly recommended: six courses centering on soba that achieve the desired balance between *assari* and *sappari.* The former applies to food that satisfies in a more sophisticated way: a delicate interplay of flavors. The latter is the satisfaction that comes from flavorful, hearty food. Buckwheat may have been cultivated first in China, but the Japanese developed it, probably in the late 1500s. Then, as now, it

was a quick, inexpensive, and delicious source of energy. The slightly sweet noodles started as food for laborers, often sold in small, plain shops or stalls, but in the late 1700s, the surroundings and the accouterments of soba shops went upscale. They remain popular through this century. There is a great deal of history and lore associated with soba (real soba noodles are usually at least 80% buckwheat), and years of training are required to be a true soba master. That's why there are many more unexceptional soba restaurants than good ones. In addition to the customs of preparation, there are many customs associated with eating soba. One that may surprise you occurs at the end of the main soba dish: Water that was used to cook the soba (called *soba yu,* which is rich with vitamins) is added to the dipping sauce and you drink the whole potion. The other custom, slurping of noodles, is encouraged. The drink of choice with this food is sake. To learn more, read *The Book of Soba* by James Udesky, available at Kitchen Arts and Letters.

KATANA

Delicacy is not among the characteristics generally thought of as American, and certainly New Yorkers wouldn't use the word delicate to describe very much of our life in this city. Since the Dutch arrived, at any rate, New York has been rough and tumble and proud of it. So, it is a pleasure to find the Japanese **Katana,** 179 Prince St. [Sullivan/Thompson] ☎ 677-1943, discreetly installed behind wooden shutters, one of the few restaurants we think could actually lower your blood pressure. Your first thought may be how simple the place looks, but if you inspect more closely, you see how sensitively the environment was created—the palm leaf matting on

JEAN-CLAUDE RESTAURANTS

At some restaurants, when the chef has a night off, you feel the air has gone right out of the room. At **Jean-Claude,** 137 Sullivan St. [Houston/Prince] ☎ 475-9232, when owner Jean-Claude Iacovelli isn't around, the place can be sorely lacking in Gallic charm. Service has always been this restaurant's drawback—in the early days it was hyperkinetic, now it can be stonefaced with forbearance. That's too bad because Jean-Claude has also set the standard in the city for amazing food values (when Jean-Claude–style restaurants appear elsewhere—Savann and Pitchoune come to mind—they're instant successes). We eat here happily just the same because the food has remained consistently excellent, and it ranks among the very best food values in town. Where else can you get a foie gras appetizer for $8? Lamb, pork loin, skate, or monkfish, all for less than $15? You'll find a limited selection of wines, and the last time we were here the choice of desserts was crème brûlée or tiramisu. Seating isn't communal, but tables are so close it is for all practical purposes. No credit cards . . . **Caffe Lure,** 169 Sullivan St. [Bleecker/ Houston] ☎ 473-2642. The crankiest waitress we encountered in 1995 worked here. Just as at Jean-Claude, you must not come expecting much in the way of solicitous service, but the seafood is terrific and nothing is priced over $13. Cash only . . . On the other hand, we went to **Soho Steak,** 90 Thompson St. [Prince/Spring] ☎ 226-0602, days after it first opened and the service could not have been more charming. With the copper sheeting on the wall, the oak ceiling, a yellow wash of paint, and flowers, the room is more turned out than at Jean-Claude. With dimmer lighting and candles on the tables, it's also more romantic, though it's hardly quiet. The filet mignon and the sirloin aren't the mammoth portions found in the city's classic steakhouses, and the beef here isn't in the same league (with dishes averaging $14, you'd hardly expect otherwise). It is, though, perfectly good food, and, as is the way with Mr. Iacovelli's places, a steal. Though this is called Soho Steak, there is a full roster of other dishes available. For wine, the Chateau Plagnac for $20 sets you up nicely. An easy call—big hit. Cash only.

the ceiling, the details on the leather chairs, the faucet in the bathroom. You can order à la carte, but we like the tasting menus, by number of courses. (Six dishes is $40, eight dishes is $60, up to 14 dishes for $120.) You will not believe the beauty of many of the presentations, small jewels served on a variety of dishware, trays, and baskets. You won't get explosions of flavor here, but we were entranced by the harmony of each plate. One gorgeous course has a little pot of watercress and shiitake mushrooms, a sardine-sized fish in the trout family, shrimp in a small circle of daikon radish, egg custard, and a single raspberry in a dice-sized white wine gelatin mold over a slice of mountain yam. Another memorable course includes a slice of tilefish, a baby oyster, cucumber sushi, and a decorative branch from the quince tree. Sake and beer are the popular accompaniments, though we like this food with white wine— the single California Chardonnay serves the purpose. A delight.

LE JARDIN

Le Jardin, 25 Cleveland Place [Spring/Kenmare], ☎ 343-9599, has a short menu (entrees average $13, wines about $18), and the

CHRISTOPHER LOVI

The pleasant garden at Le Jardin.

kitchen does the few things well. An appetizer of seafood soup, with croutons, rouille, and grated cheese, is fine under any circumstances, remarkable for the price ($5.50). The mussels are excellent and Gerard Maurice, the proprietor, makes his own country pâté. The house makes a notably flavorful steak tartare, a respectable sweetbread salad, a tasty (and generous) rack of lamb, and excellent frites. In warm weather, you'll find the restaurant proper almost empty—everyone is enjoying the pleasant garden under the grape arbor.

LE PESCADOU

No frills at **Le Pescadou,** 18 King St. [6th] ☎ 924-3434, but we'd certainly be happy to eat here anytime: The brandade (salt cod with potato and puréed garlic) is real comfort food, the fruits de mer is a delicious bonanza, they have pleasing fish soup, and snapper prepared in parchment. Entrees average $18. Service from the waiters is genial, and they work like crazy in the crowded seafood bistro.

PÃO

Pão, 322 Spring St. [Greenwich] ☎ 334-5464, hugs the edge of the island on a far western corner of Spring Street. It's a Portuguese restaurant in a small, attractive space, with nice owners (two Portuguese, one Portuguese/Dane, one American) cooking and serving. Most of the ingredients are familiar, but some of the combinations may not be. We've never had pork loin and clams together and, odd as it sounds, it works quite well. The soups are excellent: green pea with shrimp and melted cheese did wonders for us on a blustery, snowy evening, and the stone soup—red beans, potatoes, cilantro, and smoked meats—is a fortifying stew. We liked the bacalhau, which, at Pão, is composed of cod, potatoes, egg, and onion and baked in a clay dish. Another dish to try here is the shrimp set on a traditional shellfish bread pudding with lemon. The Linguica is a pork sausage flamed at the table. Puddings for dessert are traditional. The all-Portuguese wine list (most wines below $25) affords you the chance to sample some of that country's little known wines, such as the Casa de Santar '92 from the Dão region. Entrees average $13.

ZOË

Zoë, 90 Prince St. [Bway/Mercer] ☎ 966-6722, throws a great party in the let's-celebrate-the-day sense. Your hosts (the owners, Stephen and Thalia Loffredo) assemble crowd-pleasing ingredients, and the place percolates all day and evening. It has thrived by making sure you leave having dined well, wined well, and been taken care of nicely. No small feat.

Steven Levine's food is a big asset. We love the smoke-roasted Muscovy duck breast with the dominant sweet and smoky flavor. You can't go wrong starting with the browned gnocchi with morels, pancetta, and arugula, or the calamari with Vietnamese dipping sauce. Mr. Levine's chicken and mashed potatoes and his Angus steak, which comes with a rich, unctuous bourbon sauce, are exemplary. At lunch and brunch, their chicken salad is a perennial favorite, and there aren't many better burgers in town (try it with smoked mozzarella from Joe's Dairy). Main courses average $21.

A significant portion of the fun of Zoë is their exceptional wine list. It's unusual in that it's all-American (though they also have an amazing collection of single malt Scotch and not-necessarily-American after-dinner drinks). There are about 200 choices of wines. The list is broken down by grape, and there are a dozen or so half bottles available. Pricing is sometimes generous, always fair (you'll find Bonny Doon Pacific Rim Riesling for $10 in the stores; it's $18 on the list). In fact, if you choose a lower-priced wine, you can hardly pick a bad one. Top American producers are well represented—you'll find Caymus Vineyard, Ridge Monte Bello, Heitz Martha's Vineyard, Stag's Leap, and Kalin Cellars. Late in an evening, you may spot the Loffredos at a table in the corner with a number of bottles on it, tasting wines when the kitchen is winding down—enormous care has gone into this list.

We must point out, if by some chance you have never gotten to Zoë, that no one has ever heard a pin drop here—it is usually very noisy. It's not especially cushiony, and there aren't a lot of soft edges here. Fine by us. For best results, just go with some entertaining companions and let the wine flow.

MORE **Aquagrill,** 210 Spring St. [6th] ☎ 274-0505, serves seafood . . . **Jerry's,** 101 Prince St. [Greene/Mercer] ☎ 966-9464, for American food . . . **Kelley & Ping,** 127 Greene St. [Houston/Prince] ☎ 228-1212, informal, but very good Asian food . . . **Kin Khao,** 171 Spring St. [Thompson/W. Bway] ☎ 966-3939. Not the best Thai food in the city but certainly the hippest . . . **Kwanzaa,** 19 Cleveland Place [Lafayette/Spring] ☎ 941-6095, for soul food . . . **Onieals Grand St.,** 174 Grand St. [Baxter] ☎ 941-9119, is as popular for its pretty bar as for its restaurant . . . **Savore,** 200 Spring St. [Sullivan] ☎ 431-1212, serves Tuscan food . . . **Savoy,** 70 Prince St. [Crosby] ☎ 219-8570, is the Soho version of a country inn . . . **Raoul's,** 180 Prince St. [Sullivan/Thompson] ☎ 966-3518, the long-running French bistro.

WEST VILLAGE

AGGIE'S

Most people come to **Aggie's,** 146 W. Houston St. [MacDougal] ☎ 673-8994, on the weekends when it's crowded, but we think what you really want from Aggie's is to sit quietly during the week at 9:30 in the morning with the papers, by the window, forget whatever obligations you have, order a highly caloric breakfast (there aren't many places that serve up

a better one), drink plenty of coffee, go back home, and nap till lunch. In the driven atmosphere of the city, it's unlikely you will do this very often, but it's a comfort to know that you can. Cash only. The most expensive dinner entree is $13.75.

CAFE DE BRUXELLES

When we're uptown it's oysters and wine at the Oyster Bar. Downtown, our favorite bar food is at **Cafe de Bruxelles,** 118 Greenwich Ave. [13th] ☎ 206-1830, which serves delicious moules et frites. Eat the frites with their homemade mayonnaise and order Belgian beer to wash them down. We generally head straight for the bar when we come here, but the restaurant is well worth a try, particularly for the beef carbonnade and the waterzooi.

EL CID

El Cid, 322 W. 15th St. [8th/9th] ☎ 929-9332, has been delivering up lively Spanish food without benefit of atmosphere since 1988. The entrees (averaging $14) are decent, but we'd stick to the tapas ($7 average). Many prefer sitting at the bar, but at either bar or table, order their good sangria and have almost any of the tapas, including the delicious sausage, the potato and onion omelette, and the large sardines.

FLORENT

In the early days of **Florent,** 69 Gansevoort St. [Greenwich/Washington] ☎ 989-5779, this was the wonderful crossroads of worlds—limos and club boys, truck drivers, and some intrepid suits. Those days are gone, but Florent continues to serve food for after work, after partying, almost 24 hours a day. Evelyne's goat cheese salad is a favorite and the hanger steak is fine, but you really don't come here for Florent's culinary prowess. Nor do you come because it's now practically an institution. Come instead because it's fun to hang out in Florent Morellet's diner in the meat district. Cash only. Entrees average $14.

HOME

In *Knife and Fork in New York,* a guidebook to the city's restaurants from 1948, there is an entry for a restaurant called Mom's in the Kitchen that served fried chicken, brown Betty, and pork chops. Flash forward to 1993. Chef David Page and his partner, Barbara Shinn, open **Home,** 20 Cornelia St. [Bleecker/W. 4th] ☎ 243-9579. Since then, they have honed it into a classic of its kind. Mr. Page grew up in Wisconsin and learned about food on his grandfather's organic farm "before anyone knew what organic meant." (There must be a

CHRISTOPHER LOVI

David Page.

beacon to the West Village for Wisconsinites—see Village Atelier.) "What we're doing is a continuation of a long history—that's the beauty of Greenwich Village, it's timeless. There have always been little restaurants here, the neighborhood hasn't changed that much. It's one of the few solid old-time neighborhoods left." MUG is always happy to return home, especially when we can have the blue cheese fondue, one of our favorite appetizers around the city. The pork chop with cumin (you can be sure no cumin was used at Mom's in the Kitchen) is one of Home's standards, and it's easy to see why: It's a plump chop dusted with spice, familiar enough to be comforting, different enough to be interesting. Mr. Page does a chicken sausage that is notable for its substantial flavor without being too fatty, and it comes with a pleasing side of beans and smoked duck. The onion rings and the chocolate pudding are as good as they get (the onion rings, the chocolate pudding, and the roast chicken are never taken off the menu; the rest changes several times a year). At lunch, you can get a superior hamburger here, with some of Home's homemade ketchup. The biggest downside of the place is the tight squeeze, but the quality of the food makes it easy for us to overlook that. Home run. AmEx only. Entrees average $15.

LA FOCACCIA

La Focaccia, 51 Bank St. [W. 4th] ☎ 675-3754, unadorned as it is, might cause you to walk by and assume nothing much of interest is within. That would be a mistake. This is an exceedingly pleasant West Village restaurant that combines tasty food and nice service at modest prices (pastas average $11, about $15 for other entrees). Vodka penne is such a familiar dish that we hardly ever order it, but, then, it hardly ever tastes as good as it does here. There is much to like about La Focaccia. Preparations are straightforward, flavorful, satisfying. We've enjoyed the farfalle with salmon, lamb chops, risotto with peas and mushrooms, and polenta with melted Gorgonzola. As you hope with a small village restaurant, the service here couldn't be more friendly.

LE ZOO

The young owners of **Le Zoo,** 314 W. 11th St. [Greenwich St.] ☎ 620-0393, had the foresight to hire Luc Dendievel, a persuasive inducement to get you here. Mr. Dendievel handles many French dishes with ease and turns out food of quality considerably surpassing the pricing (entrees average $15). High marks for the braised leg of rabbit with mustard sauce, quail salad, crisped salmon with lentils, a cassoulet of sweetbreads, pork tenderloin, and monkfish with shallots and cabbage. Given the quality of food and the value, it isn't surprising that tables are fitted tightly in here.

MI COCINA

The last time we went to **Mi Cocina,** 57 Jane St. [Hudson] ☎ 627-8273, it was with a table of fussy eaters. A vegetarian, a fish avoider, someone who doesn't like Mexican, and a Californian who doesn't think you should eat Mexican food in NY. A recipe for disaster. Fortunately, disaster averted by Mi Cocina's stalwart food (and a few frozen margaritas). There are versions of things you find at every Mexican restaurant, but elsewhere they're not likely to be quesadillas this refined or, if you have the beef fajitas, to use beef of such quality and flavor. Mi Cocina does some excellent soups and really good guacamole. When they feature regional specialties, such as Oaxacan Mole Negro, try them. You may find representative dishes from Puebla, such as Chiles en Nogada, the pork-stuffed pepper, or Panuchos, a corn tortilla with hard-boiled egg and black bean puree from the Yucatán. Mi Cocina is fairly small and it's always crowded, but there's a reason our table of fussy eaters loved the place. Entrees average $14.

9 JONES

Ken Lipsmeyer, owner of **9 Jones St.,** 9 Jones St. [Bleecker/W. 4th] ☎ 989-1220, says that the introduction of classic American dishes to the menu of 9 Jones St. is "the culmination of what 9 Jones St. is about. We are located in the middle of the village and tried to be a 'traditional village restaurant' without knowing quite what that was." One day, he and chef Alan Harding were in the flea market where they discovered a copy of *The Epicurean,* a book written by a member of the Delmonico family in the 1890s. It is a primer on how to run a restaurant with instructions on service as well as on food. Mr. Harding is interpreting for the '90s some of the foundations of American cuisine. They have the black bean soup from The Coach House (minus the lard), Delmonico's original recipe for oyster stew, and are serving traditional cuts of meat—a double pork chop with spaetzle and mustard and a Newport steak (cut at an angle from the tip of the filet). Oysters are featured prominently, on the half shell, in the stew, and in other oyster specials. They take their cue here from the tradition from around the turn of the century of Dad doing the cooking on the maid's night off. Dad's idea was to open some oysters and cook them in a chafing dish. Both chef and owner have been looking into regional American cookbooks prior to the turn of the century. If you're not interested in historically accurate cuisine, 9 Jones has a full menu of other choices. Entrees average $15.

PÓ

Pó, 31 Cornelia St. [Bleecker/W. 4th] ☎ 645-2189, is surely the best Italian food in the city for the price (dishes average $15) and wonderfully exuberant cooking at *any* price. The restaurant Home, across the street, grafts a midwestern sensibility onto the local landscape, whereas Pó has a very urban, very New York feeling. Mario Batali, the chef, opened Pó in 1993.

Bruschetta with white beans is a delicious, recurring freebie here. You might follow that with a small but invigorating appetizer of steamed clams with a spicy mint brodetto. Mr. Batali loves beans, and they reach their apotheosis in the plain-Jane-sounding white bean ravioli. Big triangles of the pasta arrive with a dark glaze of balsamic vinegar and brown butter. It is superb. Equally good is the grilled quail with pomegranate and molasses—it's smoky, moist, sweet, beautifully presented. Mr. Batali makes an excellent ox-

tail with fennel, artichoke, and red wine. There is a solid list of Italian wines from $17. Pó is small, so you need to reserve well in advance. AmEx only.

TANTI BACI

Tanti Baci, 163 W. 10th St. [7th] ☎ 647-9651, is nestled underground and offers *really* cheap eats—pasta that is simply prepared and tasty, all for about $6.50 a plate. Many of the pastas are freshly made and come with a choice of five familiar sauces: a Bolognese, a pesto, and so on. The specials tend to be quite good but pricier. BYOB.

TARTINE

Tartine, 253 W. 11th St. [W. 4th] ☎ 229-2611, is a loose translation of French, but it captures the flavor. So, you can have escargots—good, moist, slightly livery ones—but instead of being bathed in garlic butter, they're wading in it. We don't think you'd find the herbed goat cheese croutons at L'Ami Louis, but they're a pleasing starter just the same. When the kitchen does poulet rôti, they do it well, and the delicious beef mignonette tops tender beef with assertive black pepper. Entrees average $10. The place is small and the sidewalk tables are especially nice, but try to sit on the W. 4th Street side so you can avoid people waiting on line for your table looking at you to see if you're any closer to asking for a check. Tartine takes cash only, is BYOB, and has a popular brunch.

13 BARROW

13 Barrow, 13 Barrow St. [7th/W. 4th] ☎ 727-1300, can swing wildly from mood to mood, but there's a steady hand in the kitchen thanks to John Tesar, former chef of the Inn at Quogue. You can come here and construct a number of different types of meals, choosing from the raw bar, several pizzas (the three-cheese pizza with herb crusted eggplant and truffle oil is a great starter), pastas, and more traditional appe- tizers and entrees. Traditional isn't quite right, though, since these dishes draw from many corners of the world, as is hardly news these days. Many of the ingredients are as- sociated with Asia: miso, soba noodles, star anise, lemongrass, and so on. Most of this works well: in particular the charred double-

VILLAGE ATELIER, ANGLERS AND WRITERS, AND THE BESPECKLED TROUT

Craig Bero came to New York to be an actor in 1978 from a farm near a fishing town, Algoma, in northern Wisconsin. One night, after seeing the movie *Babette's Feast,* he was walking past the corner of Hudson and Morton St. He saw "a tiny For Rent sign on an easel in the window. There was something so modest about the sign it struck a chord with me." With no restaurant ex- perience beyond the occasional waitering, he began designing **The Village Atelier,** 436 Hud- son St. [Morton] ☎ 989-1363. He set up his fam- ily's harvest table and had his grandfather send the cherry wood from the family orchard to make the wainscoting. The beams and the bath- room doors come from the farm. He did all of the cooking for the first year (until he could af- ford a chef), translating the old farm recipes, calling relatives and asking what they could tell him about how dishes he remembered were prepared. They didn't have much written down and would often describe the cooking process or the smells. This, combined with Mr. Bero's own strong memories of life on the farm, results in dishes like pan-fried yellow perch (flown in when in season) with German potato salad and Milwaukee rye bread or country roast chicken with prune stuffing. His mother, Charlotte Bero, does all of the baking for the three businesses,

rising at 1 A.M. to start making cherry pies, scones, tea breads, and jelly rolls. She rolls all the crusts by hand. 2,400 pounds of sour cherries are brought in from Wisconsin every year. En- trees average $17.50 . . . After a couple of years, Mr. Bero wanted an "everyday place, like the place where you went to have a cup of coffee and talk about fishing, something less formal." He began thinking about his great grandmother, who always served afternoon tea on the farm. The workers came in from the field and drank tea from her English china cups. He wanted to create a place where the juxtaposition of the ruggedness of the environment and the bone china teacup came together. Thus was born **An- glers and Writers,** 420 Hudson St. [St. Luke's] ☎ 675-0810 . . . Mr. Bero says, "My grandpa on my dad's side had a soda fountain where you could get candies and your fishing license." No fishing licenses, but at his general store, **The Be- speckled Trout,** 420 Hudson St. [Morton/St. Luke's] ☎ 255-1421, you can get old-style can- dies—buttons and candy necklaces. From Bern- stein's in Manitowoc, Wisconsin, comes what he calls divinity or "angel food candy," a frothy, crunchy concoction covered in chocolate, fudge, and "hard pan candies that look the way they al- ways did."

thick pork chop with ginger plum barbecue sauce and the much more delicate but no less appealing hamachi (a small Pacific tuna), with citrus juice and chive oil. The saffron risotto with vegetables and carrot emulsion is altogether a success, the pan-roasted filet mignon with porcini mushrooms and port wine glaze is fine, and so is the herb-crusted chicken. For the vegetarian in your group, the casserole of veggies (carrots, potatoes, turnips, mushrooms, chard, salsify, and fall pear) is not a casserole in the Ozzie and Harriet sense (it's not baked over with anything)—it's just well-treated vegetables prepared in a casserole. Entrees average $17.

UNIVERSAL GRILL AND MARY'S

The food is perfectly okay at **Universal Grill,** 44 Bedford St. [Leroy] ☎ 989-5621, but you don't really go for the food, you go because it's so festive—the best gay restaurant on the planet . . . Tightly packed and smoky, with a genial, largely gay and lesbian crowd, **Mary's,** 42 Bedford St. [Leroy] ☎ 741-3387, is a lot of fun. This is the old Italian restaurant, Mary's, that was bought by the Universal Grill people next door. It's an attractive townhouse space, and there's a wonderful alcove for 6–10 or so people

called the Angie Dickinson Suite. We especially like chef Lee McGrath's moist herbed chicken with its flavorful skin and the hearty pork schnitzel with red cabbage and spaetzel. AmEx only. $15 average entree.

MORE **Bar Pitti,** 268 Sixth Ave. [Houston/Bleecker] ☎ 982-3300, for pleasing Italian food . . . **Dix et Sept,** 181 W. 10th St. [7th Ave. So.] ☎ 645-8023, serves French bistro food . . . **Grange Hall,** 55 Commerce St. [Barrow] ☎ 924-5246, is popular for its American food and Odeon-like setting . . . **Grove,** 314 Bleecker St. [Grove] ☎ 675-9463, good values and a good garden . . . **Il Mulino,** 86 W. Third St. [Sullivan/Thompson] ☎ 673-3783, extremely popular Italian restaurant . . . **La Paella,** 557 Hudson St. [11th/Perry] ☎ 627-3092, for tapas and six kinds of paella . . . **Marnie's Noodle Shop,** 466 Hudson St. [Barrow] ☎ 741-3214, serves Asian noodles . . . **Paris Commune,** 411 Bleecker St. [Bank/W. 11th] ☎ 929-0509, a quintessentially comfortable Village restaurant . . . **Pink Tea Cup,** 42 Grove St. [Bleecker/Bedford] ☎ 807-6755, when you need some soulful cooking . . . **Zinno,** 126 W. 13th St. [6th/7th] ☎ 924-5182, jazz and Italian food.

EAST VILLAGE/NOHO

DANAL

It smells good when you walk into **Danal,** 90 E. 10th St. [3rd/4th] ☎ 982-6930, good enough to cause those neurons connected to pleasurable associations of home and coziness to fire rapidly and repeatedly. This is reinforced by the country bric-a-brac strewn around the room in the form of tables and chairs. You have reached the crossroads of

the East Village and Vermont, and it's rather enchanting.

The food is exactly what you expect and hope it will be: tasty American home cooking, prepared with care but not fussed over. The pork tenderloin gets charged up from the liberal dose of garlic; if you order artichoke soup, it is sure to taste mostly of artichoke. Bowtie pasta with roast duck and mushroom cream sauce, generously seasoned with thyme, is certainly not subtle, but comfort food never is. Come here for grilled chicken and pie and Danal will deliver what you came for. Entrees average $15, which keeps the tab down to very modest sums. Danal, you may already know, began as a tea shop and it serves a full tea Fridays and Saturdays at 4 P.M., by reservation only, $14.75. Perfect when it's cold outside.

FIRST

First, 87 First Ave. [5th/6th] ☎ 674-3823, is of the East Village and not: It's candlelit, modern, slightly elegant, open late. Chef Sam DeMarco may offer humble-sounding dishes, but gives them enough spin to make them work. The cabbage potato soup with corned beef dumplings and mustard oil is a tip of the hat to the neighborhood, looks bad, tastes good, like homemade but better. Crisp clam strips with saffron aioli and basil oil may be the best fried clams you ever ate. An appetizer of spicy beer-braised short ribs could almost be an entree (order carefully because there are *very* generous portions of everything). Moist pan-seared cod is lovely, a pork chop with a little barbecue sauce just requires a healthy appetite, a whole red trout with mushroom risotto needs nothing. We liked the soy honey duck with coconut lemongrass rice and the roast suckling pig (Sunday nights only). Entrees average $15. Apple tart and caramel crème brûlée are standouts. Grab a handful of the peanut brittle as you leave to extend the sweet memory of First.

GLOBAL 33

In the early 1950s, when United had their DC-6 skyliner flying, their brochure stated: "Every detail of the spacious DC-6 Mainliner 300 interior has been planned to provide you with luxurious comfort while aloft. Stroll back to the informal 'Skylounge' at the rear of the aft cabin, where you'll enjoy superb scenic views, and congenial chats with your fellow passengers." The design of **Global 33,** 93 Second Ave. [5th/6th] ☎ 477-8427, celebrates this '50s buoyancy without being kitschy or patronizing. The views here are all interior, but the spirit of the place makes it possible to have congenial chats with your fellow diners (one of the attractions of Global is its diverse crowd—there are probably people you'd like to chat with), even if it's noisy and smoky (the noise level is fueled by the bartenders who know how to mix a cocktail). It is an unexpected bonus that the food is so tasty—tapa-sized dishes (averaging $7) of things like big grilled shrimp in their shells, calamari, smoky pork tenderloin kebab, and good fries. AmEx only.

GOTHAM BAR AND GRILL

In the '80s, there was a slew of awful, cavernous restaurants in the city (remember Cafe Seiyokan?) that had mediocre food (if you were lucky) served by poorly trained and often arrogant waiters. A few bond traders go to jail, the market makes a correction, and everybody goes back to their nest. The '80s restaurants are, by and large, gone, forgotten, unlamented. Then there's **Gotham Bar and Grill,** 12 E. 12th St. [5th/University Pl.] ☎ 620-4020. It still looks like every place you hated in the '80s, but it doesn't act like it and it doesn't taste like it. The greeting is cordial. The service appears informal but is quite polished. The staff knows the menu. Alfred Portale's food is simply delicious.

Mr. Portale puts loin of venison, pumpkin, rosemary, poached pear, and wild huckleberries on the same plate, and makes it work perfectly. Order the hot smoked salmon salad and you'll see a little of the confetti from the restaurant's logo on the plate. This smashing dish has the salmon paired with white corn cake. Surrounding this is chive pesto, salmon roe, corn kernels, some burnt sienna–colored hot sauce—there are delightful contrasts of the warm cake, a cool waft of crème fraîche, the release of the roe. Great food. Perhaps the single best sandwich in the city is Gotham's grilled swordfish with pancetta, red onions, and herb aioli served between slices of ciabatta from Companio. We wonder how Mr. Portale gets the grilled octopus in the salad with chickpeas, new potatoes, and duck sausage to taste that way. Its texture is unlike any calamari we've had—firm yet remarkably tender. The hits list, which include

butternut squash risotto with roast quail and apple-smoked bacon and the roasted monkfish, considerably outnumber the misses (an herbed ricotta ravioli in braised oxtail broth that's bland and watery). We've never shared Mr. Portale's enthusiasm for constructing food vertically, but it's never for a moment gotten in the way of our enjoyment. You get familiar desserts (apple tart, chocolate cake, crème brûlée) all of which are perfectly nice without being especially memorable. Entrees average $30. We were happy enough when the go-go '80s did finally go. We're glad, though, Gotham not only survived that decade but is thriving in this one.

HASAKI

Hasaki, 219 E. 9th St. [2nd/3rd] ☎ 473-3327, is on our favorites list because of their terrific sushi at about $13. Some of the other offerings (things like beef teriyaki) are quite good as well. Most of the time, though, we're here for sushi. The place is pleasant looking and service is polite. Hasaki takes no reservations so there is almost invariably a line. Order some sake, sit on the bench outside, and wait for a table. It's worth it.

IL BAGATTO

Bubbling with Italian gusto, careening at times to the edge of chaos, **Il Bagatto,** 192 Second St. [A/B] ☎ 228-0977, offers vibrant Italian food at bargain prices, served with conquering charm. Owner Beatrice Tosti dashes through the small, packed ground-level dining room and down the stairs to the bar and lounge, taking orders, giving orders ("Whoever is smoking pot, STOP IT RIGHT NOW!" she shouts into the lounge one night), and moments later is back upstairs talking and laughing with a large table that regards her with evident affection. Her husband, Julio, and their friend, Pilar Rigon, meanwhile, are in the kitchen, cooking up things like tortellini with meat sauce, the recipe for which comes from Ms. Tosti's friend's grandmother in Emilia-Romagna (six different meats are cut by hand—no grinding—then simmered for 11 hours with veggies, wine, and porcini mushrooms). We've liked the small gnocchi with Gorgonzola, the calamari, the chicken, and the cotechino sausage they were testing out before serving, as is traditional, for New Year's. It comes with warm lentils and the lentils, it is said, bring you money. You won't spend much here—most dishes are under $15. Cash only. The Bagatto is a card in the Tarot that symbolizes willpower, diplomacy, success, and in combination with other cards can indicate a lawyer—those were the four things the owners thought they needed to start a restaurant. They can certainly claim success—Il Bagatto is like a great big bear hug.

IL BUCO

A tale of revenge was inspired by the basement at the antique store and restaurant called **Il Buco,** 47 Bond St. [Bowery/Lafayette] ☎ 533-1932. Poe is said to have gotten the idea for *The Cask of Amontillado* after a visit to this location and its netherlands. Like Il Bagatto, this is a place brimming with high spirits, so you are unlikely to leave dreaming of revenge. By day, they sell American antiques—an eclectric array of quilts, lamps, as well as some Portuguese and Spanish pottery and furniture. By night, room is made to serve the Spanish and Italian food (many tapa-sized offerings, about $9, and some full-sized entrees, about $16) as well as an intriguing collection of wines and spirits (including a bottle of vin jaune, from the Jura, something we've never seen on a menu in the city). You could share a few of the tapas such as grilled shrimp, various crostini, Spanish meatballs, or the bacalao croquettes. Try the braised pork ribs or the fine pan-seared whole striped bass. But you could also have a frisée salad, some cheese, one of their sherries—and toast Mr. Poe. Cash only.

ROETELLE A.G.

Roetelle A.G., 126 E. 7th St. [1st/A] ☎ 674-4140, anticipated the multiculti trend in the food world by many years. Instead of drawing from the East, Ingrid Roetelle (who was born in Germany and lived for a decade in Switzerland) constructed a restaurant in 1989 that would have selections from four countries: Switzerland, Germany, France, and Italy. Now, just as we're well into the whole fusion cooking movement, she's deemphasized this on her menu. There are, however, representatives from the various countries. We've always been partial to the Swiss offerings here—the fondue, the raclette, and the rösti. A more recent, and welcome, addition is the malunz, which is a kind of dumpling with Parmesan cheese. For a while, they had dropped the escargot sandwich (a sliced baguette with snails and garlic butter) but on our last visit, we were delighted to see it back. The émincé de veau, with small pieces of the meat, mushrooms, and cream is also ample reason to return. Roetelle A.G. is a welcoming restaurant with a personal vision, appealing food, and a great garden for the warm weather months. Entrees average $13.

SAPPORO EAST

Sapporo East, 245 E. 10th St. [1st] ☎ 260-1330. We've been getting our sushi fix here for years, and they've never let us down. Without fail you get utterly fresh sushi (plus soup and salad) for $9. Certainly not much in the way of atmosphere, but MUG doesn't think it's possible to find better sushi for less.

MORE **Cucina di Pesce,** 87 E. 4th St. [2nd/3rd] ☎ 260-6800, fresh, inexpensive fish . . . **Japonica,** 100 University Pl. [12th] ☎ 243-7752, popular for sushi . . . **John's of 12th St.,** 302 E. 12th St. [2nd] ☎ 475-9531, is a dark, old-fashioned Italian restaurant serving flavorful food . . . **Jules,** 65 St. Marks Pl. [1st/2nd] ☎ 477-5560, is a likable French bistro . . . **Pisces,** 95 Ave. A [6th] ☎ 260-6660, for fish . . . **Marion's Continental**

Restaurant and Lounge, 354 Bowery [Great Jones/E. 4th] ☎ 475-7621, campy fun . . . **Pedro Padramo,** 430 E. 14th St. [1st/A] ☎ 475-4581, has Mexican food worth seeking out . . . **O.G.,** 507 E. 6th St. [A/B] ☎ 477-4649, a friendly place with tasty Asian food . . . **Riodizio,** 417 Lafayette St. [Astor/E. 4th] ☎ 529-1313, Brazilian means meat . . . **Shabu-Tatsu,** 216 E. 10th St. [1st/2nd] ☎ 477-2972, for Japanese barbecue.

UNION SQUARE/GRAMERCY

AJA

Aja, 837 Broadway [22nd] ☎ 473-8388. Aja's chef, Gary Robins, impossibly long and lanky, all jutting angles, looks to us like a John Held drawing sprung to life. As such, it's easy to imagine him working out a dish, adding tamarind here (knees in), chili oil there (heels out), exploring new combinations in a kind of giddy abandon until he cannot stop himself from breaking into a Charleston. However much it is influenced by the East, there is a kind of American guilelessness to this food that only adds to its appeal. Styled up on the plate, it is remarkable how many of these creations offer unalloyed pleasure. A salad of grilled curried prawns with mint, cilantro, and blood orange vinaigrette pulses with warm and cool flavors without losing sight of the shrimp, which have been grilled just right. The succulent squab is loaded up with lots of powerful Thai chiles and kaffir lime. We've liked Mr. Robins's sake-grilled mackerel, the roast filet of beef with oyster sauce, and the caramelized striped bass with tamarind and ginger. Were we forced to try to identify everything that comes with the rack of lamb, we couldn't do it, but it's a pleasantly odd group of sidekicks that include parsnip hazelnut puree and mango pickle. Much of this food is spicy, and the dishes we've liked best have been the ones with the most heat. Mr. Robins even loads up a mango and coconut ice-cream sundae with chile and macadamia praline ("Something spicy in there," grumps our friend and leaves it half finished), but we like the teasing of sweet and fiery. As much as we love the food at Aja (not the room, which is a mess), we do have a small wish list: The first is that Mr. Robins would keep an eye on the natural flavors of some of his ingredients, particularly the vegetables. It's the listless roasted rack of venison, served with cabbage in red wine, that gives us the most pause. This combination is a step out from Mr. Robins's usual repertoire. Without the surprise ingredients and detonation of heat, though, it's the least successful dish we have tasted here. A reactionary thought crosses our mind: With all this wonderfully skewed food, if you're going to serve venison, why not do something *really* shocking—serve the venison with a classic chasseur? It's not fair, of course, to expect Mr. Robins to serve food this inventive and delicious *and* to mix idioms. Whether or not Mr. Robins gives a hoot about a chasseur, he is one of the city's most promising chefs. Average entree $27.

Gary Robins.

CHRISTOPHER LOVI

BOLO AND MESA GRILL

There is a family photograph of chef Bobby Flay, at age six, making a batch of My-T-Fine Pudding. "I remember that I enjoyed standing there and stirring the pot," he says. After deciding he wanted to become a chef, he worked for Jonathan Waxman in the mid '80s. "There were always southwestern ingredients in the kitchen—chiles and blue corn tortillas. But we didn't know what to do with them. I fell in love with them. I liked their beautiful textures and colors." Mr. Flay progressed through restaurants, learning as he went. At Miracle Grill, he was able to work the ingredients out. "It takes a long time to understand how to use the chile peppers—how to balance the heat and bring out the flavors. I talk to Mark Miller about this all the time."

Mesa Grill, 102 Fifth Ave. [15th/16th] ☎ 807-7400, is, of course, southwestern food (entrees average $23), and **Bolo,** 23 E. 22nd St. [Bway/Park Ave. S.] ☎ 228-2200, Spanish food with Mediterranean influences, "herbaceous flavors, and lots of oven to table dishes (paellas) and using lots of rice" (entrees average $24). Mr. Flay cooks at each restaurant for six-week intervals.

If you could eat just once at both restaurants, Mr. Flay recommends having the shrimp and roasted garlic tamale at Mesa Grill—one of the most requested dishes, it's never been taken off the menu. It's also the only dish on the menu made with cream. He'd also suggest "any quesadilla on the menu." At Bolo—paella and a glass of sangria.

He changes the menus in both restaurants four times a year. Ideas for new dishes come from many places: "My realm of experience, something I've eaten somewhere. I dream finished dishes. Then when I wake up I break it down to the ingredients to see how it was put together."

CAFFE BONDÍ

Caffe Bondí, 7 W. 20th St. [5th/6th] ☎ 691-8136, is owned by the Settepani family from Sicily, three sisters, two sons and a cousin—Salvatore Anzalone, the chef. Sicilian cooking combines influences from many cultures, including Arab, Greek, and Moroccan. When preparing seafood, it is not uncommon to combine something sweet with the fish, like mussels in orange and olive sauce. A signature dish of Sicily is pasta con sarde, fresh sardines, a little tomato, saffron, pine nuts, perciatelli (hollow, thin pasta), and the sweet touch of currants. The menu changes seasonally and, in season, you'll find game, wild boar, rabbit, quail roasted with tomatoes and olives, and, sometimes, pheasant. Desserts are in the hands of son Biagio, who also runs the Bruno Bakery. There are a couple of very good Sicilian wines on the all Italian wine list. Pastas average $15, entrees average $20.

C.T.

Imagine a jaunty cuisine—confident, arms swinging, optimistic, funny, impervious to any rules but its own, and that gives you an idea of the food of **C.T.,** 111 E. 22nd St. [Park/Lex] ☎ 995-8500, which is to say the food of Claude Troisgros. Only a catastrophic genetic mutation would have produced a Roannais Troisgros unworthy of his toque. M. Troisgros, however, can cook and cook marvelously well, but whether it is owing to nature or nurture (stints at the Michelin three-star pantheon of his father and uncle, Bocuse, Taillevent, Tantris, the Connaught, and 15 years on his own in Brazil), we don't know. We do know that he developed a cuisine that borrows from France, Brazil, and other points of the compass, and yet feels freshly minted. Mr. Troisgros' menu has changed over time, though he has kept a few of the most popular dishes such as the crepaze, an unlikely-sounding watercress-filled crepe with Stilton. The big taro mousse ravioli with white truffle oil and mushrooms seems the very of essence of warmth and earth flavors, and yet is so light, so unbound, that its acquaintance with the laws of gravity could be temporal. The black and blue (meaning very rare) tuna with black and white sesame seeds, daikon radish, and sesame oil is texture perfect, with the dominant taste of sesame and some grace notes of soy and ginger. Mr. Troisgros often has venison when the weather's right, and will likely roast it and serve with a reduced venison stock and a white bean or celery puree. There's a side dish to keep your eye out for: It comes in a small copper pot. Within, Brussels sprouts, lardons, mushrooms, and black truffle shavings. It is the ultimate side dish. Poire Poires Poivre—pears, pear sorbet, and black pepper—remains one of the very best desserts in town.

Mr. Troisgros also offers a few tastes of "Les Classiques Troisgros"—the family classics—well worth trying. What's not to love in the Oeufs Brouillés au Caviar (which Mr. Troisgros resists renaming Eggs Eggs Eggs): in two egg-shaped ramekins, scrambled eggs are topped with a layer of Sevruga caviar. The Troisgros original of salmon in sorrel sauce is available, and it's easy to see why this dish has remained so popular. You can also have the Troisgros seniors' signature côte de bœuf in Fleurie with marrow. Entrees average $28, with appetizers an expensive $16 or so. The Troisgros wines, not surprisingly, go well with this food, and many are at moderate prices. If you haven't been here for a while, the room is considerably improved.

EISENBERG'S

Eisenberg's, 174 Fifth Ave. [22nd/23rd] ☎ 675-5096, is one of those intact-from-another-era places that you think could vanish any day—just as their longtime waitress, Ann, did. One day we asked where she was, the tall, slender waitress in her 70s. They still don't know. Eisenberg's does make a few concessions to the times. You can get diet Coke here. You can get tuna salad with no-cholesterol mayo. They have a section on their menu called "Diet Delights," but in it is a chef's salad of roast beef, turkey, ham, Swiss cheese, and one boiled egg. In any case, most people have the hot pastrami or the tuna with regular mayo or their meatloaf. We miss Ann, and we'd miss Eisenberg's if it ever vanished.

FOLLONICO

Since we stumbled onto and then into **Follonico,** 6 W. 24th St. [5th/6th] ☎ 691-6359, one hot August night in 1993, we have returned many times, but not often enough. It was little-known then, and the restaurant was nearly empty. The welcome was not the kind of crazed desperation that comes when restaurateurs have empty rooms. It was hot out and we weren't dressed well. Still, the welcome was simple kindness itself. The Italian food was delicious. The cooking seemed both clear and sophisticated—joyously direct cooking in which elemental flavors—salt, thyme, the natural taste of red snapper, the figginess of a fig crostata—were front, center, saluted. More often than we wish, we end up in empty restaurants. They are never like Follonico, but then, not much is.

Since then, Follonico's fortunes have changed. It's never empty. It has a devoted group of diners who love its stylishly understated Italian room, who like being in the care of chef Alan Tardi and Karen Bussen, and they love the food. Another thing about Follonico that's changed is the food. It's even better, more assured. Bagna cauda, the Piedmontese "hot bath" of oil, garlic, anchovies, into which you dip vegetables is a staple on the menu. Mr. Tardi often pairs deep-fried calamari or deep-fried oysters with fried mizuma, to which he adds horseradish cream and caviar. It is an unfailing pleasure. The kitchen is not immune to the seductions of fusion cooking, but the felicitious match of foie gras with fried starfruit, quince puree, and pomegranate is surely the result of careful development. We've had roast lobster we loved and red snapper prepared in a rock salt crust that was moist, flavorful, and utterly delicious. The warm apple tart makes an ideal dessert.

Mr. Tardi always has an interesting wine list, filled with Italian wines that go well with the menu. The last time we were there, though, we thought the Thackrey Pleiades from California for $30 a vigorous, vibrant accompaniment to the food. Wines start at $18, entrees are about $22.

One thing about Follonico that hasn't changed is the warmth of the place. It's suffused with it.

MAVALLI PALACE

We received a letter once from an offended vegetarian who claimed we were anti-vegetable because we had written "Life without meat and dairy? No lamb? No crème frâiche? No thank you." And to think, the month before we had written a passionate defense of Brussels sprouts. Us anti-vegetable? Never. If it's food and it's done right, count us in. At **Mavalli Palace,** 46 E. 29th St. [Park/Mad] ☎ 679-5535, it's Indian vegetarian, and it's full of pleasures. Many people order the Masala Dosai here, the wonderful long crepe that's done to a turn. The Mavalli Masala Dosai adds potatoes and a startling level of heat from chutney. These come with sambar, a savory lentil and vegetable mix. The Kancheepuram iddly, steamed cakes of lentil and rice, flecked with cashews, ginger, and coriander, are little bombs of flavor. See for yourself if you miss meat at Mavalli Palace. We don't. Average entree $10.

PATRIA

During the summer of 1994, we spent many nights in Queens eating our way through the most popular dishes of most of the South American countries. We liked much of what we ate, but feather light it is not. South American food might not be our desert island food of choice, though if it tasted like the food at **Patria,** 250 Park Ave. South [20th] ☎ 777-6211, we'd reconsider. When Patria's chef, Douglas Rodriguez, was traveling in South America, he was fascinated by the meals he had, but the great ones always seemed to be in someone's home, not in a restaurant. He became aware that there were few great South American restaurants in or out of South America. He's now spreading the word through his inventive interpretations of South and Latin American dishes. While he likes to embellish this food, Mr. Rodriguez says some of the dishes, such as Sango Que Te Mata, a traditional Ecuadorian shrimp stew, are quite authentic. (In this case, he's named the dish after the man who introduced him to it.) His Peruvian ceviche may be more complex than what you'd find in Peru, but that will hardly stop you from enjoying it. You may also find on the menu Chilean salmon, empanadas, arepas (corn cakes that sometimes come stuffed with cheese or other things), and potatoes à la huancaina, a typical Peruvian dish with cheese and chile peppers. The last time we checked, Mr. Rodriguez also had representative (if reinterpreted) dishes from Cuba, the Dominican Republic, Paraguay, and Honduras. But after a few bites of this food, you may not care about provenance at all. Entrees average $25.

PITCHOUNE

We'll watch **Pitchoune,** 226 Third Ave. [19th] ☎ 614-8641, with interest as it progresses from an instant hit, heaped with more praise than it can bear, to a more stable and probably better restaurant. It starts off well, cooking with proficiency things like sweetbreads with a beet vinaigrette, wild mushroom risotto, pork tenderloin, pan-roasted monkfish—with entrees averaging $15. Pitchoune is very good. It does not, however, seem to us a "major player," as one writer put it, but a worthy entry into the Jean-Claude–style restaurants that are popping up around town (think of Le Zoo and Savann). We like Pitchoune very much indeed and hope it can overcome its great notices.

REPUBLIC

Republic, 37 Union Square West [16th/17th] ☎ 627-7172. A restaurant charging three or four times the amount for an entree could just as easily have opened in this space. So it is particularly good fortune for people living and working near Republic that a bowl of Asian noodles (influences from many Asian countries) is only $7 or $8 and that the food is so appealing. The wide open white space looks ready for a photo shoot, but the atmosphere is casual and relaxed. The broth noodles are all worth trying. While we haven't had everything on the menu, we haven't had anything we didn't like.

UNION SQUARE CAFE

The brevity of this piece is in inverse proportion to the pleasure we've had from **Union Square Cafe,** 21 E. 16th St. [5th/Union Sq. W.] ☎ 243-4020, and to the respect we have for what proprietor Danny Meyer has achieved here. That we are brief is simply because you likely know it well and we can only add to the general approbation. This is a case of the whole surpassing the sum of the parts, strong as those parts are. It is a touchstone of a restaurant and a *useful* one. By this, coming from a user's guide, we mean high praise. It serves so many purposes so successfully that this would be the restaurant we would have as our very own (if only to be able to reserve more easily). High marks for Michael Romano's food, wine, service, and general aura. And while the squeeze at the bar can be tight, it's still one of our favorite ways to begin a Saturday, having a burger (tuna or beef), some garlic chips, and a glass of wine. Union Square Cafe is right for so many things. It's a place to celebrate, commiserate, sign a deal, rekindle, recharge. Simply, a great place. Entrees average $26.

VERBENA

Except for an awful dish of butternut squash ravioli in a pond of orange sauce, most of the dishes at **Verbena,** 54 Irving Place

[17th/ 18th] ☎ 260-5454, are competent. They are, however, so lacking in delight, that each time we've visited, we have left utterly at a loss to explain Verbena's popularity. This is virtuous, rooty, ascetic food, with entrees averaging $26. An appetizer of endive, pickled beets, watercress, melted Taleggio with a sharp vinaigrette has too little Taleggio to make you think you're eating anything you shouldn't. A flavorful chicken wasn't cooked so much as bored to death by its accompaniment of wild rice and a "hominy" of celery root and mushroom. The sea scallops with cauliflower soufflé and oyster stew is a pretty plate—a still life that tastes like one. The beer-braised ribs are tender, though we'd prefer lusty. Foie gras is prepared right and then goes out with the wrong crowd—a coterie of salsify croutons, prunes, and pearl onions. Some of this food is served by a genuinely nice

staff, but their evil twins work here, too. Brillat-Savarin wrote that at the end of a good dinner ". . . the brain is enlivened, the physiognomy brightens, the colour rises, the eyes sparkle, and a pleasant warmth is diffused in every limb." At Verbena, you collect your coat and leave.

MORE Campagna, 24 E. 21st St. [Bway/Park Ave. S.] ☎ 460-0900, for Mark Strausman's Italian food . . . **Gramercy Tavern,** 42 E. 20th St. [Bway/Park Ave. S.] ☎ 477-0777, the enormously popular collaboration of Danny Meyer, owner of Union Square Cafe, and chef Tom Colicchio . . . **Hamachi,** 34 E. 20th St. [Bway/Park Ave. So.] ☎ 420-8608, has good sushi . . . **Periyali,** 35 W. 20th St. [5th/6th] ☎ 463-7890, upscale Greek food . . . **Sonia Rose,** 132 Lexington Ave. [28th/29th] ☎ 545-1777, pleasantly off the beaten track.

CHELSEA

ALLEY'S END

Alley's End, 311 W. 17th St. [8th/9th] ☎ 627-8899, is, in fact, at the end of an alley and should your curiosity lead you inside, you will be rewarded by chef Steve Kolyer's pleasing dishes at modest prices (average $14). You'll also enjoy the design: pleasant and laid back, ideally suited to Chelsea.

From a limited menu of six or so regular items plus a few specials, you can have Icelandic cod with artichoke hearts and cippolini, pork loin, steak, chicken, or pasta. Other options include the tender beef stew and excellent striped bass. For dessert, try their pecan pie, Valrhona chocolate cake, or banana brioche bread pudding. A well-

priced, well-chosen small list of wines (that start at $16 and top out at $25) rounds out this likable spot.

CHELSEA BISTRO AND BAR

After T-Rex and Fiasco, previously in residence, **Chelsea Bistro and Bar,** 358 W. 23rd St. [8th/9th] ☎ 727-2026, looks great. If you can, sit in the greenhouse in back. It's a perfect summer room (save the main room for cooler weather). Much praise for the food: moist snails in a green herbal sauce, a galantine of canard, red snapper that has been paired with oven-dried tomatoes, chicken with wild mushrooms and Port, hangar steak with red wine, and a special of pigeon with foie gras sauce—the best dish we tasted here. There's a great deal of variety on the plates, lots of vegetables, herbs, potatoes, and so on. Desserts are okay, but are not the restaurant's strong suit. Dishes average $19. Of Chelsea's virtues, fine dining isn't one of them, so it's lucky to have Chelsea Bistro and Bar. But, then, any neighborhood would be lucky.

ROYAL SIAM

Royal Siam, 240 Eighth Ave. [22nd/23rd] ☎ 741-1732. Reliably flavorful Thai food keeps us returning to Royal Siam. In 1995, we spent a couple of months eating at nearly two dozen Thai restaurants in the city. Royal Siam's pad Thai was among the very best. Entrees average $12.

TWIGS

Along Chelsea's restaurant row on Eighth Avenue, there are many decent if not exactly memorable places to eat. At **Twigs,** 196 Eighth Ave. [20th] ☎ 633-6735, you can always count on perfectly nice food at modest prices. We come here particularly for Twigs' salads, pastas, and pizzas. Entrees average $12.50.

ZUCCA

You might think of **Zucca,** 227 Tenth Ave. [23rd/24th] ☎ 741-1970, as the opening salvo in the transformation that the western part of Chelsea is poised to undergo. If whatever else follows is as engaging as Zucca, local residents have nothing to fear. The restaurant opened in the space that used to house Chelsea Central, entirely redone in a style apposite to the art galleries that have rooted a block away—spare without being cold and combining modern touches

(framed ripple mirrors) with a pressed-tin ceiling and tile floors.

Order the crab cake and you get a bursting taste of crab. The kitchen makes a winningly forthright chicken, and given the name of the place, you'll always find pumpkin soup here. The kitchen is perfectly capable of delicacy— when scallops are offered, they arrive to you fresh, sweet, and set over a rice pilaf in which you will find

peas, carrots, morels, and asparagus. Perfect summer food. Perfect winter food: Zucca's filet mignon with a red wine reduction. We like the ragout of escargot and spring vegetables that come with saffron cream, and fight over the quail with curly endive salad. A shellfish soup, packed with calamari, shrimp, mussels, clams, and scallops, is fresh and exudes the sea—what else can you ask of shellfish soup? West Chelsea couldn't have a better colonizer than Zucca. The chef and owner, Eric Stapleman, is the right man for the job, having originally opened Luma an avenue away. He felt somewhat constricted by the format that developed there, but he continues to cook organic when possible and doesn't use much butter in sauces. Dishes average $16.

MORE **Chelsea Commons,** 463 W. 24th St. [10th] ☎ 929-9424, a great joint with a pleasant back garden . . . **Da Umberto,** 107 W. 17th St. [6th/7th] ☎ 989-0303, the popular Italian spot . . . **Luma,** 200 Ninth Ave. [22nd/23rd] ☎ 633-8033. Scott Bryan's food has people stopping in from all over the city . . . **Meriken,** 189 Seventh Ave. [21st] ☎ 620-9684, for sushi.

MIDTOWN EAST

BANGKOK LODGE

The default style of New York restaurants is long and narrow with tables to the left and to the right and passage in the middle. It is so common a configuration that we have to remind ourselves that this is not how restaurant space is by nature, only by second nature. Unable to distinguish themselves by commodiousness or design, the standard "railroad flat" restaurant must have other attractions. **Bangkok Lodge,** 1069 First Ave. [58th/59th] ☎ 752-9277, offers solid and consistent Thai food, but the secret weapon is Marie, the cheerful French wife of the Thai chef. The people you run into here are an enjoyable mix of neighborhood locals, East Side dowagers with their furry little sidekicks, and people like us, who return time after time for the curries, the shrimp with chunks of fried garlic on top, the Bangkok Lodge lamb with spinach. Entrees average $12. Mostly we return, though, to see Marie, who scoots back and forth, chatting, laughing, bringing you another Singha. We have come here after good days and we've slunk in after terrible ones, but we have always left feeling better.

CHARLTON'S

When you want terrific steak without the Norsemen-in-the-banquet-hall trappings, consider **Charlton's,** 922 Third Ave. [55th/56th] ☎ 688-4646. The look of the restaurant is clean and handsome, and we like the maps of old New York on the walls. Charlton's serves a powerhouse porterhouse: a very  charcoaly crust surrounds tender but full-flavored meat. The T-bone is very nearly as good as the porterhouse, and

both have been cooked perfectly. The filet mignon is huge and runs true to form for this cut: It practically melts in your mouth, but the flavor makes less of an impression. Of the sides, have the creamed spinach and onion rings (and if you love garlic, the broccoli with garlic), but skip the griddled potato cake. They rotate excellent microbreweries on draft, and there's a list of wines from $24 and up to the great Bordeaux on the high end of the list. The staff here is accommodating, and while Charlton's may not have the highest profile of New York's steakhouses, it's certainly one of the most civilized. Steaks average $30.

DAWAT

The first time we ate at **Dawat,** 210 E. 58th St. [2nd/3rd] ☎ 355-7555, we ordered the bhel poori appetizer. When it came, we looked at this dish of wheat chips and puffed rice with its greenish cast and thought you might be able to discover penicillin in there. A jumpingly vibrant dish, it is made with chutneys and coriander, and it was addiction at first bite. We haven't loved every dish we've had at Dawat, but this is an Indian restaurant we'd go back to any time. Part of the fun in returning is seeing what consultant Madhur Jaffrey has developed for the special menu. On our last visit we had the raan—the tenderest possible leg of lamb, with some hints of the chile and garlic in which it was marinated before being braised and then roasted in the tandoor. The onion and black pepper kulcha, also on this menu, makes a terrific side. The whole tandoori fish is, unfortunately, overcooked and dry, and there's no thrill of flavor. A miss. From the regular menu, we like the chicken masala and the baghari jhinga—shrimp prepared with garlic, curry leaves, and mustard seeds, that yields a pink, creamy, spicy dish. Others find Dawat more comely than we do, and service has never been a strong point here. It's not cheap—entrees can be over $20 (though many are less). But a few months pass and we hear the call for fenugreek and ginger and cardamom, and we're happy to be back on 58th Street at Dawat, satisfying our urge for excellent and often unusual Indian food.

HANGAWI

August 15th is Hangawi, the Korean Thanksgiving, a day to celebrate the harvest. **Hangawi,** 12 E. 32nd St. [5th/Mad] ☎ 213-0077, is also the name of a restaurant to celebrate, offering as it does a bountiful harvest of vegetables every day in a relaxing and tranquil setting. Wear clean socks. You will be asked to remove your shoes, which turns out to be integral to the experience here. Having your shoes off makes you aware of the ground and, of course, what it offers up. If you think this sounds too crunchy and Birkenstocky, we assure you that the food at Hangawi appeals to a more general audience—the whole experience is lovely. Order the $32.95 Emperor's Meal with Steam Boat (entrees average $15, prix fixe dinners are $27.95 and $32.95) and you get a succession of orchestrated tastes. You might start with pine nut soup—cream of wheat in texture with a slightly nutty and sour taste that we like. A refresher follows in the bean sprouts dressed with a sesame oil. Then come little pancakes, the size of a sand dollar, which you hold in the palm of one hand and add beautiful strips of vegetables and greens, roll, then dip in one of the sauces. A course of crispy seaweed roll with a persimmon compote (served in the persimmon

shell) has the least clearly defined flavors, and yet we eat away contentedly. A plate of mountain roots doesn't sound like our kind of fun but there hasn't been a single complaint from our table. The pleasure continues through the tofu that comes with a spicy barbecue sauce and lemony radish. Hangawi serves one spicy and one not-so-spicy kimchi, and the former is the best kimchi we ever recall. The steam boat is a nourishing soup that brings the meal to a gentle close. For dessert, there couldn't be anything more cooling than the cinnamon broth with persimmon. There are many other possible combinations here, but they will all juggle the components of taste and texture in a quietly seductive way. The staff is happy to explain things. In fact, they seem genuinely glad that you are there. The feeling's mutual.

LE CHANTILLY

She's known to the general public as **Le Chantilly,** 106 E. 57th St. [Park/Lex] ☎ 751-2931, but in our files, her case is called "Sybil." To date, there are three distinct personalities we have been able to identify: "Sybil" comprises the extraordinary cooking of David Ruggerio and the graceful mien of a restaurant of a certain age. "Vicky" is much less assured, rather wan, and lacks interest in her surroundings. "Peggy Lou," on the other hand, is a very naughty girl who allows things to come out of her kitchen that we believe, deep down, she later regrets. The evidence of Sybil, alas, has diminished over time. It was surely Sybil who produced the dish of sea scallops, little snare drums of the sweet mollusks flanked by foie gras and a flan. It was a marvel of conception, construction, and taste. The flan was made with morels, marrow, and Cabernet, and it nearly caused a group swoon. The pumpkin soup came in a small hollowed pumpkin, and it was bolstered with a brunoise of chestnuts, mushrooms, and pancetta. It was a supreme soup and surely as far as any pumpkin could hope to go in this world.

Peggy Lou is never unpleasant, even to strangers. Lately, she has become fixated on chive. The Peggy Lou personality manifests herself most noticeably in the service. The little eddies of chaos that overtake this dining room are her way of having fun. She is able to get the staff to drop forks with amazing regularity, which they do each time as if it is the first time.

We are disheartened to see that Vicky has become the dominant personality. She inhabits the world of the hotel dining room. Blandness and indifference prevail. People come, people go. The terrine of bouillabaisse and the breast of chicken in crispy potato are manifestations of this world-weariness. Onto a pigeon have been heaped green lentils, ravioli of wild mushroom, foie gras, and Armagnac, but, for all that, it never works up into much of anything.

When Vicky or Peggy Lou are loose, watch out! When Sybil emerges, she's one of the stars of the town. $55 (with some supplements).

LESPINASSE

A talented and successful chef once said to us, "Four stars? I wouldn't wish that on anyone." By that he meant that expectations can be so high that it is impossible to live up to them consistently and for everyone. You can't be guaranteed perfection because the *Times* awarded four stars (just as you can face disappointment with Michelin three-star restaurants). So, does **Lespinasse,** 2 E. 55th St. [5th/Mad] ☎ 339-6719, live up to its reputation? Yes. Is it perfect? No. Can we

name a perfect restaurant? No. (The food of the late Alain Chapel was as close to perfect as we've ever had, and Taillevent comes close for service and ambience.)

Gray Kunz, the star chef here, as is well known by now, integrates flavors of the East into western dishes. Heretofore, we would have said that no matter what you do to a scallop, it's still a scallop. Some things simply resist transfiguration, and we'd have put the mollusk way up there on that list. That underestimates Mr. Kunz. What comes to the table is a dish that looks as if it has been on one of those spin paint machines you'd find at a fair. The scallop is ever-so-slightly breaded, served in a shell with a keffir lime reduction. The startling look of the plate is surpassed by what tastes like an infinite number of flavors erupting from the sauce as they react to the sweetness of the scallop. It's not only sweet, it's *tender*—the textural contrast of the vegetables keeps reminding you of this. We've found lately though, that the best dishes are more familiar-sounding: herbed risotto with a mushroom fricassee is sublime, and the loin and confit of rabbit with rosemary and mustard is the best rabbit we ever ate. Our experience here has been that each meal is something of a mixed bag, with the extraordinary dishes interspersed with the merely mortal. On our last visit, for instance, we had an appetizer that was a complete misfire: marinated crabmeat with avocados and melon with citrus sauce. Even worse than it sounds.

As for the room, we've never thought of New York as a Louis XV kind of town. It says deluxe but not with much conviction. The service is good but not flawless, even appearing short-staffed on one visit. Even so, this is serious cooking in a serious restaurant, and we should celebrate

Lespinasse since it satisfies and delights so often and so well. Entrees average $38.

MARCH

When the TV Food Network debuted on cable, you saw a lot of Dione Lucas in one of the early cooking shows. You may remember that Ms. Lucas demonstrates (when she isn't relentlessly plugging her sponsor, Caloric gas products) preparations of everything from chicken fricassee to shashlik to smelts. The British Ms. Lucas goes about all this with good humor and unquestioning confidence. And yet from the vantage point of today, the dishes, smothered under buckets full of cream and butter, now look positively, hilariously awful, very likely lethal. "Add the cream. If it happens to be heavy, so much the better. Then add the sour cream . . ." she advises in one show. In the smelts show, she notes that the recipe doesn't call for it, but adding a cup of lard would help. Which brings us to **March,** 405 E. 58th St. [1st/Sutton Pl.] ☎ 838-9393. Opened in March 1991, it's as good an example as any of the evolution of cooking over the past 35 or so years. Wayne Nish, the chef, who owns the restaurant with Joseph Scalice, the host, prepares delicate, subtle, and superlative food in a style as far removed from Ms. Lucas's additional cups of lard as can be imagined.

Shrimp tempura is a dish we virtually never order, but Mr. Nish gives an object lesson on what tempura can be. The shrimp has just a papering of batter and sits over a tart reduction of pomegranate and spicy carrot sauce. It is harmonious and lovely. Nish convincingly plays with texture in his confit of chicken salad with foie gras, morels, and cucumber. But it isn't only an exercise in texture—each component, strongly flavored in itself, creates an original-tasting dish, even if it's not what you understand of confit of chicken salad. This is how it is with many of Mr. Nish's creations—you don't have to work to enjoy this food, but you do have to pay attention. Roast rack of Colorado lamb with sweet mustard and herbed crust has been on the menu for a long time, and it's easy to see why it's one of the more popular choices. We hope they keep the Chilean sea bass with fingerling potatoes and black truffle cream around, too. There are prix fixe menus at $59, $70, and $85.

The grapefruit with grapefruit sorbet in gin syrup with coriander seed is a signature dessert, but other choices will complete a meal nicely. The strength of March's wine list comes from its selection of interesting, lesser-known wines, often from California. The three small rooms are all pleasant (the front room the least so), as are the welcome and the service—though on our last visit, a shadow of complacency hung in the air. We hope Mr. Scalice and Mr. Nish root it out. In general, if it's meat and potatoes or great balls of fire you want, March isn't for you. When Mr. Nish is forging ahead, though, there are enormous rewards in his cooking.

MARICHU

The ten or so tables at **Marichu,** 342 E. 46th St. [1st/2nd] ☎ 370-1866, are often filled with people from the diplomatic community of the U.N.—they're on to a good thing. Marichu (which has another restaurant in Bronxville) serves fresh and pleasing Basque cuisine, with an emphasis on seafood. The staff is genuinely courteous (cheerfully bringing the cordless house phone to diplomats' tables), and the place is simple and sparklingly clean-looking. They make an appealing ceviche here, and we like the Basque-style fish soup to start. You can't go wrong with the shrimp in garlic, either. Such a place must serve a competent paella, and they do. The squid with its black ink is notable for the tenderness of the squid and for tasting considerably better than it looks. The red peppers, stuffed with puree of bacalao is odd and striking-looking, mild flavored, enjoyable. Marichu offers some satisfying desserts, among them leche frita "little Basque (fried) delicacies" with caramel sauce, as well as the tarta de Arrese—a warm custard pie. Entrees average $20. On the wine list, some very worthwhile Spanish wines at reasonable prices, including a number of Riojas you might want to investigate and a Txakoli—a wine we'd never had before. It makes an ideal summer drink, being an unusual sparkling white that seems a cross between beer, wine, and cider. In the warm weather, you can order it in their garden.

MORTON'S OF CHICAGO

Morton's of Chicago, 551 Fifth Ave. [45th] ☎ 972-3315, is great for people who are new to food. When you (finger points to you) want to order (hand gesture scribbling on a pad), the waiter (points to himself) or waitress (points to herself) will demonstrate (hand sweeping over a trolley of Saran-wrapped food items) what food is (waiter makes chewing motion with mouth). This is a porterhouse (holds up porterhouse), this is a sirloin (holds up sirloin), this is a lobster (holds up lobster), this is an onion (holds up onion), this is asparagus (holds up asparagus). We have so often passed our Korean market and wondered what those green stalks were! The excellent porterhouse, now that we have learned the nomenclature, would be exceptional if it were intensely

beefy-tasting; the rib-eye is disappointing. (The porterhouse is $29.95, the rib-eye $25.95.) The porterhouse doesn't compensate for the many other things we don't like about the place: the atmosphere has neither the primal qualities of Peter Luger or the Palm nor any sense of elegance. Virtually every wine here is over $35—there are many good wines on the list, but putting no wines on the lower end is too greedy for our taste. Finally, we object to the side show aspect of using a live lobster, out of water all night, to show people what a lobster looks like. It strikes us as unnecessarily cruel.

OCEANA

When we want fish simple, we go to Elias Corner in Queens. When we want fish luxe, it's **Oceana,** 55 E. 54th St. [Mad/Park] ☎ 759-5941. Rick Moonen's seafood is honest, vigorous, and flavorful. It may be stretching a point to say that the dining rooms (including the revived upstairs) make you feel like you're in the Queen's Grill on the *QE2,* but you'll certainly feel like you're on a cruise ship (the posters of ocean liners on the walls aren't strictly necessary), in part because of Oceana's pleasant and attentive wait staff. You can start with the salmon tartare, which is wrapped in smoked salmon, with some osetra caviar on top. The only flaw in the grilled filet of rouget with orzo salad, tomato fondue, capers, and olives is the fish skin, which carries too much char flavor. If you like your bouillabaisse with a cutting sharpness in the broth, the Oceana East Coast bouillabaisse isn't for you—otherwise you'll love it. It's loaded up with lobster, mussels, clams, scallops, shrimp, grouper, garlic croutons, and rouille. Mr. Moonen handles the

Chilean sea bass with ginger, soy, and coriander effortlessly. The menus are $52, $80, or $135 with wine. There is another seafood restaurant in the city that has earned more praise from the city's food press. We have a far better time at Oceana.

OSCAR'S

Any chance we get, we stop in for lunch at **Oscar's** at the Waldorf, Lexington Ave. [50th] ☎ 872-4920. There is something so reassuring about this country club–style coffee shop in the middle of Manhattan. The waiters are polite, and sandwiches (like a club sandwich, $11.50) and soups (chicken noodle) are prepared exactly the way you hope, the way they must have tasted 30 years ago. It's true that Oscar's has updated some of the ingredients (the club comes with honey-pepper bacon) but that won't at all get in the way of your enjoying the simple, fresh, and satisfying light meals. Our seat of choice is the U-shaped counter where you can join a lot of weekly regulars.

OYSTER BAR

We keep meaning to eat at the **Oyster Bar,** Grand Central Station lower level, ☎ 490-6650. That is, to sit at a table and order prepared food. We mean to and then there's a seat at the counter near the oysters, and that's that. We sit, we order a dozen oysters, maybe some of the cream chowder, sorry, clam chowder, a glass of wine from their list of dozens of wines by the glass. We've come with friends and we've come with a book, and even with the cranky guys behind the counter, it's never less than wonderful.

THE PALM

When we want sirloin, we head over to **The Palm,** 837 Second Ave. [44th] ☎ 687-2953,

or across the street to its spinoff. This is the easiest way to get great steak in the city. You may have to wait a bit for a table, but it's not a tough table in the way Peter Luger is. When people talk about the Palm, they talk about the caricatures and the cranky waiters, but on recent visits, the waiters weren't especially cranky and we hardly notice the walls anymore. The point is the sirloin, and it's a point well taken. The sirloin is $29.

SHUN LEE PALACE

This is more of Chinese food expert Eileen Yin-Fei Lo's look at some of the authentically Chinese dishes to be found in the city.

BY EILEEN YIN-FEI LO

In midtown at the luxurious **Shun Lee Palace,** 155 E. 55th St. [Lex/3rd] ☎ 371-8844, a reward of pure Shanghai lineage is to be had with red-cooked pork shoulder. It consists of a shoulder, on the bone, with its fat and skin, cooked for several hours in a broth of melted rock sugar, soy sauce, cinnamon, and anise. It acquires a glistening red glaze and is exceedingly tender. The Chinese eat this pork, called *jau yau tai pong,* with its fat, which virtually melts during the cooking. At Shun Lee it is called "Braised Red Cooked Pork Shoulder." For a splendid version of a little-known Cantonese soup, have the Shun Lee Fish Soup. In Canton it would be called *sak bon yue sang tong,* or raw sea bass soup. Spinach and slices of raw sea bass are layered in a bowl; bubbling hot chicken broth is poured into it, cooking the fish and softening the spinach. The soup is topped with

Shun Lee Palace.

CHRISTOPHER LOVI

crisp pieces of Cantonese crullers, *yau jah guai*. Absolutely perfect. Entrees average $18.

SPARKS

Sparks, 210 E. 46th St. [2nd/3rd] ☎ 687-4855. The gaslight "atmosphere" isn't especially persuasive, but it's obscured anyway by the fug of testosterone. There aren't many tables for two, and there aren't many women. The groups of men are having the perfectly cooked sirloin ($29.95). Sparks wet and dry ages their meat, which seems to make it especially juicy. The steak of our dreams, though, has a lot of crust to it, which this does not. A commendable steak, if not the one we'd choose for our last night on earth. The gargantuanly girthed filet mignon turns out to be puny in the flavor department. Sparks' spinach does nothing for us, but the hash browns are perfect. The restaurant is known for its exceptional wine list (mostly in the low $30s and up), but there are a few lower-priced and, of course, many expensive Bordeaux waiting to be bankrolled and drunk.

VONG

In that "been there, done that" mentality we New Yorkers are sometimes prey to, a friend we once asked to go with us to **Vong,** 200 E. 54th St. [3rd] ☎ 486-9592, said, "But I've already been there." Her loss. Vong is wonderful and continues to get all our circuits buzzing. The $65 tasting menu is one of the best in the city, but go ravenously hungry since the kitchen is generous with its portions. Chef Jean-Georges Vongerichten says the "fragrance and clearness" of Thai food first seduced him when he cooked in Thailand, and he goes back to Bangkok once a year where it's like "eating a croissant in Paris—the flavor is in the air." Vong isn't authentic Thai food, of course, as Mr. Vongerichten readily concedes. It's "French techniques, American ingredients, and Thai spices and herbs." Much pleasure from this felicitous marriage in dishes like the chicken coconut soup (not overburdened with coconut milk), foie gras with mango, peppery black fish with cabbage and water chestnuts, and crab roll with tamarind sauce. Some wonderful desserts, too, including chocolate mousse and a fruit salad—both considerably more delicious than they sound. The place still looks great, in mint condition, really, the service is fine. The wine list is short on wines under $30, the only rub in an otherwise flawless case for multiculturalism. Entrees average $25.

MORE **Bouterin,** 420 E. 59th St. [1st/Sutton Pl.] ☎ 758-0323. Antoine Bouterin's Provençal food . . . **Cafe Centro,** 200 Park Ave. [45th] ☎ 818-1222, is an all-purpose, centrally located spot . . . **Felidia,** 243 E. 58th St. [2nd/3rd] ☎ 758-1479. Fine Italian dining courtesy of the Bastianich family . . . **The Four Seasons,** 99 E. 52nd St. [Park/Lex] ☎ 754-9494 . . . **Kokachin,** 21 E. 52nd St. [5th/Mad] ☎ 355-9300, Elka Gilmore's Asian-influenced seafood . . . **La Côte Basque,** 60 W. 55th St. [5th/6th] ☎ 688-6525, in its new quarters . . . **La Grenouille,** 3 E. 52nd St. [5th/Mad] ☎ 752-1495, for classic French . . . **Le Cirque** should be at in its new digs at the Palace when you read this . . . **Le Périgord,** 405 E. 52nd St. [1st] ☎ 755-6244, for more traditional French cooking . . . **Lutèce,** 249 E. 50th St. [2nd/3rd] ☎ 752-2225, now presided over by Eberhard Müller . . . **Monkey Bar,** 60 E. 54th St. [Mad/Park] ☎ 838-2600, John Schenk's food, David Rockwell design.

MIDTOWN WEST

ARMSTRONG'S

Armstrong's (actually, Jimmy Armstrong's Saloon), 875 Tenth Ave. [57th] ☎ 581-0606, a great joint that has been immortalized in Lawrence Block's Matthew Scudder series, serves Mexican and Cuban dishes. There is also Italian and regular American food, but here are our favorites: any of the sausages, especially the chorizos and the morcilla, wrapped up in a corn tortilla. The Alsatian sausage is also fine (though the sauerkraut is bland). We like the black bean soup, munching on the nachos that are loaded with cheese and garlic (ideal junk food), and the pork burrito. As quirky as the menu is the place itself: part neighborhood bar, part eccentrically comfortable and almost pretty restaurant. Though it's on a stretch that doesn't have much foot traffic, the place seems to have fans from all over—it's got character. $10 average entree, AmEx only.

BECCO

There's a reason why **Becco,** 355 W. 46th St. [8th/9th] ☎ 397-7597, on the theatre district's restaurant row, remains packed even after curtain time—it all works well. The food is served family-style, and most people have the antipasto and then some of the three pastas that are offered from large sauté pans brought to the table. The antipasto offerings are invariably worth having: roasted peppers, mozzarella, smoked salmon, beans, endive with a baked cheese topping, and much else. On our last visit, the three pastas were lasagna with meat sauce, farfalle with shrimp and asparagus, and rigatoni puttanesca—nothing earthshaking, but satisfying at the very least. Antipasto, salad, and the three pastas are

$19.95. If you come *really* hungry and have a second course, you might try the osso buco or a full plate of stuffed peppers. An unusual wine list in that all wines are priced at $15; there are some deft selections. (There's also a premium wine list.) Add to that on-the-ball service, and it's clear that Becco, one of the three excellent restaurants owned by the Bastianich family, has maintained its reputation as a class act.

CHRISTER'S

Our observation on returning to **Christer's,** 145 W. 55th St. [6th/7th] ☎ 974-7224, after a long absence is this: The menu (mostly Scandinavian) is somewhat less ambitious than at first, but the food is better (and we liked it in the first place). The playful, modern log cabin of a restaurant, from the Rockwell Group, is wearing well, and the fish on the wall, the gas fireplace, and the pleasant staff all add to the appeal. Christer Larsson still offers the liveliest smorgasbord in town, and the baked salmon cooked on an oak board with bacon and sweet potato puree is marvelous. We like the little neck clams in fennel and dill broth (the broth is too salty to be eaten but is a great undercoating for the clams) and the poached turbot with grilled asparagus and horseradish hollandaise. It's nice to see that after the initial flush of success, Christer's is doing things so well. Wines are from $17, and entrees average $24.

FRICO BAR

In the 1200s, monks in northern Italy created Montasio Friulano cheese. It has maintained its popularity in Italy and seems poised for similar appreciation here thanks to **Frico,** 402 W. 43rd St. [9th] ☎ 564-7272. This is an easy cheese to love, and when it's heated into a kind of pie, with crisped edges and stuffed with things like leek or mushroom and potato, you have one of the very best snacks in New York. Have it with a salad, perhaps, and one of the dozen or so draft beers here and it's perfect, inexpensive contentment. There are pastas and other Italian offerings on the menu worth trying. No surprise that the food is good since this is another Bastianich restaurant (see Becco above). The restaurant is fairly noisy, rather hard-edged, and we could live without all the televisions, but now that we've tasted them, we're not sure we could live without fricos. $7.95 for the frico, a bit more for the other entrees.

JUDSON GRILL

John Villa, at age 24, took over the kitchen at **Judson Grill,** 152 W. 52nd St. [6th/7th] ☎ 582-5252, which made him, we think, the youngest chef of any major restaurant in town. The news, though, isn't that Gen X Cooks! but that Mr. Villa is a very good cook with much promise.

He makes some exceptional dishes: a sesame tuna carpaccio, matched with red pepper relish, jicama, and oranges keeps the tuna flavor up front and adds a lot of color and texture. Trolling the Pacific Rim, he offers a light, warm weather starter of Vietnamese shrimp roll with Thai sauce and soba noodles. The sun-dried tomato and goat cheese ravioli with pesto is a gentle burst of warm flavors. Great work with the salmon, which is olive-crusted, grilled *exactly* right, and reminds us of that uniquely fresh way salmon tastes when you

eat it in Alaska. The green and black-eyed peas that come with it give an earthy counterpoint to the sea freshness. Mr. Villa does nicely with venison flank—the thin strips have a smoky char flavor, and the cinnamon and carrot oil, though it sounds suspect, enlivens the dish. The leg of lamb is superb. We've also liked the desserts, especially the chocolate sampler, the butterscotch semifreddo, a black plum Napoleon, and a tres leches cake consisting of coconut mousse, pecan tuile, and papaya and guava coulis. This is a handsome place and service is amiable and on the ball. When you're going to the theatre, it may well be the best food around. Entrees average $23.

KEENS CHOPHOUSE

You've read *Time and Again* and the sequel. You've finished *The Alienist.* You've switched to nonfiction and read *Manhattan Moves Uptown* and *Incredible New York.* You have that urge to time travel that seems to afflict many New Yorkers. Repair, with appetite, wallet, and imagination, to **Keens Chophouse,** 72 W. 36th St. [5th/6th] ☎ 947-3636. Here you will find an intact survivor from 1885, to which bits of history and lore are attached. The place was started by Albert Keen, the famous tragedian, at a time when Herald Square was a theatre district. It was a popular theatrical hangout, but women were not allowed until Lillie Langtry, the British actress, breezed in and tried to order a mutton chop. The waiters refused, but later Ms. Langtry sued and won. Everyone remembers the clay pipes (over 50,000 of them) that hang in rows from the ceiling like the delicate shards of history that they are. The pipe register has the signatures of many greats: Albert Einstein, Teddy Roosevelt, Babe Ruth, and Stanford White, among them. There are several appealing party rooms upstairs. The Lincoln Room has on the wall the theatre program of *Our American Cousin* that Lincoln was holding the night he was shot. The mutton chop is still on the menu, but, as we write this, Keens had changed their name from Keens Chophouse to Keens Steakhouse. We've continued to list the restaurant as Keens Chophouse out of respect for Ms. Langtry, who didn't blaze trails for a *sirloin*. Keens has its own ale, brewed by New Amsterdam, and there are 70 single malt Scotches at the bar. See more in the Single Malt Scotch article in the Spirits Chapter. Entrees average $27.

LE BERNARDIN

Some of our notes on **Le Bernardin,** 155 W. 51st St. [6th/7th] ☎ 489-1515.

May 1994: It is not full on a Friday night when we enter but the maître d' appears moments away from neuron gridlock anyway. He says good evening, takes our name, walks away to attend to other guests. He returns, says good evening again. We give our name again. He walks away. We fear we will never get past this point. Later we regret that we do . . . Our heart goes out to the hapless oysters that have been immersed in truffle cream sauce. We would have expected the kitchen to use briny oysters to offset the warm creaminess of the sauce. They don't. In any case, up against the cream, it's a rout for the oysters . . . Crabmeat ravioli with tarragon butter is inelegant, too sweet, almost unpleasant . . . This poor monkfish probably never amounted to much in its life, but fate could have led it to Ducasse, Mosimann, Girardet for a glorious finish. Even to Le Bernardin in earlier times. Now it has come to an ignominious, unrecognizable end in a puddle of congealed butter set atop some

loppy savoy cabbage that serves as its funeral pyre . . . We're served a poached rose fish mired in a sauce bouillabaisse that is over-reduced, medicinal, awful . . . Someone in the kitchen has gotten hold of a bottle of vinegar. The warm lobster salad, the red snapper, and the salmon all taste of it . . . The worst food we've ever had in a major restaurant.

July 1994: At a very young age, 49, Gilbert Le Coze, owner of Le Bernardin, has died of a heart attack. We recall the early days at the restaurant rather than our recent experiences there.

January 1995: We receive a fax from a subscriber to the MUG newsletter saying: "Le Bernardin may be back. Friends dined there and reported it divine." We cannot bring ourselves to go.

April 1995: Ruth Reichl gives them 4 stars. We are genuinely pleased for young chef Eric Ripert. The place sounds wonderful again.

January 1996: It's not. The food is better. It's not great. We don't like Mr. Ripert's food, as much as we try to give it the benefit of the doubt. He appears to be the one with the affection for vinegar. The loin of mackerel has so much vinegar on the plate that it's like a stun gun to the senses. The monkfish is better. The poached black bass is moist, cooked right, and set in a beet-colored chive broth that reflects the current trend for fish in broth without doing anything to explain it. The food is competent, but since entrees are about $40, that doesn't seem good enough to us. (The three-course prix fixe is $68, with many $10 and $15 supplements.) The service errors compound the problem. Food is served when someone isn't at the table. The wine bottle is empty, it is removed, and no one ever asks if we'd like anything else. Some plates are removed while we're still eating. Other plates are left to languish. The same maître d' has now taken to planting himself in the middle of the room, looking with a pained expression to a far corner, as if he alone is aware of a vexing problem, but, since he is standing *here,* cannot do anything to help *there.* That's probably true.

ORSO

Orso, 322 W. 46th St. [8th/9th] ☎ 489-7212, is always a pleasure. If you're looking for good food, Orso has it. If you're looking for pretty surroundings, Orso is attractive (in an understated way). If you're in the mood for star-gazing, Orso usually has somebody worth staring at. The Italian food ranges from pizzas ($12) to pastas ($15) to entrees such as grilled salmon, duck breast, or roast halibut (average price $19). Many people come here pre-theatre but we like to go afterward because if the show is terrible, Orso can be counted on to redeem the evening.

PONGSRI THAI

Pongsri Thai, 244 W. 48th St. [Bway/8th] ☎ 582-3392. This place has a fairly low profile, but those who know it know it's got some of the best Thai food around for miles. That must have something to do with the fact that it's owned by the same people who own the venerable Thailand Restaurant near the courthouses. The red and green curries here are exemplary, but be sure to ask them to turn up the heat if you're looking for a capsicum rush. You can't ask for a better Pad Thai. Skip the dishes with pineapple. Spicy food and a sweet staff—as far as we're concerned, a perfect match. There's another Pongsri at 311 Second Ave. [18th] ☎ 477-4100. Entrees average $10.

SAN DOMENICO

Nothing at **San Domenico,** 240 Central Park South [Bway/7th] ☎ 265-5959, suggests that the place has a sense of humor about itself. Come with yours in fine fettle and this will help you to focus on the Italian food, some of the most refined on the island, brought to you in quarters that are considerably less so.

Depending on the state of your humor, avoid at all costs—*or don't miss*—a visit to the bathroom. It conjures up how backstage must be at one of those cheesy Italian TV shows at the end of a long taping. Note the mirror cut out in the shape of a person, the harsh globe bulbs that reflect every surface inch of the orange color tiles. Listen to the piped-in music swell and dip (often the "Theme from Romeo and Juliet"), breathe in the chemical-smelling potpourri that would probably do in a test canary. Everything is slightly rundown, peeling, waiting for Fellini. After this assault, you return to your table, hoping the dining room will improve matters, but this is truly an unkissed frog of a room. Most of the hanging lamps that were here when the place opened have been removed after numerous run-ins with patrons and staff. They have been replaced with tiny spotlights, positioned far enough overhead to keep out of harm's way, their wattage and direction ideal for your dental hygienist.

The food is a different story altogether, requiring only an appreciation of first-class ingredients and the first-class preparation from chef Theo Schoenegger. The soft egg yolk ravioli with truffle butter is extraordinary. When the egg yolk empties out into the delta of the truffle butter, the resulting alluvium is one of the most decadently, wonderfully rich concoctions in town. The dish of Prince

Edward Island mussels with cannellini beans in a parsley broth isn't nearly as over the top, but it has a remarkable concentration of flavor. By contrast, the sweetbreads (billed as crispy but not), prepared with lemon, garlic sauce, and some greens, is restrained. We like the scallops, though they're slightly overdone. Same problem with the foie gras in the otherwise delicious soft polenta and foie gras combination. Your sense of humor will be needed after all for the spaghetti with basil and tomato sauce, which is lovely, but at $19 (add $4 if two of you want to split it), a *bit* much. With dishes averaging $30, this isn't exactly Manhattan's best food value. Still, where else can you get such a superb baby goat—tender, rich, stewy—or Mr. Schoenegger's olive sauce that goes with the breast of duck or the roasted veal loin. The veal comes with "bacon cream sauce" (a description we applaud for its forthrightness in this cream-fearing country) and some marvelous braised radicchio. The Dover sole with herbs and olive oil shows the kitchen's ability to make simplicity a virtue. As for wine, you can find a couple of Antinoris in the $25 range, though you're likely to pay quite a bit more for the variety available on the restaurant's extensive Italian list. Desserts are, to put it kindly, a disappointment. The crowd is everything from dates to diplomats. On matters of taste, you can pick at San Domenico, but it flies on flavor.

MORE Barbetta, 321 W. 46th St. [8th/9th] ☎ 246-9171, especially for their garden . . . **China Grill,** 60 W. 53rd St. [6th] ☎ 333-7788, expensive but tasty Asian/fusion food . . . **44** at the Royalton Hotel, 44 W. 44th St. [5th/6th] ☎ 944-8844, is hopping at lunchtime . . . **Hallo Berlin,** 402 W. 51st St. [9th/10th] ☎ 541-6248. The fellow with the pushcart by day on 5th Ave. has a restaurant by night . . . **Jezebel,** 630 Ninth Ave. [45th] ☎ 582-1045, is getting to be an old-timer but is still serving up lively soul food . . . **Joe Allen,** 325 W. 46th St. [8th/9th] ☎ 581-6464, very much part of the theatre scene . . . **La Bonne Soupe,** 48 W. 55th St. [5th/6th] ☎ 586-7650, for their onion soup and red-and-white checked tablecloths . . . **La Caravelle,** 33 W. 55th St. [5th/6th] ☎ 586-4252, for classic French . . . **Landmark Tavern,** 626 Eleventh Ave. [46th] ☎ 757-8595, the great old joint . . . **Lotfi's Moroccan,** 358 W. 46th St. [8th/9th] ☎ 582-5850, for terrific Moroccan food . . . **Palio,** 151 W. 51st St. [6th/7th] ☎ 245-4850, cool and stylish Italian restaurant . . . **Rainbow Room,** 30 Rockefeller Plaza [49th/50th] ☎ 632-5000 . . . **Remi,** 145 W. 53rd St. [6th/7th] ☎ 581-4242, very reliable Italian food in an attractive setting . . . **"21" Club,** 21 W. 52nd St. [5th/6th] ☎ 582-7200 . . . **Tout Va Bien,** 311 W. 51st St. [8th/9th] ☎ 974-9051, the been-around French bistro.

UPPER EAST SIDE

ARCADIA

Anne Rosenzweig, before she was a chef, was an anthropologist, an ethnomusicologist doing field work in Africa and in Nepal. "Part of coming into a community in a remote area" is that one of the first things people do "is bring you food and show you how to cook it. Food is part of how they live their lives and who they are." This is different from our attitude. "Food is what you eat, and then you leave the restaurant and go on to something else."

When she returned to NY, she was "consumed with learning about food." Not wanting to go back to school, she finally found a chef willing to take a woman on as an apprentice. "It was a wonderful way to learn." When it was time to open her own place, she knew she didn't want a "large, cavernous space where you can't hear yourself think," and did want a "neighborhood place that was friendly, elegant, warm and inviting." In 1985, this became **Arcadia,** 21 E. 62nd St. [5th/Mad] ☎ 223-2900, an instant success. When she started cooking, Ms. Rosenzweig says there were "maybe fewer than five women chefs in the city." (There are still very few female chef/owners. She is a founder of the International Association of Women Chefs and Restaurateurs, whose purpose it is to help women get into the field.)

On the menu since the beginning, in addition to the lobster sandwich, are corn cakes with crème fraîche and caviars, chimney-smoked lobster with tarragon butter and celery root cakes ("a luxury surf and turf"), and warm chocolate bread pudding with brandy custard sauce. "I don't even think of taking these things off the menu. They are ordered so frequently and people bring other people in to eat them." Prix fixe is $58.

In 1995, Ms. Rosenzweig opened **The Lobster Club,** 24 E. 80th St. [5th/Mad] ☎ 249-6500. "It's informal—a very neighborhood restaurant in a neighborhood that didn't have one." She's "cooking a lot back and forth" at both places. She also put together her own wine list. The regular wine list, about 50 wines (only one Chardonnay and one Cabernet), is grouped by price, since Ms. Rosenzweig thinks that's how most people select. The menu changes every two months here (entrees average $22). It is change that gives her energy. "I like the idea of change all the time. I don't have a favorite food. What's great about being in NY is that I can wake up in the morning and say to myself, 'Who has the best handmade tortillas in the city?' and the next week, 'What's the best restaurant in Astoria for grilled octopus?' and the next, 'Who's got the best bittersweet chocolate truffle?' "

AUREOLE

The single best thing we ever ate was in 1985 at the late Alain Chapel's restaurant in Mionnay. In the middle of an astonishingly great meal came a dish that looked simple enough: lobster paired with a kind of homemade potato chip. It doesn't sound in any way remarkable, but we have never before, nor since, tasted anything like it. M. Chapel's food was that way—what he sent out *mattered* to him, and it was apparent in every bite of every dish. Without ever being fussy, each dish was a culmination of his quiet, pure talent propelled by restlessness. We have thought often of that dish, once again at our most recent meal at **Aureole,** 34 E. 61st St. [Mad/Park] ☎ 319-1660. The combination of seafood and potato is one of the house specialties—a scallop sandwich, in which the mollusk is housed in a rösti sandwich. It's perfectly okay food, but it's not exactly something you'd want to stake your reputation on either—to our taste, somewhat bland and utterly lacking any magic. We think that pretty well describes Aureole, though it's a minority view, since Charles Palmer, the chef and proprietor, has one of the most popular restaurants in New

York. He also owns Alva, The Lenox Room, and the Egg Farm Dairy in Peekskill. You might see ambition, but you don't taste it.

The poached foie gras roulade with pâté of braised oxtail is among the better starters—it's got a coherent density of flavor. But then there's a special of hot lobster vichyssoise, gone from the memory before you're done spooning. The salmon in the smoked salmon appetizer is exceptional—too bad it comes with the in-flight celery and cucumber salad. The filet mignon is cooked properly, but the foie gras stuffed morels on the plate are unaccountably dreadful. Mushroom-crusted tuna is much like the steak: big portion, tame but pleasant flavor. Sauteed quail has a happier ending than the thyme-crusted guinea fowl, which is tough and dry. And while we'll take flavor over composition any time, the guinea fowl plate is also aesthetically challenged. Ask people about Aureole and they'll often mention the desserts first. Our view is that these sweets are long on construction and short on flavor: dull and tired describe the chocolate timbale, the warm apple pudding, the anjou pear with zabaglione. The white chocolate cheesecake is a bad idea gone wrong.

Aureole has never won us over on charm, either. You can spend ridiculous amounts of time on hold to make a reservation (the last time, 15 minutes). The greeting at the door is generally some variation of "go stand at the bar until we're ready." The restaurant is pretty enough, and the modest garden can be a bonus, but there's little sense of luxury, the surroundings aren't mood-transforming, nor do you get the feeling of being especially well cared for. Aureole also has some of the very worst tables in the city: Even if you find the food more to your taste than we do, be warned

that you're not likely to be happy sitting on the second floor near the top of the stairs, nor on the first floor near the bottom of the stairs to the garden when it's open. Dinner is $63 (for three courses, with some supplements).

CAFÉ CROCODILE

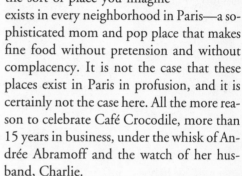

Café Crocodile, 354 E. 74th St. [1st/2nd] ☎ 249-6619, is the sort of place you imagine exists in every neighborhood in Paris—a sophisticated mom and pop place that makes fine food without pretension and without complacency. It is not the case that these places exist in Paris in profusion, and it is certainly not the case here. All the more reason to celebrate Café Crocodile, more than 15 years in business, under the whisk of Andrée Abramoff and the watch of her husband, Charlie.

The menu changes monthly, but it's always French with some Mediterranean and Middle Eastern dishes. One recurring dish is the plate of four Mediterranean appetizers. It consists of baba ghanouj and hummus, of course, as well as a cheese and spinach phyllo and a beef fritter. The brandade-indifferent will be summarily cured by Ms. Abramoff's version that uses haddock instead of cod. The snails prepared here are notable for their tenderness, set in the requisite garlic butter. Delicate tortellini were a special one night with broccoli rabe, pancetta, ricotta, and a sun-dried tomato sauce. We sometimes shy away from cassoulet, thinking it's rarely done right and not worth the heartburn. Ms. Abramoff's is rich and complex but comes sensibly portioned and is so well executed that you will have no regrets. When she sets her sights on a bouillabaisse, it is a complete success. Not only is the seafood fresh, sweet, and tender, but the stock is so flavorful that you know an inordinate amount of care has gone into it. There is a commendably ballast-free coq au vin, but it is Ms. Abramoff's rack of lamb that might be called a signature dish—perfectly cooked, lamby lamb, with a thin crust of breaded herbs. No tricks, just great, real food.

Wines start at about $18, though it's not long on interesting lower-priced wines. Service is in keeping with the place: attentive but not obtrusive. At Café Crocodile, the simple brownstone surroundings belie the care and sureness and measure of the Abramoffs, not to mention the special food. Entrees average $19.

DANIEL

Like many people who love to eat, we've spent many happy hours with food writer Patricia Wells without ever having met her. We wouldn't think of eating in France without reading through her books, and we have her to thank for stocking our most memorable picnic. Somewhere on the back roads of Alsace one December, we had a glorious lunch of aged Munster from Jacques Haxaire's barn in Lapoutroie, a bottle of Hugel Riesling, and some berawecka, a moist and dense fruit bread, the likes of which you have never seen. We hadn't, anyway. Stopping the car next to a field, we stood in the cold, gray air of Alsace, ate our cheese, drank our wine, nibbled on the fruit bread in utter bliss.

So, if Ms. Wells selected **Daniel**, 20 E. 76th St. [5th/Mad] ☎ 288-0033, as one of the 10 best restaurants in the world in 1994, that puts chef Daniel Boulud in a most rarefied league. We think Daniel is a very good restaurant but one in which you may expe-

rience disappointment as often as pleasure. When you get a special of veal tongue with crayfish salad, red beets, and watercress coulis, you understand Ms. Wells. The tender tongue makes an interesting companion to the fairly assertive crayfish, and the dish is alive not only with flavor but color and textures. The Alaskan spot prawns with cranberry beans and gratinated shellfish is another success, as is the paired braised short rib and hanger steak. The ravioli with nine herbs is a popular dish, and a good one. We like the roasted Scottish wood pigeon, which has a deep smoky, livery taste of game—that game actually tastes like game is an increasing rarity. There's no question it was brought in from the wild since we found some buckshot in it. Mr. Boulud handles the foie gras that accompanies the pigeon expertly, as you'd expect, but the sauce is distressingly sweet. Too many dishes leave us cold. Nothing much registers from the curried cauliflower and apple velouté with lobster and coriander. Roasted codfish on polenta with cardoons and glazed turnips is dull as can be—washed-out tasting—and the little runny dollops of polenta don't carry enough flavor to rescue it. We order the $31 organic chicken. Never in memory have we had a chicken as tender, but is it unreasonable to want one as flavorful as it is tender? Recently, we've had the veal loin, a terrine of wild hare, peeky toe crab salad, shrimp with celery root salad, the mashed potatoes with black truffle, and our reaction is similar in every case—we respect the technique but cannot honestly work up much enthusiasm. As for François Payard's desserts, many are delightful—most memorably the red wine tart with prunes.

A few other observations. You will be hard pressed to find wines under $40. We think with all the excellent breads available in the city right now, there's really no reason to be serving bread as plain as this. This is also not a particularly comfortable room—you are packed in too tightly, especially in the back half. Sit in the front if you can and put up with the twisting and dodging you must do to get to the bathroom in the back. Entrees average $32.

EL POLLO

The chicken at the Peruvian **El Pollo,** 1746 First Ave. [90th/91st] ☎ 996-7810, isn't as tender as M. Boulud's (see above). It's also $5 for a half chicken (instead of $31) that is juicy and bursting with flavor. They have curly fries, papa a la huancaina, and something you don't see most places: menudencias fritas—sautéed gizzards, hearts, and necks that come with a hot sauce.

PARK AVENUE CAFE

At **Park Avenue Cafe,** 100 E. 63rd St. [Park] ☎ 644-1900, we order the salmon three ways (pastrami-ized, smoked, Moroc-

can), and it's a gorgeous plate, all swirls and daubs. What are you having, asks the table on the left. Is it good? It's good. The table on the right: Is it spicy? The pastrami salmon is peppery, we say, and we realize we're now in the middle of a Ruth Reichl review. Part of the fun of reading Ms. Reichl's reviews is her cataloging of between-table (and overheard) chat. We're isolationists by nature since we find it difficult to taste, converse with tablemates, scribble notes under the table, *and* conduct intertable communication. (What's her secret?) The conditions here practically guarantee such interchanges since tables are close and presentations are dramatic. Fortunately, the taste of the food, much more often than not, lives up to the presentation. That's due to the steady hand of chef David Burke. Mr. Burke has made the exceptional swordfish chop a signature dish. At lunch, you can get a luscious variation called a minute steak of swordfish, sliced thin and tender as can be. The lemon rinds, used on the chop, turn up here as well, and crabmeat ravioli is added to this mix. This

LE REFUGE

There are not many restaurants in New York about which you can say "They get everything right." **Le Refuge,** 166 E. 82nd St. [Lex/3rd] ☎ 861-4505, gets everything right. Pierre Saint-Denis, the proprietor, has honed it into a model of its kind, where every part serves to reinforce another. When we want country French food, we go to Le Refuge. With the details of a restaurant many kilometers from Paris but without any kitsch and with no pretension whatsoever, it's all as genuinely pleasant as can be. Tables are generously spaced and candles give a glow to the rooms. We've eaten here many times over the years but think the food, lately, is better than ever. Recent highlights included escargot in puff pastry, bouillabaisse, morel-stuffed quail, a succulent duck, and roast leg of lamb with thyme and garlic. Entrees average $22, the all-French wine list starts at $20.

is very good food. So is the lamb, most recently set over mushroom risotto. For great potatoes, order a side of whipped potatoes with basil oil: These spuds were whipped into a frenzy, have the consistency of a thick soup, but are a surefire crowd-pleaser. Be warned that Park Avenue Cafe can be very noisy—the sound of Upper East Siders having a good time. Entrees average $30.

SISTINA

Sistina, 1555 Second Ave. [80th/81st] ☎ 861-7660, isn't the flashiest of the endless stream of Upper East Side Italian restaurants, and it isn't the most luxe, but it serves lovely food in the nicest way. Many customers in an evening are likely to be regulars, and the staff takes good care of them. If you are not known here, they'll take care of you, too. MUG is always happy to see that. The place has had a makeover, adding more warmth to the surroundings. We've eaten here occasionally over the years (they've been here since 1984), and Sistina is nothing if not reliable. A recent meal included grilled scallops and shrimp with scalloped potatoes, mussels with cannellini beans in what is called a marinara (that it's not the tomato sauce you might expect should not diminish your pleasure), goat cheese ravioli with artichoke sauce, chicken "Vesuvio" with peppers, and sea bass with red wine sauce and grilled radicchio. There are newer Italian restaurants around, but if they want to learn how to distinguish themselves and thrive, Sistina is as good a model as any. Entrees average $22.

VIVOLO

Vivolo, 140 E. 74th St. [Park/Lex] ☎ 737-3533. The neighborhood likes to eat on the early side, so if you show up here after 9

P.M., you can get one of the best deals in town. The place is a mahogany-paneled townhouse (upstairs is less clubby and just as nice), but it's not stuffy at all and the service is solicitous. The food is old-fashioned better-quality Italian, not at all challenging, and the more comforting for it. The after 9 P.M. prix fixe gets you a choice of salads, a choice of 20 kinds of pasta (portions are generous), dessert, and coffee for $13.95! You can have the pre-theatre special before 6:30 for $18.95, and even regular hour prices are moderate (entrees average $16). Wines are also very fairly priced.

WILLOW

When Table d'Hôte owner Lauri Gibson and executive chef Vivek Bandhu opened **Willow,** 1022 Lexington Ave. [73rd] ☎ 717-0703, loyal patrons of the Carnegie Hill restaurant and new converts from this neighborhood turned out in force. If we say that the place feels like it's been there forever, we mean this strictly as a compliment—it already has a nicely settled feeling to it, smart-looking without being tricked up. New York figures into the restaurant in several ways. The first is, the look of the place is much more New York than the New England-y Table d'Hote. Most of the dining area is on the second floor with big win-

The second floor dining area at Willow.

dows looking east—second floor perches are relatively few in town, so it provides an unusual and appealing relationship to the city while you're dining. And the restaurant takes its name from Willow Terrace, that being the name of this stretch of E. 73rd in the last century. Much of the food is quite satisfying. As of now, the most successful dishes, we think, are the robust, crispy chicken, a rack of lamb with Maytag blue cheese polenta, the mushroom ragout, and the tuna tartare. One night, the soup was a lobster bisque, without much lobster floating, but a rough, rich stock. In the pleasant column: the roasted monkfish, fried artichokes, a pumpkin and squash soup. Perhaps these will be further refined if the mashed potatoes are any indication—they had improved quite a bit between visits. Wines are from $18 (there's a passable Côtes du Rhône for $19, but mostly it's upwards of $25). Desserts are perfectly acceptable with no standout. Entrees average $22.

MORE **India Grill,** 240 E. 81st St. [2nd/3rd] ☎ 988-4646, has savory Indian food . . . **Jo Jo,** 160 E. 64th St. [Lex/3rd] ☎ 223-5656, Jean-Georges Vongerichten's place . . . **Mad.61,** 10 E. 61st St. [Mad] ☎ 833-2200, a lively place for lunch, though close quarters . . . **Matthew's,** 1030 Third Ave. [61st] ☎ 838-4343. See why Matthew Kenney is such a well-regarded chef . . . **Serendipity 3,** 225 E. 60th St. [2nd/3rd] ☎ 838-3531, a place we never grow tired of . . . **Table d'Hôte,** 44 E. 92nd St. [Mad/Park] ☎ 348-8125, the small Carnegie Hill charmer.

UPPER WEST SIDE

ALL STATE CAFE

All State Cafe, 250 W. 72nd St. [Bway/West End Ave.] ☎ 874-1883. Something of an institution on the West Side, especially inviting on a winter night when the wind whips in from the Hudson. Duck down the stairs and you smell the smoke from the wood-burning fireplace. Have a pint of beer and some of the simple and honest food. Cash only. Average dishes $10.

BARNEY GREENGRASS

In a humble dining room, **Barney Greengrass,** 541 Amsterdam Ave. [86th/87th] ☎ 724-4707, serves breakfast and lunch, and has been since 1908. They've got fans from all over—we go for the eggs with sturgeon and salmon. Figure about $15 for a full lunch. They prefer not to take credit cards.

GABRIEL'S

Gabriel's, 11 W. 60th St. [Bway/Columbus] ☎ 956-4600, is one of the best spots to eat near Lincoln Center, and we like it enough to wish we loved it. Suitable before the opera or a concert, it's more restful (though still lively) after the pre-theatre rush is over. The pastas average $17, entrees average $25. You get large portions of perfectly nice food: lentil soup, wood-grilled chicken, gnocchi, papardelle with artichokes, things like that. We've had service here that was overly chummy and at other times rather cool. Owner Gabriel Aiello treats everyone with courtesy.

GABRIELA'S

Our friend, originally from Mexico City, had been after us to try **Gabriela's,** 685 Amsterdam Ave. [93rd] ☎ 961-0574. He keeps saying how much it's like the restaurants back home, not like the typical New York Mexican restaurants. He's right. The food at Gabriela's is different and quite wonderful. The quesos fundidos (we order ours with poblano peppers), called a cheese fondue, is more of a delightful cheese puddle. Gabriela's serves delicious tacos, the one with marinated roast pork is especially recommended. The cochinita pibil (more roast pork), marinated in orange juice and achiote and spices, is succulent and meltingly tender. We think the Yucatan-style rotisserie chicken is one of the most satisfying budget meals in town: $5.95 for a half chicken plus two side dishes, tortillas and salsa. The chicken soup has a homey taste, though our homemade never had the liberal lacing of hot pepper you find here. Gabriela's isn't anything to look at, but if you like Mexican food, you'll like Gabriela's.

LA MIRABELLE

It's always a pleasure to return to **La Mirabelle,** 333 W. 86th St. [RSD/WEA] ☎ 496-0458, this little bastion of France, way west on 86th Street. There's nothing remarkable about the pink and white decor—the warmth comes from the French owner, Annick LeDouaron (whose sister owns Bangkok Lodge, another restaurant we are very fond of), and the staff. Here, go for the classics: coquille St. Jacques, the fine duck with plum sauce, coq au vin, escargots. Chocolate mousse rounds things off well. A quirky wine list with some very pricey wines, but also a Guigal Côtes du Rhône for $20. A reliable, sturdy wine, and the same goes for the restaurant. Entrees average $18.

OTTOMAN CUISINE

Ottoman Cuisine, 413 Amsterdam Ave. [79th/80th] ☎ 799-6363, serves delicious Turkish food. The owner, Mike Dumankaya, owns one other restaurant—in Istanbul. If there is something Turkish you would like that is not on the menu, call ahead and they will make it for you. We like the stuffed grape leaves with pine nuts and currants, the cacik (yogurt, dill, garlic), and zucchini cakes with green onions and cheese. The mixed grill has wonderful shish kebab, grilled chicken, and kofte (ground meat). It's all fresh and well made. Entrees are about $14.

PENANG MALAYSIA

There are other **Penang Malaysia** restaurants (one in Soho, one in Elmhurst), but we include the one at 240 Columbus Ave. [71st] ☎ 769-3988 because the Upper West Side needs it most. Malaysian food has influences from many countries, but especially from India and China. There's plenty of spice for spice lovers, but enough mild dishes on the menu to keep everyone happy. We like the food here very much. Start with the roti canai, an Indian pancake with a curry sauce for dipping, or the satay. There are a number of savory noodle dishes, fried or in soup. The beef Rendang, in a dark curry, has tender meat and a serious kick. Other good choices include the fried whole red snapper, chicken with mango and peppers, or any of the shrimp dishes. Entrees average $12.95.

SAVANN

Savann, 414 Amsterdam Ave. [79th/80th] ☎ 580-0202, is easily the best food value on the West Side, and some of the best food in that part of town, period. Chef Danforth Houle was with Jean-Claude at Caffe Lure for a year, and he is now making equally delicious food, attractively plated, for West Siders. An absolutely smashing starter is the gravlax, accompanied by a chickpea scallion pancake, crème fraîche, and caviar. We've especially liked the salmon and the duck, a mushroom risotto with vin santo, a spinach salad with lobster and an intriguing port wine and lemon sauce, and the quite respectable steak. The room is spare and dimly lit—the open kitchen casts a somewhat harsh light. Given the value (average entree price of $15), you'll hardly notice. Not when you're eating the pan-roasted cod with olive potato puree or the grilled chicken breast with spicy sweet potato and pistachio dumpling. Even the desserts, like apple tart, are enjoyable. A few more Savanns around these parts would be a fine thing.

MORE **Cafe des Artistes,** 1 W. 67th St. [Columbus/CPW] ☎ 877-3500, one of the prettiest restaurants in New York . . . **Cafe Luxembourg,** 200 W. 70th St. [Amsterdam/WEA] ☎ 873-7411, an uptown Odeon, always there . . . **Good Enough to Eat,** 483 Amsterdam Ave. [83rd/84th] ☎ 496-0163, pleasant American food . . . **Les Routiers,** 568 Amsterdam Ave. [87th/88th] ☎ 874-2742, for country French . . . **Picholine,** 35 W. 64th St. [Bway/CPW] ☎ 724-8585. Terrance Brennan's serious restaurant means, perhaps, the West Side can support fine dining . . . **Popover Cafe,** 551 Amsterdam Ave. [86th/87th] ☎ 595-8555, terrific popovers and decent cafe food . . . **Sarabeth's,** 423 Amsterdam Ave. [80th/81st] ☎ 496-6290, always popular . . . **Silk Road Palace,** 447 Amsterdam Ave. [81st/82nd] ☎ 580-6294, for Chinese food . . . **Vince & Eddie's,** 70 W. 68th St. [Columbus/CPW] ☎ 721-0068, nice American cooking . . . Jean-Georges Vongerichten, Phil Suarez, and Bob Giraldi have taken a lease at 1 Central Park West [59th/60th] and are planning a first-class restaurant, with a terrace overlooking the park. We can't wait.

HARLEM

Dana Alexander opened **Snooky's,** 63 W. 137th St. [Lenox/5th] ☎ 281-3500, in 1995, a small and pleasant cafe that works its charms on you. We've liked what we've tasted here—commendable ribs with barbecue sauce, smothered pork chops with a lot of zest in the smother, a couple of nice twists on chicken and waffles (a Harlem favorite), and the best collard greens around. Ms. Alexander sends out her carrot cake (the recipe is her grandmother's) to a number of coffee bars and restaurants around the city. There's a jazz brunch on Sundays with sets at 1 P.M. and 3 P.M. Entrees average $11 . . . Just east of the Park, some of the freshest, most delicious chicken and ribs in town at **Emily's,** 1325 Fifth Ave. [111th] ☎ 996-1212. It doesn't have the intimate appeal of Snooky's, but the food makes up for it. Entrees average $13 . . . **Londel's of Strivers' Row,** 2620 Frederick Douglass Blvd. [139th/140th] ☎ 234-6114, opened in October 1994 by owner Londel Davis. Mr. Davis, who was raised in Harlem, says, "Historically, we are a southern people, our roots and sense of hospitality emanates from there." We'd make a meal of the crisp fried chicken, the excellent hot corn bread, and the sweet, refreshing iced tea. Entrees average $12 . . . For a quick breakfast, join locals at the tiny, unprepossessing **M & G Diner,** 383 W. 125th St. [Manhattan/8th] ☎ 864-7326. Cash only. Entrees average $7 . . .

For dinner, try **Perks,** 553 Manhattan Ave. [123rd] ☎ 666-8500. Some soul food on the menu and much else, though the best reason to go may be the music: calypso, jazz, and performers like Sarah Dash and Roy Ayres. Entrees average $15 . . . Though **Wells,** 2247 Adam Clayton Powell Blvd. [132nd] ☎ 234-0700, isn't really the original Wells, this new incarnation has been drawing folks for, among other things, Monday night dancing to its big band, the Harlem Renaissance. Entrees average $11 . . . **Copeland's** has two addresses in Harlem, 547 W. 145th St. [Amsterdam/Bway] ☎ 234-2357, and 203–205 W. 125th St. [7th/8th] ☎ 666-8700. Entrees average $13 . . . Finally, there's **Sylvia's,** 328 Lenox Ave. [126th/127th] ☎ 996-0660. You can always eat well in this beloved institution (filled these days with people from around the world). There's a gospel brunch on Sundays, about $21. Entrees average $15.

BROOKLYN

CAFE CAPPUCCINO

Cafe Cappuccino, 290 Brighton Beach Ave. [Brighton 3rd St.] ☎ 718-646-6297. In spite of its name, this is a simple, pleasing Russian restaurant. We like the chicken soup, the blini, pelmeni, even a home-cooked chicken stroganoff. The crowd makes for great people-watching, filled with a fascinating cross section of Russians. Cash only. Average dish $6.

CUCINA

It's a small journey for Manhattanites to get to **Cucina,** 256 Fifth Ave. [Carroll/Garfield], Brooklyn ☎ 718-230-0711, but we think that the cooking of Brooklyn-born chef Michael Ayoub, the pretty but unpretentious setting, and the generosity of spirit from the kitchen make it one of the more delightful restaurants in New York.

You cannot go wrong with the antipasto. Choose carefully from the extensive selection, because portions here range from large to way too large. The arti-

Cucina.

choke that comes with a summer-like, intense basil dip is as memorable as an artichoke can get. The roasted red peppers are glistening and lively. Tuscan lentil salad doesn't sound like much, but Mr. Ayoub makes much of something rather humble. One night, a special appetizer of quail sounded wildly overconceived. Something about being fried with potato chip and a foie gras sauce and chestnut ravioli and who knows what else. We could have done with a little less potato chip batter, but this is a quibble: a surprising success. The kitchen does something as familiar as fusilli puttanesca, but the clear, vibrant tastes make it seem new. The char-grilled flavor of the shrimp in the farfalle pasta makes the dish jump out at you. Shrimp again, this time with ravioli and scallops, in a broth, is an achievement twice: first for the intense broth, second for the scallops that are crusty outside but still moist inside. Pasta with lobster, calamari, mussels, and clams in broth is absolutely first-rate. Mr. Ayoub's rack of lamb is done to a rosy glow and served with a sauce laced with mint jelly. You may never have expected to have mint with lamb again but you'll probably concede it's rather nice.

Desserts are completely up to par: the blueberry panne cotte, like a blueberry crème brûlée, is seductive. We liked the warm pear tarte with pistachio cream and cinnamon ice cream, but found the cinnamon ice cream too Dentyne-like. The chocolate tasting plate is another surefire choice. Pastas average $13, second courses average $17, and wines are from $21. The wine list is not a strong suit of the restaurant, and service is fair enough but not flawless. Crowds can keep you waiting for a table, and service can be slow. People come here in tie and coat, in jeans, and from all over New York—one meal explains why.

NATIONAL

The only way to appreciate **National**, 273 Brighton Beach Ave. [2nd] ☎ 718-646-1225, is to go with a group (make it at least eight people), be ready to down your vodka, get up and dance, and cross all national barriers in a haze of bonhomie. The staff will just keep bringing the decent Russian food and the vodka, and everybody in the place seems ready to party, in a wonderfully non-Manhattan way. Highly recommended—hilarious, odd, sweet, and surprisingly fun. AmEx only. $47 prix fixe for dinner and show.

PETER LUGER

If you eat steak, you already know everything you need to about **Peter Luger,** 178 Broadway [Bedford/Driggs] ☎ 718-387-7400. Lots of people order the thick slices of tomatoes and onions to start. We stick to the porterhouse, creamed spinach, and the hash

browns. It's great steak, so tender that you hardly need a knife. Gnawing on the bone seems perfectly acceptable in this rootin' Teuton atmosphere. The wine list is small; if you want beer on tap, it's Beck's. For dessert, have some pie under your schlag. When you leave, rest easy, knowing Peter Luger's is only a bridge away. Cash only. The porterhouse is about $30 per person.

PLANET THAILAND

On **Planet Thailand,** 184 Bedford [N. 7th] Williamsburg ☎ 718-599-5758, the atmosphere is like our own, but heady with spices, the Red Spot is a chile pepper, the rings calamari. Quite hospitable to human life, we think. Learning to cook at mother's knee must be intergalactic: That's how David Popermhem, P.T.'s owner (he also owns Thai Cafe in Greenpoint) learned. Even though Mr. Popermhem says it's simply "old-fashioned Thai cooking," it feels as fresh as the ingredients you see behind the counter at this former coffee shop. (Mr. Popermhem doesn't do any of the actual cooking anymore, but there are capable hands at both places.) Deconstruct the fresh spring roll, and there you will find utterly pristine ingredients, neatly packed, only waiting for a dollop of apricot sauce. Massaman curry with its cinnamon, cardamom, and cloves has Indian origins and is typical of the southern part of Thailand with its large Muslim population ("Massaman" is thought to be a version of "Muslim"). We tend to avoid it because so often it's cloying or overrich or both. Not here. Look at the color of the curry: a brocade of browns, with a remarkable range of tastes. Order it spicy and it's a masochist's delight. You are teased by the first tastes of cinnamon—sweet and lulling—followed by a rushing jab of peppers. If fish can be supernal, the fish tamarind is—a sea bass, delightfully crisped outside, as moist as can be inside. The spicy tamarind sauce is sweet, sour, and hot in perfect proportions. The beef curry is conventional but enticing—judge yourself by the number of times your tablemates' spoons go back for their rice with the sauce on it. Pad Thai is, not unexpectedly, exemplary, with a significantly higher heat factor than anywhere else in town. When you need a respite from the heat, tuck into the grilled half chicken, again marvelously moist, with an addictive herb-charred skin. Order it with the spicy but still refreshing green papaya salad, along with some sticky rice, and you will have a classic combo of the Pahk Issahn (northeastern) part of Thailand. Amaz-

ingly, most entrees here are $5.95. Cash only. When we want Thai food, the gravitational pull to P.T. is irresistible.

MORE Henry's End, 44 Henry St. [Cranberry] ☎ 718-834-1776, for American food and a wine list of over 100 American wines . . . **La Bouillabaisse,** 145 Atlantic Ave. [Clinton/Henry] ☎ 718-522-8275, for the soup . . . **Patsy's Pizza,** 19 Old Fulton St. [Front/Water] ☎ 718-858-4300, our favorite pizza in the city . . . **Waterfront Alehouse,** 136 Atlantic Ave. [Clinton/Henry] ☎ 718-522-3794, good joint, good beer . . . **The River Cafe,** 1 Water St. [East River] Brooklyn ☎ 718-522-5200. As far as we're concerned, sitting at the window here is among the city's great pleasures . . . **Totonno Pizzeria,** 1524 Neptune Ave. [15th/16th] ☎ 718-372-8606, delicious pizza.

QUEENS

ELIAS CORNER

Elias Corner, 24-02 31st St. [24th Ave.] ☎ 718-932-1510. They're not really cranky at Elias Corner, but fish here is so fresh and well prepared that you don't come here for small talk. This is serious business—seriously good fish for about $13. Menu? Forget it. There isn't one. You want tzaziki, you want taramasalata, the fried potato slices, the grilled calamari. Then all you need to know is what's in. Red snapper? Porgy? They're grilled. Have them. Don't argue. You want wine? Don't mull it over. Have the white Greek wine. You won't pay a lot. Yeah, yeah, you can have dessert. Maybe the honey doughnut thing with cinnamon. Rough and ready Elias Corner is a joy. Cash only.

HAPPY DUMPLING

BY EILEEN YIN-FEI LO

Perfectly rendered Shanghai dishes are at the **Happy Dumpling,** 135-29 40th Rd. [Main], Flushing ☎ 718-445-2163, a modest place of paneled booths. You will find no better version of those soup buns, the *siu long bau,* which Shanghai contributed to the dim sum table. Do not be put off by what they are called on the menu: "Steamed Bun with Meat Ball." Seasoned ground pork is enclosed in a small, round, swirl-topped bun with a gelatin of rich chicken stock. When the buns are steamed, the gelatin becomes a soup and the pork is cooked, thus when they are bitten into there is a burst of hot soup. Entrees average $10.

JACKSON DINER

For Indian food, nothing comes close to **Jackson Diner**, 37-03 74th St. [37th Ave./Roosevelt] ☎ 718-672-1232. They serve dishes from the north and south, and all of it is intoxicating.

The masala dosa comes filled with potatoes, peas, nuts, and a restrained (relatively) use of spice. It's very popular with the groups of young Indians who come here. Samosas, fried filled pastries (we're back north again) come with tamarind sauce, which adds a tangy fruitiness to the spice. Tandoori masala, chicken from the tandoor oven, and the Murg Kadai, a Peshawar (Pakistan) import of chicken in a tomato, ginger, and lemon sauce, both have incredibly delicious depths of spicy flavors. Roganjosh is prepared Kashmir-style, which means large boneless chunks of lamb in a masala made of red chiles, cinnamon, cardamom, and asafetida. The Chicken Tikka, prepared perfectly in the tandoor, is moist on the inside and comes with a mint sauce that is mint sauce in name only. Vegetarians have a dozen or so dishes to choose from, including aloo matar, which is described, unmemorably, as potatoes and peas in special curry. You'll remember it—there is such intensity to the taste and so much heat. Dishes come with long-grained rice sprinkled with cumin seeds, which add wafts of aroma.

Excellent breads include onion kulcha and pudina paratha, a whole wheat bread with mint. Poori, puffed-up fried bread straight from the karhai (Indian wok), is hard to resist. There are big pitchers of water on the table, which you will need. Be advised that the restaurant is as plain as plain can be—the last decorating touch was an off-Pepto paint job that didn't help. It makes no difference to us. Jackson Diner is our home spicy home. BYOB. Cash only. $8.50 average.

MIN FENG

BY EILEEN YIN-FEI LO

Min Feng, 135-32 40th Rd. [Main], Flushing ☎ 718-539-2288, serves a traditional Fujian dish that it calls simply "Conch in Foo Chow Sauce," thin slices of conch sautéed in that fermented sauce touched with sugar and rice wine. It is quite good and true, as is Spare Ribs in Special Sauce, an inadequate description for spare ribs dusted with flour and deep-fried, then sautéed with vegetables in a sauce that blends beautifully its components of soy, sugar, garlic, and Shao-Hsing wine. Even though they speak little English, the people at Min Feng are most helpful. Cash only. $10.95 for the conch dish.

SOUTH AMERICAN

El Chivito D'Oro, 84-02 37 Ave. [84th St.], Jackson Heights ☎ 718-424-0600, makes an extremely flavorful skirt steak. The owners here are Uruguayan, and while there is no exclusively Uruguayan dish on the menu, you can have the parrillada (mixed grill), $21.95, and be eating as the natives do. El Chivito D'Oro is a pleasantly modern spot that has a number of good Argentinian wines available (including Bodega Weinert) and offers a delicious dulce de leche (caramel) ice cream . . . Food may not be the first thing that comes to mind when you hear the word "Colombia," but **La Pequeña Colombia,** Roosevelt Ave. and 84th ☎ 718-478-6528, could help change that. It's hopping here on weekends; weeknights are pleasantly quiet. This large, clean, modern spot serves some of the largest portions of food on a single plate we've ever seen. And it's good, too. The plato montanero (mountain dish) consists of ground beef, fried eggs, excellent beans, an arepa, grilled banana, and tasty chicharrón (fried pork skin). This mountain of food costs $10, and you will not need to eat again for a week. La Pequeña Colombia also serves red snapper, a frequent Colombian dish, and the best chimichurri for miles. The back of the menu also endeared this place to us: listed are Colombian economic indicators (things like pulp imports and fungicide exports), population of cities, and so on . . . **La Fusta,** 80-32 Baxter Ave. [Bway], Queens ☎ 718-429-8222, is a simple, tidy, very agreeable place with some excellent food. You might try the meat empanadas, accompanied by a garlicky chimichurri, and certainly the parrillada. Here, for $16.95, you get a small grill placed on the table, with steak, sweetbreads, sausage, and other good things. They're pros with the grill—everything is cooked just right. Sit under the horseracing photos of Seattle Slew and Spectacular Bid and let La Fusta's atmosphere work on you.

THAI PAVILION

We can't say enough about **Thai Pavilion,** 37-10 30th Ave. [37th/38th], Astoria ☎ 718-777-5546. This small pleasant place is owned by Lee and Paul Arjariyawat, who do most of the cooking. We think this is among the very best places to eat Thai food in the city because the flavors are so adeptly blended and yet distinct. The steamed Thai dumplings are a must: They're large, homemade won ton skins stuffed with a sweet, spicy admixture of ground chicken, peanuts, and preserved radish topped with fried shallots. At Thai Pavilion, we've finally found a shrimp cake that we like, that's not too rubbery and uninteresting. This one has chicken in it as well, chile paste, and string beans. The tom ka kung, shrimp soup with coconut milk, is a model of clarity: the flavors of the shrimp, red and green peppers, dried chiles, galangal (like ginger), lemongrass and cilantro. Another fish soup we're crazy about is the "Thai Bouillabaisse," which is loaded with shrimp, calamari (that's been carved into a kind of design), and scallops, all in a lilting lemongrass broth. The duck salad is not for the fainthearted—boneless duck is here combined with a pretty mélange of mint, little slivers of apple, ground nuts, and much hot pepper. Thai Pavilion's nam sod, ground pork with long toothpicks of ginger, peanuts, and lime juice, is simple and fresh. The chicken with panang curry is another favorite here. Cash only. Dishes average $12. Thai Pavilion is not far from the older and well-liked **Ubol's,** 24-42 Steinway [25th/Astoria Blvd.], Astoria ☎ 718-545-2874.

ZUM STAMMTISCH

Take the subway to Germany. **Zum Stammtisch,** 69-46 Myrtle Ave. in Glendale ☎ 718-386-3014, isn't *like* an authentic German Kneipe, it really is one. The outside looks completely European without interpretation, kitsch, or respect to decade. Inside it's still authentic but not exactly kitsch-less. The place is run by Germans, and they've been turning out the schnitzel here for over 20 years. On weekends, you'll have to wait for a table in the bar area filled with a mix of locals, including a fair number of German-speaking residents. (Glendale and Ridgewood used to be heavily populated with German immigrants.) You can order good (German, of course) beer on tap and crank up the jukebox to hear Peter Alexander sing "Die Kleine Kneipe" (kitsch alert). There are two dining areas, the front being a Schwarzwald sort of spot (complete with Stammtisch—the table reserved for regulars) and the back room, which is more Bavarian in style.

The Kieler Rollmops, pickled herring rolled and stuffed with herring and onions, aren't half bad. The Sülze, head cheese with vinaigrette, is excellent, if you are partial to head cheese. The goulash soup here is pleasantly spicy and has tender meat chunks. The Bavarian Farmer Plate has Kassler Ripchen—cooked and smoked pork, Bratwurst (odd tasting), and Leberkäse (pretty good). The Sauerbraten is a mess, though, made with a cheap cut of meat and a sludgy sauce. The Klösse, which look and taste like big matzoh balls, are leaden. The potato salad with vinegar and speck is incredibly good. Wiener schnitzel is their most popular dish. Service is efficient (major surprise), and the whole experience is both satisfying and weirdly disorienting. Entrees average $12. We think the best way to get there with public transportation from Manhattan is to take the E or F to Forest Hills and hail a cab (10 minutes, $7 to the restaurant), and ask the restaurant to call a taxi for the reverse.

MORE **Green Field,** 108-01 Northern Blvd. [108th] ☎ 718-672-5202, for a Brazilian meat fest . . . **Jai Ya Thai,** 81-11 Broadway [81st] ☎ 718-651-1330, we prefer this location to the one in Manhattan . . . **Manducatis,** 13–27 Jackson Ave. [21st/47th], Long Island City ☎ 718-729-4602, for Italian food . . . **Mississippi Barbecue,** 172-14 Baisley Blvd. [172nd] no phone, and 201–05 Murdock Ave. [201st], St. Albans ☎ 718-776-3446, simple spots for delicious barbecue . . . **Stick to Your Ribs,** 5–16 51st Ave. [Vernon Blvd./5th] ☎ 718-937-3030, for ideal ribs.

SERVICES

$\longleftrightarrow$

AIR CONDITIONER REPAIR

Air Care, 58-30 Maspeth Ave. [Maurice Ave.] Maspeth ☎ 718-894-8313, started business in 1953 as Video Service repairing television sets. But they haven't dealt with TVs in years since so few people have them repaired anymore. They've been servicing air conditioners for over 30 years. David Mortman, the owner, says, "The biggest problem with ACs is dirt—air conditioners work by removing heat from the air and disposing of it on the outside. If the outside coils get clogged, it will cause the AC to work harder." Eventually, you can end up just circulating hot air in your room. "95% of machines just need a good steam cleaning. It's very rare that the compressor is broken." It's also very rare, he says, that the machine needs Freon, which is in a closed system. If a machine is losing Freon, it means there is a leak in the system, and the leak should be found and repaired—don't let someone come in and just "put gas in the machine." They need to find the leak. For a steam cleaning, the machine has to come into the shop. $85 if you bring it in, $185 if they pick up and deliver. The machine will generally be gone less than a week. Air Care will also store air conditioners over the winter.

Ace Air Conditioning, 24-81 47th St. [25th Ave./BQE] Astoria, Queens ☎ 718-406-2256. The same family has run the business since 1962, servicing Manhattan exclusively. It's $165 to steam clean the machine, give it a lacquer undercoat to prevent rusting, check thermostat and all other parts, and repair leaks. They need to take it away to do this. "Anyone who works in your apartment is not doing anything at all."

AUDIO SYSTEMS & HOME AUTOMATION

AUDIO SYSTEMS **Steve Heim** has an Associates Engineering certificate and spent three years as a recording engineer before selling audio products, which he has done for over 15 years. While he represents seven lines of equipment, he feels that the audio business in general is "too product driven," and he stresses service and results. He says people care less about the specifics than how it will sound. He "prefers to leave the brand names out of the initial discussions," acting "like a contractor who will build a system for you." If, after looking at your system, he sees he can recycle some equipment you already have, he will do that. Entry-level systems of a radio, CD player, and a pair of speakers starts at about $5,000.

HOME AUTOMATION Mr. Heim and partner, Sylvia Holland, formed **Holland & Heim,** ☎ 980-6223, and were among the first in NY to offer complete home automation. What this means is that from a single control panel you could do any number of things: have the shades lowered automatically at a particular time; adjust the room temperature; enhance your home security; automatically dim the lights, lower a screen, and mute the phone when you start to watch a movie on your VCR. The system is completely customized to your needs and habits. It's possible to retrofit a home, but, of course, the process is considerably less intrusive if you're already doing construction. The ballpark here is $10,000.

CAR SERVICES

A problem. A car service can be great for months, even years, but then you get a hostile driver or they leave you in the lurch at 6 A.M. and you strike *that* car service off your list. It's probably not reasonable to expect to have a private car service to the airport that costs less than a taxi, and we have never found a consistently reliable *and* cheap one.

Rates are from Manhattan to the airports. In most cases, rates are higher when they meet you at the airport for the ride into town (usually $5–$10 more—you'll pay the most for a driver to meet you in the terminal, less

when you go out and meet the driver in the car). Unless otherwise indicated, prices are for sedans. Tip and tolls are extra. Some services charge more around holidays.

HIGH END

Attitude New York ☎ 633-0004. When you need a client or VIP picked up or when you want a hassle-free ride for yourself, call Rosina. Attitude emphasizes personal service and reliability, and they're a favorite of celebrities. $45 per hour, 2-hour minimum, plus to and from garage time and 20% gratuity.

Bermuda Limousine ☎ 249-8400. In business for over 50 years. Our industry expert says Bermuda is the best car service in the city, though very expensive. $55 an hour,

1 1/2-hour minimum. LGA: $66, JFK: $95, NWK: $95. 15% gratuity is added.

In business for over 25 years, **Farrell,** ☎ 988-4441, is another excellent service. $45 an hour, plus 20% gratuity, two-hour minimum, plus to and from garage time. LGA: $67.50, JFK: $90, NWK: $90.

London Towncar ☎ 988-9700. In business since 1959, they've got many major corporate accounts. $48 an hour, one-hour minimum (after 10 P.M., two-hour minimum). LGA: $60, JFK: $72, NWK: $72.

Smith's Limousines ☎ 247-0711. In business since 1961. $45 an hour, no minimum. LGA: $65, JFK: $75, NWK: $75.

TWO DRIVERS

Need a great driver—reliable, polite, personable? Someone with a comfortable, clean car? Call Ray Miranda, **RAM Limousine** ☎ 718-767-6340. Mr. Miranda has one of the only 10,000 touring editions of the Lincoln Town Car. It has a cushiony suspension that will give you an especially enjoyable ride. It's Mr. Miranda's service, though, that sets him apart. LGA: $50, JFK: $65, NWK: $70. $40 an hour.

For a stylish whirl around town, it's hard to beat **The Lordship.** That's the name of Gerald the Chauffeur's ivory Austin FX. The car is in mint condition, can hold six, is carpeted and curtained, accoutered with silk cushions and fully decorated with "sporting prints" on the walls. The minibar holds a flask of Cognac to restore fatigued shoppers or give courage to nervous brides and grooms. Ger-

The Lordship.

ald himself enjoys dressing the part and can turn out in knee-high boots and visored cap, should you request it. The Taxi and Limousine Commission got wind of Gerald and the Lordship and thought maybe he should fall under its regulatory system. It ended up in court where the judge asked Gerald, "Do you regard this as a means of personal expression?" and Gerald said he did indeed. The judge then ruled that Gerald is "in the entertainment business" and the TLC lost. Gerald now refers to himself as "a moving artist." The tariff is $35/hour with a three-hour minimum. He can be reached at ☎ 917-301-3095.

A STRETCH FOR LESS

Absolut Limo ☎ 227-6588. If you need some extra leg room on your way to the airport, Absolut is good to know about because they use only stretches (*not* fresh-off-the-line) but at taxi prices. $30 an hour, one-hour minimum, plus 20% gratuity. LGA: $20, JFK: $30, NWK: $30. Don't expect an emphasis on service, and we'd use them only going to the airport (pickups at the airport are trickier). Think of it like a big taxi. If something happens and they don't show, you can hop into a small taxi.

CLEANING

APARTMENT CLEANING

Best Domestic, ☎ 685-0351, provides maids, laundresses, butlers, and office cleaners on three hours' notice. You pay the housekeeper $10 an hour, plus $15 for each cleaning to the agency. There is a four-hour minimum. Prices are slightly higher during the holidays.

Green Clean, ☎ 255-7755, uses only nontoxic, environmentally friendly products in cleaning your home or office. Malcolm Berman does cleaning for some chemically sensitive people, adjusting the products he uses depending on the sensitivity. He also cleans for people who have small children or pets or simply don't want the residue of harsh chemicals in their environment. They can also do an allergen-free vacuuming for $40. Mr. Berman trains the cleaners who work with him and sees that new jobs are properly supervised. "No one goes alone to a new job." There is an initial deep cleaning where the bathroom and kitchen are thoroughly wiped down and mildew is cleaned from tiles. This costs $20/hour with a three-hour minimum. Regular maintenance cleaning is $18/hour. Green Clean will suggest a list of products to you, sell you a customized kit for your home, or provide them at an additional $3 charge for each visit.

NY Little Elves, ☎ 674-2629, is the name of the cleaning service started by Vance Baxter Vogel in 1977. Originally, they cleaned by day and performed in the Tapestry dance company at night. Now, there are 25 employees who provide weekly and biweekly maid service to some very fussy people. Profits, in part, still go to finance one major dance or theatrical production each year. This year, a few of the cleaners participated in the production, but now the staff tends to be professional cleaners rather than actors looking for a way to make a living.

Mr. Vogel stresses attention to detail and says his staff learns "that what they thought was white when they came here, now has to be brilliant." They'll do most anything except ironing and don't encourage people to use them to do laundry as it is time-consuming, and they prefer not to have responsibility for people's clothing. Weekly maid service is $15 an hour, four-hour minimum. Services also include post-renovation cleaning, with the number of workers determined by the size of the mess you are in. On most post-renovation jobs they send someone to the site to see the situation before giving a quote. They do corporate cleaning and have what they call a "traveling super service" for residential buildings—cleaning the public areas, sweeping the gutters, handling the recycling and putting out the garbage.

CARPET, RUG, UPHOLSTERY CLEANING

Cleantex, ☎ 283-1200, cleans area rugs and wall-to-wall carpeting, draperies and furniture. They will work in your home (for wall to walls) or pick up. They'll give estimates in your home or on the phone.

Cohen Carpet Upholstery and Drapery Cleaning, ☎ 663-6902, works in your apartment: steam or dry cleaning of area and wall to walls, upholstery, and drapes. They'll quote on the phone.

Majestic Cleaners, ☎ 718-272-0010, in business since 1948, cleans upholstery, area and wall-to-wall carpets, drapes, curtains, window treatments, bedspreads, and comforters, including down. Majestic will rehang drapes or window treatments when they return them to your home. They quote on the phone, pick up, and deliver.

CHIMNEY CLEANING

Kings County Chimney & Furnace Cleaning, ☎ 718-891-0766. William Barreto's company cleans and repairs chimneys and relines them if necessary. They clean by forcing a wire brush down the top of the chimney, then come inside and pull the damper down and clean above the hearth. A reputable chimney sweep should not make a big mess, but Mr. Barreto (who's been doing this for 15 years) advises covering any furniture that is close to the fireplace. If a fireplace is used 12 or more times a year, the chimney should be cleaned on an annual basis because creosote, a gummy substance that is released from the burning wood, can build up in the chimney. It's flammable and should be removed. It takes up to an hour to clean a chimney, and the average charge is $75.

VENETIAN BLIND CLEANING

Crosstown Shade and Glass, 200 W. 86th St. [Amsterdam/Bway] ☎ 787-8040. Mini with 2 tapes is $14; 2-inch with 2 tapes is $11. Pickup by appt., with a $20 pickup and delivery charge. A 2-inch blind is washed, recorded, and retaped for $30.

If your blinds do not need a major washing or repairs, **NY Little Elves** (see above) will also do the blinds in your house. They do not take them down. The little elves can either vacuum with an industrial machine or dust slat by slat.

K&L Window Fashions, 40-20 22nd St., Long Island City ☎ 718-392-7373, charges $5 per tape with a $35 minimum. They pick up and deliver in Manhattan on Mondays. It will take a week to get your blinds back. If you need other repairs, washing, retaping, and recording, a 1-inch Levolor (72 inches long) with 2 tapes is $36; the same for a 2-inch blind is $24.

Ultrasound machines can do a good job of blind cleaning. They work by vibration, literally shaking the dirt off the blinds. But, if the dirt has been on the blinds a long time and they are hanging in a sunny window, the grime can become baked onto the paint. This will show up as a smudge after the ultrasonic cleaning. Also, if the dirt has gotten wet, either through rain or attempted washings, it will not be removed by ultrasonic cleaning.

WINDOW CLEANING

Prestige ☎ 517-0873. Tom Lorenzo, the owner, has been in the window cleaning business for 31 years. He does most of the work himself. Free estimates. Upper East Side and parts of the Upper West Side only. There is a $40 minimum, with individual windows costing $6 and up depending on type.

Shields Window Cleaning, ☎ 929-5396, is a small, residential window cleaning company run by Pat Shields, who's been doing windows for 14 years. He charges $6 per tilt in window, with a $35 minimum. Larger or older windows (which may require belt work) range from $8–$10.

Red Ball Window Cleaning, ☎ 861-7686, has been in business since 1928 and under the guidance of Miss Clark for the last 25 years. Depending on the size and condition of the windows, the basic prices are $5.50–$6 per 3 × 6 foot window. There is a $35 minimum on the East Side (where they're located), a $42 minimum on the West Side, and a $42 minimum below 8th St.

CLOTHING

DRY CLEANERS

When special garments require cleaning, consider one of the following:

Chris French Cleaners
57 Fourth Ave. [9th]
☎ 475-5444

Hallak

　　1232 Second Ave. [64th/65th]

　　☎ 879-4694

Meurice French Dry Cleaners

　　31 University Place [8th/9th]

　　☎ 475-2778

Mme. Paulette

　　1255 Second Ave. [66th]

　　☎ 838-6827 and

　　1317 Second Ave. [69th]

　　☎ 988-2080

MORE Turn to **Studio Gina Bianco,** ☎ 924-1685, for exceptional care of rare, antique, or couture clothing. Ms. Bianco, who was called in by the Ford's Theatre for help with Abraham Lincoln's greatcoat, will also help you decide what to do with a Balenciaga or a raccoon coat. They do bridal restoration (when you want to wear great-grandmama's gown) and archival packing of new gowns. She and her staff use "nonaggressive cleaning techniques," dye, repair, restitch, and reconstruct where necessary. They reline garments for museum purchase or for private collections. They work on millinery. "We try to keep a balance between the aesthetic and the conservation techniques." While they occasionally do simple repairs, "most projects are at least half a day's work." The cost is $50/hour.

　　Pickup and delivery services: **Valet Express,** ☎ 505-1379. You put your laundry into one of the company's blue nylon bags, leave it with your doorman (or a neighbor), and your clothes are returned to you on the next business day. They do dry cleaning as well. Laundry is $1.25/lb. for wash and fold. Shirts on a hanger are $2 . . . **White and White,** ☎ 800-400-9448, picks up and delivers. Laundry is $1/lb. Shirts are $1 on a hanger.

DYEING

It's difficult, though not impossible, to find a cleaners that will do clothes dyeing. The reason most have stopped offering the service is that synthetics used for clothing (including stitching), don't take dye. One place that does it is **Mme. Paulette,** 1255 Second Ave. [65th/66th] ☎ 838-6827. Owner John Mahdessian warns, though, that dyeing "is the last alternative in salvaging" a loved garment. Only 100% natural fibers can be dyed—silk, cotton, wool, or linen. Even some of these, especially wools, will not withstand the heat required. Zippers may have a nylon coil or be on a polyblend tape. Dye will not take on these, in which case, Mme. Paulette may have to replace the zipper. Most linings in jackets are rayon (not dyeable by this process) and may have to be replaced. These services add to the cost. The good news is that you can choose any color in the Pantone book. If you're dyeing the garment because of a stain, though, Mr. Mahdessian says that it will not necessarily disguise it. In some cases, the stain will have to be removed first by a process called dye stripping, which removes all the color (as well as the stain), or by bleaching for white things. As there are so many factors involved, Mr. Mahdessian analyzes each garment that comes in for dyeing and gives you his best guess on the outcome. The work is done on site and takes about two weeks. The cost, $145 for 2 lbs., covers dyeing only. You will be asked to sign a release and leave a deposit.

GLOVES

These two companies specialize in cleaning gloves. The first is **Glove Masters,** 808 E. 139th St. Bronx, NY 10454 ☎ 718-585-3615. Drop your leather or suede gloves (ladies' or men's) into an envelope with $10 for a short pair, $20 for over the elbow, wait a week to ten days, and get them back good as new. They also do leather and suede jacket cleaning . . . When Joan Collins wore a fancy pair of white leather gloves on a *Cosmo* cover a few years ago, they got stained with makeup. They were sent to **Robison & Smith,** 335 N. Main St. Gloversville, NY 12078 ☎ 518-725-7181, and came back in pristine condition. You send them your gloves and ask them to call you with a quote, then you send a check. In general, wrist gloves are $9, elbow gloves are $11.

HAT CLEANERS

Carlos NY Hats, 45 W. 38th St. [5th/6th] ☎ 869-2207. By appt. Carlos Lewis cleans ladies' and men's felt hats. The trims and linings are removed, the hat is washed, cleaned, reblocked, and trims and lining are replaced. The average price is $27 ("unless it's in bad shape"), and it takes about a week. You drop your hat off at his showroom (where you can see his full line), and he sends it to his facility in Brooklyn for the cleaning.

   Champion, 94 Greenwich Ave. [12th/ 13th] ☎ 929-5696. Champion has been at this spot since 1927—but Mike and Zoya DeLuca have run the business for 15 years. The shop makes no concessions to modernity or decor, but they do renovate, clean, and block hats for men and women. They replace linings and leather bands and can resize hats. The hats piled up in the window are for sale and can be altered to suit your taste. Brims can be cut and shapes can be changed. $25 to clean, $35 and up to clean and block, depending on the condition of the hat. They can't do women's hats that have unusual shapes.

Mr. Horace Weeks is the proprietor and hat master at **Peter & Irving,** 36 W. 38th St. [5th/6th] ☎ 730-4369. The business has been around for over 60 years, and Mr. Weeks has been there since the late '60s. He cleans, blocks, and restores straws and felts for women and men. He can replace the inside leather band and put new bands on the outside. When we visited, he was working on copying a straw hat in felt for one client, dyeing a gray man's hat for another, and restoring a top hat for a horse carriage driver. All work is done in the shop, which seems to con-

CHRISTOPHER LOVI

Mr. Horace Weeks.

tain the entire history of millinery in the hundreds of wooden hat blocks that sit on floor-to-ceiling shelves. Cleaning and blocking a regular man's hat is $27.50, a cowboy hat $35. Generally, it takes two to three days, but overnight rush orders can be arranged. MUG thinks if you don't own a hat, it's worth buying one just to have Mr. Weeks clean it.

KNITS

Perry Process, 1315 Third Ave. [75th/ 76th] ☎ 628-8300. This business started in 1942, when knits entered the clothing industry for more than underwear and stockings. Perry worked closely with the knit manufacturers to develop ways to care for these garments. They not only clean but block and alter them (they have the special sewing machine, called a merrow machine, for this). You can make an appointment with their blocker, who will tell you if he can block the garment to fit. Charles Reiner, the owner, advises that wool is the best material for maintaining the look of a knitted garment. Cottons do tend to stretch, but many times these can be altered. All sweaters are boxed rather than hung, and sweater repairs are made.

LEATHER CLEANING

See Leather in the Feature chapter.

REWEAVERS

These are people who repair moth holes, tears, and rips to the fabric itself. There are three types of reweaving. In the *French method,* one tries to duplicate the weave of the garment. *Inweaving,* or *piece weaving,* is used when there is a hole in the garment too large for French weaving. A small piece of fabric is placed in the hole and woven around the edges. *Stoting* is used when there is a long vertical tear. In this case the edges are closed with a method that is not completely invisible. Each tear or rent must be seen and evaluated by these experts who will tell you what you can and cannot expect.

French-American Re-Weaving, 119 W. 57th St. [6th/7th] ☎ 765-4670. This establishment has been fixing clothes for New Yorkers since 1930. Ron Moore, the manager for 25 years, is most helpful and articulate on the odds of a successful repair. They repair both knits and wovens and maintain a "yarn bank" to work on sweaters, since people often don't have the little yarn card that came with the sweater. The level of "invisibility" of the repair depends on how complicated the weave of the fabric is. Most repairs take about two weeks.

Alice Zotta, 2 W. 45th St. [5th/6th] ☎ 840-7657. Ms. Zotta learned to do reweaving as a 13-year-old child in Vicenza, Italy, where she apprenticed in the Marzotta fac-tory. Ms. Zotta has been doing reweaving for 35 years. Repairs average two weeks.

SHOE REPAIR

Anania, 34 W. 46th St. [5th/6th] ☎ 869-5335. Top quality shoe repair. They take their time, but you'll see the quality when you get your shoes back. $50 and up for a whole sole on men's shoes.

Two other reputable shoe repairers are **Jim's,** 50 E. 59th St. [Park/Mad] ☎ 355-8259, and **Manhattan Shoe Repair,** 6 E. 39th St. [5th/Mad] ☎ 683-4210. Whole soles at Jim's start at $45. At Manhattan Shoe Repair, from $41.

TAILORS, DRESSMAKERS, AND ALTERATIONS

Abe's Tailor Shop, 1013 Sixth Ave. [37th/38th] ☎ 921-1193. Joseph D'Attoma is tailor-in-residence at this Garment Center institution. His father "put a needle in his hand" when he was 12. Forty years later, Mr. D'Attoma is still at it—altering men's and women's clothing. He does all the fitting himself, and all hems are hand sewn. Pant hems are made with a special liner so the pant falls properly over the top of the shoe. Pant cuffs start at $11, shortening sleeves begins at $20, and jacket shortening at $35. Alterations take from 2–14 days, depending on the job. If it's an emergency, they'll work with you.

H.K.T., 136 Waverly Place [6th/Gay] ☎ 675-0818, short for Hong Kong Tailor, is a shop that does good quality alterations and custom tailoring for men and women, re-lining of coats, hemming (by hand), nipping and tucking. There are stylebooks in the front of the shop to help you decide on styles and to communicate with the tailor. Some fabrics are available, and they will also work with fabric you bring them. Not much English spoken. Shortening pants with a cuff is $13, without a cuff it's $10.

Deborah Anderko's skills are bred in the bone—her grandfather was a tailor and her mother was "in the business." Ms. Anderko went one step further by graduating from F.I.T. She runs a cozy shop at 147B E. 90th St. [Lex] ☎ 289-2988, where she does all the work herself. Alterations include changing buttons, hemming slacks ($12–$18), and shortening jacket body lengths for both men and women. She also custom makes clothing. You can bring in a pattern, pictures, or sketches of a garment. She can advise you on fabric or she will shop for you. "If a customer is nervous, I make a muslin pattern first." This adds about $60 to the bill. She makes dresses, skirts, slacks, bridal dresses, and evening gowns. She prefers not to do fine tailoring on suits and doesn't work on lingerie or swimsuits.

John's European Tailoring, 118 E. 59th St. [Lex/Park] ☎ 752-2239. John was trained in tailoring from the age of 12 in Greece. The current location dates from 1985, but he has worked as a tailor and custom suitmaker for more than 30 years. He and his partner do alterations to men's and women's tailored clothing as well as custom tailoring. He has some swatch books in the front of the shop and sells a line of English wools for jackets and pants. Shortening a pair of pants is $10.

Harriet Kurzon, ☎ 661-9467, by appt. Ms. Kurzon has 60 years' experience doing alterations. She learned by doing and has done for many people in the fashion industry. She works on day and evening wear, and

if she has a specialty, it's alterations for larger women. She works from her apartment and has access to workrooms in the garment center when she needs them.

Oriental dresses can be made to order at the **Oriental Dress Co.,** 38 Mott St. [Pell/Mosco] ☎ 349-0818. For more information, see the Fabric article in the Stores chapter.

Peppino Tailors, 780 Lexington Ave. [60th/61st] ☎ 832-3844. Like most good tailors, Peppino learned the trade when he was a child, in his case in Italy. He was with Oleg Cassini for seven years. Now, in his own shop, he employs as many as eight tailors during the busy seasons (spring and fall). They do alterations for men and women. In addition to the usual gamut of repairs, he will work on beaded garments, although he cautions that these can be time-consuming and expensive. $11.50 to shorten a pair of slacks.

Rosette Couturiere is in a small atelier at 160 W. 71st St. [Columbus/Bway] ☎ 877-3372. An appointment is best during the week. Sat. drop-ins okay from 10–6. Brenda Barmore was trained in dressmaking in her native England, and she and her staff work mostly on women's clothes (but will do hems on men's pants and sleeves) and specialize in coming up with creative solutions to problems like lengthening sleeves. They also shorten, let out, and take in, and work on a lot of wedding dresses, vintage and new. A wall above her desk is full of snapshots of brides and women in Rosette creations. They make custom clothing for women (suits start at $475 for labor). One photo shows a client who bought a sari that they transformed into a three-piece outfit. Straight skirt hems start at $22 and are done by hand, pant hems begin at $18. Most things take between 7–10 days.

TIES

Tiecrafters, 252 W. 29th St. [7th/8th] ☎ 629-5800, is run by Andy Tarshis. All of the ties (they clean silk scarves, too) that come to him are dry cleaned and hand finished at his miniplant on W. 29th St. The hand spotter, James Singleton, eyeballs the ties to identify each spot. Was it tomato sauce or coffee? Each offender is treated with its own solvent. Ink can be the hardest to remove. The staff hand presses the ties, making sure that the edges roll and are not creased. Stitching and tacking are done by hand as well. Ties are boxed and shipped back to you via UPS. Tiecrafters also widens, narrows, shortens, and lengthens ties. They custom make ties (including bow ties) either in your fabric ($30) or theirs ($40), as well as cummerbunds and braces. The custom ties are often ordered by tall and short men to get the proper length and by wedding parties who want to coordinate their attire. $5.75 to clean a tie, $8.50 to alter, and $11.50 to clean and alter the same tie. Many people mail their ties in. Pickup and drop off can be arranged for a $5 fee each way. There is a second location at 245 E. 57th St. [2nd/3rd] ☎ 759-9057.

MORE For more clothing-related businesses, see the Garment Center article in the Stores chapter.

COPY SHOPS

CHEAPEST It's not hard to find copy shops charging 5¢ a copy. Kinko's is 8¢ for the first 100 copies. In general, the price goes down as the number of copies goes up. You can get it down to 2 ½¢ a copy if you have at least 500 copies and take the job to **Wholesale Copy Club,** 1 E. 28th St. [5th] ☎ 779-4065.

COLOR COPIES **Clicks,** 49 W. 23rd St. [5th/6th] ☎ 645-1971, is worth knowing about because you can make color copies yourself from one of their 10 Canon 500 copiers. This means you can play with images (you can mirror the image, contour it, adjust the color, etc.) for 75¢ per copy including tax—which is the best price we've found.

OPEN ALL NIGHT See Copying in the Open Late/24 hours article in the Information chapter.

DELIVERY

AIR CONDITIONERS You can order an air conditioner by calling any of these buying services and they'll deliver it: **Peninsula Buying Service** ☎ 838-1010; **Home Sales Dial a Discount** ☎ 513-1513; **Price Watchers** ☎ 718-470-1620.

BEVERAGES **Dream Beverage** delivers a dozen or more kinds of waters (sparkling, still, flavored) to your home. Prices are good, there's no delivery charge, but there is a two-case minimum ☎ 718-655-5200 . . . **Grill Beverage** will deliver beer—no charge for five cases or more ☎ 463-7171. **B & E** has a delivery charge, $10 or so, depending on where you are ☎ 243-6812.

BOOKS **Books and Co.,** 939 Madison [74th/75th] ☎ 737-1450, will deliver gift books (and that would certainly include a gift to yourself) in Manhattan for free, with no minimum.

FOOD See Food Delivery in the Food chapter.

GIFTS **The Gifted Ones** does gift baskets of all kinds—just the thing when you're short on time or short of ideas. There are gift baskets in all ranges and for most any occasion. Prices go from $40–$150. From the Get Well line, you might choose the "Apple a Day" basket for $39.99, a wooden apple basket with cookies, candies, crossword puzzles, playing cards, and a can of chicken soup. There are birthday baskets, summer beach baskets, and baskets for new babies. They're at 150 W. 10th St. [Waverly] ☎ 627-4050. Delivery is extra; in Manhattan it's $10 . . . **Manhattan Fruitier,** ☎ 686-0404, will, for $50, deliver a basket of 8–9 lbs. of seasonal fruit (the fall basket might include three types of apples and pears, grapes, persimmon, pomegranate, and oranges), decorated with dried hydrangeas and greens. Larger baskets, which include biscotti, chocolate, and cheese

sticks in various combinations, are available and cost up to $150. They'll do same-day delivery in Manhattan if you call by 1 P.M., and they can arrange overnight shipping anywhere in the U.S.

HAIRDRESSER Many of the top salons will arrange for a stylist to come to your home. This can cost up to three times the price of a salon cut. **Frederic Fekkai,** ☎ 753-9500, and **Louis Licari,** ☎ 517-8084, are two that will make a home appointment.

VIDEOS **Palmer Video,** 295 Park Ave. South [22nd/23rd] ☎ 982-4000, delivers within a few blocks, from 5–10 P.M., free membership, $1 delivery . . . **Palmer Video,** 444 Second Ave. [25th] ☎ 213-2355, delivers within a few blocks, from 5–10 P.M., free membership, $1 delivery . . . **Video Stop,** 367 Third Ave. [26th/27th] ☎ 685-6199, has free membership, delivers from Houston to 49th East to about 8th Ave. $1 per trip . . . **Fliks Video To Go,** 175 W. 72nd St. [Columbus/Amsterdam] ☎ 721-0500, will deliver from 59th St. to 80th St. on the West Side. Membership is free; several prepaid delivery plans . . . **Video Connection,** 2240 Broadway [80th] ☎ 724-2727. You need a lifetime membership ($9.95) and it's a $1 delivery charge. They deliver from 70th–90th, RSD to CPW . . . **Video Room,** 1487 Third Ave. [84th] ☎ 879-5333. Membership is $89 a year, $79 for renewals. Free delivery 365 days a year with 12 free rentals. 96th to 58th on the East Side, 96th to 58th on the West once a day.

EXTERMINATOR

Betty Faber has a Ph.D. in entomology and is a specialist on the subject of the cock-

roach. She once ran a study in the American Museum of Natural History on the natural habits of cockroaches, numbering each iridescently on their wings and giving them the run of the place. She is now busy building the entomological collection at the Liberty Science Center. To keep roaches away, she says: "I always emphasize cleanliness. Try to separate your apartment as much as possible from others. Of course, if you are living next to a slob, there's not much you can do. Start by filling holes with steel wool and caulk any openings. Roaches need water, so fix any leaks you may have. Don't overwater your plants. Some people put a little detergent down the drain every night. They don't like soapy water so they won't go into the drain to take a drink. When you turn on the kitchen light at night, see where they run to. Then take your flashlight and look into those places. Spray only where they are. Roaches love your animal's dried food, so don't leave dried cat or dog food out. Painting helps. Roaches put down signposts that say 'This smells like home,' and the painting covers them up. Boric acid works well and is best when it's dry. Put it in places where you are not going to be, like behind radiators or in corners, between the wall and the floor. You have to treat this like a detective story." Dr. Faber doesn't like spraying unless it's absolutely necessary. "If you spray a lot it can make you sick. We did learn a lot from DDT. The new sprays don't last long." Manufacturers purposely make the spray smell bad so you won't overspray. Dr. Faber appears as Betty Bug at "the yuckiest site on the Internet," where you can learn about cockroach biology and ask her specific questions. "People ask all kinds of things, like 'Can you microwave a cockroach?' " She says, "Not for very long." On the web at www.lsc.org.

TRADITIONAL

Hercules Exterminating, ☎ 718-945-0922. Things are changing in the exterminating business. Even a traditional company such as Hercules says, "Spraying is not the way to go. Twenty years from now who knows what problem it will cause." The state of the art product today is Max Force gel, a repellant that gets put into cracks and into the behind-the-stuff places where roaches hide. Hercules also "tries to look at the whole picture." They may tell you "what to clean up, what holes to fill in." On the first visit, you will have to empty all cabinets and wash things before you put them back. Subsequent visits are scheduled depending on the level of the problem. The initial visit is $75 for a small apartment, $25 monthly afterwards. Hercules also deals with ants, moths, bees, wasps, squirrels, and mice.

ECOLOGICALLY ORIENTED

Shelley Mandell has been in the exterminating business since 1986. For five years she used traditional methods, mostly for Manhattan restaurants. After researching alternative methods to do her job, she changed the name of her business to **Sterile Peril** ☎ 718-965-1918. As an ecologically conscious exterminator, she uses only all-natural, noncarcinogenic materials that are low in toxicity (for humans). Sterile Peril's first visit to your home can be a labor-intensive affair for you. Since most infestations are in kitchens and bathrooms, you have to empty all of the cabinets. This does two things. First, you start to push the roaches back into the walls. Ms. Mandell works by injecting (not spraying) her specially prepared formulations into cracks and crevices. This keeps them away from people and pets and gets them closer to where the bugs actually are. No chemicals touch food or dishes. Emptying the cabinets also allows for cleanup of any eggs that may be there. When the roaches begin to make their way back, they walk over the chemicals and head off to meet their maker. If you wait a year between visits, you will have to empty cabinets. That's unnecessary with biannual visits. Generally, a one bedroom is about $175 for an initial visit and $140 for subsequent visits. She does much work with chemically sensitive people, including recovering cancer patients, those with HIV, asthma or other breathing difficulties, and in households where there are children and/or pets.

FIREWOOD

Make sure when you order that it's seasoned rather than treated. Seasoned wood is wood that's been dried long enough to burn well. Treated wood is wood that's still green but has been chemically treated to burn. It will burn, but it burns faster than naturally treated wood.

A face cord is 4 feet high, 8 feet long, and 1 log deep. Half a face cord is 4 feet high, 4 feet long, and one log deep. There are extra charges for those who live in walk-ups and want the wood stacked in the apartment.

AA Armato Wood & Ice, ☎ 737-1742, delivers in bundles only. 10–12 split logs in a bundle sell for $8. There is a five-bundle minimum.

Aspen Tree, ☎ 718-492-7025, delivers a half ($75) or a full ($140) face cord.

Hicks, ☎ 800-696-7167, bundles of 12–16 pieces, $15 each, with a minimum of five bundles. Half a face cord is $100, a full face cord is $173.

FLORISTS

UPPER EAST SIDE
Ronaldo Maia, 27 E. 67th St. [Mad/Park] ☎ 288-1049. Mr. Maia, born in Brazil, opened his shop in 1968. Since then, he has been an Upper East Side fixture, creating distinctively beautiful flower arrangements.

Renny, 159 E. 64th St. [Lex/3rd] ☎ 288-7000. Renny Reynolds is among the best-known NY florists. He specializes in full, lush, fresh arrangements without a lot of greenery. There is a $50 minimum for delivery.

MIDTOWN EAST
Denis Flowers at the Hotel Intercontinental, 526 Lexington Ave. [48th/49th] ☎ 355-1820. Are there florists in town with more fans than Helen Denis has? There can't be many. Ms. Denis has been in this location since 1970 and before that had a shop on Third and 48th for 34 years. She did Bette Davis's flowers (as well as flowers for Henry Fonda and Mary Martin). The shop does dozens of offices every week, while Ms. Denis's brother takes care of the flowers for the Intercontinental. They do topiaries and lots of shaped arrangements like teddy bears, cats, Santas, and so on. Delivery minimum $35. A nice staff that obviously adores Ms. Denis, and, if you drop by, you will, too.

Fiori in the St. Regis, 2 E. 55th St. [5th/Mad] ☎ 832-2430, provides the lovely arrangements used in the hotel. They take phone orders, or you can stop by. There is a delivery charge of $10, and arrangements run $15–$75. Phillip Haight is the designer.

Zezé Flowers, 398 E. 52nd St. [1st] ☎ 753-7767. Owner Zezé Calvo is much sought after for homes as well as corporate clients. Mixed arrangements that sometimes incorporate pods, vines, and fruit. $50 delivery minimum.

CHELSEA

At **Bloom,** 16 W. 21st St. [5th/6th] ☎ 620-5666, an exceptionally pretty store, they don't use any "fillers, carnations or baby's breath," just good-quality garden flowers in free-flowing arrangements. $60 delivery minimum.

VILLAGE

VSF Inc., 204 W. 10th St. [Bleecker/W. 4th] ☎ 206-7236, stands for Very Special Flowers, and they are—a popular florist, in a pretty New England–style store with lots of dried flowers, topiaries, and artfully arranged fresh ones. English country garden arrangements using many Dutch flowers and much dried work. $50 minimum for delivery.

Larkspur, 39 Eighth Ave. [Jane] ☎ 727-0587. The owners will tell you that their specialty is simply "terrific flowers . . . nothing gimmicky. We use beautiful flowers and let them speak for themselves. We like a lot of color." Their regular clients (many corporate) know that that is modest. They won the 1993 Gold Medal from the New York Flower Show. Stop in and see why. $50 minimum for delivery.

Rebecca Cole's **The Potted Garden,** 27 Bedford St. [6th/Downing] ☎ 255-4797, is quirky and charming. She doesn't use mums or tropicals, only what grows in a garden. Containers are as important as the flowers to Ms. Cole, who "scours the world" looking for interesting ones. You might find something planted in a toy truck or in an antique sap bucket. A minimum of $45 to make an arrangement, but she will deliver any flowers or plant for a $10 charge.

SOHO

Elan Flowers, 108 Wooster St. [Prince/Spring] ☎ 343-2426. Elan's creativity (a wide range of styles including some beautiful monochromatic arrangements) has put them at the top of many people's lists. They do weddings (including bridal headpieces), parties, corporate installations, photo shoots, and other events. Their flowers are mostly Dutch and French.

BY PHONE

You get beautiful flowers from **Cornucopia,** 28 W. 27th St. [Bway/6th] ☎ 696-4323, and they're likely to smell good, too. Owner Dorothy Pfeiffer says that so many flowers are overbred that they lose their scent. So, she's made it a practice to include scented flowers, lots of roses, and herbs. The bouquets are put into clay pots, sometimes colored ones, which add to the spray of color. With the bouquet comes a card explaining what the flowers and scents are and how to care for them. $50 and up.

Matthew Hopkins of **MDH Decor,** ☎ 627-2086, provides decor for corporate or private special events. You can see his work in Pino Luongo's restaurants and the Reebok Sports Club. His designs are contemporary, elegant, and often elaborate. He

DRIED FLOWERS

There are dried flowers and then there are dried flowers from **Cut & Dried**, 968 Lexington Ave. [70th/71st] ☎ 772-7701. Madi Heller runs this light-filled shop with her husband, Felix Blume. Ms. Heller imports her own flowers from Europe, choosing them for their color (natural, not dyed or "enhanced") and their form. Mr. Blume does the arranging. There are bouquets and topiaries in the shop, but Ms. Heller will gladly work to match your furnishings. Mr. Blume's creations are lively, blending subdued and full colors, with just the right leaves—a thin, wavy, mini Italian ruscus leaf or a wide, flat, pale green salal palm leaf. The arrangements should last about two years in the "grease-based dust" of Manhattan. Small bouquets start at $50. Ms. Heller and Mr. Blume also teach dried floral arranging by appointment.

also works for private individuals who use floral arrangements on a regular basis. Party minimum, $250.

Alessandra-Pesany, ☎ 683-3655. Robert Pesany arranged flowers at Mädderlake (now closed) for six years. Mr. Pesany still creates his open, airy arrangements, using as many rare flowers as possible. $75 minimum for delivery.

Stacey Daniels Flowers ☎ 914-762-8372. She can do the usual gift arrangements, flowers for the home, for corporations, and so on, but she seems to thrive on the unusual. She likes events—parties and weddings especially—and will create unique bridal headpieces with antique flowers, beads, jewels, or laces. For parties, she can arrange the whole look: tablecloths, lighting, and music. Her silk flower arrangements can be seen at Bergdorf Goodman. Pieces start at $150 and can be shipped anywhere.

ORCHIDS
See Orchids in the Feature chapter.

24-HOUR
Not Just Roses sells not just roses until 5 P.M. After 5, it's roses only. They will deliver in Manhattan 24 hours a day ☎ 247-6737.

FRAMING

WHAT TO LOOK FOR We spoke with one museum archival framer who said works of art (or any work that is valuable to you) should be framed with these things in mind: a strong frame, protecting the work, and esthetics. The work should not come into contact with either the frame or the glass. With works on paper, this means that they should be hinged to a backing somewhat larger than the work itself. The best hinges are made of Japanese mulberry paper. These hinges are similar to those used in stamp collections. Gluing or taping a work to the backing isn't done, as this may cause damage to the work. The backing itself should contain no wood pulp (wood pulp has acid in it, which will leach into your work and cause brown staining). The best backing is made from 100% rag content. In order to keep the work from touching the glass, a mat is used. The size of the mat is a question of esthetics but, again, should be made of 100% rag content and should be at least 4-ply or 3/32-inch thick. (An 8-ply mat, 1/8 inch and up, is recommended for charcoals, pastels, and some watercolors.) With a colored mat, you should also be sure that it's acid-free. Plexiglas is desirable in many cases since it's somewhat porous—this can cut down on mold forming. You can now get Plexiglas with a UV filter to prevent light damage to the work. However, if you are framing a pastel or chalk piece, glass is preferable because Plexi sets up static electricity that can lift the powder from the paper. A strainer, a sort of frame-within-a-frame, may be added to support the primary frame. Finally, the back is sealed off with a bug-repelling black photography tape or with brown paper.

Bark Frameworks, 85 Grand St. [Greene] ☎ 431-9080. By appt. only. Bark is considered by many to be the ultimate in framing. They have published a small series of leaflets, *Notes on Framing,* available to clients, which details the issues of conservation and protection involved in framing. The three frame designers at Bark are students of the history of frames and framing. Jared Bark designs complex frames from many elements. He uses profiles and variations from 16th and 17th century Dutch and Italian frames. The work of James Barth and Jamie Dearing has a more modernist sense. They have a range of patinated and gilded frames as well as copper and brass cladding over wood.

Charles Carrico, 24 Fifth Ave. [9th] ☎ 228-5014. By appt. only. Mr. Carrico does a lot of work for museums and corporations and specializes in framing works of the 20th century. Mr. Carrico said, "When you frame, everything you do should be re-versible. The artwork should be able to come out of the frame in the same condition that it went into the frame." He prefers a sleek, rectangular look in woods—some blonds, some gold-leafed, and some reddish African bubinga. For collectors with valuable or fragile works, Mr. Carrico will make a house call, make the frame in his shop, and complete the work on site so that the piece doesn't have to leave your home or business.

If you are framing an "important period piece," particularly 19th and early 20th century American, you may want to consider the trove of period frames, both originals and replicas, at **Eli Wilner Frames,** 1525 York Ave. [80th/81st] ☎ 744-6521. Stanford White and James McNeill Whistler are two of the frame designers represented in this collection where the frame can sometimes cost more than the work inside it. Mostly gilt and ornate.

Gallery Frames, 524 Broadway [Spring] ☎ 226-7430. Orlando Condeso started as a printmaker and still runs Spring Press, which prints fine art editions. The frame samples are tucked away in drawers because, according to Mr. Condeso, "The factors to be considered in framing are so diverse that I don't want to add to the confusion of the client." He asks if the client has an idea of what the piece should look like when it is framed; then, keeping the technical considerations in mind, Mr. Condeso will show frame samples that

meet all the criteria. Best of all, Mr. Condeso has a mirror set at a 45° angle above the layout table, which gives the effect of viewing the piece on a wall—albeit, in reverse.

Goldfeder/Kahan Framing, 37 W. 20th St. [5th/6th] ☎ 242-5310. When Eric Kahan and Elizabeth Goldfeder set out to open a framing business, they wanted "the ultimate frame shop," and they got it. The showroom, where Ms. Goldfeder meets customers, is spacious and well lit, there is a display that shows the different design periods of frames, and a selection of styles from simple metal sections to hand-carved, hand-rubbed, 22 carat gold with finished corners. There are rag mats, fabric mats, and a French mat painter on staff who will customize colors and line arrangements for you. After you've made your selection, your work is sent downstairs to the framing laboratory, a climate-controlled clean room where workers don taffeta frock coats, hair bonnets, and special sneakers. The air in the clean room is filtered three times each minute and is kept static free by an increased humidity. This means that your art is sealed in the frame in one of the cleanest environments in NYC. Ms. Goldfeder likes explaining the processes to customers, and they'll work to budget.

House of Heydenryk, 417 E. 76 St. [1st/York] ☎ 249-4903, was established in 1935 by Mr. Heydenryk, a fourth-generation framemaker from Holland, who brought the Old World skills of hand-carving and gold-leafing to the increasingly modern 1930s New York art scene. His admiration for the painters of the time caused him to donate frames to them, which are now showing up on museum walls. On the ground floor are full samples, not just cor-

ners. Upstairs carvers are carving, gold leafers are leafing and burnishing, and others are painting beautiful scrollwork on frames. "There are only two machines here—two saws—otherwise, everything is done by hand." They restore and repair old frames and make copies of antique ones. Only archival materials are used in the actual framing. Most of the reproduction frames range from $500–$1,500. Antique frames can be as low as $50 for a small piece and go to $30,000.

J. Pocker & Son, 135 E. 63rd St. [Lexington] ☎ 838-5488. Robyn Pocker is the third generation of Pockers to frame New York. If you want to see a wide range of corner samples, this is the place. What's on the wall is only part of the stock. Ms. Pocker says, "It's important to know when conservation framing is called for." She showed us several variations on the theme of black frame with gold trim suitable for framing a diploma. In addition to the frames, Pocker's has some French mats with hand-washed colored panels that look like the ones often seen on old master drawings in museums. Lots of decorators have work done here, attracted by the array of choices and the attentive service. The big variety they carry enables them to do very high-end framing, but they also give you a lot of style for a wide range of budgets. They frame archivally and nonarchivally.

Minagawa Art Lines, 25 Great Jones St. [Lafayette/Bowery] ☎ 982-8711. By appt. only. Do not expect to see a wall of corner samples when you visit Yasuo Minagawa in his workshop space. He will discuss your work with you and make recommendations. The Paula Cooper Gallery, The Drawing Center, Chuck Close, and Jennifer Bartlett trust his judgment. Mr. Minigawa builds his wood frames and then applies the finish. Some are stained, some are lacquered. There is also the M.A.L. line of less expensive wooden frames. The walls of the office hold works which have been given to him by clients and is a satisfying gallery visit in itself.

Poster Portfolio, 438 Sixth Ave. [9th/10th] ☎ 777-7716, is a good, inexpensive place for framing posters. They also work with corporations and offices that want poster decoration. They will provide your business with a free consultant who will work within your budget and make decoration suggestions.

FURNITURE REPAIR & RESTORATION

The ECR in **ECR Antiques Conservation and Restoration,** 515 W. 29th St. [10th/11th] ☎ 643-0388, is Eli Rios, described by more than one of the people we spoke with for this article as "one of the finest craftsmen in New York." He has 22 years experience in furniture restoration and a background in chemistry. Chemistry? The first step in furniture conservation is the "surface analysis." Examining a 200-year-old gilt mirror frame with him in his large workshop, he points out, "This discoloration comes from a candle flame and much of this is nicotine." He determines that the original gilding on the mirror is actually two different kinds, meant to give two different colors and now requires two different cleaning solvents. All manner of restoration is done on mostly expensive old pieces, including regluing, refinishing, replacing veneers, cleaning ormolu, and carving. Estimates are free, pieces are brought to the shop by a trucking company and work begins after a 50% deposit is paid. The average dining room chair—tightened, cleaned, and polished—starts at $125. Workers can be sent to your home for reconditioning and polishing. Finally, if you're considering specific antiques at auction or from a shop, Mr. Rios (for $125/hour) will examine the piece with you and give an analysis of the item, its period and condition, a repair estimate, and will suggest a bidding price.

Joe Biunno, 129 W. 29th St. [6th/7th] ☎ 629-5630, began restoring furniture in his father's little shop when he was 18 years old. Twenty years later, Mr. Biunno has 15 highly skilled employees—carvers, polishers, painters, gilders, mold-makers and casters, and a metalworker. Restoration is only a part of the business. After he restores your dining room chair, he can make seven more like it. He keeps a library of chair legs in case you want him to build chairs from scratch. The best way to get an estimate is to send him a Polaroid of your piece. Work is $60/hour. Reproduction chairs (including the finishing) start at $1,100. They have no truck, so if the piece does not fit in a cab, he'll recommend a trucker to you. Mr. Biunno is a specialist in furniture locks and keys. "At least once a year I get called to open a chest where no one can find the key and the piece is too valuable to jimmy the drawer." He keeps a collection of furniture key blanks, but won't charge if he can't open it.

Baggott Frank Conservation, 430 Broome St. [Crosby/Lafayette] ☎ 226-6244, is the husband and wife team of Tom Frank and Grace Baggott. Mr. Frank does restoration work on high-end antiques for private individuals, antique shops, and institutions. He works mostly by himself, only occasionally hiring an assistant. Repairing a chair starts at $400. Ms. Baggott sells fine-quality furniture-care products. A wood cleaner, Vulpex, is $20.75/half pint. (This may sound expensive, but you dilute it with 20 parts water.) A conservation-quality furniture wax, Renaissance, is $24/can.

When you visit Steve Olsen's shop, **Timeless Antiques,** 440 E. 75th St. [1st/York] ☎ 772-3857, you are able to see his handiwork. He and his partner, Michael McPhail, work on a wide variety of furniture styles. Along with the Biedermeier, they repair collectibles and items that have no value other than sentimental. They do French polishing in your home and are willing to do small repairs there. Otherwise, things go to the shop. When faced with a furniture problem, Mr. Olsen does a little detective work. "It's best if you know how the problem developed." Is the ring on the table from water or from alcohol? It makes a difference in how he repairs it. He does not discourage small jobs. Generally work is $60/hour, and he "will advise if it is worth doing."

Perry & Gundling, ☎ 675-2361, take pieces to their shop in NJ. Bill Gundling is the studio manager for the Craft Students' League woodworking classes. They do simple repairs from reattaching legs to more complex restorations. They will work on site for small repairs, wall systems, and paneling. Estimates are $20–$30, which is deducted from the cost of the job. Unlike many other restorers, Perry and Gundling will do small jobs. "But we are up front with people. Sometimes the cost of the repair can be more expensive than the piece."

Phoof, 71 Gansevoort St. [Greenwich/Washington] ☎ 807-1332, is a one-stop shop for furniture. This store of American furniture from the 1940s and 1950s has an upholstery and refinishing shop upstairs. They strip, sand, reglue, refinish, polish, and relaminate Formica. Prices are in the mid-range. They can give you a rough estimate over the phone and, should you decide to go ahead, a firm estimate on seeing the piece. Pickup and delivery service is another $55 on your bill. They prefer to do work in their shop instead of your home, but you can go in to approve finish and color at various points in the work cycle.

Scottie Donohue, ☎ 477-0519, learned her trade at Sotheby's. She works only in your home, which means that valuable pieces don't have to be transported and that "the client sees what is going on" and why furniture restoration can take so long. She prefers to work on 18th and early 19th century antiques. She does all repairs, stripping, creating new joins if they are needed, reveneering, replacing of trim, finishing and polishing while protecting your walls and floors with coverings. She has hardware repaired and polishes brass trims herself. She admits that sometimes things are so black and damaged that "even I can't always see what will be the end result of a good restoration. But it's very satisfying to bring something from dire to beautiful." She will give you a time estimate when she sees the condition of your piece, and charges $250 per day.

GLASS, MIRRORS, PORCELAIN

GLASS

When Augustine Jochec was growing up in Czechoslovakia, his family were considered to be "enemies of the state." Young Jochec was sent to apprentice in the glass factory at age 15 as those so classified had no say in the professions or education of their children. The irony of this is that Mr. Jochec, who escaped in 1968, had the benefit of training in a well-established craft in Czechoslovakia, and he is now a friend to all who love glass objects. His business, **Glass Restorations,** 1597 York Ave. [84th/85th] ☎ 517-3287, has been in NYC since 1970. The walls around the grinding machines are hung with the many wheels needed for his trade. Getting rid of nicks and chipped edges on large pieces may start with the rough Carborundum wheel, each grinding using a finer and finer wheel. Profile wheels are used to repair chips on cut-glass pieces, the wheel matching the shape of the cut in the bowl or decanter. When something is broken, Mr. Jochec advises bringing it in for repair as soon as possible. Dirt and dust can settle into cracks over time and can't be completely removed. We saw two Steuben dolphins, both having lost their back fin. One was able to be reset and glued. On the other, Mr. Jochec had to cut a new fin (from "scrap Steuben glass"), polish it, and then set it. In both cases the repairs were seamless. He often has to replace candle cups on candelabras, because people let the candle burn down into the cup and the heat cracks it. What Mr. Jochec calls "sick glass," that is, glass decanters that have gotten cloudy on the inside, can be repolished. The "sickness" is not on the surface of the glass (which is why you can't clean it), but is the result of a chemical reaction between the glass and wine (among other things). Repolishing the inside of a decanter starts at $80–$120. He will open stuck stoppers in decanters and will repair the stopper if you break it trying to get it out. Grinding the edges of crystal glasses is $18–$20. Repairs can take from a few days for glasses to several weeks for complicated jobs.

Exquisite Glass, 123 Allen St. [Delancey/Rivington] ☎ 674-7069. There are not many professional etchers left in the city; fortunately, there's Buz Vaultz. When we visited recently, he showed us some glass panels with variations on geometric and floral patterns that are used in kitchen cabinet doors. Mr. Vaultz can transfer virtually any design to glass by cutting away a special tape he places over the back of the piece—creating a drawing. Then a spray of very fine sand eats away a little of the surface of the untaped areas. He also does small decorative projects with a new photographic transfer technique that allows him to place insignia, crests, even photographs, on glass or mirrors. (He recently made a valentine for a client that reproduced a musical score onto glass.) Mr. Vaultz makes screens and room dividers, door panels and decorative mirrors, and monograms crystal bowls and glassware. While most of his work comes through architects and designers, he does accept private commissions. Depending on the complexity of the project, prices start at $25 a square foot. Generally, there is a 2–4 week wait for pieces.

New York Carved Arts, 115 Grand St. [Wooster/Bway] ☎ 966-5924. Jean Claude Fevrier is the master craftsman and owner of this business that was founded in 1931 by two Frenchmen and later sold to his father. Mr. Fevrier taught himself the skills needed to create a Lalique look. His work differs from some other sandblasted glass in that he creates varying depths of glass in his patterning, sometimes breaking through to the other side and making holes. His work is on display in the chapel of the Seamen's Church Institute at the Seaport. He works on small pieces (door panels or a personal memento) or larger ones (security doors, decorative panels, room screens or doors). Occasionally, he adds gold or silver leafing to a piece.

Anton Laub Glass, 1873 Second Ave. [96th/97th] ☎ 734-4270, replaces glass and mirror pieces, such as the panels in china cabinets and other furniture pieces. They can replace missing mirror pieces from Venetian mirrors and the curved glass panels in lanterns. People who collect compacts come here for mirrors.

Allstate Glass, 85 Kenmare St. [Mulberry] ☎ 226-2517. This bustling, friendly business has been here since 1923 and in the hands of Sydelle Phillips for the last 25 years. They provide a variety of glass tops for interior use. Most jobs are cut and polished in their shop attached to the store. If it's necessary, someone will come to your home to measure and bring samples. After the work is done, they will install or hang. Beveling and polishing is done on site, etching is sent out. Small pieces can be done while you wait. Prices are among the best in town.

Rosen Paramount Glass, 45 E. 20th St. [Bway] ☎ 532-0820, specializes in custom cut glass and mirrors. Stanley Rosen is the third generation in his family to be in this business. On a busy Friday afternoon, we watched him talk with a steady stream of clients, giving advice about what kind of glass to use in a variety of household projects. There is a cutting and polishing shop on site. Several store displays show the thicknesses of glass, various finishes, textures and tintings, and degrees and styles of beveled edges for mirrors. They can sandblast a design into a piece of glass to dress up a tabletop or door and will work with your design or show you some of theirs. All artwork is approved by the client before sandblasting begins, and often they provide a sample. Mr. Rosen recommends glass 1/4 inch in thickness for protecting the wood or other surface of a table. If the tabletop itself is made of glass, it needs to be a minimum of 3/8-inch thick.

MIRRORS

Sundial Schwartz, 1582 First Ave. [82nd/83rd] ☎ 717-4207. The Greenspan family has owned the combined Sundial and Schwartz businesses since 1976. One dates back to 1945, the other to 1915. Most of their work is done with contractors and architects, but son David Greenspan will consult with you in your home on wall mirrors, glass tops, mirrored bars, splashbacks—any "interior mirror or glass use." Besides cutting, polishing, and beveling mirrors, the Greenspans resilver and create a variety of antique finishes and do sandblasting. One designer told us that Sundial Schwartz is "not afraid to be a little creative" with mirrors. They will try something new instead of just saying it can't be done. They carry black, bronze, and gray mirrors, as well as the clear. An Italian polishing machine sees to it that the edges don't have what Marilyn Greenspan calls "that crystally look." All estimates are free, many can be given over the phone, and the average interior job takes 10–14 days. Wall mirrors are installed and medicine cabinet mirrors can be replaced.

J. Dixon Prentice, 1036 Lexington Ave. [74th] ☎ 249-0458. The ratio of floor space for customers to floor space for goods is the smallest in the city. As in a suburban driveway, you may have to back out if the previous customer wants to leave. However, they do specialize in antique mirrors, trying to have on hand everything from Art Deco enameled hand mirrors ($300 range) to large pier glasses (thousands).

Goldfeder/Kahan Framing, 37 W. 20th St. [5th/6th] ☎ 242-5310, will provide you with a custom sized and shaped mirror in a frame or will frame a mirror you bring to them. They will help you with a special project, providing regular, beveled, or antiqued glass to be placed in one of the large selection of frames in their comfortable showroom. This company builds frames to last. Mirrors are backed with corrugated polypropylene for scratch and moisture protection. Only rust-resistant stainless steel wires and hardware are used. The braces that hold the mirror in place are screwed into the frame (not stapled) for extra solidity. They even paint inside the front-frame bevel so that the unevenness of the stain is not reflected in the glass. Some smaller mirrors in a Florentine stand are $75.

The **True Mirror** is the brainchild of John Walter ☎ 741-1651, by appt. When you look into an ordinary mirror, the images you see are reversed. Raise your left hand and the mirror image raises your right hand. By setting two mirrors together at a right angle (and figuring out how to eliminate the seam between them) the True Mirror raises your left hand. It's very disorienting and trying to,

say, put on lipstick with this mirror isn't recommended. Mr. Walter says, "Many people have a bad reaction when they look into it for the first time. You finally see what others see when they look at you." The silver coating is on the surface of this mirror, instead of behind the glass, which heightens the three dimensionality of the image. The mirror comes in an 18″ × 18″ box that is mounted on the wall. It requires special care so that you don't scratch the silver coating. It costs $275.

David Dear, an ingenious designer, often plays with context for humorous effect. His wonderful Duck Mirror pairs an oval mirror with cast duck feet. It has been seen in a number of galleries and stores in town. Currently, it's available at Mxyplyzyk, 125 Greenwich Ave. [Jane/Horatio] ☎ 989-4300, for $100.

PORCELAIN

Rena Krishtul went to a fine arts college in the then Soviet Union, where she was trained to be a designer in a pottery and glass factory. A self-described "antiques freak," she says that after she came to the U.S. with her husband, Anatole, "We would go out every weekend. We couldn't afford anything but the broken pieces," which they restored on their kitchen table in Forest Hills. They would sometimes sell the restored piece back to the dealer they bought it from, thereby becoming a "secret source" for galleries and dealers. Now **ARK Restoration,** 350 Seventh Ave. [29th/30th] ☎ 675-7994, has a lovely, calm reception room with display cabinets, a "clean" room where they do the painting and a "dirty" room for working in clay. They specialize in restoring broken porcelain and ceramics, especially the old and the valuable from Europe, China, and Japan. They have a kiln that allows them to make replacement parts like covers, necks, and bases. They also make replacements of missing pieces for historical china services. "We get the white pieces from factories in Europe that have kept the old molds." Then they match the decorations. While it's true that most of their work is on the valuable and the rare (they recently restored a large vase broken in the Kobe earthquake), they don't turn away from the sentimental and the personal. Small repairs start at $25.

Hess Restorations, 200 Park Ave. South [17th] ☎ 260-2255, has been in business, albeit with different owners, since 1845. The original Mr. Hess was a German immigrant, and according to Marina Pastor, who owns the shop with her mother, Nina Korabelnikov, most of the current restorers are European. "It's a time-consuming apprenticeship to learn it properly," and it requires a combination of "creativity, patience, and craftsmanship." Hess puts back together broken china, porcelain, jade, ivory, wood, and lacquer items. Ms. Pastor will tell you what you can expect to see after repairs and will advise you on what grade of repair is proper for your piece ("museum" or "com-

mercial" repair—"museum" has the least amount of interference with the piece, so you see the cracks). When things are broken, she advises wrapping each piece separately so there is no further grinding of the edges. Repairs start at $50.

At **Sano Studio,** 767 Lexington Ave. [60th/61st] ☎ 759-6131, Jadwiga Baran and two workers repair porcelain, pottery, and enamel pieces. None of the repairs use heat techniques, so whatever is worked on can be used only for display purposes. You will not be able to put it in the oven or the dishwasher or serve hot food on it. Ms. Baran had an art education in Poland, came to the U.S. in 1966, and spent a few years looking around for a way to make a living. She found a job at Sano Studio, developed her restoration skills, and now owns the business. "If a piece is replaceable, it is better to replace it," she advises. But with old, sentimental, or one-of-a-kind pieces, replacement is not an option. It is possible, in some cases, to remake missing parts. Be careful how you gather and pack the pieces. "The more pieces, the more charges." There is a binder full of thank you letters from places like the Smithsonian Institution and private art collectors. Work is $50 an hour.

HOME RENOVATION & REPAIRS

Bathrooms!

BATHROOM

WHAT TO CONSIDER

Interior designer **Ellen Berns** (ASID), ☎ 517-7155, has written and lectured on bathrooms as well as remodeled and designed them. She cautions that it is a place where there can be a domino effect. You think you are just going to do a little, but if there isn't proper

preparation, or if things are too old, it can become a big job. (Case in point: You think you'll replace that one cracked tile but, if the tiles are old, they're also friable—crumble-prone—and removing the one can cause surrounding tiles to crack and break.) She also advises that some things require permission and permits from your building, landlord, or the city. Jacuzzis, for example, may relieve stress, but they add to the paperwork: city permits are necessary in addition to okays from the building. To avoid delays, she advises not starting demolition until 90% of the materials have been delivered and approved. It may take longer to get started, but it's less wasteful of time and material as you go along. In large projects, it can take a day to demolish and up to two months to put it back together. There are now regulations about how much water a flush toilet can use (new code for toilets is a 1.6 gallon flush) and, in most cases, the standard 3/4-inch piping for risers will not bring you enough water for bidets, Jacuzzis, or fancy showers. Ms. Berns strongly recommends white fixtures—your resale value will be higher.

Contractor Norman Sukkar adds the following about bathrooms: A new city code says that bathroom outlets must contain a circuit breaker (ground fault). Since it is not possible to put this in the light fixtures, new ones don't have them. He says that if the wiring in the old outlet is secure, it will cost about $150 to put in a new outlet that meets the code. In most bathrooms, "the things that look the worst are the sink and the tile." Figure about $1,000 labor to retile in 4″ × 4″ white tiles, and add another $300–$600 for a floor. Removal and installation of a new sink runs about $350. He warns against vanities made of pressboard. "Hot water, steam and pressboard don't mix." At maximum, you will have this for 3–4 years even if it is covered in melamine. You can get a new toilet for $100–$150. Labor to install them ranges from $150–$400.

FOR $1,500
Florence Perchuk is a Certified Kitchen Designer ☎ 932-0441. She says that $1,500 should allow you to change the sink, toilet, and faucets and pay for the plumber to install them. A nice pedestal sink can start at $200 at a plumbing supply store. New faucets will start in the same range. A little more money will get you an inexpensive and attractive light fixture. In a bathroom, a down-facing (and therefore focused) light is preferable to an up-facing light. Fluorescent lighting has long been a staple in the bathroom, but new warm white bulbs eliminate the harshness. Halogen lighting is becoming more popular since it's bright and long-lasting. Some fixtures use either halogen or incandescent bulbs. She says that the $1,500 makeover will have "an instantaneous effect in updating a bathroom."

FOR $2,500
All of the above plus changing the medicine cabinet, shelving, towel bars, and other accessories. Ms. Perchuk says that bathroom construction "is a microcosm of house construction" because of the systems that are included there. Having a designer work with you on a renovation, small or large, helps to organize and orchestrate the construction as well as protect the rest of the premises, since most bathrooms are an interior space. The designer also knows which craftsman comes first in makeovers when there is going to be various kinds of work done. Both Ms. Berns and Ms. Perchuk consult—Ms. Berns charges $150 per hour, and Ms. Perchuk, $225. For projects that require more than a consultation, fees can be worked out on a per-project basis.

SOURCES: SINKS, MEDICINE CABINETS, FAUCETS
SHOWROOMS & STORES What you need to know to change a faucet: How many holes come up through your sink—one,

two, or three. The third hole is usually for a spray device. A two-holed sink can generally be converted into a one-handled faucet by a plumber; a plate is placed on the sink under the faucet to cover the holes . . . **AF Supply,** 22 W. 21st St. [5th/6th] ☎ 243-5400, is one of the best showrooms in New York City. Large, quiet, and well-laid-out, with an overwhelming selection of sinks, faucets, and hardware. Concinnity and Kohler brands among others, plain and fancy faucets, hardware in brass, chrome, and rubber. The price range is from moderate to expensive in all products, and the staff of salespeople can tell you what measurements to bring in and what to look for when making bathroom changes . . . In the D & D Building, 150 E. 58th St. [Lex/3rd], there are showrooms for **Kohler,** ☎ 688-5990, on the 4th floor and on the ground floor, **Davis & Warshow** and **American Standard** ☎ 593-0435. Open weekdays. You can shop in both places on your own (without a decorator). Sinks, tubs, toilets in many colors as well as faucets. Consultants are available for a $250 fee, deductible from your purchase . . . **Hastings,** 230 Park Ave. South [19th] ☎ 674-9700, has a lot of stylish lines, including Il Bagno and a Philippe Starck sink. Sinks and faucets are set up against a section of tiled wall so you can see the ensemble. Hastings also sells a wide variety of ceramic tile, and there is a large table in the middle of the showroom on which to make tile layouts. Things here are high end (sinks can be over $2,000), so you may feel that you are doing more than a makeover . . . **Krup Kitchen and Bath,** 11 W. 18th St. [5th/6th] ☎ 243-5787, is crowded with kitchen appliances and bathroom fixtures. They are happy to show you manufacturers' catalogs for things not on display. Discounts are offered. Styling is mostly up-to-date . . . **Kraft,** 306 E. 61st St. [2nd/3rd] ☎ 838-2214, is a two-story showroom for bathroom fixtures. They have lots of small accessories like wire shelving, chrome wastebaskets and toilet brush holders, as well as a large array of door handles. Best to shop here with a decorator or architect because, according to Ms. Perchuk, "They are more geared to the professional." . . . **NY Replacement Parts,** 1464 Lexington Ave. [94th/95th] ☎ 534-0818. The staff knows a lot and will help novices, although you may find yourself in the midst of a lot of professionals. Basic and some fancy fixtures, a handsome display of taps and faucets, heated towel bars, and door handles by Domus including some of the lever type ($80–$100 range without locks) that are easier to open with wet hands than the standard round knob. They carry replacement parts for faucets and other fixtures . . . At the lower, and perhaps more practical, end, **Rickel's,** 200 W. 79th St. [Amsterdam] ☎ 580-9331 and 305 E. 86th St. [1st/2nd] ☎ 427-2145, has what you need to make repairs to toilets and sinks as well as Moen faucets for less than anyone in town. There is also a line of mix-and-match faucets and handles at moderate prices . . . **Simon's Hardware & Bath,** 421 Third Ave. [29th/30th] ☎ 532-9220, has a large bath-supply area. They have one of the best assortments of bath hardware (towel bars, robe hooks, soap and glass holders, tub grab bars) in town, as well as some modestly (and not so modestly) priced good-looking sinks and faucet sets. There is a section for about a dozen different shower heads, including the sunflower-sized one used in the Savoy Hotel in London. (The showers at the Savoy are the best we've ever had.) You need at least 60 lbs. of pressure to be able to use it, which leaves most of us out. A plumber can measure your pressure for you. Just about everything is marked, not the case everywhere else . . . **Howard Kaplan Bath Shop,** 47 E. 12th St. [Bway] ☎ 228-7204. A Francophile's delight. Antique French basins, some in reproduction, with faucets, sink brackets, soap dishes, shelving, and other small decorative pieces. Things here tend to be very expensive. Be sure to consult with your architect/plumber/contractor to be sure these beauties can be connected to your plumbing.

PLUMBING SUPPLY HOUSES At these places, no frills and not much in the way of displays. Mostly you will be choosing fixtures from a catalog with more or less of an explanation. Discounts, though, range from 25% to 40% off retail. **F & M Plumbing Supply,** 631 E. 9th St. [B/C] ☎ 674-0545, has been around since 1946. They spend most of their time working with architects and contractors but find that with the decline of the '80s "spend a big number" mentality, more and more customers are individual homeowners. Consult with Steven Margolies, since he's a pleasure to talk with and knows what he's doing. F & M carries Kroin fixtures, which are in the MoMA Design collection, and other European companies like Hansa and Grohe. The high-arching Kroin KV1 with a swivel head lists for $495, sells for $297 here. Mr. Margolies can help you find a "side job type" plumber to install the fixtures if your skills are rusty, and will advise on how much

it should cost you . . . **George Taylor Specialties,** 100 Hudson St. [Franklin] ☎ 226-5369, is another plumbing-supply house worth knowing about. They sell at discount, and carry only lines that are well made. They're helpful to novices. Price Pfister faucets start at under $100. Styling leans to the traditional, and there is a small display area for sinks and a tub. Sinks start at $45 for a small wall-hung bathroom model, and $180 for a pedestal. They specialize in replacement parts and tools for repairs.

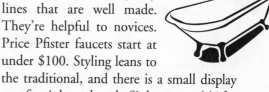

LIGHTING

Lighting by Gregory, 158 Bowery [Broome/Kenmare] ☎ 226-1276, has the largest selection of bathroom lighting that we saw, and they're very helpful . . . **Lightforms,** 509 and 510 Amsterdam Ave. [84th/85th] ☎ 496-2090 & ☎ 875-0407, stocks all the bulbs you're likely to need, as well as switches and dimmers . . . **Light Inc.,** 1162 Second Ave. [59th] ☎ 838-1130, has a good selection of bathroom fixtures, bulbs, and electrical hardware.

TOOTHBRUSHES AND SHAVING ACCESSORIES

After you've designed over 1,000 toothbrushes, you probably should call yourself something like "toothbrush king," except that Stuart Kalinsky, designing for **Alan Stuart, Inc.,** has also done huge numbers of shaving brushes, nail brushes, combs, mirrors, soap dishes, and almost any other accessory you can think of for the bathroom. Still, it's the toothbrushes that have gotten him the most attention. There are brushes with animal patterns, fruit, Las Vegas-y glitters, and iridescent, loopy dots and blobs.

The latest brushes are called "shakees" and have tiny metallic cows or cocktail glasses floating inside a cylindrical handle. They glow in the dark. The bristle heads screw off and can be replaced, an ecologically sound way to keep a favorite brush. There is a line of wood and sisal bath brushes. A selection of Mr. Kalinsky's products can be seen at **Bed, Bath and Beyond,** 620 Sixth Ave. [18th] ☎ 255-3550, **Ad Hoc Softwares,** 410 W. Broadway [Spring] ☎ 925-2652, **Origins,** 402 W. Broadway [Spring] ☎ 219-9764, the shop at the **Folk Art Museum,** Columbus Ave. and 65th St. ☎ 496-2966, and Bergdorf's.

SHOWER CURTAINS

Bed, Bath and Beyond has an extensive shower curtain collection . . . **ABC Carpet & Home,** 888 Broadway [19th] ☎ 473-3000, will custom make shower curtains for approximately $100 labor plus the cost of fabric and a plastic liner from their third-floor bath shop . . . **Gracious Home,** 1220 Third Ave. [70th/71st] ☎ 517-6300, has a wide selection of shower curtains in many styles including traditional, French provincial, and modern, many in fabric and with wastebaskets and other accessories to match. Across the street at their other store, they have some sinks and faucets, but there are better displays and better prices elsewhere . . . **Little Rickie's,** 49 1/2 First Ave. [3rd] ☎ 505-6467. Little Rickie's buyer (and that's a job we covet) always has a line of fun shower curtains . . . Our favorite, though, is from **Moss,** 146 Green St. [Prince/Houston] ☎ 226-2190, where they carry the Psycho Curtain ($75). It's a shadow of Anthony Perkins holding up a knife.

CARPENTERS

WHAT TO KNOW Anyone working in your home should have workmen's compensation and enough insurance to cover possible damages. Matthew Shank, an interior designer, advises that you put a 10% penalty in writing if the work is not finished by the agreed-upon date. Keep a copy of the drawing. Put every change in writing. Check and watch over measurements. Specify drawer mechanisms, hinges, pulls. Ask to see mockups if you are not sure you and the carpenter are interpreting the drawing the same way. Ask for a sample of the finish or stain on a scrap of your wood.

Joseph Flores, ☎ 280-0946, does more cabinetwork than construction, but can put up new walls, hang doors, and install fancy floors. His work is contemporary in style. Lately, he's been installing a lot of bookcases, shelving, and wall units. He also builds chairs and kitchen tables. He will also do hourly work ($30) if that makes more sense on your job or for repairs. We saw a mahogany bookcase he did to match the owner's piece of antique furniture. The bookcase appears to be built in, but is actually screwed together so that it can be moved.

At **The Little Wolf Cabinet Shop,** 1583 First Ave. [82nd/83rd] ☎ 628-1966, John Wolf has taken over this custom unpainted furniture business from his father, who established it in 1956. Dad is still involved drawing sketches. About half of their work is for designers and architects, the remaining half for individuals. Work takes about six weeks to complete. They do no finishing here, but will recommend finishers who will work in your home. The showroom is full of armoires, entertainment centers, and wall units showing various carpentry details. They do Formica work, too.

Garett Fitzgerald, ☎ 369-5401, has a cabinetry shop located in a former dairy in East Harlem. Mr. Fitzgerald brings training in engineering and a stop-off as a furniture restorer at Sotheby's to his carpentry skills. He specializes in "top end demanding work for demanding customers." Most often, he works through architects and designers. Everything is built in his workshop and delivered finished to the site.

Jay Dosembet's small company, **Constructor, Ltd.,** ☎ 925-6494, has been in business less than two years, but Mr. Dosembet has developed a reputation in the garment industry for building showrooms, runways, display stands, and the House of Horrors party space and dance floor for the Ghost party at the 1995 Seventh on Sixth. In domestic situations, he has built closets, home offices, and hangs a lot of shelving. He will do small jobs (hanging a shelf is $20 an hour, supplies in the $50–$100 range). "Design is important to me," and Mr. Dosembet brings his hip, contemporary sense to projects.

FINISHING

Dominick Guida, ☎ 673-3836, has made a specialty of finishing (not refinishing) large pieces of furniture on site. "This means there is no spraying like they do in factories." Everything has to be brushed on. Mr. Guida has 20 years experience working in "occupied apartments," where there are rugs or newly done floors after a renovation. With a good piece of wood, he likes to varnish and to allow nature and time "let the wood come through." He can also paint furniture on site and, with his fine-art background, is good at mixing colors and does some painted finishes, including glazes. He charges by the foot, and costs depend on the type of finish and combinations of finish you are using.

CONTRACTORS

WHAT TO KNOW Get several estimates and references. Call the Dept. of Consumer Affairs, ☎ 487-4398 (which licenses contractors—yours should be), to find out if there have been any complaints lodged against your contractor. See their work. Ask to see their Workman's Comp Certificate (which reduces your liability), ask how much liability insurance they have. All subcontractors should be licensed. Study up on materials and appliances you'll be using or buying. The more you learn, the easier it'll be to sort through the differences in cost from one estimate to another. The estimate should break the job down into components and should state what materials are going to be used. Paying: You can work out a payment plan for the job, and it should be spelled out in the contract. Get a "proof of payment" clause to ensure your contractor has paid all subcontractors and vendors (otherwise you may be liable). You have a right to cancel the contract up to midnight of the third business day after the date on the contract. Even on a small job, the contractor is likely to be around for longer than you anticipate. Pack valuables, breakables and anything that dust will damage and store them, if possible, out of the way.

Bailey Construction, ☎ 866-4352, is Dee Martin and Gunnar Bauska, husband and wife, in business for 15 years. Ms. Martin, who is an architect, calls Bailey Construction "a small, family company, an old-fashioned, hands-on residential contractor." They contract out electric and plumbing, but have a long association with the tradesmen they use. They take no more than two jobs at a time so that they can keep them under control, and specialize in jobs that require "real know-how"—intricate carpentry, cabinetry, slab, stone or marble work, and joinery.

R. Greenberg Construction, ☎ 566-4536. "We are a small outfit that tries to do only custom work. We give the customer the best that they can afford. We have put in $75,000 kitchens and put up Ikea cabinets." He generally takes jobs starting at $50,000 but will sometimes work smaller. They do full renovations and do not like to work room by room. On larger jobs, Mr. Greenberg encourages people to move out, if at all possible. "We tell people, 'The Sheetrock dust is going to be in your bed,' and they think they can put up with it. They say, 'We can rough it. We hike and camp.' But construction is different, and after a while the mess in your home wears you out. . . . Everyone wants Sub Zero—it's $3,000—we try to tell them we'll put it in, but the GE is half the price. We take on only two or three projects at a time; any more and we can't be effective and scheduling can't be maintained."

DONALD KAUFMAN COLOR COLLECTION

Mr. Kaufman, a color consultant for the last 10 years to such places as the Getty Museum, Takashimaya, the Museum of Broadcasting, and portions of the Wallace wing at the Met, decided to apply his museum experience to paint for private homes. He formulated a group of 30 complex colors for interior use. This means that as many as 11 different pigments are used in the formulation of the final color (though no black or umbers are used—they're light absorbers). These are then added to commercial bases. The results are unusually luminous colors, available in several different finishes.

Is it worth an extra $50 or so a gallon? Every interior designer we spoke with said yes. Glenn Gissler uses DK Colors "as often as possible"—on up to 90% of his projects. "These colors have luminosity and richness and nuance. There is a full spectrum of colors that react to whatever light is hitting it. So, if the sunset comes into the room and one evening it is purple and another evening it is orange, the paint will reflect differently." He thought originally that you had to "be an aesthete or particularly sensitive to color" to appreciate this paint, but says that's not the case. Naomi Leff says the color makes a "sophisticated and discreet difference. With all the color on the market, it is hard to find the beauty and dustiness you like, especially in the dark tones. Paint stores say they can copy his colors, but they can't."

All ordering is done by phone. Paint comes in two ways—either in blended gallons or in the form of color concentrate, which is then added to a gallon of commercial base. A packet contains enough color for a gallon of paint. A set of 30 large, brushed-on swatches are available for $20. ☎ 201-568-2226, to order. You can see the color sets at **Archivia Bookstore,** 944 Madison Ave. [74th/75th] ☎ 439-9194.

ELECTRICIANS

WHAT TO KNOW Electricians are licensed by the Dept. of Buildings. Licensing is a long process, and the rules governing electricians are byzantine. Consequently, much work is done by people who don't have a license. City regulations, though, say that a licensed electrician is needed for "installation of anything having to do with light, heat, and power, regardless of voltage." A spokesman at the Dept. of Buildings confirms that "a licensed electrician is required for *any* electrical work." The license holder must file the work with the city.

The Electric Connection, 333 W. 39th St. [8th/9th] ☎ 268-9220, has been around since 1984. Neil Fairey (licensed) and his staff make a specialty of doing the kind of small interior project that most people face: hanging fixtures, ceiling fans, chandeliers, dealing with stereo or computer wiring. They do troubleshooting and repairs when, say, lights start flashing for no apparent reason. "Electrical work tends to be fiddly work that often involves some damage. We try to explain what's at stake." They charge $75 for the first half hour, which covers travel time. After that, $50/hour.

Jim Da Silva, ☎ 619-0413, is a licensed electrician who works for contractors and builders when buildings are being rewired. He also does projects like adding on a room or installing an electric range. Generally a $100 minimum, but he tries to accommodate people with small jobs (changing a fixture or changing an outlet).

FLOORING

WHAT TO KNOW The floor experts all agree that if you maintain a wood floor properly, the time between refinishings can be greatly increased, and depending on how it is used, you may never have to refinish. Wood floors that are not polyurethaned should be waxed three times a year. With and without polyurethane, the most important thing you can do is regularly dust them with a soft mop that has been sprayed with a static dust attractor. There are water-based and oil-based polyurethanes. The advantages of the water-based products are: they're environmentally friendly, they dry in a couple of hours, and they're non-yellowing (which

is important over light and white stains). The disadvantage is that they are not quite as durable as the oil-based ones. The oil-based polys take longer to dry and have more odor.

It is often hard to imagine what a big floor will look like looking from a small sample on the wall. **I. J. Peiser's Sons,** 475 Tenth Ave. [36th] ☎ 279-6900, has done much to help by setting up a 4,000-square-foot showroom with large (in some cases 10' × 12') samples of flooring patterns. All of the patterns, borders, antique effects, pre-finished flooring, even brass and marble inlays, are installed on the floor. Smaller 10' × 2' areas illustrate the "species" samples in different finishes. The color range of the woods is stunning, everything from pale bird's-eye maple, the gold of yellowheart, to dark ebony. Another area shows a range of stains on standard oak flooring. Basic oak floors start at $12–$15 per square foot, and prices can rise steeply for more unusual woods and treatments. Peiser's also has refinishing crews. When they refinish, they come out to measure before giving an estimate. Basic sanding, scraping, and polying starts at $3 per square foot.

The showroom at **Janos P. Spitzer Flooring,** 133 W. 24th St. [6th/7th] ☎ 627-1818, is a pleasantly woody place. The Brazilian cherry floor is as tight as can be, and the walls are hung with representations of floor designs that Spitzer has laid. They always make a sample first so you'll know exactly what you're getting. Parquetry and marquetry, simple and complicated, and all manner of finishes are there, including one with inlaid brass strips. New floors start at $15 per square foot for American white oak, a wood Mr. Spitzer calls "the best in the world for flooring" because of its durability and the fact that it is not photosensitive. Moving up through exotic woods and layouts can take you to $100 per square foot and beyond. Sanding, staining, and polyurethaning an existing floor costs $5 square foot. "We go to great lengths to sand very flat and perfectly smooth." They use a minimum of three coats of polyurethane, "more and more the new water-based products." Without staining, it's $4 per square foot.

At **Downtown Floor Supplies,** 338 Lafayette St. [Bleecker] ☎ 982-2600, Oliver Keeley says, "Flooring is hard work," but if you have little cash and lots of patience, he will walk you through the steps, rent you the machines, and sell you the materials. There are wood samples to show you various finishes and stains. They have a full line of oil- and water-based polyurethanes. A sander/edger machine rents for $30 for 24 hours. Pickup and delivery is $20 extra. If you are using an oil-based poly, which can take at least 6–8 hours to dry between coats, you will need a machine for two days. Downtown will also do the job for you. Sanding, putting on a sealer, and two coats of poly will cost $1.50 per square foot.

HANDY PERSONS

Suzanne Langenwalter is the Jill behind **Jill-of-all-Trades.** When things overwhelm you and your "To Do" list is unmanageable, she steps in to help out—on a one-time basis or more. She can do small household repairs, errands, connect and program the VCR, and other bothersome tasks like helping you unpack and get a household up and running after a move. Working for individuals and small businesses, she can set up systems on the Mac. She does a lot of organizing of closets and cabinets and generally gets you back on track. Costs range from $20–$45/hour, depending on the job; 2-hour minimum ☎ 228-7084.

David Jensen's skills fall somewhere between handyman and contractor. While he has done complete renovations, he prefers smaller jobs. He has put up partitions and dropped ceilings and repaired floors. "Many people just need someone to put up some quick shelving or to rearrange parts of their built-in systems." After meeting with you, he will write a proposal and give a written free estimate. If drawings are necessary, he will provide them. If they are complicated there will be a fee for them. There is a $200 minimum for work. He is "up front if the job is too small" ☎ 308-6997.

HARDWARE AND ARCHITECTURAL PIECES
HARDWARE

The hardware at **Archetype Gallery,** 115 Mercer St. [Prince/Spring] ☎ 334-0100, is handcrafted by artists—nothing is machine made. Knobs and drawer pulls are made of cast bronze, or painted, bejewelled wood. Our favorite: great-looking small brass heads (they look like a cross between a human and an alien). They're made by artist Michael Aram and come in two sizes. The small is $7, the large $11.

The Outwater Idea Center, 223 West Broadway [White] ☎ 966-6366, has some innovative products. Door and drawer handles include the Biomorph series, with irregular, blobby shapes in a variety of metallic finishes. There are casters in many sizes; lots of decorative moldings meant to be used as baseboards, chair rails, and ceiling trims; plastic "glass" blocks; and some wall rack ideas for kitchen storage. They will sell to you, but would prefer to sell to your contractor or architect, which explains the two-tier price structure.

Simon's Hardware and Bath, 421 Third Ave. [29th] ☎ 532-9220. A huge stash of hardware: drawer knobs and pulls, door-knobs and push plates, hooks, switchplates, towel bars. Traditional brass, up-to-the-minute brushed aluminum and chrome, verdigris, and plastic pieces are arranged on wall racks.

ARCHITECTURAL PIECES

Architectural Salvage Warehouse, 337 Berry St. [4th/5th], Brooklyn, is run by the Landmarks Commission. Decreases in staff mean that it is not open all of the time. Call ☎ 487-6740 to find out when it is open or to make an appointment to go there. It is intended as a resource for the historical-building owner and contains both interior and exterior pieces. There is domestic woodwork in the form of doors, shutters, newel posts, window frames, and fireplace mantels. There are building cornices, areaway fences, exterior stonework, bathtubs and sinks, and the occasional sculpture.

Bill's Architectural Salvage, 699 W. 131st St. [Bway/RSD] ☎ 281-0916, by appt., has what you need to restore a simple row house. While, "there are no Tiffany windows" or anything fancy, there are about 500 doors, plumbing fixtures, gates, hardware.

Irreplaceable Artifacts, 14 Second Ave. [1st/Houston] ☎ 777-2900. Seven floors of architectural ornaments from demolished buildings—cornices, friezes, plaques, columns. You can also expect to find doors, fireplaces, lighting fixtures, iron gates, fencing, and vintage plumbing. If this isn't enough, they have a warehouse in Newark that you can visit by appt.

Urban Archaeology, 285 Lafayette St. [Prince/Houston] and 143 Franklin St. [Hudson/Varick] ☎ 431-6969. Bathroom fixtures, sinks, terra-cotta, gates, grates, cab-inets, showcases, tile, and two lines of re-productions—one of lighting and one of bathroom fixtures. "Anything that can be taken off a building."

INTERIOR DESIGNERS

WHAT TO KNOW The American Society of Interior Designers, ☎ 685-3480, has a free referral service to over 200 professionals who have passed national qualifying exams. Both residential and commercial designers are available. For a $40 donation, they will suggest 3–4 designers for you to contact, after you fill out a form giving them information about the size and scope of your job. They try to match the client to the designer, but you are under no obligation to hire their suggestions. You should be planning on spending a minimum of $35,000 on a project.

Karen Fisher, a decorating editor for many home magazines, was always fielding questions from her friends about designers. Her company, **Designer Previews,** ☎ 777-2966, is her way of letting you see the work of over 100 designers and getting some tips for interviewing them. When you come to her office, she puts on a slide show for you "a visual Rorschach"—where you say what you do and don't like. You go away with the names of two or three designers to interview, and if these don't work out, she will make another selection for you. This service costs $100. Ms. Fisher points out that the whole process of decorating has become very costly. A one-bedroom apartment with no renovation will be a minimum of $35,000.

There are three basic methods of payment for an interior design job. No matter how you pay for the job, your expectations should be detailed in writing, specifying what you are paying for and what the designer is responsible for doing. It can be a flat fee, hourly (if the job does not require too much oversight or detailed planning—like drawings), or percentage fees. The designer either tacks an agreed upon percentage to all goods and services, or the client pays the retail fee and the designer, who buys at a lower rate, keeps the difference.

The Kips Bay Show House, ☎ 861-4308, is a good place to go to see designers' work. It's usually in April, at a different address each year. The $15 admission also gets you the designer sourcebook, which tells you who did what.

THE DESIGNERS

Aero Studios, 132 Spring St. [Wooster/ Greene] ☎ 966-4700, is a full-service design firm that does large-scale commercial work (the East Side David Barton gym and the Soho Grand Hotel) as well as small residential jobs. The two principals, William Sofield and Thomas O'Brien, and the six other designers on staff often take a team approach to projects, using the expertise of each. The store on Spring St. has some things that you can take away with you, others can be customized. Go upstairs to the gallery to see their mix of custom furniture and antiques.

Sig Bergamin, ☎ 861-4515, is a native Brazilian who continues to work in his native land as well as in NYC. Many of his projects, like Bar Anise, show an esthetic drawn from his heritage: "lots of color, lots of linen and cottons (no velvets because it is too hot), lots of Portuguese furniture." Other projects have an English feel: using leather chesterfield sofas or putting a round table for dining in the corner of the living room. Mr. Bergamin and his staff of five will do small jobs such as one-room apartments.

Glenn Gissler, ☎ 727-3220, is a younger

Glenn Gissler's restrained sophistication.

designer who works primarily with residential clients. "It's often their first experience working with a designer. I try to get them on the path to quality furnishings." He likes to know about the bones of the apartment or house first. What are its problems? Does it require renovation or redecoration? He works in diverse styles, based on your lifestyle, the architectural features of the building, and where you are in your life. A "realistic" starting budget is $40,000–$50,000, and he sometimes works on a consulting basis. MUG likes Mr. Gissler's cool, clean sophisticated rooms in restricted palettes.

Katherine Gormley, Architect, ☎ 517-4121, works on large and small projects in NY apartments. Ms. Gormley and associate Emily Abrahams don't like to "impose a decorated or artificial quality to the rooms." They have an eye for textiles and objects and believe "homes should reflect the lives and histories of the people who live in them and their personalities—quirky or elegant, or indeed both." Depending on the project, they work by percentage or an hourly ($100) rate.

Victoria Hagen Interiors, ☎ 888-1178. Ms. Hagen says her "point of view is modern," but we'd say not in any rigid sense. She mixes pieces unpredictably and wittily, one time inserting a working clock face into the

ANDREW BOARDWIN

back of a dinette chair. She leaves the dwellers space and light by keeping surfaces relatively clear and using light, reflective colors. She has creative solutions to the realities of daily life, such as where to put recycled newspapers. Ms. Hagen does no consulting work and takes on projects where more than one room will be redone. Plan on a generous six-figure budget.

Mariette Himes-Gomez, ☎ 288-6856, does residential and commercial interior design all over the world. Her work has a "refined simplicity, clean lines, and clear architectural definition." While her designs are not period, she does have an "understanding of period detail." She has recently created a line of furniture—chairs, tables, sofas, lamps, and lanterns—that can be seen by appointment in her showroom. Ms. Himes-Gomez uses a combination of flat fee and percentage in her charges.

Lembo/Bohn Design Associates, ☎ 645-3636. Joseph Lembo and Laura Bohn have been in partnership for 16 years. They have designed public spaces in Saudi Arabia and Japan and collections of fabric and wall coverings produced by Donghia. Their residential style is "modern, clean, spare, and Zen, but comfortable." Projects begin at $100,000, but they also do much consulting work. This means they give you the specification package with sourcing if you request it. The consultation fee is $250 per hour. Most people contract for 10–20 hours, and they get the style and direction as well as drawings.

If you just want some guidance and sources and your budget is limited, there is **Barbara Landsman,** ☎ 800-486-7336, who has been giving decorating advice over the telephone since 1986. You send her your floorplan, swatches (if you have any), photos or video of your rooms, and tell her what you are trying to achieve. Include a SASE so she can return things to you. She will make a phone appointment with you, which costs $100. You can talk as long as you need to, though there is a two-room limit. Many people record the call to be sure they get all of the ideas she offers.

Tonin MacCallum, ☎ 831-8909, does not consider herself "a signature designer." Thirty years' experience in the business has taught her to be client-oriented. When she meets with you she asks how you live and what your family life is like—"They're not the same thing"—and what's your realistic budget. She charges $200 an hour for design, and the retail price for purchases. There is no minimum job.

Nancy Mullin, ☎ 628-4629, is ASID, CKD (certified kitchen designer), and a licensed home improvement contractor, a combination that means you only have to deal with one person. She's most comfortable working in a traditional style. "Most of my work is in prewar buildings. I try to make them look the way they would if they'd had the advantage of our technology."

A kitchen by Nancy Mullin.

She has developed a seven-page questionnaire that helps to detail for both of you what is important. The initial consultation is $100—applied to the cost of the job. There is a design fee starting at $1,000 and then a percentage on materials and labor.

Benjamin Noriega-Ortiz, ☎ 465-1198, who worked with John Saladino, is diffident about describing his own style. He tailors his work to the client and will work in any style, but likes rooms that are "simple, calm, and serene." He works by the hour, and hourly charges start at $150.

The **Gladys Remler Design Group,** ☎ 734-5055. Ms. Remler says, "It costs money to decorate, and if your budget is small you may want to do it in phases." To that end, they do a room at a time, help you to buy "important" pieces of furniture, and do small offices. "We know people are busy, and we respect their time and money." There is no charge for the introductory meeting, and they work on the percentage system.

Tod Williams/Billie Tsien, ☎ 582-2385. Their exceptionally beautiful work

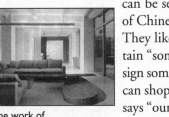

The work of
Tod Williams/Billie Tsien.

can be seen at the Museum of Chinese in the Americas. They like projects that contain "some possibility to design something." While they can shop for you, Ms. Tsien says "our strength is in making things, so rather than buying a dining room table, we would like to design a dining room table." They have a "modernist style, somewhat quirky," with a richer palette than many modern designers. Their interest in materials leads them to uses for homosote (made from recycled newspapers), new finishes for masonite and barra board. They will do small jobs (like a dining room table) to a full renovation. No minimum price for a job.

MORE If you're renovating your kitchen or bathroom, see the Bathroom section of this Home Renovation & Repairs article. Two designers you might want to consider are Florence Perchuk, a Certified Kitchen Designer, and Ellen Berns, an architect (and a thoughtful and careful designer) . . . For children's room designers, see the Furniture article in the Stores chapter.

PAINTERS

WHAT TO KNOW Advice from Mary Louise Guertler, an interior designer at McMillen Inc.: "You need to supervise the little details." Don't assume that the painters remember you want the inside of your medicine cabinet painted. Be there to answer all of their questions, or *you* may be the cause of delays in the project. Get an estimate in writing that is broken down by room and gives a step-by-step plan—spackling, skimming, painting, how many rolls of wallpaper they are going to use, etc. The painter should explain how much and what kind of preparation he is going to do on the walls. If colors are being matched you want at least a 24-inch square painted on the walls to look at. A good painter brings all of his own supplies, comes on time, finishes on time, and gets his materials out when he is finished. Each of the painters listed also hangs paper.

Master Craftsmen Decorators, ☎ 718-885-1807, is Louis Criscola's painting company. With the help of several employees, Mr. Criscola provides wood graining, marbling, and other finishes, paperhanging, and restoration work on old plaster moldings. About half of Mr. Criscola's work is "straight, flat out" painting without the fancy finishes, but even here he feels it is important to get rid of the irregularities in walls as much as possible. He will do a single room.

Robert Star Painting, ☎ 737-8855. Robert Robinson has been a painting contractor since 1982. He now has a staff of painters, some of whom specialize in finishes such as glazing, ragging, and faux bois. He does mostly high-end work and does much work with designers at prestigious firms. He knows that "painting is an intrusive and a dirty job," and tries to do things that make it seem less so. "The quality of the work is a given for me, it's the level of service that distinguishes us."

Roth Painting, ☏ 758-2170, does a wide range of painting jobs from the easiest, "painting an apartment for rerenting" up to special, decorative finishes. As with most of these painters, unless you are a client already,  he does not paint less than a single room. Giving people an estimate requires that they ask a lot of questions since there are so many variables: how many colors, the sheen level of each, the scope of the work, how much access the painters will have to an apartment, the client's time frame, and "the acid test—the condition of the walls."

Ira Smolin Painting, ☏ 831-0205. Mr. Smolin has been a residential painting contractor for 15 years. "You have to be conscious of more than good quality. You have to keep the place clean and be very conscious that people are living there." Mr. Smolin does not look down on small jobs, like painting a single room or papering a bathroom. His partner, Marat Kadyrov, does glazing, marbling, gold leafing, and trompe l'œil.

Lillian Heard, ☏ 718-230-8693, specializes in Venetian plaster, a fresco-like technique. A 1989 trip to Italy interested her in the polished plaster walls she saw in palaces with their transparent colors. Working with a small trowel, her "plaster" is actually a thin layer of marble dust suspended in an encaustic polymer. Any color can be added, and the result can be solid or mottled. Other additives like mica dust can give an opalescent quality. Finished walls can be coated with beeswax for a polished, somewhat more iridescent effect. Many people choose this for kitchens and bathrooms, as it is water-resistant. Ms. Heard recently completed Dakota Jackson's showroom. Cost varies with the amount of labor involved, and starts at $15 per square foot. Ms. Heard also does gold and silver leafing on baseboards and wood trims.

PLUMBERS

WHAT TO KNOW Plumbers are licensed by the Dept. of Buildings. According to the Director of Public Affairs at the D.O.B., "You need a licensed plumber for any work that requires a permit," not for maintenance work. "If it's just to change a washer, a license is not needed." The city has been removing some minor jobs from the filing list, so their rule of thumb is: "If it's not hazardous, not dangerous, it's not a problem." Licensed plumbers are needed for "adding a bathroom to a basement, enlarging a half bathroom to a full bathroom, making all water and gas connections, or installing a tub or sink. It is legal to charge sales tax when the work is a repair. Only one plumber in a firm needs to be licensed to satisfy the city regulations.

Lichtenberger Plumbing, 304 Spring St. [Hudson/Renwick] ☏ 807-8811. In business since 1900, their 20-person staff does everything from changing a washer to repiping a high rise. Their white and blue trucks are stocked with "common and repair fittings," so the chances are "80–85%" that the worker will have what he needs when he gets to you. The charge is "portal to portal." $76.40/hour. They service below 96th St.

Sandy's Plumbing ☏ 475-6510. Since

1972 Joel Cohen has been a licensed plumber. He and his 16 employees do everything from high-end alterations to fixing leaks in walls and changing bathroom fixtures. They work anywhere in Manhattan. Repairs are charged by the hour, $100 for mechanic and helper. (If the part is not in the truck, the "helper goes shopping while the mechanic keeps working.") For alterations, they give an estimate and a contract.

TILES

See the Tiles article in the Stores chapter.

JEWELRY REPAIR

Rissin's Jewelry Clinic, 4 W. 47th St. [5th/6th] ☎ 575-1098. Joe Rissin began making and repairing jewelry when he took an art metal class in high school. He apprenticed with Anton Kun, a renowned jewelrymaker and a hard taskmaster, who taught him "if you do it right, you don't have to do it over." Mr. Rissin repairs antique pieces, both fine and costume. He fabricates intricate clasps for better pieces. "A good clasp is one you can hear click from 10 feet away." His wife works with him to do restringing. Soldering a base and putting a new post on pierced earrings is about $14. He works in stones and metals and also repairs eyeglasses.

KNIFE SHARPENING

Since 1874, **Henry Westpfal & Co.,** 105 W. 30th St. [6th/7th] ☎ 563-5990, has been in the knife sharpening trade. The store continues to be owned by Westpfals, and the current grinder, John Chapman, learned his craft at their hands. You can do a lot of damage to your knives by taking them to a local store that sharpens by putting the blades into a machine. The only good way is the "wet wheel" method, in which the blade is carefully pressed against a spinning wheel that is frequently lubricated with water. Sharpening without water can "burn" the metal. The touch of the grinder is important as well: The wrong touch can harm the blade. In addition to knives, they will sharpen scissors, pinking shears, toenail and cuticle nippers, and straight blades. For a small knife, figure $2.50–$4.50 for sharpening. Chef's knives can run $9. Closed weekends.

LAMPS & LAMPSHADES

All of the following lamp repair shops can rewire European lamps for American systems and vice versa. They can mount a lamp, which means take something not a lamp and make a lamp from it, and can replace parts.

Grand Brass Lamp Parts, 221 Grand St. [Elizabeth] ☎ 226-2567, sells brass and glass lamp parts, including many mounts, ceiling covers, chain lengths, harps, and sockets. They will build a lamp from their parts and do all manner of repairs. Replacing a socket starts at $12.

Just Shades, 21 Spring St. [Elizabeth] ☎ 966-2757, sells made-up shades, almost exclusively in ivory, although there are some black and leopard print ones. They advise you to bring the lamp in, so you can try a variety of styles and sizes on it. If you can't find something that suits, they will make up a shade for you. A custom shade in a modest size with basic trim starts at $120.

Louis Mattia, 980 Second Ave. [51st/52nd] ☎ 753-2176. The shop is full of many articles Mr. Mattia has collected over the years that he thought would make a nice lamp. Metal pieces that he turns into wall mounts, heavy copper pots that look like stills, a large copper brazier from who knows where. Vases and pottery globes sit on the long, dusty tables next to a collection of glass lamp parts. There are hurricanes, ceiling globes, bobeches, and drawers and drawers of replacement crystals for chandeliers. In short, the shop is full of treasures. Mr. Mattia is something of a treasure himself—a former machinist who turned his abilities with metal to making lamps and lamp parts— he's a gentleman and a craftsman of great skill. Of course, he rewires and repairs. To change a socket or replace a wire costs $20.

Oriental Lamp, 816 Lexington Ave. [62nd/63rd] ☎ 832-8190 and 223 W. 79th St. [Bway/Amsterdam] ☎ 873-0812. Ron Murakami stepped into his father's and grandfather's business in 1988. Oriental sells new lamps and shades and provides a full range of repair and customizing services. They can rewire or replace parts and are proud of the quality parts that they use, like solid brass sockets. All work is done in their own shops. Custom shades can be made from your fabric or theirs. They have a painter who puts designs on shades. Since there are so many variables in the process, it is impossible to quote prices over the phone. Mr. Murakami prefers you to bring the lamp in, and they will give you an estimate.

Restoration and Design Studio, 249 E. 77th St. [2nd/3rd] ☎ 517-9742. Paul Karner (see more in Silver & Metal Repair in this chapter) repairs many kinds of lamps and does rewiring.

At **Unique Custom Lampshades,** 247 E. 77th St. [2nd/3rd] ☎ 472-1140, each item really is unique as they do only custom work. Lampshade frames are made to order by a framemaker in Brooklyn. No fabric shades or trims are glued; all are hand sewn. Skilled craftswomen pleat, smock, ruche, and create effects with fabric. "Shades made this way are meant to last 10–20 years," according 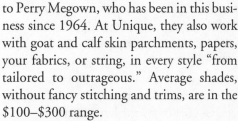 to Perry Megown, who has been in this business since 1964. At Unique, they also work with goat and calf skin parchments, papers, your fabrics, or string, in every style "from tailored to outrageous." Average shades, without fancy stitching and trims, are in the $100–$300 range.

Ruth Vitow, 351 E. 61st St. [1st/2nd] ☎ 355-6881, will only admit to being in the shade and lamp business "for fifty years. Any more than that and people start guessing about your age." Her showroom is a wonderful place to browse. She has many things she has collected to use as lamp bases, including blue and white Chinese vases, handblown glass from an artisan in New Jersey, twisted wooden spindles. She has a store of parts and can change arms on sconces and rework chandeliers. Mounting a lamp starts at $100.

MESSENGER

We've been very impressed lately by the messenger service called **Thunderball** ☎ 675-1700. They've been in business for just a few years, but they've grown to 4 foot messengers, 25 on bikes, and 4 drivers. Delivery starts at $7 and goes up depending on distance. Generally, it's about $10 a shot. The owners say they try to hire "smart, articulate people who are familiar with Manhattan," and we think it shows. They're courteous on the phone, and we've found when they say they'll be there within 30 minutes, they are.

ORGANIZERS

Carol Trefethern, ☎ 233-0156, does interior organization, furnishing, and project management. For people who have little time to devote to a move, she takes charge of the whole operation, so that you are dealing with only one person. She'll also watch carefully over the whole budget. She can come up with a game plan for finding new living or work space, hire a contractor when it's a big job, oversee everything: construction, paint, floors, fabric, carpeting, lighting, and do any needed shopping. She can even interview housekeepers, handymen, nannies, personal secretaries, and hone down a list to present a few good choices to you. She has an office in L.A., and often works with bicoastal clients. By the hour: $110.

Linda Rothschild is the president of the NY Chapter of Professional Organizers, and her company, **Cross It Off Your List,** ☎ 725-0122, "provides services for people who don't have time to do everything." She helps people to move; organizes closets (with or without construction), file cabinets, and kitchens; and does space planning. She has a small staff of people who help you pay your bills, run errands, stand in line.

Terry Ward of **Get Your Act Together,** ☎ 860-0257, works mostly with people who are overwhelmed by clutter, especially paper clutter. After she gets you through the initial pile up, she sets up simple filing systems so that it's easier for you to pay your bills, gather the information you need to do your taxes, and generally makes life easier. Ms. Ward will do the same for your closets and cupboards. $50/hr.

Life Support Systems, ☎ 362-2399, is run by Audrey Lavine. She will organize papers, get your computer set up and running, plan an event, help with a move, catalog books and tapes, make room for the baby, sort out insurance claims, and set up home offices, regular offices, and studios. Cost is $60–65/hr. for basic organizing, $50/hr. for moving. If it is a huge job, she will negotiate a day rate.

PARTIES

CATERERS

Charlotte's Catering, ☎ 732-7939, is run by Alicia and Mikael Möller (Charlotte is no longer with the company). Not only is Charlotte's an excellent caterer, but they're an exceptionally nice group to boot. According to one person in the food industry we spoke with, "They are good at everything from the talking to the finished product." Charlotte's does big corporate and small private parties, and according to Ms. Möller, "We like to make every client feel special." There is a $500 minimum charge on weekends.

The Cleaver Co. ☎ 431-3688. Mary Cleaver's company will do everything from finding a location (if you don't want to use your home) to decorations, entertainment, staffing, and providing food. Cleaver has done dinner parties for two people and has worked for as many as 2,000. They also have a retail store at 229 West Broadway [White], where party foods can be bought and ordered for nonstaffed catered events. (We've eaten their shop food many times for takeout lunches, and it's always excellent.) This caterer can provide custom cakes and platters for corporate or private gatherings. No minimum charge.

Creative Edge Parties, ☎ 741-3000, is highly regarded for their combination of delicious food and great attitude. Carla Ruben, president of the company, says that people feel overwhelmed when they have to give a party, so "we break the planning down into steps and take the anxiety out of it." They will assist you with flowers, invitations, lighting. They catered the opening of the Matisse exhibit at MoMA and will work a 20-person cocktail party or a 12-person dinner party. They do not do any drop-off work—there is a chef present on every job. $700 minimum.

Fletcher Morgan ☎ 989-0724. They can plan and carry out your entire party—small to large dinner and cocktail parties for businesses and homes as well as cater drop-off business lunches for as few as six people. There is no minimum charge.

Glorious Food ☎ 628-2320. For over 20 years, Sean Driscoll's Glorious Food has been setting the party standard in New York. Glorious and Tentation are top of the line.

Parties by Rossi ☎ 463-0872. Chef Rossi has been catering parties for over 10 years. She does many small parties in people's homes, as well as weddings, bar mitzvahs, and corporate events. She specializes in American regional cuisine. "I love the southwestern, Creole, southern, and, recently, New England dishes." Lately, she has been using organic and free-range food from country sources. $500 minimum. She will do drop-off trays for cocktail parties.

Spoonbread Catering ☎ 734-0430. Norma Darden and her sister Carole run this operation that serves tasty food, some of it with their southern flair, as well as African, West Indian, Latin, and other national and ethnic specialties. They catered the inauguration of Mayor Dinkins, among many other events, but are happy to cater a dinner party for 12 or a sit-down banquet for 500. You can read about the Dardens in their family history/cookbook *Spoonbread and Strawberry Wine.*

Tentation ☎ 353-0070. This (with Glorious Food) is the other blue-chip caterer. It's the North American outpost of the venerable French caterer Potel & Chabot. They do dinners for 8 to 2,000 people, working with corporate and private clients. When they do a party, they take care of everything: flowers, music, linens, location scouting, etc. Minimum of $1,500.

FLORISTS

See Florists in this chapter.

HELP

Best Domestic, ☎ 685-0351, can provide butlers and maids for your parties with a minimum of four hours' notice. Butlers can assist with serving, take messages, attend to guests, and do some housekeeping. Butlers charge $15 per hour, with a four-hour minimum. Maids, who help prepare the meal, serve, and assist in the after-party cleanup, are $10–$12 per hour, also with a four-hour minimum. The agency charge is an additional $12.50 per person, per call. Before major holidays, many people like help taking out the fine china, washing up the crystal, and polishing the silver. They can send you a good housekeeper or houseman to help with this chore.

ICE DELIVERY

These places need one day's notice for delivery: **Casamassima & Sons,** ☎ 355-3734, delivers a 40-lb. plastic bag of ice for $9.20, and there is a $15 minimum delivery charge . . . **Mountain Ice,** ☎ 397-1500, delivers 40-lb. bags at $12.99 or a 39-lb. plastic tub with a lid that you can serve from for $16.80.

MUSIC

The **Mannes College of Music** can provide musicians who play "everything from Cole Porter to Mozart." Students and graduates can be hired to perform solo, in trios or quartets, jazz or classical. $70 per hour per musician, $5 of which goes to finance Mannes's program of sending musicians into hospitals. Arrangements can be made by calling Elizabeth Aaron at the college at ☎ 580-0210, ext. 40 . . . Mr. John Blanchard will help you to select current talented students or more experienced graduates from the **Manhattan School of Music.** Classical and jazz musicians are available. Rates start at $65–$85 per hour per musician, with a $100 minimum and some extras if you should want, say, a harp (add $75 for cartage). He can be reached at ☎ 749-2802 ext. 486.

PAPER AND PLASTIC

Rubenstein's, for many years at the corner of Broadway and 17th, is now at 24 E. 17th St. [5th/Bway] ☎ 924-7817. You can find very basic holiday decorations as well as plastic and paper plates, plastic glasses, and napkins. Colored 9-inch plastic plates are $4 for a pack of 20. Dinner napkins are $4 for a pack of 50.

PARTY SPACES

If you're throwing a big bash outside of your home, your caterer or your party planner will have a long list of available sites. You can also call **Paint the Town Red** ☎ 677-3176, which has 600 party spaces in their data bank. Howard Givner and his five employees try to get as much information from you as possible, not only about date and number of guests, but about things like atmosphere and style. After that, you get a list of locations with contact names and numbers, and do your own booking. The service is free to you (they make their money from the spaces) . . . A similar service is available from the people who put out the **Locations** sourcebook. For this company, you need to fax them your particulars. Their fax is ☎ 861-0939.

RENTALS

Candelabras, chairs, coat racks, linens, tables, and a whole range of more esoteric party items: cotton candy machines, piñatas, wishing wells are available from: **Party Time** ☎ 682-8838. $75 minimum for rental; there's a booklet available listing their stock . . . **Service Party Rental,** ☎ 288-7384, has a $350 minimum in December, $100 rest of the year . . . You can also try **Broadway Famous,** ☎ 269-2666, $150 minimum and **Something Different,** ☎ 201-742-1779, also with a $150 minimum.

WINES AND SPIRITS

When you want to buy in quantity for a party, try one of the top-value wine stores: **Warehouse Wines,** 735 Broadway [8th/Waverly] ☎ 982-7770; **Garnet,** 929 Lexington Ave. [68th/69th] ☎ 772-3211; **Gotham,** 2519 Broadway [94th] ☎ 932-0990; or **Union Square Wines,** 33 Union Square West [16th/17th] ☎ 675-8100. See more in the Wine Stores article in the Spirits chapter.

PERSONAL CARE

KID'S BARBERS

Cozys Cuts for Kids, 1125 Madison Ave. [84th] ☎ 744-1716. A big, bright shop that specializes in kid's cuts. $22.

    The Tortoise and the Hare, 1470 York Ave. [78th] ☎ 472-3399, says if a child is particularly nervous, they'll cut hair while the child sits in a parent's lap. $20.

    Short Cuts, 104 W. 83rd St. [Columbus/Amsterdam] ☎ 877-2277, shows videos during the haircut. If the child has a favorite one, you can bring it in. $18.

LADY BARBER

Kathleen Giordano is known around town as the **Lady Barber** ☎ 826-8616. Ms. Giordano, who is licensed as a Master Barber, does not have a shop with a red-and-white pole. She cuts your hair in your office. Many men find that they can continue working during the cut. $50.

MAMIE'S SKIN CARE

There are more lavish skin care centers in the city, but there can't be any that produce a more peaceful glow than an hour under Mamie McDonald's gentle care at **Mamie's Skin Care Center,** 29 Washington Square West [MacDougal] ☎ 260-9372. You enter into a professional office space, fill out a brief form, and then go into Mamie's retreat. For $70 you will get an exceptionally good facial massage with aromatherapy. She does herbal body wraps ($125), a homeopathic facial, and glycolic acid treatments. This is the exfoliating sugar cane derivative that improves

BODY SUGARING

Body sugaring is an ancient method of hair removal. You might want to get sugared because it is considerably less painful than waxing. The recipe, which comes from Egypt, is nothing more than sugar, water, and lemon that has reached the ribbon stage of candymaking (before it hardens). You can be sugared by Tamara, who runs **Skin Shape** ☎ 718-531-4552. The sugar mix is applied over small areas by hand and manipulated by her until she expertly flips the pancake of sugar off you, removing hair with, we found, much less pain and reddening of skin than with other methods. There is no sticky residue as there is with waxing, and the sugar substance will not stain or harm your clothing. It does take more time than waxing and costs slightly more. She will bring her portable table and the body sugaring process to you. $65 minimum.

skin tone, $70. There's music in the background to help you relax, but it's Mamie herself who makes it special—she's professional, fun, and soothing. Her hours are Tues.–Sat., 9:30–7.

MASSEURS

Cărapan, 5 W. 16th St. [5th/6th] ☎ 633-6220, is the new age spa that looks good (subdued warm lighting), smells good (herbs and spices in the air), and feels good (leaving here relaxed and invigorated is practically guaranteed). Massages are $75.

Jonathan St. George, ☎ 254-9890, studied at the Swedish Institute. He does sports, medical, deep tissue, and shiatsu, and works with people recovering from injuries. On the first visit, he does an evaluation, including postural analysis. $50 at his office, $75 if he comes to you.

You can find a masseur at the **Swedish Institute,** a school where massage therapists are trained in Swedish massage and shiatsu for certification by NY State. House calls start at $85 an hour and can go up, depending on the distance the therapist has to travel and how much equipment they need to bring to you. Call ☎ 924-5900, ext. 120.

Joni Yecalsik, ☎ 673-3227, has been a massage therapist for over 20 years. She worked with the Joffrey Ballet when they were headquartered in NY and went on tour with them as their masseuse. She works on a table (with oil) and does a combination of myofascial (deep tissue) with some shiatsu. If she comes to you it's $125, unless you have your own table, in which case it's $100. If you go to her, it's $75 an hour.

SPAS

There aren't a lot of day spas in New York where you'd actually want to spend the day,

though the Peninsula comes close. That doesn't mean you can't get some therapeutic, and relaxing, treatments. There are enough around town to satisfy the Patsy and Edina in all of us. F = Facial; M = Massage (massages are generally 60 minutes).

Anushka, 241 E. 60th St. [2nd/3rd] ☎ 355-6404. They offer facials, body wraps, massage, waxing, and electrolysis, but specialize in cellulite treatments. Men and women. F $60, M $65.

Dorit Baxter, 47 W. 57th St. [5th/6th] ☎ 371-4542. Tiny rooms, friendly staff, lots of privacy. Treatments include mud, seaweed, paraffin, facial, haircuts, and massage. F $60, M $60.

Elizabeth Arden, 691 Fifth Ave. [54th/55th] ☎ 546-0200. Through the Red Door, a variety of massages, facial treatments, haircare, manicures, and pedicures. Their specialty is the wax treatments for face, legs, or arms. The nail room has tall windows, one of which gives you a view of the sculpture garden at MoMA. Men and women, but mostly women. F $65, M $60.

Estée Lauder in Bloomie's ☎ 980-9040. Okay for a quick stop (facials, massage, waxing), but small and no atmosphere. F $60, M $60.

Four Seasons Hotel, 57 E. 57th St. [Mad/Park] ☎ 350-6420. The usual Four Seasons high standards, very pleasant (though not extraordinary) surroundings, commensurate prices: F $105, M $105. For those prices, you get use of the steam, sauna, and whirlpool, but *not* use of the gym.

Georgette Klinger, 501 Madison Ave. [52nd/53rd] ☎ 838-3200 and 978 Madison Ave. [76th] ☎ 744-6900. Specializing, since 1940, in facials for men and women, using their own products. Each client is worked on in a small, utilitarian, private room. After your facial, you have a meeting with a consultant who will recommend products. F $72, M $70.

Kozué, 795 Madison Ave. [68th] ☎ 734-8600, facials and Ki therapy (we'd better let them explain this) in the second-floor spot. F $64, M $64.

La Casa Day Spa, 41 E. 20th St. [Bway/Park Ave. So.] ☎ 673-2272. Nice staff, pleasant (though in no way luxurious) surroundings. Massage, body wraps, facial, flotation tank (better than a tank—a small room), and sauna. F $75, M $70.

Mario Badescu, 320 E. 52nd St. [1st/2nd] ☎ 758-1065. Problem-skin care (certainly not decorating) is their strong suit. They have about 175 products (using natural ingredients) and a lot of people who love them. The spa (it's more of a clinic, really) does free skin evaluations and lots of facials. F $60. No massage.

Millefleurs, 130 Franklin St. [Varick] ☎ 966-3656. Massage, body wraps, facials, aromatherapy, manicures, and pedicures. F $75, M $70 and up.

Origins Feel Good Spa at Chelsea Piers

☎ 336-6780. F $60, M $60. Massages include a 30 minute "warm up," $35; reflexology, 45 minutes for $45; an hour craniosacral massage, $75; and a one-hour massage with two masseuses, $120. The menu of facials offers acupressure along with the more routine deep cleansing. They're $65 for 75 minutes.

Osaka Health Center, 50 W. 56th St. [5th/6th] ☎ 682-1778. Shiatsu, sauna, aromatherapy, Japanese hot and cold tubs, massage. No facials. M $75 for 90 minutes.

Peninsula, 700 Fifth Ave. [55th] ☎ 247-2200. As much luxe as you'll find in town. Spa services include the usual facials, wraps, and massages. The catch is, though, that you have to buy a package of at least three to be able to use the pool, sun deck, and gym. F $90–$105, M $90.

Susan Ciminelli Day Spa, 601 Madison Ave. [57th/58th] ☎ 688-5500, does scrubs, aromatherapy, reflexology, facials. They also do lymph drainage, reflexology, and reiki (which, they say, is an ancient technique that is supposed to relieve tension). F $75, M $75.

PETS

ADOPTING A PET When you adopt a pet, most animals will be up-to-date on shots and will have been spayed or neutered.

The **ASPCA,** 424 E. 92nd St. [1st/York] ☎ 876-7700, is now a "no kill" facility, which means they have more animals there for adoption. $45 for a cat and $55 for a dog . . . **Bide-a-Wee,** 410 E. 38th St. [1st/FDR] ☎ 532-4455. They have mostly "mixed breeds in dogs and domestic shorthairs in cats." As they say, "you are not buying an animal, you are adopting an animal." $55 for

animals under 6 months, $30 for those over 6 months . . . **Center for Animal Care and Control,** 326 E. 110th St. [1st/2nd] ☎ 722-3620. A former ASPCA facility, now a city shelter for lost, stray, or abandoned animals. Many cats and dogs and occasional exotics like potbellied pigs and snakes. $55 for a cat, $60 for a dog. This is a kill facility . . . **Humane Society,** 306 E. 59th St. [1st/2nd] ☎ 752-4840. $55 for cats and larger dogs, $65 for smaller dogs and more for purebreds. Cost includes three weeks of follow-up care . . . **New Yorkers for Companion Animals,** ☎ 427-8273, is a rescue group that takes animals from the streets and saves some from the city shelter. They are cared for in foster homes until they are adopted. Most animals are 1–2 years old; no puppies or kittens. $45 . . . **Place for Cats,** 230 E. 52nd St. [2nd/3rd] ☎ 751-2093. A not-for-profit rescue and adoption organization. Cats and kittens are kept in foster homes until they are adopted. Kittens must go in pairs, unless you have a young cat in your home. $65 for kittens and $90 for altered cats.

BEHAVIORIST Dr. Peter Borchelt, ☎ 718-891-4200, has a Ph.D. in animal behavior and has been practicing since 1978. He works mostly with dogs and cats (though he's put some birds, gerbils, and rabbits on the couch, too) with behavior problems that fall outside the bounds of the usual obedience classes. Figure two to three hours on the first house call (somewhat less for a cat) for Dr. Borchelt to get a history of the pet, work on a diagnosis, and give you techniques to deal with it. $200–$250, depending on the animal and the problem. His associate, Dr. Linda Goodloe, has a telephone consultation line, ☎ 721-1231, where 30 minutes of advice is $25.

BOARDING AND DAY-CARE Canine Country, 207 W. 75th St. [Bway/Amsterdam] ☎ 877-7777, boards dogs only. There is a large playroom that the dogs are in all day. (Aggressive dogs are not accepted.) The animals are in individual kennels at night and for meals. Cost goes by weight of dog and ranges from $27–$40/night . . . **Paws Inn,** 189 Ninth Ave. [21st/22nd] ☎ 645-7297, is lodging primarily for dogs and cats, although they have boarded ferrets, bunnies, and pigs. It is cageless 24 hours a day, and there are "corralled-off play areas with sofas and TVs." (MUG could not resist asking what they watch—most popular are Rikki Lake and Spanish soap operas.) There is a fenced-in, carpeted roof deck for exercising. They separate dogs by size and disposition. Cats are in a separate room. You can visit anytime except 4:30–6:30—dinner and workout time. Overnight, day-care and half-day care. Overnight care for a dog starts at $38 . . . At **Dog Wash** (see below) Glen Gaylinn has nine 4′ × 8′ dog runs. The dogs are separated and have room to move around. Overnight boarding ranges from $19–$34, depending on size . . . **Run Spot Run,** 415 E. 91st St. [1st/York] ☎ 996-6666, is centered around a big playroom where dogs have the run of the place. When it comes to meals and to sleeping, though, they are in private quarters. In addition to day-care and boarding, grooming and training services are available. Day-care is $15–$19, boarding is $25–$45 per night for the first week. Rates drop a bit for subsequent weeks.

CLEANING Two drop-in places for your pet. **Beverly Hill's Laundermutt,** 45 Grove St. [Bedford/Bleecker] ☎ 691-7700. It's do-it-yourself bathing for your dog or cat, though staff is available to do it for you or to give you assistance. Washing little angel yourself will cost $15–35. This includes use of the Victorian tubs, shampoos, towels, the dryers, and guidance from the staff. Full service runs $30–$75; $5 nail clipping . . . **Dog Wash,** 177 MacDougal [W. 8th/Waverly] ☎ 673-3290. There are seven bath bays in a concrete structure with slightly angled basins that the dog stands on—owner Glen Gaylinn's got a patent pending on his invention. The water is sprayed through a hose, after which the dog is blown dry by specially designed equipment. Each wash is $14, which includes soap. If you want one of the staff to wash your dog for you, the price is $27. There is a full-time groomer on staff, and four times a year they have a vaccination clinic. A vet comes in and charges $15 per shot, with no office visit charge. "We want to make responsible, humane pet care easy and at an affordable price."

COMPLAINTS To report a vicious dog, one suspected of rabies, or of being mistreated: ☎ 718-649-8600.

DEATH OF A PET Most older pets are in a chronic-care situation with a vet and are put to sleep. In case of accident or the unforeseen, the first thing to do is to call the vet. They are affiliated with animal cremation and burial services. If it is late at night and the vet is gone, the technician can tell you what to do . . . **Aldstate** is a pet crematorium in Brooklyn ☎ 718-748-2104. Many people make arrangements with them ahead of time, and they are there from 8:30–6:30 . . . The **Pet Loss Support Program** at the Animal Medical Center (see below) is one of the first support groups of its kind in the country. They meet every other week, and payment is by contribution. Talk to Susan Cohen ☎ 838-8100, ext. 269 . . . At the ASPCA, Paula

Anreder ☎ 876-7700, ext. 4355, can provide compassionate **grief counseling** when you lose an animal companion. You talk to her on the telephone or come in for a one-on-one session. She works with many children as well as adults. This is a free service (but a donation would be nice).

DOG RUNS These are the official Parks Dept. dog runs. **Fish Bridge Park** (under renovations), Dover St. [Pearl/Water]. **Washington Square Park,** W. 4th St. [Thompson]. **Tompkins Square Park,** E. 9th St. [B]. **Thomas F. Smith Park,** 11th Ave. [23rd]. **Madison Square Park,** E. 25th St. [5th]. **Robert Moses Park,** E. 42nd St. [1st/FDR]. **Peter Detmold Park,** west of the FDR [51st]. **DeWitt Clinton Park,** W. 52nd St. [10th/11th] and W. 54th St. [10th]. **Theodore Roosevelt Park,** Columbus Ave. [81st]. **Carl Schurz Park,** E. 86th St. [east of EEA]. **Riverside Park** at W. 87th St. and at W. 105th St. **J. Hood Wright Park,** W. 173rd St. [Haven]. There's a non-affiliated public dog run at **Hudson River Park,** West Thames [Little West St.] and a private dog run at **LaGuardia Place,** Mercer St. [Houston].

EMERGENCY Animal Medical Center, 510 E. 62nd St. [York] ☎ 838-8100, is a superb facility. As one vet said to us, "If they can't fix it, no one can." Open 24 hours.

GROOMERS Karen Stampanato, ☎ 279-4053, works in the East Side Animal Clinic as a groomer, but she also comes to your house (Weds. only). She washes small dogs on the kitchen counter and larger dogs on the floor. She spends an hour on each dog, "unless they are tangled." If you have her wash your dog every week, it's $30, otherwise it's

$50. Haircuts start at $45 . . . **Terrie Vitolo,** ☎ 718-388-1442, has been a professional dog groomer since 1965. She will come to your home to care for a pet—but small breeds only. She specializes in caring for elderly pets as well as nervous ones. There's a lot of pampering, there are no cages, and Ms. Vitolo says she uses a tearless shampoo and only nontoxic flea products. $30 an hour. Ms. Vitolo draws raves for her work.

LICENSES Every dog must have a license. To get one, call the Dept. of Health at ☎ 566-2456. It costs $8.50.

TRAINING **Bash Dibra,** ☎ 718-796-4541, is sometimes known as the "dog trainer to the stars," but he had a very un-star-like beginning. Escaping Albania as a child, he and his family were held in a Yugoslavian camp for seven years. The very young Bash was able to befriend the attack dogs who patrolled the camp. Now, he trains dogs and has written two books on the subject. A one-hour session is $150. He is also founder of the **Delta Society,** ☎ 800-869-6898, which trains owners and their dogs to volunteer time in hospitals and care facilities and also trains dogs for work with the blind, the hearing impaired, and those in wheelchairs . . . **Robin Kovary,** ☎ 243-5460, who does film and photo shoot work with animals, has studied with many different trainers and trains all kinds of dogs—even pit bulls and rottweilers. Training takes place in your home, and 8 sessions usually do the trick . . . **Ginny Schroeder,** ☎ 982-4982, and her sister, Susan, run **The Lucky Puppy,** which does dog training in your home. They train all breeds and advise that it is best to start early so that "you can live together peace-

fully." On average, a dog can be trained in 6–8 weeks. Lessons are $100 each. Ginny walks dogs in small groups on the Upper East Side and can arrange for boarding at her facility in Pennsylvania . . . **The Well-Mannered Dog,** ☎ 516-493-3471, is run by Toni Kay, who apprenticed with dog trainer Brian Kilcommons. She still comes to Manhattan from time to time, but has moved most of her business to Long Island. She will take your dog for two weeks of training, at the end of which you must spend a session, about 90 minutes long, with her and your newly well-behaved dog. Prices start at $75/night, more if the dog is aggressive . . . The **ASPCA** does group training classes at 424 E. 92nd St. [1st/York]. All classes are 8 weeks, one hour per week, and cost $230. Puppy kindergarten is for dogs 11–16 weeks old at the start of the class. It teaches problem-solving techniques and the facts of puppy development to the owners and basic obedience to the puppies. It is limited to six dogs and all the members of their household who want to attend. A beginning obedience class is for dogs 17 weeks or older, and an advanced beginner class works on canine good citizenship. These classes have up to 8 dogs in them, who are on the leash during the training. For those who wish to volunteer pet partner time in nursing homes, hospices, and special health facilities, the ASPCA has training certification in the Therapy Dog class ($200). To arrange for classes, call Jacque Schultz at ☎ 876-7700, ext. 4421.

TRANSPORTATION **Pet Taxi,** ☎ 755-1757 or ☎ 917-887-2800, is the life-simplifying idea of Larry Reilly. His yellow minivan has an artificial grass floor and crates if you request them. He will take your pet (and you) to the vet, the groomers, or to the airport. He works by reservation and also offers 24-hour emergency service for injured or sick pets. He has a stretcher, gloves, and muzzles. Fees are $40 round-trip in Manhattan, $46 to LGA one-way, $56 to JFK one-way. Mr. Reilly will taxi your pet out of the city to a boarding facility.

VETS WHO MAKE HOUSE CALLS Dr. **Amy Attas** ☎ 581-7387 can vaccinate, examine, trim nails, clean ears, take blood, and even provide chemotherapy at home. The service is extremely helpful for people with more than one pet. (Have you ever tried getting two cats at once to a vet?) Dr. Attas stresses that in order to best advise you about your pet, she likes to know when there will be changes in habits or lifestyle. She says a vet can often tell you what effect this will have on the pet and can help you to alleviate any negative effects. Dr. Attas has an arrangement

with a hospital where she treats and admits serious cases, but most situations can be handled in your home. She travels to all house calls with a technician. A house call is $80 plus the transportation cost to your apartment . . . **Dr. George M. Korin,** ☎ 838-2569, likes the continuing relationship between himself and the pet (and its owner) and the sense of follow-up outside of a clinic and waiting room situation. Home visits allow him to spend more time with an animal than the 15-minute schedule that many clinics permit. He does routine preventive health care. If necessary, he will temporarily rearrange your furniture to set up an examining area. He brings a technician when it's necessary and can take blood, do a urinalysis, and skin tests. Dr. Korin is affiliated with two hospitals when surgery is required. Pickup and delivery service is offered for hospital care. $50 for house call, $45 for the exam, plus tests.

PHOTO RESTORATION

Whether you have a Steichen or albums of family photos, a little precaution pays because photos are fragile. Here are some sources for photos that need help.

PHOTO RESTORATION
Galowitz Photographics, Inc., 50 E. 13th St. [University/Bway] ☎ 505-7190. Alan and Phyllis Galowitz are photographic retouchers at the top of their field. The Galowitzes do not work on the original image, "except in the most minor way." Instead, they make a good copy to "prolong the life of the image." Mr. Galowitz tries to do as little retouching as possible since "too much looks artificial and does not look historically accurate." Much can be done to restore a

faded image with the use of filters and papers. When the Galowitzes return your photo to you, everything is in the proper inert archival storage materials. Many peo-

Photo restoration by Galowitz Photographics, Inc.

ple do not realize that the old-style photographic album is often made of materials that are destructive to photographs. (The "press and stick" albums are so bad for photographs that some of the manufacturers tell you not to use them for photos.) The Galowitzes are also agents for Light Impressions, a catalog company that sells archival materials, so you can find acid-free boxes, album covers, pages, and mounts at their shop. Album covers start at $19, with pages starting at $5 per package.

PHOTO CONSERVATION

Nora Kennedy and Peter Mustardo's conservation business is called **The Better Image** ☎ 908-730-9105. Between them, Mr. Mustardo and Ms. Kennedy have worked for major museums in New York, Washington, D.C., and abroad. They work only on photographs—everything from family photos to contemporary art photography. They do not do any chemical restoration, but only physical repairs like mending tears or flattening curled photographs. Ms. Kennedy says some of the family photos, especially the enlargements, are in "terrible condition." She knows how much these mean to people, like the man who drove two hours each way for Ms. Kennedy to assess the condition of his grandmother's photo. You don't have to make this effort, since they will make arrangements to consult with you in Manhattan. A written report follows that describes the condition of your photo, sets out possible treatment (sometimes there is more than one option), and gives a cost estimate. No work is done without your permission. The Better Image charges $100 per hour; reports start at $50.

Fine Art Conservation Services, ☎ 914-757-3812. Nancy Wu says, "A truly good conservator has a sensitivity to what you are working with: paper quality, tonal quality, how did the photographer work? She should have good tactile skills, be able to make a good mend, and have an eye for how far to go without intruding on the original piece." Ms. Wu remounted Rita Hayworth's personal photo albums, eliminating the nonarchival material. She has worked on photos by Dorothea Lange, Stieglitz, Moholy-Nagy, and works for Sotheby's, Christie's, the ICP, and is a recommended restorer by many of the museums in NYC. Ms. Wu is in NYC one day a week and meets with clients at the Houk Friedman Gallery, 851 Madison Ave. [70th/71st] ☎ 628-5300, where she charges $75 an hour for a consultation (deductible from the bill if you go forward with the project). If she comes to you, consultations are a minimum of $150 an hour.

COMPUTER RESTORATION

Your photo may be scratched, cracked, scribbled on, hole punched, or otherwise messed up, but with the help of **Final Image,** 2404 Broadway [88th] ☎ 595-7155, an offshoot of West Side Camera, you may wind up with a photo that is miraculously fault-free. Your photo is scanned into a computer and then the type of computer retouching system used by advertising agencies and fashion magazines is put to work. Since the original photo is scanned, it is never touched again and is returned to you. All of the work is done on the computer screen. They can fill in missing areas, correct the color on faded photos, or even put in something that was not there. In some cases, they've been asked to remove people from photographs (mostly ex-husbands, wives, lovers). The service is $150 per hour, and an estimate is given when you bring work in. For $14.95 per page, you can use their Creation Station to make enlargements or copies using a photo—you don't need a negative. The machine can also enhance the sepia and contrast, and you can add text.

MORE Besides Light Impressions at Mr. Galowitz's shop, you can also find archivally safe products at **B & H,** 119 W. 17th St. [6th/7th] ☎ 807-7474. It's **Talas,** 568 Broadway [Prince] ☎ 219-0770, though, that is the specialist: They sell archival material for every conceivable purpose (not just photography). They have many sizes of acid-free storage boxes and proper negative storage envelopes. Their catalog, available for $4, is comprehensive.

SILVER & METAL REPAIR

Brandt & Opis, 46 W. 46th St. [5th/6th] ☎ 302-0294, repairs copper, silver, brass and pewter items, plates gold, silver, and brass, and polishes all metals. They do not work on jewelry. Like most of the other businesses in this article, this is a working shop. Things are lightly coated with the rouge dust from the polishing machines. Replating is done by electroplating. A final polishing is added. Polishing of flatware costs $4 a piece. They will replate old flatware starting at $5 a piece. Minimum labor charge is $25. They sell Hagerty bags and silver-care products. In business since 1955, it's been owned by Roland Markowitz since 1973.

Jean's Silversmiths, 16 W. 45th St. [5th/6th] ☎ 575-0723. This is a treasure trove of silver objects and estate jewelry, specializing in sterling. Cases are crammed with old silver bowls, pitchers, salt and pepper shakers, flatware (organized by manufacturer and pattern), and much else. They polish and remove monograms (when possible), and in general are a good source of information on care of silver. They do not do any plating, but do make repairs (sterling only).

Restoration and Design Studio, 249 E. 77th St. [2nd/3rd] ☎ 517-9742, is run by Paul Karner. He repairs many kinds of objects, but specializes in repairing lighting fixtures in many types of metals, including rewiring. He can recreate missing pieces—old sockets, joints, wooden handles for coffee pots—making the rules to fit the problem at hand. He sends out plating, but does polishing. He also works with brass, bronze, copper, and other metals. Free estimate if you bring in the piece.

Thome Silversmith, 49 W. 37th St. [5th/6th] ☎ 764-5426, has been in business since 1931, and does work for Cartier, Sotheby's and Fortunoff, among others. They do restoration of antique and modern silver pieces. Mr. and Mrs. Routh run the place. They send out engraving and work with someone who lines silver boxes with velvet. Plating and polishing are done on site.

STEREO REPAIR

F & C Electronics, 233 W. 77th St. [Bway/WEA] ☎ 874-7722. They'll repair your stereo, generally within two weeks. Free estimates, but you must bring in and pick up your equipment. They also repair televisions and VCRs.

You can have your stereo repaired by the **Sound Smith** (see VCR repair in this chapter) by taking it to Park Ave. Audio, 425 Park Ave. S. [29th/30th] ☎ 685-8101, or any of the four Harvey Electronic stores (request that it be sent to Sound Smith). Repairs are picked up every Tuesday.

STORAGE

Here are some of the things to keep in mind when you consider storing any of your possessions.

1. *Security of your things.* Do they use a computerized entry system? Are there closed-circuit cameras that record? Alarm and sprinkler systems? Do the guards seem attentive or barely breathing? Theft, flooding, and fire can be serious problems in storage facilities. Given the value of what it is you want to store, does the facility appear adequate? You will need to provide your own padlock and key. Chances are, you can get a less expensive set outside of the storage facility.

2. *Insurance.* The insurance is your responsibility; the storage company is not insured. All the companies will recommend an insurer, but be sure to read the fine print carefully. One insurance policy covers you against theft, fire, and other disasters, *except* for jewelry, furs, money, artwork, documents, flood, or "climatic conditions" like rust or mildew. Check whether the policy covers the replacement cost of goods or their depreciated value. Generally speaking, home owners or tenant's insurance gives you off-premises theft coverage for an amount up to 10% of the value of your policy.

3. *Your own security.* This is more of an issue than you might think. The fact is, many of the city's storage places are not located in highly trafficked areas. If you're going to be needing access at odd hours, keep this in mind.

4. *Space size.* Most people think they need more than they do. A 5 x 5 x 8-foot space (200 cubic feet) can hold a bike, a trunk, a wardrobe, and boxes, and 5 x 10 x 8 feet (400 cubic feet) will hold the contents of a studio apartment.

5. *Temperature.* When we asked an attendant at Chelsea Storage if the building was air conditioned, he said, "It's an old building. It doesn't get hot in the summer." That may be acceptable for storing certain things, but it's not going to be helpful for wine or phonograph records. Some places, Manhattan Mini Storage for one, do have climate control at some locations and on certain floors. It costs more. Most have heat, but ask. Make sure the lighting is adequate.

6. *Cost.* Here's a rough guide of what you can expect to pay at storage facilities around town. In addition to the monthly charge, expect a one-month security charge. A 5 x 5 x 8-foot room averages $75, a 5 x 8 x 10-foot room averages $95.

7. *Hours.* Most places are open 10–12 hours a day. Two Manhattan Mini Storages offer unlimited access, 24 hours a day: one is at Varick and Spring, and the other at W. 29th and 11th Ave.

8. *Access.* You should make sure there are no access charges—that you can enter your space as often as you wish without a fee. Check the parking situation: Are there loading docks where you can load and unload your possessions? How many elevators? Find out if they loan out hand trucks and rolling platforms. They should, and you'll need them.

TIME-SAVING SERVICES

It's Easy, ☎ 586-8880, waits in line for you at the Motor Vehicles Bureau, the Passport office, and at consulates for visas. They expedite learner's permits. When a transaction, such as a first-time passport, requires a personal appearance, they'll make an appointment for you and help keep the waiting time to a minimum. If you have lost a driver's license (personal appearance), they drive you to a DMV office that's less crowded. They also book appointments for road tests at sites in Brooklyn and Yonkers that are less busy. Passport renewal is $35 (plus the $65 for the passport).

Passport Plus, 20 E. 49th St. [5th/Mad] ☎ 759-5540, is another way to avoid hours on line waiting to get a passport renewed (or to get a new one). They also deal with visas and getting duplicate birth, death, and marriage certificates, but only for those filed in the five boroughs. They can help with a driver's license, and you can get a passport photo done right in their office. In addition to the government fees, passport renewals are $50 for a one-week service, $150 for same-day service. Forty-eight hour and next-day service are also available.

Red Tape Cutters ☎ 406-9898. This service will handle just about everything having to do with the DMV, including getting new plates, duplicate titles, car registration (they tell you about documents and signatures needed and will bring you the forms. You return them to the messenger and the whole process can be completed in 24–48 hours). If you have one of the new driver's licenses with a computer image of you and a nine-digit ID number, they can renew your license. Until you get one of these new licenses, you have to appear in person. They also do boat registrations, renew your passport, take care of birth and death certificates, parking and moving violations, and take your car for inspection. If your car is towed, they will check the status of your car with the Parking Violations Bureau. They can retrieve your car about three hours after they check on the status. Fees range from $75 for a simple, nonrush passport renewal to $225 for a complicated tow-job retrieval. (Most towing retrievals are about $100.)

For more help, see Organizers in this chapter.

TYPEWRITER REPAIR

Abalon Office Equipment, 227 Park Ave. [45th/46th] ☎ 682-1653, does repairs, refurbishes old cases, and if they don't have a ribbon, they will get one for you.

Osner Business Machines, 393 Amsterdam Ave. [78th/79th] ☎ 873-8734, repairs manual, electric, and electronic typewriters. They also work on checkwriters and calculators, sell typewriting ribbons and cartridges and calculator paper.

Tytell, 116 Fulton St. [Nassau/William] ☎ 233-5333, will "make up a typewriter in any one of 145 languages," restore old typewriters, and it "carries every ribbon that was ever made."

UPHOLSTERERS

The upholsterers we've listed will all work with individuals who come unaccompanied by an interior designer. They can all do more than upholster a chair or sofa; they can make pillows, curtains, shower curtains, drapes, bedspreads, duvet covers, comforters, headboards, window treatments, valances, swags, balloon and Roman shades, slipcovers, and tablecloths. Most will also do wall upholstery and will arrange for pickup and delivery. This is a labor-intensive business. Everyone has to do this work by hand. The upholsterers here work with Dacron and/or down filling and use staples to hold the fabric to the furniture frame. There are craftsmen who do Old World construction, using webbing, horsehair, and cotton batting padding under the foam, who hand stitch the ticking and hand tack the fabric to the frame. These methods are more expensive, and you will need an interior designer to gain access to the people who use them.

Diamint, 324 E. 59th St. [1st/2nd] ☎ 754-1155, has been in business since 1962, and under the proprietorship of Sylvia and Michael Gonzales for 15 years. They do work for Sotheby's, D & D Building folks, and Asprey, but work happily with individuals. Diamint is a workshop, which means they will help you to get fabric by giving you sources, but they don't sell it—they prefer you to come in with your fabric. They will come to your home for a cost-and-yardage estimate, and they prefer not to pick up your piece until they are ready to work on it. When they pick it up, they will give you a time estimate, often 4–6 weeks, (which is better than many).

Interiors by Robert ☎ 718-641-0815. Robert Boccard upholsters, makes draperies, window treatments, headboards. His work has been featured in many showrooms and designer magazines. The reason many designers especially like him is that his workroom is meticulously clean, an important consideration if you have a fabric that would show dirt. He also works hard to satisfy customers, whether they're designers or not. Mr. Boccard is careful to wrap finished pieces in protective covering. You must have your own fabric, though he will advise on how much to buy. He does pickup and delivery.

Polarolo, 11 E. 12th St. [University/5th] ☎ 255-6260. Richard Polarolo, a third-generation upholsterer, runs this somewhat chaotic shop. The Polarolos have been in business for 70 years, 50 years at this location. He also refinishes wood furniture and does machine and hand caning.

Richard's Interior Design, 1390 Lexington Ave. [91st/92nd] ☎ 831-9000. Richard Harary has more than 25 years experience in decorating and upholstering, including restoration of chairs for Gracie Mansion. He and his staff provide full decorator service: in-home consultations are $200 an hour, but you can bring in Polaroids, measurements, color samples, and the staff will work with you in the store at no cost. Mr. Harary imports directly from some European mills in an effort to keep down the cost. He has many brocades, mohair velvet, and jacquards as well as prints. Aware of some of the problems of NYC living, he upholsters walls, which has the additional benefits of reducing noise and helping insulation. Drapes can be lined with soundproof lining. Emphasis here is on service.

Versailles Drapery and Upholstery, 37 E. 18th St. [Bway/Park Ave So.] ☎ 533-2059, is a large loft studio crammed with fabrics and furniture waiting their turn. The three Fischer brothers who run the place have been in the business for over 30 years. Customers include Sotheby's and Hirschl and Adler. It's a workroom—not a showroom or a decorator service. If you bring in your own fabric, they will work with you. In some cases, though, if you know the pattern number and mill, they are willing to order it for you. They'll give you a general price quote on the phone and will make a house call to give you a more precise quote and advise on fabric quantity. Not the place if you're in a rush.

MORE Monte Coleman, 49 E. 10th St. [University/Bway] ☎ 995-2649. While, technically, he doesn't do upholstery, he does do marvelous slipcovers and drapes. You must have your own fabric. His slipcovers are contemporary, fresh, and slick, but there is a lot of old-fashioned attention to detail: He puts hem trims in by hand. He has been featured frequently in design magazines, and does much work for top design team Patino-Wolf. (But he'll do a job as small as a pillow.)

VCR REPAIR & HELP

REPAIR

We wondered why VCRs break down so much these days and why getting them repaired can be such a problem. **The Sound Smith,** located upstate, is run by Peter Ledermann. He understands VCRs better than almost anyone—which is why the Harvey Electronics stores send many VCRs to him for repair. Mr. Ledermann says, "Once, VCRs were expensive and well built." A machine that cost $700 before 1986 would now cost well over $1,000. VCRs today are often in the $200–$300 range, and with the decline in price came a decline in quality. That's why they break down as much as they do. "Each machine," he says, "can have hundreds of parts. Many of the parts are plastic, even in the expensive machines." But it's the design errors that are most responsible for problems. So, instead of replacing a badly designed part that will likely break again, Mr. Ledermann often creates new parts or makes modifications so the machine will work longer and "not end up in landfill." Most VCR problems are mechanical, and, in any case, mechanical problems have to be fixed first before you can determine if the other sections are working and the condition of the head or the circuitry. So, when you get a "free estimate," Mr. Ledermann says, the person is often giving you the worst-case estimate and playing the odds that he will be covered. If the work costs less, they're ahead. Your machine can be serviced by Mr. Ledermann by taking it to any of the four Harvey's in the city (you can request that it be sent to him). There's a one-year guarantee.

Nick Veltri at **American Video Service,** 516 Amsterdam Ave. [85th] ☎ 724-4870, has been repairing electronic components since 1978 and sees this new generation of machines as a devolution. They are now so lightweight that most of the repairs brought to him are because the machines have fallen off the top of the television when a tape was inserted. He does most repairs on home machines for $59.95, which includes parts, labor, and a cleaning. There is a three-month guarantee on parts and labor.

HELP

VCRs may be the worst designed best idea in history, but there are people who can help. **Aaron Brown,** ☎ 201-743-7267, will consult with you about which machines to buy, install them, integrate your television and audio systems, and instruct you in how to use them. $50–$75 an hour.

Suzanne Langenwalter of **Jill of All Trades,** ☎ 228-7084, (see more in Handy Persons in the Home Renovation & Repairs article in this chapter) will connect and program your VCR for you.

WATCH & CLOCK REPAIR

Aaron Faber, 666 Fifth Ave. [53rd] ☎ 586-8411, has a service and restoration department for any vintage watch. One-year warranty.

Time Will Tell, 962 Madison Ave. [75th/76th] ☎ 861-2663, gives a year-and-a-day guarantee on their repairs. Opinions and repair estimates are free. They have a large selection of replacement watchbands.

Time Pieces, 115 Greenwich Ave. [Jane/Horatio] ☎ 929-8011. Warranty of two years for clocks and one year for watches. Quartz watches and clocks, six-month warranty.

SPIRITS

<—————————————————————————>

BARS

A list of favorite bars, watering holes, pubs, lounges, locals, and other places to meet, talk, argue, catch up, drink, smoke, contemplate, or just be gloriously in your cups.

ALL STATE CAFE

Down the steps into the **All State Cafe,** 250 W. 72nd St. [Bway/WEA] ☎ 874-1883, you are enveloped in that old-style fug of bar, restaurant, smoke, fireplace, and years of conversation. That it's not a destination bar adds immeasurably to its appeal. It's just a small den of comfort to those who know about it, who are happy to occupy a bar stool or stand by the fireplace and slake their thirst before returning to the world outside.

ANGEL'S SHARE

When whiskey ages for many years, nearly one-third of it evaporates, and this evaporated portion of it is known as the "angel's share." It's also the name of a magical small bar. You get to **Angel's Share,** 8 Stuyvesant St. [3rd Ave.] ☎ 777-5415, by climbing the stairs to a Japanese restaurant, taking a left at the top of the stairs, and entering the unmarked door. Within, an attractive small space, Raphaelesque angels on a mural over the bar, a few tables, and perhaps 10 seats at the bar. The young bartenders mix drinks with a delicacy, precision, and ritual that is captivating. No drink is served without a small dram spooned onto the back of the bartender's hand for a taste of their own handiwork. They have a nice, small wine list, but most people come for their martinis, frozen cocktails (excellent), and a list of over 40 single malt Scotches. There are windows over the street life below but, for once, the view is considerably less compelling than the show behind the bar.

BAR D'O

A bar to insinuate yourself into—the olive-colored baize (at least that's how it looks, but it's too dark to be sure) couches and ottomans encourage lounging, and the candles cast the room more in intrigue than romance. Performances some nights (Joey Arias channels on Tues., Sat., and Sun. at 10:30). A downtown mixed crowd with minimal attitude. A useful prototype for the neighborhood bar of the future. **Bar D'O,** 29 Bedford St. [Downing] ☎ 627-1580.

BEMELMANS BAR

The Carlyle Hotel, 35 E. 76th St. [Mad/Park] ☎ 744-1600, more than any other landmark that comes to mind, neatly sums up the Upper East Side. What better way to soak up that atmosphere than sitting at the **Bemelmans Bar,** enjoying Ludwig Bemelmans's murals, sipping a cocktail, and perhaps listening to Barbara Carroll. One of those places where you feel nothing could ever go wrong.

CUB ROOM

The bar at the **Cub Room,** 131 Sullivan St. [Prince] ☎ 677-4100, isn't a place we like much during prime time, since the charms of the room get overwhelmed by the crowds. But come off peak, nestle into the furniture, and enjoy the many attractive features of the room. Order one of the well-made cocktails, sit by the illuminated globe, and watch the world pass in front of the full-length bay windows on Prince St.

D.B.A.

d.b.a., 41 First Ave. [2nd/3rd] ☎ 475-5097. When so much passion goes into procuring the best beers in the world and serving them properly, the results can only be a beer lover's paradise, which d.b.a. certainly is. In addition to the brews, d.b.a. has a formidable collection of other spirits: single malt Scotch, tequilas, and bourbons. See more in the Beer article in this chapter.

GLOBAL 33

Global 33, 93 Second Ave. [5th/6th] ☎ 477-8427, is a jigger of Saarinen, a dash of James Bond, the fizz of the East Village. This

The scene at Global 33.

is not a place to go when you're looking for solace, since everyone else will be having a buzzing good time. This is a place to go to when life is treating you well and you're with friends and several cosmopolitans would only improve matters. That the inexpensive tapas are also delicious makes it a place where you can pass the better part of an evening enjoying the food, the excellent cocktails, and an agreeable mix of mostly downtown types.

KEENS

There was a time, perhaps, in Keens's long history (it opened in 1885), when people came here simply for the nostalgia of it. The bar at **Keens,** 72 W. 36th St. [5th/6th] ☎ 947-3636, though, is such a good one, that you can simply ignore all the history and enjoy it as the excellent and vibrant place that it is. Keeping an eye on things at all times is Miss Keens, as she lies naked, thoughtful, draped over a lion's head rug. Keens attracts a wide variety of types to its quarters, including many regulars, and certainly one of the allures is the over 70 single malt Scotches that are available. They also have their own ale, light and somewhat fruity, made for them by New Amsterdam.

KING COLE BAR

It always comes back to the ingredients, and **The King Cole Bar** at The St. Regis Hotel, Fifth Ave. and 55th St. ☎ 753-4500, has perfect ones—it would be hard to find a better bar in the city. Looming over the small, attractive, wood-paneled room is the Maxfield Parrish mural (1906). Look behind the bar and you'll see everything is just so. There are small bowls of nuts and chips, and the bartenders periodically plop down little boxes of matches. Stand there with your coat draped over your arm and someone will offer to check it. Drinks are expertly poured (they're expensive), and whether you sit at the bar or at one of the tightly packed tables, you will certainly contemplate your next visit and leave stirred, not shaken.

MOLLY'S

We like the Irish bar **Molly's,** 287 Third Ave. [22nd/23rd] ☎ 889-3361, because it's one of the few places in the city where you can order a fine pint of Guinness and drink it standing in front of a wood-burning fireplace. Stay for a few rounds, for the simple Irish fare in the restaurant, and let Molly's work some of its Irish charm. You'll see the word *shebeen* on the outside of the place. This means, roughly, a speakeasy. It's a seductive come-on.

Ñ

Lacking distinguishing architectural features (unless polka-dot walls qualify), **Ñ,** 33 Crosby St. [Broome/Grand] ☎ 219-8856, nevertheless falls easily into our list of favorite bars, but we're hard-pressed to say exactly why. It's a small and narrow, fairly dark place on quiet Crosby St. Perhaps we like it because people who are here haven't just stumbled in—they like the place. That helps. So does the excellent sangria and agreeable staff. Tapas are there if you're hungry. Perhaps it's that Ñ is so *unforced* that we always have a good time here—exactly what you want from a bar.

OLD TOWN

The owners of the **Old Town,** 45 E. 18th St. [Bway/Park Ave. S.] ☎ 529-6732, have done a lot to keep this 1892 bar looking as good as old. The room is double height, with the requisite tin ceilings, the equally requisite massive bar, tile floor, and stout (Murphy's) on tap. The men's room, famous for the large urinals, has been redone more to the period, and they plan to replace the concrete in front with bluestone. Time travel doesn't get any easier or more pleasant.

PALIO

Palio, 151 W. 51st St. [6th/7th] ☎ 245-4850. A stark modern cube to which the Sandro Chia mural adds immeasurably to the room's character and unique vibes. You can sit at one of the few tables scattered around the room's periphery or at the horseshoe-shaped bar. Peo-

The bar at Palio.

CHRISTOPHER LOVI

ple smoke cigars or tuck in for a plate of pasta or just unwind. Have a glass of one of the excellent open Italian wines—an Amarone, perhaps—and you've found the spot for a superb nightcap.

PENINSULA BAR

You need to work a bit to get to the **Peninsula Bar** at the Peninsula Hotel, 700 Fifth Ave. [55th] ☎ 247-2200, through various hallways, elevators, and flights of stairs but at least a couple of things make it worth it. The bar itself is a fairly standard-issue hotel bar, but when the weather's fine, step out onto the small balcony facing north or go out onto the larger terrace and enjoy the full sweep of Fifth Avenue north to south.

RAINBOW PROMENADE BAR

The **Rainbow Promenade Bar,** 30 Rockefeller Plaza [49th/50th] ☎ 632-5000, offers the panorama of the city we love, plus superb classic and newly invented cocktails. Even though he's no longer behind the bar, Dale DeGroff oversees the Promenade's cocktail menu. See more on Mr. DeGroff in this chapter under Cocktails.

THE ROOM

The Room, 144 Sullivan St. [Houston/ Prince] ☎ 477-2102. A two-room bar, simple and modern—one room being the bar proper and the other set up with chairs, tables, and couches. The owner sees to it that this is a very welcoming place, and since he doesn't offer food, if you're hungry, he'll hand you a stack of take-out menus and encourage you to order in.

ROYALTON ROUND BAR

The **Royalton Round Bar,** 44 W. 44th St. [5th/6th] ☎ 869-4400, the circular, inti-

mate, blue-padded pouf of a bar, serves mostly vodka and champagne. That it's somewhat hidden adds to its allure.

SPLASH

Splash, 50 W. 17th St. [5th/6th] ☎ 691-0073, is certainly the most popular gay bar in town. While we don't think there is a single great gay bar in the city, we'd pick Splash, along with **Barracuda,** 275 W. 22nd St. [7th/8th] ☎ 645-8613, more of a neighborhood bar with a lounge in the back, and the stylish **Rome,** 298 Eighth Ave. [24th/25th] ☎ 242-6969, as favorites. For lesbian bars, **Crazy Nanny's,** 21 Seventh Ave. South [Leroy/Carmine] ☎ 366-6312, **Henrietta Hudson,** 438 Hudson St. [Morton] ☎ 924-3347, and **Julie's,** 204 E. 58th St. [2nd/3rd] ☎ 688-1294.

TEMPLE BAR

We love the **Temple Bar,** 332 Lafayette St. [Bleecker/Houston] ☎ 925-4242, but one more drop of attitude and we swear we won't go back. We'd miss, though, the pretty bar and the lounge with its spots of light and the house's decent cocktails.

WALKER'S

You probably could have won a bet with Stanford White. Which will be around longer, you say to him, your Madison Square Garden (designed in 1890 and built in 1892) or Walker's, this sweet little tavern near the Ninth Ave. El? Easy money. **Walker's,** 16 N. Moore St. [Varick] ☎ 941-0142, which opened in 1890, continues to offer libations in a low-key, old New York atmosphere that remains stubbornly (thank goodness) resistant to signs of hip or change.

BEER

A rundown of the town's top taps and brew purveyors.

WHERE TO BUY

B & E, 511 W. 23rd St. [10th]
☎ 243-6812. This is the best place in Manhattan to buy beer. Absolutely incredible variety and some bottles we haven't seen anywhere else on the island.

Dean & DeLuca, 560 Broadway [Prince] ☎ 221-7714, has special German beers and a good selection of microbreweries.

Fancy Grocery, Bleecker and Christopher, no phone. Overrun with bottles. An amazing selection.

Pioneer, 289 Columbus Ave. [74th] ☎ 874-9506. Not as good as it once was, but a large selection of bottles.

Grill Beverage, 350 West St. [Houston] ☎ 463-7171, does keg delivery.

BARS, BREWERIES, AND RESTAURANTS

T: Tap **B:** Bottles (Some taps change frequently.)

UPTOWN

Bear Bar, 2156 Broadway [75th]
☎ 362-2145 **T:** 6 **B:** 130.

Carnegie Hill Brewery, 1600 Third Ave. [90th] ☎ 369-0808 **T:** 6.

Kinsale Tavern, 1672 Third Ave. [94th] ☎ 348-4370 **T:** 35 (incl. Fuller's ESB and the Belgian Hoegaarden White) **B:** 116.

Ruby's Taphouse, 1752 Second Ave. [91st] ☎ 987-8179 **T:** 26 **B:** 20. The taps change according to the season: Maibock, Weizen, etc.

West Side Brewing, 340 Amsterdam Ave. [76th] ☎ 721-2161 **T:** 6 brewed on site.

Yorkville Brewery, 1359 First Ave. [73rd] ☎ 517-2739 **T:** 4 seasonal beers.

MIDTOWN

American Festival Cafe, 20 W. 50th St. [5th/6th] ☎ 332-7620 **T:** 2 **B:** 20. They do monthly beer dinners.

Armstrong's Saloon, 875 Tenth Ave. [57th] ☎ 581-0606 **T:** 12 (incl. Sam Smith's Oatmeal Stout) **B:** 10.

Bull and Bear, Lexington and 49th St. ☎ 872-4900 **T:** 4 (New Amsterdam makes a special Bull and Bear ale for them) **B:** 18.

Cafe Centro Beer Bar, 200 Park Ave. [45th] ☎ 818-1333 **T:** 10 (incl. a guest tap of the week) **B:** 29. Generally, a beer dinner a month.

Charlton's, 922 Third Ave. [55th] ☎ 688-4646 **T:** 6 **B:** 30.

East Side Alehouse, 961 Second Ave. [51st] ☎ 752-3615 **T:** 16 (Catamount, Park Slope, Harpoon, Sierra Nevada) **B:** 50 (all domestic microbreweries). A sampling called "Surf the Taps" gets you four 4-oz. glasses for $5. They "proudly do not serve Bud, Coors, or Miller."

Frico Bar, 402 W. 43rd St. [9th] ☎ 564-7272 **T:** 11.

Ginger Man, 11 E. 36th St. [5th/Mad] ☎ 532-3740 **T:** 66 **B:** 120. Beers from Belgium, the Czech Republic, England, Germany, Scotland, Slovakia, and the U.S.A., including some of the rarer Belgian and German wheats and bocks.

Jekyll & Hyde, 1409 Sixth Ave. [57th/58th] ☎ 541-9505 **T:** 24 **B:** 220.

Jimmy Walker's, 245 E. 55th St.
[2nd/3rd] ☎ 319-6650 **T:** 15 **B:** 10.

Joe Allen, 326 W. 46th St. [8th/9th]
☎ 581-6464 **T:** 8 **B:** 45.

Landmark Tavern, 626 Eleventh Ave.
[46th] ☎ 757-8595 **T:** 7 (incl. Murphy's Irish Stout and McSorley's Ale and Double Dark) **B:** 4.

Maggie's Place, 21 E. 47th St. [Mad]
☎ 753-5757 **T:** 15 **B:** 4.

Manchester NY, 920 Second Ave. [48th]
☎ 223-7484 **T:** 18 (incl. Fuller's London Pride and ESB) **B:** 45.

Stock and Tankard, 587 Third Ave.
[38th] ☎ 661-3181 **T:** 24 (all American micros).

Typhoon Brewery, 22 E. 54th St.
[5th/Mad] ☎ 754-9006 **T:** 12 (from brewmaster Lou Farrell) **B:** 24.

DOWNTOWN

Boxer's, 190 W. 4th St. [6th/7th]
☎ 633-2275 **T:** 12 **B:** 15.

Burp Castle, 41 E. 7th St. [2nd/3rd] no phone **T:** 9 **B:** 60.

RAY DETER OF D.B.A.

Ray Deter tasted cask-conditioned ale for the first time on his honeymoon in England. "For the first time I was drinking real beer." He was so enthusiastic that his wife gave him a home-brewing kit. Impressed by how easy it was to produce good quality beer at home, he joined the NYC Homebrewer's Guild, "which is fertile ground for many professionals in the NYC beer scene," and he became "more and more fanatical." When his friend Dennis Zentek asked him to open a bar with him, though, he resisted, unsure that a bar that specialized in quality beers would work. His wife encouraged him to quit his "mundane, horrible job in litigation management" on Wall Street, and d.b.a. opened in October of 1994. Mr. Deter says, "We hedged our bets. We put Coors Light on one of the taps." The real mission, Mr. Deter says, is to look "for the best beers available in the world" to attach to his 14 taps. Freshness is a criterion, although not the only one, since "it's possible to have a fresh beer that doesn't taste very good." He takes Belgian beers whenever possible, like Rodenbach or Boonkriek Ale. You might find Liberty Ale from San Francisco, ("a world-class beer") or Old Thumper ESB from the Shipyard Brewery in Maine. Guinness is a staple. Cask-conditioned ales are on two of the hand taps. English or English-style brews are always represented by selections like Bateman's XXXB, Fuller's ESB, Young's Oatmeal Stout, or Young's Ramrod. Four of the taps are hand taps from England. This means that the beer is pumped by hand into the glass instead of being forced from the keg by carbon dioxide gas. When the taps arrived from England they came in pieces with no instructions. It took a plumber, a cabinetmaker, Garrett Oliver—the brewmaster of Brooklyn Brewery—and Mr. Deter to put it all together again. Mr. Deter has an eye for rare bottled beers, such as a vintage 1986 Framboise Boon Lembeek or a Lindeman's Cuvée René (an aged gueze). Bad bottles he's tasted? A beer flavored with white chocolate. There are regular tasting evenings at d.b.a. And they still have a cask of Coors Light in the basement that they don't think they'll be needing.

Bridge Cafe, 279 Water St. [Dover]
☎ 227-3344 **T:** 6 **B:** 10.
Broome St. Bar, 363 W. Broadway
[Broome] ☎ 925-2086 **T:** 8 **B:** 24.
Cafe de Bruxelles, 118 Greenwich Ave.
[13th] ☎ 206-1830 **B:** 20 Belgian beers.
C3, 103 Waverly Pl. [MacDougal]
☎ 254-1200 **T:** one monthly selection
B: 11. They do a series of beer dinners
(5 beers with 5 courses).
Chelsea Brewing Co., Pier 59, 18th St.
and the Hudson River in the Chelsea
Piers complex. ☎ 336-6440. **T:** 6 (pale
ale, wheat raspberry, nut brown, red,
blonde with seasonal variations) **B:** 0.
Chumley's, 86 Bedford [Barrow]
☎ 675-4449 **T:** 23 (all domestic
micros).
d.b.a., 41 First Ave. [2nd/3rd] ☎ 475-
5097 **T:** 14 **B:** 80 bottles.
Gramercy Tavern, 42 E. 20th St.
[Bway/Park Ave. S.] ☎ 477-0777
T: 8 (domestic micros) **B:** 11.
Greenwich Pizza and Brewing, 418 Sixth
Ave. [9th] ☎ 477-8744 **T:** 12 **B:** 80–90.
Heartland Brewery, 35 Union Square
West [16th/17th] ☎ 645-3400 Brew-
master Jim Migliorini does six brews.
Jekyll & Hyde, 91 Seventh Ave. South
[Barrow/Grove] ☎ 255-5388 **T:** 24
B: 220.
Jeremy's Ale House, 254 Front St.
☎ 964-3537 [Peck Slip/South] **T:** 17.
Knitting Factory, 74 Leonard St. [Bway/
Church] ☎ 219-3055 **T:** 18 **B:** 12.
McGovern's, 305 Spring St. [Green-
wich/Hudson] ☎ 243-8804 **T:** 6 **B:** 25.
Nacho Mama's Brewery, 40-42 Thompson
St. [Broome] ☎ 925-8966 **T:** 6 brewed
on site. Three of the taps have cask-
conditioned ales.

North Star, 93 South St. [Fulton]
☎ 509-6757 **T:** 8 (incl. Newcastle Brown
Ale and McEwan's Export) **B:** 14.
Patria, 250 Park Ave. South [20th]
☎ 777-6211 **B:** 13–15 varieties of
Central and South American beers.
Peculier Pub, 145 Bleecker St. [6th/
Bway] ☎ 353-1327 **T:** 12 **B:** over 420.
Pugsley's, 85 West St. [Washington/
Albany] in the Marriott Financial
☎ 385-4900 **T:** 10 (all micros, mostly
from nearby microbreweries).
riverrun 176 Franklin St. [Greenwich/
Hudson] ☎ 966-3894 **T:** 15 **B:** 10.
The Room, 144 Sullivan St. [Houston/
Prince] ☎ 477-2102 **T:** 6 **B:** 35.
Silver Swan, 41 E. 20th St. [Bway/Park]
☎ 254-3611 **T:** 8 **B:** 93 (mostly imports
with the emphasis on German, includ-
ing 15 weizens).
Slaughtered Lamb, 182 W. 4th St.
[Barrow/Jones] ☎ 627-5262 **T:** 12
B: 90.
Water Club, 500 E. 30th St. [E. River]
☎ 683-3333 **T:** 2 **B:** 20.
Z Bar, 206 Ave. A [13th] ☎ 982-9173
T: 13 **B:** 40.
Zip City, 3 W. 18th St. [5th/6th] ☎ 366-
6333. Three brews at a time.

HOME BREWING

Little Shop of Hops, 9 E. 37th St.
[5th/Mad] ☎ 685-8334 and 79 New St.
[Beaver] ☎ 952-4374.
Milan Labs, 57 Spring St. [Lafayette/
Mulberry] ☎ 226-4780.

CLUBS

If you want to join the **Beer Bar Club,**
stop in at the Beer Bar at Cafe Centro and

complete a form. This gets you their newsletter, *Brews News,* with event info . . . The **NYC Homebrewers Guild** meets on the third Tues. of every month at Brews, 156 E. 34th St. [Lex/3rd] ☎ 889-3369.

BYO WINE

When you want to bring a bottle of wine to a meal in a restaurant (we're talking about fine restaurants that have a liquor license), it should be a special occasion and a special bottle of wine. It is a good idea, at least, to call ahead—some restaurants insist on it. Some restaurants will allow you to bring the wine only if it's not on their list. In spite of what some restaurateurs say, it *is* legal to bring a wine to a restaurant that has a liquor license and for them to charge a corkage fee. No restaurant, however, is *required* to allow you to do so, and if they permit you to bring a bottle, it is as a courtesy. We asked Danny Meyer, owner of Union Square Cafe and Gramercy Tavern, for his advice on tipping under these circumstances. He suggests tipping on the value of a wine you would have ordinarily ordered. Below are some of the top restaurants that, with varying degrees of enthusiasm, will permit you to bring a bottle of wine in. Call first! (The price following the restaurant is the corkage fee based on each 750 ml bottle. If you are well known to the restaurant, other rules may apply.)

An American Place, $15.
Arcadia, $10–$15.
Aureole, $35.
Bolo, $15.
Bouley, $28.
Cafe des Artistes, $10.
Chanterelle, $25.
Four Seasons, $10.
Gotham Bar and Grill, $18.
Gramercy Tavern, $15.
Hudson River Club, $15.
Jo Jo, $25.
La Caravelle, $20.
Lespinasse, $30.
Montrachet, $15–$25.
Oceana, $14.
Remi, $10.
Tribeca Grill, $15–$25.
Union Square Cafe, $15.
Vong, $15.

COCKTAILS

"One of sour, two of sweet, three of strong, four of weak." That's a Colonial American recipe for a good cocktail that Dale DeGroff, for many years the Head Bartender and now Beverage Director of The Rainbow Room, likes to quote. "This still works out pretty well" as a guide when he is making up new cocktail recipes. Mr. DeGroff devises at least two cocktail menus each year for The Rainbow Room. Each menu is a combination of classic cocktails and his own inventions. He has a library of cocktail recipe books that he consults, looking for drinks that "have a dramatic name (like Blood and Sand), have stood the test of time, and that taste delicious." The Snowball, which he had on the menu during the winter of 1996, "is a very old recipe, and the combination (white rum, sugar, egg white, and ginger ale) is delicious." When he came across The American Beauty Cocktail, he thought the combination of ingredients (brandy, sweet vermouth, dry vermouth, port, and orange) didn't sound at all promising—until he mixed himself one. Now it is one of the most requested cocktails at Rainbow. Challenged once by a customer bored with gin and tonic to come up with a new gin drink, Mr. De-Groff devised the Fitzgerald, a combination of gin, lemon juice, Angostura bitters, and syrup. Mr. DeGroff plans and oversees occasional martini events and an annual cocktail dinner—five courses are paired with five different cocktails.

COCKTAIL SHAKERS

Vintage shakers can be found at **Chartreuse,** 309 E. 9th St. [1st/2nd] ☎ 254-8477. There are some with a glass shaker imprinted with recipes for things like Highballs and Old Fashioneds, as well as more elegant glass and metal shakers. Prices range from $28–$40

. . . **Moss,** 146 Greene St. [Houston/Prince] ☎ 226-2190, can be relied on for the Arne Jacobsen stainless steel martini set designed in 1967. The 40-oz. mixer comes with a strainer and a spoon. Murray Moss says, "It was an inventive use of stainless steel at the time—both technically and aesthetically." The set is still made in Denmark and costs $115.

CORDIALS & CIGARS

We asked our friends at *Wine Spectator* and *Cigar Aficionado* magazines to give us some suggestions for good after-dinner combinations, which they were kind enough to do: **Fonseca 20 year tawny port** with a **Fonseca 10-10 cigar.** Dominican Republic tobacco, Churchill-size, it has medium body with a mellow, long flavor. $4.75 each, box of 24: $102.60. At Arnold's. The Fonseca is $45 at Morrell . . . **Booker Noe Single Barrel Bourbon** varies in proof because it's bottled from individual casks. It's full-bodied, big, bold, and robust. Pair it with **Arturo Fuente Don Carlos Reserva** in the robusto size. The sweetness of the Cameroon wrapper matches the sweetness in the bourbon. They come and go fast, so reserve at Arnold's, $7.50 each, box of 25: $180. The bourbon is $43.99 at Union Square Wines . . . **Dalwhinnie single malt Scotch** ($33.90 at USW) comes from the highest elevation of a distillery in Scotland. It is an elegant and light-bodied malt. The **Davidoff Special T** is Dominican Republic tobacco in a Connecticut wrapper. The torpedo shape is a benchmark for skilled cigarmakers because it is so difficult to roll. Cigar smokers believe it delivers the most mouth-filling flavor by the nature of its design, without having the Churchill size. This cigar is a medium body, complex smoke. At Arnold's, they're $10.30 each, box of 20: $195.70 . . . **Bacardi Spe-**

cial Reserve Rum is a golden, aged, sipping rum. The **La Gloria Cubana Medaille D'Or #1** comes from a famous Miami cigarmaker who blends a truly smooth cigar with the finest tobacco from the Caribbean and South America. It has the classic Lonsdale shape. You must reserve at Arnold's, which gets them in three times a year. Box of 25: $75. The rum is $16.99 at USW . . . The **Hine Antique Cognac** ($75 at USW) and a **Macanudo Vintage #5.** A corona gorda size, it's smooth and mild with delicate nuances that won't fight with the subtle aromatics of the brandy. At JR, they're $8.25 each, box of 20: $119.95 . . . **Bonny Doon's Muscat Canelli Vin de Glacière** and an **Avo XO Intermezzo.** Another corona gorda size with a full-flavored, round, balanced taste made with aged tobacco and a Colorado shade Connecticut wrapper. At Arnold's, $7.75 each, box of 25: $178.10. The Bonny Doon is $15.99 at USW . . . **Chateau Suduiraut Sauterne** and a **Padron Anniversary Series Diplomatico.** It's a Churchill made with vintage Nicaraguan tobacco. This is a limited-production cigar with a rare combination of full body and finesse. Arnold's suggests reserving for these, $7.05 each, box of 25: $161.50. At Acker Merrall, the 1988 is $47.50, the 1975 is $110. ☞ Acker Merrall, 160 W. 72nd St. [Columbus/Amsterdam] ☎ 787-1700. Arnold's, 323 Madison Ave. [42nd/43rd] ☎ 697-1477, JR Tobacco, 11 E. 45th [5th/ Mad]. Morrell, 535 Madison Ave. [54th] ☎ 688-9370. USW = Union Square Wines, 33 Union Square W. [16th/17th] ☎ 675-8100.

PORT

For the casual Port drinker (serious Port fans usually have a preference for one of the top vintage producer's house styles and won't look far afield), here are some thoughts from wine and spirits expert Paul Pacult, publisher of the *Spirit Journal,* on some good alternatives to vintage Ports. (Mr. Pacult holds about 10 Port tastings a year. He can be hired by private groups to conduct tastings of Ports or other spirits. If you want the *Spirit Journal,* it's $49 a year. Write 421-13 Rte. 59, Monsey, NY, 10952.)

GOOD DEALS "We are in a buyer's market for Port right now. Sales have been down and prices have been reduced to move volume out of stuffed warehouses," according to Mr. Pacult. Here are some of his Port picks with a high dollar-to-taste ratio: **Taylor Fladgate First Estate Vintage Character** for $13.99 at Astor Wines, 12 Astor Pl. [Lafayette] ☎ 674-7500. Vintage character means the Port, unlike a vintage Port from a single year, is a blend of different Ports from different vintages. These are usually not the "crème de la crème" of each vintage, but should be blended to give a "good solid Port" at a good price . . . **Cockburn Fine Ruby Port** is a "good place to begin"— $8.99 at Garnet, 929 Lexington Ave. [68th/69th] ☎ 772-3211. **Dow Vintage Character** "is an excellent value—one of the best." It's $14.99 at Garnet. **Sandeman's Founders Reserve** is another vintage character that he recommends. It's $10.99 at Garnet . . . Mr. Pacult points out that the aged tawnies are often overlooked. **Taylor Fladgate Special Tawny** is "aged in wood and develops a woody flavor." It's $10.95 at Sherry-Lehmann, 679 Madison Ave. [61st/62nd] ☎ 838-7500 . . . The **Delaforce Aged Tawny** His Eminence's Choice is "one of the top ten Port values." $9.99 a half bottle at Crossroads, 55 W. 14th [5th/6th] ☎ 924-3060.

CALIFORNIA "Port snobs are sniffing at the California Ports, but they are missing out," says Mr. Pacult. Two names to consider: **Ficklin Vineyards** makes a Tinta Port that is "superb" at $9.99, as well as the occasional vintage Port. They use the same grape varieties used in Portugal. Sample their wares at Washington Square Wines, 545 LaGuardia Pl. [Bleecker/W. 3rd] ☎ 477-4395. $5.99 for half bottles of the Tinta. You can find the vintage Ficklin at Carnegie Spirits, 849 Seventh Ave. [54th/55th] ☎ 477-4395 . . . **Windsor Vineyards** does mail order only, but many consider their nonvintage Port a steal. Call ☎ 800-204-9463. The three-bottle minimum, including tax and shipping, comes to just over $43.

WHERE TO DRINK **Il Buco,** 47 Bond St. [Bowery/Lafayette] ☎ 533-1932, has 7 Ports by the glass . . . **Keens,** 72 W. 36th St. [5th/6th] ☎ 947-3636, has 12 different vintage Ports, sold by the bottle, from a $75 Graham 1983 to a $325 Taylor 1963 . . . **The North Star Pub,** 93 South St. [Fulton] ☎ 509-6757, has 7 by the glass . . . **Union Square Cafe,** 21 E. 16th [5th/Union Sq. W.] ☎ 243-4020, has 7 Ports by the glass, including a Warre '75 for $14 . . . **Zoë,** 90 Prince St. [Bway/Mercer] ☎ 966-6722, also has 7 Ports by the glass, and if you ask, they will arrange an individual tasting for you.

SINGLE MALT SCOTCH

We asked single malt Scotch experts Gary Regan and Mardee Haidin Regan, authors of *The Book of Bourbon and Other Fine American Whiskies,* Chapters Publishers, to tell us about their list of favorite single malts. We follow their suggestions with a few places of where to taste and where to buy.

BY GARY REGAN AND
MARDEE HAIDIN REGAN
"Recommend your favorite malts," the man said, "between five and ten bottlings." But the beauty of single malt Scotch is that it's easy to have a very legitimate twenty favorites, each for a different time of day, a different climate, a different occasion. So, instead of our ten absolute favorites (which would tax us horribly), we will recommend eleven great single malt Scotches—since we couldn't bear to leave any one of these bottlings out—that represent different Scotch-producing regions and different styles within the regions.

ISLAY (EYE-LUH) Lagavulin: This 16-year-old malt is very dry, extremely peaty, and full of the flavors of the sea. It's not a beginner's malt, but it is one for which there is no known substitute. Sip a dram after dinner with a fine cigar ($39.95 at Crossroads—all prices are for 750 ml.) . . . **Laphroaig** (LA-froyg): The 15-year-old bottling is an intense example of the medicinal/sea air Islay-style of malt that's not quite as harsh as its 10-year-old brother. Sip it with a tiny splash of water after a long walk in cold weather in front of a roaring radiator ($48.99 at Garnet) . . . **Bowmore:** The 17- 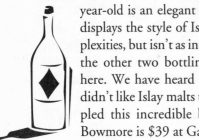 year-old is an elegant Islay malt that displays the style of Islay in its complexities, but isn't as intensely peaty as the other two bottlings mentioned here. We have heard of people who didn't like Islay malts until they sampled this incredible bottling. (The Bowmore is $39 at Garnet.)

CAMPBELTOWN Springbank: The 21-year-old bottling is a great example of a Campbeltown style. Look for the saltwater characteristics that define this region, along with sherry and caramel in the palate ($99.95 at Soho Wines).

HIGHLANDS Glenmorangie (glen-MOR-ngy): The 18-year-old is one of the finest complex Highland Malts on the market. The light, flowery, peppery style of this distillery is very distinctive, and in this particular bottling, the malt has gathered a variety of spices and fruits—look for blackcurrant, you'll find it. Sip the 10-year-old before dinner, and save the 18-year-old for postprandial fireside chats ($34.99 at Garnet) . . . The **Macallan** 18-year-old is a Highland Malt with a style all its own. Aged entirely in Sherry casks, this malt is smooth, rich, and has a way of reminding one of candy apples and cassis. Another great after-dinner malt ($43.99 at Garnet) . . . **Highland Park** is distilled on the island of Orkney, but is considered a Highland malt. This whiskey offers the smoky/briny characteristic of island malts and the toffee/heathery/honey sweetness usu-

ally associated with the heavier Highland whiskies. Perfect for all occasions ($35 at Soho Wines) . . . **Longmorn:** Fairly new on the market, this incredibly complex 15-year-old malt is full of light aromatics—new-mown grass, wildflowers—and a light dusting of highland peat. The finish is extremely long and elegantly dry ($46.99 at Crossroads) . . . **Oban:** At 14 years old, this malt is the definitive representative of the Western Highlands, and it is surely one of the world's most versatile whiskies. The nose offers a gentle breeze of bracing sea air, and its complex palate displays a hint of peat and hints of orange zest. Here's a bottling that we love to turn people on to—it hasn't failed us yet ($31.99 at Garnet).

LOWLAND Auchentoshan (OK-en-TOSH-en) is a prime example of a Lowland malt—light, clean, and crisp. This whiskey is a wonderful apéritif or mixed 50/50 with water, and is a good drink for a summer afternoon ($39.95 at Soho Wines) . . . **Glenkinchie** (GLEN-kin-SHEE), on the other hand, while having the characteristic clean palate of a Lowland malt, is fruity, spicy, and has enough depth of character to make it a dram worthy of a fine snifter. Savor it neat, after dinner ($28.50 at Soho Wines).

WHERE TO TASTE Angel's Share, 8 Stuyvesant St. [3rd Ave.] ☎ 777-5415, offers over 40 single malts . . . **d.b.a.,** 41 First Ave. [2nd/3rd] ☎ 475-5095, has over 50 single malts, with a tasting every other month under the guidance of John Hansell, who publishes *The Malt Advocate* . . . **Bridge Cafe,** 279 Water St. [Dover] ☎ 227-3344, has 44 single malts on the menu and will set up a flight for you . . . **East Side Alehouse,** 961 Second Ave. [51st] ☎ 752-3615, has 45 single malts. They'll set up a five-Scotch flight, price depending on the particulars . . . **Keens,** 72 W. 36th St. [5th/6th] ☎ 947-3636, has 70 single malts at the bar at all times. Each evening the bartender picks two that he pairs for a suggested tasting. There is a short guide to single malts for perusing, and they will sell half shots so you can make up your own tasting. Keens arranges tastings with master distillers on an irregular basis—call for details. When they have a tasting, a distiller talks, shows slides, and Keens makes up special (and substantial) hors d'oeuvres for the Scotch event . . . **Landmark Tavern,** 626 Eleventh Ave. [46th] ☎ 757-8595. The Landmark, around since 1868, serves 20 single malts at the bar. Monday night is single malt night. When you buy one, you get a half shot free . . . **North Star Pub,** 93 South St. ☎ 509-6757, has 60–65 single malts and self-guided single malt tastings, with three half shots in a flight. One constant tasting is their Tour of Scotland: 1 Highland, 1 Lowland, 1 Islay. (They've also done 3 ages of a single Scotch, aromatic malts, etc.) Their resident expert is Deven

Black . . . **Stock and Tankard,** 587 Third Ave. [38th] ☎ 661-3181, has 50 single malts . . . At **Third Floor Cafe,** 315 Fifth Ave. [32nd] ☎ 481-3669, 60 single malts, and once a month there is a guided Scotch "nosing." Flights available by region or one from each of the four regions . . . **Zoë,** 90 Prince St. [Bway/Mercer] ☎ 966-6722, has 25 Scotches on the menu, a three-Scotch flight is presented with a map on which you put your tasting notes.

WHERE TO BUY Park Avenue Liquor Shop, 292 Madison Ave. [40th/41st] ☎ 685-2442, has this one locked up with over 200 single malts (though not the lowest prices). They do tastings several times a year. Talk to Herb Lapchin to get on the mailing list . . . **Soho Wines and Spirits,** 461 W. Broadway [Houston/Prince] ☎ 777-4332, has 60 or so . . . **Union Square Wines,** 33 Union Square West [16th/17th] ☎ 675-8100, has over 50 available . . . **Garnet,** 929 Lexington Ave. [68th/69th] ☎ 772-3211, has about three dozen in stock.

"21" WINE CELLAR

"21" Club, 21 W. 52nd St. [5th/6th] ☎ 582-7200. The restaurant, opened as a speakeasy in 1929, accommodated its clients' desires for privacy by having shelving behind the bar that would flip up at the touch of a button. The wrong knock at the door would cause patrons to place their glasses on the shelves, and look innocent while the glasses smashed on the cellar grate below. The inventory and some very special clients were also hidden in the cellar. Mayor Jimmy Walker had his own booth built there. Wal-

ter Winchell, a regular drinker at the club, fell into a fit of pique one evening when he didn't get his regular table. His column the next day suggested that the authorities should look into the "21" Club. Local officials decided to give the club a pass, but federal agents came in. They spent 12 hours trying to find the entrance to the cellar rooms. The 18-inch-thick brick-and-steel frame door did not sound hollow when they tapped on it, the seal was so tight there was no draft, and water thrown on the door did not reveal any seam. What's more, going over the plans of the building and measuring off the floor space did not show them any missing area. What we know, and they didn't, is that the cellar of "21" is actually under 19 W. 52nd, and the door is made from the wall between the buildings.

You can have a private party in the wine cellar, the original speakeasy, which has a table that can seat up to 12 people. You are in a room containing Jimmy Walker's booth and surrounded by 35,000 bottles of wine. The price of $400 per person for a party of 12 includes a seven-course meal with appropriate wines chosen by the chef, flowers, red light-bulbs, and the chance to play with the straight wire "key" that unlocks the massive door to the speakeasy. Tradition has it that wines are kept long past the time that an habitué (Joan Crawford, John Huston, Richard Nixon) is in any position to make use of them.

WINE BARS

Mad.61, 10 E. 61st St. [Mad] ☎ 833-2200. 25 to 30 wines by the glass. Most of what is available on the wine list can be had by the glass. They have tastings (3 oz.) of Chardonnays and Chiantis, and flights (using a 1.5-oz. glass). They rotate the selection frequently and seek out "up and coming vineyards."

Oyster Bar, Grand Central Terminal, 42nd St. and Vanderbilt Ave. ☎ 490-6650. You can sample about 41 wines by the glass—a complete range including wines from Alsace, Rioja, and Hungary, as well as dessert wines.

Soho Kitchen and Bar, 103 Greene St. [Prince/Spring] ☎ 925-1866. Though the food here is only average, they have the largest Cruvinet in the city, which allows them to keep 101 open bottles of wine fresh and ready to sell by the glass. The choice ranges from inexpensive Chilean Cabernets to the upper reaches of the Bordeaux superstars. They offer many flights—four to eight different wines from a single category served in small 1.5-oz. tasting glasses. You can also make up your own flights.

Third Floor Cafe, 315 Fifth Ave. [32nd] ☎ 481-3669. 14 wines by the glass that include well-chosen small, domestic vineyards and Bordeaux.

WINE CLASSES

For a one-evening tasting to a more formal wine education, see Wine in the Learning chapter.

WINE STORES

Acker Merrall & Condit, 160 W. 72nd St. [Columbus/Bway] ☎ 787-1700

Astor Wines and Spirits, 12 Astor Pl. [Lafayette] ☎ 674-7500

Beekman Liquors, 500 Lexington Ave. [47th/48th] ☎ 759-5857

Burgundy Wine Co., 323 W. 11th St. [Greenwich/Washington] ☎ 691-9092

Cork and Bottle, 1158 First Ave. [63rd/64th] ☎ 838-5300

Crossroads, 55 W. 14th St. [5th/6th] ☎ 924-3060

First Ave. Wines and Spirits, 383 First Ave. [22nd/23rd] ☎ 673-3600

French Wine Merchant, 480 Park Ave. [58th] ☎ 935-0533

Garnet Wines and Liquors, 929 Lexington Ave. [68th/69th] ☎ 772-3211

Gotham Liquors, 2519 Broadway [94th] ☎ 876-4120

K & D Wines, 1366 Madison Ave. [95th/96th] ☎ 289-1818

Luria Colony, 1217 Madison Ave. [87th/88th] ☎ 722-6700

McAdam Buy Rite, 398 Third Ave. [28th/29th] ☎ 679-1224

McCabe's, 1347 Third Ave. [77th] ☎ 737-0790

Morrell and Co., 535 Madison Ave. [54th/55th] ☎ 688-9370

Nancy's Wine for Food, 313 Columbus Ave. [74th/75th] ☎ 877-4040.

Park Ave. Liquor Shop, 292 Madison Ave. [40th/41st] ☎ 685-2442

Quality House, 2 Park Ave. [32nd/33rd] ☎ 532-2944

Rosenthal Wine Merchant, 318 E. 84th St. [1st/2nd] ☎ 249-6650

Schapiro Wine Co., 126 Rivington St. [Essex/Norfolk] ☎ 674-4404

Sherry-Lehmann, 679 Madison Ave. [61st/62nd] ☎ 838-7500

67th St. Wines and Spirits, 179 Columbus Ave. [68th] ☎ 724-6767

Soho Wines and Spirits, 461 W. Broadway [Houston/Prince] ☎ 777-4332

Sutton Wine Shop, 403 E. 57th St. [1st] ☎ 755-6626

Union Square Wines, 33 Union Square West [16th/17th] ☎ 675-8100

Washington Square Wines, 545 LaGuardia Pl. [Bleecker/W. 3rd] ☎ 477-4395

BEST PRICES Garnet, Gotham, K & D, Union Square Wines, Warehouse Wines.

REGIONAL STRENGTHS *California:* Astor Wines, Crossroads; *Bordeaux:* Sherry-Lehmann; *Burgundy:* Burgundy Wine Company, Rosenthal; *Long Island:* McAdam Buy Rite; *Kosher:* McCabe's, Schapiro Wine Co.; *Champagne and Sparkling Wines:* Garnet.

SELECTION Sherry-Lehmann, Morrell, Astor Wines, Garnet.

OUR FAVORITE Union Square Wines for its combination of excellent selection and prices.

SPORTS

←――――――――――――――――――――→

BASEBALL & SOFTBALL

WHERE TO PLAY

There are 134 **public diamonds** in Manhattan for baseball and softball. Leagues, companies, church groups, or two teams from any or no affiliation can apply to play on them by sending a SASE to the Manhattan Borough Office, 16 W. 61st St., New York, NY 10023. There is an $8 charge for adult teams that play on a turf field. There is no charge for asphalt fields and for children's teams . . . **Chelsea Piers Field House,** ☎ 336-6500, has four batting cages, 1 for lefties, 3 for righties. 12 pitches for $1 . . . **Hackers Hitters & Hoops,** 123 W. 18th St. [6th/7th] ☎ 929-7482. Two batting cages for balls pitched at 50 or 80 mph. 12 pitches for $2 or 30 minutes for $29, with a $3 admission charge after 5 P.M. . . . Nine batting cages at the **Randalls Island Practice Center,** ☎ 427-5689, 15 pitches for $1.75, from slow to fast . . . **New York Women's Baseball League.** Connie White is president of the New York Women's Base-

ball League and the first woman in American history to play in the stadium at Cooperstown. The teams play real hardball, with major league rules, and it's the only league of its kind in the northeast United States. Players on the teams find that they are picking up where they left off. "Most played in Little League until they were 12. Then the opportunities for women to play ran out." ☎ 718-549-2431 for more info.

LITTLE LEAGUES

There are 10 leagues in Manhattan with regular play from late March to mid-June. Yearly fees are around $80. Call the District Administrator of the leagues to find the one nearest you. ☎ 201-822-8278.

THE YANKEES

Ticket sales: ☎ 307-1212. **Group sales:** ☎ 718-293-6013. To get a **game schedule:** ☎ 718-293-4300. **Web address:** www.yankees.com. **Party facilities:** Six Hall of Fame suites, named for famous players, each can handle 22–30 people during the game. ☎ 718-293-6013. The Great Moments Room is available for pre- or post-game parties only. 50–125 people ☎ 718-579-4431 . . . **Tours of Yankee Stadium:** Weekdays only from 10–4 for groups of 12 or more. In season, no tours on game days. $6 adults, $3 children ☎ 718-293-4300, ext. 552 . . . To get your name on the Center Field **Scoreboard:** Send a SASE to Scoreboard Dept., Yankee Stadium, Bronx, NY 10451 for an application. For $45 (the money goes to a charity), John Franzone will announce your personalized message while it appears on the Yankee Fan Marquis, a color message board.

THE METS

Ticket sales, group sales, game schedules, and **special events:** ☎ 718-507-8499. Call for info on DYNAMETS! Dash Days (the kids get to run around the bases after the reg-

ular game), fireworks nights, and Old Timers Day . . . The Clubhouse on the Mezzanine level can be used for pre-game birthday parties for groups from 15–60. Birthday children are saluted on the scoreboard . . . Other pre-game party facilities are the Executive Suite for groups of 25–60 and the Left Field Terrace for groups of 36–144 . . . In order to have a **birthday greeting on the scoreboard** if you are not having a party at Shea, you must write to Shea Promotions Dept. NY Mets, Shea Stadium, Flushing, New York 11368. The first 25 requests received are acknowledged . . . During the game, the Team Mets Clubhouse converts to a **playroom** with toys and games for smaller fans fatigued by the game and a TV for parents to keep track of the action.

Baseball!

BASKETBALL

WHERE TO PLAY

Corporate Sports ☎ 245-4738. A small league that plays one night a week. Men only.

Greater NY Pro-Am League, ☎ 431-5265, is where some pro and college players keep in shape in the off-season. You need to try out, and it can be difficult to get on a team. It's for players 21 and older. They also train referees, scorekeepers, and statisticians.

NY Urban Professionals Athletic League, ☎ 877-3614. Men's and women's leagues play full-court games in the summer and winter seasons and half-court three-on-three in

spring and fall. Membership costs vary with the season.

Yorkville Sports Association, ☎ 645-6488, has a youth program for ages 8–18 and adult corporate leagues for women and men.

Yorkville Youth Athletic Association, ☎ 570-5657, is a league for children in grades 3–9. About $60 a year.

The Knicks. It can be frustrating getting to a Knicks game if you don't have season tickets (☎ 465-6050). In September, the remainder are sold at the box office ☎ 465-6040 and through Ticketmaster ☎ 307-7171, and they are gone in very short order.

The **NY Knicks Fan Line** ☎ 465-5867

gives you scheduling and fan club information and connects you (eventually) to Ticketmaster . . . Birthday greetings can be flashed on the Garden Vision "Sweet Spot" for a $25 charity donation. ☎ 465-6555 gives you all the particulars.

BIKING

BIKE CLUBS

The NY Cycle Club, ☎ 886-4545, has been around since 1939. Membership is $21 for a year, and this gets you a monthly bulletin with the listings of the club's rides. There are day trips on weekends for riders at all levels, as well as some midweek rides. Rides range from 15–100 miles (1 1/2–8 hours) . . . **Century Road Club Association,** ☎ 222-8062, has been around even longer—since 1898. It's a club for racers, and there are races in Central Park most every Sat. at 7 A.M. from March–Nov. Membership is $50 (this includes a bike jersey and a newsletter) . . . **Five Borough Bicycle Club,** ☎ 932-2300, ext. 243, is a not-for-profit organization associated with the American Youth Hostels. The basic membership of $10 per year gets you the bimonthly newsletter and information on all club activities. There are all levels of expertise. Day and weekend rides range from 15–150 miles. They teach repair classes.

BIKE STORES

Bicycle Habitat, 244 Lafayette St. [Prince/Spring] ☎ 431-3315
Bicycle Renaissance, 430 Columbus Ave. [81st] ☎ 724-2350
Bronx Bicycle Discount Center, 912 E. Gun Hill Rd. [Bronxwood/Paulding] ☎ 718-798-3242
Conrad's, 25 Tudor City Pl. [1st/2nd] ☎ 697-6966

Emey's, 141 E. 17th St. [Irving/3rd] ☎ 475-7409
Frank's Bike Shop, 553 Grand St. [Columbia/Mangin] ☎ 533-6332
Gene's Bicycle Shop, 242 E. 79th St. [2nd/3rd] ☎ 249-9344
Larry and Jeff's Bicycles Plus, 1400 Third Ave. [79th/80th] ☎ 794-2929 and 1690 Second Ave. [87th/88th] ☎ 722-2201
Stuyvesant Bicycles, 349 W. 14th St. [8th/9th] ☎ 254-5200

BIKES & PUBLIC TRANSPORTATION

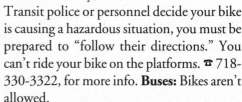

Subways: Bikes are allowed on the subway, but if the Transit police or personnel decide your bike is causing a hazardous situation, you must be prepared to "follow their directions." You can't ride your bike on the platforms. ☎ 718-330-3322, for more info. **Buses:** Bikes aren't allowed.

Metro North Trains: Metro North allows you to take bikes on certain trains during off-peak service. At Grand Central, go to Window 27 and buy a lifetime bike pass for $5. Or write to Ron Valinoti, Metro North Station Services, 420 Lexington Ave., 11th fl., New York, NY 10017. You'll get a copy of the rules for traveling with a bike. For more info ☎ 532-4900 . . . For info on **LIRR** rules, call ☎ 718-990-8228. It's similar to Metro North: You need a permit, available for $5, and you can't take bikes on trains during rush hours and on some holidays . . . To take a bicycle on **Amtrak,** call ☎ 630-7635. It's not always possible since bikes have to go as baggage, and not all trains have a baggage car.

BIKE LOCKS

Generally, people will tell you that the Kryptonite lock (about $80) is the top bike lock. The company that makes it had withdrawn their guarantee for New York, but has now reinstated it with their **New York Lock.** This means that if the lock is broken, you get reimbursed for the value of the bike up to $1,000. Kryptonite's offer has a number of limitations: The guarantee is good only for a year, is void if the thieves use power tools, and so on. And everyone will tell you that no locks or chains are 100% effective in keeping your bike from getting stolen. You can also try through-hardened chain locks (ask for the Quadra chain for about $100).

LEARNING

Terry Chin, ☎ 718-680-5227, gives private classes in bike riding and bike repair in Central Park. Most people who come to him for riding lessons are 25 years and older, including some seniors. A private session is two hours and costs $70. One session is usually enough to get someone riding. Group classes are held on Sundays. Four lessons, two hours each, cost $56. Bikes can be rented if you don't have one. "It usually takes four lessons to learn everything taught in a private session." He also teaches a four-hour bike repair class in the park once a month for $40.

MORE **Transportation Alternatives,** ☎ 475-4600, is an organization that, among other things, works to improve biking conditions in the city. They are also a good source of information about all things having to do with biking. They advocate for new bike lanes and bike racks, encouraging both recreational and utilitarian bike use.

BOWLING

Bowlmor Lanes, 110 University Pl. [12th/13th] ☎ 255-8188. Open bowling on M, W, Th, Sa, Su. $3.25/game. Shoe rental, $1.
Leisure Time, 625 Eighth Ave. [40th] ☎ 268-6909. Open M–Th 10 A.M.–11 P.M.; F, Sa 10 A.M.–1 A.M. League bowl M–Th between 5–8 P.M., so the lanes are closed to others during those hours. $3.75/game, shoe rental, $2.

CHELSEA PIERS

MUG isn't as smart as it thinks it is. When we first heard about the plan to transform the Chelsea Piers, 23rd St. and the Hudson River, into a sports and entertainment complex, we thought, "You can't get there. Who's going to use it?" As it turns out, the answer is: We would. It *is* off the beaten subway path, but the people behind this swift and startling waterfront resurrection have included good reason after good rea-

The Roller Rinks at Chelsea Piers.

son to spend time at this enormous facility.

We suggest you start with a walk along "Sunset Strip," a north to south interior walkway in the Field House, to get a sense of the history of the piers. You do that by looking at the large photos that line walls showing what the original 1910 Warren and Wetmore design looked like. See where many immigrants docked before their ferry ride to Ellis Island and where the *Titanic* was bound (the *Carpathia* came into Pier 54). The *Lusitania* left from Pier 54 in 1915 before being torpedoed off Ireland. The prime, and then the decline, of the piers is in black and white before you.

We'd head next to the water, perhaps out to the little park on Pier 62, the site's northernmost pier. The park is the only disappointment in the complex (too little, hardly a park at all), but you can ignore that for the access to the Hudson. Then, pick an activity.

WHAT YOU CAN DO

The Chelsea Piers covers 1.7 million square feet. There's plenty to do. Since many of the facilities are reserved at various times for leagues and classes, though, you might want to call ahead to make certain what you want to use is available.

BASKETBALL ☎ 336-6500. The two b-ball courts in the Field House can each be rented (when they're not in regular use) for $100/hr.

BATTING CAGES ☎ 336-6500. Four batting cages, 1 for lefties, 3 for righties. 12 pitches/$1.

GOLF ☎ 336-6400. The four-level driving range has a system that automatically tees up each ball. You're facing the Hudson, and the range is enclosed by elegantly rigged netting that preserves the views. It's $15 for 108 balls. If you're using the driving range, you can spend some time working on your putt at their putting green. For more serious improvement, you can take lessons from the Jim McLean Golf Academy, all at the same site. Private lessons are $80/hr.

GYMNASTICS ☎ 336-6500. There is an extensive gymnastics area in the 80,000 square foot Field House. Classes for children and adults. Kids sign up for 17-week sections ($325). Adults pay $20/class.

ICE-SKATING ☎ 336-6100. Ice-skating is the reason why the whole development got started. Sky Rink needed a new home, and out of the search grew this complex. There are two rinks, one for general skating and one for hockey. $9 for adults, $6.50 for kids. Skate rental, $3.50. It's open 24 hours a day.

ROLLER SKATING ☎ 336-6200. There are two regulation-sized rinks on Pier 62. $3.50 for adults, $2.50 for kids.

WORKING OUT ☎ 336-6000. Everything is big at Chelsea Piers, including the 150,000 square foot Sports Center, a mega gym. There are rows and rows of cardiovascular equipment, aerobics studios, a quarter-mile indoor track, a rock climbing wall, volleyball courts (including sand volleyball), a 25-yard pool with whirlpool and sundeck. This is a membership club, but there are also day passes for $26.

MORE Also at Chelsea Piers are film and television production facilities and sound-stages; the Crab House restaurant; the Chelsea Brewing Co. ☎ 336-6440; the Spirit of NY cruises ☎ 727-2789; and the first Origins Feel-Good Spa, ☎ 336-6780.

EXERCISE EQUIPMENT

Some of the best options on exercise equipment for the home.

WHAT TO CONSIDER Eric Ludlow, a senior trainer at World Gym, says you need to decide whether you want equipment for *aerobic* or *resistance* training. He advises people to try out a lot of machines in the gym or in the store and to buy what they find they would most likely use if they were going to the gym. Then, "get the best piece of equipment you can afford. You will use it more and appreciate it more." According to Tom Heavey, general manager of the uptown Crunch, "The first and most important thing to think about is what kind of *warranty* you are getting with the product." Many people find themselves spending a lot of money for a piece of equipment with a 30-day warranty, only to find themselves putting hundreds of dollars worth of parts into the product a year later when it breaks down. Find out who services the product—the store or the manufacturer—and whether there is a service contract available. Of course, keep in mind how much *space* you

---

D A R T S

All you need is a dart board and 3 darts per player. You can get them at **All Fun and Games,** 160 W. 26th St. [6th/7th] ☎ 366-6981. Bristle boards run $32–$65. A set of 3 brass darts starts at $5. Avid players usually move up to darts made from tungsten because they are thinner and you can get 3 in the bull's eye and other tight high-scoring areas. Tungsten darts start a little higher and can cost as much as $165. It's possible to customize your darts with the over 700 flights (the part of the dart that used to be a feather) designs available here. Soft-tip dart games, which have a nylon tip dart and keep score electronically, are $200–$350. Another source is **The Dart Shoppe,** 30 E. 20th St. [Bway/Park] ☎ 533-8684 ... **To Play • Kettle of Fish,** 130 W. 3rd St. [6th/MacDougal] ☎ 533-4790, is dart central in New York, and darts are big at **Muffins Pub,** 699 Second Ave. [37th/38th] ☎ 599-9349; **McAleer's,** 425 Amsterdam Ave. [81st/82nd] ☎ 874-8037; and **The Pour House,** 1712 Second Ave. [89th] ☎ 987-3790. For more info, call the **NY Dart Organization** ☎ 718-499-3745.

have. Don't forget to double check the *voltage*. Make sure it's 110v (which most homes are wired for) rather than 220v. In deciding which type of equipment to buy, Jonathan Bowden of Equinox and On Location Fitness says, "The best is the one you're most likely to use."

TREADMILLS Treadmills outsell the other forms of serious aerobic equipment. You can get a simple treadmill, on which you are going to primarily walk, starting at about $1,695 (for a Pacemaster brand). Otherwise, figure on paying $2,800–$4,300. Eric Ludlow: "You want one with an adjustable grade from 0%–10%, at least." The mph should go from 0–10. If a machine can do both of these two things, it will have a stronger engine and will probably last longer. There are many bad home units—watch out for narrow belts. Tom Heavey: "Even if you are just walking, you can increase your cardiovascular fitness by adding some grade" without going any faster. Mr. Heavey calls the various calorie and pulse monitors "bells and whistles," and thinks that their "accuracy may be questionable." Jonathan Bowden likes Trotter treadmills, most of which are in the $3,000–$4,000 range. The top of the line is the Trotter 685 for $7,595.

 STATIONARY BIKE Tom Heavey: "Schwinn Air Dyne is a good one to think about. It uses no power and works the upper body. A good piece of equipment for older exercisers." ($599 at Gym Source.) Eric Ludlow: In a stationary bike you want to be sure it has "sturdy, secure welds" and "is fairly heavy." You want the seat to be "comfortable right away" and be a comfortable distance from the handlebars. The "resistance should be smooth and not jerky," and the increments of resistance should be small. The Lifecycle bikes, found at many gyms, start at $900 and go up to $2,500. The Tectrix Bike Max provides an unusually smooth ride for $2,200. Top of the line, at least for bells and whistles, is the Tectrix virtual reality bike, which has a video monitor depicting animated rides through the country. You control which route you take. (Go off the road into a pond and you hear a splash of water.) The bike rocks from side to side, adding to the "realism." It has an unreal price tag of $8,000. *Recumbent bikes* are especially good for people who need lower back support. The Lifecycle 5500R for $1,995 is a good choice and is available at the Gym Source.

STAIRSTEPPERS There are many kinds of stairsteppers available, but Mr. Ludlow thinks that they may have peaked in their popularity in the gym. Now he sees people "mix it up more" in their use of equipment. Surprisingly, the Tectrix (more so than the Stairmaster) is the hot machine: It's a very smooth climb with a big step. Their Climb-Max PC is $2,195. Richard Miller, owner of the Gym Source, says gyms spend a lot of money each year (about $400) maintaining and repairing Stairmasters, largely because of the chain drives. Tectrix uses a steel cable that eliminates a lot of the maintenance problems and provides a smooth workout as well.

CROSS-COUNTRY SKIERS Eric Ludlow: The Nordic Track is a good home unit, but "it takes longer to get proficient. It requires more coordination but is less traumatic to the joints." It even took him a while to be able to use it. Tom Heavey: It uses no power and not much space. It gives "a tremendous upper and lower body workout," but "takes time and practice." The cross-country ski movement is not a natural one for most people. Responding to this problem, Nordic-Track now provides an instructional video with purchase. The basic model (which has variable resistance) starts at $300. Though NordicTrack has most of the market for these, there is an alternative called Precor, available at the Gym Source.

MULTISTATIONS These can take up a significant amount of space, and you give up some of the precise alignments found on individual pieces of equipment. Jonathan Bowden says that the "biomechanics of the muscles" aren't optimally served unless you exactly fit the form and frame on which the machines were designed and tested. Nevertheless, they can offer a good range of resistance exercises. Consider the Hoist 1200 for $2,395 or, even better, the Paramount Personal Fitness Center, since it has a horizontal bench, at $2,695. Cybex, the excellent manufacturer of the resistance equipment found in many gyms, does make a multistation home unit, but it is not considered a successful multistation and is not recommended.

BASIC EQUIPMENT Jonathan Bowden says you can do very nicely with some simple things: a step (the kind used in step classes) with extra risers so you can use it as a step, as a bench, or an incline bench. It stores easily. (Cost: $99.95.) He'd add to that a Lifeline Gym ($49.95) that consists of a resistance cable and bar. It weighs very little and fits easily into a suitcase. For people who don't need much resistance training, a couple of dumbbells would suffice. Otherwise, he recommends the Power Block ($199), two blocks of cleverly interconnected dumbbells that take up about as much room as two good-size toaster ovens. (You probably want them in the 5-lb. rather than 10-lb. increments.) The idea of changeable weight dumbbells seems like a good one, but most people get aggravated having to stop a workout to change the weight. The Power Block makes weight adjustment easier.

WHERE TO BUY Eric Ludlow: Any store where you are considering buying should let you use the equipment "for at least five minutes." There should be a manufacturer's warranty and a store warranty . . . **The Gym Source,** 40 E. 52nd [Mad/Park] ☎ 688-4222, is the top choice in town. Health clubs and trainers rely on them extensively for their selection and service. In addition to sales, they offer service contracts to take up where the warranties leave off. They also do equipment rental, so if someone needs a piece of equipment at a hotel or other site, they can arrange it . . . **NordicTrack,** 650 Madison Ave. [60th] ☎ 688-3883 and 200 Park Ave. S. [Union Sq.] ☎ 614-6800.

FISHING

For information on fishing tours and where to get a fishing license, see the Fish article in the Feature chapter.

GOLF

COURSES

General info on the options for playing golf in the five boroughs with some comments from golfers who use the area courses. Course yardage is calculated from the middle tees. You can play on these city courses with or without a permit, but the permit saves you money if you play more than a couple of times a year. The permit is $6 annually, payable at any of the courses with proof of NYC residency. Permits are good until Dec. 31.

THE BRONX

Van Cortlandt, Bailey Ave. and Van Cortlandt Park S. ☎ 718-543-4595. 18 holes, 5,913 yards. With permit: $15 weekdays, $17.50 weekends. Without permit: add $6. Instruction: $31/half hr. 100 years old in 1995—oldest public course in the U.S.A. ☞ "If you don't have a car, this is the easiest one to get to . . . Weekends are very crowded here . . . The reservation system can be a little confusing at times, but it's better than the previous system—which was no system. You need two people to reserve a time, then you will be paired up at the course . . . It is a narrow course, and #2 is the signature hole: 620 yds, par 5, the longest hole in the Metropolitan Golf Assn. . . . Wear your running shoes . . . The course is used by non-golfers for their own purposes, and while there are fewer burning automobiles now that American Golf Corporation has taken over, there are still times when you will want to move along . . . The closest 18 holes to the Upper East Side, reachable by public transportation, although some women might not feel comfortable taking the subway there. Walk-on singles have a good chance of golfing."

Mosholu, Jerome Ave., opposite E. 213th and Holly Lane ☎ 718-655-9164. 9 holes, 3,263 yards. With permit: $15.50. Without permit: $19.50. Driving range with buckets: $5 and $8. Instruction: $35/half hr. ☞ "Easy to get to from the East Side . . . Many beginners play here so it is slower playing and is in worse shape than some of the other city courses."

Pelham/Split Rock, Shore Rd., north of Bartow Circle ☎ 718-885-1258. Both courses are 18 holes. Pelham, 6,405 yards; Split Rock, 6,239 yards. With permit: $19.50 weekends, $17.50 weekdays. Without permit: add $6. Instruction: $25/hr. Putting green and short (40 yards) pitching green. ☞ "Can be reached by bus . . . Both are nice courses . . . The layout of Split Rock is nicer than Van Cortlandt. There are elevation changes and doglegs . . . Split Rock is one of the more difficult."

BROOKLYN

Dyker Beach, Seventh Ave. [86th St.] ☎ 718-836-9722. 18 holes, 6,260 yards. With permit: $17.50 weekdays, $19.50 weekends. Without permit: add $6. Instruction: $40/half hr. with Tom Strafaci. ☞ "Dyker Beach and Van Cortlandt are my favorites. There are generally good players, and the course has a good layout . . . Watch out for 'outings'—busloads of players who will slow down the course. Ask when you make your reservations how many outings they have that day, and how close they will be to you . . . The subway puts you within a few blocks of the course. The pro, Tom Strafaci, has taught a lot of New Yorkers. A much-loved figure, he held the course record at Shinnecock Hills until the PGA played there in

1986, and he still holds the course record at Dyker Beach . . . A good course."

Marine Park, 2880 Flatbush Ave., near the Belt Pkwy. ☎ 718-338-7149. 18 holes, 6,609 yards. With permit: $15.50 weekdays, $17.50 weekends. Without permit: add $6. Instruction: $30/half hr. ☞ "Long and windy 'links'-style course . . . A decent course which is built on the site of an old dump. If you take too big of a divot, you will hit a refrigerator."

QUEENS

Forest Park, Forest Park Dr., near the Interboro Pkwy. ☎ 718-296-0999. 18 holes, 5,431 yards. With permit: $15.50 weekdays, $17.50 weekends. Without permit: add $4. No instruction ☞ "It is a forest with too many trees, the greens are not in good shape, and it's too crowded . . . A decent course on the shorter side."

Clearview, Belt Pkwy and Willets Point Blvd. ☎ 718-229-2570. 18 holes, 6,263 yards. With permit: $15.50 weekdays, $17.50 weekends. Without permit: add $6. Instruction: $35/half hr. ☞ "Hard to get to without a car, but a nice course. On weekends, though, you can have 6-hour rounds . . . A well-conditioned course, not too long, kind of flat, and not as interesting as some of the others . . . Okay course . . . Caters to beginners with wide fairways."

Douglaston, 6320 Marathon Pkwy. [Commonwealth Blvd.] ☎ 718-428-1617. 18 holes, 5,100 yards. With permit: $15.50 weekdays, $17.50 weekends. Without permit: add $6. Instruction: $44/hr. ☞ "The most played of the city courses. It racks up the most rounds played each year . . . It can provide a good round of golf."

Kissena, Booth Memorial Ave. [164th] ☎ 718-939-4594. 18 holes, 4,425 yards. With permit: $15.50 weekdays, $17.50 weekends. Without permit: add $6. Instruction: $30/half hr. ☞ "The lowest on the totem pole of the city courses. It's not a course people take seriously. It's short and often not well kept."

STATEN ISLAND

Silver Lake, 915 Victory Blvd. [Forest Ave.] ☎ 718-447-5686. 18 holes, 5,736 yards. With permit: $15.50 weekdays, $17.50 weekends. Without permit: add $6. No instruction. ☞ "While it is easier to get to than La Tourette on Staten Island (see below), La Tourette is so much nicer . . . A nice little course . . . Decent."

La Tourette, 1 London Rd. [Forest Hill & Rockland Aves.] ☎ 718-351-1889. 18 holes, 6,500 yards. With permit: $17.50 weekdays, $19.50 weekends. Without permit: add $6. Instruction: $35/half hr. ☞ "The nicest of the city courses because of its layout and the variety of the holes . . . The best city course with the best overall condition through the years . . . The layout is more interesting, it has a decent distance, and is scenic . . . Nice people in the pro shop."

South Shore, Huguenot Ave. [Raily St.] ☎ 718-984-0101. 18 holes, 6,317 yards. With permit: $15.50 weekdays, $17.50 weekends. Without permit: add $6. Instruction: Talk to Mario Rapaglia. ☞ "At the far edge of Staten Island. Too far to get to . . . Another one on the lower end of the totem pole."

DRIVING RANGES

Chelsea Piers, 23rd and the Hudson River ☎ 336-6400, has a 200-yard driving range. 52 stalls are on 4 levels. They all hit into the outdoors. M–Sa, 8 A.M.–10 P.M.; Su, 9–9. $15 for 108 balls.

Golden Bear Alley Pond Park, Northern Blvd. [231st] Queens ☎ 718-225-9187. Driving range: $10 for 102 balls. Miniature golf: $3.50/children, $5/adults.

Golfport, 51-24 2nd St., Long Island City ☎ 718-472-4653, is a short-distance driving range with 10 stalls. You can hit 60 yards out into a back netting. Open year round and night lit. $8 gets you 70 balls.

Flushing Meadows-Corona Park, foot of Passerelle Ramp at Willets Point #7 station ☎ 718-271-8182. Pitch and Putt only. $6.75 weekdays, $7.75 weekends. No reservations.

You can practice your golf swing on a driving range at 4 A.M. in New York City. The place is the **Randalls Island Practice Center** ☎ 427-5689. There are people (and not a few) who are on this 24-hour driving range (with 106 spots) at just that hour on any given day. Go at more traditional hours and you will find it is surprisingly sylvan, given the hug of the Triborough on the perimeter. It's fairly quiet, too, offering the golfer a chance to hit some balls and put the city pretty well out of mind. There's mini golf as well, and though there are absolutely no gizmos, wheels, or clown faces on the course, it's actually a lovely course of 36 holes. They've got batting cages, too. The best way to get there is by using their shuttle van. It stops in front of Modell's on

Randalls Island Practice Center.

Third Ave. between 86th and 87th; M–F 4–8; Sa, Su 10–5 on the hour. It's $7 round trip for the shuttle. Golf lessons are available, a bucket of 40 balls is $5, 80 balls for $8. The late hours are scaled back off-season.

Turtle Cove, 1 City Island Rd. [Belden] ☎ 718-885-2646. Driving range only. $8.50 for 115 balls.

SHOPPING

Most people who want golf equipment go to Queens or New Jersey and drive around to big stores to find the best deals. You need to shop where they have a place for you to swing the club. But there are some good choices in the city. At the top of most people's list is **Richard Metz Golf,** 425 Madison Ave. [49th] ☎ 759-6940. The hushed atmosphere belies the amount of activity here—over 8,000 lessons are given each year—in an atmosphere that re-creates a pro shop at a golf course. Three full-time PGA pros teach in the canvas-enclosed rooms at every level from beginner to accomplished. They have videotape replay, computer-swing analysis, and use Mr. Metz's method of the "graduated swing." A series of ten half hour lessons is $350, and you have a year to use up the series. The retail shop sells the better clubs at 20–30% off retail, as well as other golf paraphernalia. Repairs and regripping are offered. They've been in business since 1968. About a third of their instructees and customers are now women . . . **The Fifth Ave. Golf Center,** 581 Fifth Ave. [47th/48th] ☎ 754-0110, is also a teaching store, more crowded than Richard Metz. There is a putting green where you can try out putters and a semiprivate teaching room. The lessons are videotaped. (Bring a blank tape and you can take it home to review it.) At first, the technique of the golf swing is stressed, and you "don't have to worry about where the ball goes" because you are hitting into a net. Lessons are $40/half hr. A package of 4 lessons is $140. In addition to clubs, bags, and balls, the shop carries books and maps of courses . . . **Nevada Bob's,** 989 Sixth Ave. [36th/37th] ☎ 736-4653 and 143 E. 54th St. [Lex/3rd] ☎ 888-3400, is part of a chain of golf stores. The Sixth Ave. store, with three levels, is the larger of the two and one of the largest golf stores in Manhattan. A special section has clubs for left-handed players . . . **New York Golf Center,** 131 W. 35th [Bway/7th] ☎ 564-2255, has a huge selection. You should be able to go from these two to **Larry's Golf Shop,** 21 W. 35th St. [5th/6th] ☎ 563-6895 (sometimes a little cheaper than the two big stores, but does not have as big a selection), and **Golftown,** 25 W. 32nd St. [Bway/5th] ☎ 563-0506. If you are looking for price, Nevada Bob's and The New York Golf Center are very competitive. NY Golf also has great range in pricing—you will be able to find a set of irons anywhere from $200–$6,500. The sales help at New York Golf Center is knowledgeable . . . **The World of Golf,** 147 E. 47th St. [Lex/3rd] ☎

755-9398, is in a converted townhouse without much space. Clubs and equipment are crammed in . . . **Chelsea Piers,** 23rd St. and the Hudson River ☎ 336-6400, has a full-service pro shop.

MORE The NYC Golf Club, ☎ 692-4653, is the idea of Eric Lynch, who decided to eliminate some of the drawbacks of the game for golfing Manhattanites. The NYC Golf Club makes prearranged tee times at about 20 different town, country, and semiprivate courses in NY and beyond. Transportation is provided in the "Golf-mobile," a custom-built large van that holds up to three foursomes and their equipment. Additional transportation options are available. They offer golf outings 7 days a week. Membership costs $179 per season, with an additional $50–$75 for transportation and greens fees on each outing. Cart rental is extra. The NYC Golf Club runs its own Golf School in Port Imperial, NJ. A five-minute ride on the NY Waterways Ferry from 38th St. and Twelfth Ave. puts you a chip shot from the school. A series of 12 two-hour lessons is $425, which includes a playing lesson. All equipment is provided.

HIKING

ORGANIZATIONS

NY/NJ Trail Conference, 232 Madison Ave. [37th] ☎ 685-9699, was established in 1920 as an all-volunteer organization to build and maintain trails in NY and NJ. They sell maps and books dealing with southern New York State and northern New Jersey. If you need to find a hike leader, they will send you their list of hiking clubs that can help you. There is a lending library for

members and a newsletter that lists hikes and events in and around NYC. You can also request their leaflet "You Don't Need a Car," which tells you how to take public transportation to hiking trails . . . **Appalachian Mountain Club,** 5 Tudor City Place [2nd Ave/41st] ☎ 986-1430, an organization of hikers, has been in existence for over 100 years. They are a conservation and recreation organization that wants you to enjoy the outdoors, but wisely. A modest yearly membership fee gives you access to the AMC huts in the White Mountains as well  as their facilities in the Delaware Water Gap and Fire Island. There is a triquarterly schedule of hundreds of events—guided hikes, workshops, canoe trips, ski trips, etc., many of which are planned for New Yorkers who do not own cars . . . The **Sierra Club** sponsors hikes in the NY area. ☎ 473-7841 for more info.

EQUIPMENT

Eastern Mountain Sports, 611 Broadway [Houston] ☎ 505-9860, sells everything you need to go into the woods: boots, binoculars, raingear, backpacks, special watches, and more.

Patagonia, 101 Wooster St. [Prince/Spring] ☎ 343-1776, brings high technology to outdoor clothing. They have a range of Gore-Tex jackets meant to keep you warm and dry at various temperatures and altitudes. Some boots and cooking equipment, etc.

REPAIR

Down East Service Center, 50 Spring St. [Lafayette/Mulberry] ☎ 925-2632. Leon Greenman, Down East's owner, has hiked and climbed extensively and has drawn his own maps of hiking trails in NY state. These maps are printed on Tyvek, a supple plastic that can't be torn and is waterproof. There are many maps and books available in Mr. Greenman's tidy little shop, and he is a valuable resource of trail information. Down East's main claim to fame is repair and customization of outdoor equipment. They repair holes in tents, zippers, backpacks, and send out your hiking boots for resoling. Mr. Greenman customizes outdoor gear with Cordura nylon, webbing, and high-quality metal hardware. His creative solutions have brought photographers and set and costume designers to him for special bags and other items.

HORSEBACK RIDING

WHERE TO RIDE

Claremont Riding Academy, 175 W. 89th St. [Amsterdam/Columbus] ☎ 724-5100. Lessons: $35/half hr. Riding: $33/hr. every day. You need to be an "experienced English rider." Built in 1892, it's the oldest continuously operated stable in the U.S. The emphasis is on instruction, but 6 miles of bridal paths in Central Park are available for riding (though there are a number of restrictions). They have a large facility in NJ called the Overpeck Riding Center, ☎ 201-944-7111, accessible by bus or car. Thirty acres, a large indoor arena, lessons, boarding, and showing programs.

Riverdale Equestrian Center, Broadway and 254th St. ☎ 718-548-4848. Rusty Holzer, an olympian on the United States Virgin Island jumping team, and Ashley Nicoll, who was on the Canadian dressage team, teach here. Liberty Lines East Side line, BXM3, takes you to the end of their driveway, $4. Riding and lessons are $60/hr. Open Tues.–Fri., 8–8, Sat., Sun., 8–5. A new indoor ring allows year-round riding.

Pelham Bay Stable, Pelham Bay Park, 9 Shore Rd., the Bronx ☎ 718-885-0551. Lessons: $30/hr., $20/hr. for a group. Riding: M–F, $20/hr. Pony rides: $1. Pleasant riding in Pelham Park . . . Nearby is **C Hooks,** 1680

Pelham Pkwy. S., the Bronx. Chickens roam freely, dusty, a small stable, no phone. They do some trail riding, but no lessons.

Other places to ride include: **Jamaica Bay Riding Academy,** 7000 Shore Pkwy. [Bway Ridge/70th] Brooklyn, ☎ 718-531-8949. Trail rides: $23/45 min. Lessons: $45/hr. Some trails are right on Bergen Beach . . . **Lynne's Riding Academy,** 88-03 70th Rd. [Sybilla] Forest Hills ☎ 718-261-7679. Riding: By appt., $20/hr. Lessons: $30/half hr., $45/hr. Groups of 3 or more ride on the wooded trails in Forest Park.

EQUIPMENT

Miller's, 117 E. 24th St. [Park/Lex] ☎ 673-1400, has mostly English saddles, riding clothing, and much riding-inspired clothing. They also sell the riding sneaker, a very comfortable alternative to the traditional boot.

Since 1879, **Vogel Boots and Shoes to Measure,** 19 Howard St. [Lafayette/Crosby] ☎ 925-2460, has made riding boots and shoes. See the Shoes article in the Stores chapter.

Hermès, 11 E. 57th St. [5th/Mad] ☎ 751-3181, sells everything from pochettes printed with scenes of the track at Chantilly, for $75, to a red hunt jacket for $2,000. They have a full saddle shop with saddles, horse brushes, blankets, etc.

Winston-Taylor's, 11 E. 44th St. [5th/Mad] ☎ 687-0850, makes custom riding clothing. They make hunt frocks using traditional English fabrics, riding breeches, jackets for hunt balls, and sometimes the Pink Coat (which is the red coat you associate with riding) for the Master of the Hunt.

ICE SKATING

WHERE TO SKATE

4 World Trade Center, on the second level ☎ 524-4386. Adults: $7; Kids: $3.50; Skate rental: $3.50.

Ice Studio, 1034 Lexington Ave. [73rd/74th], 2nd floor ☎ 535-0304. Indoors, complicated schedule, so call. 1 hour: $5; 1 1/2 hours: $6; Skate rental: $2.75. This is a small rink that does a lot of teaching. Private lessons $35/half hr.

Lasker Rink, 110th St. and Lenox Ave. ☎ 396-1010. Adults: $3.50; Kids: $1.75; Skate rental: $3.25. M–W, 10–3, Th–Su, 10–10.

Rivergate Ice Rink, 401 E. 34th St. [1st Ave.] ☎ 689-0035. Outdoors. M–F, 12–10, Sa, Su, 10–10. Adults: $6.50; Kids: $3.25; Skate rental: $3.25.

Rockefeller Center ☎ 332-7654. 4-hour periods beginning at 9 A.M. (8:30 on weekends) with 1/2-hour breaks to clean the ice. Weekdays: Adults: $7, Kids: $6. Weekends: Adults: $8.50, Kids: $6.75. Skate rentals: $4.

Sky Rink at Chelsea Piers [23rd St. and the Hudson River] ☎ 336-6100. Two indoor rinks, one for general skating and one for hockey. Adults: $9; Kids: $6.50; Skate rental: $3.50.

Wollman Rink, mid-Park at 62nd St. ☎ 396-1010. M, 10–5, Tu, W, Th, 10–9:30, F, Sa, 10–11, Su, 10–9. Adults: $6.50; Kids: $3.25; Skate rentals: $3.25.

WHERE TO BUY

See Rollerblading in this chapter.

KAYAKING

New York is always a surprise. It never occurred to us that kayaking is a city sport, but it is in this city. Many of the kayakers we spoke with remarked on the pleasure of being in their kayaks in the middle of the Hudson, looking back at the city.

WHERE TO START

If you're looking for a place to start, try the **Metropolitan Canoe and Kayak Club** ☎ 724-5069. You'll talk to Ralph Díaz, who also publishes *Folding Kayaker*. As Mr. Díaz writes: "This is a bi-monthly newsletter devoted to folding sea kayaks. This highly stable type of sea kayak has a long tradition of major crossings, expeditions, and military use that underlines its basic toughness and seaworthiness. Their skin over frame construction harkens back to the Eskimo kayak and allows an intimacy with your surroundings not possible in any other craft. For city dwellers, folding kayaks offer the advantage of disassembling into duffle-sized bags for easy storage in crowded apartments and uncomplicated movement by public transportation to the many good paddling sites around Manhattan. The boats in their bags qualify as ordinary baggage for air travel, opening up other vistas as well." *Folding Kayaker* regularly reviews boats and equipment, discusses safety and paddling techniques, etc. Subscription is $28/yr.

WHERE TO BUY

The NY Kayak Co., ☎ 924-1327, is run by Randy Henriksen, who sells folding kayaks that range in price

CHRISTOPHER LOVI

Kayaking New York–style.

from $1,400–$4,500. On the lower end are the small, lightweight, single touring models. The more expensive are heavy duty, "expedition," double kayaks. Right now, the most popular seller is the Feathercraft K-Light, a 30-lb., $1,800 model that Mr. Henricksen says is "a very, very good boat. The engineering is just fantastic." The kayak folds up into a backpack, and it's "easy to catch a taxi with it. You can ride a bike with it on your back." A dedicated kayaker might want a custom kayak, which Mr. Henriksen makes. You can have a West Greenland–style kayak, which means an authentic Eskimo-style craft that the Eskimos used to hunt seal. Mr. Henriksen uses canvas for the skin (rather than seal skin) and fir and oak for the frame. He says using this kind of kayak is a different experience. "It's absolutely silent, flexes in the water, and is a lively boat." These are made for one person and are actually custom designed for a particular body. Prices start at $3,000.

WHERE TO LEARN

Mr. Henricksen offers kayaking lessons. In a group, it's $120 for six two-hour lessons or, for private instruction, $40/hr., with a two-hour minimum.

WHERE TO LAUNCH

There are 11 **Parks Dept. official launch sites,** three of which are in Manhattan. These are the 79th St. Boat Basin, Riverside Park at 148th St., and Inwood Hill Park at the foot of Dyckman St. The Parks Dept. issues a kayaking permit for $2 a season, available from the Parks Dept. office in the Arsenal in Central Park, ☎ 360-8111, or the **Downtown Boathouse,** on the Hudson at

N. Moore St., ☎ 966-1852. This is an all-volunteer, nonprofit storage and launch site. It can hold about 100 boats and is currently open only on weekends. When there are enough volunteers, they will extend the hours. Still to come are a boat-building shop, a children's sailing program, and a toy-boat pond. Membership is $50, annual storage is $200. For more info, talk to Jim Wetteroth.

MORE **The Hudson River WaterTrail Association** is nonprofit group whose mission it is to create a kind of Appalachian-style waterway trail on the Hudson from the city up to Troy. What they hope will happen, according to Josh Bloomgarden of the Association, is to have a string of launch sites and campsites all along the way. They publish a quarterly newsletter as well as *The HRWA Paddler's Guide to the Hudson River.* Membership is $25 a year. For more info, write to the HRWA, 247 Grove St., #1, Jersey City, NJ 07302, or visit their Web page at: http://www.envirolink.org/elib/orgs/hrwa/hrwa.htm.

KITING

WHERE TO GO
People fly kites in Sheep Meadow and in Hudson River Park, but the air currents are generally best suited for simpler, single-line kite models—the more complicated models don't always get enough wind. Jones Beach, near Parking Lot 6, is where serious kiters go.

WHERE TO BUY
Big City Kite Co., 1210 Lexington Ave. [82nd] ☎ 472-2623, is kite central in New York. Kiting magazines are available at the shop, and David Klein, the owner, has a handy sheet of "Kite Flying Tips." There is also a kite buggy—a cart for you to sit in and be pulled along by your kite ($599). The three-dimensional cellular kites ($18–$31) are especially eye-catching. They sell plenty of line, winders, Mylar tail, and the other accessories for the sport. Mr. Klein will take orders for custom kites for birthdays, anniversaries, or corporate events. He will also set up kite shows for corporate picnics—starting at $300 per day.

MOST POPULAR KITES
The 4½-foot delta wing is the most popular model at Big City Kite because it's the easiest to fly and comes in a lot of color combos. Most kites are made of nylon taffeta or the stronger rip stop nylon. The only kites made of paper these days are some from India and Japan, which have unusual shapes and wood-block print designs. Chinese kites are hand-painted silk and look like butterflies or dragons. Simple kites run from $16.50, many kites are $25 or so, and competition kites can go for over $100.

MAKING KITES
Big City Kite works with the Central Park Conservancy and school groups in kitemaking workshops. Call Big City for more info.

KITE HISTORY
The Cradle of Aviation Museum in Garden City (closed now during a renovation) is situated on the airfield where Lindbergh started his transatlantic flight. A permanent exhibi-

tion is planned to detail how kites contributed to the development of the airplane. Kitemakers from all over the world have been asked to duplicate historic kites—ones made by the Wright Brothers, Alexander Graham Bell, and so on—many of which will be flyable. If you want more information, or if you have info, call Nick D'Alto at ☎ 516-221-5396.

LAWN BOWLING

The Dutch brought a bowling game to the island in 1626, said to be Manhattan's first sport. When Bowling Green Park was established in 1733, the English played on Bowling Green. The game the English played is the lawn bowling still played in Central Park. When Richard Keoseian used to walk past the lawn bowlers in Central Park, he assumed it was an exclusive private club. It's not—it's a public facility, and he's now the president of the Metropolitan Lawn Bowling Club of NY. If you wish to join, you will need $90 for the season. Every year in May there are free introductory classes. While learning, which Mr. Keoseian says you can do quickly, you can use the club equipment. This will allow you to determine the size and weight bowl that is best for you. Players wear whites and flat shoes. The green is located in the park at W. 69th St., just north of Sheep Meadow. Write to Mr. Keoseian at 171 W. 71st St., New York, NY 10023.

MARTIAL ARTS

Here's a survey of some of the martial arts classes in the city. We got much good advice from John Burke, producer of *Martial Arts World* on MSG and over 150 instructional videotapes on martial arts featuring important teachers. These videos are available through ESPY-TV ☎ 800-735-6521.

WHAT TO KNOW

Learning the martial arts requires a sense of commitment. These are complex activities—requiring much time to refine technique and become proficient. Since there is a significant amount of physical activity in all except T'ai Chi, you need to be in pretty good shape before starting lessons. Be sure that the school where you study carries liability insurance to cover possible injuries if there is full contact involved in the training.

Look for one that does not rush you through the belt levels. Better ones want to be sure you have mastered all the techniques needed before upgrading. Most schools charge by the month, lowering the per-class fee the longer the period of sign-up. But be wary of schools that ask you to sign a long-term contract; most of the good schools ask you to pay month to month. Children can participate in most of the martial arts (where it is not appropriate we note it), but Mr. Burke strongly advises parents "to observe two full classes" before enrolling your child, and at least one alone without the child. The best teachers are the ones who teach both the martial and the art component of each activity. Look for schools where the head *sensei* or *sifu* is still actively teaching. These schools may be smaller and have fewer amenities, but the quality of instruction given by these masters can more than make up for the inconveniences. Besides learning the techniques of the form, you're entering another culture — commands and responses are given in the language of the discipline. There is some meditation at the beginning and close of each class. You'll need to learn proper forms of address and behavior—for instance, all students take part in cleaning the *dojo* (school). Rank, or *kyu,* is important and shown by belt color. A progression of white, yellow, green, brown, and black is used, with some variations from school to school. There are 9 levels, or *Dan,* of black belt. In general, we are describing the most basic form of each martial art. Some, like karate and kung fu, have hundreds of variations.

T'AI CHI comes from China. Roughly translated, it means the balance of yin and yang. One set of yin/yang in T'ai Chi is hard and soft, another is energized and relaxed. When done correctly, the fluid, continuous, detailed movements of the "forms" or exercises look soft but signify a body under exceptional control. Adjacent muscle groups can be controlled in opposite manners. We have seen teachers demonstrate how the forearm can be held rigid while the wrist and hand move in a graceful manner. T'ai Chi teaches that the body and mind are connected. As exercise, it can be performed by anyone of any age, requires no equipment or special place. Bob Murphy, a teacher who is also a student of Chinese medicine, says, "It enhances circulation of the blood and energy, regulates blood pressure, strengthens the bones and sinews, teaches awareness of the body, and, above all, patience." In beginning classes there is no body contact or

stressful movement. When you add the word *Chuan* after T'ai Chi it means the "fist form" of the exercises.

CHRISTOPHER LOVI

Shum Leung moving through a T'ai Chi form.

Schools and Teachers: **Master William C.C. Chen,** 725 Sixth Ave. [23rd/24th] ☎ 675-2816, has been teaching for 40 years, the last 30 on the same block. Beginners, Push Hands (T'ai Chi for two), and San-Shou (boxing), the latter by invitation only, are taught by Master Chen. **Master Yu Cheng Hsiang,** ☎ 718-353-5663, teaches Yang style at 380 Broadway [White]. It is more spirited and stresses line and point. **Bob Murphy,** who has been studying for 20 years, the last 11 with Master Yu, also teaches here through the Open Center ☎ 219-2527. It's an ongoing course where beginners are welcome at all times. Most of the teaching in the U.S. is the Yang style. Rarer forms are Wu and Chen. Mr. Burke says, "NYC is lucky to have **Shum Leung** who teaches in the Wu style" at 147 W. 24th St. [6th/7th] ☎ 633-6134. "This is a softer, flowery, more circular way that can be quite pretty. After one gains experience, it is done with a little sound and, when performed fast, can be used as self-defense."

AIKIDO, "the most peaceful of the martial arts," comes from Japan. It is derived from the Samurai art of jujitsu. Yes, Aikido teaches you to throw someone to the ground, but it also teaches you how to then walk away. There is a lot of throwing and somersaulting on the mat, and while it looks simple, learning can be a bruising experience. You learn how to throw and be thrown, how to fall and roll, and how to balance your body. Exercising, in pairs or groups of four, is in near-silence, with some low-voiced commentary from the teachers. There are no tournaments or competitions, and while it is vigorous, there is no full-body contact.

Schools and Teachers: **Yoshimitsu Yamada** is at Aikido of Uyeshiba, 142 W. 18th St. [6th/7th] ☎ 242-6246, the headquarters of the U.S. Aikido Federation. Sensei Yamada, an 8th Dan black belt, has been teaching for 30 years. There is not much of a sign outside, but there is a good-sized, bright white practice room with a Japanese shrine at one end. Courses offered on all levels to men, women, and children (ages 12–18) by a large teaching staff (men and women), including Y. Yamada. In all, the most beautiful class we saw. **Nobuyoshi Higashi,** a professor at SUNY Stony Brook, teaches the Tomiki system at the Kokushi Budo Institute of NY in the basement of the Buddhist temple at 331 Riverside Drive [105th] ☎ 866-6777. A serious school with a nice atmosphere.

KARATE, loosely translated as "open-handed art," was brought to Okinawa from China where it had been developed by a Buddhist monk traveling from India. The peasants of the Middle Ages were not permitted to carry weapons, and karate became a weaponless method of self-defense. Classes are made up of rigorous calisthenics, including push-ups of increasing difficulty (culminating in the one-finger push-up), followed by work on forms done singly or in pairs. Breaking boards is generally reserved for public displays and is taught at advanced levels only. Many teachers arrived in NYC in the '50s and '60s, bringing dozens of styles *(ryu)* with them. The students of these original teachers are now teaching. Karate is not for all kids. Since at least 2–3 sessions a week are required to attain and maintain proficiency in karate, many of the schools are like clubhouses with other social and communal activities. Karate schools and associations tend to be larger than some of the other arts, with the founder teaching less, if at all.

Schools and Teachers: Sensei **Masataka Mori,** 8th Dan, teaches all the classes at Shotokan Karate of NY, 2121 Broadway [74th] ☎ 799-5500. There are fewer calisthenics here and more work on karate forms. Kaicho (Grand Master) **Tadashi Nakamura** heads World Seido Karate Honbu, 61 W. 23rd St. [5th/6th] ☎ 924-0511. He is actively teaching at all levels, except for children. This is one of the largest and nicest facilities in Manhattan, though Nakamura is tough.

KUNG FU ("good talent"), sometimes called "the grandfather of all the martial arts," is derived from a physical regimen practiced by Chinese monks in the Shaolin temple. The movements come from precise observations made of animals. It is done very fast and reenacts a fight. There is an element of boxing here and some of the styles carry animal names: the Tiger Claw, Snake, Dragon, Crane, and Leopard. About 20 styles are taught in NYC. Classes are strenuous affairs, beginning, in some cases, with a full hour of stretching exercises, followed by practicing forms and routines.

Schools and Teachers: The Eagle Claw technique—Ying Jow Pai—uses more grabs and holds. **Shum Leung** teaches it at 147 W. 24th St. [6th/7th] ☎ 633-6134. Classes are about 3 hours long. Sifu Shum, who has been teaching in NYC since 1971, teaches every class. He moves among the students during practice and class, correcting and guiding. The dragon sifu **Yip Wing Han** teaches in the basement of a store at 291 Grand St. [Eldridge/Allen] ☎ 964-2019. The Wing Chun style, developed by a Buddhist nun, Wu Mui, has "compact, specific motions" for defending yourself against a bigger person. Bruce Lee used much of Wing Chun in his style. **Chung Kwok Chow** teaches at 303 Park Ave. S. [23rd] ☎ 914-234-0281.

KENDO, the Japanese sport of sword fighting, has been handed down from the Samurai class. And kendo participants look like Samurai warriors in their culottes, hard chest protectors, and helmets with a grill opening. The sword is a bamboo pole *(shiai).* There are exercises in sword control and quick changes of direction on foot. In competition, contact is made with the poles, and there is a system of point scoring. The Ken-Zen Institute, 152 W. 26th St. [6th/7th] ☎ 741-2281, is under the direction of **Daniel T. Ebihara,** and the U.S. BudoKai Kan, 110 W. 14th St. [6th/7th] ☎ 807-7336, is run by **Rico Guy.** Kendo should be reserved for older kids. Most places that teach Kendo also teach Iado, in which there is no confrontation or fighting. It is, however, performed solo with a real sword and is a series of very stylized moves.

TAE KWON DO ("hand foot art") is sometimes called the Korean Karate. It uses a full range of hand and foot techniques, with high, extended kicks. The technique most pictured is a flying kick, which, when done properly, is forceful but with the body so completely in balance that you land solidly on your feet. **S. Henry Cho**'s school at 46 W. 56th St. [5th/6th] ☎ 245-4499, has 8 teachers and classes at all levels, including children's. Master Cho, a 9th Dan Black Belt, author of *Secrets of Korean Karate,* and member of the Black Belt Hall of Fame since 1971, teaches 5 classes each week himself, one to children. There is no body contact, even in sparring classes, unless protective gear is worn.

JIU JITSU is an eclectic Japanese method of fighting that draws from Judo, Aikido, and Karate, but is a more rugged form with many different styles. Stretching and acrobatic calisthenics are warm-ups for a series of two-person workouts using punching, throwing, and flipping. Some are performed standing and some on the floor. There can be full body contact. Professor **Higashi** (see Aikido) teaches the kokushi ryu, a style he has developed during his 30 years of teaching. Men and women in the same classes.

JUDO, an Olympic sport and one of the first martial arts to reach America for use in the military, comes from Japan. It uses knowledge of the body's center of gravity, timing, and balance to make it possible for a small person to throw a larger person. There is no punching or kicking, but it is fair to grab on to the clothing of your opponent, so special, stronger *Gi* (the judo kimono and pants) are worn. When done well, the throws happen very fast. Kids can start any time, good for teens. For judo, you want Professor Higashi (see Aikido).

RACETRACKS

Aqueduct, Rockaway Blvd. and 110th St. ☎ 718-641-4700. Racing Wed.–Sun. from the third week of October through the end of April. $2 for the grandstand, $4 for the clubhouse.

Belmont Park Racetrack, Hempstead Turnpike and Plainfield Ave. ☎ 718-641-4700. There is racing Wed.–Sun. in May, June, July, September, and October. $2 for the grandstand, $4 for the clubhouse.

ROLLERBLADING

The Rollerblade company would like you to refer to the sport as "in-line skating," but that's only for those of you who use facial tissues and listen to personal stereos.

TEACHERS
Lisa-Michelle Buckley, ☎ 642-5969, gives private Rollerblading lessons to children. See more in the Trainers article in this chapter.

    Kate Gengo, ☎ 718-782-9175, teaches at Chelsea Piers and privately, mostly to adults. She also competes nationally in Aggressive Skating competitions. When she teaches, though, it's the basics of safety and balance. How long it takes you to learn depends on "how many miles you put on your skates." $30/hr.

    Alan Slesinger, 800-492-9003, says blading is a "quick and efficient way" to negotiate the "ocean of asphalt" that we live on. Mr. Slesinger teaches individuals and groups (of no more than six), choosing park areas "which are safe and where people feel se-

cure." He breaks the sport down to its basic elements, starting with "how the skates work." Private lessons are $45/hr., groups, $20/hr.

WHERE TO BUY
Blades has 6 locations including one at Sky Rink in Chelsea Piers. ☎ 336-6199, **Gymnasium Inc.,** 133 W. 42nd St. [6th/Bway] ☎ 354-2800, **Paragon Sports,** 867 Broadway [18th] ☎ 255-8036, **Peck & Goodie,** 919 Eighth Ave. [54th/55th] ☎ 246-6123.

MORE Anthony Pepe at **TranSports,** 207 E. 85th St. [2nd/3rd] ☎ 249-7657, custom makes a motorized skate. "It's more like skiing than skating, because you don't pick up your feet." There is a tiny motor mounted on the back of the skates, and you have a gas throttle with a shut-off switch in your hand. Mr. Pepe scoots around at about 45 mph when he takes them out for fun on weekends. $1,300.

RUNNING

Our favorite place to run in the city is the reservoir. You're supposed to run counterclockwise, but we ignore the rules and run

clockwise. The reason is that you get much better views of the skyline to the south when you are running southward on the east side of the reservoir. Here are some of the city's running clubs (which would doubtless disapprove of our disregard of the rules. Sorry!).

RUNNING CLUBS

Achilles Track Club
☎ 921-4495. Disabled runners
Big Apple Triathlon Club
☎ 914-247-0271. Advanced
East Side Racewalk Team
☎ 516-731-5255. Advanced
Front Runners
☎ 724-9700. Mostly gay and lesbian

Heights-Inwood Track Club
☎ 942-3821. All levels
Millrose Athletic Association
☎ 663-5641. All levels
Natural Living Running Club
☎ 799-1243. All levels
Go Run NY
☎ 923-5473. All levels
New York Road Runners Club
☎ 860-4455. All levels
Warren Street
☎ 807-7422. All levels
West Side Y
☎ 787-1301. All levels

SAILING

LEARNING TO SAIL

You can learn to sail at the **Great Hudson Sailing Center,** at the Chelsea Piers, 23rd St. and the Hudson River ☎ 741-7245. From April to October, they give weekend sailing lessons, broken down into four 4-hour sessions. $425.

Volunteers in the **Coast Guard Auxiliary** teach at Hunter College and the Marine Information Office at the Battery. There is a basic powerboat class and a basic sailing class, both are 13 weeks. An advanced class in Coastal Navigation has one or the other as a prerequisite. Classes are free, with a nominal charge for textbooks and other materials (about $60). The classes are not given at regular intervals, but to find out scheduling information, you can talk to David Friedman, the Public Education Officer for Flotilla 5-10. ☎ 355-1564.

Hayden Planetarium, Central Park West and 81st St. ☎ 769-5900, teaches Navigation in Coastal Waters and Beginning and Advanced Celestial Navigation classes. $110.

For more on sailing, see Boating in the Arts and Diversions chapter.

SKATEBOARDING

For skateboard supplies, go to **Supreme,** 274 Lafayette St. [Houston/Prince] ☎ 966-7799. You'll find skateboarders on the Manhattan side of the Brooklyn Bridge, around Astor Place at night, and on Sixth Ave. between 42nd and 59th Streets.

SKIING

SNOW REPORTS

CONNECTICUT
Mohawk Mountain ☎ 203-672-6100
Mt. Southington ☎ 203-628-0954
Powder Ridge ☎ 800-622-3321
Ski Sundown ☎ 203-379-9851

MAINE
Saddleback ☎ 207-864-3380
Shawnee Peak ☎ 207-647-8444
Sugarloaf ☎ 207-237-2000
Sunday River ☎ 207-824-6400

MASSACHUSETTS
Berkshire East ☎ 413-339-6617
Blue Hills ☎ 617-828-5070
Bousquet ☎ 413-442-2436
Brodie ☎ 413-443-4751
Butternut ☎ 413-528-2000
Catamount ☎ 800-342-1840
Jiminy Peak ☎ 413-738-5500
Mt. Tom ☎ 413-536-0516
Otis Ridge ☎ 413-269-4444
Wachusett Mountain ☎ 800-754-1234

NEW HAMPSHIRE
Attitash ☎ 603-374-0946
Cannon Mountain ☎ 603-823-7771
Gunstock ☎ 800-486-7862
Waterville Valley ☎ 603-236-4144
Wildcat ☎ 800-643-4521

NEW JERSEY
Campgaw Mountain ☎ 201-327-7800
Craigmeur ☎ 201-697-4500
Hidden Valley ☎ 201-764-6161
Vernon Valley/Great Gorge ☎ 201-827-2000

NEW YORK
Belleayre ☎ 800-942-6904
Bristol ☎ 716-234-5000
Gore Mountain ☎ 518-251-2523
Greek Peak ☎ 800-365-7669
Holiday Mountain ☎ 914-796-3161
Holiday Valley ☎ 716-699-2644
Hunter ☎ 800-367-7669
Mount Peter ☎ 914-986-4992
Ski Plattekill ☎ 800-633-3275
Ski Windham ☎ 800-729-4766
Sterling Forest ☎ 914-351-4788
Whiteface ☎ 518-946-7171

PENNSYLVANIA
Alpine ☎ 717-595-2150
Big Boulder ☎ 800-475-7669
Blue Knob ☎ 814-239-5111
Blue Mountain ☎ 800-235-2226
Camelback ☎ 800-233-8100
Elk Mountain ☎ 800-233-4131
Hidden Valley ☎ 800-443-7544
Jack Frost ☎ 800-475-7669
Montage ☎ 717-969-7669
Mt. Tone ☎ 717-798-2707
Seven Springs ☎ 800-523-7777
Shawnee ☎ 717-421-7231
Ski Liberty ☎ 717-642-9000
Ski Roundtop ☎ 800-767-4766
Whitetail ☎ 717-328-5300

VERMONT
Bromley ☎ 802-824-5522
Jay Peak ☎ 802-988-2611
Killington ☎ 802-422-3261
Mad River Glen ☎ 802-496-2001
Mt. Snow ☎ 802-464-2151
Okemo ☎ 802-228-5222
Pico ☎ 802-775-4345

Smuggler's Notch ☎ 802-644-8851
Stowe ☎ 802-253-3600
Stratton ☎ 802-297-4211
Sugarbush ☎ 802-583-7669

GETTING TO THE SLOPES

BY EVELYN KANTER

You don't need a car to enjoy slopes in the Catskills, Adirondacks, or even Vermont. There are daily and weekend bus and train trips that are cost-effective and convenient.

What you save via a reduced-price group ticket, plus what you don't spend for gas and tolls, reduces transportation cost to pennies. Plus, it's more restful to let somebody else drive while you doze, read, or socialize. Reservations are a must. Skiers who show up minutes before departure may get left behind because there's no space.

Island Tours goes to Ski Windham on Sunday, Monday, Wednesday, and Friday. Pick-up: Grand Hyatt, 42nd near Lexington, 6 A.M. $60 weekends, $50 weekdays, includes lift ticket, ski movie, and bagels in morning, action movie and snacks on way home. For beginners, the tab includes a lesson. Weekend trips include accommodations and meals. ☎ 718-343-4444.

Paragon Sporting Goods day trips to Hunter Mt. on Wednesdays and Saturdays from the store, 17th and Broadway. $55 with ticket, $28 without. Ski or snowboard rentals are $19.95. Reserve gear ahead of time and they load it for you. A group lesson is a bargain at $10. ☎ 225-8036.

At the bottom of the list for service and value is **Scandinavian Ski Shop,** 40 W. 57th St. [5th/6th], going to Hunter Mt. on Saturdays, Sundays, and holidays at 7 A.M. $57 does not include gear ($19) and they don't load it for you. A much better deal is Scandinavian's weekend trips to Stowe, Sugarbush, and Maine's Sugarloaf. ☎ 757-8524.

Blade's West, 120 W. 72nd St. [Columbus/Bway], takes primarily snowboarders to Hunter Mt. Thursdays and Sundays, departing 7 A.M. Rentals are $20; transportation, breakfast, and movie is another $55, with choice of an all-area lift ticket or limited-area pass and snowboard lesson. ☎ 787-3911.

Adirondack Trailways leaves 40th St. Port Authority terminal mornings for Belleayre, which has free cross-country skiing. That's because Belleayre's groomed trails are at the bottom of the mountain, so there's no need to buy a lift ticket.

Or be pampered by **The Sagamore,** the resort on a private island on Lake George. Take Amtrak from Penn Station to Albany. Sagamore's van drives you to the hotel and shuttles you daily to nearby Gore Mountain. Or cross-country ski on the snow-covered golf course. ☎ 800-358-3585.

STROLLERCIZE

Elizabeth Trindade created Strollercize, a regimen for new moms, using the stroller and the weight of the baby inside. They meet mostly in Central Park. You can take a single class ($15) or buy a series for a lower per-class price. For more info, ☎ 759-4689.

SWIMMING

We began to feel a bit like Neddy Merrill in John Cheever's short story "The Swimmer" as we pool-hopped, in our case, around Manhattan. The only criterion was that the pool be open to the public either by membership or by the day. Prices are average yearly prices. Many have one-time initiation fees in the $300 range. Almost every place listed runs specials that change monthly and may have corporate discounts.

LOWER MANHATTAN

Bally's Jack La Lanne, 233 Broadway [Barclay/Park] ☎ 227-5977. M–F, 6–9, Sa, Su, 9–5. 64' × 18'. 1 free lane, 2 for laps. $19–$33/month, 3-yr. commitment. ☞ Dingy and depressing. One of the worst.

Battery Park Swim & Fitness Center, 375 South End Ave. [Liberty] ☎ 321-1117. M–F, 8–6:45, Sa, Su, 9–6. 50' × 25'. 4 lanes. $863/yr. ☞ Being completely glass-enclosed makes it one of the nicest for atmosphere.

Executive Fitness Center, NY Vista Hotel, 3 World Trade Center ☎ 466-9266. M–F, 6–9:30, Sa, Su, 8–7. 50' × 20'. 4 lanes. $1,100/yr. ☞ You can't argue with the views, though it's crowded after work and at lunch.

Hamilton Fish Pool, 128 Pitt St. [Ave. C] ☎ 387-7687. Generally 11–7, but varies with programs. 100' × 50'. 11 lanes. No fee. ☞ A great restoration success—the best outdoor pool in the city.

NY Health & Racquet, 39 Whitehall St. [Pearl] ☎ 269-9800. M–F, 6–10, Sa, 9–6. 65' × 35'. 2 lanes. $1,195/yr. ☞ The best of the Health & Racquet pools.

Stuyvesant High School, 345 Chambers St. [West] ☎ 374-0973. After 7 P.M. weekdays, 1–7 weekends. 75' × 45'. $100 membership, 5-month waiting list. ☞ Great design makes this one of the best in the city—for serious swimmers.

The Terrace Club, 380 Rector Pl. [SEA] ☎ 945-3665. M–Th, 7–9:45, Sa, Su, 9–5:45. F, closed. 45' × 20'. 1 lane. $795/yr. ☞ Clean, light because it's in an atrium.

VILLAGE, CHELSEA, GRAMERCY

Asser Levy Recreational Center, FDR Drive at 23rd St. ☎ 447-2020. M–F, 7–9:30, Sa, Su, 8–4:30. Scheduled hours for lap swim and general swim. Outdoor: 126' × 50', indoor: 63' × 64'. 3 lanes indoors, none outdoors. $25/yr. ☞ Can be crowded, but this is a terrific facility and value.

Carmine Street Pool, Clarkson St. and Seventh Ave. ☎ 242-5228. M–F, 7–9:30, Sa, 2:30–5:30. Outdoor: 100' × 75', indoor: 60' × 34'. 3 lanes. $25/yr. ☞ Indoor pool is old and is not in good shape.

Chelsea Piers, 23rd St. and Twelfth Ave. ☎ 336-6000. M–F, 6–11, Sa, 7–10, Su, 8–8. 75' × 45'. 6 lanes. $300 initiation, $100/month. ☞ A very appealing pool with plenty of windows through which to enjoy the views of the Hudson.

McBurney YMCA, 215 W. 23rd St. [7th/8th] ☎ 741-9210. M–F, 6–9:30, Sa, 10–7, Su, 9–5. Pool closed when classes offered. 48' × 20'. 6 lanes. $708/yr. ☞ Okay, but basic facility needs sprucing up. A new Olympic-size pool should open at the end of 1996. Historical note: Merrill is said to have met Lynch at this pool.

NY Health & Racquet, 24 E. 13th St. [5th/University] ☎ 924-4600. M–F, 6–11, Sa, Su, 8–9. No lanes. 35' × 20'. $1,195/yr. ☞ Well-maintained, but much too small for laps.

NYU-Coles Sports & Recreation Center, 181 Mercer St. [Houston/Bleecker] ☎ 998-2020. Variable hours. 82' × 45'. 6 lanes. $58 for 12 visits. ☞ You must be affiliated with NYU, a Village resident, or take an SCE swim class to use the pool. There's a six-month waiting list for one of the better downtown pools.

Printing House Fitness & Racquet Club, 421 Hudson St. [Leroy] ☎ 243-7600. M–F, 6:30–10, Sa, Su, 8–7. No lanes. 20' × 30'. $1,395/yr. ☞ Seasonal outdoor pool June 1–Sept. 30. One of the few health club outdoor swimming pools, nice views, good for dipping.

Szold Place, E. 10th St. at Szold Place [C/D] ☎ None. 35' × 29'. $25/yr. ☞ Surrounded by city-owned housing, the pool is old and not very attractive. Just the basics here.

MIDTOWN EAST

Atrium Club, 115 E. 57th St. [Park/Lex] ☎ 826-9640. M–F, 6:30–10, Sa, Su, 9:30–6. 40' × 30'. 5 lanes. $105/month. ☞ Airy, bright, windows around pool, though no views.

Bally's Jack La Lanne, 45 E. 55th St. [Mad/Park] ☎ 688-6630. Daily, 6–10. Pool closed between 2–2:30 daily. 14' × 36'. No lanes. $19–$33/month, 3 yr.-commitment. ☞ Big thumbs down.

E. 54th St. Recreational Center, 348 E. 54th St. [1st/2nd] ☎ 397-3154. M–F, 3–10, Sa, 10–5. 48' × 54'. 8 lanes. $25/yr. ☞ A city pool in serious need of help.

Excelsior Athletic Club, 301 E. 57th St. [2nd] ☎ 688-5280. M–F, 5:30–10, Sa, Su, 7:30–6. 40' × 20'. 4 lanes. $950/yr. ☞ Attractive, glass-enclosed pool. Roof opens in summer.

NY Health & Racquet, 132 E. 45th St. [Lex/3rd] ☎ 986-3100. M–F, 6–10, Sa, Su, 9–6. 45' × 30'. 2 lanes. $1,195/yr. ☞ Fine, well-kept but can be crowded.

NY Health & Racquet, 20 E. 50th St. [5th/Mad] ☎ 593-1500. M–F, 6–10, Sa, 9–6. 50' × 20'. 2 lanes. $1,195/yr. ☞ Serviceable, though somewhat closed-in feel.

NY Sports Club, 614 Second Ave. [33rd/34th] ☎ 213-5999. M–Th, 7–11, F, 7–9, Sa, 11–6:45, Su, 9–7. 13' × 25'. No lanes. $249 initiation, $58/month. ☞ Small facility, small pool, cramped, not particularly inviting.

UN Plaza Hotel Health Club, First Ave. and 44th St. ☎ 702-5016. 6:30–10:15. 4 lanes. 40' × 24'. $1,352/yr. ☞ Spectacular views in terrific facility. Day rate: $25.

Vanderbilt YMCA, 224 E. 47th St. [2nd/3rd] ☎ 756-9600. M–F, 6–10, Sa, Su, 8–7. 75' × 40'. 6 lanes. $708/yr. ☞ Excellent pool, clean, one of the best in the city. Day rate: $15.

Vertical Club, 335 Madison Ave. [43rd/44th] ☎ 983-5320. M–F, 6–9:30, Sa, Su, 9–6. 75' × 20'. 3 lanes. $1,499/yr. ☞ Long, narrow pool, good for laps.

YWCA, 610 Lexington Ave. [52nd/53rd] ☎ 755-4500. M–F, 6:30–9, Sa, 8–4, Su, 10–2. 75' × 36'. 6 lanes. $55 membership, $550/yr. or $12/hr. ☞ A good facility: clean, large, well-lit, friendly staff.

MIDTOWN WEST

Athletic & Swim Club at Equitable Center, 787 Seventh Ave. [51st/52nd] ☎ 265-3490. M–F, 6:30–9, Sa, 9–5. 75' × 32'. 4 lanes. $1,656/yr. ☞ High ceilings and smart lighting help hide the underground ambience of this otherwise excellent, though expensive, pool.

Club La Raquette, 119 W. 56th St. [6th/7th] ☎ 245-1144. M–F, 7–10:45, Sa, Su, 9–6:45. 40' × 20'. 3 lanes. $1,100/yr. ☞ On the top floor of the Parker Meridien. Small pool, but tons of light and *spectacular* views. Day passes are $25.

Inn on 57th St., 440 W. 57th St. [9th/10th] ☎ 581-8100. 10–8, summer only. 25' × 11'. No lanes. $15/weekdays, $25/weekends. ☞ Unremarkable pool, but it's outdoors and the view's good.

John Jay College, 899 Tenth Ave. [58th] ☎ 237-8000. M–F, 11–7, but lap swim times vary. 75' × 20'. 4 lanes. $300/yr. ☞ Clean, well-lit, good to know about.

Manhattan Plaza Health Club, 482 W. 43rd St. [9th/10th] ☎ 563-7001. M–F, 7–9:30, Sa, Su, 9–6:45. 75' × 35'. 4 lanes. $875/yr. ☞ One of the top pools in the city.

NY Health & Racquet, 110 W. 56th St. [6th/7th] ☎ 541-7200. M–F, 6–11, Sa, 9–8:30, Su, 9–5:30. 50' × 35'. 4 lanes. $1,195/yr. ☞ Underground feeling, but one of the better HRC pools, with two aquacizers (like running tracks) underwater in the pool.

NY Sports Club, Crowne Plaza Hotel, 49th and Broadway ☎ 977-8880. M–F, 6–9:30, Sa, 9–8, Su, 9–6. 50' × 20'. 4 lanes. $349 initiation, $75/month. ☞ Perfectly nice, clean, and airy.

The Peninsula Spa, 700 Fifth Ave. [54th/55th] ☎ 903-3910. M–F, 6–9, Sa, Su, 8:30–7. 42' × 19'. No lanes. $2,600 initiation, $180/mo., with family rates available, or $200/day with spa facilities. ☞ Lovely overall, pool is fine, but not especially so for laps.

Sheraton Manhattan, Seventh Ave. and 51st St. ☎ 581-3300. M–F 6–9:30, Sa, Su, 8–8. 50' × 25'. 2 lanes. $600/yr. or $20/day. ☞ Good pool, perfect for an urban getaway, with an outdoor area for sunbathing.

Vertical Club, 139 W. 32nd St. [6th/7th] ☎ 465-1750. M–F, 6–10, Sa, Su, 9–6. 80' × 15'. 4 lanes. $1,499 for 2 yrs. ☞ Very nice pool, excellent for laps. Sauna, steam, and whirlpool are poolside.

Vertical Club, 351 W. 49th St. [8th/9th] ☎ 265-9400. M–F, 6–9:30, Sa, Su, 9–5:30. 82' × 26'. 4 lanes. $1,299/yr. ☞ Hi-tech, large, glass-enclosed. Not bright, but otherwise excellent.

West 59th St. Recreational Center, 533 W. 59th St. [10th/11th] ☎ 397-3159. M–F, 3–10:30. Sa, 12–5:30. 60' × 25'. 4 lanes. $25/yr. ☞ The facility's creaky, but the pool is okay—much better than the E. 54th St. Center.

UPPER EAST SIDE

Asphalt Green, 555 E. 90th St. [York] ☎ 369-8890. M–F, 5:30–10, Sa, Su, 8–8. 175' × 60'. 8 lanes. $828/yr., $15/day pass. ☞ One of the most beautiful facilities in the city.

Gold's Gym, 1635 Third Ave. [91st/92nd] ☎ 987-7200. M–F, 5–12 A.M. Sa, Su, 6–11. 50' × 30'. 5 lanes. $950. ☞ Low industrial ceiling over basement pool, but bright and clean enough. Jacuzzi and sauna poolside.

John Jay Pool, 77th St. at Cherokee Place [E. of York] ☎ 794-6566. Generally 6–8, but variable. 145' × 50'. No lanes. ☞ Large urban pool due for a renovation.

Lenox Hill Neighborhood Assoc., 331 E. 70th St. [1st/2nd] ☎ 744-5022. Widely varying swim hours. 60' × 20'. 3 lanes. $325/yr. ☞ An old pool with some character.

NY Health & Racquet, 1433 York Ave. [76th] ☎ 737-6666. M–F, 7–10, Sa, Su,

9–9. 35' × 20'. No lanes. $1,195/yr. ☞ Tiny basement afterthought pool.

92nd St. Y, 1395 Lexington Ave. [91st/92nd] ☎ 427-6000. M, Th, 6:30–9:45, F, 6:30–4:45, Sa, 6–8:45, Su, 9–4:45. 75' × 36'. 3–4 lanes. $884/yr.☞ Nice enough pool, clean. Several hot tubs poolside.

Vertical Club, 330 E. 61st St. [1st/2nd] ☎ 355-5100. M–F, 6–11, Sa, Su, 9–9. 42' × 27'. 3 lanes. $1,499/2 yrs. Overall facility is overwhelming, the pool somewhat underwhelming. Huge Jacuzzi poolside.

UPPER WEST SIDE

Aerobics West, 131 W. 86th St. [Columbus/Amsterdam] ☎ 787-3356. Widely variable hours. 20' × 40'. 3 lanes. $900/yr. In The Jewish Center: closed Fri. afternoons and Sats. ☞ Friendly place, plenty of light, but not a great pool.

Club 30, 30 Lincoln Plaza [62nd/63rd] ☎ 247-8404. M, W, Th, F, 6:45–9:45, Sa, Su, 8–6:45, closed T. 40' × 18'. 5 lanes. $945/year. ☞ Clean and attractive, better than average. Great sun deck.

Lasker Pool in Central Park, South of Lenox Ave. at 106th St. ☎ 534-7639. Generally 9–7, but variable. 225' × 195'. $25/yr. ☞ Huge pool in the park—what else?

Paris Health Club, 752 West End Ave. [96th/97th] ☎ 749-3500. M, W, 6–10:45, T, Th, F, 6–9:45, Sa, Su, 8–7:30. 50' × 20'. 6 lanes. $806/yr. ☞ Decent, crowded pool with an underground feeling.

Reebok, 160 Columbus Ave. [67th] ☎ 362-6800. M–F, 5–11, Sa, Su, 8–8. 75' × 28'. 3 lanes. $950 initiation, $140/month. ☞ Considering the scope of Reebok City, the pool is very good (with an underwater sound system), but not extraordinary.

Top of the One, 1 Lincoln Plaza [63rd/64th] ☎ 595-5121. M–F, 6:30–9:30, Sa, Su, 8–7. 40' × 20'. Variable lanes. $945/yr. ☞ A pleasant facility and the only one with a wood-burning fireplace in the large, adjacent lounge!

YMCA, 5 W. 63rd St. [CPW/Bway] ☎ 787-1301. M, F, 6:30–10, T, W, Th, 6:30–9, Sa, 8–8, Su, 9–5. 2 pools: one is 75' × 25', 4 lanes, used for lap swimming; the other is 60' × 20', which is used for lessons. $684/yr. ☞ The tile adds a grace note to the aquatics.

INSTRUCTION

Doug Stern gives group swimming classes at Columbia Prep School, 5 W. 93rd St. [Columbus/CPW]. He teaches everyone from water phobics to experienced swimmers who want to improve their skills or learn new strokes. The phobics class comes with a money-back guarantee if he does not have you swimming by the end of the last class. One of his tricks is the use of swim goggles that allow you to keep your eyes open in the water, and consequently "gives you one less thing to be afraid of." The Different Strokes class teaches the breast stroke, the butterfly, and the backstroke. A 1 1/2-hour class (6–7 sessions, depending on the course) is $205. Mr. Stern has also developed deep-water running in conjunction with the NY Road Runners Club. It's just what it sounds like. You use a waist flotation device and run in the water, which provides resistance—helping you to build muscle and improve circulation— without the pounding you get when you run on pavement. This reduces the risk of knee, hip, or back problems. If you have suffered an injury, this kind of running can help in the healing process. It also helps you to increase speed on land. Most people, in fact, use the deep-water running to supplement their regular running program. The deep-water running sessions take place at John Jay College, 899 Tenth Ave. [58th/59th]. Mr. Stern says the activity is very easy to learn, and there are coaches at each session to get you started. Musical accompaniment ranges from "The Ride of the Valkyries" to swing to rock. $15 a session, or $80 for a series of 7 classes. Call Mr. Stern at ☎ 222-0720 for schedules.

TENNIS

DOWNTOWN

NY Health and Racquet Tennis and Yacht, Wall St. Piers 13 and 14 ☎ 422-9300. 6 A.M.–midnight. Eight indoor Har-Tru courts under a bubble. $795 per year, $500 initiation, hourly $25–$60. Hourly rates for non-members: $50–$120. Seasonal rates available. Fee for guests. Does game arranging, lessons, tournaments. ☞ Very attractive facility, and great locker rooms. The way the courts are lined up end-to-end down the length of the pier gives you a sense of privacy.

NY Health and Racquet Village Tennis Court, 110 University Pl. [12th/13th] ☎ 989-2300. 7 A.M.–11 P.M. Two hard rubber Supreme court surfaces plus practice court with ball machine. The courts are on a rooftop under a bubble. Yearly membership rate is $294, plus the hourly charges of $31–$83. Seasonal rates available. No initiation fee. HRC has more membership options than we've listed: tennis and health club, tennis only, and limited hour tennis. ☞ Solid HRC facility.

TEAM MERCHANDISE

Gerry Cosby started **Gerry Cosby Sporting Goods,** now in Madison Square Garden ☎ 563-6464, in 1938, eight years after playing goalie on the winning 1930 World Championship Games team. Mr. Cosby is retired, but his son, Michael, runs the shop. This store specializes in authentic team clothing for baseball, football, basketball, and hockey as well as some boxing attire. If you need a shirt like those worn by Phil Simms or Bobby Bonilla or Patrick Ewing, this is the place. Other stores may sell official clothing, but Gerry Cosby sells for all teams in the entire league, not just local teams or recent winners.

They also sell jerseys, hats, jackets, and other souvenirs like pennants, key chains, and so on ... **Mets Store Clubhouse Shop,** 575 Fifth Ave. [46th/47th] ☎ 986-4887 ... **Yankees Clubhouse Shop,** 110 E. 59th St. [Park/Lex] ☎ 758-7844 and 393 Fifth Ave. [36th/37th] ☎ 685-4693 ... **Collector's Stadium,** 214 Sullivan St. [3rd/Bleecker] ☎ 353-1531, sells mostly baseball cards, but they also keep in stock baseball caps from most of the current teams as well as official replicas of teams from the turn of the century to the 1920s. There are a couple of styles of Brooklyn Dodger caps, which, not surprisingly, are among their best sellers.

MIDTOWN WEST

Manhattan Plaza Racquet Club, 450 W. 43rd St. [9th/10th] ☎ 594-0554. M–F, 6 A.M.–midnight, Sa, Su, 7 A.M.–midnight.

The outdoor courts at Manhattan Plaza Racquet Club.

Five hard surface courts. Outdoor from May–Sept, otherwise under a bubble. $750 annual, $250 initiation. Family and corporate options. Hourly rates, in addition to membership, $28–$50. For court time, you generally need to book a week in advance. ☞ Just about everything at this club, including tennis, is first class.

Crosstown Tennis, 14 W. 31st St. [5th/Bway] ☎ 947-5780. Daily 6 A.M.– 10 P.M., except Sa, 6 A.M.–8 P.M. Four indoor air-conditioned Decoturf II courts. $38–$95/hour, depending on season and day of week. Season rates for 36 weeks, $1,300–$3,249. $80 for lessons with a pro (includes court). No guest fees, no initiation fee. ☞ In average shape, nothing posh, but certainly serviceable.

Midtown Tennis Club, 341 Eighth Ave. [26th/27th] ☎ 989-8572. M–F, 7 A.M.–midnight, Sa, Su, 8 A.M.–midnight. Eight Har-Tru courts: 4 outdoor courts are under a bubble in winter. The 4 indoor courts are air-conditioned. $35–$70 by the hour. Seasonal rates for early Oct–early May, $1,085–$2,170. Lessons, clinics, leagues, and social events, children's program. ☞ Not especially pretty, but courts are well maintained.

MIDTOWN EAST

Sutton East Tennis Courts, 488 E. 60th St. [Sutton/York] ☎ 751-3452. 7 A.M.–midnight. Eight indoor clay courts in a bubble under the 59th St. Bridge. No net separators between courts. $1,176–$2,912 for the 28-week season, Oct.–Apr. $32–$104 hourly. Lessons, game arrangement, tournaments, and tennis parties, many children playing after school. ☞ An unappealing approach to the club along 60th St., but inside the courts are in beautiful shape.

The Tennis Club at Grand Central, 15 Vanderbilt Ave. [42nd/43rd] ☎ 687-3841. M–F, 7 A.M.–10 P.M. 8 A.M.–5 P.M. during the winter season, and closed summer weekends. Two indoor Decoturf courts. $1,100–$2,750 seasonally, $3,850 yearly, $65–$75 hourly. Many slots are booked seasonally. No match-up service. ☞ A no-frills atmosphere, but we love the idea of playing in Grand Central.

U.N. Plaza-Park Hyatt Health Club, First Ave. and 44th St. ☎ 702-5016. Daily, 7 A.M.–11 P.M. One indoor Supreme court surface. Fifty-two 1-hour sessions, $2,860. Lessons, $60/hr. Hourly, $55–$60. No match-up services. Pool and exercise room are freebies. ☞ Spacious, quiet, clean, private feeling, top-notch facility. Great views over the river and of the U.N.

Town Tennis Member Club, 430 E. 56th St. [Sutton/1st] ☎ 752-4059. Daily, 8 A.M.–10 P.M. Three outdoor Deco-Turf II courts, two of which are lit for night play, and a 3/4 court with a backboard, used for practicing. Initiation: Seniors (40 and over!) $3,000; Intermediates (under 40) $2,000; nonresident $1,100. Annual dues: $3,350 for seniors and intermediates over 30; $2,700 for intermediates under 30; $1,150 for nonresidents. $24 for singles per court per hour. ☞ A circuitous route through an apartment building takes you to a smart-looking club with an attractive cafe and sitting area. But you're supposed to be recommended to the club by a member, and they want bank references!

The Vertical Club, 330 E. 61st St. [1st/2nd] ☎ 355-5100. 6 A.M.–10 P.M. Six indoor and two outdoor (on the roof) courts. Supreme surface. $3,000 for the first year; $1,000 each year thereafter gets you use of the courts and all of the other facilities in the building. Hourly court fees are $20–$25 additional. Lessons, game arranging, tournaments, and social events. ☞ The price is steep, but the VC is a top facility.

UPPER WEST SIDE

Columbus Tennis Club, 795 Columbus Ave. [97th] ☎ 663-6900. Daily, 7 A.M.–9 P.M. Nine outdoor Har-Tru courts, lighted for nighttime playing. Season is mid-April through Oct. Individual, $1,750; individual weekday, $1,400. Family, junior, and corporate memberships available. No additional fees for court time, and you can play as many times as you can schedule a game. They do game arranging. ☞ Distinctly urban environment, just feet from Columbus Ave.

Trinity Tennis Club, 101 W. 91st St. [Columbus/Amsterdam], inside the Trinity School ☎ 932-6827, ask for Sonia. 7 A.M.–midnight, except school hours. Two courts, the indoor is Ball-tex carpeting, the outdoor is Ball-tex mesh. Thirty-five-week season runs from mid-Sept. to mid-May. You buy the same hour each week. Costs from $660–$1,440, vary by the time slot. ☞ Perfectly adequate courts.

UPPER EAST SIDE

Tower Tennis Courts, 1725 York Ave. [90th], on the 3rd floor of the East River Tower ☎ 860-2464. Summer: Tu–Th, 6 P.M.–10 P.M. Winter: 7 A.M.–midnight. Two Decoturf II courts under a bubble. Winter costs $1,000–$2,900 or $60–$80 per hour, but this is available only when there are cancellations. Lessons, bulletin board for those seeking to arrange games. ☞ Plain but spacious sitting areas, but an away-from-it-all sense in finding a tennis court on an apartment building floor. Virtually no summer play since there's no air-conditioning.

OTHER

East River Tennis Club, 44-02 Vernon Blvd. [44th Ave.], Long Island City, ☎ 718-937-2381. Daily, 7:30 A.M.–10 P.M. Eighteen Har-Tru outdoor courts, covered with a bubble in winter, two additional courts in summer. Rates start at $1,750 plus $23 for singles. ☞ Nice facility, with a pool and great views of Manhattan. Limited shuttle bus service from 57th St. and Third Ave.

Tennisport, 51-24 Second St. [Borden], Long Island City, ☎ 718-392-1880. M–F, 7:30 A.M.–10 P.M. Sa, Su, 7:30 A.M.–8 P.M. Thirteen outdoor Har-Tru courts, 16 indoor red clay courts. $2,800 annually, plus $15 per hour during peak, and $12 off-peak. Off-peak annual fee: $1,400 with same court fees. Under 35, $800 per year (during non-peak). $10 per hour court time. Lessons, $70, and game arranging available. ☞ A good, serious place, a short walk from the Vernon Ave. stop on the #7, IRT.

USTA National Tennis Center, Flushing Meadows, Corona Park, ☎ 718-760-6200. Twenty-two outdoor Deco-Turf II courts, lit for night play. Nine indoor Deco-Turf courts enclosed in a permanent structure. Indoor weekdays, 32-week, one-hour rates: $896–$1,280. Hourly rates: $28–$40. Indoor rates are reduced from May 15–Oct. 1. Many programs, including one for wheelchair tennis. $57–$67 for private lessons, group instruction available. Construction of a new stadium is underway. It is scheduled to be ready for the 1997 Open. After that, the current stadium will be "downsized," and 47 courts will be available to the public. The controversial construction will create 11 courts where you can use your city permit. Air-conditioned. ☞ A superb facility.

Roosevelt Island Racquet Club, 281 Main St., Roosevelt Island ☎ 935-0250. 6 A.M.–midnight. Twelve air-conditioned clay courts under a bubble. Hourly rates available from $24–$40, plus per person guest fees of $10 or $20, depending on time of day. Memberships are $750 a year plus $500 initiation, $250 of which is payable on joining, the other $250 due on renewal. There are a few other plans available, and Roosevelt Island residents get a break on the price. Membership entitles you to the lowest court rates, priority reservations, game arranging, free use of the ball machine. ☞ Just

a tram ride away (the club is next to the tram station), and the facilities are in tip-top shape. This is a beautiful facility, and the staff couldn't be nicer.

CITY COURTS

One $50 permit gives you access to the 98 courts in Manhattan. There are 30 in Central Park [93rd/W. Dr.]; 10 at Riverside Park at 96th St.; 8 at Riverside Park at 119th St.; 12 at East River Park [near Delancey]; 10 at Ft. Washington Park [Henry Hudson Pkwy./172nd]; 9 at Inwood Hill Park [207th/Seaman]; 8 at Frederick Johnson Playground at 151th St. [7th Ave.]; Randalls Island has 11. Permits are issued at the Arsenal, Fifth Ave. and 64th St. ☎ 360-8131, and at Paragon Sporting Goods, 867 Broadway [17th/18th] ☎ 255-8036. If you are going to Paragon, you will need to take a photo I.D. with you. The Arsenal is now set up to take your picture. You need to fill out an application and make payment in cash or by personal check. The city courts are open from April–November, and permits go on sale at the end of March. The only courts that can be reserved are some in Central Park, ☎ 280-0205, in season only.

TRAINERS

The American Council on Exercise, ☎ 800-529-8227, is a national certification organization for trainers. They also answer questions about fitness and training and will supply you with the names of three certified trainers in your zip code. Debbie LaChusa, SP at ACE, suggests that you "interview trainers the way you would anyone else you

are going to hire." Be sure they are certified by a national organization. This helps ensure that they know proper ways to do the exercises. Choose a trainer who works with people with similar needs to yours (pregnant women or those preparing for a 10K). Liability insurance is also important. Trainers who work in gyms may not be covered by the gym liability if they are there as free-lancers or if they are working in your home.

Lisa-Michelle Buckley's **ABC** (Athletic Bodies for Children), ☎ 642-5969, is a program of personal training for children. She has been teaching children privately and in the public schools (as a kindergarten teacher) for more than a dozen years. Ms. Buckley teaches Rollerblading, swimming, gymnastics, and skiing in step-by-step programs that help children achieve proficiency and healthy bodies. A certified swim instructor, she teaches children as young as 2 years to swim. Skiing or Rollerblading can start at age 4 or 5, "depending on the child's size and development." Gymnastics can begin as early as 9 months in her "Mommy and Me" program that shows parents how to exercise their babies. With older children, her teaching is a combination of fitness and fun. Ms. Buckley says that to have any effect on the Nintendo generation, "it's gotta be fun." She does slip in good nutrition, because "I know I would have been better off if the Twinkies hadn't been in the house." We watched Ms. Buckley and a young student during a Rollerblading class, and she certainly has a way with kids. Instruction is $50/hr., and a 10-session package is $350. She will travel with families on ski or swim vacations as an instructor.

Jonathan Bowden is a personal trainer (and a contributing editor to *Fitness* and *Crosstrainer* magazines) who caters to the personalities of the people he works with because "the same motivation does not work for everybody," and, in fact, the "same exercises do not work for everybody." As a former musician who traveled with a lot of Broadway shows, he started **On Location Fitness**, ☎ 757-3922, to help people in the entertainment industry and business people who were away from home and had interrupted their fitness routines. He has branched out to include New Yorkers who need to establish a routine or who can't get to the gym. Out of necessity, he has become an expert in creating a workout with a minimum of equipment, using light hand weights, rubberized tubing, and step items that are "easy to store, inexpensive, and multipurpose. I can put your gym behind a door." Mr. Bowden will meet with you to tailor a fitness program that takes into consideration your goals, the amount of time you have to exercise, whether you are deskbound for long periods, or whether you travel a lot and have interruptions in your routine. $75/hour.

Elissa Levy's **NYFIT** (Focused In-Home Training), ☎ 769-1900, provides more than just exercise routines. The staff includes a personal trainer, massage therapists, a yoga instructor, and nutritionists. All are certified, licensed, and insured. Most of their clients are people who don't, for whatever reason, feel comfortable going to a gym. During the first visit, they develop a program for you. If your goal is to lose weight, you have a session with the nutritionist. Kofi, a personal trainer with NYFIT, began to develop his methods when he was a decathlete in training for the English Olympic Team. He sees flexibility as the "neglected area of fitness," and tries to balance cardiovascular work, muscular strength, and flexibility in developing a strong body for you. He works with many older people "who have either not exercised enough or at all" and who don't want to be involved in the gym scene. $75/hour.

Martha Coopersmith has been running exercise programs for 20 years. Her company, **The Bodysmith**, ☎ 249-1824, now has 11 female trainers as well as Ms. Coopersmith. They work only with women "and a few husbands." When you call as a new client, they take an exercise and brief personal history. They work with pregnant women. "Since it's almost a luxury to have a personal trainer, it should be what you want." They will work in your home, office, or apartment-house gym. $70–$80/hour. Ms. Coopersmith also produces an informative newsletter for her clients called *What the Health.*

VOLLEYBALL

Big City Volleyball League ☎ 288-4240.
 After-work league for men and women.
 120 teams.
Corporate Sports ☎ 245-4738. Men only.
NY Urban Professionals Basketball and Volleyball League ☎ 877-3614.
 Women and men.
Yorkville Sports Association ☎ 645-6488
Women Athletes of NY ☎ 759-4189

There are three courts on the hard surface closed road at 68th St., mid-park, in Central Park. For a free permit, send a SASE to Parks and Recreation, Permit Office, 16 W. 61st St. New York, NY 10023. When you play, you need to bring a net and ball. For the adjacent sand volleyball court, you sign up on the day you want to play on site.

WALKING

The Walking Center of NYC, 140 W. 79th St. [Columbus/Amsterdam] ☎ 580-1314, gives 1½-hour classes in Central Park on weekends, which combine work on body alignment with a cardiovascular walk. $10/class. They do private sessions and will give seminars to organizations.

STORES

↔

BEAUTY & FRAGRANCES

AROMATHERAPY & ROOM FRAGRANCE

There are other **Aveda** stores, but we like the one at 233 Spring St. [6th/Varick] ☎ 807-1492 on an otherwise noncommercial block, which is perfumed by the scents from the store. At the Aroma Bar, which recalls a 19th century apothecary, you are asked to smell 25 or so scents. Those you like are set aside and a custom "pure-fume" is created. This mixture can be made into a cologne or spray mist, used to scent a cleansing base, moisturizer or massage oil, or left in oil form for you to use in room diffusers. Price is based on the oils used—figure about $30. Little jars of ground coffee are scattered around for you to smell (preventing "nose fatigue"). There are some pre-mixed products (like their refreshing citrusy "Insightful" mist), and there is also a line of hair- and body-care products and cosmetics.

Down the steps at **Erbe,** 196 Prince St. [Sullivan/Macdougal] ☎ 966-1445, the herbal fragrances are based on recipes of Italian Renaissance monks. They do herbal facials ($65) and a lot of custom products for skin care using herbs and essential oils. Rose, rosemary, and lavender distilled tonic waters ($17 for 7 oz.) are good facial refreshers.

Jean La Porte L'Artisan Parfumeur, 870 Madison Ave. [70th/71st] ☎ 517-8665, makes appealing room fragrances. We'd been using their "blue" fragrance for years until they discontinued it. Now we'll have to get used to one of their other eight enticing room sprays. They sell Jean LaPorte perfume, eau de toilette, bath oils, soaps, burning oils, and candles. The room sprays are $65 for 4.3 oz., small scented candles are $15.

At **Origins,** 402 W. Broadway [Spring] ☎ 219-9764, there is no custom blending, but there are "sensory therapy" products like Peace of Mind, a peppermint lotion that you rub on your temples and behind your ears for "on-the-spot" relief. It helped us cross Sixth Ave. at Bleecker without the usual stress. Mint Condition, a body wash, used in a tepid shower, offers midsummer refreshment. In the Inhalations line, meant to be used in a diffuser, Sanitation Dept. is a blend of Egyptian geranium and spearmint. It is supposed to calm.

Scent from Heaven, 333 Bleecker St. [Christopher] ☎ 741-2595, is a shop that resembles a very elegant chemistry lab. The walls are lined with brown dropper bottles and vials of scents. There are nearly 200 different perfume oils and essential oils that can be combined into individualized fragrances—to be worn on their own or added to a line of unscented bath and personal-care products. Scents can be added to a jojoba- and aloe-based moisturizer, shampoo, conditioner, bath gel or massage oil.

BATH, BEAUTY CARE, & MAKEUP

Ad Hoc Softwares, 410 W. Broadway [Spring] ☎ 925-2652. Scented soaps in beautiful colors, bath and personal-care products from around the world tempt the sybarite or the fatigued. They carry our favorite rose-scented bath oil, Coté Bastide; Occitaine, the wonderful vegetable oil soaps from the southwest of France; Thymes Unlimited body lotions; and Carboline from Italy. You'll also find an assortment of bath brushes and body scrubbers.

Bath Island, 469 Amsterdam Ave. [82nd/83rd] ☎ 787-9415, uses their 80 essential oils to custom scent all manner of personal-care products—body and hair shampoos, bubble baths, bath oils, hand and body lotions.

The Beauty Response Center, 575 Fifth Ave. [47th] ☎ 984-4164, does cosmetics testing before products are released to the market. The reason to sign up is that you get a number of free existing products while you test new skin, hair, and fragrance items. You make an appointment, fill out a form, and they give you something to use for a week or more. When you return, you will be asked a few questions about it. Every time you go, they give you freebies—a bag, say, of L'Oréal. Most visits are 10 minutes or less.

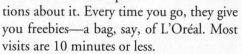

Floris of London, 703 Madison Ave. [62nd/63rd] ☎ 935-9100. English flower scents in soaps, perfumes, room sprays, shaving creams, and other beauty products and toiletries for men and women.

Fragrance Shoppe, 21 E. 7th St. [2nd/3rd] ☎ 254-8950, blends perfumes from essential oils and custom scents body lotions and bath products. Their signature scent is called Rain—lily of the valley, musk, and rose.

Kiehl's, 109 Third Ave. [13th/14th] ☎ 677-3171. How could anyone not love Kiehl's? They have great products, the staff is so agreeable, and they invariably send you away with a freebie or two. Their line of personal-care products is also available at Bergdorf's, Barneys, and Douglas Pharmacy, 1388 Second Ave. [71st/72nd] ☎ 879-3800. But you'll miss a key part of the Kiehl's experience: the charm of this old-fashioned store and the courtesy of the staff. Millard Fillmore was president when Kiehl's opened in New York in 1851.

The Makeup Center, 150 W. 55th St. [6th/7th] ☎ 977-9494. Come here for a makeup lesson (normally $25, but often on special at $15) in a relaxed atmosphere and in a private room. You'll get an individualized face chart showing where to place color, and tips on how to apply. The Makeup Center sells their own cosmetics, but there is no hard sell for you to buy after the lesson. If you don't like department store makeup counters, this is the place to come for the privacy and attention.

my Essentials, 1300 Madison Ave. [92nd] ☎ 987-8030 and 1034 Lexington Ave. [74th] ☎ 570-1317, has men's and women's personal-care products (including the Molton Brown line) as well as their own line of bath, skin care, and makeup products. Essential oils can be custom blended into lotions and sprays.

The Revlon Store, GM Bldg., 767 Fifth Ave. [58th/59th] ☎ 486-8857. Follow signs in the concourse to the Revlon Employees' Store (in spite of the signs, it's open to the public— weekdays only). You'll find not only Revlon but also Almay, Max Factor, Ultima II, and Charles of the Ritz makeup, skin- and hair-care products, and fragrances, at well below retail. You never know what else you'll find.

PERFUMES & COLOGNES

When you're looking for selection, it's the department stores, of course. When you're looking for the best values, here are three stores where you will save 20%–50% (occasionally more) off department store prices. Prices in parentheses indicate what you're likely to pay in the department stores.

Guy America, 20 E. 17th St. [5th/ Bway] ☎ 255-7770. We found Dior Poison, 100 ml for $32 ($74), and Joop for men, 125 ml for $33 ($55) . . . **Hema,** 313 Church St. [Lispenard/Walker] ☎ 431-5110. On the last visit, Fendi, 50 ml was $22 ($37) . . . **Jay's Perfume Bar,** 14 E. 17th St. [5th/ Bway] ☎ 243-7743. At Jay's, Chanel No. 19, 100 ml for $37.50 ($67.50), and Davidoff Cool Water, 125 ml for $40 ($57.50).

BOOKS

OUR FAVORITE BOOKSTORES

Academy, 10 W. 18th St. [5th/6th] ☎ 242-4848. An ideal secondhand bookstore. Perfectly plain-looking, small enough not to be overwhelming, but plenty of good stuff to keep you browsing. The last time we were there, we watched a staff member tenderly restoring a book with almost fierce concentration. It's the attic you wish you had. At **Skyline,** 13 W. 18th St. [5th/ 6th] ☎ 759-5463, across the street, more of the same.

Barnes & Noble. If you're flipping through this book at a bookstore, chances are you're at Barnes & Noble. (Now go directly to the cashier and pay for it.) New Yorkers may miss many of their favorite small booksellers, but so much space devoted to books, in an atmosphere designed

to keep you *involved* with books, is amazing and wonderful.

Books and Co., 939 Madison Ave. [74th/75th] ☎ 737-1450. You can spend a dreamy hour or two just moving along the center aisle of interesting selections, with the floor creaking below your feet. Books and Co. has an invariably great reading series.

Coliseum, 1771 Broadway [57th] ☎ 757-8381. One of MUG's favorite bookstores in the city. It's not long on atmosphere, but it has everything else: It's well stocked in nearly all areas, it has spacious aisles with signs that make it easy to find things, a downstairs with deals on hardcovers and paperbacks, and it's open late. It hasn't got Barnes & Noble's pull-up-a-chair-and-hang-out style—it's just about books.

Gotham, 41 W. 47th St. [5th/6th] ☎ 719-4448. A beloved bookstore replete with atmosphere and history. A beacon and an oasis since 1920 for the literati, bibliophiles, browsers, wise men (and women) fishing. Upstairs is the art book department with a small gallery where they present exhibitions from time to time.

Rizzoli, 31 W. 57th St. [5th/6th] ☎ 759-2424. There are other Rizzolis, but not to us. And there can't be many more beautiful than this Rizzoli, particularly the second floor. Note the details on the ceiling, walk to the windows, and look out onto 57th St. They are especially strong on art books.

St. Marks Bookshop, 31 Third Ave. [9th] ☎ 260-7853. It isn't as atmospheric as its previous headquarters, but a serious bookstore with East Village style.

The Strand, 828 Broadway [12th] ☎ 473-1452. It may seem overwhelming when you're looking for an out-of-print book, but the staff is incredibly knowledgeable and once you get the knack of it, it's really not that hard to find things. One of the best deals in town is the selection of reviewers' copies of new books (1/2 off). A literary and city landmark.

Three Lives, 154 W. 10th St. [Waverly Pl.] ☎ 741-2069. A perfect small bookstore stocked with things you want to read, run by lovely people who are always talking about books with their loyal customers.

SPECIALTY BOOKSTORES
Our suggestions on where to start for each topic.

Academic: **Columbia University Bookstore,** 2926 Broadway [115th/116th] ☎ 854-4131. **Papyrus,** 2915 Broadway [113th/114th] ☎ 222-3350.

Architecture: **Urban Center Books,** 457 Madison Ave. [50th/51st] ☎ 935-3592.

Art: **Hacker Art Books,** 45 W. 57th St. [5th/6th] ☎ 688-7600. **Ursus Books,** 981 Madison Ave. [76th/77th] on the mezzanine floor of the Carlyle Hotel ☎ 772-8787 and 375 W. Broadway [Spring/Broome] 3rd floor ☎ 226-7858.

Biography: **Biography Book Shop,** 400 Bleecker St. [W. 11th/Perry] ☎ 807-8655.

Children: **Bank St. Books,** 610 W. 112th St. [Bway] ☎ 678-1654. **Books of Wonder,** 132 Seventh Ave. [17th/18th] ☎ 989-3270.

Computers: **McGraw-Hill,** 1221 Sixth Ave. [48th] ☎ 512-4100.

Design: **Archivia,** 944 Madison Ave. [74th/75th] ☎ 439-9194. **Morton,** 989 Third Ave. [58th/59th] ☎ 421-9025.

Fashion: **Fashion Design Books,** 234 W. 27th St. [7th/8th] ☎ 633-9646.

Food: **Kitchen Arts and Letters,** 1435 Lexington Ave. [93rd/94th] ☎ 876-5550.

Foreign Languages: **French and European Publications,** 610 Fifth Ave. [49th] ☎ 581-8810.

Gay and Lesbian: **A Different Light,** 151 W. 19th St. [6th/7th] ☎ 989-4850.

History: **Argosy,** 116 E. 59th St. [Park/Lex] ☎ 753-4455. **Ideal Book Store,** 1125 Amsterdam Ave. [115th] ☎ 662-1909. **The Liberation Bookstore,** Lenox Ave. and 131st St. ☎ 281-4615.

Military: **The Military Bookman,** 29 E. 93rd St. [5th/Mad] ☎ 348-1280.

Mysteries: **The Black Orchid,** 303 E. 81st St. [1st/2nd] ☎ 734-5980. **Murder Ink,** 2486 Broadway [92nd/93rd] ☎ 362-8905, 465 Second Ave. [76th/77th] ☎

517-3222, 1 Whitehall [Stone] ☎ 742-7025. **The Mysterious Bookshop,** 129 W. 56th St. [6th/7th] ☎ 765-0900. **Partners & Crime,** 44 Greenwich Ave. [6th/7th] ☎ 243-0440.

New York: **NY Bound,** 50 Rockefeller Plaza [50th/51st] ☎ 245-8503.

Out of Print: **Academy,** 10 W. 18th St. [5th/6th] ☎ 242-4848. **Antiquarian Book Arcade** in the Chelsea Antiques Building, 110 W. 25th St. [6th/7th] ☎ 620-5627. **Gotham,** 41 W. 47th St. [5th/6th] ☎ 719-4448. **Gryphon,** 2246 Broadway [80th/81st] ☎ 362-0706. **The Strand,** 828 Broadway [12th] ☎ 473-1452. **Pageant,** 114 W. Houston St. [Thompson/Sullivan] ☎ 674-5296. **Skyline,** 13 W. 18th St. [5th/6th] ☎ 759-5463. **Stubbs Books and Prints,** 153 E. 70th St. [Lex/3rd] ☎ 772-3120.

Pets: **The Dog Lover's Bookshop,** 9 W. 31st St. [5th/Bway] ☎ 576-4333.

Photography: **A Photographer's Place,** 133 Mercer St. [Prince/Spring] ☎ 431-9358. **Chartwell Booksellers,** 55 E. 52nd St. [Mad/Park] ☎ 308-0643.

Psychology: **Brunner/Mazel,** 19 Union Square West [15th/16th] ☎ 924-3344.

Reference: **Reference Book Center,** 175 Fifth Ave. [22nd/23rd] ☎ 677-2160.

Science: **Technical Books,** 10 W. 19th St. [5th/6th] ☎ 206-1310.

Science Fiction: **Forbidden Planet,** 840 Broadway [13th] ☎ 473-1576. **Science Fiction Shop,** 168 Thompson St. [Bleecker/Houston] ☎ 473-3010.

Sports: **Sportswords,** 1475 Third Ave. [83rd/84th] ☎ 772-8729.

Theatre, Film, TV: **Applause,** 211 W. 71st St. [Bway/WEA] ☎ 496-7511. **Drama Bookshop,** 723 Seventh Ave. [48th/49th] ☎ 944-0595. **Richard Stoddard Performing Arts Books,** 18 E. 16th St. [5th/Union Sq. W.] ☎ 645-9576.

Travel: **Complete Traveller,** 199 Madison Ave. [35th] ☎ 685-9007. **Rand McNally,** 150 E. 52nd St. [Lexington/3rd] ☎ 758-7488, **Traveller's Bookstore,** 22 W. 52nd St. [5th/6th] ☎ 664-0995.

MORE

Bookbinding. See Bookbinding in the Paper and Pens article in the Feature chapter. **Book plates.** See the Gifts and Collectibles article in this chapter. **Center for Book Arts.** See the Paper and Pens article in the Feature chapter. **False Book Panels.** See the Leather article in the Feature chapter.

CANDLES

Archetype Gallery, 115 Mercer St. [Prince/Spring] ☎ 334-0100, has a beautiful assortment of colors in beeswax, made for them by artist Bernie Roth, $3.25 each. They will make up custom-colored beeswax candles to order. A dozen minimum.

Candlelande, 305 E. 9th St. [1st/2nd] ☎ 260-8386. This gothic and appropriately dark shop sells extravagant candelabra—some new, many old, and many from churches. Wrought iron pieces are full of curlicues and can hold votives or large pillar candles. Their own line of hand-dipped candles is composed mostly of large dramatic pillars and ball shapes in deep blue and black.

The Candle Shop, 118 Christopher St. [Bleecker/Bedford] ☎ 989-0148, and **Can-**

dleshtick, 2444 Broadway [90th/91st] ☎ 787-5444, have a full range of candles— thin tapers to fat pillars in white and colors, many scented. Candleshtick, in particular, has many aromatherapy candles.

For the best deals: If you are willing to buy in bulk, **Empire Restaurant Supply,** 114 Bowery [Grand/Hester] ☎ 226-4447, sells a gross (144) of 12-in. tapers for $54, which is 38¢ each. Most stores charge about $1.50 for a 12-in. taper, so you've saved $162. At **Lechters Hardware,** all over town, they sell 12-in. tapers in a good assortment of colors for a reasonable 89¢ . . . We've never come up with a better price on tea lights than $1.49 for 10 at Woolworth's.

CANVAS BAGS

Globe Canvas, 177 Mott St. [Kenmare/ Broome] ☎ 226-4922. Frank DeMartini started in business in 1948 as a sailmaker. As times changed, he kept adjusting his business, and in 1963 he developed the first messenger bag. This was followed by backpacks and duffels. Kathleen DeMartini, his daughter, has added beach bags and pocketbooks to the line, and there is a custom bag for deejays, with pockets for recordings, headphones, and mikes. All of the bags are made of heavy water-resistant canvas with waterproof liners. Most of the styles come in two or three sizes, and they're very durable—great schoolbags. Prices generally range from $40–$60. Hours are Mon–Fri, 2–7 P.M.

Manhattan Portage makes a wide variety of bags, including camera, messenger, carry-on, duffel, shoulder bags, and knapsacks. Construction is high quality and comes with a lifetime warranty. It's all made right on West 29th St., and they'll do custom bags with your company logo. Call them at ☎ 594-7068. Note that this is the headquarters, not a store. You can buy MP products at, among many others, Down East, 50 Spring St. [Lafayette/ Mulberry] ☎ 925-2632. Prices start at $29 for a mailbag, $38 for a basic knapsack, and a briefcase-style bag costs $65 or more.

CLOTHING

GOOD DEALS

Aaron's, 627 Fifth Ave. [17th], Brooklyn ☎ 718-768-5400. Take the N or the R to Prospect Ave.—well worth a trip for women's clothing. Designer merchandise starts marked down and gets progressively more so as a season goes on; final markdowns can be as much as 70%. Clothes are arranged by designer, are clearly organized, and the selection is large. Bill Blass, Scaasi, Eileen Fisher, Tahari, Tomatsu, Liz Claiborne, and others. Communal dressing rooms.

Aida's and Jimi's Merchandising, 41 W. 28th St. [Bway/6th] ☎ 689-2415. Girls' clothing from 3 months to 12 years, boys to size 7. They don't always have every size in every style, but if you call them, they'll tell you how much of a selection they have in the size you want. Open for off-price shopping all year. Some brand names, lots of cute things.

Alberene Scottish Cashmeres, 435 Fifth Ave. [39th] ☎ 689-0151, sells only 100% Scottish cashmere. They have sweaters for men and women, as well as capes, berets, gloves, watch caps, turtlenecks, woven scarves, and throws. The quality is superb.

Blue Duck, 463 Seventh Ave. [35th] ☎ 268-3122. The shearling coats and jackets here (mostly women's) are lightweight, supple, and silky. The skins come from Europe or New Zealand, but the coats are made in Brooklyn. Since they are so close to their production facilities, Barry Novick and Gail Khan can customize sleeve and body lengths. Styles range from classic to downtown chic. The showroom is open by appointment from mid-September to the end of their season, or until the skins run out, about mid-January. Coats start at $600. Expect to wait two weeks for a special order.

Carlisle, 439 W. 55th St. [9th/10th] ☎ 246-2555, makes upscale tailored women's sportswear. Their hidden space is reached by taking the freight elevator to the 12th floor. Clothes are arranged in groups and by size. Most of the garments are tailored in Hong Kong, and the fabrics and sewing are good quality. Ignore the price tags on the garments and pick up a price list at the desk. Sizes 6–16. Communal try-on room. Tues.–Fri., 8:30–4.

Century 21, 22 Cortlandt St. [Bway/Church] ☎ 227-9092. It's no longer anything like a secret, but with patience, luck, and repeat visits, you can still land great bargains—on our best forays, we've gotten designer clothes at more than 80% off. Weekday mornings are best.

Carl Goldberg is **Cego Custom Shirt-**

maker, 174 Fifth Ave. [22nd/23rd] ☎ 620-4512. He's been making custom shirts for over 10 years. The shirts are hand cut, with 13 soft and hard collars to choose from, French or regular cuffs and front, 100% cotton from oxford to fine Swiss. His stitching is especially fine. Mr. Goldberg often has a group of fabrics from which he can make two shirts for $150—a great deal.

Forget the cat; there's no room to swing a vole at **Designer's Promise,** 93 Nassau St. [Fulton] ☎ 513-1532. Narrow aisles and jam-packed racks of mid-range designer clothing at prices topping out between $80–$100. We saw Anne Klein II, Gruppo Americano, and Tomatsu. Smaller sizes are in abundance, only a few things size 10 and above. Many of the evening wear and what once were called "dressy dresses" are in plastic bags, which adds to the challenge of the search, but finding an Anne Klein russet long dress with a filmy off-the-shoulder treatment ($79.99) was worth the effort. The store has a hat department carrying names like Eric Javits and Mr. John at substantial discount.

Glove St., 304 Fifth Ave. [31st/32nd] ☎ 594-2223. LaCrasia, a New York glovemaker, frustrated by the lack of outlets for gloves these days, has opened her own shop in front of the glove factory. Many of the styles here may surprise you, like the bright colors and prints on stretch fabrics. There is a $5 rack. Leathers and printed suedes are $70 and up. If it's possible (if they have the piece goods) they can make gloves to order for men as well as women.

Jamak, ☎ 787-0278, by appt. Day to dinner clothes for professional women. Gruppo Americano and similar lines for 50% or more off retail. Some alterations.

Kavanagh's, 146 E. 49th St. [Lex/3rd] ☎ 702-0152, is an exceptional resale shop. Mary Kavanagh, former director of personal shopping at Bergdorf Goodman, says she "spent years filling the closets of women with with designer clothing. Now I'm emptying them." Her customers were asking her where they could sell clothes that had been worn a couple of times. So Ms. Kavanagh fitted out a lovely shop with carpet, soft lights, and a small sofa, put in private dressing rooms, and arranged the consigned clothing around the walls. Galanos, Beene, Chanel (before and after Lagerfeld), Valentino, Armani, Bill Blass, and Oscar de la Renta make up some of the stock in trade. Clothes are arranged by category and by size so it is easy to shop. There are some accessories, mainly scarves and bags, and some vintage couture. Prices start at $20 for a scarf and go to $950 for a Chanel suit. Ms. Kavanagh, who has an eye for fine workmanship, likes the garments to have their original labels, buttons, and cuff links.

Le Firme, 37 W. 57th St. [5th/6th] ☎ 888-3433. Italian designer clothing for men and women at substantial savings. Silk ties are a feature, and the price goes down when you buy more than one.

Nice Price SSS Sales, 134 W. 37th St. [Bway/7th] is closed every Monday to restock. They open Tuesdays at noon with new merchandise. Mostly women's, but sometimes men's and children's clothing from moderate to better designers. First-quality merchandise with an occasional damages rack. Prices are wholesale and below. No try-ons. Occasional pandemonium when a line like Joan Vass is being sold. Other labels that show up on a regular basis are Mevisto, Ballinger-Gold, Pringle cashmeres, Michael Simon sweaters, Kenar,

Kikit, and BCBG. ☎ 947-8748 will put you in touch with their frantic recorded message info line telling you what brands they are selling each week.

Tahari Outlet, 525 Seventh Ave. [38th/39th] ☎ 921-5164. Upscale women's suits, dresses, separates, and a few knits in sizes 2–14. A large loft space arranged by category and price but not by size, so you may have to do a little looking. All prices are wholesale or below. Communal dressing room.

Upland Trading Co., 236 E. 13th St. [2nd/3rd] ☎ 673-4994, is an outpost for Barbour, an English company specializing in quality outerwear, mostly for men. Jackets are made from durable fabrics that are waterproof, wind-resistant, abrasion-resistant, even thornproof. There is every length from the waist-length jacket you wear with your waders to a trench coat. The fine quality Hanro underwear from Switzerland is always sold at off price.

FROM THE ATELIERS

Chelsea Atelier, 128 W. 23rd St. [6th/7th] ☎ 255-8803, is the former Chelsea Designers, but the atelier in question is that of Suzanne Zeldin. Working in natural fibers only, without buttons or zippers (she does use elastic), results in garments where beautiful colors and a flowing cut are emphasized. A number of her customers have had breast cancer surgery and find that many of the dresses meet their needs beautifully. Silk velvet, silks, and linens are dyed in small batches. Despite their luxurious appearance, many can be machine washed, and they travel well. You can also find Christina Lightfoot's hand-painted silk tunics and jackets. Ms. Lightfoot has an extraordinary way with color. Her tunics start at $280, but there is much in the shop for less.

Ruth Hunt, ☎ 201-626-8899, went to F.I.T after she left her 27-year career as a Seventh Ave. model. She won the millinery prize and designs hats and ensembles. "I specialize in glamour," she says, and she'll put together a dress and a hat, say, that will glam up an event. She will also arrange for a fashion show or "hat tea" for your club or group. When she puts on a show she uses both "full-figured and slim models."

It looks like a tailor shop, but the storefront windows are too clean and the single sample garment displayed has no chalk lines. There is a cutting table and a fitting form, and the tailor at **Koos + Co.,** 215 W. 10th St. [Bleecker/7th] ☎ 463-8009, is none other than Koos Van Den Akker, the master fabric collagist. Deciding to give up his wholesale operation and work more directly with individual customers, Koos personally makes every garment on the rack. You'll find his trademark loose-fitting and comfortable clothing showing the sure hand and eye of the artist designer. The sewing is impeccable. Silks are pieced with seersucker gauzes, lace strips, or novelty rayon weaves into short-sleeved shirts. Funky screen print panels are appliquéd onto iridescent gauze in a long-sleeved shirt. One new jacket was inspired by a client—she wanted a garment to remember her father using his ties. Koos appliquéd 24 ties onto a wool jacket. Prices start at $200 for a short-sleeved blouse. Dresses and pants are available. If the ready-made garments don't suit because of size or color, you can consult with Koos.

Judy Straeten spent 12 years working at the Costume Institute at the Metropolitan Museum of Art, where clothing made by Mariano Fortuny often passed through her hands. Fortuny stopped making his famous pleated dresses in the 1950s, and "the pleating technique is supposed to be lost." But she kept trying to figure it out. Ms. Straeten feels that the technique of her pleated silk dresses is similar to Fortuny's. Two styles of dress—a single layer and a tunic model—can be had sleeveless or with short or long sleeves. The dresses are hand-dyed, so it's possible to choose colors. Ms. Straeten has also developed three styles of hand-stenciled velvet mantles to complete the outfits. Two are copies of Fortuny styles, the stencils are her own designs. Pricing starts at $1,500. Ms. Straeten is represented by Diana Burke ☎ 539-3947.

Lee Anderson, 23 E. 67th St. [5th/Mad] ☎ 772-2463, is a shop with an intimate couture feel. Ms. Anderson and her assistant, Jeffrey Moss, create two collections each year "with some holiday." The price (these are "investment clothes"), with dresses starting at $500 and suits at $1,100, includes tailoring. Fabrics lean to the all-natural wool, silks, wool crepes, and georgette for winter; cotton piqué, linen, and organdy for summer. The designs are clean and functional, with enough detail, especially on collars and cuffs, to distinguish them. Some accessories, including millinery by Mr. Moss, and vintage jewelry are also available.

George Preston, ☎ 620-5272, by appt. A former art historian and gallery curator, Mr. Preston works like a printmaker when it comes to clothing. His shapes are simple squares and rectangles that he hand paints, dip dyes, and/or prints with patterns he has adapted from historical textiles. Everything is fresh and modern in feel, and his forgiving shapes are adaptable. His signature sarong suit comes with a sarong skirt, a silk blouse, and either a tailored jacket or a shawl. Fabrics are silks or a silky polyester. Garments are produced in limited editions of six, each with a slightly different cut or decoration. Each comes with a printed card telling you about the motif he used (one is based on a morning glory that is in the wallpaper at the Jumel Mansion) and a little map showing you how to make the ties and knots in sarong skirts, shawls, and head wraps. Dresses start at $200 and go up to $1,100 for a three-piece suit.

FORMALWEAR
See Formalwear article in this chapter.

HATS
See Hats article in this chapter.

VINTAGE CLOTHING
Darrow Vintage Clothing and Antiques, 7 W. 19th St. [5th/6th] ☎ 255-1550, is where to go when you are looking for a more couture vintage garment. Darrow Canniz-

S Ł O W I K

Plenty of people are star watchers. Our particular thrill is watching *rising* stars—seeing someone with talent and passion turn that into a thriving enterprise. In fashion, watch for the name Słowik, the line of designer Steven Leszczynski Slowik.

People in the fashion industry know him because, though in his mid-thirties, he's, nevertheless, been around. He's worked as senior designer at Calvin Klein, for Albert Capraro, Kasper for J. L. Sport, and Albert Nippon. Since 1988, he's designed Ferragamo's ready-to-wear and continues now as their consultant. He's an American, born in Detroit, who went to school in NY (Parsons) but moved to Florence for his work at Ferragamo. When it came time to launch his own line, under his name, he moved to Paris. "Paris is a creative center of Europe, and there's still a draw here to my craft of making clothing. There's something in the air, some energy, some feeling. This combines with the historic side of Paris, and I feel this is very inspiring.

"The thing I wanted to show was the idea of separates—separate pieces of clothing that a woman can mix together in various ways to cre-

ate different looks to suit her day. These clothes are for active women, women who travel, who demand a lot from their clothes. They travel well and pack well."

Many of the fabrics Mr. Slowik uses contain Lycra or elastin, giving an element of stretch and ease of movement, though that's not to say that every piece is tight and stretchy. There's a mix of textures and color: fabrics such as velvet (used for day and evening) are combined with gazar cady or satin duchesse stretch. Many of the fabrics, manufactured in Italy, are "highly technical" as they say, meaning these mixtures (nylon and silk or double crepe cotton) are *composed*— they're new textures, fabrics that you really haven't seen before. As for color, from a base of black, white, vanilla, and cement, Mr. Slowik mixes in a highly personal selection of chartreuse, verdigris, beet red, sky blue, coral, lavender, mauve, and clementine. You can see the work for yourself at Barneys, Bendel's, Bloomies, Saks, and Bagutta, 422 W. Broadway [Spring] ☎ 925-5216. Dresses run $500–$600, $750–$950 for a jacket, pants are in the $250 range, shirts go from $175–$350.

zaro says she loves coats, and she has a special rack of gabardines from the '40s to be worn in the spring. She tries to always have on hand some Pucci dresses and scarves as well as couture from Adele Simpson, "a forerunner of Prada," with her clean lines and shocking colors (dresses are $200–$300). She also likes accessories from Trifari and Miriam Haskell. Half of the shop is men's wear. "About 90% of the suits are unused. Most men who come in buy two." The average suit is $150.

The Fan Club, 22 W. 19th St. [5th/6th] ☎ 929-3349, Gene London's store is pure fun but leave yourself some time to go through the many racks. Clothes are arranged by type, not by size, so all of the evening dresses are on one rack, all of the sequined sweaters on another. Many of the garments rely heavily on glitter of one kind or another, and you can find pieces such as a hammered metal-trimmed Stavropoulos jacket across the aisle from a gold-dust-glued-on-tulle prom dress. Some alterations. Prices range from $20 for a machine-knit rayon scarf to $250 for a couture piece.

Patricia Pastor Vintage Fashions, ☎ 734-4673, by appt. Patricia Pastor, former assistant to Perry Ellis and a long-time clothing collector, used to have a Madison Ave. shop but now works privately with clients. While she does have a large number of designer and couture items for sale (1920s–1960s), she doesn't limit herself to that. She always "buys from a design point of view," knows her fabrics, and has a weakness for those "which can no longer be reproduced." She doesn't sell anything that can't be worn and only carries items in good condition. Everything is cleaned before sale. Her large stock is stored in a warehouse and, when you visit, you can see photographs (front and back view) of each piece. Forties blouses with beaded collars start at $100, there are many suits (including dinner suits) in the $250–$650 range, and coats go from $300–$800. Ms. Pastor makes a specialty of shawls, has some bags, and some men's ties from the '40s.

The Metropolitan Antiques Building is run by Alan Boss, the man who brings you the 26th St. flea market. They have shows of vintage clothing several times a year. 110 W. 19th St. [6th/7th] ☎ 463-0200 for schedule. Admission charged.

UNDERNEATH IT ALL

A beneficent spirit seems to imbue **Underneath It All,** 444 E. 75th St. [York] ☎ 717-1976, a shop created by survivors of breast cancer for other survivors of breast cancer. What Carol Art Keane found, after cancer therapy, was that there were few places catering to her specific needs, and none with the kind of clothes or service that she wanted. A friend of Ms. Keane's, who had also had breast surgery, echoed her sentiment: "There's nothing pretty out there," her friend said. The idea for a store developed and it opened in 1993. It's a lovely, supportive environment to buy clothes and accessories. The needs of women undergoing cancer therapy are also sensitively cared for here.

The setting is something like dress shops of yore. The boutique is comfortably elegant with a sitting area, carpeting, wallpaper, and fitting rooms. (You wouldn't be surprised to find Kay Thompson bustling in and out.) It's one-stop shopping: bras, lingerie, swimwear, wigs, hats, turbans, even baseball caps. There are breast forms of all types, including one with dark tones for women of color. Underneath It All has clothing styles for women older or younger, conservative or trendy. The styles change seasonally. They carry Gottex bathing suits and got the company to give them extra material so that the suits could be altered for the needs of their clients. Swimwear runs from $65–$165, bras are $15–$45, wigs are $200–$250. You select a wig for style and color, and then their stylist adapts the piece to you. There is a makeup artist who does makeovers on women undergoing chemo-

therapy. The store does alterations on everything they sell and will customize existing clothing for you.

They're open M–F, 10–6, but it's best to call ahead for an appointment. Husbands or significant others are welcome. It's clear when you visit that in addition to taking care of a woman's wardrobe and accessories, much trading of stories takes place among customers and the genuinely caring and understanding women who run the place. They've been there.

COSTUMES

Abracadabra, 10 Christopher St. [Greenwich/Gay] ☎ 627-5745, has 4,000 or so costumes that rent from $35–$400, plus a security deposit equal to the price of the costume. A list of costumes is available. They have children's costumes that start at toddler age (though there is no list of these). You can buy beards, wigs, glue, makeup, fun false eyelashes, glitter hair gel, masks, and rubber attachments (latex brains, Dracula teeth, devil horns).

Animal Outfits for People, 2255 Broadway [81st] ☎ 877-5085, by appt. only. Chet Doherty will rent from his stock of 150 animal costumes, which can be worn individually (a bumblebee or gorilla) or with some close friends in a Chinese dragon or a cow. Prices are $100 and up.

Creative Costume, 330 W. 38th St. [8th/9th] ☎ 564-5552, has been renting and selling costumes since 1982. They do custom outfits for rental, but need two weeks' notice (and two months to be ready for Halloween). They carry no costumes for children, but do all sizes for adults. There

are roughly over 2,000 costumes in stock, and you can browse through them. $25–$200 to rent, which includes free alterations.

Frankie Steinz Costumes, 24 Harrison St. [Hudson/Greenwich] ☎ 925-1373, by appt. Ms. Steinz designs and constructs most of the costumes here. There are over 1,000 costumes, which she will alter to fit you. Price is $50–$250 for 48-hour rental, including all the accessories. Lots of imaginative costumes and good workmanship with excellent details. We love the Captain Hook and Mae West (complete with a large picture frame hat). Ms. Steinz has some authentic 1950s prom dresses, too. Many kids costumes are available (sizes 2–12), including a mermaid, a flapper, a Mad Hatter, and a spaceman.

Gordon Novelty, 933 Broadway [21st/22nd] ☎ 254-8616, is more or less wholesale, but they do sell costumes to the public around Halloween. A huge selection of rubber masks ($30–$100) as well as wigs and accessories.

ELECTRONICS & APPLIANCES

Buying electronics and appliances is nobody's favorite pastime in the city, but here are a few places where you may not be completely miserable.

STORES

Bernie's Discount Center, 821 Sixth Ave. [28th/29th] ☎ 564-8582. A no-frills store that has low prices on large and small appliances such as refrigerators, stoves, dishwashers, toaster ovens, coffeemakers, and microwaves, as well as some electronics.

Harvey Electronics emphasizes service. They don't always have the best prices but they may try to match a competitor's price, if you bring in the ad. Three locations: 2 W. 45th St. [5th/6th] ☎ 575-5000, 119 W. 57th St. [6th/7th] ☎ 489-0800, inside ABC, 888 Broadway [19th] ☎ 228-5354.

J & R, 31 Park Row [Ann/Beekman] ☎ 238-9100. The best selection of electronics in the city. They don't sell major kitchen appliances, but they carry telephones, cellular phones, copiers, and much else.

Sound City, 58 W. 45th St. [5th/6th] ☎ 575-0210. Low overhead and a good kind of wheeler-dealer attitude is something of a throwback to the '60s and '70s in NY— it means you get low prices with minimal hassle.

Stereo Exchange, 627 Broadway [Houston/Bleecker] ☎ 505-1111. A mom-and-pop organization with access to every brand. They're real experts, and they stand behind their stuff.

Zabar's, 2245 Broadway [80th/81st] ☎ 787-2000, for smaller kitchen appliances like food processors, juicers, breadmaking machines.

BY PHONE

Economy Buying Group, 211 E. 43rd St. [2nd/3rd] ☎ 682-2716. They sell major kitchen appliances, televisions, VCRs, camcorders, and some audio equipment. They'll help you if you don't have model numbers. You can go and look through the catalogs with them, but there is no merchandise on display.

Home Sales Dial-a-Discount, ☎ 513-1513, for major appliances and televisions.

LVT Price Quote Hotline, ☎ 516-234-8884, sells over 4,000 items, small and large appliances, audio equipment, but no computers. You must have brand and model number.

Peninsula Buying Service, ☎ 838-1010. Large appliances, televisions, VCRs, air conditioners, a limited range of audio equipment.

Price Watchers, ☎ 718-470-1620. All major brands of large kitchen appliances, VCRs, televisions, camcorders, and air conditioners. No audio.

FABRIC

Beckenstein Fabrics is down to two stores from three on Orchard Street (ladies' fabrics is gone). The men's store is at 121 Orchard St. [Delancey/Rivington] ☎ 475-6666.

Wool suitings, tweeds, and tropicals, as well as shirting fabrics. The majority of fabrics run from conservative to bland to dreary. They have a home fabrics store at 130 Orchard St. [Delancey/Rivington] ☎ 475-4887, which has more prints and chintzes than Zarin's, as well as some tapestries and jacquards. Downstairs, a sale area where short yardages are further discounted.

Chinese Fabric: Silks or, more precisely, half silk and half polyesters are at **Oriental Dress Co.,** 38 Mott St. [Pell/Mosco] ☎ 349-0818. The goods are 30 inches wide and have traditional Chinese motifs woven into the brocades. Some are sequined with dragons or chrysanthemums, a few are embroidered. Starting at $20 yard, they can be used for pillows or garments. In the back of the shop, traditional Chinese dresses are made to order. A long-sleeved long dress starts at $240.

Harry Zarin Fabric Warehouse, 72 Allen St. [Grand/Broome] ☎ 226-3492, is fabric heaven. The crowded 2nd floor warehouse has an enormous stash of fabrics, many of which are of extremely high quality and quite beautiful, most of which are at steal prices. Zarin's is arranged by type of fabric. All tapestries, for example, are grouped together. They carry a lot of jacquards, velvets, some matelessés, chenilles, and prints. The stress is on fabrics for upholstery.

Indian Fabric: 74th St. in Jackson Heights [Roosevelt/37th]. Walking along this mini-bazaar of a block just off the E,F,R,G, and 7 lines, you'll find a dozen or so Indian fabric shops, all selling traditional clothing as well as yard goods. It's impossible to single out one or two stores, though they all try to have something the others don't. Largely silks and rayons with some polyesters thrown in, most are put up in six-yard lengths—enough for a sari. The Indian textile tradition always renews and updates itself—many of the prints are exceptional. The listed price is not always the actual price. Sari lengths begin at $15 for polyester; nice things can be had for $35, extraordinary things for more.

Joe's Fabric Warehouse, 102 Orchard St. [Delancey] ☎ 674-7089, is the smallest of the Lower East Side shops and is devoted to decorating and upholstery fabrics. While there seems to be a lot of duplication among these stores, Joe's has the advantage of natural light—helpful in color matching.

Mendel Goldberg Fabrics, 72 Hester St. [Allen/Orchard] ☎ 925-9110, is a model of a fabric shop. A large but not overwhelming selection, well organized, well lit, well staffed. Mostly goods for women's wear, there are a lot of European woolens in style-conscious plaids and stripes. There are some wool challis, mohair blends, linens, and linen blends from France, and a good selection of fancy linings. Prices are reasonable and below.

Ragfinders, 263 W. 38th St. [7th/8th] ☎ 354-4111, buys the sample and leftover yardage of designers like Carolina Herrera, Ralph Lauren, and Liz Claiborne. They then sell to fabric stores and small boutiques—but they will also sell to you.

FIREPLACE EQUIPMENT

A few sources for fireplace equipment: **Danny Alessandro/Edwin Jackson,** 307 E. 60th St. [1st/2nd] ☎ 421-1928, sells mantels in wood and marble, tools, screens, and andirons. There is a section of antique tools and an equal number of reproductions and modern styles. Prices begin at $200, although there is not much of a choice in this range—more in the $300 to $400 area. Screens start at $150 and can go up steeply . . . **Irreplaceable Artifacts,** 14 Second Ave. [Houston] ☎ 777-2900, has mantelpieces on four floors in wood, marble, cast iron, and limestone. You can also ask to see photos of the selection in their Newark warehouse . . . **A & R Asta Fireplace and Accessories,** 1152 Second Ave. [60th/61st] ☎ 750-3364. Mantels, tools, electric flames, and irons. The staff is friendly, but the lay-out of the store makes it hard to see things. Not everything is marked . . . **William H. Jackson,** 210 E. 58th St. [2nd/3rd] ☎ 753-9400, sells very high-end accessories for the fireplace, including mantels, tools, brooms, and bellows. They've been in business since 1927 . . . **Gracious Home,** 1220 Third Ave. [70th/71st] ☎ 516-6300, has brass and black fireplace tools in sets ranging in price from $20–$80. They also have gates, screens, and grates.

See more in the Firewood and Chimney Cleaning articles in the Services chapter.

FORMALWEAR

WHAT TO KNOW Do you want a **single-** or **double-breasted** jacket? **Notch lapel, peak lapel,** or **shawl collar?** Shawl collars are popular lately. When salespeople refer to **Super 100s,** they're talking about the wool from Australian merino sheep. It's the finest wool from these sheep and makes garments that are softer and more durable. Rental price almost always includes the tux and accessories: shirt, bow tie, cummerbund, studs, and cuff links. Most places have shoes that you can rent for a small additional charge. For weekend use, most allow you to pick up on Thursday and return on Monday.

DESIGNER Barneys. Lots of black-label Armani (white, too), Ermenegildo Zegna, Boss, Corneliani. The black-label Armanis are about $2,000. If you want the really high-end goods, bypass the formalwear area in the downtown store and head for the designer boutiques. The 7th floor in the uptown store has about the nicest space in town for tux shopping. **Bergdorf for Men** has, in their (too) small formalwear shop, Donna Karan, Armani, Hugo Boss, and a Brioni for $3,200.

THE CARRIAGE TRADE A. T. Harris, 11 E. 44th St. [5th/Mad] ☎ 682-6325, are the traditional outfitters to the carriage trade. Lord West is their only brand. $500 for the tux and, for an additional $50, you get all the accessories (including suspenders) except shoes. Rentals are $135 . . . **Brooks Bros.:** $340–$700, classic cuts, of course.

MID-RANGE TUXES Gilcrest, 900 Broadway [20th] ☎ 254-8933. We like Gilcrest for their helpful staff and their stylish Bäumler tux from Germany for $549. Rentals are $85–$115 . . . **Mel's Lexington Formalwear,** 12 E. 46th St. [Mad] ☎ 867-4420, has an especially pleasant decor, good mid-range tuxes ($400–$700), lots of accessories. Rentals are from $95–$135. They deliver and pick up in midtown . . . **Bloomies:** We liked the DKNY double-breasted loose-construction tux—$485 for the jacket, $245 for the pants . . . **Baldwin,** 52 W. 56th St.

[5th/6th] ☎ 245-8190, is low on ambience, has a friendly enough staff, and we were taken with their Versace tux for $850. Rentals run $95–$150 . . . **Ted's Formal Wear,** 83 Orchard St. [Broome] ☎ 966-2029, has tuxes from $199–$750, and we especially like their fun stock of accessories. Rentals are $89.

GOOD DEALS When your shopping karma's right, **Century 21,** 22 Cortlandt St. ☎ 227-9092, can have some great deals on designer tuxes. When we were there last, they had Hugo Boss for $429.97, Byblos for $449.97, and a Gianni Versace for $699.97 . . . **Eisenberg & Eisenberg,** 85 Fifth Ave. [16th] ☎ 627-1290, since 1898: Most tuxes around $325 with a lot of familiar names: Bill Blass, Perry Ellis Portfolio, Ralph Lauren Chaps. Small selection of accessories. Rentals are $85–$115 . . . **Today's Man,** 625 Sixth Ave. [18th/19th] ☎ 924-0200, was the biggest surprise to us. A great choice for inexpensive tuxes: a full range of sizes of Perry Ellis Portfolio for $300, Bill Blass, Christian Dior, and After Six for $149. If you want two tuxes and the price for one is $149, the total price for two is $199. Not great on accessories. Alterations are extra . . . **Syms,** 42 Trinity [Rector] ☎ 797-1199, is not bad for basic $159 tuxes.

USED **Alice Underground,** 481 Broadway [Broome] ☎ 431-9067 and 380 Columbus Ave. [78th] ☎ 724-6682 . . . **Andy's Chee-pee's,** 16 W. 8th St. [5th/MacDougal] ☎ 460-8488 and 691 Broadway [E. 4th] ☎ 420-5980. Tuxes at $55 . . . **Antique Boutique,** 712 Broadway [W. 4th] ☎ 460-8830 and 227 E. 59th St. [2nd/3rd] ☎ 752-1680. Motown castoffs at $60 . . . **Family Jewels,** 832 Sixth Ave. [29th] ☎ 679-5023.

$85–$300 of widely varying quality . . . **Gentlemen's Resale,** 303 E. 81st St. [1st/2nd] ☎ 734-2739. We found an excellent used tux here not long ago for $125. We'd check here first.

ACCESSORIES The Cognac cigar, Gummi Bears, and a matchbook cover are some of the delightful cuff links from Danielle Shriber's **Prairie NY** company. They can be found at The Gift Co., 1023 Third Ave. [60th/61st] ☎ 421-4435, Peter Elliott, 1070 Madison Ave. [81st] ☎ 570-2300, Saks, and Takashimaya. Picture links run about $45; silver starts at $100 . . . **Archangel Antiques,** 334 E. 9th St. [1st/2nd] ☎ 260-9313, maintains a large selection of antique cuff links . . . **Tiecrafters,** 252 W. 29th St. [7th/8th] ☎ 629-5800, makes custom bow ties, cummerbunds, and braces in your fabric or theirs.

BEST FREEBIE **Jack Silver,** 1780 Broadway [57th/58th] ☎ 582-3389. So that you can put your money toward a better quality mid-range tux (and not spend it on all the accessories right away), if you buy a tux from them they will let you *borrow* any accessories you need (including shoes) until you're ready to buy them. Rental $85–$135.

FOR WOMEN Mom's Night Out, 970 Lexington Ave. [70th/71st] ☎ 744-6667. Patricia Shiland rents party dresses to pregnant women in sizes petite to full bloom. These pretty dresses and gowns are designed and made for her shop. Good fabrics such as silk chiffon are used in high-fashion designs. $75–$185 for a 3–5 day rental. There is a catalog for women who can't get to the shop, and dresses can be shipped to you. Jewelry, purses, and some shoes are also available for rental. Maternity lingerie and hose are for sale. Appt. preferred . . . **Jana Starr,** 236 E. 80th St. [2nd/3rd] ☎ 861-8256, carries vintage dresses from the '20s to the '50s. She has about 100 one-of-a-kind party dresses on hand at any one time in sizes 8–12, starting at $200.

FURNITURE

ABC **ABC Carpet & Home,** 888 Broadway [19th] ☎ 473-3000. The fourth and fifth floors of ABC have estate furniture, antiques, and a wide array of pieces from different countries and periods. Great for one-stop shopping. Check also the Dungeon (the basement floor), where they put furniture and linens that have not sold quickly enough from the floors upstairs. Prices are greatly reduced. All of the furniture is "as is," but often there is little or no damage.

AMERICANA See article on Americana in the Feature chapter.

ANGLO-INDIAN **British Khaki** by Robert Lighton, 62 Greene St. [Spring/Broome] ☎ 343-2299. Teak chairs, beds, tables, and writing desks made in southern India.

ANTIQUES. A small sampling of what's available. Since these stores tend to cluster with other like-minded ones, we group them by district.

Atlantic Ave. District in Brooklyn. Between Hoyt and Nevins, a collection of antique shops. Most specialize in 19th century American and English furniture. Many places will refinish and reupholster for you—sometimes this is included in the marked price. When it is included, the price tag says so. **Time Trader,** 368 Atlantic Ave. [Bond/Hoyt] ☎

718-852-3301 is huge, with a mind-boggling array of chair sets, dressers, and tables, and a cockatoo for entertainment . . . **Circa Antiques,** 377 Atlantic Ave. [Hoyt/Bond] ☎ 718-596-1866, specializes in 19th century furniture from Europe and America. Everything from beautifully carved sofa frames, which start at $2,000 (upholstering can be arranged), side tables, and dining tables to silver and crystal . . . **Doc's,** 490 Atlantic Ave. [Nevins/3rd] ☎ 718-858-0069, has small furniture items, chests, chairs, and some collectibles.

Chelsea District. You won't find enormous selections of furniture at the fleas, but there is some, and you can find good deals. See the Flea Markets article in the Districts and Spaces chapter . . . While you're in Chelsea, head west to **John Koch Antiques,** 514 W. 24th St. [10th/11th] ☎ 243-8625. It's a warehouse floor full of antiques worth scouting through—chairs, tables, hutches, vanities, dressers, armoires—you have to thread your way through the helter-skelter shop, but prices are reasonable and some of the pieces are beautiful. Mr. Koch buys estates, so you never know what you'll find (everything from the jelly glasses to the armoire).

Kentshire District. Kentshire Galleries, 37 E. 12th St. [University/Bway] ☎ 673-6644, is seven floors of breathtaking English 18th and 19th century antiques with equally breathtaking prices . . . There is a slew of other mostly high-end antiques stores on

10th, 11th, and 12th streets, and Broadway, including **Philip Colleck of London,** 830 Broadway [12th/13th] ☎ 505-2500, for 18th century English furniture—"anything that might have been in an English house."

Lafayette District. Urban Archaeology, 285 Lafayette St. [Prince/Houston] ☎ 431-6969; **1950,** 440 Lafayette St. [Astor Pl./W. 4th] ☎ 995-1950; and **Lost City Arts,** 275 Lafayette St. [Prince/Houston] ☎ 941-8025, are three of the big players here. Urban Archaeology has architectural elements, a line of reproduction bath and lighting pieces, and beautiful showcases for sale that look like they came from the Museum of Natural History in Vienna. 1950 is a huge store of '50s furniture (lots of enormous board room/dining room tables), and at Lost City, among the fun antiques is their line of reproduction Warren McArthur furniture. Aluminum frames and mohair upholstery are the signature style markers here.

Soho District. Depression Modern, 150 Sullivan St. [Houston/Prince] ☎ 982-5699, for '30s and '40s Deco . . . **Fred Silberman,** 83 Wooster St. [Spring/Broome] ☎ 925-9470, for moderately priced Art Deco . . . More Art Deco at **Wooster Gallery,** 86 Wooster St. [Spring/Broome] ☎ 219-2190 . . . At **Eileen Lane Antiques,** 150 Thompson St. [Houston/Prince] ☎ 475-2988, Swedish and Austrian Biedermeier, Jugendstil, and Art Deco. Go also for the huge selection of onyx lamps . . . **Frank Rogin,** 21 Mercer St. [Howard/Canal] ☎ 431-6545, doesn't have a lot of pieces, but what's there is an excellent selection of 20th century furniture.

Upper East Side. No end of places, but the place we'd drop a few million with pleasure is **Delorenzo,** 958 Madison Ave. [75th/76th] ☎ 249-7575. You can buy some Eileen Gray and mostly early 20th century

French designers here, but if we could have anything, it would be the Ruhlmann armoire. ($1,400,000).

ART FURNITURE Art et Industrie, 52 Thompson St. [Spring/ Broome] ☎ 966-6800, represents artists that make "sculpture in the guise of furniture." . . . **Franklin Parrasch Gallery,** 20 W. 57th St. [5th/6th] ☎ 246-5360, represents many contemporary furniture artists. . . . **Peter Joseph,** 745 Fifth Ave. [58th/59th] ☎ 751-5500. The top art furniture gallery in the city, probably the country. Lately, though, it's been needing a fresh breeze. . . . **Jean Paul Viollet,** ☎ 718-782-1727, came to Brooklyn from a village in the French Alps with a desire to revive the furniture techniques of 1930s France. He makes one-of-a-kind pieces of very-high-end furniture, using unusual woods, specializing in marquetry, and with materials like parchment and shagreen (sharkskin). Parchment has a translucent effect when used as wall covering and in screens. Shagreen covers tables and lamps, giving them a slightly scaly look. Shagreen in particular requires painstaking care. In its natural state, it is nubby with calcium. It has to be ground and sanded to a smooth surface. These skins are rather small, and in general only the centers (where there is a round, raised calcium dot that cannot be removed) are used. Mr. Viollet places the pieces so that these dots make their own pattern. Coffee tables start at $5,000.

AUCTIONS Furniture of all kinds at the city's auction houses. See more in the Auctions article in the Information chapter.

BALINESE FURNITURE Sing Ken Ken, 401 Washington St. [Laight] ☎ 226-1641.

Vanessa Murphy's 6th floor reconverted loft space is filled with new and antique furniture imported from Bali, largely of teak. Many of the pieces use a slatted construction. Some, like a bench ($550) and table ($850), fold up for easy storage. There is a steamer chair with brass trim, desks, and cabinets . . . Rattan, wicker, and bamboo are staple ingredients for furniture and accessories at **Coconut Company,** 131 Greene St. [Houston/ Prince] ☎ 539-1940. Everything from the sofas to the drinking glasses has a colonial look to it.

CHILDREN'S FURNITURE

SAFETY Both the federal government and the juvenile products industry regulate children's furniture. A seal is displayed by all products that meet the industry's safety regulations. Deb Albert at the Juvenile Products Manufacturing Association cautions, "No baby product is meant to be a babysitter. New products are so technologically sophisticated that parents have a sense of security that they shouldn't have because a baby is still a baby." The American Academy of Pediatricians has published *Caring for Your Baby and Young Child* ($15.95 in paperback), which gives guidelines for choosing baby and children's furniture. The pediatricians are "unalterably opposed to walkers" because of the high incidence of accident with this product. The book can be ordered by calling ☎ 800-433-9016. (You get a 20% discount by ordering directly.)

STORES FOR INFANTS **Albee Baby Carriage,** 715 Amsterdam Ave. [95th] ☎ 662-5740, says they have "everything but the baby," and this is pretty accurate. The display is a bit chaotic, but the assortment of cribs, dressers, and changing tables is large

and they stress solid pieces with safety decals (we did not see a single dresser without drawer stops here). They also were the only store to carry an old-fashioned wooden high chair in addition to the molded vinyl models seen everywhere else . . . **Baby Palace,** 181 Seventh Ave. [20th/21st] ☎ 924-3700. The small street frontage belies a cavernous store with lots of cribs, youth beds, and a good selection of strollers. This was the only store in our survey where everything had a price tag. Most cribs are in the $300 range, and all cribs include the mattress with free delivery and setup (in Manhattan). Dressers, changing tables, and toy chests had safety features . . . **Bellini Juvenile Furniture,** 473 Columbus Ave. [82nd/83rd] ☎ 362-3700. A small, stuffed store with a half dozen very upscale, mostly white cribs that are hard to see because they are filled with bedding, toys, etc. This is their own line of coordinated infant furniture. Prices are not marked, but cribs range from $399–$725, a high-density foam mattress is $90, and delivery and setup is approximately $35. The back room has a selection of strollers, a few high chairs, car seats, gates, and safety nets to put around railings . . . **Ben's for Kids,** 1380 Third Ave. [78th/79th] ☎ 794-2330. Modest selection of better cribs and furniture for infants up to 4 years. There is no delivery charge or service charge for putting the crib together. You might want to note that we priced a Ragazzi Shaker Dreams crib here: $375 plus a $75 Simmons foam mattress. The same crib set up at Portico Kids was $570 plus $130 for Simmons foam plus $80 delivery and setup. (A savings of $330 at Ben's.) Prices are clearly marked . . . **Hushabye,** 1459 First Ave. [76th] ☎ 988-4500. A good selection of better furniture. Lots of platform rockers, dressers, changing tables. (A

Status crib here with green slats is $400 plus $100–$150 for the mattress, and $35 for delivery and setup. At Schneider's, the same Status crib is $400, including the mattress; delivery and setup is $15.) . . . **Schneider's,** 20 Ave. A [Houston/E. 2nd] ☎ 228-3540. A huge selection with use-your-imagination display. Cribs are lined up in the middle of the room with high chairs, changing tables, and chests around the side walls . . . **Wicker Garden Baby,** 1327 Madison Ave. [93rd/94th] ☎ 348-1166. The ultimate in turn-of-the-century charm. White wicker cribs, dressers, and changing tables can be hand painted in Pamela Scurry's designs. They advise a 16-week advance notice for painted furniture. A look with prices to prove it—cribs in the $1,000 range . . . At **Plain Jane,** 205 W. 80th St. [Bway/Amsterdam] ☎ 595-6916, the stock is anything but plain. Suzanne O'Brien and Melanie Williams decided that linen selection for infants needed some sprucing up. They use vintage and modern fabrics in creating charming infant comforters, crib bumpers, and dust ruffles, as well as a variety of pillows and slipcovers. Items can be purchased directly from the shop or made to order. A bumper runs from $120–$140.

OLDER KIDS **A Bear's Place,** 789 Lexington Ave. [61st/62nd] ☎ 826-6465, has some upholstered kid's furniture—a roll armchair in a cowboy print is $400, a two-seat sofa is $600. A wing chair and a chaise longue have also been scaled down, and several fabrics are available . . . **Children's Room,** 140 Varick St. [Spring] ☎ 627-2006. Bunk beds, beds, storage units, and desks for older kids. Styling is Scandinavian utilitarian . . . **Frederick Mattress,** 107 E.

31st St. [Park/Lex] ☎ 683-8322, has a modest selection of bunk beds. They can help you with nonstandard-sized mattresses for bunks and trundles . . . **R. V. Cole Furniture and Design** 114 E. 32nd St. [Lex/Park] ☎ 481-5566. Straightforward styling of sturdy, solid, wood bunk beds, beds, dressers, desks, and bookcases. Many of the designs combine a bed with storage space: under-bed drawers and cabinets (even a trundle bed). No infant furniture . . . **Portico Kids,** 1167 Madison Ave. [86th] ☎ 717-1963. Attractive infants' and children's furniture at Madison Ave. prices. The small upholstered pieces are cute (a club chair starts at $450 and can go to $1,000, depending on fabric choice), but the staff can be uninterested. We were surprised that many of the stylish dressers did not have stops to keep the drawers from falling out onto a curious child.

CUSTOM ROOMS AND FURNITURE
Charm and Whimsy ☎ 683-7609. Esther Sadowsky began painting furniture for children over 10 years ago when her nephew was born. Since then, her business has evolved to the creation of rooms that are fantasy environments for children, like a western theme room complete with a covered wagon bed. She does a lot of problem solving along the way. When she had to design a very small space for a little girl, she turned it into a doll's house. Toys were stowed in the house and the bed was on the roof—which she bordered with a picket fence guard rail. An initial consultation is $150. She also paints cribs, changing tables, dressers, and other furniture that you have purchased or that she purchases for you. She does wall murals and painted ceilings . . . **Kimberley Fiterman,** ASID ☎ 633-0660, is

a designer who specializes in designing rooms for children. She tries to help parents "carve out a space for the child without giving up their own space." The infant grows into a child so fast that the needs of the room keep changing. Her rooms accommodate those changes, in many cases without a lot of expense. Ms. Fiterman finds that many new lines of children's furniture never make their way into NY stores, so she has researched many other resources. Ms. Fiterman will work on a consulting basis at $100 an hour or on a fee basis of 30% of the budget if you want her to design a room . . . Ten years ago when Hope Winthrop was having her second child, she was unhappy with the children's furniture that she saw in stores. She did like some hand-painted *doll's* furniture that she found in a toy store, located the painter, and together they created **Boston & Winthrop** ☎ 410-6388, by appt. They offer sturdy wood furniture in traditional styles that is painted and trimmed to your specifications (with a trailing vine pattern, say). You can send or bring them your color scheme, swatches of wallpaper or linen pattern, and they will match the color and design on dressers, armoires, beds, chairs, and accessories. A catalog and price list is available. A twin bed with rails and slats is $495, a small table and chairs, $350.

CONTEMPORARY FURNITURE & MODERN CLASSICS

Full House, 133 Wooster St. [Houston/Prince] ☎ 529-2298, for a big selection of '40s, '50s, and '60s furniture—including Noguchi tables, Herman Miller, and Scandinavian pieces.

Todd Hase and his wife, Amy, have a shop at 51 Wooster St. [Broome/Grand] ☎ 334-3568. Mr. Hase designs the chairs,

sofas, and settees with more than looks in mind. The construction is of high quality, with sprung backs, hand-tied springs, and a cotton batting covering over the springs. Styling is clean and sophisticated without being astringent.

Knoll, 105 Wooster St. [Prince/Spring] ☎ 343-4000, produces modern classics, including work designed by Saarinen, Mies van der Rohe, and Frank Gehry.

Modern Age, 102 Wooster St. [Spring/Prince] ☎ 966-0669. All modern, mostly Italian designs. Sofas, chairs, shelving, and lighting.

Poltrona Frau, at Galleria Frau, 141-145 Wooster St. [Houston/Prince] ☎ 777-7592 and **Sofa So Good,** 106 Wooster St. [Prince/Spring] ☎ 219-8860. For leather.

Palazzetti, 152 Wooster St. [Houston/Prince] ☎ 260-8815, sells reproductions of modern classics that are in the public domain, like Marcel Breuer's daybed and an Eileen Gray sofa and side table.

See, 920 Broadway [20th/21st] ☎ 228-3600, has works from contemporary furniture designers.

You can read whatever significance you want into the metal shark suspended ominously overhead in **Traumbau,** 47 Second Ave. [2nd/3rd] ☎ 614-0257, but it certainly gets your attention. Uwe Bruggeman is the

Inside Traumbau.

designer and fabricator of these sleek (yet not too hard-edged) metal home furnishings (and flying fish)—having begun working in metal in Hamburg, Germany, about 15 years ago. He says, "The challenge of metal furniture is to give the dense steel a lighter appearance—to make it appear to be fabric or smoke." Small side tables that have brushed aluminum tops and U-shaped legs are $225–$250 each. Larger console tables or dining tables with stainless steel tops and hot rolled steel legs are priced according to size. A 5-foot table approximately 30 inches wide is $650. A three-tiered table called the "pregnant ellipse"—a shape generated by Mr. Bruggeman working with a pantograph—is a wonderful postmodern version of the Noguchi kidney table. It holds a set of stereo components perfectly. $225. Mr. Bruggeman specializes in built-in stainless steel kitchen cabinets. He makes everything to order, and there is a 4–6 week wait. And the fish—when Mr. Bruggeman takes a break from furniture, he creates metal sharks. He studies them and works from photos to achieve the natural curves and arcs of the body while swimming. At last check, a Blue shark and a Hammerhead inhabited the shop with a titanium Perlon shark in the window.

DESIGN CENTER **New York Design Center,** 200 Lexington Ave. [32nd] ☎ 679-9500. This is a user-friendly, 16-story building filled with furniture and decorating showrooms. When you enter you are asked to sign in and are given the 96-page directory to the building. You can wander the carpeted halls and go in and out of a dizzying number of middle- to high-end furniture showrooms. Styles of furniture run from traditional to country to contemporary and office. You'll find upholstered goods, cabinetry, tables, chairs, some lighting, wall treatments, textiles, and window treatments. The 16th floor is the **clearance center** for floor samples or merchandise that hasn't been sold. Some showrooms are closed to the general public, but there is an easy way to obtain access to these. You make an appointment with the American Society of Interior Designers, which maintains an office on the 4th floor, and a designer will meet with you for consultation and take you to showrooms. There is no charge for this service, and your purchase price will be 20% above net or roughly 15%–30% below retail. The ASID office isn't staffed all the time, so call ahead.

IKEA 131 E. 57th St. [Lex] ☎ 308-4532. The bus to their Elizabeth, NJ, store runs on weekends from 11 A.M.–3 P.M. approximately every 45 minutes, from in front of the store on E. 57th.

OFFICE FURNITURE Try **David's Office Equipment,** 327 Canal St. [Mercer/Greene] ☎ 966-5418, when you're looking for a single, used, inexpensive file cabinet, chair, or desk . . . When you want the largest selection of used office furniture you've ever seen, you want to go Long Island City. **Office Furniture Service,** 47-44 31st St. [48th] LIC ☎ 718-786-7776, is an enormous space in the Factory Building, where they sell, repair, and refinish furniture. Delivery available . . . **Adirondack Furniture Outlet,** 31-01 Vernon Blvd. [31 Ave.] LIC ☎ 718-204-4550, has several floors of both used and new office furniture. They do not recondition the used stuff, but much of it is in good shape.

PACE WAREHOUSE OUTLET CENTER 11-11 34th St. [11th] LIC ☎ 718-721-8201.

Weekdays only. Take the N train to Steinway, then the Q104 bus to last stop at corner of 34th and 11 St. (You will be two blocks from Socrates Sculpture Park and a block from the Noguchi Museum.) One floor of the sizable Pace Warehouse has been given over to a showroom. This is where floor models from Manhattan come to rest, along with other samples and some damaged goods. All the categories of Pace furniture are represented here, and the savings are substantial. Some upholstered seat side chairs were $195, others were $595. Sofas from $900 to several thousands for leather sectionals. Side tables from $250 to large, glass-topped dining tables. Delivery arranged. The main showroom is at 321 E. 62nd St. [1st/2nd] ☎ 838-0331.

PHOOF Phoof, 71 Gansevoort St. [Greenwich/Washington] ☎ 807-1332, is run by Jeanette Iannucci, Victor Mendolia, and Mark Shannon—three people with a passion for the decor of the late '30s to the late '60s. They specialize in Haywood-Wakefield furniture, as well as lamps and period accessories. Phoof also has a refinishing and upholstery shop where they recondition some of the pieces that then go on sale. They will also work on your pieces. (See more in the Furniture Repair article in the Services chapter.)

ROOM SCREENS Amanda Weil, ☎ 229-0655, by appt. Ms. Weil combines her abilities as a photographer and a furnituremaker in her striking room screens. Large black-and-white images are printed on a transparent material and toned with blue, gold, or copper. They are then sandwiched between glass panels and framed with wood or steel. A three-panel screen can also be put on wheels. Ms. Weil uses her own photographs exclusively, but she will work with you on subject matter. Trees and leaves are the most requested subjects. A custom screen averages $4,000. Side and breakfast tables, sconces and lanterns use the same technique . . . See also Exquisite Glass and NY Carved Arts in the Glass, Mirrors, Porcelain article in the Services chapter.

WYETH It's not often that we walk into a store and want to buy everything or just move in, but at **Wyeth,** 149 Franklin St. [Varick/Hudson] ☎ 925-5278, all they have to do is invite us. This store has a stock of 20th century antiques and reproductions that have been selected with an exquisite eye and displayed with the same sensibility. It's the result of the work of three brothers—John Birch, the designer and buyer; Philip, who manages the store; and Paul, who does restoration and fabrication. You'll find Castiglione lamps displayed side by side with antique French wicker chairs and sofas. Highly polished chrome table fans from the '40s sit atop American oak tables. Mr. Birch says his taste runs to the "clean, simple, and strong . . . not ornamental." He likes using metal in home decor, especially nickel. The brothers like to take pieces designed for one function and transform their use—such as an aluminum saddle rack transformed into a sideboard. The Birches are also reproducing some of the furniture designs of Pierre Chareau, famous as the architect of the Maison de Verre in Paris. The brothers have re-created small tables in pitted steel with maple tops and similar mahogany-topped stools. There are small patinated steel table lamps with alabaster shades and a group of wicker chairs from Chareau designs. The club chairs and rocker are of variegated wicker in warm tones from honey to tea ($1,000–$1,750). A group of them surrounds an aeronautic-looking German glass top table from the '50s with a cast aluminum base. Great stuff.

GAMES

BOARD GAMES

For board games, we always go to one of the two **Game Show** stores, 474 Sixth Ave. [11th/12th] ☎ 633-6328 and 1240 Lexington Ave. [83rd] ☎ 472-8011. Both stores have an excellent selection and a knowledgeable staff . . . **The Compleat Strategist,** with three locations in the city, 11 East 33rd St. [5th/Mad] ☎ 685-3880, 320 W. 57th St. [8th/9th] ☎ 582-1272, and on the concourse at Rockefeller Center ☎ 265-7449, emphasizes adventure, war, and fantasy/science fiction games.

David Galt, ☎ 769-2514, has been interested in games just about all of his life. He has a collection of historical gameboards, some of which were once exhibited at the New York Historical Society. If you are planning a party, he will make up a game for you. He devises word games, card games, and board games for adults and children, private and corporate events. From $50–$200 for games that do not require special equipment. He needs at least a few days' notice, more if you want something intricate.

CASINO SUPPLIES

Marion & Co., 147 W. 26th St. [6th/7th] ☎ 727-8900. This store supplies casinos all over the country with blackjack tables, raffle drums, card dealing shoes, precision dice, bingo equipment, roulette wheels, and blackjack tables. They specialize in monogrammed poker chips ($16–$55 per 100 chips) and cases to carry them in. Marion & Co. supplies these chips to large gift catalogs, so you save money by going to the source . . .

Manhattan Gaming, 66 W. 39th St. [6th] ☎ 997-0880, sells roulette wheels, slot machines, poker chips, and they give lessons in blackjack and craps. A one-hour lesson ($25), besides teaching you the game, also deals with table etiquette and "bankroll management."

CHESS

The Village Chess Shop, 230 Thompson St. [W. 3rd/Bleecker] ☎ 475-9580, is more like a chess club than a shop. Tables are set with boards and chess pieces waiting for players. Chess sets are carved in exotic stones or woods and can represent soldiers in the Napoleonic campaigns or the Simpsons. Chess boards are available in different square sizes and in alabaster, glass, ceramic, and wood. Boards start at $100. Chess clocks and computer chess games and trainers. But in chess it's practice, practice, practice. To that end, the shop is open noon to midnight, and you can play for $1 per hour.

The new kid on the block is **Chess Forum,** 219 Thompson St. [W. 3rd/ Bleecker] ☎ 475-2369. So far, the assortment of chess sets and boards is about the same as at the Village Chess Shop, and there are tables for playing.

GARDENING

The Gardener's Touch, 1545 Second Ave. [80th/81st] ☎ 288-1418, is run by Jim Manning, a landscape designer, who has filled his store with garden books, tools, pots, garden sculpture, Farmer McGregor–style watering cans, bird feeders, and notecards with floral themes—everything you need for "terrace, backyard, or windowsill." If you buy 10 Dutch Master daffodil bulbs ($4.99), he will give you all the information you need to end up with 10 blooming daffodils in your apartment in a few weeks. There are window box herb gardens and gift-boxed hyacinths, crocuses, and amaryllis for indoors.

Folly, 13 White St. [Bway/Church] ☎ 925-5012, sells antique garden ornaments like large urns, sculptures, benches, and trellis-work at hefty prices.

Grass Roots Garden, 131 Spring St. [Wooster/Greene] ☎ 226-2662. The store looks like an urban jungle with everything from ground covers to apartment trees. Bring Larry Nathanson and his staff some of your particulars, such as the kind of light you get, your ceiling height, and a snapshot of where you'd like plants to go, and they will give good advice on what you can grow. If you want them to come to your home for a consultation, it's $75–$100.

Lexington Gardens, 1008 Lexington Ave. [72nd] ☎ 861-4390, sells antique and new garden statuary, urns, planters, and some furniture. There are also indoor French plant racks and a variety of decorative items (candle holders, small dishes, and pots) with more or less of a gardening theme. The store is large but crowded with goods, and moving about can be difficult. Help appears reserved for those known to the proprietors.

Nurseries: Chelsea Garden Center, 401 W. 22nd St. [9th] ☎ 929-2477 . . . **Dimitri's Nursery,** 1992 Second Ave. [101st/102nd] ☎ 831-2810. Not the greatest neighborhood but worth the trip for great prices and variety . . . **Farm & Garden Nursery,** 2 Sixth Ave. [White] ☎ 431-3577 . . . and **Union Square Greenmarket.**

Smith & Hawken, 394 W. Broadway [Spring/Broome] ☎ 925-0687. The urban gardener used to windowsills and containers gets a breath of fresh air from the lovely pots, tools, and bloom-ready bulbs sold here.

GARMENT CENTER

BUTTONS Hersh 6th Avenue Button, 1000 Sixth Ave. [37th/38th] ☎ 391-6615, in business at this location for over 80 years, is run by Angel Cosme. The staff is known for their friendliness, and the place is the informal information central of the Garment Center. If they don't know where to find something, chances are it's not findable. Hersh sells everything you need for sewing (including things now impossible to find anywhere else): thread, seam binding, needles and pins of all kinds, a wide range of scissors (including pinking shears, trimmers, cutting shears), seam rippers, zippers, sleeve pressers, and many other such items. Zippers can be cut to size and repaired. They sell buttons, old and new, and make custom button covers. These are made from findings (the hardware that goes into making jewelry and buttons) covered with stones (colored

CHRISTOPHER LOVI

An abundance of buttons at Hersh 6th Avenue Button.

bits of glass), beads, or other things that you slip over your plain buttons. They also custom dye buttons—done for garmentos all the time. What it means to you is that you must purchase a gross of buttons, pay the price for the buttons ($7 to $45), then add a $5 dye charge . . . Tender Buttons tends to get more attention uptown, but **Gordon Button,** 222 W. 38th St. [7th/8th] ☎ 921-1684, carries a large assortment in this well-lit shop. Peter Gordon will make up stone buttons for you if he does not have the right color in stock, or he will sell you the findings and you can fill them with stones or beads from one of the trim shops.

BUTTONHOLES **Buttonhole Fashion,** 580 Eighth Ave. [38th/39th] ☎ 354-1420. Melvin and Betty Reich have been making buttonholes for over 40 years—slash, "keyhole" (the kind usual on coats and heavier fabrics that have a rounded cut after the slash) and "bound" (the opening is covered with something, usually fabric). They will set (put in) snaps and grommets and set pockets for you. It's a big, busy loft with

some production work going on and garmentos waiting for samples to be worked on. Mr. Reich has a lot of old-fashioned Garment Center character . . . **Moonlighting,** 63 W. 38th St. [5th/6th] ☎ 398-6711, on the other hand, is the new guard. The small, bright shop is run by the charming Janise Beckwith, who has a degree from F.I.T. She makes plain buttonholes, can knock off a garment you have (to replace a skirt that's wearing thin, say, or re-create a dress in a different color), and if she's not too busy with production work, she will make original garments for you.

MILLINERY **Manny's Millinery Supply Center,** 26 W. 38th St. [5th/6th] ☎ 840-2235. The simplest way to get started is to buy an untrimmed body (hat shape), get some advice on which of their trims (veiling, ribbons, feathers, flowers, etc.) will look best on it and you, and on how to apply it. Manny's will block the hat for you. They also sell millinery texts for professionals and do-it-yourselfers, all the necessary supplies, a good looking assortment of hatboxes, and a group of hat pins. In winter the store is filled with straws for summer, and, about July, the felts and velours come back. The back of the store is a selling area for trimmed hats by small designers. The prices on these are very reasonable . . . **Concord Merchandise,** 1026 Sixth Ave. [38th/39th] ☎ 840-2720, sells forms and trims, but does not do any blocking.

TRIMS **Tinsel Trading,** 47 W. 38th St. [5th/6th] ☎ 730-1030. Arch Bergoffer started his business in the '30s selling tinsel (gold trim) to the U.S. military for uniform trim from a loft on 36th St., and then expanded for the needs of the garment industry. He bought gold and silver cords, tassels, ball fringes, sequins, metallic threads, and woven metallic ribbons from France, handmade raffia flowers from Italy, straw millinery trims from Switzerland, and anything else he saw in European catalogs brought to him by traveling salesmen. When things went out of style he boxed them up and put them in the basement. After Mr. Bergoffer died, his granddaughter, Marcia Ceppos, inherited the business and came across the boxes in the basement. She said, "It took a while to sink in. Some of these boxes had not been opened for 50 years." Ms. Ceppos has brought these small treasures (most of which cannot be duplicated and some of which are in short supply) out of hiding and into the shop. Now costume designers and restorers shop here. "The most amazing thing," Ms. Ceppos says, "is he never went to Europe. He bought all this from little pictures in catalogs." She also has the catalogs . . . **Metropolitan Impex,** 966 Sixth Ave. [35th/36th] ☎ 502-5243, has been in business since 1933 selling domestic and imported trims for millinery and artificial flowers. Come in with or without a picture or idea for a bridal headpiece, and "if you can explain it, we can make it"—which includes matching the color of a dress. Some models are on display and are for sale—about $35. They sell rhinestones and the very simple-to-use machine you need to apply them, sew-on beads and pearls, shoulder pads, crinolines, and hoops. There is much in the way of tiaras and costume jewelry. Upstairs, they have a private showroom for imported wedding dresses (appt. necessary). Service is knowledgeable, if sometimes brusque . . . **M. & S. Schmalberg,** 470 Seventh Ave. [35th/36th] ☎ 244-2090, has some fabrics

for sale, both knits and wovens at reasonable prices. But Schmalberg's real claim to Garment Center fame is the array of artificial flowers. They will make up flowers for you from your own fabric for about $5 per flower . . . **M & J Trimming,** 1008 Sixth Ave. [37th/38th] ☎ 391-8731 and their **Decorator Collection,** 1014 Sixth Ave. [37th/38th] ☎ 391-8731. Since 1936, M & J has been a mine for braids, tassels, cords, varieties of fringes (including beaded and leather), frogs, lace and eyelet trim by the yard, ribbons, lace collars, and inserts, iron-on rhinestone appliqués, patches of all kinds, flocked letters, feathers, beads, ruffles, and buttons. Sammy and the crew explain at Garment Center pace how to use or apply the trims you are interested in. The decorator collection is a place where you can take in your fabric and some ideas and Janice Hardial and her well-trained staff will advise you on color and type of trim for your project. They can recommend pillowmakers and upholsterers, too.

BEADS Sheru Beads, 49 W. 38th St. [5th/6th] ☎ 730-0766, is for people who make their own jewelry. You'll find here fashion beads, findings, some European Lucites, semiprecious stones, Austrian rhinestones, 700–800 designs in metal stampings, and drawers of wood beads. Get there early (before noon—lunch time and afternoons get busy) to get a space at the counter and some help from the knowledgeable staff. You may have to ask for seed beads, for instance, as not everything is on display (you may find this impossible to believe since Sheru is visual overkill). They sell wholesale to the public . . . **Toho Shoji,** 990 Sixth Ave. [36th/37th] ☎ 868-7465, sells jewelry findings and beads for do-it-yourself costume jewelry. Things are clearly laid out in this bright, two-year-old store. They'll help when they're not busy. It's more expensive than Sheru Beads, but not as chaotic.

RIBBONS Hyman Hendler & Sons, 67 W. 38th St. [5th/6th] ☎ 840-8393. Since 1910, Hendler has been collecting an encyclopedic array of ribbons: satins, velvets, grosgrains, woven and printed designs, and wired. There is so much ribbon here, in heap after heap, that it seems unlikely that anything has ever been discarded once it arrived. One-yard minimums and it's best to check prices before the ribbon is cut as, counter to appearances, this is not a discount shop. Prices drop when you buy by the roll . . . **Ribbon So Good,** 28 W. 38th St. [5th/6th] ☎ 398-0236. The ribbons have been collecting here for only a couple of decades, but you will still have to navigate the nar-row central passageway between towering stacks of ribbons to find what you need. Friendly staff, good prices.

SNAPS Sure Snap, 505 Eighth Ave. [35th/36th] ☎ 921-5515. This company makes snaps and other metallic trims, but they will set snaps for you in your garments or leather goods. There is a small display of the products you can choose from—metallic or colored enamel snaps, tack buttons (the kind used on jean jackets), eyelets in a variety of sizes (used lately on lace-up garments), and plastic snaps on woven tape for bodysuits. There are also fireman clips—very popular right now—as well as some 361 (approx. 7/8" diameter) snaps in nautical and heart shapes. Work often can be done while you wait. $6 minimum.

LEATHER See Leather in the Feature chapter.

GIFTS & COLLECTIBLES

Our list of places to consider when you need a gift but don't know what to get.

GIFTS

Ad Hoc Softwares, 410 W. Broadway [Spring] ☎ 925-2652, is a favorite of ours for small kitchen items, housewares, and for its great collection of bath products from around the world.

Archetype Gallery, 115 Mercer St. [Prince/ Spring] ☎ 334-0100, especially for their jewelry and glassware.

Aris Mixon, 381 Amsterdam Ave. [78th/ 79th] ☎ 724-6904. Thoughtfully chosen napkin rings, candles, picture frames, sta-tionery items, and small home decor items.

Avventura, 463 Amsterdam Ave. [82nd] ☎ 769-2510. For tableware and Venetian glass jewelry.

Century 21, 22 Cortlandt St. [Bway/ Church] ☎ 227-9092. Ties, sweaters, and designer clothes at steep discount.

Chelsea Antiques Building, 110 W. 25th St. [6th/7th] ☎ 929-0909. Twelve floors (plus the basement) of potential gifts and, on the weekends, more at the fleas.

Craft Caravan, 63 Greene St. [Spring/ Broome] ☎ 431-6669. Multicolored African trading beads, strings of amber, crocheted wire baskets, and indigo textiles.

Felissimo, 10 W. 56th St. [5th/6th] ☎ 247-5656. One of the few places in the city where the shopping is actually a pleasure. A broad range of gift items, mostly for the home, all chosen with care.

Gifted Ones, 150 W. 10th St. [Waverly] ☎ 627-4050. Fun gift baskets for any occasion.

La Maison Moderne, 144 W. 19th St. [6th/7th] ☎ 691-9603. You never know what you'll find—perhaps North African tea glasses, candles, French perfume bottles, small clocks and boxes, sealing wax and stamps, and many tassels.

Little Rickie, 49 ½ First Ave. [3rd] ☎ 505-6467. Elvis has never left the building. Wall-to-wall kitsch, and great fun.

L S Collection, 469 West Broadway [Houston/Prince] ☎ 673-4575. You're sure to find something among the housewares and many other objects from around the world.

Mabel's, 849 Madison Ave. [70th] ☎ 734-3263. Animal motif everything: furniture, slippers, frames, mugs. Good quality merchandise that's not too cute or kitschy. But how about a few price tags?

Manhattan Fruitier, 105 E. 29th St. [Park/Lex] ☎ 686-0404, for reliably excellent fruit baskets.

Moss, 146 Greene St. [Houston/Prince] ☎ 226-2190. Cocktail shakers, bowls, glassware, fly swatters, tabletop items, a *Psycho* shower curtain, a superbly designed ironing board. Murray Moss unerringly picks the best of available 20th century design.

Myron Toback, 25 W. 47th St. [5th/6th] ☎ 398-8300. A small collection of silver frames, silver clips, and silver key chains at a fraction of what you'd pay elsewhere.

Mxyplyzyk, 125 Greenwich Ave. [13th] ☎ 989-4300, for small household goods, bath products, stationery items, lighting, and some decorative things like bowls and clocks. Everything here is selected with an eye for good design and materials you want to touch.

The Spectrum Store inside The Lighthouse, 111 E. 59th St. [Lex/Park] ☎ 821-9384, specializes in products for the sight-impaired and for the blind, but many of their products are so well designed that they would benefit anyone. A saucepan has a lid that won't fall off when you are draining hot liquids. There are talking clocks and calculators with large numerals, and large-type reference books, like dictionaries, atlases, and cookbooks.

Takashimaya, 693 Fifth Ave. [54th/55th] ☎ 350-0100. The tableware makes especially good gifts.

Tender Buttons, 143 E. 62nd St. [Lex/3rd] ☎ 758-7004. Buttons (including some antique) for the fashion-conscious type on your list. They might like a new set of blazer buttons, some '20s jet pieces, or a Krazy Kat or two. Tender Buttons also make cuff links from buttons.

T Salon, 142 Mercer St. [Prince] ☎ 925-3700, for Mariage Frères teas and tea jellies, antique tea services, and tea cakes.

William Wayne, 845 Lexington Ave. [64th/65th] ☎ 737-8934 and 40 University Place [9th] ☎ 533-4711. Lacquered trays, glassware, napkins, decorative items. The house specialty is any item with a monkey on it.

PERSONALIZED GIFTS

BOOKPLATES You choose the ink color and typeface for a name, and **Bowne & Co.,** 211 Water [Seaport] ☎ 748-8651, will print it on either stock Ex Libris designs or a plate of your own design. The first 75 bookplates from a stock design are $50, the next 75 (printed at the same time), $25. They also print calling cards, place cards, and personalized postcards.

CHOCOLATES 5th Ave. Chocolatière, 510 Madison Ave. [52nd/53rd] ☎ 935-5454. John Whaley takes customer requests for all manner of things, just so long as they can be molded into his imported Belgian chocolate. The items are then personalized with a handwritten message in icing. It can be written on telephones, computer screens, tennis rackets, musical notes, Christmas cards, etc. He has over 5,000 molds: "If you can think of it, we probably already have it." If he doesn't, he will make a mold to order. Business cards and other personal or promotional materials can also be reproduced in chocolate molds. A 1 ½ lb. mold with wording is $26.

CRYSTAL & GLASSWARE Buz Vaultz at **Exquisite Glass,** 123 Allen St. [Delancey/Rivington] ☎ 674-7069, etches bowls, glasses, and other crystal pieces for weddings or other occasions—both corporate and private. The most requested item: two champagne flutes engraved with bride and groom's name and date of wedding, $45 for the engraving (you provide the glasses). Anything from a wedding invitation to a corporate logo can be etched into glass or a mirror. See more in Glass, Mirrors, and Porcelain in the Services chapter.

GOLD STAMPING Douglas and Sons, 25 W. 43rd St. [5th/6th] ☎ 557-0088, is now Charles Douglas with help from his daughter and some gold stampers. Mr. Douglas stamps monograms in gold on leather and vinyl goods. Most of the work is done on briefcases and attachés, but they will also monogram wallets, put names on books, and title your photo albums. Ladies' handbags are tricky because of the many ways in which they can be made. "If there is any danger of spoiling it, I discourage it." Gold stamping costs $12.50 a line—a line being 5 1/2″ long in a given typeface.

GUGGENHEIM FONT PINS When Frank Lloyd Wright designed the Guggenheim Museum, he designed the font that letters the front of the building. In 1991, the museum commissioned Gwathmey Siegel & Associates and Vignelli Associates to complete the alphabet and then further commissioned artist Jane Bohan to turn them into wearable pins. Each letter is 1″ high and is plated in 18 karat gold over brass. They have a tie tack back, cost $45 each, and are sold only in the Guggenheim shops.

KIDS Art & Tapisserie, 1242 Madison Ave. [89th/90th] ☎ 722-3222, is an improbable name for a toy shop, but this one has lots of nifty things. The standout, we think, is the stool with the child's name cut out in puzzle pieces. These letters can be removed and replaced into the bench. In natural ($78) or white ($88) wood, both with multicolored letters. Rectangular, heart, or baseball-shaped.

LIMOGES BOXES ARK Restoration, 350 Seventh Ave. [29th/30th] ☎ 675-7994, is a supplier of hand-painted Limoges boxes to places like Asprey. Rena Kristul will custom paint a box for you, or you can choose from one of their stock designs starting at $150; custom work is more.

METAL ENGRAVING Seymour Multz has been "on the street" (W. 47th) since 1959, engraving since he was 18, when he was apprenticed to a Grand St. company. **Jay-Mor Engravers,** 50 W. 47th St. [5th/6th], Booth 18/19 ☎ 719-1993, does machine engraving on watches and wedding bands. "The longest one was 110 letters from a Shakespeare quote, but the date is the most important thing, so you don't forget it later on." There are about 50 fonts to choose from and several monogram arrangements. It's 75¢ per letter, $10 minimum. It generally takes a day. Mr. Multz also produces engraved plaques for business use and private commemorations.

PAPER Products like napkins, coasters, matchbooks, and guest towels can be imprinted at **Rubenstein's,** 24 E. 17th St. [Bway/5th] ☎ 924-7817. Printed white napkins are $19.90 per 100.

POKER CHIPS **Manhattan Gaming,** 66 W. 39th St. [5th/6th] ☎ 997-0880, monograms poker chips for 10¢ a chip . . . **Marion & Co.,** 147 W. 26th St. [6th/7th] ☎ 727-8900, supplies casino shops all over the world. Poker chips come in three qualities and can be monogrammed. Plastic ones are $14 for 100; clay and nylon are $35 for 100; and all-clay casino quality are $55 for 100. Prices include the monogramming.

COLLECTIBLES

Since anything can be a collectible, this is only a small survey of what's out there. For fine things, you might start with Faces of Time, described below. After that, we've organized some collectibles by item.

Sheila Shwartz's studio, called **Faces of Time,** 32 W. 40th St. [5th/6th] ☎ 921-0822, by appt., is crammed with her complete accessory collection. She calls her business Faces

M O N O G R A M S

Edward Sacher or, as he prefers, **Edward the Monogrammer**, has taken up residence in the Maxene Cleaners, 750 Columbus Ave. [97th] ☎ 666-8349. He provides a full range of monogramming services on all manner of household and personal linens and clothing: towels, bedsheets, pillowcases, men's shirts and handkerchiefs, coat linings, napkins. There is a book of styles to choose from, or you can develop your own monogram with him. He does all the work himself, which is hand-guided, and he can embroider original artwork. You bring him something you want to have copied, like a theatre program or a child's drawing, and he will put it on the back of your jeans jacket or lapel of your robe. Cost for this depends on the complexity

of the design and the number of colors involved, but starts at $90 . . . **Hoofbeats, Ltd.,** 232 E. 78th St. [2nd/3rd] ☎ 517-2633. Suzanne Chinard and her embroidery machine will put monograms, names, or sobriquets on just about anything you can think of. She also sells products for monogramming of very good quality. Robes for all sizes are in 100% cotton terry or a soft velour. $48 for toddlers (including monogram, up to $120 for a long adult robe). Baby pillows, wool and cotton blankets, bibs and Irish linen towel sets are available. Baseball hats are stitched across the front ($21.50 for hat and one word). She will also embroider things that you bring her, such as doctors' lab coats, shirts, or home linens.

CHRISTOPHER LOVI

Faces of Time.

of Time because when she started designing jewelry 30 years ago, she used vintage watch faces. Ms. Shwartz still does this work and sells some vintage watches, but she specializes in creating new jewelry and other items from old elements collected from the '40s and '50s and earlier. You'll find everything from beautiful rope necklaces made up of French jet and topaz beads, others of American Lucite beads from the '30s, binoculars, birdcages, linens, gaming chips, lots of sporting items, and dresser items: cuff links, atomizers, shaving mirrors, and so on. She showed us a beautiful collection of things for the desk covered in shagreen (a light aqua-colored sharkskin), many with silver fittings. There are lots of silver candlesticks, toast racks, sugars and creamers, cake stands, and epergnes from the 1850s and 1860s. On one of the Victorian sofas is a collection of Teddy Bears. In her "packrat's paradise," a closet-sized room, are many jeweler's trays filled with small items— all of which are marked and categorized. Most of her things are limited editions or one-of-a-kind. If you can't find what you're looking for, Ms. Shwartz likely knows where it can be found.

AUTOGRAPHS **Gary E. Combs Autographs,** ☎ 242-7209, by appt. Mr. Combs, who's dealt in autographs for 25 years, sells them either archivally framed or unframed— most framed pieces come with a photograph or engraved portrait. Mr. Combs says his strong points are Americana and music. He has autographs from George Washington, Abraham Lincoln, Jackie Onassis, Harry Houdini, and Charlie Parker. Prices range from under $100 to thousands.

BASEBALL MEMORABILIA An amazing collection of baseball memorabilia has been turned into wonderful posters by **David Spindel,** 18 E. 17th St. [5th/Bway] ☎ 989-4984. They're 22" × 28" and $9.95 each or three for $19.95, plus postage and handling.

CARS **L'Art et L'Automobile,** 121 Madison Ave. [30th/31st] ☎ 684-6185, was started by race car driver Jacques Vaucher as a mecca for people interested in classic and unusual automobiles. They specialize in original art and posters having to do with cars and racing, as well as toys, models, and books. By appointment only.

CHILDHOOD **Alphaville,** 226 W. Houston St. [Varick/Bedford] ☎ 675-6850. Things you played with and would like to play with again: erector sets, tops, original Mr. and Mrs. Potato Heads, a Fire Chief Pedal Car, and vintage games.

COOKIE JARS The place to start is on the 8th floor of the Chelsea Antiques Building, 110 W. 25th St. [6th/7th] ☎ 751-7356, in the shop that sells little else. Prices from $75.

DECOYS **Grove Decoys,** 36 W. 44th St. [5th/6th] ☎ 391-0688, sells duck decoys, antique fish lures, and antique reels.

DOLLHOUSES **Dollhouse Antics,** 1343 Madison Ave. [94th] ☎ 876-2288; **Manhattan Dollhouse,** 176 Ninth Ave.

[20th/21st] ☎ 989-5220; **Tiny Dollhouse,** 1146 Lexington Ave. [79th/80th] ☎ 744-3719; **Mini Mansions,** 1710 86th St. [17th/18th] in Brooklyn ☎ 718-331-7992; **Sleppin's Dollhouses,** ☎ 718-229-5152, in Flushing, by appt.

DOORSTOPS **James II Galleries,** 11 E. 57th St. [5th/Mad] ☎ 355-7040. 19th century doorstops in glass, wood, and brass.

EASTER EGGS **Ukranian Museum,** 203 Second Ave. [12th/13th] ☎ 228-0110.

FIESTA WARE **Mood Indigo,** 181 Prince St. [Sullivan/Thompson] ☎ 254-1176.

GENERAL **Darrow's Fun Antiques,** 1101 First Ave. [60th/61st] ☎ 838-0730. A great resource for, as they say, fun stuff: animation art, Steiff animals, Beatles and Barbie memorabilia, political buttons, and World's Fairs items . . . **World Collectibles Center,** 18 Vesey St. [Church/Bway] ☎ 267-7100, for old magazines, toys, rock and political memorabilia, Marilyn, and Elvis.

GLASSWARE **Authentiques,** 255 W. 18th St. [7th/8th] ☎ 675-2179, for highball glasses and jelly glasses imprinted with anything you can think of: playing cards, dice, and Yosemite Sam.

PAN AM MEMORABILIA at the Barricini candy store, ☎ 684-9381, ground level of Grand Central opp. Track 18. In the store, ask for the catalog of Pan Am memorabilia.

PLASTIC HANDBAGS Janice Berkson, ☎ 941-1468, by appt., specializes in plastic

handbags from the '50s. She has about 100, some of which have never been used. There are a number of clear plastic ones, which allow you put in a scarf or handkerchief to match your outfit. From $100–$700, with many about $200.

POSTERS **J. Fields Gallery,** 55 W. 17th St. [5th/6th] ☎ 989-4520, sells vintage film and '60s psychedelic posters (many original) . . . **Chisholm Larsson Gallery,** 145 Eighth Ave. [17th] ☎ 741-1703. All original French railroad, WWI and WWII propaganda, Polish and Swiss . . . Movie and theatre posters are in the Movies, Theatre, TV, and Video article in the Arts and Diversions chapter.

POTTERY **Gwenda G,** 1390 Lexington Ave. [91st/92nd] ☎ 534-8437, sells Roseville Pottery.

SNOW DOMES **It's a Mod, Mod Mod World,** 436 E. 9th St. [1/A] ☎ 460-8004; **Mood Indigo,** 181 Prince St. [Thompson/Sullivan] ☎ 254-1176; **OK Harris Gallery,** 383 Broadway [Broome/Grand] ☎ 431-3600, for the limited edition ones designed by artist Don Celender.

TEAPOTS **The Museum Gallery,** 410 Columbus Ave. [79th/80th] ☎ 873-9446.

TV & FILM **Children of Paradise,** 154 Bleecker St. [Thompson] ☎ 473-7148, has dolls of stars like Gumby and Pokey and Cher, lunchboxes, mugs, and wind-up toys with entertainment characters on them . . . **Television City,** 64 W. 50th St. [5th/6th] ☎ 246-4324, sells some vintage games and lunchboxes, as well as current merchandise.

VENETIAN GLASS **Gardner & Barr,** 213 E. 60th St. [2nd/3rd] ☎ 752-0555. Venetian glass from the late 19th to the early 20th centuries. Pairs of goblets, as well as some singles, bowls, compotes, vases, candlesticks, and some chandeliers.

HATS

WOMEN'S HATS

Carlos NY Hats, 66 W. 38th St. ☎ 869-2207, by appt. The Philadelphia Museum of Art has his snail hat, but you can have one of his straw pillboxes or top hats trimmed with velvet flowers. Carlos does much work for special events like weddings and bar mitzvahs, and working with him is a pleasure.

When you walk into **Ellen Christine Millinery,** 255 W. 18th St. [7th/8th] ☎ 242-2457, you are likely to see Ms. Christine sitting at the front banquette sewing a hat. Her stock in trade is mostly vintage. In fact, she "has no interest in clothing after 1947." So, you're likely to find toques and cloches from the '20s and Edwardian-style pouf-topped hats with wide brims. When she is working on a new hat, she uses vintage fabrics. Summer hats are wonderfully beflowered and besprigged. Some antique men's hats. Prices run from $35 for a fabric hat to $450 for an Edwardian beaver.

Georgia Hughes, ☎ 369-6021, sells her very good-looking and handcrafted hats from her residence/showroom on the East Side. Though they have Edwardian touches, they are also very contemporary, comfortable, and meant for use. They are available in better stores, but the advantage of going to Ms. Hughes is that she will measure your head and let you pick the shape, the trim, and the color, possibly giving you an original. She mines NY for extravagant fabrics—brocades, velvets, woven soutaches, which she puts on handmade frames. Prices start at about $250.

See **Ruth Hunt** in the Clothing article in this chapter.

"Classic, tasteful, quality hats" are what **Eric Javits** says he likes, and we think that's exactly what he designs. It's also the reason that everyone looks good in an Eric Javits hat. Mr. Javits says that when he designs, he likes to "keep things as simple as possible, using a minimum of trim and colors that people need to use, like a lot of neutrals." He knows that when you're having a bad hair day you don't want to have to fuss with a hat, either. "A hat does what your hair does." His creations are unobtrusive and light in weight. "Function is the fashion when it comes to today's headgear." He says that when you put the right hat the right way on your head, "a harmony will happen." The best sources for these harmonic convergences are Saks and Bendel's.

Lola Ehrlich of **Lola Millinery,** 2 E. 17th St. [5th/Bway] ☎ 366-5708, says she "does what she pleases," working mostly in straw or fur felt but occasionally, when the mood strikes, out of some unusual material, like window screening. "You can make a hat out of anything." When she finishes one of the more "fanciful ideas" and puts it in the shop, she says, "We always think it won't sell, but there is always someone who is interested." Most of the work done in the shop is custom. Bring your outfit, swatches, or a picture. Average hat is $200.

You can shop at **Makins Hats,** 212 W. 35th St. [7th/8th] ☎ 594-6666, all year round, just BYOBag. There are both funky and conservative styles for men and women. Sample hats, some one-of-a-kind pieces. Some days the sale area is fuller than others. $45 and up. Cash only. You'll find Makins hats (at higher prices) at Barneys.

Tracey Tooker, 1211 Lexington Ave. [82nd] ☎ 472-9603. Ms. Tooker's designs are lovely, festive, and traditional.

Diana Burke Fine Millinery, ☎ 539-3947, by appt. Ms. Burke represents milliners Sheryl Leggi, Maria Stephanatos, Tia Mazza, and herself. They make one-of-a-kind pieces, working up sketches for you as part of the consultation. Styles range from the standard to the outrageous. If you would like a hat show for a charity event, they will set one up for you.

MORE In the back of **Manny's Millinery Supply Center,** 26 W. 38th St. [5th/6th] ☎ 840-2235, are hats by young designers. Prices are moderate.

MEN'S HATS

Hat shopping for men is easy: go to **J.J. Hat Center,** 310 Fifth Ave. [31st/32nd] ☎ 239-4368. You can choose from over 10,000 hats and caps, which they've stocked up on in their 81 years in business. They sell Stetson, Borsalino, collapsible top hats, boaters, and many styles of caps. They have a catalog ... **Worth & Worth,** 331 Madison Ave. [43rd] ☎ 867-6058, has a small but natty selection.

JEWELRY

The **Jane Bohan Studios** was founded by Ms. Bohan in 1983. Her rings, earrings, and bracelets are distinguished by three-dimensional surface texture patterns on sterling silver, 18 karat gold, or platinum. All of the metals have a satin finish, so the silver is "white looking," and the gold is not shiny. Gemstones include fresh water and baroque pearls, garnets, blue-colored iolite, and citrine. The look recently has been for delicate, petite work that goes well with the spare look in contemporary clothing, but Ms. Bohan says these things go in cycles and she is beginning to make some larger rings. Her creations can be seen at Works Gallery, 1250 Madison Ave. [89th/90th] ☎ 996-0300, where a pair of earrings in a silver-and-gold combination with a stone can start at $200.

Janet Goldman and Jimmy Moore, known in the trade for their accessories showroom, now have a shop called **Fragments,** 107 Greene St. [Prince/Spring] ☎ 226-8878,

Fragments.

in the same building that houses the showroom. Costume pieces, semiprecious and precious stones, and gold and silver work are all represented in the stylish, well-designed shop. They frequently feature new designers. Prices start at $35. An excellent resource to see work by a wide range of working jewelers.

Patti Horn is known for her delicate, highly finished pieces. The pewter bases are plated to look like antique silver or gold or an oxidized gold plate. Semiprecious stones (garnet, carnelian, tiger's eye, citrine, or moonstones) are always in settings. Necklaces with as many as 10 linked set stones, still have a lightness to them. "We use a premise of an antiquated look with detail and warmth." The best selection can be seen at Barneys.

Vass Ludacer makes men's and women's jewelry in about equal proportions. Cuff links, heavy rings, and pocket knives can be found at Paul Smith, 108 Fifth Ave. [16th] ☎ 627-9770. Hal Ludacer was not trained as a jeweler, and he says that is probably why he likes the element of chance in his pieces. There are pits and cracks in his heavy metal pieces. He doesn't polish these out, enjoying the irregularities. Many of the pieces are stamped with updated versions of silversmith's hallmarks, a skull, or letters that spell out Et Tu Brute? He jokingly refers to "The Frankenstein Collection"—a group of rings, bracelets, and hearts that look like "the metal has been wounded and then stitched up with gold." Barneys also carries his work.

Robert Lee Morris, 400 W. Broadway [Spring/Broome] ☎ 431-9405. Mr. Morris opened his shop, Artwear, in Soho when the neighborhood was known for its light manufacturing. He promulgated the idea of jewelry that blurred the boundaries between art, craft, and fashion, stressing wearability, usability, and excellence. These days, in a more serene setting, Mr. Morris crafts large-scale metal pieces for body wear and some home decorating items like candlesticks, bowls, and flatware.

Ted Muehling, 47 Greene St. [Broome/Grand] ☎ 431-3825. Jewelry designs that require you to stop and take notice. Mr. Muehling takes nature, and the sea in particular, as his inspiration. A drawer full of metal brooches recall the curves of seashells. A linked necklace has small leaves and the bulbous shapes of air bladders on seaweed. He works in gold-plated bronze, sterling silver, and "every karat of gold in the smaller pieces. All the colors of gold are beautiful and different." He uses a matte finish in

A necklace by Ted Muehling.

most pieces. The jewelry is never flashy, but not necessarily understated. Mr. Muehling also features the work of **Gabriella Kiss,** including some striking black hair combs from horn, embellished by some highly realistic gold bugs, and a trio of silver insect brooches.

Max Nass, 118 E. 28th St. [Park/Lex] ☎ 679-8154. A crowded little store in which all manner of jewelry is sold—strands of beads, metalwork, some new, but mostly old pieces from the '20s and '30s. If you don't like what you see, they will make adaptations. They do restringing and repairs.

Reinstein/Ross, 29 East 73rd St. [5th/Mad] ☎ 772-1901 and 122 Prince St. [Greene/Wooster] ☎ 226-4513. Susan Reinstein and Brian Ross use classical goldsmithing techniques in their pieces. Unusual gemstones show up regularly—such as melon, pink, and purple-colored sapphires.

Emeralds tend to be in paler shades. The tiny designs have a Byzantine influence.

Jordan Schlanger uses engineering techniques as well as traditional jewelrymaking techniques to create things like his hollow form line. The eggshell-thin metal is strong but light, allowing him to make sizable pieces that do not weigh you down—the earrings made this way will surprise you with how comfortable a large piece can be. The flexibility of the linked necklaces and bracelets is remarkable. They lie on the body like fabric. The best selection of Mr. Schlanger's works can be seen at Saks and Takashimaya.

Wild C.J. Accessories is a counter located on the bottom floor of Designer's Promise, 93 Nassau St. [Fulton] ☎ 513-1532, where they make up rhinestone and colored stone costume jewelry to order. They have the findings for many styles of earrings and pins. You pick the color stone you want, and they glue the stones into the findings while you wait. About $15 for earrings with no extra charge for the gluing.

Winky & Dutch, 44 W. 24th St. [Bway/6th] ☎ 243-1919, is a company that makes fun, kitschy jewelry like camera cuff links, scissor tie pins, hula key chains, charm bracelets, and Dutch handpainted crystal sportstones that feature a Scotty or a comet. To explain the Winky part: winkies (or flickers or lenticulars) are the images that flicker back and forth when you move them. (If you behaved yourself in your childhood checkups, you might have gotten a winky ring from your doctor.) Winky & Dutch bought out the winky stock of the Vari-Vue company in Mt. Vernon when it closed in 1987, and they've been turning the winkies into key chains and pins and so on ever since. Winky & Dutch is not a store but the studio where these things are made. They sell some of their goods to places like Little Rickie but other things to very upscale spots like Charivari. They will sell directly to you, at wholesale prices, if you call ahead and arrange a time to visit. Ask for Jim.

Caro Yamaoka Pearls, ☎ 421-2850, by appt. This business was established in 1947 to sell Japanese cultured pearls. Mr. Yamaoka's daughter-in-law, Gerda Yamaoka, is now taking care of things. She sells good-to-excellent quality cultured pearls from Japan and the South Seas (larger than the Japanese) at wholesale prices. Pearls are graded by size and matched according to color. A string of 6–6 1/2 millimeter pearls (enough to make an 18-inch-long necklace when strung and knotted with a plain clasp) runs $600–$800. Excellent quality in the same size is around $1,200. A string of 7–7 1/2 millimeter pearls is around $2,000. Quality of pearls is determined by their roundness, texture (they should be smooth with no dimples or nicks in the skin), and luster. They come in several shades—white, pale pink, and pale yellow. It is very easy to see the difference in colors when they are side by side. (Ms. Yamaoka also has some gray pearls from Tahiti.) There are many customers who build a necklace year by year, often starting with the smallest pearls, which become the back of the necklace, and adding graduated larger pearls each year. Pearl post earrings are also available. Ms. Yamaoka offers a lifetime service on her necklaces. "It is better to wear pearls, and they should be restrung every year, especially if you wear them a lot." She will restring any necklace bought from her for free. She will restring any other necklaces for $1 per inch.

Mark Spirito's stone and metal pieces occupy a corner counter at Bergdorf's. Mr. Spirito describes his work as "very clean, very graphic, and large scale." He works mostly in silver, but sometimes uses a combination of silver and gold, 18 karat gold, or silver with vermeil (a gold plate). The designs are minimal, eliminating detail and "do not try to evoke anything." He considers the stones to be "the most important feature of the work," and the color of the stones another important aspect of his collection. Garnets, iolites, aquamarines, and many colors of tourmaline are used.

MORE Zak Tools, 55 W. 47th St. [5th/6th] ☎ 768-8122, sells jewelrymaking tools. While you may not see any immediate need for a diamond polisher, they do have the small fine pliers that you need to make simple repairs. The large counter at the doorway sells all manner of jewelry displays and gift boxes. Sectioned trays covered in velvet come in sizes for earrings and pins and can be inserted into a box for utilitarian jewelry storage.

LAMPS & LIGHTING

LAMPS

Karl Barry Studio, based in Brooklyn, has a showroom at 160 Varick St. [Vandam/Charlton] ☎ 718-596-1419, by appt. His lamps are in the Arts and Crafts style, influenced by Frank Lloyd Wright. The bases are brass or copper with various patinas, shades are hand-leaded stained glass with copper plate. Small and large table lamps, floor lamps, sconces, lanterns, and chandeliers. Mr. Barry will do custom orders. Prices from $395.

Vicente Wolf, the interior designer, has designed a series of lamps, including a number of table lamps, some chandeliers, floor models, and a few sconces. Mr. Wolf says that, unlike most things he designs, these lamps were done "as if I were designing for myself." They are "contemporary but soft" and some have "a sense of humor." Mr. Wolf also uses gilded iron and oak stained and pickled to create various wood finishes. The lamps are available through MSK Illuminations, 969 Third Ave. [58th] ☎ 888-6474. $250–$600.

Luz Lampcraft, 790 Greenwich St. [W. 12th/Bethune] ☎ 255-1909. Lanie Kagan's lamps (mostly table) are pure geometry: spare and elegant. The shades are rectangles, squares, cylinders, or triangles made from beautiful papers, cork, and woven birch strips. The legs are thin black metal or stainless steel. From Japan, there are grass paper shades and our favorite—a thick, crinkled paper made from a relative of the mulberry bush. Lamps are $100–$375. Some models can be seen at Zona or Mxyplyzyk, but to see all 30 models, call Ms. Kagan at her studio.

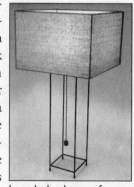

Lamp by Luz Lampcraft.

David Bergman, ☎ 475-3106, designs lighting as an offshoot of his architectural business. His materials are the kind of copper tubing used in plumbing, copper screening, and the MR-16 halogen bulb. The ceiling fixtures are minimal and hip, leaving the halogen bulb exposed on the end of bent tubing. There are floor and table lamps that Mr. Bergman calls calla lillies, in which the bulb is shaded with copper screening in the shape of the flower. The standing lamps have bases made from recycled soybeans and newsprint—a material that looks surprisingly like granite—and comes in black or green. Prices from $320 to $790. By appt. in Mr. Bergman's studio or at Stimuli, 330 E. 9th St. [1st/2nd] ☎ 477-1476.

Many of the mulberry bark paper and bamboo "light sculptures" designed by Isamu Noguchi in the '40s and '50s can be seen at **The Isamu Noguchi Garden Museum,** 32–37 Vernon Blvd., LIC ☎ 718-721-1932. The complete collection is available through Akari Associates, who will send you a catalog ☎ 718-721-2308. Most of the table lamps are between $100 and $200. Prices for the larger floor lamps and some of the ceiling fixtures are about $500.

LIGHTING

TRADITIONAL & MODERN LAMPS

The department stores, of course, plus **Bettina Gates,** 1360 Third Ave. [77th/78th] ☎ 535-5008 . . . **Gracious Home,** 1220 Third Ave. [70th/71st] ☎ 517-6300 . . . **Lee's,** 1755 Broadway [56th/57th] ☎ 581-4400, 1069 Third Ave. [63rd] ☎ 371-1122 . . . **The Lighting Center,** 1097 Second Ave. [58th] ☎ 888-8383 . . . **Lighting Depot,** 490 Sixth Ave. [12th/13th] ☎ 675-3300.

GOOD DEALS

Most people tell you to go to the Bowery for lighting deals, and you can find some steals here. Also much dreck. There is a lot of turnover of lighting stores there, but a big player has emerged on the street, reminding us of the way J & R took over Park Row. It's **Lighting by Gregory,** 158 Bowery [Delancey/Broome] ☎ 226-1276, and we lost count of how many stores they have in a two-block area. Enough for you to find what you

need, anyway. Some of it is priced to sell, some is high end . . . Try also **Bowery Lighting,** 132 Bowery [Grand] ☎ 941-8244; **NY Gas Lighting,** 145 Bowery [Grand/Broome] ☎ 226-2840; and **House of Lights,** 185 Bowery [Delancey] ☎ 505-0300. One other, **Lamp and Lighting Liquidators,** 135 Bowery [Grand] ☎ 219-2059, is dumpy but has some bargains . . . On Canal Street, we like **CL Lights,** 317 Canal St. [Church/Bway] ☎ 219-8076, because they have a wide selection and Canal St. prices. **Canal Electric,** 369 Canal St. [W. Bway] ☎ 274-8813, is a good second.

PERIOD

Artisan Antiques, 81 University Pl. [11th] ☎ 353-3970, has an enormous collection of Art Deco, all of it expensive . . . **Barry of Chelsea,** 154 Ninth Ave. [19th] ☎ 242-2666, has lamps from the Deco period and earlier in an old neighborhood store with atmosphere, $100 and up . . . **Price Glover,** 59 E. 79th St. [Mad/Park] ☎ 772-1740, for antique British lamps . . . **Oldies Goldies and Moldies,** 1609 Second Ave. [83rd/84th] ☎ 737-3935, has an interesting collection of antique lamps, among other nifty things . . . **Uplift Lighting,** 506 Hudson St. [Christopher] ☎ 929-3632, is a store full of mostly Deco chandeliers, lamps, and sconces that can be beautiful or kitschy, sometimes both.

LAMPSHADES

Some of the lamp stores we have listed also carry shades. Here are some additional places that specialize in shades and in custom work. **Just Shades,** 21 Spring St. [Elizabeth] ☎ 966-2757 . . . **Charlotte Moss,** 1027 Lexington Ave. [73rd] ☎ 772-3320 . . . See more in the Lamp & Lampshades article in the Services chapter.

NEON

Let There Be Neon, 38 White St. [Church] ☎ 226-4883, is worth stopping in, even if you're not in the market for neon. In addition to making custom neon pieces, the space doubles as an art gallery, and you're always sure to see some engaging neon art pieces.

TRACK

Track by Jack, ☎ 340-9111, for custom track work. Also try **Lighting By Gregory,** 158 Bowery [Delancey/Broome] ☎ 226-1276.

LAMP PARTS

Canal Electric, 369 Canal St. [W. Bway] ☎ 274-8813 . . . **Grand Brass Lamp Parts,** 221 Grand St. [Elizabeth] ☎ 226-2567 . . . **CL Lights,** 317 Canal St. [Church/Bway] ☎ 219-8076.

LAMP REPAIR & RESTORATION

See Lamps & Lampshades in the Services chapter.

LIGHTBULBS

These places have, in addition to the common GE variety, a large inventory of hard-to-find or unusual bulbs: **CL Lights,** 317 Canal St. [Church/Bway] ☎ 219-8076 . . . **Just Bulbs,** 938 Broadway [22nd] ☎ 228-7820 . . . **The Lighting Center,** 1097 Second Ave. [58th] ☎ 888-8383 . . . **Lighting Plus,** 676 Broadway [Great Jones/Bond] ☎ 979-2000.

MAGIC

Flosso-Hornmann Magic Co., 45 W. 34th St. [5th/6th] ☎ 279-6079, is the oldest magic store in the world. It also has an incredible resource, in the form of Jack Flosso, who can trace the roots of the store back to the 1860s in Essen, Germany. Mr. Flosso knows just about every trick in the book and as much about magic and magicians as anyone alive. There is a small museum in this small space consisting of glass cases filled with mementos of Mr. Flosso's and other well-known magicians' careers. He will help beginners and pros alike and can recommend magicians, clowns, and balloon performers for events. He'll also demonstrate tricks you are interested in purchasing. His recommendation of a good starting book for children is *Now You See It* (child of 12 or so). This store is one of the greats.

Tannen's Magic Studio, 24 W. 25th St. [Bway/6th] ☎ 929-4500, is the *largest* magic store in the world and has been in business since 1934. They have tricks, books, videos, magic show kits for kids, and apparatus for routines. They give private magic lessons ($150/hr.), as well as a four-class workshop ($198), hold a yearly convention open to the public in October, and have a catalog available for $15. In the summer, Tannen's runs a magic camp for children.

Abracadabra, 10 Christopher St. [Greenwich/Gay] ☎ 627-5745, has novelties, costumes, and makeup, as well as magic. There are two professional magicians on staff (Ed and Rick), and they have lots of patience with children learning magic and a good assortment of tricks for adults.

See more in the Magic article in the Learning chapter.

ODDS & ENDS

This is an odd lots store, sort of. Their business card describes it as a "strange art supply store." Whatever it is, **Canal Surplus** 363 Canal St. [W. Bway/Wooster] ☎ 966-3275, is a gold mine if you are an artist, a designer, scientist, tinkerer, craftsmaker, or just love odd stores, as we do. The best way to give you a sense of the place is to tell you some of what they sell: cleaning brushes, washers, springs, beads, magnets, Pyrex beakers, leather pieces, rhinestone buttons, beeswax, luggage snaps, many things made out of brass (garlands, snakes, and badges). They sell basic science projects plans for $1 that include 10 or so plans to do things like make a doorbell or get electricity from a lemon. They will search for an item if you ask them to. A messy, unusual, wonderful shop.

We love the air freshener called **Go Away Evil,** but not for the smell. Even though it says on the can that it does not have supernatural powers, we're sure it must and thought it could be a useful exorciser for houseguests who have overstayed their welcome. The company that makes it, M & A Amateau, also makes Go Away Evil soap, candles, and perfume. They're up on E. 115th. For more info ☎ 369-7390.

OFFICE SUPPLIES

For Computers, see the Computers article in the Feature chapter.

For Office Furniture, see the Furniture article in this chapter.

For Office Machines, see the Electronics & Appliances article in this chapter.

For Paper, see Paper & Pens in the Feature chapter.

For Typewriter Ribbons, see Typewriter Repair in the Services chapter.

ORNAMENTS

Kids might like ornaments with Disney and other animated characters on them. You can find these at **Animated Classics,** 399 Bleecker St. [W. 11th/Perry] ☎ 255-7604 . . . **Aris Mixon,** 381 Amsterdam Ave. [78th/79th] ☎ 724-6904, is a great place for gifts year round, and they have an impeccable selection of ornaments and other Christmas goodies . . . **Authentiques,** 255 W. 18th St. [7th/8th] ☎ 675-2179, sells vintage Christmas ornaments . . . **Matt McGhee,** 22 Christopher St. [Greenwich/Waverly] ☎ 741-3138, is *it*. Ornaments of every imaginable shape, size, and price, including many German hand-blown and hand-painted ones. We doubt you'll leave empty-handed . . . A place where we always seem to find something is **Somethin' Else,** 182 Ninth Ave. [21st/22nd] ☎ 924-0006. They have lots of Christmas things, including ornaments, throughout the store . . . **Williams Sonoma Outlet Center,** 231 Tenth Ave. [23rd/24th] ☎ 206-8118, generally has some good deals on ornaments and wrapping paper on the second floor.

MORE Two large importers of Christmas ornaments usually open their doors to the public in the month between Thanksgiving and Christmas. They are **James A. Cole,** 41 W. 25th St. [Bway/6th] ☎ 741-1500, and **Kurt Adler Santa's World,** 1107 Broadway [24th/25th] ☎ 924-0900. Call before going.

PRINTS

Pageant Book and Print Shop, 114 W. Houston St. [Thompson/Sullivan] ☎ 674-5296, has prints and engravings—views from around the world, natural history, maps, early views of New York City, and architecture.

Old Print Shop, 150 Lexington Ave. [29th/30th] ☎ 683-3950. Specializes in Americana through about 1950.

Stubbs Books and Prints, 153 E. 70th St. [Lex/3rd] ☎ 772-3120. Mostly architectural prints, with some botanical.

SHEET MUSIC

Sam Ash, 163 W. 48th St. [6th/7th] ☎ 398-6070, has a pretty fair selection of contemporary music . . . **Brown's,** 44 W. 62nd St. [Columbus] ☎ 541-6236. Classical, especially piano and vocal, some mainstream pop . . . **Carl Fischer,** 62 Cooper Square [Astor Pl.] ☎ 677-0821. Band and choral, about 200 Broadway vocal selections, pretty good on pop music, lots of stuff in file cabinets . . . **Colony,** 1619 Broadway [49th] ☎ 265-2050. A grubby Broadway institution, fittingly strong on musicals and standards . . .

Frank Music, 250 W. 54th St. [Bway/8th] ☎ 246-5757. Lots of classical sheet music on file . . . **Musical Score Distributor,** 625 Broadway [Bleecker/Houston] ☎ 475-0270, is a loft-sized warehouse that doubles as a shop, stocking mostly classical (including choral works) and some Broadway. Catalog available . . . **Patelson,** 160 W. 56th St. [6th/7th] ☎ 582-5840. Virtually all classical music, painstakingly organized, in an ideal setting for an Ernst Lubitsch film.

SHOES & BOOTS

WOMEN'S

For women's shoe advice, we turned to Mary Trasko, the ultimate shoe maven and author of *Heavenly Soles: Extraordinary Twentieth Century Shoes.* If you love shoes, you'll love her book. It's available from Abbeville Press in paperback for $19.95 ☎ 800-278-2665.

Ms. Trasko says, "This is not a time when singular talents in footwear are appreciated. The vast majority of shoes sold in stores are merchandised into a few top marketing trends of the season and, therefore, shoppers find the same styles and silhouettes everywhere. Shoe departments at Barneys, Bergdorf's, and Bloomingdale's have at least two departments for women's shoes, usually selling designer and bridge and/or more casual footwear. In one stop, you can find more styles from trendsetting houses (such as Gucci or Prada), along with up and coming designers newly discovered by the buyer for the department, plus seasonal 'must-haves.' "

Christian Louboutin, 30 E. 67th St. [Mad] ☎ 737-3333. Witty, wonderfully crafted shoes from the Parisian designer. While the shoes are pricey, a stylish loafer or a marvelously fanciful pair of evening pumps decorated with feathers or fringe will be unique and special for seasons to come. They won't date like this season's silhouettes.

Manolo Blahnik, 15 W. 55th St. [5th/6th] ☎ 582-3007. Always beautifully crafted and madly chic, Blahnik's faithful cult of shoe enthusiasts don't mind paying the price his shoes command. Here one can still buy fine embroideries, mules in satin and silk, and evening styles that bring back luxe and elegance.

Belgian Shoes, 60 E. 56th St. [Mad/Park] ☎ 755-7372. European-looking boutique with house shoes (slippers) only. $250 for leather, $275 for velvet. Colored leather. Men's and women's. Choose 20–30 emblems (some come with emblems; if you add one it's an extra $75).

At 59th St. and Lexington Ave., you are in the shoe district. You can shop at **9 West,** 714 Lexington Ave. [57th/58th] ☎ 486-8094 (but many locations), which have basic, comfortable, fashion-oriented shoes ($60–$80) of decent quality for the price . . . **Zara,** 750 Lexington Ave. [59th], is the NY store of this international chain of trendy, well-priced shoes and clothing. The shoes average $75 . . . **Robert Clergerie,** 41 E. 60th St. [Mad/Park] ☎ 207-8600, has a

great following for the well-made shoes (around $300), that are fashionable but refined. A few are more fun and eccentric.

Patrick Cox, 702 Madison Ave. [62nd/63rd] ☎ 759-3910. The whole spectrum from elegant and witty to more basic fashionable. A little bit of the East Village on the Upper East Side.

Otto Tootsie Plohound, 413 W. Broadway [Prince/Spring] ☎ 925-8931. Fashion shoes of decent quality at prices from $150–$250. A large selection. The men's store is at 137 Fifth Ave. [20th/21st] ☎ 460-8650.

MEN'S

The Wright Arch Preserver Shoe Shop, 344 Madison Ave. [43rd/44th] ☎ 687-3023, has a great selection of Alden Shoes. Alden often uses the extremely durable cordovan leather (horse leather), and they produce great-quality classic English-style shoes that only get more beautiful as they age. They also have shoes in calfskin and suede and with some in sizes as wide as EEEE. Alden Shoes for women (not often seen) are available at **Lynn Boot + Shoe,** 16 W. 46th St. [5th/6th] ☎ 819-0092.

a. testoni, 665 Fifth Ave. [52nd/53rd] ☎ 223-0909. These are beautifully constructed Italian shoes of exceptional quality. There are two lines: the regular line is $300–$400, the "black label" line is about $600. They have sales in January and July, with prices cut up to 50%, sometimes more.

John Lobb at Hermès, 11 E. 57th St. [5th/Mad] ☎ 751-3181. These are top-quality shoes (at top prices) in conservative styles. Figure about $600.

Church's English Shoes, 428 Madison Ave. [49th] ☎ 755-4313, for classic English shoes.

Barneys and **Bergdorf's,** of course, for a wide range of quality shoes (the uptown Barneys has a better selection than the downtown), and **Brooks Brothers** for Alden and other classic English style shoes.

MADE TO ORDER

In business since 1879, **E. Vogel,** 19 Howard St. [Crosby/Lafayette] ☎ 925-2460, knows shoes and boots. Run by the third- and fourth-generation Vogels, they've stayed in business because they make top-of-the-line traditional boots and shoes for men and women, and provide the service that goes along with it. Once you come into the store and they measure your feet, they will do custom shoes for you with a phone call and will ship anywhere. This level of craft and service comes at a price: $650 for the first pair of shoes, and $550 after that. Boots range from $500 to $900. It takes 16 weeks or so for delivery of your first pair, though rush is available. Cordovan leather shoes start at $850, riding boots from $550–$1,000.

John Lobb (see above). Fitters come twice a year from Paris to take measurements for custom shoes. A wooden last is made of your foot and kept "on file." Prices start at $1,850.

T.O. Dey, 9 E. 38th St. [5th/Mad] ☎ 683-6300. They've been making custom shoes here since 1926. Any style in over 300 colors of leather. Shoes start at $650 and take 6–7 weeks.

For horseback riding boots, see Horseback Riding in the Sports chapter.

EXTRA WIDE

Eneslow, 924 Broadway [21st] ☎ 477-2300. Men's and women's up to EEEE.

Salamander Shoes, 335 E. 86th St. [1st/2nd] ☎ 369-3045. Men's and women's up to EEEE.

Tall Shoe Sizes, 3 W. 35th St. [5th/6th] ☎ 736-2060. Women's up to 14 EE

Treadeasy, 24 W. 39th St. [5th/6th] ☎ 840-2239. Men's up to EEEEEE; women's up to EEEEE.

For shoe repair, see Shoe Repair under Clothing Care in the Services chapter.

TABLEWARE

Seeing Cindy Sherman as Madame de Pompadour on Limoges china was not what we expected to find putting together this article on tableware, but it certainly was a highlight. It's part of the concept of **Artes Magnus,** ☎ 674-3043, a company started by four art collectors—Richard and Barbara Lane and Bill Ehrlich and Ruth Lloyds—in which "contemporary artists design fine pieces for the tabletop that are consistent with their work." We asked Ms. Sherman how the work evolved, and she told us that she went to Limoges to see the original molds and there were some dishes designed either by or for Mme. de Pompadour. Ms. Sherman started with the tureen, working some fish into the gold pattern after discovering Mme. de P.'s maiden name was Poisson. Then, she devised a "character type loosely based on her." It was "not a full make up," but the whole design was meant "to accentuate the gaudiness of her period." When everyone saw how it looked, the project extended to dinnerware and a tea set. The Sherman 30-

Cindy Sherman limited edition Limoges porcelain.

Piece Dinner Service is $4,200. You can also own a Tom Otterness Seder plate ($6,000) and Elijah cup ($2,000) or a Cesar thumbprint serving platter ($750). All are manufactured in limited editions signed and numbered by the artist. Kiki Smith has done a sterling silver fingerbowl, and there's a cake plate by Lucas Samaras. If you break a piece, they'll replace it at cost.

Artists have also been designing for **Rosenthal** china. In two series of espresso cups, European painters have provided designs for the same cup shape (starting at $50). The most fanciful series is the Rosenthal Collector's cups where artists play with the shape as well as the decoration of coffee cups and saucers ($325). Some pieces, like a serving plate designed by Roy Lichtenstein ($350), are in limited editions (in this case 3,000). The best display is at Bloomingdale's, but if you have trouble finding pieces you are looking for, you can talk to Christina Norsig of Rosenthal USA ☎ 532-6702.

GOOD DEALS If we were looking to buy good tableware at the best prices, we'd shop at **Brodean**, 377 Broome St. [Mott/Mulberry] ☎ 219-2424, by appt. only. It's tiny but it's just you and Andrew Mellon and staff. The over 70 china, crystal, and flatware patterns are prettily displayed on a wooden pharmacist's hutch. The napkins and flatware are in the little drawers (crystal is everywhere). There's a sofa where you can sit and contemplate the displays and a table to set with the pieces you are considering. Mr. Mellon sells, among others, Royal Worcester, Swid Powell, Arabia, Hermès, Puiforcat, and Annie Glass. Many are discounted. Five-piece place settings start at $40.

Rogers and Rosenthal, ☎ 827-0115, was located on Canal St. for over 40 years. Now, without catalog or showroom, they take phone orders only, and thus have some of the very best prices on tableware in town. Jerry Rosenthal often answers the phone, replacing pieces for old clients or setting up a bridal registry. Most things are shipped from the factory, and they're honest about ship dates.

Lanac, 73 Canal St. [Allen] ☎ 925-6422. It's almost impossible to see the display, nice as it seems to be. The aisles leading to the glass cases filled with china, crystal, and lots of Lenox are jammed up with cardboard boxes and are impassable. They do carry Bernaudaud, Wedgwood china, Fitz & Floyd, and Villeroy & Boch, among others. There is a catalog available, help is courteous, and prices are discounted.

You can get some good deals on tableware at the **auction houses.** Call Lubin's, 110 W. 25th St. [6th/7th] ☎ 924-3777; Christie's, 502 Park Ave. [59th] ☎ 546-1000; Tepper Galleries, 110 E. 25th St. [Park/Lex] ☎ 677-5300; and Sotheby's, 1334 York Ave. [72nd] ☎ 606-7000.

Jean's Silversmiths, 16 W. 45th St. [5th/6th] ☎ 575-0723. Try Jean's when you need to replace missing pieces. See more on this store in the Silver and Metal Repair article in the Services chapter.

Unique Tableware, 340 E. 6th St.

[1st/2nd] ☎ 533-8252, has simple, colorful, and reasonable Portuguese tableware.

GENERAL At **ABC Carpet & Home,** 888 Broadway [19th] ☎ 473-3000, vintage and contemporary plates, fine china, silver, crystal and everyday things like Portuguese pottery are hodgepodged together in the signature display style of this store. Christofle, Baccarat, Mottahedah, Aynsley, and some vintage linens are on the main floor.

Michael C. Fina, 3 W. 47th St. [5th/6th] ☎ 869-5050, has a comprehensive display area on the lower level for all tabletop items. While there is some discounting, nothing is marked, so you will need to ask the sometimes aggressive sales help. Given the number of brides-to-be shopping here, the atmosphere can be less than restful. This is a good place to get an overview of what's available.

CONTEMPORARY MacKenzie-Childs, 824 Madison Ave. [69th] ☎ 570-6050, is an emporium for the delightfully eccentric designs of Victoria and Richard MacKenzie-Childs. Looking like they were made for Alice's Tea Party, several ice cream–colored patterns cavort on the same ripply-rimmed dish (a checkerboard overlaid with flowers and dots or stripes). Like Alice's dishes, they seem to be rushing off the table. The teapots would house several dormice quite nicely. Starting in the $30s for a single plate or cup.

At **Sara,** 952 Lexington Ave. [69th/70th] ☎ 772-3242, they say they specialize in Japanese pottery, but these dishes (*sara* is the Japanese word for dish) and other accouterments of the Japanese table are finely crafted, often delicately rendered, and displayed like works of art by owner Kumi Oniki. Small handblown glasses come in a variety of shapes, some with gilded feet.

Round liqueur glasses that seem to have strips of confetti floating inside the glass material ($50 each) are displayed on square gold chopstick rests. If you're buying a gift, the store will wrap it in special Japanese paper.

See, otherwise a furniture store at 920 Broadway [20th/21st] ☎ 228-3600, carries designer designed tableware. Izabel Lam's flatware and glass dishes are influenced by her experiences as a scuba diver. The undulations of water flowing over sea plants inspired the handles on her knives and forks. Her dishes look as though running water had lifted a corner of the glass, their surfaces rippled and textured. At See, you can also find flatware designed by Robert Lee Morris (Mr. Morris's flatware is also at his store at 400 West Broadway [Spring/Broome] ☎ 431-9405) and china by Andrée Putman, Vicente Wolf, hand-painted plates by Noble Tile and Vessel, Taitu, and Rosenthal.

Jon Waldo, ☎ 777-4838, by appt., customizes dinnerware. Mr. Waldo paints images and words representing your interests on classic plates. Plates and bowls start at $60.

Ceramica, 59 Thompson St. [Spring/Broome] ☎ 941-1307, sells only Italian Majolica. The hand-painted plates, platters, bowls, cups, and serving pieces are distinctive in their heavy designs using primary colors. The subtle variation from dish to dish is part of their charm. Priced according to amount of painting and rarity of design, dinner plates start at $35. One-of-a-kind items turn up with regularity.

Ellen Evans/Terrafirma, 152 W. 25th St. [6th/7th] ☎ 645-7600. This is a working pottery studio that has transformed two small front rooms into a show and sales area. Both firsts and seconds are available. Ms. Evans's style often combines glazed and unglazed terra-cotta in serving pieces. Unglazed fruits, stems, and leaves climb or curl around the edge of the plate. Dinner services are fully glazed and come in solids, sponge, lace, or the new ivy or animal skin patterns. You can mix and match and buy any piece in any quantity. If they don't have it, they'll make it. Plates from $21. Ms. Evans's work can be seen at ABC, and often as background in *Gourmet*.

Wolfman-Gold & Good, 117 Mercer St. [Prince/Spring] ☎ 431-1888, known for their all-white table, have now added shades of green and bisque to the dish department. Solid-color plates have scalloped rims. They're always a good source for platters, some plain, some with raised fruit designs (starting at $65). Sets of antique spreading knives with colored Bakelite handles, six pieces in the original, somewhat tattered boxes are $85.

ANTIQUES Charterhouse Antiques, 115 Greenwich Ave. [7th/8th] ☎ 243-4726. Tons of old china with some cut and depression glass thrown in. Dishes are stacked on dishes on every surface, including the floor, which makes seeing the merchandise a challenge. But Jim Ray knows his stock and can tell you something about the plates. Each has a small, dusty, precisely lettered label with the date, price, and whatever else is known about it. Specialties are blue and white chinas and English versions of Imari ware. Prices from $1 for small cut-glass plates to several hundred for French porcelains. Individual plates as well as services can be found. Much in the $40–$60 range.

Maya Schaper Cheese and Antiques, 106 W. 69th St. [Columbus/Amsterdam] ☎ 873-2100. Ms. Schaper has been selling food-related antiques for 30 years. She has some antiques in the shop, but will use her 30 years of experience in the field to search for particular items.

GLASSWARE Riedel is generally considered the finest wineglass maker. They have three levels of glasses: the Sommelier, mouth-blown with a separate glass for each type of wine, is not for most people's everyday use at about $70 a glass; the Vinum, machine-blown, prices out at $19 a glass; and the new Ouverture series has generic red and white wineglasses for $8.99 each. Available at Morrell ☎ 688-9370, Sherry-Lehmann ☎ 838-7500, and 67th St. ☎ 724-6767.

Avventura, 463 Amsterdam Ave. [82nd/83rd] ☎ 769-2510, is owned by Marc Hurwitz, whose discerning eye is responsible for the selection and display. Dishes, flatware, and decorative items are arranged tightly but visibly. What's striking, though, is the selection of glassware—outstanding Murano tableware; small black-and-white bowls and plates made in the glass cane technique familiar in millefiore ($100–$250); and stemware from Italy and England in traditional and nontraditional shapes.

LINENS Extraordinary table linens are the business of **Françoise Nunnallé,** ☎ 246-4281, by appt., who is passionate about them. All antique and in excellent condition, laces, embroidery, cutwork, and drawn work cloths come from Europe, but the damask comes "only from Czechoslovakia." Oversized napkins, anywhere from 28″ to 42″ square are sold in sets of 10–12, and almost all are monogrammed. Cloths start at $650, napkins at $400/doz. Ms. Nunnallé will search for particular sizes of cloths and will try to match your monogram. She also has a collection of antique soup tureens (starting at $1,500), many with the original ladles and trays. Worcester, Meissen, and Creamware.

Nina Ramsey's **Archipelago** produces sure-handed designs. Her linen and cotton organdy napkins are simply designed—they're mostly white with wide pastel borders, and some have "couture" details like covered buttons or tailored bows. Trying to bring back "dinner games," her Persona napkins have a different personality trait heavily embroidered in each corner: "lucid, enigmatic, flip, provocative" reads one napkin. Archipelago is sold in Bendel's and

Charlotte Moss, 1027 Lexington Ave. [73rd/74th] ☎ 772-3320.

NAPKIN RINGS Designer **Mark Rossi** continues his wonderful line of napkin rings—the best selection of which is at Bergdorf's. His original crossed knife, fork, and spoon has been much copied, and Mr. Rossi has many new styles in shapes of stars, acorns, flowers, shells, turtles, monkeys, and so on. He's also now done pearl-trimmed napkins and placemats. But it's the napkin rings he loves: "I always thought the napkin ring was the final touch to the table."

TELESCOPES & BINOCULARS

Clairmont-Nichols, 1016 First Ave. [56th] ☎ 758-2346, is a licensed optician that also sells quality optical instruments like telescopes, binoculars, and magnifying glasses. The telescopes are clustered near the front door—everything from the squat Celestron to elegant teak or chrome models custom made with Zeiss lenses. Leonard Malsin, the owner, says that from New York "you can see Jupiter, Saturn, Venus, and Mars, a dozen galaxies, and, of course, the moon." There is a little "veranda" in front of the store and they take the scopes outside for

you to look through. You get some simple night sky charts when you purchase a telescope that show you what you can expect to see throughout the year. They carry binoculars for birding, boating, opera, and for night vision. Telescopes start at $250, a custom teak one is $2,650. Binoculars start at $100. A very good birding scope made by Swarowski is $800. Mr. Malsin recommends opera glasses with a three to four power so that you can see the whole stage. Fancy ones with mother-of-pearl cases are about $300, simpler cases start at $125.

THRIFT SHOPS

There are an awful lot of thrift shop junkies out there, but perhaps no one who knows more than the person who wrote the book on the subject, Vicki Rovere. She's the author of *Worn Again, Hallelujah,* the guide to New York's thrift shops. We asked her to put together for MUG readers a list of her favorites from the more than 300 places in her book.

BY VICKI ROVERE

For sheer volume, try the flagship **Salvation Army Thrift Store** at 536 W. 46th St.

[10th/11th] ☎ 664-8563. One huge selling floor for furniture and major appliances, another floor for everything else. As you stride amidst the clothing racks stretching to the horizon, you can be trailed by a plastic shopping basket with a man's tie attached, toss in your finds, and pull it along after you. Surprise! Visa and MasterCard are accepted for sales over $25.

Pretty Plus Plus, 1309 Madison Ave. [93rd] ☎ 427-4724. The only consignment shop in New York City dealing exclusively in women's large sizes (14–4X). Lots of dressy dresses, some furs and leather jackets, caftans. Labels include Givenchy, Trigère, Dior, Michael Kors, Adrienne Vittadini.

Another rarity, also located on the Upper East Side, is a men's consignment store, **Gentlemen's Resale,** 303 E. 81st St. [1st/2nd] ☎ 734-2739. In this genteel, narrow store, you'll find lots of suits and shoes, as well as coats, shirts, and silk handkerchiefs. Hermès ties are $50, others $1–$4. Labels include Armani, Valentino, and Ralph Lauren. One unusual feature is that exchanges are allowed within 24 hours of purchase, a policy instituted because women sometimes take clothes home for their husbands to consider.

For atmosphere and furniture, try **Calvary/St. George's Furniture Thrift Shop,** 277 Park Ave. South [22nd] ☎ 979-0420. Housed in a wing of Calvary Church, this vaulting space has the comfy, calming aura of a barn-turned-antiques-store. Most of the furniture, both antique and more humble, is wood, rather than upholstered—I found only a couple of sofas. Wind your way through the narrow aisles past trunks, chests of drawers, mirrors, headboards, breakfronts, chairs, lamps, wall art, and a few appliances. They repair and refinish worthy pieces of donated old furniture.

The cheeriest and most spacious of several children's consignment shops in Manhattan is the relatively new **Good-Byes Children's Resale Shop,** 230 E. 78th St. [2nd/3rd] ☎ 794-2301. Clothes range from $5–$50, averaging around $10 (rompers and Oshkosh jeans, for example). They're all in good condition and neatly organized on racks. The stock includes baby furniture, toys, books, and some maternity dresses. In the middle of the store, a play area with a card table and coloring books has thoughtfully been provided.

Out of the Closet, 220 E. 81st St. [2nd/3rd] ☎ 472-3573, is an appealing combination of elegance, clutter, and atmosphere: The front building was formerly a farmhouse, the back an 1850 stable. They've got almost everything—clothes, art, and antiques, books and records, and furniture.

Jonah's Whale, on the fringe of the theatre district at 935 Eighth Ave. [55th/56th] ☎ 581-8181, is crammed with books, wall art, lamps, and other nonclothing items.

For uncluttered elegance, visit **Renate's** at 235 E. 81st St. [2nd/3rd] ☎ 472-1698—but call for an appointment first. You'll find only European designer clothing here—Chanel, Armani, Ungaro, Jil Sander at about a third of the retail price. Women's clothes only.

I'd give the prize for social pioneering to **Harlem Restoration Thrift Shop** at 461 W. 125th St. [Amsterdam/Morningside] ☎ 864-6992, which doesn't segregate the women's clothing from the men's.

There are thrift shops or flea markets in Coney Island, Bay Ridge, Riverdale, City Island, the Rockaways, and Tottenville at the far end of Staten Island. (You could actually tour the city with *Worn Again, Hallelujah!*) Roosevelt Island, though, might be the easiest excursion. Take the subway, bus, or tram, stroll along the esplanade, and stop in at **Cabrini Thrift Shop** at 520 Main St. ☎ 644-8332. It's especially well stocked with sports equipment, which makes sense when you notice all the surrounding fields and open space.

In Bayside, Queens, **The Worthy Pause Thrift & Gift Shop** at 40–08 Corporal Kennedy St. [39th–40th] ☎ 718-279-8191, is run by an animal charity. Many of its items, largely bric-a-brac and collectibles, have animal themes.

A number of stores in Greenpoint and Williamsburg sell clothing by the pound. At least some items among these mountains of garments are thrift-shop grade, and priced much lower.

Domsey's, the largest and best known of these enterprises, has two adjoining spaces, one is a department store of secondhand clothing on hangers (e.g., 26 feet of dressy dresses at $5 a piece), the other a warehouse brimming with bulk clothing at $2.25 a pound. Huge rolling bins, laundry carts, a conveyor belt, and industrious patrons rummaging through the piles set the scene.

Domsey's Warehouse Outlet and Annex, 431 Kent Ave. [Bway/8th], Brooklyn, for pound goods and 496 Wythe Ave. [9th/10th] Brooklyn for the store ☎ 718-384-6000.

In Brooklyn, the **P.S. 321 Flea Market** on 7th Ave. in Park Slope [1st/2nd] is specifically a weekend recycling market—all vendors sell used goods—with a good-natured community feel.

And if you're looking for formal wear (for women and children) and don't mind a ferry ride, head out to **Discount Bridal Center,** 2381 Hylan Blvd [Otis/Locust] ☎ 718-351-6968, in New Dorp, Staten Island. I measured 24 feet of wedding dresses, and a comparable amount of other fancy clothes, including women's large sizes.

Worn Again, Hallelujah also includes store hours, travel directions, hours for accepting donations or consignments, and other useful information for each store. It's available for $10 at most bookstores (or by mail order for $11.50 from Ms. Rovere, 339 Lafayette St., New York, NY 10012).

TILES

You can drive yourself to distraction by the quantity of lovely tiles at **Country Floors,** 15 E. 16th St. [5th/University] ☎ 627-8300. Everything from childlike doodles in bright colors to delicately drawn Chinese miniature paintings with plenty of fruits, flowers, animals, and one-of-a-kind pieces . . . Nearby is **Ann Sacks Tile and Stone,** 5 E. 16th St. [5th/University] ☎ 463-8400, which is beautiful to look at, if not quite as over-the-top as Country Floors . . . **Waterworks,** 237 E. 58th St. [2nd/3rd] ☎ 371-9266, has tiles (both floor and wall) that are highly decorative; many are in high relief, like the one with three lemons bursting from the surface . . . **Nemo Tile,** 48 E. 21st St. [Park/Bway] ☎ 505-0009, is much larger than it appears from the street. They sell ceramic tiles for all uses (wall, counter, floor, and decorative) and in a variety of sizes (from 1/2-inch square to 12-inch square). Shiny and dull finishes as well as painted tiles. In the back of the store, they sell replacement tiles and tile cleaners . . . **Tiles,**

A Refined Selection, 42 W. 15th St. [5th/6th] ☎ 255-4450, specializes in handmade, artist-designed tiles. These come mostly from small manufacturers and studios. Some, like Pewabic Pottery, are keeping alive Arts and Crafts techniques. Others, like Surving Studios, are sculpting high-relief chameleons, geckos, and frogs on colored backgrounds . . . **Paris Ceramics,** 150 E. 58th St. [3rd/Lex] ☎ 644-2782. Stones and tiles from Roman times to the present and reproductions of mosaic floors from Pompeii . . . **Laura Shprentz** makes custom tiles by hand for fireplaces, counter backsplashes, and to spice up areas of more moderately priced tiles. Some of her pictorial pieces can be framed for display. Her tiles are distinguished by a depth of color that she achieves from a method of adding colors at each step in the process. Contact her at Spiral Studios ☎ 995-1359.

TOYS

What follows are some of the special, sometimes lesser known, toy shops in the city.

Building Blocks, 1413 Third Ave. [80th/81st] ☎ 772-8697, sells educational toys only.

Classic Toy Store, 218 Sullivan St. [Bleecker/W. 3rd] ☎ 674-4434, specializes in new and old cars, planes, and soldiers.

At **Dinosaur Hill,** 302 E. 9th St. [1st/2nd] ☎ 473-5850, look for hand puppets and marionettes and many toys with a dinosaur theme.

The **Enchanted Forest** is the genuinely enchanted children's store at 85 Mercer St. [Spring/Broome] ☎ 925-6677. It makes for delightful browsing and has a lot of unusual, inventive, and just plain fun gifts for kids. Look for the handmade bears by Irene Heckel.

Jan's Hobby Shop, 1557 York Ave. [82nd/83rd] ☎ 861-5075, sells model ship kits and the paints, tools, and fittings you need to make them come to life.

Kidding Around, 60 W. 15th St. [5th/6th] ☎ 645-6337 and 68 Bleecker St. [Lafayette/Bway] ☎ 598-0228. Sweet-looking dolls in a variety of skin tones, sections devoted to musical toys, art supplies, science experiments, and infant development toys. A small clothing section.

Red Caboose, 23 W. 45th St. [5th/6th] ☎ 575-0155, for model trains and everything that goes with them.

B. Shackman & Co., 85 Fifth Ave. [16th] ☎ 989-5162. A wonderful old-timey collection of dollhouse furniture, mechanical metal toys, cut-out dolls, tiny porcelain tea sets, tops, stickers, the Magic Rock Garden, and seasonal novelties and decorations.

MORE A Bear's Place, 789 Lexington Ave. [61st/62nd] ☎ 826-6465 . . . **Uncle Futz,** 408 Amsterdam Ave. [79th/80th] ☎ 799-6723 and 1054 Lexington Ave. [75th] ☎ 535-4686 . . . **Penny Whistle Toys,** 448 Columbus Ave. [81st/82nd] ☎ 873-9090 and 1283 Madison Ave. [91st/92nd] ☎ 369-3868. These three stores sell generally good-quality (often educational) toys in pleasant surroundings.

WALLETS

W. H. Gidden has been making beautiful leather products since 1806, and they're the official saddlemaker to the Queen. The wallets are simply beautiful and last and last. Available at Bergdorf for Men, $165–$400.

Il Bisonte, 72 Thompson St. [Spring/Broome] ☎ 966-8773 and 22 E. 65th St. [5th/Mad] ☎ 717-4771, make the popular Italian cowhide wallets with their well-

known bison stamp. $68–$148. Good selection and service.

Peter Herman Leather Goods, 118 Thompson St. [Prince/Spring] ☎ 966-9050. Italian leather wallets, $85–168, with some interesting designs and some snazzy hardware.

See more in the Leather article in the Feature chapter.

WATCHES & CLOCKS

VINTAGE WRISTWATCHES Aaron Faber, 666 Fifth Ave. [53rd] ☎ 586-8411. Edward Faber told us that over 500 million wristwatches are now manufactured in a year. He sees this as an indication of how "obsessed and governed by time" we have become. The wristwatch came into style around 1915, and the peak collectible period extends to 1960. "High-grade European and American rarities" are available at his store. There is a service and restoration department for any vintage watch, and there is a one-year warranty. Pocket watches are coming into vogue for men again, and Mr. Faber has a collection of them starting at $125 up to $15,000 . . . **Time Will Tell,** 962 Madison Ave. [75th/76th] ☎ 861-2663. Stewart Unger is the proprietor of this small, bustling store. He offers a range of watches—everything from a $65 quartz watch with a pig on the dial to high-quality vintage watches at prices in the five figures. Gruens, Elgins, and extraordinary Audemars Piguets sit beside the modern sculptural minimalism of Alfred Brodman's designs. Mr. Unger's enthusiasm for watches has been passed on to his staff. Everything is in working condition when it leaves the store, and there is a one-year-and-

a-day warranty on all vintage watches. He gives opinions and repair estimates on old (and new) watches, does repairs, and supplies new watch straps. Mechanical watches can be tested for accuracy on the Vibrograph, a machine that measures the ticking mechanism of the watch and gives a paper readout, just like an EKG. He is a coauthor, along with Edward Faber, of *American Wristwatches—Five Decades of Style and Design,* a $75 text on the subject, available here . . . Vivian Swift is a watch historian at Christie's. **Christie's** has watch and clock auctions a couple of times each year. Ms. Swift is available for appraisals privately ☎ 914-738-1862. Christie's will give free appraisal on any watch you wish to sell or auction . . . **Cartier,** 653 Fifth Ave. [52nd] ☎ 753-0111, offers a search service for people looking for vintage Cartiers. Call Ellen Devera at ☎ 446-3483.

CLOCKS Fanelli Antique Timepieces, 790 Madison Ave. [66th/67th] ☎ 517-2300. Joe and Cindy Fanelli have been collecting and dealing in clocks since 1967. Their stock includes carriage clocks, which are eight-day clocks designed to be carried in a carriage. They also have some grandfather clocks and some even larger display clocks. Currently, there is a collection of cuckoo clocks. A small selection of vintage wristwatches is on hand. Everything has been overhauled and comes with a one-year guarantee. Mr. Fanelli is the author of *A Century of Fine Carriage Clocks*—$59.95 at the store ... **Time Pieces,** 115 Greenwich Ave. [W. 13th] ☎ 929-8011. This is a small shop crammed with mantel and dresser, alarm, wall, and cuckoo clocks, as well as vintage pocket and wristwatches. Everything on sale is in working order. Clocks have a two-year warranty and watches a one-year warranty. They do repairs after giving you a free estimate. The repairs carry the same warranties as the items on sale.

MODERN WATCHES M & Co. Labs, based here in the city, is the design firm started by Tibor Kalman. The company makes wristwatches, clocks, and pocket watches that are great fun and good looking (though not cheap). The wall clocks are $95, the watches are $175–$195 (higher for sterling). We especially like the watch called History, which has icons for the numbers representing water, frogs, pants, media, and other things to give you a "handy wrist reference for the History of Everything (so far)." Call ☎ 343-2408 for more info ... **Fossil** makes hundreds of new watch styles every year, many of which are retro-looking, and which come in tin cases. Very popular watches now, they generally cost less than $100. Macy's has the best selection ... Swatch collector George Wohl wanted a way to get immediate info on prices and values of old Swatches, so he founded the **New York Collectors of Swatch.** They have monthly meetings and publish a newsletter. ☎ 246-4830 for info. Annual dues are $30.

CHARACTER WATCHES Maggie Kenyon, ☎ 675-3213, by appt. The Mickey Mouse watch face, done in 1933, kept the Ingersoll Co. in business (Macy's sold 11,000 of the Mickeys in one day)—it eventually became Timex—and started the character watch craze. Ms. Kenyon has some of the 1933 Mickeys for sale, along with Betty Boop and Dick Tracy. Her product watches include the Ritz Cracker watch, the Spam timepiece, one from Tabasco, and the rare Tom Mix Ralston Purina. Sports watches commemorate Mickey Mantle, Nolan Ryan, and Muhammad Ali. Political watches depict most of the presidential winners and losers. Ms. Kenyon only sells things that are in perfect condition. $200 and up into the thousands.

GOOD DEALS Not many people know that the **Bulova Factory Store,** 26-15 Brooklyn Queens Expressway (it's on a service road, actually) ☎ 718-204-3599, is open to the public. It's not where the Bulova sign is, it's in Woodside near LaGuardia. Best to get there by car. You can find dozens of Bulova styles here (some discontinued, some small lots, some slightly imperfect) for 50% to about 66% off retail. We saw an Accutron, retailing for $475, that they were selling for $135.31. There are also plenty of inexpensive models selling for less than $40. Weekdays only ... **Yaeger Watch Corp,** 578 Fifth Ave. [47th] ☎ 819-0088, has a couple of thousand quality watches in stock at any one time, for 30–40% off the retail price, with a one-year guarantee. They will quote prices on the phone, if you have the make and model. If they don't have what you're looking for, they'll order it for you . . . **Chelsea Watch Outlet,** 62 W. 22nd St. [5th/6th] ☎ 627-0130, sells Timex, Casio, Lorus, some Seiko and Citizen at 30–60% below retail all the time. Lots of character watches and sports watches with stopwatch features, Timex Indiglo, and the thin digital Timex travel clocks ($9 here, $24 elsewhere). Battery and band replacement service while you wait.

INDEX

←——→

Page numbers in bold indicate primary entries in text.

BY CATEGORY

BY LOCATION

STATEN ISLAND

A – Z

A